D#246979

D0634620

TH[

GREAT TOWNS

OF THE

WEST

2/10/86 RH

DATE DUE

SEP 25 1986		
FEB 2 4 1996		
GAYLORD		PRINTED IN U.S.A.

San Diego, California

Library of Congress Cataloguing in Publication Data

Vokac, David.
  The great towns of the West.

  Includes index.
    1. West (U.S.) — Description and travel — 1981 - —
Guide-books. 2. Alberta — Description and travel — Guide-
books.   3. British Columbia — Description and travel —
Guide-books.   I. Title.
F595.3.V64   1985   917.8'0433   84-26918
ISBN 0-930743-00-8

Copyright© 1985 by David Vokac
All rights reserved. No part of this book may be reproduced in any form without permission
in writing from the publisher. Inquiries should be addressed to:
West Press
P.O. Box 99717
San Diego, Ca. 92109

Second Edition
2 3 4 5 6 7 8 9 10

Preface

The West has captured the imagination of people everywhere. Our continuing fascination with the area is demonstrated each year when millions of visitors travel great distances to experience superb natural attractions like Yellowstone, Yosemite, and Banff National Parks. Recent explosive growth of major cities throughout the region further illustrates the West's increasing drawing power.

Much has been written about these natural wonders and vibrant cities. However, information about special places apart from the time-honored attractions remains scarce. Towns like Aspen, Santa Fe, and Carmel are still treated with indifference in major guidebooks, in spite of their renown. These and other out-of-the-way towns that successfully blend inspiring natural settings with the comforts and artistry of civilization are among the West's greatest achievements—and least discovered treasures. They are leisure-time bonanzas for all who are lucky enough to find them.

As a youth, I was dramatically introduced to the West during a summer-long, family "grand tour" of the region a few years after World War II. We moved to Cody, Wyoming — "The Eastern Gateway to Yellowstone National Park" — the next year. I have been captivated by the geography and culture of the West ever since. Seizing every opportunity to explore it, I visited — and revisited — all of the renowned parks and cities in both the Western United States and Canada. During these trips, I also discovered a number of enchanting towns that were ignored altogether, or casually described with random information in available guidebooks. Meanwhile, as a college student, I worked with the U.S. Forest Service during summers in Wyoming prior to receiving a Master's degree in Geography and Area Development from the University of Arizona. As a professional urban planner, I served as the community planning coordinator for the City of Denver, and as the chief of park development for San Diego County.

My abiding interest in the West, and my work in Western planning, eventually led to this book. Three years of full-time, entirely independent effort have made it as honest, accurate, and complete as possible. For everyone who ever wondered what special places and pleasures might lie beyond the cities and just over the next mountain, *The Great Towns of the West* has the answers.

This book is dedicated
to Joan
whose inspiration, loyalty, and expert help made it possible.

THE WEST

N

BRITISH COLUMBIA

Courtenay

Banff
⊙ CALGARY

Vernon

⊙ VANCOUVER

Penticton

ALBERTA

Port Townsend

Chelan

Whitefish

⊙ SEATTLE

Sandpoint

Coeur d'Alene

Bigfork

Seaside
Cannon Beach

WASHINGTON

MONTANA

⊙ PORTLAND

Newport

Bend

McCall

Red Lodge

OREGON

Cody

Grants Pass
Ashland

Ketchum

Jackson

IDAHO

WYOMING

Mendocino

⊙ SALT LAKE CITY

Nevada City   Tahoe City

Steamboat Springs

Estes Park

Calistoga
St. Helena
Sonoma

South Lake Tahoe

NEVADA

Vail

⊙ DENVER

Sonora

Aspen

Breckenridge

⊙ SAN FRANCISCO

UTAH

Crested Butte

Monterey
Pacific Grove
Carmel

Telluride

COLORADO

CALIFORNIA

St. George

Durango

Cambria

San Luis Obispo

Taos

Solvang

Santa Fe

Ojai

Sedona

⊙ LOS ANGELES

Prescott

Palm Springs

ARIZONA

NEW MEXICO

⊙ SAN DIEGO

⊙ PHOENIX

Pacific Ocean

Scale in miles
0   100   200
One inch equals approx. 200 miles

4

Contents

Introduction

Picture — somewhere in the West — majestic peaks towering just beyond a tranquil lake, a crystal-clear river, or a rushing stream. Think of pine-forested mountains overlooking the Pacific Ocean, and far below — a long, driftwood-strewn beach; a remote sandy cove; or a secret harbor. Now, imagine human-scale towns, with style and pleasures normally found only in cities, in the midst of these idyllic settings. Welcome to the great towns of the West!

This book was written to help you find these remarkable places and their unforgettable surroundings, and enjoy them to the fullest. It will be useful both for easily comparing towns and their features while you plan your trip, and for helping you decide what to do after you arrive.

A wealth of new information is presented in this guidebook, which is different from other efforts in two important ways. First, traditional guidebooks are almost always written for families. Typically, descriptions are provided only for features of interest to both children and adults. The material in this guide is oriented toward adults. As a result, attention is focused on leisure pursuits primarily of interest to adventurous couples and individuals. Wineries and remote hot springs receive as much attention as museums and amusement parks. Second, conventional guidebooks usually focus on either large regions or individual subjects. Regional guides inevitably suffer from their inability to provide more than representative cross-sections of random, sketchy information about places apart from major cities or parks. Single-subject guides typically ignore all but one aspect of any community, such as country inns, gourmet restaurants, or campgrounds. The material in this guidebook deals exclusively with the West's elite collection of great towns and their surroundings. By thus limiting the scope, it was possible to identify, describe, and evaluate **all** of the special places and pleasures in each town. Subjects normally included in guidebooks — attractions, restaurants, and lodgings — are presented in careful detail. In addition, several subjects that have never been addressed together in a single book — weather, shopping, nightlife, camping, and special events — are given the same thorough attention.

Following are some general comments about the selection of the great towns, major categories of information, location criteria, the rating system, prices, and related topics.

Selection of the West's Great Towns

There are almost 7,500 named settlements in the West. Every one of them was considered during the search for great towns throughout a vast 1.8 million-square-mile region that includes eleven American states and two Canadian provinces. The term "great" is not used lightly in this book. As defined in Webster's, it can mean "much higher in some quality or degree; much above the ordinary, or average... illustrious, superior, remarkable... highest in its class." A systematic process of elimination was used to find every Western town with these characteristics reflected in its size, location, natural and urban features. First, each town's population was considered. Numerous studies have concluded that the most desirable population for an urban place is less than fifty thousand people. At the other extreme, villages with less than one thousand people are almost always too small to have all essential urban services and facilities. After eliminating cities and villages from further consideration, the two thousand towns that are "the right size" were evaluated in terms of "independence." All towns less than ten miles from the nearest small city (of at least fifty thousand population), and farther (up to at least forty miles) from the largest metropolitan centers, were excluded. This was done because suburban communities are inevitably dominated by, and assume some of the characteristics of, the nearby city. The "natural setting" of each remaining town was then assessed. Mountains and the Pacific Ocean are the outstanding landforms and the ultimate attractions of the West. All towns more than a few miles from one or the other of these features were omitted. Next, "environmental problems" like open-pit mining operations or smokestack industries near downtown caused additional towns to be rejected. Finally, to identify "destination towns" — places desired by visitors as well as residents — the quantity and quality of lodgings and amenities were evaluated. All of the 132 towns that survived the entire process of elimination through this step were field-checked. A comprehensive survey was conducted in each town. Fifty towns achieved superior scores.

Collectively, these are the most sought-after towns in the most exciting and dynamic region of the continent. Individually, each offers unique enchantment that makes it a worthy destination for a weekend — or a lifetime.

Weather Profile

Weather plays a crucial role in molding patterns of recreation and leisure. Because of this, a great deal of care was taken in obtaining and presenting detailed weather information. The weather profiles for each town are intended to be the most complete in any guidebook.

Numeric data is provided about average high and low temperatures, rainfall, and snowfall for each month. The "Vokac Weather Rating"© (VWR) uses all of this (plus the frequency of precipitation) to measure the probability of "pleasant weather" — i.e., warm, dry conditions suitable for outdoor recreation by anyone dressed in light sportswear. The typical weather that can be expected each month is systematically rated from "0" to "10." A "0" signifies "bad" weather with almost no chance that shirt-sleeves and shorts will be appropriate. Every increment of one on the VWR represents a 10% greater chance of pleasant weather. For example, a "5" is used where there is a 50% chance that any given day in the month will be pleasant. A "10" connotes "great" weather, with a predominance of warm, dry days almost 100% assured. An easy-to-follow line graph is used to display each monthly VWR. Ratings of "7" or above indicate a high probability of desirable conditions for outdoor activity. Ratings of "6" or less suggest an increasing likelihood that the weather may restrict outdoor activities and/or require special clothing. As an added convenience, each month on the graph has been subdivided into four segments, roughly corresponding to weeks. Readers interested in "fine-tuning" the VWR may find the smaller segments helpful. For example, if the ratings for October and November are "9" and "4," the position of the connecting line during the last week (segment) of October indicates a "7" rating. The implication is that weather during the last week in the month is normally still "good," but no longer as "fine" as it was earlier in the month. The data has also been translated into concise narrative forecasts that describe what the weather will probably be like in each month, and in each season, of the year.

Attractions and Diversions

All notable attractions in each town are identified and described. Included are places like wineries, nude beaches, and libraries that are typically missing from conventional guidebooks because they are of interest primarily to adults. In addition, all kinds of diversions like bicycling, ballooning, horseback riding, and river running are described, and sources for equipment rentals and guides are named. As a convenience, certain popular categories of attractions and diversions are always listed alphabetically under headings such as "boat rentals," "golf courses," "warm water features," and "winter sports."

Shopping

Distinctive shops are among the most popular features of almost every great town. Yet, they are uniformly ignored in conventional guidebooks. In this book, all notable shops that feature locally produced gourmet foods or unusual items (especially those reflecting local artistry or craftsmanship) are described under "Food Specialties" and "Specialty Shops" for each town. The desirability of each downtown as a place to shop and browse is also discussed.

Nightlife

Life after dark is of particular interest to most adults. The overall quality of places to go and things to do for an evening is summarized for each town. All first-rate live theaters, saloons, and other sources of distinctive nightlife are named. Each is described in terms of featured entertainment as well as furnishings and decor.

Restaurants

Both the quantity and quality of dining places are discussed, along with the predominant food style, for each town. All noteworthy restaurants are described in terms of food and atmosphere. Service is not mentioned because it can vary so much over time — or even on a given evening. Prices are summarized in categories from "low" to "very expensive" (see the discussion of "prices" later in this chapter). Meals served (B = Breakfast, L = Lunch, D = Dinner) are identified under the restaurant's name, along with days closed, if any. Hours of operation and special services (like approved credit cards) are not described, because they change frequently in most restaurants. Places that cater especially to families, fast-food shops, and most chain restaurants are generally excluded because of the adult orientation of this book and the emphasis on distinctive dining.

Lodging

A systematic effort was made to identify and describe all of the best and all of the bargain accommodations in each town. Most of the conventional motels and other sanitized lodgings clustered along highway strips and near freeway off-ramps are excluded. These places seldom reflect the charms of an area and are even less frequently bargains. Each town is summarized in terms of the number and quality of lodgings, and the average percentage by which rates are reduced or increased apart from summer. Each uncommon lodging is portrayed in terms of amenities, both natural (like a lakeside location or an oceanfront beach) and man-made (i.e., outdoor pool, whirlpool, tennis courts, etc.). Room decor and generally available room features are discussed. For the first time in any guide, thousands of individual rooms with special views and/or furnishings are singled out. All lodgings with one or more exceptional accommodations include specific listings in which each room (starting with the best) is identified by number (or name), described, and priced. Every effort was also made to include and depict all of each town's safe and clean bargain accommodations (priced at $30 per night or less). The "regular room" price which completes each listing is the lowest price charged during prime time (on a summer weekend) for two people in a room with one bed.

Campgrounds

Two kinds of campgrounds are included: all places with a special natural setting (by a river or an oceanfronting beach, for example), and places with complete facilities (including hot showers) that are convenient to a great town. Natural and man-made attractions, as well as sanitary and individual site features, are consistently described. The base rate that concludes each listing is the minimum price charged for two people occupying a tent site during prime time.

Location

It is hard to be lost for very long in any of the great towns because of their compact "human scale." To simplify locating features without a map, every listing in this guide is addressed according to a street number and both distance and direction from downtown. The term "downtown" includes all features within approximately one-quarter mile of the busiest, most intensely developed portion of the business district. Because the same definition is used for each town, it is easy to compare numbers and kinds of features within and among downtowns, and to quickly estimate distances between any listings in each town. (Cambria, Newport, and Vail each have two downtowns. Distances and directions are given from the nearest of the two centers in these towns.)

Ratings

All features in each town are rated in a star system. Three ratings are used. (1) A star preceding an entry connotes an especially notable example or source of a product or service. It is worth going out of the way for, if you are interested in that thing. (2) An entry is included, but not starred, if it is a good (but not exceptional) example or source of the product or service. (3) Places and activities that were not included were judged to be of only average or lower quality, readily available in many other places, or lacking in some important characteristic.

Evaluations of each feature were made anonymously, and independently of any payment or favor. As a result, each listing is rated on merit alone, and solely reflects the judgment of the author. A special effort was made to assure that ratings are comparable among all features and towns. For example, if a restaurant is starred, it is not merely one of the best available locally. It would be regarded as a place for a special dining experience in any town lucky enough to have it. Each individual feature was consistently evaluated both in terms of its overall quality and how well it succeeds in being what it purports to be. Thus, if a restaurant proclaims that it is a temple of haute cuisine, its rating was based both on the quality of the food and decor and on its success or failure to live up to a lofty aspiration. All rating information is somewhat perishable in any guidebook. After all, chefs move on, bed-and-breakfast inns change ownership, and shops discontinue certain merchandise over time. However, longer-than-normal staying power can be expected from the listings in this guide because they are each area's most notable features.

Prices

Information is provided about the cost of all lodgings, campgrounds, and restaurants. Because prices change along with the economy and the whims of management, there are no assurances that the specific prices quoted in the lodgings and campgrounds sections will be in effect. The numbers will continue to illustrate comparable values, however, since price levels usually remain constant. For example, a "bargain" motel (with rooms costing $30 or less in 1984) can be expected to remain a relative bargain in later years — even though the price of a room increases — because other places will typically increase their prices by about the same percentage as the bargain motel. All prices in this book are quoted in American dollars. For consistency and simplicity, all Canadian prices have been converted into American dollars at the rate of $1.25 Canadian = $1.00 American.

All quoted prices were obtained for every lodging listed in this book during a systematic telephone survey conducted in August, 1984. As a result, the "high season" (summer) prices for any lodging or room can be conveniently compared to those of any other accommodations in town, or in other towns. Each price is a per-night rate for two people in a room with one bed. Rates for one person are usually a few dollars less, and rates for two beds may be a few dollars more per night. Prices are for European plan accommodations (no meals) except as noted in the text for facilities that include one or more meals in their daily rates. The campground prices are the lowest quoted in 1984 per car with two persons for a site without electrical or other special hookups. It should be assumed for both lodgings and campgrounds that the use of on-premises facilities (like swimming pools, saunas, etc.) is included in the price of a room or campsite, unless fees or rental charges are noted in the description.

A basic price code was designed to provide a fast, accurate picture of the cost of an average meal in each restaurant. The same code is used for all listed restaurants. As a result, the cost of different kinds of fine dining can be compared within any great town, or contrasted with the cost of similar restaurants in any other great town. Four categories are used to define the cost per person for a "normal" dinner (soup or salad, average-priced entree, and beverage) not including wine, tip, or tax. The categories and related prices are:

Low : less than $8
Moderate : $8-$14
Expensive : $14-$20
Very Expensive : more than $20

Some Final Comments

All information has been carefully checked, and is believed to be current and accurate. However, the author cannot be responsible for changes in name, address, phone number, prices, or quality of listed places and services since these are beyond his control. No malice is intended or implied by the judgments expressed, or by the omission of any facility or service from this guide.

As with any guidebook, this one will be challenged about towns and features that were included, and those which were left out. A reader may disagree with the absence of a favorite town, or the fact that a place remembered fondly in one of the great towns has been excluded. Regardless, *The Great Towns of the West* will achieve its purpose if it encourages you to go beyond the cities and famous landmarks to discover and experience the special pleasures of these enchanting places.

The author welcomes your comments and questions. Please write:

c/o West Press
P.O. Box 99717
San Diego, California 92109

Prescott, Arizona

Elevation:

5,354 feet

Population (1980):

20,055

Population (1970):

13,631

Location:

91 mi. NW
of Phoenix

Prescott is a large and lively link to the Old West. Surrounded by a mountain-rimmed ponderosa pine forest, it is the heart of a mile-high "sky island" above the Arizona desert. The handsome setting complements the town's genuine Western spirit. Ranchers, miners, cowboys, and Indians come into town as they always have. Some of the Southwest's finest museums showcase frontier artifacts dating back to the days when this was a territorial capital during and after the Civil War. Scores of historic buildings are carefully maintained. Many continue to house their original businesses in delightfully unchanged settings. A relatively mild four season climate features particularly idyllic weather in late spring and early fall. Summer is normally hot, and wetter than any other time of year. This is the most popular season anyway, when visitors seek a haven from nearby desert heat. A wild and woolly Western 4th of July celebration, the Prescott Frontier Days, is the year's biggest event and one of the nation's oldest and largest rodeos. From spring through fall, hiking, camping, and gold panning are enjoyed in the surrounding forest, as well as boating and fishing on numerous small man-made lakes.

During the Civil War, gold was discovered in these highlands. Within a year, by 1864, the town of Prescott was formed, and Arizona became a territory with this as its first capital. In 1867, the capital was moved to Tucson, then back to Prescott in 1877 where it remained until 1889. By the time the capital was permanently moved to Phoenix that year, Prescott was already a major town in the Southwest, claiming more than four thousand residents and a diverse economy serving a large trading area. On July 14, 1900, a fire started when a drunken miner overturned a kerosene lamp. Much of the heart of the business district was burned. Buildings lost in the fire were quickly replaced by bigger and better structures, which accounts for the turn-of-the-century feeling evident today.

Most of the symbols of Prescott's rich history are reassuringly maintained. The stately old Yavapai County courthouse continues to preside over a classic tree-lined square in the heart of town. Other impressive public buildings and monuments, fine museums, a few specialty shops featuring Southwestern goods, the area's best restaurant, and a beautifully restored hotel are all within an easy stroll. Whiskey Row is also on the square with one of the most authentic lineups of turn-of-the-century bars in the entire West. It is as popular as ever for drinking, dancing, and live entertainment. There are plenty of restaurants and lodgings around town. Several exhibit the unassuming, old-fashioned Western style that is Prescott's greatest charm.

Prescott, Arizona

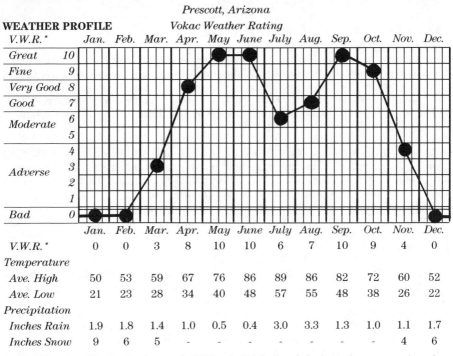

WEATHER PROFILE   *Vokac Weather Rating*

V.W.R.*	Jan.	Feb.	Mar.	Apr.	May	June	July	Aug.	Sep.	Oct.	Nov.	Dec.
V.W.R.*	0	0	3	8	10	10	6	7	10	9	4	0
Temperature												
Ave. High	50	53	59	67	76	86	89	86	82	72	60	52
Ave. Low	21	23	28	34	40	48	57	55	48	38	26	22
Precipitation												
Inches Rain	1.9	1.8	1.4	1.0	0.5	0.4	3.0	3.3	1.3	1.0	1.1	1.7
Inches Snow	9	6	5	-	-	-	-	-	-	-	4	6

V.W.R. = Vokac Weather Rating: probability of mild (warm & dry) weather on any given day.

Forecast

Month	V.W.R.*		Temperatures Daytime	Evening	Precipitation
January	0	Bad	cool	chilly	infrequent snowstorms
February	0	Bad	cool	chilly	infrequent snow flurries
March	3	Adverse	cool	chilly	infrequent rainstorms/snow flurries
April	8	Very Good	warm	cool	infrequent rainstorms
May	10	Great	warm	cool	negligible
June	10	Great	hot	warm	negligible
July	6	Moderate	hot	warm	occasional rainstorms
August	7	Good	hot	warm	occasional rainstorms
September	10	Great	warm	warm	infrequent rainstorms
October	9	Fine	warm	cool	infrequent rainstorms
November	4	Adverse	cool	chilly	infrequent snow flurries/rainstorms
December	0	Bad	cool	chilly	infrequent snow flurries

Summary

Mile-high Prescott is a true four season town, which is unusual in Arizona. Each season is relatively mild by Western standards. In **winter**, when all of the year's nominally bad weather occurs, bitter cold days and heavy snowstorms are rare. Normally. Pacific storms leave a total of about two-and-a-half feet of snow during the entire season. These snowfalls usually disappear quickly as daytime temperatures return to well above freezing. Unfortunately, the combination of light snowfalls and alternatingly slushy and frozen ground precludes development of commercial winter recreation facilities. **Spring** is perhaps the most pleasant season, with sunny and warm days, cool evenings, and the year's lightest rainfalls. **Summer** days are often hot. But, they are balanced by comfortably warm evenings that are a welcome relief from the sweltering heat of the nearby desert. Occasional thundershowers bring out the aromatic tang of the surrounding pine forest and give the air a special stimulating quality. **Fall** is delightful until after Halloween. Comfortably warm temperatures and only infrequent rainstorms make enjoyment of all kinds of outdoor recreation easy.

ATTRACTIONS & DIVERSIONS

★ **Courthouse Plaza**   *downtown at Gurley/Montezuma Sts.*

The stately three-story Yavapai County Courthouse (1916) is in the center of a landscaped square block downtown. The plaza also includes a gazebo, lawns and charming tree-lined walkways reminiscent of Prescott's Yankee heritage. In front of the courthouse is a large equestrian sculpture. The dramatic bronze monument was erected by the State of Arizona as a tribute to Bucky O'Neill and the first United States Volunteer Cavalry — Teddy Roosevelt's "Rough Riders."

Golf

Antelope Hills Municipal Golf Course   *6 mi. N on US 89*   *445-0583*

Gentle mountains and wide-open rangeland provide a scenic backdrop for a relatively level 18-hole golf course open to the public year-round. Facilities include a clubhouse, pro shop, driving range, club and cart rentals, bar and food service.

Prescott Country Club Golf Course   *14 mi. E on AZ 69*   *772-8984*

The view of distant mountains across a broad valley is a feature of this 18-hole championship course open to the public year-round. A clubhouse, club and cart rentals, a driving range, bar and grill are available.

Granite Basin   *8.5 mi. NW via Iron Springs Rd.*

A picturesque area of granite cliffs and boulders deep in a pine forest offers good hiking and climbing opportunities, plus picnicking and camping adjacent to a fishing pond.

★ **Granite Dells (Point of Rocks)**   *4 mi. NE on US 89*

Fanciful granite boulder formations line the highway for about two miles. The area includes a small, photogenic reservoir — Watson Lake — which is popular for boating and fishing. Campsites and picnic facilities are on slopes near the lake.

★ **Library**   *downtown at 215 E. Goodwin St.*   *445-8110*

The Prescott Public Library occupies a large, contemporary building. The well-furnished interior includes a comfortable reading area with picture window views of Thumb Butte and downtown from alcove seats. Closed Sun.

Lynx Lake   *7 mi. SE: 4 mi. via AZ 69 & 3 mi. on Walker Rd.*

A small trout-fishing reservoir surrounded by ponderosa pines provides camping, picnic areas, a concession stand and boat rentals.

Prescott National Forest   *W and S of town*   *445-1762*

Luxuriant stands of ponderosa pine blanket most of the rolling terrain in this large forest. Several small, pine-shaded reservoirs, and some unusual granite outcroppings, can be easily accessed by paved or dirt roads. Hiking, camping, fishing, boating and hunting are enjoyed.

★ **Sharlot Hall Museum**   *downtown at 415 W. Gurley St.*   *445-3122*

An intriguing collection of homes and furnishings from Arizona's territorial years has been assembled in a landscaped complex that includes a museum center, the two-story log territorial governor's mansion (1864), the John C. Fremont House (1875), the late Victorian-style Bashford House (1877), plus a memorial rose garden and a pioneer herb garden. Closed Mon.

Smoki Museum   *.6 mi. E on Arizona Av. N of Gurley St.*   *445-9840*

A stone building patterned after early pueblo structures houses a fine collection of pottery and other artifacts from Yavapai County Indian ruins, plus paintings portraying ceremonials and legends. Open daily in summer, except Mon.

★ **Thumb Butte**   *4 mi. W via Thumb Butte Rd.*

The most imposing landmark visible to the west from downtown is a huge granite outcropping that looks like a closed hand with its thumb extended. The area includes picnic facilities, running water, and a trail to the top of the butte which rewards hikers with fine views of Prescott. Signs along the trail have been provided for easy identification of vegetation.

The Trolley   *downtown on the Plaza*   *778-7197*

Prescott's "Little Flower" looks much like one of the town's original trolleys. It's a fun way to get around town, or to sightsee. Closed Sun.

Warm Water Feature

Yavapai College Pool   *1 mi. NE at 1100 E. Sheldon St.*   *445-7300*

Year-round swimming is available to the public in this large indoor pool.

★ **Whiskey Row**   *downtown on W side of plaza on Montezuma St.*

A solid block of brick buildings on the west side of the plaza has housed the liveliest lineup of businesses in Prescott since the turn of the century. A concentration of first-rate saloons has always been the star attraction. In addition, Western art galleries, Indian arts and crafts shops, and good restaurants give even teetotalers an excuse to savor the genuine Western spirit of these proud landmarks.

SHOPPING

Downtown, centered around the handsome Courthouse Plaza, has always been Prescott's most delightful area to stroll and shop. Parking is free and many of the stores in the blocks near the plaza are as interesting inside as their turn-of-the-century facades suggest.

Food Specialties

Dent's   *downtown on the plaza at 113 S. Cortez St.*   445-9092

Assorted ice cream specialties are a feature of this pleasant cafe. As an added attraction, the homemade cinnamon rolls are outstanding when they're fresh.

★ **Overall Baking**   *.6 mi. NE at 504 E. Sheldon St.*   778-9834

Quality is emphasized for a limited selection of delicious breads and pastries, including some unexpected specialties like brioche, in this tiny takeout bakery. Closed Sun.-Mon.

The Upper Crust Bakery   *2 mi. NW at 1042 Willow Creek Rd.*   778-5876

A full range of traditional American breads, cakes and pastries are offered in this large bakery in a shopping center.

Village Sweet Shoppe   *1.5 mi. NW at 722 Miller Valley Rd.*   445-5353

This large modern donut shop features fine cinnamon rolls and apple fritters as well as an impressive array of donuts. Booths and coffee are available.

Specialty Shops

Prescott Newsstand   *downtown at 123 N. Cortez St.*   778-0072

A notable assortment of magazines, paperback books and newspapers are nicely displayed in this bright new store.

The Worm   *downtown on Whiskey Row at 128 S. Montezuma St.*   445-0361

A good selection of books (including many of regional interest), U.S.G.S. topographic maps, and posters are sold in this pleasant little shop.

NIGHTLIFE

One of the nation's finest collections of authentic "Wild West" saloons and bars is within an easy stroll of Courthouse Plaza. Whiskey Row, the solid block of brick buildings on the west side of the plaza, is still the heart of where the action is, just as it has always been. Thankfully, no concessions have been made to make these classic turn-of-the-century watering holes more socially acceptable as tourist attractions.

★ **Bird Cage Saloon**   *downtown on Whiskey Row at 134 S. Montezuma St.*   445-9882

Casual live entertainment is offered at different times. Patrons in comfortable booths have a good view of a handsome back bar and front bar, plus an elaborate mounted bird collection.

Boiler Room   *downtown at 116 N. Montezuma St.*   445-9001

Live entertainment attracts crowds on weekends to a big, plain saloon past a boiler in the basement of an old building.

★ **Copper Penny Saloon**   *downtown at 134 N. Cortez St.*   778-0850

This old-time working-class saloon has a splendid back bar, stamped ceiling, and a lot of well-worn character, plus pool and ping-pong. There is live music on weekends.

★ **Matt's**   *downtown on Whiskey Row at 112 S. Montezuma St.*   778-7003

Live music and dancing are featured most nights in this classic Victorian saloon with a stamped tin ceiling, mounted animal trophies, a hardwood back bar, plus atmospheric murals and nude paintings.

★ **The Palace**   *downtown on Whiskey Row at 118 S. Montezuma St.*   *no phone*

This is one of the West's incomparable saloons. A feeling of authenticity is everywhere — in the commodious old bar, nostalgic pictures, stuffed wild animals, well-worn furnishings, and the lofty stamped metal ceiling. Even the presence of new electronic games can't mar the timelessness of the fascinating interior. Instead, they blend easily with the older features of barroom decor and remind the visitor that this is a real "working" bar — not a museum. Closed Mon.

Prescott Center for the Performing Arts *downtown at 113 E. Gurley St.*   778-3113
The Elks Opera House, a turn-of-the-century theater, has been restored. Performances are offered on weekends throughout the year.

★ **Prescott Mining Co.**   *2 mi. W at 155 Plaza Dr.*   445-1991
Sofas and overstuffed chairs gathered around a fireplace provide a comfortable setting for quiet conversations. Several wines are available by the glass. One of the area's favorite restaurants adjoins.

Western Bar   *downtown on Whiskey Row at 130 S. Montezuma St.*   445-9863
Live music and dancing draw crowds most nights to a room enhanced by stamped metal and wood trim decor.

RESTAURANTS

Restaurants are plentiful and plain. Emphasis is on reasonably priced American homestyle cooking — e.g., bacon, eggs, and biscuits (this is one of the homemade biscuit capitals of the West) for breakfast, and steak and potatoes for dinner. Decor is also refreshingly unpretentious and unabashedly Western.

Berry's Pies   *.3 mi. W at Gurley St./Grove Av.*   778-3038
L-D.   *Low*
Many kinds of pies are the new owner's specialty. The plain, pleasant restaurant is located in an older converted home.

Dinner Bell Cafe   *downtown at 321 W. Gurley St.*   445-9888
B-L-D. Only B on Sun.   *Low*
Generous portions of well prepared, reasonably priced all-American dishes are served in an endearing no-frills cafe.

Dry Gulch Steakhouse   *3 mi. NW at 1630 Adams St.*   778-9693
D only.   *Moderate*
This rustic little steakhouse and bar is very popular in spite of its out-of-the-way location. A large, family-oriented branch is located 11 mi. SE on AZ 69.

Maude's   *downtown on Whiskey Row at 132 S. Montezuma St.*   778-3080
B-L. Closed Sun.   *Moderate*
Homemade soups, breads, and desserts are served amidst pleasant wood-and-plants decor in this popular little restaurant.

★ **Palace Hotel Restaurant**   *downtown at 116 S. Montezuma St.*   778-6225
B-L-D.   *Moderate*
Carefully prepared American specialties are presented in a splendid new restaurant overlooking the plaza from the second floor of a national historic landmark building. A series of plush-carpeted rooms are handsomely detailed in oak trim, and are furnished with well-spaced tables, comfortable bentwood chairs, and many plants. Updated rusticity also prevails in the adjoining view bar.

Pine Cone Inn   *2 mi. S on US 89 at 1245 White Spar Rd.*   445-2970
L-D.   *Moderate*
For many years, one of the area's largest and most enthusiastically supported restaurants has featured a classic American menu emphasizing hearty steaks and baked goods made on the premises. Old-fashioned comfort prevails in the dining room. Live music and dancing are available later in a big adjoining lounge.

Prescott Mining Co.   *2 mi. W at 155 Plaza Dr.*   445-1991
L-D. No. L on Sat.   *Moderate*
This large, well-regarded restaurant specializes in prime rib, steaks and seafood. "Instant Old West" decor is complemented by many plants, comfortable booths, and a night-lighted view of the adjacent creek. The very comfortable lounge includes some cleverly updated artifacts.

Prescottonian Coach House   *1 mi. E on US 89 at 1317 E. Gurley St.*   445-7207
L-D. Closed Sun.   *Moderate*
Continental and American specialties are served in modern Western-style dining rooms with fireplaces. There is also a well-furnished fireplace lounge.

The Terrace House *downtown at 234 S. Cortez St.*   776-0381
B-L-D.   *Moderate*

Steaks are the highlight of an American menu featured in this new restaurant located in an attractively converted historic house. The cozy upstairs dining rooms are especially comfortable.

Willow Creek Inn *4 mi. N at 2516 Willow Creek Rd.*   445-0090
L-D.   *Moderate*

A century-old house was recently converted into a casual restaurant offering an eclectic variety of meals. One of the large rooms is an inviting bar.

LODGING

Accommodations are plentiful, and plain with two delightful exceptions. There are few bargains in summer or on weekends year-round. Prices are usually at least 20% less than those quoted from fall through spring except on weekends.

Apache Lodge *.9 mi. E on US 89 at 1130 E. Gurley St.*   445-1422

This old, single-level motel is a **bargain** except on weekends in summer. Each modest unit has a phone and cable color TV with movies.

regular room —   Q or K bed...$36

★ **Hotel Vendome** *downtown at 230 S. Cortez St.*   776-0900

This newly restored small hotel is in a quiet location near the heart of town. Each beautifully updated room features plush, blue-toned decor, and has a phone, cable color TV, and either a very modern or a nostalgic bath. Complimentary fruit juice and coffee are served in the stylish wine bar downstairs.

#31 — corner, big modern "garden" tub, fine view of Thumb Butte from   Q bed...$55
#17 — corner, spacious, antiqued bathroom, tree view windows,   Q bed...$55
regular room —   Q bed...$55

★ **Loba Lodge** *5 mi. SE on Senator Hwy.*   445-1987

Rustic elegance has been achieved in a delightful collection of distinctive cabins that blend neatly into a secluded sylvan setting in the mountains near town. Each big well-furnished unit has a complete kitchen, full bath and a wood-burning fireplace (the only ones in the Prescott area).

"Log House" #17 — unique 6-sided log cabin by remote creek,
2 fireplaces, loft,   2 T & D beds...$60
"Upper Gatehouse" #11 — 1 BR, corner stone fireplace, deck,   T & D beds...$59
#8,#7 — 2 BR cabins, fireplace, screened porch,   2 T & Q beds...$59
regular room — studio apt., Franklin fireplace, screened porch,   D bed...$39

Mission Inn *.9 mi. E on US 89 at 1211 E. Gurley St.*   445-5660

An outdoor pool is a feature of this older single-level motel. Each modest room has a phone and a cable color TV.

regular room —   K bed...$42
regular room —   Q bed...$37

Motel 6 *.9 mi. E at 1111 E. Sheldon St.*   778-0200

The **bargain** motel chain is represented in Prescott by a nicely maintained facility with an outdoor pool.

regular room —   D bed...$22

Prescottonian Motel - Best Western *1 mi. E on US 89 at 1311 E. Gurley St.*   445-3096

The largest motel in town is a modern, conventional facility with an attractive restaurant and lounge. Each spacious, well-furnished room has a phone and cable color TV.

#208 — private view,   K bed...$42
#308 — some view & privacy,   K bed...$42
#247 — some view,   2 Q beds...$42
regular room —   Q bed...$42

Sierra Motel *1.6 mi. S on US 89 at 809 White Spar Rd.*   445-1250

This motel has some large newer units with gas fireplaces. There is an outdoor pool. Each nicely furnished unit has a phone and cable color TV with movies.

#48 — spacious, corner widows, refr., gas fireplace, pvt. tree view,   K bed...$42
#29 — spacious, kitchenette, gas fireplace,   K bed...$46
#24 — spacious, kitchenette, gas fireplace,   Q bed...$46
regular room —   Q bed...$33

CAMPGROUNDS

Several campgrounds dot the pine-forested mountains within a half hour drive from town. The best are beside small scenic reservoirs.

Granite Basin   *8.5 mi. NW: 5.5 mi. NW on CR 255 & 3 mi. NW on FR 374*   *445-1762*
This small Prescott National Forest facility is in a pine forest near a tiny reservoir. Fishing is popular. Pit toilets are available. There are no showers or hookups. Each pine-shaded site has a picnic table and fire area.   base rate...$2

Lynx Lake   *6.5 mi. SE: 4 mi. E via AZ 69 & 2.5 mi. S on CR 197*   *445-7253*
This Prescott National Forest facility in a pine forest near a small reservoir (Lynx Lake) features boating (no motors), rental boats, a boat ramp, and fishing. Flush and pit toilets are available, but there are no showers or hookups. Each pine-shaded site has a picnic table and fire area.   base rate...$3

Watson Lake   *4 mi. N on US 89A*   *445-9978*
This private facility is on a gentle slope above a small picturesque reservoir (Watson Lake) with some memorable rock formations. Fishing is popular, and there are boat rentals and a boat launch. Flush toilets, hot showers (fee), and hookups are available. Each site has a picnic table. Some are oak- or pinon pine-shaded and have lake views.   base rate...$4

SPECIAL EVENTS

George Phippen Memorial Western Art Show   *plaza*   *Memorial Day Weekend*
More than one hundred artists participate in an invitational Western art show and sale.

★ **Prescott Frontier Days**   *plaza & fairgrounds*   *July 4th weekend*
Some claim that the rodeo was originated in Prescott on July 4, 1888. Regardless, this annual celebration has become an enormously popular event with a championship rodeo, plus horse racing, parades, shootouts and fireworks.

★ **Smoki Ceremonials**   *fairgrounds*   *1st or 2nd Sat. in August*
Every year since 1921, during the dark of the moon in August, a group of white men and women perform various traditional dances and ceremonials intended to preserve Southwestern Indian lore.

OTHER INFORMATION

Area Code: *602*
Zip Code: *86301*
Prescott C. of C.   *downtown on the plaza at 117 W. Goodwin St.*   *445-2000*
Prescott Natl. Forest - Supervisor's Office   *.3 mi. S at 344 S. Cortez St.*   *445-1762*

Sedona, Arizona

Elevation:

4,223 feet

Population (1980):

5,368

Population (1970):

2,022

Location:

109 mi. N
of Phoenix

Sedona is an increasingly civilized presence in the West's most flamboyant townsite. It sprawls amid a luxuriant pinon pine and juniper forest deep in a gigantic amphitheater. All around, multicolored sandstone cliffs, spires, and monuments soar up to 2,000 feet high. The inspired setting has fostered an artists' colony worthy of the location, and some remarkable architecture. In addition, the town enjoys the region's mildest year-round climate. Every season is appealing. Spring and fall are especially desirable, when balmy weather is coupled with the fleeting splendor of blossom-time around Easter and autumn colors near Halloween. Crowds are heaviest in summer, as vacationing hordes are drawn to the clear, cool stream that flows through Sedona, and provides welcome relief from the oppressive heat of the nearby desert. To the north are sixteen miles of overhanging galleries of mature oak and other shade trees above deep pools and rapids along Oak Creek Canyon. Throughout the year, panoramic golf courses, backcountry jeep tours, and other distinctive diversions give everyone an opportunity to experience the magnificent scenery of the area.

Sedona was founded in 1902 with the establishment of a post office. But, until the 1950s, the rugged topography and the difficulty of hauling water from the creek discouraged development beyond a tiny village serving isolated ranches and western movie crews in the area. Construction of the paved road through Oak Creek Canyon, a nearby freeway, and deep wells finally cleared the way for growth. Among those attracted were a large number of artists intent on capturing the area's grandeur in a variety of media.

Today, Sedona sprawls into two counties, and is both a major artists' colony and a destination resort. Outstanding architectural achievements like the sublime Chapel of the Holy Cross built into the red rocks, and Tlaquepaque, a peerless shopping complex, are artistic tributes to the inspiring location. Sophisticated galleries and studios throughout the area showcase renowned Southwestern arts and crafts. Nightlife is relatively scarce, but gourmet dining is plentiful. Even for breakfast, Sedona has one of the West's best collections of fine restaurants. Accommodations are notably diverse, ranging from lavish bungalows with fireplaces and in-room whirlpools, or plush contemporary rooms with panoramic views, to rustic cabins in gardens above the stream, or scenic campgrounds deep in the canyon.

Sedona, Arizona

WEATHER PROFILE — *Vokac Weather Rating*

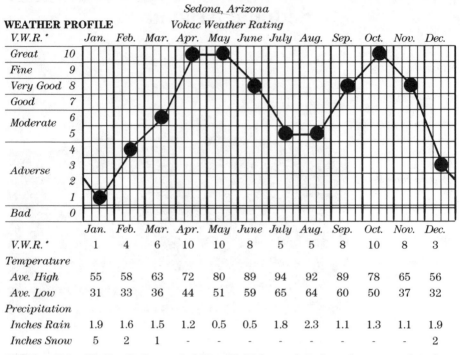

V.W.R.*	Jan.	Feb.	Mar.	Apr.	May	June	July	Aug.	Sep.	Oct.	Nov.	Dec.
V.W.R.*	1	4	6	10	10	8	5	5	8	10	8	3
Temperature												
Ave. High	55	58	63	72	80	89	94	92	89	78	65	56
Ave. Low	31	33	36	44	51	59	65	64	60	50	37	32
Precipitation												
Inches Rain	1.9	1.6	1.5	1.2	0.5	0.5	1.8	2.3	1.1	1.3	1.1	1.9
Inches Snow	5	2	1	-	-	-	-	-	-	-	-	2

V.W.R. = Vokac Weather Rating: probability of mild (warm & dry) weather on any given day.

Forecast

Month	V.W.R.*		Temperatures Daytime	Evening	Precipitation
January	1	Adverse	cool	chilly	infrequent rainstorms/snow flurries
February	4	Adverse	cool	chilly	infrequent rainstorms/snow flurries
March	6	Moderate	cool	chilly	infrequent rainstorms
April	10	Great	warm	cool	infrequent rainstorms
May	10	Great	warm	warm	negligible
June	8	Very Good	hot	warm	negligible
July	5	Moderate	hot	warm	occasional rainstorms
August	5	Moderate	hot	warm	occasional rainstorms
September	8	Very Good	hot	warm	infrequent rainstorms
October	10	Great	warm	cool	infrequent rainstorms
November	8	Very Good	warm	cool	infrequent rainstorms
December	3	Adverse	cool	chilly	infrequent rainstorms/snow flurries

Summary

Sedona is unique among the West's great towns outside of California in having no really bad weather. The town is both high enough to escape the extreme heat of the nearby desert and low enough to miss the heavy snowfalls of the adjacent plateaus and mountains. In this special setting balmy weather is the rule, except during the short **winter**. Then, occasional Pacific storms may result in light snow in town which disappears quickly in the cool dry air that normally follows. **Spring** is one of Sedona's two outstanding seasons with warm sunny days, cool evenings,and negligible rainfall. These conditions give way to long hot days, warm evenings and occasional dramatic rainstorms in **summer**. **Fall** is the other special season, with comfortably warm and sunny days, cool evenings, and infrequent rainstorms. This delightful weather typically continues until Thanksgiving, so there is plenty of time to appreciate nature's annual fall color spectacle along Oak Creek Canyon.

ATTRACTIONS & DIVERSIONS

★ **Chapel of the Holy Cross**   *4 mi. S via AZ 179 & Chapel Rd.*   *282-4069*
Uniquely perched between two red sandstone pinnacles is a remarkable "sculpture church." It was completed in 1956 through the inspiration of Marguerite Brunswig Staude. The wonderfully understated sanctuary is open daily to visitors.

★ **Coconino National Forest**   *surrounds town*   *282-4119*
The most prominent feature of this huge forest is Mt. Humphreys (12,670 feet), the highest point in Arizona. In winter, its massive slopes support a major skiing complex (The Arizona Snow Bowl). Magnificent Oak Creek Canyon is the forest's most renowned attraction. High above, on the Mogollon Rim, several lakes are hidden in a vast ponderosa pine forest. Hiking, horseback riding, fishing, boating, swimming in Oak Creek, and camping are popular.

Flying
   Skyhawk Enterprises   *2.5 mi. SW at Sedona Air Center*   *283-3100*
One way to enjoy the area's natural grandeur is by scenic air tours, available by advance reservation.

Golf
★   **Oak Creek Country Club**   *7.2 mi. S on AZ 179 & Bell Rock Blvd.*   *284-1660*
This relatively level 18-hole golf course, designed by Robert Trent Jones, is surrounded by gigantic red rock formations. It is open to the public year-round, and has a pro shop, club and cart rentals, a restaurant and bar.

★   **Poco Diablo Resort Golf Course**   *2.3 mi. S on AZ 179*   *282-7333*
A spectacularly beautiful executive 9-hole course is open to the public year-round. A pro shop, club and cart rentals, and adjoining full resort facilities are available.

★ **Hozho Tours**   *.7 mi. S at 431 AZ 179*   *282-9548*
Scenic trail rides, archeological tours, a jeep tour of the Red Rocks, or guided fishing trips can be arranged by advance reservation with this new tour service.

★ **Jerome**   *29 mi. SW via US 89A*
One of the West's great copper mining towns had a population of 15,000 by the 1920s. But, when the copper mines stopped operation in 1953, it quickly became a ghost town. In recent years, Jerome has been "reborn" by artists and dreamers attracted by the picturesque old buildings and the dramatic location high on a mountain slope overlooking the Verde Valley. Several distinctive studios and galleries, restaurants and bars occupy restored buildings downtown. The nearby Jerome State Historic Park includes a museum in the mansion of one of the early mining magnates.

★ **Lamb's Shop Jeep Tours**   *uptown at 207 N. US 89A*   *282-5000*
Sedona is the starting point for fascinating jeep tours through pinon pines, cypress, and juniper forests to unique rock formations, gorges, and colorful cliffs and buttes around town. Two-hour backcountry trips are offered daily year-round.

Library   *uptown on Jordan Rd.*   *282-7714*
The Sedona Public Library, in a small building with a striking redstone facade, has a view of the color country. Closed Sun.

★ **Montezuma Castle National Monument**   *24 mi. S via AZ 179*   *567-3322*
Perched about fifty feet above Beaver Creek in a concavity of a massive limestone precipice is a five-story cliff dwelling that is one of the best preserved prehistoric Indian structures in the Southwest. While access into the "castle" is not allowed (as a preservation measure), a self-guided trail offers good views of the exterior and a scale model of the interior. The visitor center and monument are open daily. Nearby Montezuma Well is a large spring-fed limestone sinkhole, which is also worth a visit.

★ **Oak Creek Canyon**   *for 16 mi. N along US 89A*
Starting in uptown Sedona, the highway parallels a large, clear creek spectacularly lined for sixteen miles by overhanging trees and a continuous display of colorful towering sandstone formations. Convenient picnic facilities, hiking trails and deep natural pools for swimming abound. Five U.S. Forest Service campgrounds are attractively sited among oaks and other hardwoods along the creek. Trout fishing is very popular along this entire section. At the north end of the canyon, the highway climbs via a series of dramatic switchbacks to Oak Creek Vista, a lookout park more than 2,000 feet above town atop the Mogollon Rim. Beyond is the world's largest ponderosa pine forest.

★ **Red Rock Crossing**   *6.5 mi. SW via US 89A and Red Rock Loop Rd.*
From an idyllic picnic area adjacent to Oak Creek, the view to the majestic Cathedral Rocks is, deservedly, among the most photographed scenes in the West.

★ **Schnebly Hill Road**   *for 7 mi. E on Schnebly Hill Rd.*
A graded dirt road (which starts just east of where AZ 179 crosses Oak Creek) provides panoramic views of town and "color country" as it climbs breathtakingly quickly to the top of the Mogollon Rim.

Shrine of the Red Rocks   *2.4 mi. SW on Airport Rd. off US 89A*
The open-air religious site on Tabletop Mountain offers inspiring views across town to colorful monoliths, cliffs, and canyons to the north.

★ **Slide Rock**   *8 mi. N on US 89A*
Numerous western movies have featured this famous natural water slide that ends in a rock-bound swimming pool on Oak Creek. Slide Rock and Grasshopper Point (four miles to the south) are extremely popular for swimming in the summer. Serious hikers will discover more secluded swimming holes elsewhere along the creek.

SHOPPING
Sedona has recently achieved fame as a Western arts center. Distinctive studios and galleries featuring one-of-a-kind items are scattered throughout the area. Many of the best shops are concentrated between the original uptown shopping district with its casual Western flair, and Tlaquepaque, a triumph of planning, design and landscaping with one of the best collections of specialty shops in the West.

Food Specialties

Eat Your Heart Out   *uptown at 317 Jordan Rd.*   282-1471
Gourmet takeout items, including an impressive variety of desserts, are featured. This inviting new deli/cafe also offers limited alfresco dining, weather permitting. Closed Sun.

Sedona Bakery   *6.7 mi. S on AZ 179 in Castle Rock Plaza*   284-2253
Various pastries and breads are served to go, or at a few coffee tables in the area's most complete bakery. Closed Sun.

★ **The Sedona Fudge Co.**   *uptown at 203 N. US 89A*   282-1044
Many delicious fudges are finished in an exhibition work area. Samples are available.

Sedona Ice Cream Parlour   *uptown at 117 N. US 89A*   282-7287
Assorted ice cream treats and candies are served amidst old-fashioned soda fountain atmosphere.

Specialty Shops

★ **Artesania Plaza**   *.3 mi. S at 221 AZ 179*
A new shopping complex overlooking Oak Creek features fine arts and crafts beautifully displayed in several distinctive contemporary galleries.

★ **Crimson Shadows**   *uptown at 450 N. US 89A*   282-1411
This studio/gallery features fine Western paintings and sculptures.

★ **Elaine Horwitch**   *.6 mi. S at jct. of AZ 179 & Schnebly Hill Rd.*   282-6290
In addition to a beautiful location by Oak Creek, this large gallery has an impressive collection of modern wall hangings and sculpture.

★ **Garland Building**   *.6 mi. S at jct. of AZ 179 & Schnebly Hill Rd.*   282-4070
Unusual redrock buildings house galleries with art and pottery, Indian jewelry, and a large selection of Navajo rugs.

★ **Hozho**   *.7 mi. S at 431 AZ 179*   282-6232
This new Santa Fe-style complex is a striking showcase of Southwestern decor with an intriguing collection of fine art galleries and specialty shops.

★ **Ratliff-Williams Fine Arts Gallery**   *.8 mi. S at 330 AZ 179*   282-7489
Contemporary Western paintings and sculptures are beautifully displayed in a handsome wood-toned building. Windows frame Oak Creek and canyon country views that are as delightful as the finest paintings. Closed Sun.

Sedona Arts Center — the Barn   *uptown on N. US 89A*   282-3809
A barn building showcases local talent through arts and crafts sales and exhibits, workshops, and performing arts programs. Closed Mon.

★ **Son Silver West**   *1.8 mi. S at 663 AZ 179*   282-3580
Fine sculptures and paintings, including Western and traditional works by nationally known artists, are featured in this atmospheric Southwestern gallery complex.

★ **Tlaquepaque**   *.5 mi. S at 211 AZ 179*   *282-4838*
This carefully planned, beautifully landscaped, five acre architectural showplace of charming Spanish-colonial-style shops should not be missed. Flowered courtyards, fountains, sculptures, and appealing displays are at every turn. Since construction began in 1971, Tlaquepaque's exemplary collection of galleries, restaurants, and unique specialty shops has given an enormous boost to Sedona's significance as a major Southwestern art center.

The Worm   *uptown at 105 N. US 89A*   *282-3471*
Books about the Southwest are emphasized in a small store that also has a good selection of general interest books.

NIGHTLIFE
Bars and lounges with atmosphere ranging from casual to refined are scattered throughout the area. A few provide picture windows or outdoor decks that highlight the awesome surroundings. Several offer live entertainment — especially Western music.

The Fireplace Deck   *uptown at 210 N. US 89A*   *282-5180*
The Canyon Portal Motel has a small lounge and an adjoining large outdoor deck with a fireplace above Oak Creek. It is a good place for watching the changing hues of surrounding cliffs and canyons.

★ **Oak Creek Owl**   *.8 mi. S at 329 AZ 179*   *282-3532*
Grand piano music is featured several nights weekly in a plush little Southwestern-style lounge adjoining one of Arizona's best restaurants.

★ **Oak Creek Tavern**   *uptown at 121 N. US 89A*   *282-7921*
This old-fashioned Western bar has appealed to residents and visitors alike for decades. Casual decor is distinguished by a giant mounted polar bear in the back, comfortable booths, a rock fireplace, pool tables and foosball. The prestigious Cowboy Artists Association of America was founded here by some of Sedona's famous resident artists.

Poco Diablo Lounge   *2.3 mi. S on AZ 179*   *282-7333*
The Poco Diablo Resort has a newly remodeled lounge, called Brandy's. Contemporary decor includes comfortably padded armchairs well suited to quiet conversations.

Shawn's   *2.3 mi. W on US 89A*   *282-7585*
Live music and dancing are offered most nights in this large casual nightclub.

RESTAURANTS
Sedona is now experiencing the kind of multiplication of fine dining facilities that occurred in the earlier proliferation of quality galleries. The area's best restaurants offer both gourmet cuisine and personalized atmosphere. As an added feature, several notable restaurants serve excellent breakfasts — a rare treat in the West.

The Atrium   *.5 mi. S on AZ 179 in Tlaquepaque*   *282-5060*
B-L. Closed Wed.   *Moderate*
Casual dining in a greenhouse garden setting is featured, and breakfast is served all day.

Fiddlers   *2.7 mi. W at 2545 W. US 89A*   *282-1900*
B-L-D.   *Moderate*
An eclectic menu offers a limited variety of nicely prepared dishes. Hanging plants and local art enhance comfortably padded booths in this new restaurant.

★ **The Hideaway**   *.3 mi. S just beyond Y on AZ 179*   *282-4204*
L-D.   *Low*
Fine Italian specialties, pizza, and homemade pies are accompanied by classical music and an Oak Creek view. A dining balcony over the stream is particularly inviting because of the adjacent forest of sycamores.

★ **House of Joy**   *29 mi. SW via US 89A on Hull Av. - Jerome*   *634-5339*
D on Sat. & Sun. only. Closed Mon.-Fri.   *Moderate*
Complete gourmet dinners are skillfully prepared from the freshest available ingredients and served by reservation only on two nights each week. The memorabilia-filled dining rooms of this celebrated gastronomic haven catered to different appetites years ago when this was a brothel.

★ **L'Auberge de Sedona**   *downtown off US 89A at 301 Little Lane*   *282-1661*
B-L-D.   *Expensive*
A charming new inn offers gourmet French cuisine. The lovely creekside dining room is outfitted in country French decor.

★ **Oak Creek Owl**   *.8 mi. S at 329 AZ 179*   *282-3532*
D only. Closed Jan.   *Expensive*
Sedona's premier gourmet haven is still the place for romantic Continental dining —
amidst a whimsical collection of owls in paintings, sculptures, stained glass and wood
carvings. Plush furnishings and classical music are particularly captivating in the back
room overlooking a lush garden.

★ **Oaxaca**   *uptown at 231 US 89A*   *282-4179*
B-L-D.   *Low*
Mexican specialties are offered, including distinctive Mexican-style breakfasts that are
delicious and bountiful. Spanish-colonial atmosphere is complemented by expansive
canyon views through gracefully arched windows. A new view deck provides alfresco
dining.

★ **The Plump Hen**   *1.3 mi. W on US 89A in La Posada Plaza*   *282-7360*
D only. Closed Mon.-Tues.   *Moderate*
Innovative gourmet dinners and homemade baked goods are served amidst intimate
Southwestern atmosphere in a unique gallery/restaurant.

Poco Diablo Resort   *2.3 mi. S on AZ 179*   *282-7333*
B-L-D.   *Moderate*
The new Willows Restaurant offers a limited variety of American specialties in a pleasant
contemporary dining room with a panoramic view of the golf course and countryside.

Ranch Kitchen   *.3 mi. S at Y of AZ 179/US 89A*   *282-9971*
B-L-D.   *Low*
Homemade baked goods (pies, breads and pastries such as large raisin-filled cinnamon
rolls) are the highlight of this plain old-fashioned family restaurant.

★ **Rene at Tlaquepaque**   *.5 mi. S on AZ 179 in Tlaquepaque*   *282-9225*
L-D. Closed Tues. Closed Jan.   *Moderate*
Fine French and American cuisine complements some of the West's most resplendent
Spanish-colonial decor. A well-played grand piano contributes to an air of romantic
refinement.

Rincon del Tlaquepaque   *.5 mi. S on AZ 179 in Tlaquepaque*   *282-4648*
L-D. No D on Sun. Closed Mon.   *Low*
Mexican food is served in appealing Mexican-style dining rooms and on a sycamore-
shaded patio.

★ **Shugrue's**   *2.5 mi. W at 2250 W. US 89A*   *282-2943*
B-L-D. No B on Mon.   *Moderate*
A long-time favorite now offers a full range of freshly prepared specialties in a new, larger
restaurant. Classical music, comfortable armchairs and booths, distinctive table settings,
a fireplace, and fine wall hangings set the tone for this Southwestern-style gallery/
restaurant. A plush firelit piano bar adjoins.

Stretch's Airport Restaurant   *2.5 mi. SW at Sedona Airport*   *282-9804*
B-L-D.   *Moderate*
Hearty American fare including a variety of homemade pies is served in cheerful dining
rooms with an abundance of plants and picture windows overlooking the small plane
runway on Tabletop Mountain.

LODGING
Most of the area's finest motels and resorts are oriented toward the spectacular
surroundings. Visitors have a choice of some of the most unforgettable views in the West.
While there are very few bargains from spring through fall, rates are often at least 30% less
in winter apart from weekends.

★ **Arroyo Roble Hotel - Best Western**   *uptown at 400 N. US 89A*   *282-4001*
This new and modern five-floor motel overlooking Oak Creek has a large outdoor pool and
whirlpool, plus grand canyon country views to the east. Each room has a phone and cable
color TV.

   #501 thru #504 — spacious, lg. pvt. balc., panoramic view,   K bed...$70
   regular room — most have canyon views,   Q bed...$65

Canyon Portal Motel   *uptown on US 89A*   *282-7125*
Conveniently located in the heart of uptown Sedona, this motel has an outdoor pool and scenic red rock views, plus a small dining room and a lounge with a view deck. Each room has a phone and cable color TV.
> #16 — pvt. balc., fine view over pool,   K bed...$48
> regular room — many have good canyon views,   D, Q, or K bed...$48

★ **Cedars Resort**   *.3 mi. S at AZ 179 & US 89A*   *282-7010*
On a slope above Oak Creek, this motel has some **bargain** units. Several large, well-furnished rooms were recently added with memorable views and creek sounds. Each room has cable color TV.
> #38,#39 — end unit, spacious, panoramic canyon view beyond creek,
>   pvt. balc.,   K bed...$64
> #12,#11 — end unit, spacious, creek/canyon view beyond pvt. balc.,   2 Q beds...$64
> regular room — no view, faces highway in older buildings,   D bed...$28

★ **Garland's Oak Creek Lodge**   *8.3 mi. N on US 89A*   *282-3343*
Comfortable log cabins are carefully sited on nicely landscaped, tree-shaded grounds above Oak Creek in one of the prettiest spots in Arizona. A modified American plan prevails with breakfasts and dinners featuring produce from their garden and orchard.
> #4 — lg. cottage with fireplace, pvt. view over Oak Creek,   D bed...$98
> #5,#11 — spacious, cottage with fireplace, porch, red rock views,   D bed...$98
> regular room —   D bed...$82

★ **L'Auberge de Sedona**   *.3 mi S off US 89A at 301 Little Lane*   *282-1661*
This just-opened creekside motor lodge includes a charming country French restaurant. Each of the cabins is luxuriously appointed with French antiques and reproductions and has a phone and cable color TV. Gourmet breakfast and dinner are included on the modified American plan.
> #2 thru #7 — 1 BR, by the creek, canopied   Q bed...$150
> regular room — 1 BR, creek view, canopied   Q bed...$150

La Vista Motel   *uptown at 320 N. US 89A*   *282-7301*
This older, recently rehabilitated motel is near Oak Creek. Each unit has cable color TV.
> #7 — canyon view, kitchenette,   Q bed...$48
> regular room —   D bed...$42

Lomacasi Cottages   *1.5 mi. N on US 89A*   *282-7912*
Well-maintained older units in several buildings are scattered over six nicely landscaped acres along Oak Creek. Each unit has color TV. Closed Dec.-Mar.
> #6,#4 — spacious duplex, next to Oak Creek,   Q bed...$40
> #9,#10 — 1 BR cottage, kit., stone fireplace,   Q bed...$50
> regular room — motel unit by the creek,   Q bed...$40

Oak Creek Terrace   *4.4 mi. N on US 89A*   *282-3562*
A small, single-level motel above Oak Creek has some rustic rooms with a wood-burning fireplace and cable color TV.
> regular room —   D bed...$50

★ **Poco Diablo Resort - Best Western**   *2.3 mi. S on AZ 179*   *282-7333*
This beautifully situated, contemporary resort is one of the most complete in the West. Amenities include a 9-hole golf course, lighted tennis courts, racquetball, two outdoor pools, a whirlpool, plus a restaurant and lounge. Each unit has a phone, cable color TV and a refrigerator.
> #301,#302 — lg., fireplace, in-room whirlpool, pvt. red rock view
>   past golf course,   K bed...$118
> #303,#305,#307,#311 — lg., fireplace, in-bath whirlpool,
>   fine red rock view,   2 Q beds...$98
> #317,#323 — pvt. view of creek from   2 Q beds...$98
> #418,#416 — in-bath whirlpool, some golf course view,   K bed...$88
> regular room —   Q bed...$78

Red Rock Lodge   *.5 mi. N on US 89A*   *282-3591*
An outdoor pool with a scenic canyon view is a feature of this small, single-level older motel. There are some **bargain** units.
> regular room —   D or Q bed...$29

★ **Rondee - Best Western**   *uptown on US 89A*   *282-7131*
This well-maintained, modern motel in the heart of town has a large, outdoor view pool and whirlpool, plus a restaurant and lounge. Each nicely furnished room has a phone, cable color TV, and a patio or balcony.

#32,#33 — spacious, balc., fine view of Oak Creek and canyon,	K bed...$66
regular room —	2 D or K bed...$66

★ **Sky Ranch Lodge**   *2.4 mi. SW on Sedona Airport Rd.*   *282-6400*
Recently opened, this delightfully contemporary ranch-style motel has an outdoor pool and whirlpool. There are several **bargain** units, plus units with patios perched at the rim of a cliff high over town. Each spacious, attractively decorated room has a phone and cable color TV.

#50,#46,#42,#38 — stone corner fireplace, kit., pvt. patio, awesome view,	2 Q beds...$45
#49,#45,#41,#37 — as above,	K bed...$45
regular room —	2 D or Q bed...$30

Slide Rock Inn   *6.5 mi. N on US 89A*   *282-3531*
This small, single-level motel in Oak Creek Canyon features some rustic fireplace units (no TV).

#21 — fireplace, some view,	2 D beds...$45
#9 — fireplace,	Q bed...$45
regular room —	D or Q bed...$36

CAMPGROUNDS
Only a few miles from town, numerous inviting campgrounds line the wonderfully usable stream in colorful Oak Creek Canyon. The best feature shady, well-spaced sites an easy stroll from scenic swimming and fishing holes.

★ **Cave Springs Campground**   *11.5 mi. N on US 89A*   *282-4119*
This Coconino National Forest facility is in a natural garden setting that includes some fern grottos at the base of boulder formations by Oak Creek. Features include swimming and fishing in Oak Creek, and a nature trail. Flush toilets are available, but there are no showers or hookups. Each spacious site has a picnic table, fire ring, and a raised fire grill. None of the sites are by the creek, but all are near it, and some are surrounded by lush clumps of ferns.   base rate...$7

Manzanita   *6.2 mi. N on US 89A*   *282-4119*
The nearest Coconino National Forest campground to town is a small creekside facility offering swimming and fishing in Oak Creek. Flush toilets are available, but there are no showers or hookups. Each tree-shaded site has a picnic table, banked fire ring, and a raised fire grill. There are a few creekside locations.   base rate...$7

SPECIAL EVENTS
★ **Easter Sunrise Services**   *Tabletop Mountain*   *Easter Sunday*
A truly inspirational panorama is the backdrop for Easter Sunrise Services held each year at the Shrine of the Red Rocks on Tabletop Mountain (Airport Mesa) in West Sedona.

★ **Autumn Arts Festival**   *in town*   *late September*
When the leaves start turning to red and gold along Oak Creek, residents stage a festival of western films made in the area, followed by an artisans' festival.

★ **Festival of Lights**   *Tlaquepaque*   *mid-December*
The lights of thousands of luminarias are blended with live music to herald the arrival of the distinctively Southwestern Christmas season in Tlaquepaque.

OTHER INFORMATION
Area Code: *602*
Zip Code: *86336*
Sedona-Oak Creek Chamber of Commerce *uptown at US 89A/Forest Rd.*   *282-7722*
Coconino Natl. Forest-Sedona Ranger Station *.3 mi SW at 225 Brewer Rd.*   *282-4119*

Calistoga, California

Elevation:

365 feet

Population (1980):

3,879

Population (1970):

1,882

Location:

74 mi. N
of San Francisco

Calistoga is the only Western town esteemed for both water and wine. Surrounded by vineyards and wineries at the northern end of the renowned Napa Valley, it is also the site of a remarkable cluster of small hot springs resorts and a bottling plant that ships the town's mineral water worldwide. The little valley is sheltered by the oak-covered foothills of towering Mt. St. Helena. An uncommon amount of good weather is enjoyed from late spring, which coincides with the release of new vintages, through early fall, when the harvest and crush attract the greatest influx of visitors. During this period, and on weekends throughout the year, lodgings are usually full to capacity. Throngs are increasing in response to growing interest in both premium wine and the sybaritic pleasures of hot springs resorts. Other unusual local attractions include a major glider port, a natural geyser, and a petrified forest. The nearby hills and picturesque valley also offer fine bicycling and hiking opportunities. Still, the town's major preoccupation is with more relaxed diversions — like wine tasting, soaking in hot mineral water whirlpools, and taking ash baths.

Calistoga was founded in 1859 by Sam Brannan, California's first millionaire land developer who was also the publisher of San Francisco's first newspaper. Recognizing the potential of the area's warm springs, volcanic mud, and hot water geysers, he purchased a square mile near Mt. St. Helena and developed what was intended to become the "Saratoga of California," rivaling the famous New York resort. He, and others, also cultivated the grapevines that are now part of vineyards producing premium wines recognized as some of the world's finest. For more than a century, Calistoga's economy was based on the health-related aspects of the natural hot springs and in growing, harvesting, and processing premium grapes. In recent years the complementary sybaritic relationship between fine wine and hot springs spas has begun to attract visitors in pursuit of pleasure as well as cures.

Today, major improvements are being made to existing facilities, while growth remains determinedly low-keyed. Constriction of the valley to as little as one-half mile between steep foothills has focused the town's development around a compact and charming downtown. Recent skillful renovations have successfully restored a turn-of-the-century feeling to the classic main street. Almost all of the major hot springs spa and lodging facilities, plus the few good specialty shops, and most of the scarce-but-excellent restaurants and bars are located within easy walking distance of this appealing thoroughfare.

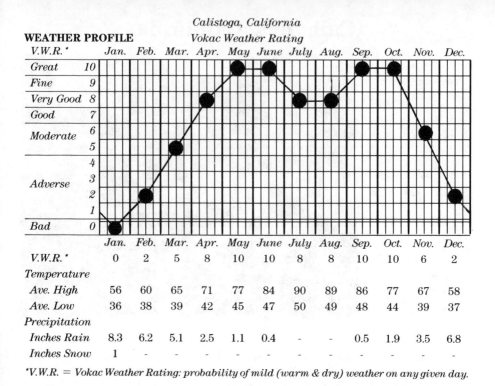

Calistoga, California
WEATHER PROFILE — Vokac Weather Rating

V.W.R.*		Jan.	Feb.	Mar.	Apr.	May	June	July	Aug.	Sep.	Oct.	Nov.	Dec.
V.W.R.*		0	2	5	8	10	10	8	8	10	10	6	2
Temperature													
Ave. High		56	60	65	71	77	84	90	89	86	77	67	58
Ave. Low		36	38	39	42	45	47	50	49	48	44	39	37
Precipitation													
Inches Rain		8.3	6.2	5.1	2.5	1.1	0.4	-	-	0.5	1.9	3.5	6.8
Inches Snow		1	-	-	-	-	-	-	-	-	-	-	-

*V.W.R. = Vokac Weather Rating: probability of mild (warm & dry) weather on any given day.

Forecast

Month	V.W.R.*		Temperatures Daytime	Temperatures Evening	Precipitation
January	0	Bad	cool	chilly	frequent downpours
February	2	Adverse	cool	chilly	frequent downpours
March	5	Moderate	warm	cool	occasional downpours
April	8	Very Good	warm	cool	infrequent downpours
May	10	Great	warm	cool	infrequent rainstorms
June	10	Great	hot	warm	negligible
July	8	Very Good	hot	warm	none
August	8	Very Good	hot	warm	none
September	10	Great	hot	warm	negligible
October	10	Great	warm	cool	infrequent rainstorms
November	6	Moderate	warm	cool	infrequent downpours
December	2	Adverse	cool	chilly	frequent downpours

Summary

At the northern end of the Napa Valley, Calistoga's weather is moderated somewhat by marine air pouring through the gap in the Coast Ranges at the Golden Gate. As a result, there is almost no snow in **winter**. The season is usually cool and wet, with frequent heavy rainfalls contributing well over half of the year's normal precipitation. **Spring** is delightful, with warm days, cool evenings, and fewer and lighter rainfalls as the season progresses. **Summer** days are hot and sunny, evenings are warm, and there is a virtual assurance that no precipitation will disrupt outdoor activities. **Fall** is perhaps the most desirable season. Warm sunny days, cool evenings, and infrequent rainfalls provide ample opportunities to get out and share in the celebration of the area's most renowned collaboration between man and nature—the bountiful grape harvest.

ATTRACTIONS & DIVERSIONS

★ **Bicycling**

Hauschildt's   *downtown at 1255 Lincoln Av.*   942-4666
Bicycle riding is very popular on scenic byways throughout the relatively flat Napa Valley. Individual or tandem bicycles can be rented here by the hour or day.

Flying

★   **Calistoga Soaring Center**   *downtown at 1546 Lincoln Av.*   942-5592
The unique thrill of soaring can be experienced behind a professional glider pilot on flights that originate and land near the middle of town. Because nearly ideal soaring conditions prevail much of the year in the upper Napa Valley, this is one of the West's major centers for the sport.

Golf

Mt. St. Helena Golf Course   *.5 mi. N at 1434 Oak St.*   742-9966
A relatively level 9-hole course adjacent to the Fairgrounds offers scenic views of nearby Mt. St. Helena. It is open to the public with a practice range, club and cart rentals, and a snack shop.

★ **Old Faithful Geyser**   *2.5 mi. N at 1299 Tubbs Lane*   942-6243
One of the few regularly erupting geysers in the world is appropriately located next to Calistoga. Super-heated water erupts to a height of sixty feet or more every forty minutes — approximately. The novel attraction is in a private park.

★ **Petrified Forest**   *5 mi. W at 4100 Petrified Forest Rd.*   942-6667
This private park contains fossil redwood logs buried millions of years ago when ash covered a redwood forest uprooted by the concussion of the volcanic eruption of nearby Mt. St. Helena. The texture and fiber of redwoods up to 126 feet long and four feet in circumference are remarkably preserved.

Pioneer Park   *downtown on Cedar St. 1 blk. W of Lincoln Av.*
The tiny Napa River passes through this handsome little park. Several picnic tables under majestic shade trees overlook the stream. Unfortunately, signs now warn visitors that it is against the law to drink alcoholic beverages like wine in the park.

Robert Louis Stevenson State Park   *6 mi. N on CA 29*
In addition to a scenic road through this undeveloped park, there is a five mile hiking trail to the top of Mt. St. Helena (4,343 feet elevation). From the top of the extinct volcano (the area's highest landmark) the Pacific Ocean, Bay Area, and Sierra Nevada are visible — on a clear day. A memorial one mile up the trail notes the cabin site where Robert Louis Stevenson honeymooned in 1880 and got his inspiration for *The Silverado Squatters*.

Sharpsteen Museum Complex   *downtown at 1311 Washington St.*   942-5911
The museum features dioramas and exhibits prepared by one of Walt Disney's talented artists dedicated to Calistoga's offbeat history. Nearby are an authentically furnished 1860 cottage and a peaceful little garden by the Napa River.

★ **Spring Lake Park**   *14 mi. SW via Petrified Forest/Calistoga Rds.*
At the far edge of the beautiful hill country to the southwest of town, a large park has been developed around little Santa Rosa Creek Reservoir. It is a deservedly popular water recreation site in summer because of a big, picturesque swimming lagoon with a sandy beach. Rental rowboats, sailing, fishing, and bicycle and hiking paths are other attractions.

Warm Water Features

★   **Calistoga Spa**   *downtown at 1006 Washington St.*   942-6269
Swimming in 85° mineral water in this private spa's big old "Roman Olympic" (150' x 60') outdoor pool is open to the public during the summer. Closed Oct.-Apr.

★   **Mineral Springs Spas**   *downtown*
Seven hotels and motels have an array of hot springs spa facilities apart from their accommodations to tempt the public. All are within walking distance of downtown. Guests can luxuriate in indoor and outdoor warm mineral water pools; hot mineral water whirlpools; steam baths; blanket wraps; and massage in a variety of genial settings. The most unusual spa feature is the ash/mud bath, in which local volcanic ash is mixed with mud and hot mineral water to fill "mud relaxation tubs." Several places package all of the above features into a single sensationally sybaritic session lasting between one and two hours.

★ **Pacheteau's Hot Springs Pool**   *downtown at 1712 Lincoln Av.*   942-5589
The public is invited to swim in 90° mineral water in a big outdoor pool built decades ago
against a picturesque hillside. Closed Nov.-Mar.

★ **Wineries**
Calistoga is at the northern end of the world famous Napa Valley wine producing district.
While the heart of the "wine country" is St. Helena, Calistoga is also surrounded by some
of the state's most outstanding vineyards and wineries. Several provide delightful tasting
facilities for visitors.

★   **Chateau Montelena**   *2.7 mi. N at 1429 Tubbs Lane*   942-5105
This renowned winery was established in 1880 in a castle-like building with imported
facing stone and side walls built of native stone up to twelve feet thick. Oriental water
gardens including pavilions, a junk, and islands connected by foot bridges focus attention
on a pretty little five acre lake. Tasting and sales 10-12 and 1-4 daily. Tours by
appointment.

★   **Cuvaison**   *3 mi. E at 4550 Silverado Trail*   942-6266
Established in 1970, this winery uses state-of-the-art equipment to concentrate on three
premium wines. Idyllic vineyard views are a bonus of oak-shaded picnic grounds next to
the winery. Tasting and sales 10-4 Wed.-Sun. No tours.

Hans Kornell Champagne Cellars *4.5 mi. SE off CA 29 on Larkmead*   963-2334
Since 1958, this winery has been devoted to the production of traditional, bottle-
fermented sparkling wines. Tours, tasting (one kind of sparkling wine), and sales 10-4
daily.

★   **Sterling Vineyards**   *2 mi. SE at 1111 Dunaweal Lane*   942-5151
In 1973, a monastery-like winery with a resplendent white facade opened on a 400-foot
knoll overlooking much of the Napa Valley. Worthwhile self-guided tours of the post-
modern facility are reached by parking at the base and riding (for a fee) an aerial tram up
the hill. Afterward, visitors can relax indoors or outdoors in one of the nation's most
impressive settings for wine tasting. Sterling concentrates on only four premium wines,
and is the largest completely estate-bottled winery in the country. Tasting, sales, and self-
guided tours 10:30-4:30 daily (Apr.-Oct.); Closed Mon.-Tues. (Nov.-Mar.)

SHOPPING
Almost all of the stores in Calistoga are clustered downtown. There are no outlying
shopping centers. The highly strollable main street contains several intriguing specialty
shops, in addition to notable dining, drinking and lodging establishments.

Food Specialties
★ **All Seasons Market**   *downtown at 1400 Lincoln Av.*   942-9111
Delectable homemade pastries, ice creams and preserves are sold in this new shop, along
with an assortment of other gourmet provisions. Lunches and light dinners are served. In
a side room, one of the West's largest premium wine selections is on display, and wine
tastings by-the-glass or in-series-by-type of wine are offered every day.

The Calistoga Wine Stop   *downtown at 1458 Lincoln Av.*   942-5556
A good assortment of local and regional wines are sold in a cheerful little shop in the
Calistoga Depot complex.

★ **Continental Pastry and Coffee Shop**   *downtown at 1353 Lincoln Av.*   942-0279
Some of the most outstanding pastries in the West are the specialty of this ingratiating
little bakery. Ice cream is also served at the few tables by a picture window view of main
street. Closed Mon. (also Tues. in winter).

Hauschildt's Ice Cream Parlor   *downtown at 1255 Lincoln Av.*   942-4666
Many ice cream flavors and complete fountain service are features of this small shop with
a deck by the Napa River.

★ **Napa Valley Walnut Farms**   *.5 mi. S at 414 CA 29*   942-4339
Shelled walnuts from local trees are the specialty here. Sales continue from the beginning
of harvest (mid-September) until sold out — usually around Easter.

Specialty Shops
★ **Calistoga Bookstore**   *downtown at 1343 Lincoln Av.*   942-4123
An excellent selection of titles for all ages is displayed, and coffee or tea is available in a
comfortable reading area. Poetry, discussion, and live music are occasionally offered in
this big, appealing bookstore.

Calistoga Depot   *downtown at 1458 Lincoln Av.*
In 1868, this depot was completed as the terminus of the Napa Valley Railroad which
served San Franciscans who came by steam ferry and train from Vallejo to enjoy the spa
facilities. The tracks were removed beyond St. Helena about 1970. The depot was
renovated in 1978 into Calistoga's first specialty shopping complex. Closed Tues.

Earthsongs   *downtown at 1414 Lincoln Av.*   *942-0154*
An old drug store has been converted into an inviting new shop. Much of the eclectic
mixture of California-style arts and crafts is handmade, along with some nods to high-
tech like the bionic chair.

NIGHTLIFE
Calistoga has almost no regular evening diversions except for a few surprisingly
distinctive lounges.

★ **Mount View Hotel**   *downtown at 1457 Lincoln Av.*   *942-6877*
A pianist usually plays music for listening or dancing in the evening, but the stellar
attraction is the sleek 1930s art deco lounge itself. Recent skillful renovation has fully
restored the room into one of the valley's most romantic havens.

★ **Promothermes Lounge**   *.6 mi. NE at 1880 Lincoln Av.*   *942-4636*
Live music is featured on weekends in a revitalized relic of the 1940s that is a feast for
nostalgia buffs. The streamline-moderne decor is remarkably authentic, with curves
everywhere, a wall of glass bricks, a procession of mirrors — even a stainless steel back bar
and a white leather bartop — plus comfortably upholstered armchairs.

★ **Silverado Restaurant and Tavern**   *downtown at 1374 Lincoln Av.*   *942-6725*
Comfortably Old Western decor is accented by a magnificent 1895 polished hardwood
back bar. A number of premium wines are always available by the glass from a wine list
that has been nationally acclaimed as one of the best in the country. Formal wine tastings
are featured most Tuesdays. Quality tap beer hasn't been neglected either, with Henry
Weinhard's Private Reserve and Anchor Steam heading the list.

RESTAURANTS
Restaurants in Calistoga are scarce, but most are very good, and almost all are
concentrated on the main street. The best feature notable lists of the valley's wines to
complement predominantly Continental or New California cuisine.

★ **Bosko's Italian Restaurant & Wine Shop**   *downtown at 1403 Lincoln Av.*   *942-9088*
L-D.   *Moderate*
Contemporary Italian specialties include a selection of well-made hot and cold pastas,
salads, and desserts, plus Napa Valley wines by the glass. Exposed brick walls, open
rafters, twirling fans, and sawdust on the floor have been incorporated into a casual and
inviting deli/dining room. There is also takeout service.

★ **Calistoga Inn**   *downtown at 1250 Lincoln Av.*   *942-4101*
D only. Closed Mon.   *Expensive*
A light touch with fine fresh ingredients results in some of California's best seafood and
Continental specialties. Guests are surrounded by simple elegance in an attractively
restored inn where polished hardwood floors and wainscoting five feet high contribute
to a turn-of-the-century feeling.

★ **Cinnabar**   *downtown at 1440 Lincoln Av.*   *942-6989*
B-L-D.   *Moderate*
Light Continental cuisine is served in a handsomely remodeled Victorian-style bistro.
Distinctive breakfast omelets are featured all day. Wines by the glass are poured at an
alcove bar.

★ **Las Brasas**   *downtown at 1350 Lincoln Av.*   *942-4056*
L-D.   *Low*
The super-hot fire of an exhibition mesquite grill is used to prepare deliciously distinctive
Mexican entrees featured in a stylish and lively new dining room.

Mark West Lodge   *12 mi. W at 2520 Mark West Springs Rd.*   *746-2592*
D only. Sun. brunch.   *Expensive*
Gourmet French meals are once again served in casually elegant surroundings of a
charming century-old landmark that has been beautifully restored after a recent fire. The
grapevines next to the building may be the oldest in the country.

★ **Mount View Hotel**   *downtown at 1457 Lincoln Av.*   *942-6877*
L-D. B on Sat. & Sun.   *Expensive*
Continental cuisine in nouvelle style is featured. The meticulously renovated art deco
dining room is a plush haven of nostalgic tranquility. During the summer, a barbecue is
also offered several nights weekly in the delightful poolside patio.

Promothermes of America   *.6 mi. NE at 1880 Lincoln Av.*   *942-4636*
B-L-D. No D on Sun. Closed Mon.-Tues.   *Moderate*
A variety of well-regarded French specialties are offered in Jacques, the casually elegant
dining room in this newly remodeled, French-owned spa resort.

★ **Silverado Restaurant and Tavern**   *downtown at 1374 Lincoln Av.*   *942-6725*
B-L-D.   *Moderate*
Creative California cuisine highlighted by delightful homemade baked goods is served in
comfortable country atmosphere where well-spaced tables are accented by fresh flowers
and linen. One of the most extensive wine lists in the nation is available to guests in the
dining room and in the handsome adjoining bar.

LODGING
Because this is a hot springs mecca, most of the town's limited accommodations are
oriented around a wide range of spa facilities. Surprisingly, most lodgings are relatively
plain, and almost no rooms provide views of the scenic valley. Reservations should be
made well in advance for visits on weekends in summer or during grape-harvest time.
There are no bargains in summer. However, mid-week rates, and rates from late fall
through early spring, are often at least 30% less than those shown.

★ **Calistoga Spa**   *downtown at 1006 Washington St.*   *942-6269*
Guests may use either the covered whirlpool or the large hot mineral pool in the
courtyard. Optional (fee) spa facilities include mud, whirlpool, or steam baths; blanket
wraps; and massage. Recently constructed rooms in a newer wing are spacious with
wood-paneled interiors, open beam ceilings, and comfortable furnishings. All have
kitchenettes (no ovens) and cable color TV. (Nov.-Feb. every fourth day is free.)
      #17 — end unit, windows on 3 sides, some privacy, mt. view,   Q bed...$40
      regular unit —   Q bed...$40

Dr. Wilkinson's Hot Springs   *downtown at 1507 Lincoln Av.*   *942-4102*
This nicely maintained modern motel has indoor and outdoor mineral pools free to
guests. Kitchenettes are optional. Complete bath/health club facilities are available for a
fee. Each unit has a phone and color TV.
      deluxe room — refrigerator,   K bed...$52
      regular room —   Q bed...$43

★ **Golden Haven Spa**   *downtown at 1713 Lake St.*   *942-6793*
A contemporary motel in a quiet residential area has a naturally heated indoor pool, plus
an outdoor redwood whirlpool with sundecks. Complete (fee) bathhouse/health club
facilities are optional. All well-furnished rooms have cable color TV with movies, and a
refrigerator.
      #27,#20 — in-room raised whirlpool,   K bed...$75
      large room —   K bed...$50
      regular room — small,   Q bed...$36

Hideaway Cottages   *downtown at 1412 Fairway*   *942-4108*
A large outdoor pool and whirlpool in a tranquil location are features of this newly-
restored old cottage colony. Each unit has cable TV.
      "El Paso" — 1 BR, kitchen,   Q bed...$40
      regular room —   Q bed...$34

Larkmead Country Inn   *4.5 mi. S at 1103 Larkmead Lane*   *942-5360*
One of the valley's most beguiling bed-and-breakfast inns is surrounded by vineyards. This
gracious Victorian structure with an Italianate flavor is meticulously furnished with
Persian rugs, antiques, and fine old paintings. Rooms have vineyard views and private
baths. A Continental breakfast is included, as is a decanter of wine.
      "Chablis" — corner, sitting porch with vineyard view,   2 T beds...$85
      regular room —   2 T beds...$80

★ **Mount View Hotel**   *downtown at 1457 Lincoln Av.*   *942-6877*
A large outdoor pool and whirlpool occupy a garden courtyard highlighted by striking fountain sculptures behind this small landmark hotel. Carefully restored rooms and suites are each individually furnished in styles that reflect the hotel's art deco origins. Guests are served complimentary fresh croissants, orange juice, and coffee each morning in a pleasant downstairs room, and a bottle of Calistoga water is placed in each room.
  #221 — corner, nice view over pool, fine period furnishings,   Q bed...$75
  regular room —   D bed...$45
Nance's Hot Springs   *downtown at 1614 Lincoln Av.*   *942-6211*
This homespun, vintage motel features a large enclosed hot mineral water whirlpool. Each simply furnished unit has a phone, cable color TV, and a kitchenette. Complete bathhouse facilities, including volcanic ash mud baths, are available for a fee.
  regular room —   K bed...$38
★ **Promothermes of America**   *.6 mi. NE at 1880 Lincoln Av.*   *942-4636*
A large outdoor pool and an indoor hot mineral water whirlpool are features of this newly remodeled motor hotel, along with a well-regarded new French restaurant and a nostalgic lounge. A complete new high-tech European spa facility (highlighting ash/mud baths) is available for a fee. Each room has a color TV.
  deluxe room — Roman tiled tub,   Q bed...$50
  regular room —   D bed...$40
★ **Roman Spa**   *downtown at 1300 Washington St.*   *942-4441*
Luxuriant gardens surround motel buildings, an outdoor mineral pool and whirlpool, a building housing a Finnish sauna and hot indoor mineral whirlpool for guests, and complete (fee) bathhouse facilities. Each unit has a cable color TV. Complete kitchens are optional. (Nov.-Feb. every fourth day is free except weekends and holidays.)
  #42,#46 — new, end units, refr., lg. in-bathroom
             whirlpool tub with shower,   Q bed...$74
  regular room — newer motel unit, refr.,   Q bed...$42
  regular room — older section,   D bed...$32

CAMPGROUNDS

Campgrounds are scarce in the area. The best is a deservedly popular facility that is beautifully situated along a stream deep in a luxuriant forest of oak and pine.

★ **Bothe-Napa Valley State Park**   *3.8 mi. S on CA 29*   *942-4575*
A mixed evergreen forest along a picturesque little stream provides an ideal location for this state operated campground. An outdoor pool and scenic hiking trails are other features. Flush toilets and hot showers are available. There are no hookups. Each of the well-spaced sites has a picnic table and a fire area. Many sites are tree-shaded, and several are by the creek.   base rate...$5
Napa County Fairgrounds   *.5 mi. N via Fairway on Oak St.*   *942-5111*
This county operated facility is conveniently located near downtown. There is a fee for an adjoining 9-hole golf course. Flush toilets, hot showers, and hookups are available. Each closely-spaced site has a picnic table, and a few are tree-shaded.   base rate...$5

SPECIAL EVENT

Napa County Fair   *fairgrounds*   *July 4th Week*
All of the traditional features of an old-fashioned country fair and 4th of July celebration are present in this five-day event.

OTHER INFORMATION
Area Code: *707*
Zip Code: *94515*
Calistoga Chamber of Commerce   *downtown at 1458 Lincoln Av.*   *942-6333*

Cambria, California

Elevation:

60 feet

Population (1980):

3,061

Population (1970):

1,716

Location:

220 mi. NW
of Los Angeles

Cambria is a whimsical village tucked into a pine forest by the sea. This southern gateway to the fabled Big Sur coast has become a refuge for artists and dreamers attracted by spectacular mountain-backed seascapes. A surprising number of museum-quality galleries and gourmet restaurants highlight the two small downtown areas. Surrounded by pine-covered hillsides and pastoral countryside, Cambria is still unspoiled by either shopping centers or commercial "strip" development along the highway approaches to town. The tranquil setting also benefits from a mild year-round climate. Summer and fall are especially desirable, with natural air conditioning providing fine weather for exploring remote beaches and rugged coastal mountains. The ocean is too cold for swimming, but beachcombing, clamming, and fishing are popular and hiking, backpacking, and camping are enjoyed in the area. Excellent summer weather also attracts capacity crowds to nearby Hearst Castle, the area's most famous attraction.

Shortly after the Civil War, the first permanent settlement was established along Santa Rosa Creek by farmers and dairymen. They were lured by the year-round stream in a sheltered valley at the base of the Coast Range Mountains. By the 1880s, Cambria was an established dairying and mercury mining center. Soon, however, the town went into a long period of decline that was finally reversed during the 1950s with better accessibility and creation of a preeminent attraction nearby. Major improvements began on California State Highway 1 (CA 1), and Hearst Castle was opened to tourists as a state-operated facility at that time.

Population has begun to increase again as the result of Cambria's recent emergence as both a low-keyed tourist destination and an arts and crafts center. Most of the town's businesses are clustered along the old main road in two charming districts. The original commercial center, "east village," has an idyllic sheltered location a mile inland from the ocean. Much recent development has also occurred in "west village" along Main Street nearer to the ocean. Numerous sophisticated galleries and specialty shops feature local arts and crafts in both centers. Romantic restaurants serving gourmet cuisine in quaint cottages or in ocean-view dinner houses are another of the village's attractions. Nightlife is scarce, but it is distinctive and diverse. In sharp contrast with most other California destinations, there are no big motel-chain or convention-oriented complexes. Instead, visitor facilities individually complement the serenity and natural beauty of this special place. Several luxurious small motels with ocean views are concentrated along Moonstone Beach Drive near west village.

WEATHER PROFILE

Cambria, California

Vokac Weather Rating

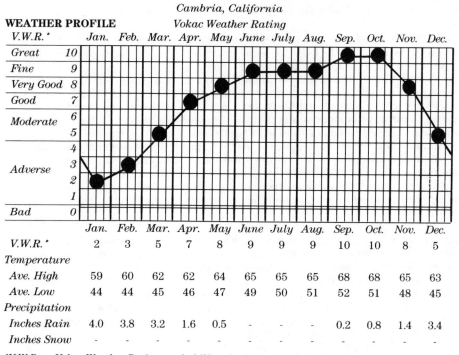

V.W.R.*	Jan.	Feb.	Mar.	Apr.	May	June	July	Aug.	Sep.	Oct.	Nov.	Dec.
V.W.R.*	2	3	5	7	8	9	9	9	10	10	8	5
Temperature												
Ave. High	59	60	62	62	64	65	65	65	68	68	65	63
Ave. Low	44	44	45	46	47	49	50	51	52	51	48	45
Precipitation												
Inches Rain	4.0	3.8	3.2	1.6	0.5	-	-	-	0.2	0.8	1.4	3.4
Inches Snow	-	-	-	-	-	-	-	-	-	-	-	-

*V.W.R. = Vokac Weather Rating: probability of mild (warm & dry) weather on any given day.

Forecast

Month	V.W.R.*		Temperatures Daytime	Evening	Precipitation
January	2	Adverse	cool	cool	frequent rainstorms.
February	3	Adverse	cool	cool	occasional rainstorms
March	5	Moderate	cool	cool	occasional rainstorms
April	7	Good	cool	cool	infrequent rainstorms
May	8	Very Good	cool	cool	negligible
June	9	Fine	warm	cool	none
July	9	Fine	warm	cool	none
August	9	Fine	warm	cool	none
September	10	Great	warm	cool	negligible
October	10	Great	warm	cool	infrequent rainstorms
November	8	Very Good	warm	cool	infrequent rainstorms
December	5	Moderate	cool	cool	occasional rainstorms

Summary

With a sheltered location by the ocean, Cambria has one of the mildest climates in the West. **Winter** is cool, with some fog but seldom a frost of any consequence. Occasional rainstorms that occur during this season contribute more than half of the average annual precipitation. Pleasant **spring** months offer uniformly cool days and evenings, with occasional fog and moderate-to-brisk winds, plus inconsequential rainfalls. **Summer** is consistently appealing, with brisk days, cool evenings, and no rainfall. In this classic naturally air conditioned seaside recreation area, the ocean unfortunately remains too cold for swimming. The most desirable season is **fall**, when the warmest and sunniest days of the year occur. Splendid weather usually prevails until the rainy season begins again in earnest after Thanksgiving.

ATTRACTIONS & DIVERSIONS

Bicycling
    Cambria Pines Lodge   *.5 mi. S of east village at 2905 Burton Dr.*   *927-4200*
Bicycles can be rented at the lodge to tour scenic coastal highways and byways.

★ **Big Sur Coast**   *N for approximately 80 mi. on CA 1*
The awesome combination of a mountain wilderness rising abruptly from an unspoiled sea inevitably delights those who visit the fabled Big Sur. A paved two-lane highway provides one of the West's most thrilling scenic drives and access to all of the features of this rugged coastline as it clings precariously to the western slopes of the Santa Lucia Mountains. Travelers should allow at least a full day to begin to appreciate the remote beaches and lush forested canyons, well-tended state parks, and unconventional galleries and restaurants that complement the breathtaking scenery along the Big Sur coast.

★ **Cambrionia**   *in west village on Main St.*
A custom-built miniature Victorian mansion is uniquely perched atop Townes Antique Emporium. It is much-photographed for both its surprising location and intricate detailing.

Harmony   *6 mi. SE on CA 1*
This is a tiny old dairying community in the attractive rolling hill country inland from Cambria. The creamery buildings have been converted into a whimsical medley of shops, galleries, and restaurants amidst gardens and objects of art.

★ **Hearst Castle**   *8 mi. NW on CA 1 - San Simeon*   *927-4621*
"La Casa Grande" has a ridge-top position that gives it the appearance of a castle from the distant highway. The imposing 137-foot high cathedral-like main structure was William Randolph Hearst's private residence. It is now the focal point of the Hearst San Simeon State Historical Monument that also includes guest residences, terraced gardens, pools, sculpture, and unusual plants and animals. The extravagent collection of eclectic antiques and furnishings were accumulated during Hearst's lifetime of world travel. As the result, a tour of this unique estate is unforgettable. Visitors may only take conducted tours, of which there are four, each lasting about two hours. Reservations are often required during the summer.

Horseback Riding
    Rancho San Simeon Stables   *5 mi. NW off CA 1*   *927-8970*
Rental horses are available for riding along scenic trails between the mountains and the sea.

★ **Library**   *in west village at 900 Main St.*   *927-4336*
The Cambria Public Library occupies a charming contemporary building. Skylights, sculptures, and padded seating in a greenhouse-styled window alcove all contribute to a bright and inviting interior. Closed Sun.-Mon.

Nitt Witt Ridge   *just above west village*
On a ridge a short walk above town is a whimsical bric-a-brac mansion. It was built incrementally since 1928 out of everything from bike parts to beer bottles by Art Beal, affectionately known as "Captain Nitt Witt." This classic example of folk art construction is listed in the National Register of Historic Landmarks. While it is a private residence that can only be viewed from the street, it is worth finding as another expression, along with Hearst's Castle, of what individuality is all about. '

★ **San Simeon Beach State Park**   *1.8 mi. NW at Moonstone Beach Dr./CA 1*
Picturesque sandy beaches, blufftop trails, and ocean-view picnic sites are features of this inviting day use park.

★ **Shamel County Park**   *.5 mi. W of west village on coast*
This day use facility has a parking area adjacent to Cambria's finest sandy beach, an outdoor swimming pool open in summer, and pleasant shady picnic sites.

Sportfishing
    Virg's Sport Fishing   *8 mi. NW on CA 1 - San Simeon*   *927-4676*
Full, half day, and twilight ocean fishing trips can be chartered here except in winter, or at the Morro Bay Embarcadero location year-round. Shore fishing is also popular off the rocky coast and sandy beaches near Cambria.

Winery

★ **Mastantuono Winery**   *21 mi. E on CA 46*   *238-0676*
A new roadside store gives visitors an opportunity to sample some central California premium wines produced from grapes grown in the owner's nearby vineyards. Tasting and sales 10:30-6 (10-5 in winter).

SHOPPING
Cambria is in an early stage of becoming one of the major arts and crafts centers of the West. Several fine galleries and specialty shops already display the works of local artisans. Almost all of the shops in the area are clustered in two tiny business districts — on Burton Drive (east village) — and about a mile west along Main Street (west village).

Food Specialties

★ **Linn's Fruit Bin**   *5 mi. E on Santa Rosa Creek Rd.*   *927-8134*
Seasonal fresh fruits and vegetables are displayed and sold, along with a variety of outstanding fruit and berry preserves made in this picturesque farmhouse shop. An assortment of gift packages will be mailed anywhere. Closed Tues.-Wed. from fall to spring.

Oliver's Twist   *in west village at 724 Main St.*   *927-8196*
Gourmet produce is the specialty, including excellent displays of local wines, local and international preserves, and more.

★ **The Upper Crust Bakery & Tea Room** *in east village at 2214 Main St.*   *927-8227*
Cinnamon rolls, donuts, croissants, and other international pastry specialties and breads are all deliciously made from scratch in one of the West's great bakeries. A few tables and coffee are available. Closed Mon.

Specialty Shops

Artistic Glass   *in west village at 788 Main St.*   *927-4045*
Glass is skillfully blown into all types of art objects and functional items that can be personally engraved on the premises.

Cambria Book Co.   *in west village at 784-C Main St.*   *927-3995*
This pleasant upstairs store has a small, well-organized selection of books, particularly paperbacks. Comfortable chairs are provided for browsers.

Cambria News Center   *in west village at 755 Main St.*   *927-4882*
Many metropolitan newspapers are displayed along with magazines and paperbacks.

★ **Seekers**   *in east village at 4090 Burton Dr.*   *927-4352*
This outstanding gallery features extraordinarily beautiful displays of museum-quality hand-blown glass, porcelain, ceramics, and wood carvings by local and other California artists.

★ **The Soldier Factory**   *in west village at 789 Main St.*   *927-3804*
Fascinating toy soldiers, dragons, unicorns, and other whimsical creatures in a choice of polished or painted pewter are made and sold at this factory/showroom.

NIGHTLIFE
Peace and quiet reign in Cambria, even in the evening, but there are a few places with after-dark "action." Collectively, they offer a good range of casual entertainment and individualistic atmosphere.

Cambria Pines Lodge   *.5 mi. S of east village at 2905 Burton Dr.*   *927-4200*
Dancing and entertainment are featured most nights in a large, comfortable lounge off the lobby of an atmospheric old wooden lodge. Live theater is also occasionally offered.

★ **Camozzi's Saloon**   *in east village at 2262 Main St.*   *927-8941*
Games and occasional live music and entertainment have enticed residents and visitors into this appealingly funky old saloon for many years.

★ **Golden Lion Pub**   *in west village at 774 Main St.*   *927-8842*
Live music and games are featured nightly amidst congenial English pub atmosphere. Dozens of imported and domestic beers are available, along with some traditional English dishes like steak-and-kidney pie, and pasties.

★ **Old Cayucos Tavern** *14 mi. SE on CA 1 at 130 N. Ocean Av. - Cayucos*   *995-3209*
First-rate live entertainment happens frequently in this landmark saloon, and pool, darts, and shuffleboard are available anytime. A working fireplace and a couple of bigger-than-life pictures of cowgirls are part of the rustic decor. All-American fare is offered in the adjoining dining room, including some unusual specialties like turkey nuts and deep-fried artichoke hearts.

★ **Pewter Plough Playhouse**   *in west village at 824 Main St.*   927-3877
Live theater and art films are always worthwhile here, partly because of the whimsical charm of this stylish, intimate playhouse.

RESTAURANTS

A concentration of fine restaurants is one of Cambria's most compelling attractions. Creative gourmet cuisine is readily available, and atmosphere is remarkably varied — ranging from antique-filled old cottages to California-contemporary dining rooms with views of gardens, pine forests, or the ocean.

★ **Barbara's**   *in east village at 2094 Main St.*   927-4830
B-L. Closed Sun.   *Moderate*
The cinnamon rolls, muffins, and biscuits baked here are delicious, as are the distinctive omelets and other homemade dishes served in this pleasant little cafe.

★ **The Brambles**   *in east village at 4055 Burton St.*   927-4716
D only.   *Moderate*
An oakwood pit and oven are featured for preparing steaks, prime rib, and fresh seafoods. Homemade baked goods are another specialty of this long-time favorite where dinners are served amid antiques in one of Cambria's original many-roomed 1890s clapboard cottages.

★ **Bridge Street Cafe**   *in east village at 4286 Bridge St.*   927-8459
B-L-D. Closed Wed.   *Moderate*
An extensive menu highlights notable seafoods, including crab prepared several ways. This new restaurant occupies a rustic cottage that was recently converted into several casual little dining rooms.

★ **Caffe Porta Via**   *in east village at 2248 Main St.*   927-8742
D only. Sun. brunch. Closed Mon.   *Moderate*
This romantic little restaurant specializes in skillfully-prepared Italian cuisine, plus steaks and seafoods, and offers an excellent Sunday champagne brunch. There is also a cozy wood-crafted bar area.

Cambria Pines Lodge   *.5 mi. S of east village at 2905 Burton Dr.*   927-8742
B-L-D.   *Moderate*
American fare is featured in a refurbished rustic-wood lodge that is an enduring town landmark. Picture windows in the dining room provide views of peacocks in an adjacent sylvan garden.

The Flying Frog Restaurant   *in east village at 4090 Burton Dr.*   927-5656
L-D.   *Low*
Contemporary American fare and good adaptations of Mexican dishes are served in a cheerful new two-level restaurant with an inviting front bar.

The Golden Lion   *in west village at 774 Main St.*   927-8842
L-D.   *Low*
English specialties like Cornish pasties, sausage rolls, and steak-and-kidney pie complement classic pub atmosphere in a room with a large fireplace and live music nightly.

★ **Grey Fox Inn**   *in east village at 4095 Burton Dr.*   927-3305
B-L-D.   *Moderate*
Continental specialties and homemade baked goods are served in the graceful and intimate dining room of a charming old cottage, and on a beautiful vine-covered outdoor terrace when weather permits.

The Hamlet at Moonstone Gardens   *2 mi. NW of west village on CA 1*   927-3535
L-D. Closed most of Dec.   *Moderate*
American and Continental dishes compete with the ocean view from this large, recently-built restaurant. The dining area is outfitted with an interesting mix of contemporary and antique decor. Tables are also set in an exotic garden/nursery when weather permits. A good selection of premium wine-by-the-glass is available at the wine bar.

★ **Harmony Valley Inn**   *6 mi. SE of east village on CA 1 - Harmony*   927-4205
L-D. Closed Mon.-Tues.   *Expensive*
American cuisine is given a distinctive light touch, and served amid antiques in several well-appointed dining rooms of a remodeled old creamery building.

Ian's　*in east village at 2150 Center St.*　　　927-8649
D only.　　　　　　　　　　　*Expensive*
Limitations of the New California dishes offered here are offset by outstanding post-Modern decor in this new restaurant. Pastel colors, crisply elegant table settings, and artistically arranged prints and plants have been used to create wonderfully tranquil dining rooms.

Moonraker *1.1 mi. NW of west village at 6550 Moonstone Beach Dr.*　　927-3859
B-L-D. Closed Wed.　　　　　　*Expensive*
Contemporary American dishes and fine ocean views can be enjoyed all day in a casual, pleasant restaurant overlooking Moonstone Beach.

★ **Picnique in the Pines**　*in west village at 727 Main St.*　　927-8727
B-L-afternoon tea. Closed Mon.　　　*Moderate*
Delicious homemade croissants, scones, popovers, and pies, plus gourmet pates, crepes, and unusual salads, are compelling reasons to try this artistically decorated new dining room. There are also a few tiny sidewalk tables, and meals will be packed for carryout picnics.

Sea Chest　*.8 mi. NW of west village at 6216 Moonstone Beach Dr.*　　927-4515
D only. Closed Mon.-Tues.　　　*Moderate*
Shellfish and seafood are specialties of this popular, intimate restaurant with casual, nautical decor above Moonstone Beach. There is a fine ocean view from the Oyster Bar.

The Way Station　*14 mi. SE via CA 1 at 78 N. Ocean Av. - Cayucos*　　995-1227
L-D. B on Sat. & Sun. only.　　　*Moderate*
American specialties are served in a handsome Victorian setting or in a pleasant backyard garden. Many premium regional wines are offered by the glass in the adjoining bar.

LODGING

Accommodations reflect the serenity and natural beauty of this special place. Major motel chains with large facilities are thankfully absent. Reservations are often essential in summer and on most Saturday nights. There are no bargains in summer. However, from fall through early spring, non-weekend rates are usually at least 20% lower than those shown.

Cambria Pines Lodge　*.5 mi. S of east village at 2905 Burton Dr.*　　927-4200
The 1920s lodge and cabins above the village in a Monterey pine forest are being renovated. Recent additions include Cambria's best and largest heated pool and whirlpool, plus saunas, attractively enclosed in a glass-walled structure with a knotty-pine beamed ceiling. A restaurant and lounge are also available. Each room has cable color TV.
　　#27,#26 — spacious, wood-toned decor, pitched roof, fireplace,　　K bed...$85
　　regular room — small cabin or lodge room,　　　　　　　　D bed...$45

Cambria Village Motel　*in east village at 2618 Main St.*　　927-4021
This small, older single-level motel is within easy walking distance of east village. Each recently renovated room has a cable color TV.
　　#5 — end, raised brick fireplace,　　　　　　　　　　Q bed...$38
　　regular room —　　　　　　　　　　　　　　　　　Q bed...$34

★ **Fireside Inn - Best Western** *1.3 mi. NW at 6700 Moonstone Beach Dr.*　　927-8661
This contemporary single-level motel is only fifty yards from Moonstone Beach and has a large outdoor pool and whirlpool. Each spacious, well-furnished room has a phone, cable color TV with movies, and a refrigerator.
　　#126,#128,#127 — gas fireplace, in-bath whirlpool, ocean
　　　　　　　　　view across road,　　　　　　　　K bed...$65
　　#104,#101,#103,#102 — gas fireplace, ocean view across road,　　K bed...$60
　　regular room —　　　　　　　　　　　　　　　　Q bed...$50

The Hampton's Cabins　*in east village at 2601 Main St.*　　927-8969
Each of the small, older cabins in this complex has a tiny kitchen and color TV.
　　regular room — small cabin,　　　　　　　　　D or Q bed...$32

★ **Moonstone Inn** *.7 mi. NW of west village at 5860 Moonstone Beach Dr.*   *927-4815*
A beautifully maintained small motel across the road from Moonstone Beach has been furnished in English Tudor style to serve as a bed-and-breakfast country inn. A few rooms have ocean views and there are numerous nice touches: a wine and cheese hour in a glassed-in patio with a whirlpool overlooking the ocean, Continental breakfast in bed, crystal ice buckets, and fresh flowers. Each room has cable color TV and a phone.

    #8 — ocean view across road,   K bed...$83
    regular room —   Q bed...$73

Pickford House   *.8 mi. S of east village at 2555 MacLeod Av.*   *927-8619*
A new bed-and-breakfast country inn on a hill south of town has captured some of the tranquility and craftsmanship of Cambria. Each unit is decorated in the style of the silent film era and each has a bath. A light breakfast in the morning is complimentary, as is a drink with appetizers each evening by the fireplace in an inviting downstairs bar.

    "Pickford Room" — Victorian decor in pinks/blues, gas
                   fireplace, good mt. view,   K bed...$90
    "Valentino Room" — sleek satin decor in maroon colors, gas
                   fireplace, fine view,   2 D beds..$90
    regular room —   D bed...$60

★ **San Simeon Pines Resort** *1.7 mi. NW at N end of Moonstone Beach Dr.*   *927-4648*
This redwood ranch-style motel in a nicely landscaped pine forest has direct access to adjacent San Simeon Beach State Park and the ocean. A landscaped outdoor pool, beautiful par-3 (9-hole) golf course, and an outdoor games area are free to guests. Several rooms are in an unusual, deluxe, adults-only section. Each of the spacious, well-furnished rooms has color TV.

    #76,#87 — newer, pitched roof, brick fireplace (presto logs),
                  windows on 3 sides, surf view,   K bed...$67
    #62 — newer, fine pvt. view of surf,   K bed...$64
    regular room —   Q bed...$44

CAMPGROUNDS

Campgrounds are scarce in the area. The best offers relatively primitive facilities in a choice location a short stroll from unspoiled ocean beaches.

★ **San Simeon State Beach**   *3 mi. N of west village on CA 1*   *927-4509*
This large, state owned campground occupies some gentle slopes an easy stroll from a long adjoining ocean beach. Beachcombing, fishing, and hiking are popular. Chemical pit toilets are provided. There are no showers or hookups. Each of the well-spaced grassy sites has a picnic table and a fire ring/grill. There are few trees, but some of the hilltop sites have fine ocean views.   base rate...$5

OTHER INFORMATION

Area Code: *805*
Zip Code: *93428*
Cambria Chamber of Commerce   *west village at 767 Main St. - CA 1*   *927-3624*
Los Padres National Forest - Pacific Valley Station   *on CA 1*   *927-4211*

Carmel, California

Elevation:

200 feet

Population (1980):

4,707

Population (1970):

4,525

Location:

132 mi. SE
of San Francisco

Carmel is one of the world's loveliest collaborations between man and nature. On the southern side of the Monterey Peninsula, it is a unique seaside village of intense natural beauty above a slope of fine, white sand that extends into the surf of Carmel Bay. Homes and shops are carefully sited in a forest of pines and rare Monterey cypress. Gnarled branches of these picturesque trees frame views of the fabled Big Sur coastline to the south. The mild climate is almost as remarkable as the setting. Because snow and frost are rare, lush vegetation and outdoor activities are enjoyed year-round. The verdant, flowery landscapes of spring and the warm days of summer and fall are especially appealing. During these seasons, capacity crowds share a wealth of outdoor recreation — beachcombing, sunbathing, sailing, fishing, bicycling, hiking, horseback riding, tennis, and some of the world's most famous golf courses.

Father Junipero Serra built a mission on a site overlooking the mouth of the Carmel River in 1770. However, it wasn't until after the turn of this century that artists and writers began to build homes among the pines. They were attracted by the captivating location and the potential for a simple lifestyle. The sensitivity of these artists and dreamers fostered the charm that is still being nurtured.

Fairy tale cottages and fanciful houses and shops are one highly visible part of the legacy. Another part is the residents' continuing determination to retain the beauty and serenity of this place in spite of its overwhelming popularity. As a result of their efforts, the village still does **not** have: traffic lights, parking meters, neon signs, billboards, street lights outside the business district, buildings more than three stories high, or home mail delivery. It **does** have a compact and fascinating downtown with an astonishing proliferation of notable places to stroll, shop, eat, drink, and sleep. Today, in an area smaller than one square mile, more than seventy distinctive galleries display everything from local to international arts and crafts at prices ranging from modest to mind-boggling. A wonderful assortment of uncommon specialty shops compete for the stroller's attention. The same area has the West's greatest concentration of gourmet restaurants featuring outstanding examples of most of the cuisines of the world. Here also, a profusion of architecturally unique buildings provide romantic lodgings. Carmel's artistic style has even favorably influenced recently-constructed nearby shopping centers, restaurants, and lodgings, which are among the most distinctive anywhere.

WEATHER PROFILE *Vokac Weather Rating*

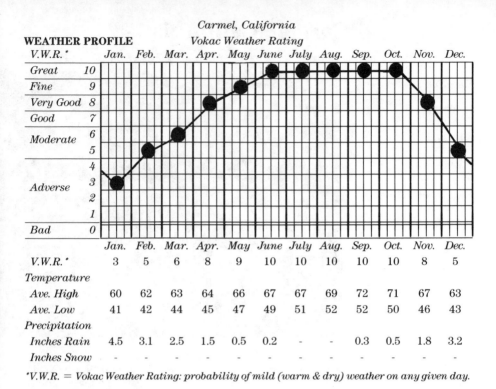

V.W.R.*	Jan.	Feb.	Mar.	Apr.	May	June	July	Aug.	Sep.	Oct.	Nov.	Dec.
Great 10												
Fine 9												
Very Good 8												
Good 7												
Moderate 6 / 5												
4												
Adverse 3 / 2												
1												
Bad 0												

	Jan.	Feb.	Mar.	Apr.	May	June	July	Aug.	Sep.	Oct.	Nov.	Dec.
V.W.R.*	3	5	6	8	9	10	10	10	10	10	8	5
Temperature												
Ave. High	60	62	63	64	66	67	67	69	72	71	67	63
Ave. Low	41	42	44	45	47	49	51	52	52	50	46	43
Precipitation												
Inches Rain	4.5	3.1	2.5	1.5	0.5	0.2	-	-	0.3	0.5	1.8	3.2
Inches Snow	-	-	-	-	-	-	-	-	-	-	-	-

*V.W.R. = Vokac Weather Rating: probability of mild (warm & dry) weather on any given day.

Forecast

Month	V.W.R.*		Temperatures Daytime	Evening	Precipitation
January	3	Adverse	cool	cool	frequent rainstorms
February	5	Moderate	cool	cool	occasional rainstorms
March	6	Moderate	cool	cool	occasional rainstorms
April	8	Very Good	cool	cool	infrequent rainstorms
May	9	Fine	warm	cool	infrequent showers
June	10	Great	warm	cool	negligible
July	10	Great	warm	cool	none
August	10	Great	warm	cool	none
September	10	Great	warm	cool	negligible
October	10	Great	warm	cool	infrequent rainstorms
November	8	Very Good	warm	cool	infrequent rainstorms
December	5	Moderate	cool	cool	occasional rainstorms

Summary

Spectacularly located by the sea on the southern curve of the Monterey Peninsula, Carmel has one of the West's most desirable climates. Pleasant weather for most outdoor activities is the rule, except during **winter**. Then, days and evenings are cool, but seldom include a frost of any consequence. Occasional heavy rainstorms during this season contribute well over half of the average annual precipitation. **Spring** marks the beginning of many months of mild weather for enjoying outdoor activities in light sportswear. The appeal of warm days, cool evenings, and diminishing showers is offset somewhat by sea breezes and coastal fog common during this season, however. **Summer** weather is excellent. In addition to uniformly warm days and cool nights, there is no rainfall. But, coastal fog is recurrent in this naturally air conditioned seaside playground at this most popular time of year. **Fall** is an improvement of summer, with less fog and daytime temperatures early in the season that are normally the year's highest. Splendid conditions continue until around Thanksgiving, when the rainy season begins again in earnest.

ATTRACTIONS & DIVERSIONS

★ **Bicycling**

Valley Cycle Center *4 mi. SE on Carmel Valley Rd. at Valley Hills Ctr.*   *624-5107*
This place rents bicycles by the hour and has information on local routes, including one of the world's finest bicycle rides — the Seventeen Mile Drive that winds through Pebble Beach from Carmel. Even though it is primarily an auto route, bicyclists are allowed to use it at most times and are not required to pay the non-resident vehicle toll.

★ **Big Sur Coast**   *S for approximately 80 mi. on CA 1*
California Highway 1 is a narrow, paved two-lane road that winds and dips along the flanks of a mountain wilderness rising precipitously from an unspoiled shoreline. This is one of the nation's most exhilarating scenic drives. Numerous hiking trails lead from roadside parking areas into groves of redwoods and fern-shaded canyons, and to remote sandy beaches and coves. Well-located state parks along the route offer splendid camping and picnicking opportunities. Unique galleries, restaurants, and lodgings blend harmoniously with the unforgettable scenery.

★ **Carmel Beach Town Park**   *.3 mi. W at the foot of Ocean Av.*
Between the business district and the ocean at Carmel Bay is a town park featuring a pine-studded slope of fine, dazzlingly white sand. The picturesque beach backed by this splendid sand dune is a wonderful place for strolling, picnicking and sunbathing. Ocean swimming is unpopular because of the undertow and cold water.

★ **Carmel Mission**   *1 mi. S off CA 1 at 3080 Rio Rd.*   *624-3600*
Mission San Carlos Borromeo del Rio Carmelo is one of the most authentic links to early California history. Established on a site overlooking the mouth of the Carmel River in 1770 by Father Junipero Serra ("father of the California missions"), it was his residence and headquarters until his death in 1784. He is buried beneath the church floor in front of the altar. The carefully restored mission's museum has a notable collection of his memorabilia and other early relics.

★ **Carmel River State Beach**   *1 mi. S on Scenic Rd.*
A photogenic ocean beach composed of fine, sparkling white sand is an inviting attraction for beachcombers, picnickers, and sunbathers. Swimming is regarded as unsafe because of currents, but most bathers would find the water too cold anyway.

Golf

★   **Pebble Beach Golf Links**   *2 mi. NW on Seventeen Mile Dr.*   *624-3811*
The home course of the Crosby Pro-Am Tournament is ranked as one of the ten best 18-hole championship golf courses in the nation. It is also one of the most picturesque anywhere. With reservations, it is open to the public with all facilities and rentals.

★   **Rancho Canada Golf Course**   *2 mi. SE on Carmel Valley Rd.*   *624-0111*
Two scenic 18-hole championship golf courses are open to the public year-round with all facilities and rentals.

★   **Spyglass Hill Golf Course**   *3 mi. NW on Stevenson Dr.*   *624-3811*
This Robert Trent Jones-designed championship 18-hole golf course in Pebble Beach is ranked among the nation's top forty. The spectacularly beautiful facility is open to the public with reservations. All facilities and rentals are available.

★ **Horseback Riding**
Horses can be rented by the hour or longer for scenic rides in Pebble Beach, the Big Sur, or Carmel Valley. For more information and reservations, contact:

Big Sur Trail Rides	*667-2666*
Pebble Beach Equestrian Center	*624-2756*
Whiffletree Ranch	*659-2670*

★ **Library**   *downtown at Ocean Av. & Lincoln St.*   *624-4629*
The Harrison Memorial Library, behind a tiny garden park on the main street, is an outstanding little public library. High arched windows on one side of the large main room allow sunlight to fill the vaulted space, and provide a charming view of a colorful garden. A great stone fireplace is used during the winter, and upholstered chairs in the periodical reading area are very popular. Closed Sun.

★ **Point Lobos State Reserve**   *4 mi. S off CA 1*   *624-4909*
One of the most beautiful spots on the Pacific coast, the reserve includes six miles of
rugged picturesque coastline. There are headlands, Sea Lion Rocks, a natural grove of
Monterey cypress, and Bird Island is just offshore. Unfortunately, poison oak is also
naturally abundant, so hikers should be wary while using scenic shoreline trails.
Numerous viewpoints are good places to watch the antics of sea lions and sea otters.
Whale watching is also popular from the headlands when the awesome animals pass by
here close to shore on their annual 12,000 mile migration to Baja California each winter.
Other attractions include a choice of shady or sunny picnic sites, tidepools teeming with
marine life, secluded sandy beach coves, and shoreline fishing spots.

★ **Scenic Road**   *S for approximately 2 mi. from foot of Ocean Av.*
Whether walking, bicycling, or driving, this aptly named street delights everyone who uses
it. Through green tunnels created by overhanging branches of majestic pines, past tiny
rockbound coves and white sand beaches, unusual residences and colorful flower
gardens, the route follows the shoreline to a panoramic viewpoint overlooking the mouth
of Carmel River and the Big Sur beyond.

★ **Seventeen Mile Drive**   *just N via Carmel Way*
One of the world's great scenic drives meanders through Pebble Beach and along the
magnificent coastline between Carmel and Pacific Grove. It is a toll road except to
bicyclists and residents. In addition to unforgettable seascapes, highlights include Pebble
Beach's stately homes and legendary golf courses. Gnarled trees clinging to rocky
headlands at The Lone Cypress and Cypress Point are among the West's most
photographed landmarks.

Warm Water Features
  Blackthorne Spas   *11 mi. SE off Carmel Valley Rd. at 4 Pilot Rd.*   *659-3241*
Several nicely landscaped hot tub enclosures, featuring open air privacy, redwood decks,
hydrotherapy jets, soft music, and showers are rented by the hour every day until
midnight.

Winery
★   **Chateau Julien**   *6 mi. E at 8940 Carmel Valley Rd.*   *624-2600*
One of the central coast's newest wineries is concentrating on the production of several
premium wines, primarily from grapes grown elsewhere in the county. Impressive
craftsmanship is apparent in the handsome new chateau-style winery building. Visitors
may sample various wines during tours, by appointment only. Tasting, tours, and sales
8:30-5 weekdays, 10-5 Saturday, 12-5 Sunday.

SHOPPING

The enormously popular downtown area of Carmel is unique. No other place has so many
distinctive specialty shops, galleries, and restaurants in so little space with as little
conventional commercialism. By banning tall or massive buildings, parking structures
and meters, bright lights, and billboards, emphasis has been successfully focused on
artistic landscaping and personalized architectural details. As a result, an enchanting
human scale has evolved that still somehow accommodates ever-increasing hordes of
shoppers and strollers.

Food Specialties

Bagel Bakery   *1.5 mi. SE at 173 Crossroads Blvd.*   *625-5180*
An assortment of New York-style bagels are served to take out, or in a small cafe with
coffee, omelets, and other light fare.

Bud's of San Francisco   *1.5 mi. SE at 121 Crossroads Blvd.*   *624-4446*
The Monterey Peninsula's first outlet for this highly-regarded San Francisco ice cream
offers a variety of chilly treats in a small new takeout shop.

★ **Carmel Bakery**   *downtown on Ocean Av. near Lincoln St.*   *624-6265*
It's fun just to look at the whimsical creations made of edible bakery products, and to taste
samples that are usually provided. But the real feature is a fine assortment of
international pastries (like scones and croissants), breads, and cakes. They may be
purchased to enjoy with coffee at one of the few tables, or to go.

Carmel Vintage Shoppe   *downtown at Dolores St. & 7th Av.*   *624-3895*
Premium California wines are well-represented and attractively displayed in this shop.

★ **Carmel Wine & Cheese Co.**   *1.5 mi. SE at 145 Crossroads Blvd.*   614-2486
A noteworthy selection of California wines is beautifully displayed, and selected wines can be sampled at the tasting bar. There are also many cheeses, pates, and other gourmet items like Lavash — an Armenian sandwich sold by the inch.

★ **The Cheese Shop**   *downtown off Ocean Av. near Junipero Av.*   625-2272
A good selection of cheeses and several splendid pates are highlights among the many gourmet foods and premium California wines featured here.

★ **Mediterranean Market**   *downtown at Ocean Av. & Mission St.*   624-2022
A tantalizing array of imported and domestic food delicacies provides a treat for the senses in this colorful store. Specialties include cheeses, sausages, breads, and a good selection of wines.

★ **Monterey Baking Co.**   *1.5 mi. SE at 107 Crossroads Blvd.*   624-0929
Delicious croissants and other European pastries are featured along with sourdough and French breads at the most notable new outlet of a burgeoning bakery chain.

★ **Mrs. M's Fudge**   *downtown at 6th Av. & Mission St.*   624-5331
Fudge in all kinds of enticing flavors is made on the premises and attractively displayed in this shop.

★ **Nielsen Brothers Market**   *downtown at San Carlos St. & 7th Av.*   624-6441
Top quality produce and a full line of gourmet foods are showcased in this epicurean haven. A fine selection of premium California wine is another specialty, and tastes of several are sold at the wine bar each day.

Sylvia's Danish Pastry Shop   *1.5 mi. SE at 3650 the Barnyard*   624-1198
Danish and French pastries are served in a pleasant little European-style tea room with coffee, or to go.

Specialty Shops
★ **The Barnyard**   *1.5 mi. SE off CA 1 and Carmel Valley Rds.*   624-8886
Here is the state of the art in recreational shopping. Profusions of flowers, music, and intriguing fountains and sculptures lend enchantment to a cluster of Western barn-style buildings housing more than sixty fine specialty shops, galleries, and restaurants.

★ **Books, Inc.**   *downtown on Ocean Av. near Mission St.*   625-2550
The largest bookstore in the area displays a full line of hardcovers and paperbacks in a bright, well-organized environment.

★ **Carmel Art Association Galleries** *downtown at Dolores St. & 6th Av.*   624-6176
One of Carmel's most esteemed art complexes is set apart by a beautifully landscaped garden setting. Eight galleries exhibit paintings, graphic art, and sculpture by association members, some of whom are renowned.

★ **Carmel Plaza**   *downtown at Ocean Av. & Mission St.*
A compact two-level complex in the heart of downtown offers an assortment of specialty shops and restaurants built around a handsomely landscaped interior courtyard.

★ **Crossroads**   *1.5 mi. SE off CA 1 & Rio Rd.*   625-3165
Carmel's newest major shopping complex is a colorful mosaic of contemporary California architecture and landscaping. A prominent Westminster chiming clock and bell tower is the centerpiece for what will eventually be an array of more than one hundred distinctive specialty shops and restaurants.

★ **Highlands Gallery of Sculpture**   *3 mi. S at CA 1/Fern Canyon Rd.*   624-0535
This captivating little gallery is devoted entirely to sculpture by more than a dozen well-known sculptors. Large pieces in wood, stone, and metal are displayed to maximum advantage in an adjacent oak-shaded garden.

★ **Thunderbird Bookshop**   *1.5 mi. SE at 3600 the Barnyard*   624-1803
One of the West's most remarkable bookstores has a large and excellent book selection. Shelves also line one wall in a casual adjacent dining room, where patrons are free to eat, drink, browse and read.

★ **Other galleries**   *throughout downtown*
There are about seventy galleries in Carmel offering an awesome assortment of works in all media. Many are excellent. Most are concentrated within two blocks of Ocean Avenue between Mission and Monte Verde Streets. A complete list and map is available from the Chamber of Commerce.

NIGHTLIFE

Carmel has several intimate, romantic places to enjoy a quiet drink, and dancing to live music is featured in nearby Carmel Valley. Movies, live theater, and concerts also contribute to life after dark throughout the year.

★ **The Cypress Lounge**   *2 mi. NW off Seventeen Mile Dr.*   *624-3811*
In the Lodge at Pebble Beach, dancing to live music is featured on weekends in the plush lounge. Jackets are required.

★ **Forest Theater**   *downtown at Mt. View Av. & Santa Rita St.*   *624-1531*
Carmel's oldest theater has been in existence for more than seventy years. It is still the setting for theater classics and occasional new plays on Thursday thru Saturday evenings. The natural outdoor locale has a special magic enhanced by two big outdoor firepits.

★ **Forge in the Forest**   *downtown at 5th Av. & Junipero Av.*   *624-2233*
One of Carmel's most popular watering holes has an ornate wooden bar and intriguing copper walls that gleam in the light of the room's fireplace. A pub menu is served here and on an intimate fireplace-warmed patio.

★ **Highlands Inn**   *4 mi. S on CA 1*   *624-3801*
The resort's incomparable new cocktail lounge has a window-wall with an awe-inspiring seacoast panorama. A grand piano is played nightly for patrons ensconced in glove-leather armchairs.

★ **Hog's Breath**   *downtown off San Carlos St. between 5th & 6th Avs.*   *625-1044*
The tiny bar in Clint Eastwood's well-known restaurant smells seductively like a wine cellar. Drinks are also served with hors d'oeuvres in the flickering firelight of a romantic courtyard backed by an artistic wall-sized mural of a Carmel scene.

Maxwell McFly's   *downtown on Ocean Av. near San Carlos St.*   *624-2515*
An attractive back bar, stained glass, and antique fans come together nicely in this popular watering hole.

The Other Place   *1.5 mi. SE at 3770 the Barnyard*   *625-0340*
Recently opened above Andre's, both the Other Place and Sundeck Garden Bar feature adult ice cream drinks and fresh fruit cocktails in a contemporary plants-and-wood setting. Furnishings include free-form redwood tables and benches and padded bar stools. Light meals are served all day.

Sade's   *downtown on Ocean Av. at Lincoln St.*   *624-9990*
The oldest bar in Carmel offers cozy atmosphere and comfortable sofas with an unusual outlook on the main street.

Studio Theatre Restaurant   *downtown on Dolores St. near Ocean Av.*   *624-1661*
A choice of two entrees accompanies the productions featured Thursday thru Sunday evenings in this intimate dinner theater.

Sunset Center Theater   *downtown at San Carlos St. & 9th Av.*   *624-3996*
Carmel's charming old cultural center has a theater that features plays, films, concerts, and lectures at different times year-round.

RESTAURANTS

Fine dining is an enduring passion in Carmel. Residents and visitors alike zealously seek out new "finds," and relish returning to old favorites among a mind-boggling array of delightful alternatives. The village probably has the most remarkable concentration of notable restaurants in the West.

Adobe Inn (Bully III)   *downtown at Dolores St. & 8th Av.*   *625-1750*
L-D.   *Moderate*
The specialty is prime rib cut to order. A salad bar, steak, and seafood are also offered. Comfortable English pub atmosphere is enhanced by intimate views of oak trees and cypress just beyond a window-wall. "Early Bird" dinners are very popular, as is a handsome lounge featuring well-prepared short order items.

★ **Andre's**   *1.5 mi. SE at 3770 the Barnyard*   *625-0447*
L-D. Closed Tues.   *Expensive*
Fresh fish and wild game are among Continental specialties served amidst luxuriant plants and Old World stained glass, chandeliers, and hardwoods. One dining room features the intimate elegance of well-appointed enclosed booths.

★ **Anton & Michel**   *downtown on Mission St. between Ocean & 7th Avs.*   *624-2406*
L-D.   *Expensive*
Gourmet cuisine carefully prepared by Swiss chefs is complemented by a dignified Old
World setting overlooking the Court of the Fountains. There is also a pleasant lounge with
a fireplace.

The Bayou Cafe   *downtown at Mission St. & 5th Av.*   *624-6769*
L-D. Closed Wed.   *Expensive*
Authentic New Orleans-style cuisine has finally found a Carmel showcase in this bright
and lively new restaurant.

Butcher Shop   *downtown on Ocean Av. between Dolores & Lincoln Sts.*   *624-2569*
D only.   *Expensive*
Cooking is over an oak wood pit broiler. The place is often jammed with customers in spite
of an overabundance of tables crowded into a dimly-lit combination dining room/bar.

Carmel Cafe   *downtown at Mission St. & 6th Av.*   *624-1922*
B-L.   *Moderate*
This small American-style cafe is a popular destination for country breakfasts, omelets,
and other light fare plus homemade desserts.

Carmel Epicurean   *downtown at Dolores St. & 7th Av.*   *625-4332*
L-D. No D on Mon.   *Moderate*
An eclectic menu of light Continental fare is featured in a comfortable new restaurant
that also sports an extensive wine list.

★ **Casanova**   *downtown on 5th Av. between San Carlos & Mission Sts.*   *625-0501*
B-L-D.   *Expensive*
Country fresh French and Italian cuisine is served amidst casual elegance in several tiny
rooms or on the enclosed garden patio. The homemade pasta, baked goods, and desserts
are especially notable.

★ **Chez Danielle**   *downtown off San Carlos St. near 7th Av.*   *625-1151*
B-L.   *Moderate*
Hidden away in a charming courtyard is one of the West's best breakfast places. Omelets,
crepes, and specialty dishes like "The Cloud" are outstanding. The tiny stylish restaurant
is thoroughly contemporary, with courtyard views and bunches of flowers for accents.

★ **Chez Felix**   *downtown on Monte Verde St. between Ocean & 7th Avs.*   *624-4707*
D only. Closed Sun.   *Expensive*
Traditional French cuisine is skillfully prepared from ingredients selected fresh each
morning and served amidst intimate French Provincial decor in a long-established little
restaurant.

★ **Clam Box**   *downtown on Mission St. between 5th & 6th Avs.*   *624-8597*
D only. Closed Mon. & 3 wks. at Christmas.   *Moderate*
The fresh seafood served here is regarded as some of the best on the entire peninsula.
Everything is carefully prepared, including homemade baked goods and desserts, in this
extremely popular little place.

★ **Creme Carmel**   *downtown at San Carlos St. & 7th Av.*   *624-0444*
L-D.   *Expensive*
The short menu changes frequently, but the New California-style dishes are always fresh,
innovative, and delicious in this refreshingly understated new restaurant.

Em Le's Restaurant   *downtown on Dolores St. near 5th Av.*   *625-6780*
B-L.   *Moderate*
The nutty waffles served here are the reason to try this unassuming little coffee shop for
breakfast. Homemade pies are the other specialty among conventional American fare.

★ **Fish House on the Park**   *downtown at 6th & Junipero Avs.*   *625-1766*
D only. Closed Tues.   *Expensive*
Fresh, locally caught or imported seafood delicacies are featured. Continental specialties
are also offered. Plush contemporary furnishings are enhanced by a view of Carmel's
serene downtown park. A tropical saltwater aquarium distinguishes an adjoining cozy
lounge.

Flaherty's   *downtown on 6th Av. near Dolores St.*   *624-0311*
L-D.   *Moderate*
Simply prepared fresh seafood is the crowd-pleaser in a disarmingly plain little restaurant
where the lively, congested atmosphere resembles a modern Eastern-style seafood house.

★ **French Poodle**   *downtown on Junipero & 5th Avs.*   *624-8643*
D only. Closed Sun.   *Expensive*
Highly regarded French cuisine including homemade pastries is formally presented in this
plush, romantic restaurant. Jackets are required.

Friar Tuck's Restaurant   *downtown at Dolores St. & 5th Av.*   *624-4274*
B-L.   *Moderate*
Assorted omelets served with homemade biscuits or blueberry muffins are a breakfast
highlight in this modest cafe presided over by an enigmatic replica of the friar himself.

From Scratch   *1.5 mi. SE at 3626 the Barnyard*   *625-2448*
B-L.   *Moderate*
Fresh, innovative dishes live up to the restaurant's name. The pleasant country-style
dining room is enhanced by a large working fireplace and patio-view windows.

General Store   *downtown at 5th & Junipero Avs.*   *624-2233*
L-D.   *Moderate*
New California cuisine is served in a casual, comfortable dining room, or on an artistically
landscaped patio with a fireplace.

Giuliano's   *downtown on Mission St. near 5th Av.*   *625-5231*
D only.   *Expensive*
Northern Italian cuisine is the specialty in a pink-and-pretty little dining room where full
linen service and mirrored walls lend casual elegance to closely-spaced banquettes and
tables.

★ **Glen Oaks**   *25 mi. S on CA 1 - Big Sur*   *667-2623*
D only. Sun. brunch. Closed Mon.   *Expensive*
Skillfully prepared Continental and American cuisine is presented in a beautifully
appointed firelit dining room in this acclaimed restaurant.

★ **Highland's Inn**   *4 mi. S on CA 1*   *624-3801*
B-L-D.   *Expensive*
Contemporary American dishes accompany what is arguably the world's finest seascape
view from a public restaurant. The plush, comfortable new dining room is big, so guests
should request on a window table when making reservations, especially for the extremely
popular Sunday brunch. All of the new public rooms in this famous country motor inn are
brilliant examples of the state of the art in contemporary architecture and decor.

★ **Hog's Breath Inn**   *downtown off San Carlos St. between 5th & 6th Avs.*   *625-1044*
L-D.   *Moderate*
Clint Eastwood's wood-and-stone one-of-a-kind restaurant offers good American food in
intimate firelit dining rooms, or in an adjoining romantic courtyard warmed by fireplaces
and heat lamps and overseen by a charming Carmel mural.

Jack London's Bar & Bistro   *downtown off San Carlos St. near 5th Av.*   *624-2336*
L-D.   *Moderate*
A popular rendezvous, this likably cluttered little bistro serves light meals into the wee
hours.

★ **Katy's Place**   *downtown on Mission St. between 5th & 6th Avs.*   *624-0199*
B-L.   *Moderate*
The owner of this glorified coffee shop has a wonderful way with hearty American fare
made from fresh local ingredients like Monterey Bay prawns. Delicious omelets and other
breakfast specialties are served all day.

★ **La Boheme**   *downtown on Dolores St. near 7th Av.*   *624-7500*
D only.   *Moderate*
One meal is served family-style nightly. The European country cooking involves careful
preparation of the freshest available produce. Colorful, congested Old World atmosphere
is a distinctive accompaniment to the delicious food.

Le Bistro   *downtown on San Carlos St. between Ocean & 7th Avs.*   *624-6545*
B-L-D. No D on Sun.   *Low*
Light European specialties are emphasized, including egg crepe omelets, buttermilk waffles, and fondue. Many plants, a fireplace, and a tiny patio enhance this convivial sidewalk cafe.

Le Coq d'Or   *downtown on Mission St. near 5th Av.*   *624-4613*
D only.   *Moderate*
A limited variety of carefully prepared French gourmet entrees and baked goods made on the premises are features of this casually elegant, congested little restaurant.

★ **L'Escargot**   *downtown at Mission St. & 4th Av.*   *624-4914*
D only. Closed Sun.   *Expensive*
Classic French gourmet cuisine is the highlight of a restaurant with a long-standing reputation for fashionable excellence. The tastefully appointed dining room exudes plush Gallic charm.

★ **The Lodge at Pebble Beach**   *2 mi. NW via 17 Mile Dr. on Cypress Dr.*   *625-1880*
L-D. Closed Mon.   *Expensive*
The Cypress Room is the Lodge's original grand dining room, and formal elegance still accompanies an outstanding view of the famed golf course and Carmel Bay. Downstairs in the Club XIX, the atmosphere is casual for lunch, with terrace service available. In the evening, gourmet French dinners are presented in a setting of formal opulence. Jackets are required for dinner.

★ **The Marquis**   *downtown on San Carlos St. at 9th Av.*   *624-8068*
D only. Closed Sun.   *Expensive*
Flaming dishes are featured, along with Continental gourmet cuisine and homemade pastries. The atmosphere is formally elegant with some romantic touches like long white tapers in silver candle holders.

★ **Patisserie Boissiere**   *downtown on Mission St. between Ocean & 7th Avs.*   *624-5008*
B-L-D.   *Moderate*
An excellent selection of French baked goods is always displayed, and a Continental breakfast is served all day in this charming little restaurant with a fireplace, fresh flowers, and patio dining.

The Peppercorn   *1.5 mi. SE in the Barnyard*   *625-1070*
B-L.   *Moderate*
Breakfast omelets are served all day, along with other light foods and homemade desserts in a congested contemporary cafe with a picture window view of gardens in the Barnyard shopping complex. A high-tech kitchenware shop adjoins.

Pine Inn   *downtown on Ocean Av. between Lincoln & Monte Verde Sts.*   *624-3851*
B-L-D.   *Expensive*
Carmel's downtown landmark hotel offers American specialties in a large dining room furnished in posh Victorian decor or in an innovative contemporary courtyard covered by a spectacular glass dome. A comfortable lounge adjoins.

Plaza Cafe   *downtown on Ocean Av. near San Carlos St.*   *624-4433*
B-L-D.   *Moderate*
Contemporary American and European dishes are given a light touch in an attractively updated coffee shop with casual indoor and outdoor seating.

★ **Quail Lodge**   *4 mi. SE off Carmel Valley Rd.*   *624-1581*
D only.   *Expensive*
Continental cuisine is served in the Covey, a showplace of contemporary elegance with beautifully appointed, well-spaced tables overlooking a lake and lush gardens of the renowned lodge. Jackets are required.

★ **Raffaello**   *downtown on Mission St. between Ocean & 7th Av.*   *624-1541*
D only. Closed Tues. and Dec.   *Expensive*
Acclaimed Northern Italian haute cuisine is the forte, along with notable homemade desserts. The fireplace-and-candlelight atmosphere is formally elegant, and jackets are required in one of Carmel's favorite and most prestigious restaurants.

★ **The Rio Grill**   *1.5 mi. SE at 101 Crossroads Blvd.*   *625-5436*
L-D.   *Moderate*
Exquisitely prepared New California cuisine attracts enthusiastic crowds to this paragon of Post-Modern dining. Changing specials highlight seasonally fresh ingredients in innovative ways. An abundance of crisp white linens and casually elegant table settings blend smoothly with pastel colored walls accented by bold floral pictures. Premium wines can be purchased by the glass in the dining rooms and in the popular lounge.

Robata Grill and Sake Bar   *1.5 mi. SE at 3658 the Barnyard*   *624-2643*
D only.   *Moderate*
Modern Japanese dishes, including a colorful sushi bar showcased at a massive redwood counter, are served in rooms comfortably furnished with padded booths and redwood tables. Outside, an open firepit is a feature of the landscaped patio.

Royal Danish Bakery   *downtown on San Carlos St. near 7th Av.*   *624-3667*
B-L.   *Moderate*
Light meals and Scandinavian pastry are served in a little coffee shop or on a charming landscaped patio above the street.

St. Tropez   *downtown on Junipero Av. between 5th & 6th Avs.*   *624-9018*
D only. Closed Tues.   *Moderate*
Hearty French dishes and showy homemade desserts are served in congested, nicely-appointed dining rooms.

★ **Sans Souci**   *downtown on Lincoln St. between 5th & 6th Avs.*   *624-6220*
D only. Closed Sun.   *Moderate*
Gourmet French cuisine is served amid comfortably elegant decor accented by a wood-burning fireplace, classical music, and well-spaced tables set with tall white candles and fresh flowers.

Shabu Shabu *downtown on Mission St. near Ocean Av. in Carmel Plaza*   *625-2828*
D only. Closed Tues.   *Expensive*
Japanese specialties are cooked in a traditional clay pot at the table. Distinctive wooden cubicles provide an illusion of privacy in this lovely Japanese country-style restaurant.

★ **Simpson's**   *downtown at San Carlos St. & 5th Av.*   *624-1238*
D only.   *Expensive*
Classic, traditional American fare including fresh homemade baked goods has been served in this big, bustling, very popular restaurant since 1946.

Swiss Tavern Restaurant   *downtown on Lincoln St. near 5th Av.*   *624-5994*
D only.   *Moderate*
Traditional Swiss dishes are offered amidst European decor in a modest little upstairs dining room.

★ **Tuck Box Tea Room** *downtown on Dolores St. between Ocean Av. & 7th Av.*   *624-6365*
B-L & afternoon tea. Closed Mon. & Tues. Moderate
Everything served on the limited menu is fresh and homemade. The thatched-cottage motif of this tiny English tea room is as picturesque as the food is good. There is almost always a waiting line, even when the quaint little courtyard is used.

Ventana Inn   *28 mi. S off CA 1*   *667-2331*
L-D.   *Expensive*
International dishes are served in a handsome contemporary dining room. The main attraction, however, is an expansive patio where meals and drinks are served with an unforgettable view of the Big Sur coast.

Wagon Wheel   *4 mi. SE on Carmel Valley Rd.*   *624-8878*
B-L.   *Moderate*
Generous portions of hearty American food are offered in a rustic little Old West-style coffee shop that is especially popular for breakfast.

Will's Fargo   *12 mi. SE on Carmel Valley Rd.*   *659-2774*
D only. Closed Mon.   *Expensive*
Steaks cut to the customer's specifications have been the specialty here for a quarter of a century. These and a few other entrees are served with simple American-style accompaniments and homemade baked goods in casual, comfortable dining rooms.

LODGING

The wonderful little inns of Carmel capture the romantic spirit for which the village is renowned. Most of these beguiling havens are within an easy stroll of both the heart of town and the beach. Even the larger motel-style accommodations are distinctively decorated, prettily landscaped, and oriented toward seascapes or town views. Rooms in town are all relatively expensive and inevitably full on weekends and throughout summer. Reservations at these times are appropriate. While there are almost no bargain rooms, off-season non-weekend rates are often reduced at least 20% below those shown.

★ **Adobe Inn**   *downtown at Dolores St. & 8th Av.*   624-3933
This newer contemporary motor inn features a small pool and sauna, and has a covered garage, a restaurant, and lounge. Each spacious, lavishly furnished room has a wood-burning fireplace, refrigerator, cable color TV, phone, and private patio or deck nestled among oaks and pines. A complimentary Continental breakfast is offered.

    #29,#30,#37 — fine ocean views,   K bed...$88
    regular room —   K bed...$80

Candlelight Inn   *downtown on San Carlos St. between 4th & 5th Avs.*   624-6451
The grounds are nicely landscaped and there is a small pool in this attractive motel. Each room has a phone, cable color TV, and a refrigerator.

    deluxe unit — fireplace,   K bed...$75
    regular room —   Q bed...$65

Carmel River Inn   *1.5 mi. SE on CA 1*   624-1575
The small Carmel River is adjacent to this modern motel. Each room has a phone and cable color TV.

    "riverside rooms" — 2nd (top) floor, view deck above river,   K bed...$38
    regular room — cottage,   Q bed...$32

Carmel Sands Lodge   *downtown at San Carlos St. & 5th Av.*   624-1255
This contemporary motel has an outdoor pool and a popular restaurant. All rooms have cable color TV and a phone.

    #20 — gas fireplace, balc. above st., some ocean view,   K bed...$70
    #21 — four-poster bed, balc. above st., gas fireplace,   Q bed...$68
    regular room —   D bed...$48

★ **Carriage House Inn** *downtown on Junipero Av. between 7th & 8th Avs.*   625-2585
Early American furnishings, handmade quilts, original oil paintings, brass beds, and bay windows are some of the embellishments in this newer, elegant little motor inn. All of the beautifully furnished rooms have wood-burning fireplaces, sunken-tiled baths, refrigerators, cable color TV, and phones. A complimentary Continental breakfast is brought to the room, along with the morning paper.

    #8 — corner, many large windows with pvt. oak view,   K bed...$95
    #3 — unusually spacious, spectacularly furnished,   K bed..$100
    regular room — small,   K bed...$70

Cypress Inn   *downtown at Lincoln St. & 7th Av.*   624-3871
Built around a delightful courtyard, this large older inn exudes Mediterranean charm. All rooms have color TV and phones, and a complimentary Continental breakfast is offered. The romantic tower room, usually booked months in advance, is probably the only **bargain** in Carmel.

    "Tower" — tiny room, shared bath, 270° view over downtown,   D bed...$20
    #219 — corner suite with big windows, pvt. tub/shower,   K bed...$80
    regular room — pvt. bath,   D bed...$39

Forest Lodge   *downtown at Ocean Av. & Torres St.*   624-7023
A tiny motor lodge in a choice location features three units in three buildings. Each has a bath, phone, cable color TV, and refrigerator.

    "Guest House" — spacious, big fireplace, view window/alcove,   Q bed...$90
    "Garrett" — upstairs, windows on 3 sides, village/ocean view, 2 D beds...$75
    regular room "Cottage" — 1 BR, kitchenette,   Q bed...$75

★ **Highlands Inn**   *4 mi. S on CA 1*   624-3801
One of the world's most magnificent coastal panoramas is the highlight of this large,
wonderfully updated resort hotel high above the Big Sur coast. The new public rooms —
lobby, restaurant, lounge — are outstanding examples of opulent contemporary decor
beautifully blended with an awesome setting. The landscaped grounds also include a large
outdoor pool and whirlpool, plus saunas. Each spacious, luxuriously furnished new unit
has a phone and cable color TV with movies.
    #19,#18,#9,#8,#17,#4 — fireplace, kit., lg. pvt. balc., raised in-bedroom whirlpool,
                pitched roof, floor/ceiling windows, awesome
                coastal view,   K bed..$190
    regular room — in lodge, some have a view or a fireplace,   Q bed...$95

Hofsas House   *downtown at San Carlos St. & 4th Av.*   624-2745
Behind the alpine-chalet facade is a large, attractively furnished modern chateau with a
scenic outdoor pool and a sauna. Each of the spacious rooms has cable color TV and a
phone.
    "fireplace unit" (there are 4) — gas or Franklin fireplace, pvt. balc.,   K bed...$88
    regular room —   Q bed...$55

★ **Horizon Inn**   *downtown at Junipero & 3rd Avs.*   624-5327
This is a small contemporary motel with colorful landscaping, an outdoor pool, and some
fine panoramic views. All rooms have a phone, cable color TV, and a refrigerator. A
complimentary Continental breakfast is brought to the room.
    #19,#21 — end, pvt. balc., gas fireplace, panoramic view,   K bed...$105
    #1 — end, pvt. balc., gas fireplace, fine view,   K bed...$92
    regular room —   K bed...$72

★ **Jade Tree Inn**   *downtown at Junipero & 6th Avs.*   624-1831
On a rise above the village center, this large contemporary motel features panoramic
views, and has an outdoor pool. Each room has cable color TV and a phone.
    #58 — gas fireplace, balc., panoramic view to ocean,   K bed...$65
    #55,#57,#59 — gas fireplace, balc., fine view,   K bed...$65
    regular room —   Q bed...$42

★ **La Playa Hotel**   *downtown at Camino Real & 8th Av.*   624-6476
Carmel's hideaway hotel is in a tranquil location convenient to both the beach and
downtown. Completely remodeled in 1984, the large landmark is a showplace of lavish
dining and drinking facilities, and dramatically landscaped grounds with an outdoor pool.
Each beautifully furnished room has a phone, cable color TV, and a refrigerator.
    #170,#172 — fireplace, near the pool,   K bed..$115
    regular room — some have town or ocean view,   Q or K bed...$90

★ **Lodge at Pebble Beach**   *2 mi. NW via 17 Mile Dr. on Cypress Dr.*   624-3811
This large, world famous resort has a magnificent oceanfront location and a remarkable
variety of amenities, including (for a fee) an 18-hole golf course, par-3 golf, fifteen tennis
courts, and horseback riding. An outdoor pool, sauna, beach and hiking trails are free to
guests. There are also acclaimed restaurants. All of the well-furnished rooms include a
refrigerator, cable color TV, and a phone.
    "fireplace room" —   2 Q beds...$160
    regular room —   Q bed...$160

Monte Verde Inn *downtown on Monte Verde St. between Ocean & 7th Avs.*   624-6046
A lovely old inn in the heart of the village has a garden patio and a variety of distinctive
rooms, each with a private bath.
    #2 — top corner room, bright, pvt. ocean view,   Q bed...$55
    #4 — spacious, fireplace, kit., pvt. balc., view of oaks/town,   Q bed...$75
    regular room —   2 T or D bed...$50

Ocean View Lodge   *downtown at Junipero & 3rd Avs.*   624-7723
A small, nicely landscaped motel offers spacious units comfortably furnished in Early
American decor. Each unit has a fully equipped kitchen, a living room with a wood-
burning fireplace, cable color TV, and a phone.
    #6 — good ocean view,   Q bed..$100
    #4 — some ocean view,   K bed...$90
    regular unit —   Q bed...$85

★ **Pine Inn** *downtown on Ocean Av. between Lincoln & Monte Verde Sts.*   *624-3851*
Carmel's main street landmark is a handsome turn-of-the-century hotel. Elegant Victorian furnishings grace the lobby, public areas, and restaurants. A newer courtyard restaurant with a dramatic roll-back roof is especially notable. All of the tastefully decorated rooms have cable color TV, a phone, and bath.

"Fireplace Suite" — refr., ocean view,	K bed...$110
regular room —	D bed...$50

★ **Quail Lodge**   *4 mi. SE on Carmel Valley Rd.*   *624-1581*
This renowned resort is a study in contemporary luxury. Deep in Carmel Valley, no expense was spared to create an ultimate leisure retreat. Manicured grounds provide a lovely setting for a picturesque 18-hole golf course, four tennis courts, three outdoor pools, a whirlpool, and rental bicycles. The main building houses a fine restaurant and lounge. Each of the expansive, sumptuously furnished rooms includes cable color TV with movies, and a phone.

"balcony room" (there are 6) — gas fireplace, pvt. balc., wet bar/refr.,	K bed...$185
regular "terrace" room —	K bed...$155

★ **Sandpiper Inn**   *1 mi. SW at 2408 Bayview Av.*   *624-4334*
Antiques and fresh flowers fill this small, beautifully maintained half-century-old bed-and-breakfast inn. In a quiet residential area just fifty yards from Carmel Bay, some rooms have fine ocean views. All rooms have private baths and wood-burning fireplaces. A Continental breakfast in the morning and sherry in the evening are complimentary. Ten-speed bicycles are available to guests.

"Dollhouse" — top, corner, some ocean view,	Q bed...$90
"Garden View" — garden view,	Q bed...$95
regular room —	Q bed...$85

Svendsgaard's Inn   *downtown at San Carlos St. & 4th Av.*   *624-1511*
The beautifully oak-shaded grounds of this contemporary motel include an outdoor pool. Each room has a cable color TV, phone, and refrigerator.

#4,#18 — pvt., gas fireplace,	K bed...$72
#10,#17,#37 — gas fireplace, kitchenette,	K bed...$80
regular room —	Q bed...$45

Tally Ho   *downtown at San Carlos St. & 4th Av.*   *624-2232*
Sunny gardens surround this tiny modern country inn. All units are individually furnished, have private baths, and cable color TV.

#5 "Veranda" — fireplace, kitchenette, ocean view deck,	Q bed...$90
"Penthouse" — big fireplace, kitchenette, pvt. view deck,	K bed..$145
regular unit —	Q bed...$75

★ **Tickle Pink Motor Inn**   *4 mi. S on CA 1*   *624-1244*
Spellbinding coastline views are the unforgettable attraction of this contemporary motel. All units have cable color TV, phone, and refrigerator. A complimentary Continental breakfast is offered.

#21,#20 — top fl., spacious, fireplace, lg. balc., pvt. seascape view,	K bed...$115
#28 — split level, fireplace, windows on 2 sides, pvt. seascape view,	Q bed...$115
#14 — 1 BR, enormous suite, fireplace, deck, awesome view,	K bed...$159
#15 — as above, but no fireplace,	K bed...$93
regular room — tree view,	Q bed...$93

★ **Tradewinds**   *downtown at Mission St. & 3rd Av.*   *624-2800*
This delightfully contemporary motel features a large outdoor pool in a lush garden setting. All of the spacious rooms have cable color TV and a phone. A complimentary Continental breakfast is brought to the room.

#D,#19,#20 — gas fireplace, wet bar, pvt. town view balc.,	K bed...$85
regular room —	Q bed...$65

★ **Ventana Big Sur**   *28 mi. S. off CA 1*   *667-2331*
One of the finest examples of Post-Modern architecture and decor in California occupies a hillside high above the awesome Big Sur coast. A large pool, saunas, whirlpools, restaurant and lounge, plus a sunny terrace with a fantastic coastal panorama are features. Each spacious, artistically appointed unit is of unfinished cedar, with a private tree-view terrace, color TV, and phone. A complimentary Continental breakfast is brought to the room.

special unit — Franklin fireplace, wet bar,	K bed...$185
regular room —	Q bed...$145

The Village Inn   *downtown at Ocean & Junipero Avs.*   *624-3864*
This modern motel has tastefully furnished rooms with cable color TV and a phone.

#19B — top, end, gas fireplace, kit., park/downtown views,	K bed...$52
#32 — end, windows on 2 sides, trees/main street views,	K bed...$52
regular room —	Q or K bed...$52

Wayfarer Inn   *downtown at Mission St. & 4th Av.*   *624-2711*
Each of the units in this charming inn/motel has color TV and a phone. Continental breakfast is complimentary.

#16 — top, corner, fireplace, refr., some ocean view,	Q bed...$80
#5 — fireplace, kit., some view,	Q bed...$90
regular room —	Q bed...$55

CAMPGROUNDS
There are only a few campgrounds within many miles of the village. However, one of the West's finest is relatively close in the fabled Big Sur with complete facilities and a magnificent location by a small river deep in a redwood forest near the ocean.

★ **Andrew Molera**   *24 mi. S on CA 1*   *No Phone*
The state operates this uncommon little facility by the Big Sur River as a walk-in campground for tenters only. Trails lead to nearby remote and picturesque ocean beaches, and fishing and swimming in the river are popular. Pit toilets are available. There are no showers. Each site is well-spaced, and some are tree-shaded.   base rate...$3

★ **Pfeiffer - Big Sur State Park**   *27 mi. S on CA 1*   *667-2315*
One of California's most acclaimed state operated campgrounds is strung along a lovely little river in a luxuriant forest accented by majestic redwoods. Numerous well-maintained hiking trails provide easy access to surrounding mountains, a waterfall, and scenic unspoiled beaches along the fabled Big Sur coast. The river is popular for swimming and fishing. Flush toilets, hot showers, and hookups are available. Each well-spaced site in this big facility has a picnic table and a fire area. Most are tree-shaded and some are by the river.   base rate...$5

Saddle Mountain Rec. Park *6 mi. SE via Carmel Valley & Schulte Rd.*   *624-1617*
This privately operated campground has a (fee) pool and a recreation room. Flush toilets, hot showers, and hookups are available. Each site has a picnic table and fire area.
base rate...$10

SPECIAL EVENT
★ **Carmel Bach Festival**   *downtown at Sunset Center*   *late July*
One of the West's most important musical events takes place in the Golden Bough Theater and at Carmel's lovely cultural center. Three weeks of classical concerts and recitals are performed by some of the world's finest musicians before large and enthusiastic audiences.

OTHER INFORMATION
Area Code: *408*

Carmel Business Association *downtown at San Carlos St. & 7th Av.*   *624-2522*
Greater Carmel Chamber of Commerce   *SE on Carmel Valley Rd.*   *659-4000*
Los Padres Nat. For. - Carmel Off. *1.5 mi. SE at CA 1/Carmel Valley Rd.* *624-2246*

Mendocino, California

Elevation:

60 feet

Population (1980):

1,008

Population (1970):

400+

Location:

155 mi. NW
of San Francisco

Mendocino is a lovely little town with a thoroughly romantic appeal. It lies gently on an isolated grassy promontory overlooking a ruggedly beautiful coastline. Whitewashed redwood buildings exude authentic charm in their current roles as studios and galleries, specialty shops, gourmet restaurants, and quaint inns. Many of the buildings have withstood well over a century of rough winter storms sweeping across these unprotected headlands. Fortunately, the weather isn't always bad. In fact, it is predictably fine during the summer, when days are inevitably brisk and occasionally foggy, and there is almost no rainfall. During this season, capacity crowds enjoy exploring the village, beachcombing secluded coves and headlands, hiking scenic coastal trails, or canoeing on the adjoining stream that spills out of a lush green forest of redwoods and firs. People seeking tranquility can find it here during other seasons when the crowds are gone. From fall through spring, a more leisurely pace and the warmth of much-used fireplaces offset normally cool, damp weather.

The town was settled in the 1850s by lumbermen from New England. They recognized the commercial potential for a sawmill on the headland above a deep water anchorage by a river with access to vast adjacent redwood forests. After nearly a century as a mill town, Mendocino began fading into oblivion after the last mill closed during the Depression. Its demise was averted by artists and others who were attracted by the natural beauty of the area, its isolation, and the low cost of housing. They were followed by a more affluent breed of urban escapist. Together these new residents carefully restored and preserved this authentic cluster of clapboard relics. In the 1970s the State of California gave a strong boost to the effort by acquiring the blufftop meadow that had been the millsite between downtown and Mendocino Bay. Both the meadow and nearby Big River Beach will now remain in a natural state free from any development.

Today, a concentration of Yankee-Victorian wood frame buildings is accented by a picturesque profusion of water towers, picket fences, and boardwalks. Some of the carefully refurbished structures house unique specialty shops and galleries displaying fine locally-produced arts and crafts. Others have become romantic restaurants offering gourmet cuisine, or enchanting places to go for live entertainment or a quiet drink. Several of the most impressive old buildings are now distinguished bed-and-breakfast inns lavishly outfitted with local arts and crafts or authentic period pieces.

Mendocino, California
WEATHER PROFILE   *Vokac Weather Rating*

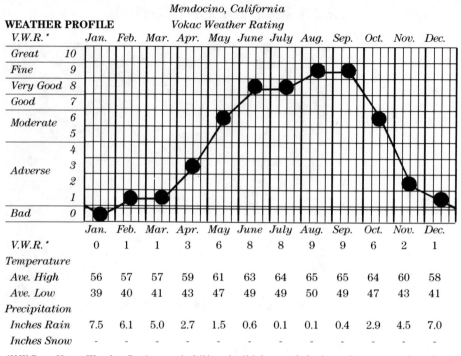

V.W.R.*		Jan.	Feb.	Mar.	Apr.	May	June	July	Aug.	Sep.	Oct.	Nov.	Dec.
Great	10												
Fine	9												
Very Good	8												
Good	7												
Moderate	6												
	5												
	4												
Adverse	3												
	2												
	1												
Bad	0												

	Jan.	Feb.	Mar.	Apr.	May	June	July	Aug.	Sep.	Oct.	Nov.	Dec.
V.W.R.*	0	1	1	3	6	8	8	9	9	6	2	1
Temperature												
Ave. High	56	57	57	59	61	63	64	65	65	64	60	58
Ave. Low	39	40	41	43	47	49	49	50	49	47	43	41
Precipitation												
Inches Rain	7.5	6.1	5.0	2.7	1.5	0.6	0.1	0.1	0.4	2.9	4.5	7.0
Inches Snow	-	-	-	-	-	-	-	-	-	-	-	-

V.W.R. = Vokac Weather Rating: probability of mild (warm & dry) weather on any given day.

Forecast

Month	V.W.R.*		Daytime	Evening	Precipitation
			Temperatures		
January	0	Bad	cool	chilly	continual rainstorms
February	1	Adverse	cool	chilly	continual rainstorms
March	1	Adverse	cool	chilly	continual rainstorms
April	3	Adverse	cool	cool	frequent showers
May	6	Moderate	cool	cool	occasional showers
June	8	Very Good	cool	cool	infrequent showers
July	8	Very Good	cool	cool	none
August	9	Fine	warm	cool	none
September	9	Fine	warm	cool	infrequent showers
October	6	Moderate	cool	cool	occasional rainstorms
November	2	Adverse	cool	cool	frequent rainstorms
December	1	Adverse	cool	chilly	continual rainstorms

Summary

Sprinkled across an unprotected headland on the remote and rugged Northern California coastline, Mendocino is almost perpetually cool, and fog is common year-round. **Winter** days are normally cool and evenings are chilly. Because of the moderating infuence of the seaside location, there is seldom a frost of any consequence, and snowfalls are rare. Continual rainstorms during the winter months keep people indoors, however, and contribute more than half of the year's precipitation. **Spring** days and evenings are also cool, but more usable because of diminishing rainfall. **Summer** is the only season with a fine weather outlook. Occasional fog or brisk winds are balanced by an almost assured absence of rain, and the year's warmest days are suitable for comfortably exploring this hauntingly beautiful area. Unfortunately, the ocean is always too cold for swimming. **Fall** is also uniformly cool, with increasingly frequent and heavier rainfalls as the season progresses.

ATTRACTIONS & DIVERSIONS

Bicycling
Mendocino Cyclery   *downtown at 45040 Main St.*   937-4744
Bicycles can be rented here by the hour or longer to tour coastal highways and byways which make up in scenic quality whatever they lack in quantity or safety.

Boat Rentals
★ **Catch-a-canoe**   *.7 mi. S off CA 1 at 44900 Comptche-Ukiah Rd.*   937-0273
Canoe rentals are available from April to October by the hour or day for trips up the Big River. It's actually a gentle little river that flows through a narrow, undeveloped canyon where redwood and fir are interspersed with sandy beaches and swimming holes. Because the river is tidal for several miles, you can plan your trip to allow the flow of the tides to carry you up and back for an extraordinary experience.

★ **California Western Railroad**   *11 mi. N at foot of Laurel St. - Ft. Bragg*   964-6371
The "Skunk" line offers one of the West's most scenic train rides. It twists through forty miles of rugged mountains highlighted by groves of redwoods along the Noyo River to Willits. More than thirty bridges, trestles, and tunnels are along the route — which is inaccessible by car. Diesel trains operate daily year-round. The round trip takes about seven hours. Half-day tours can be reserved during the summer months when open observation cars are used.

Golf
Little River Inn Golf Course   *3 mi. S on CA 1*   937-5667
This challenging 9-hole course overlooking the ocean is open to the public. Facilities include a pro shop, driving range, putting greens, cart rentals, and a restaurant.

★ **Jug Handle State Reserve**   *5 mi. N on CA 1 - Caspar*   937-5804
At Jug Handle Creek is a remarkable "ecological staircase" phenomenon. Five wave-cut terraces form a staircase with each step holding an ecosystem much older than the one below. On the partially submerged bottom terrace are tide pools with a wealth of marine life. A five-mile self-guided nature trail explores all five terraces.

Mendocino Coast Botanical Gardens   *7.5 mi. N on CA 1*   964-4352
Two miles of self-guided hiking trails meander through these large privately-owned gardens. From a coffee shop, paths wind through natural woods and meadows interspersed with a profusion of rhododendrons, wild lilac, fuchsias, and other seasonal blooms. A fern canyon, rustic bridges, and picnic facilities are scattered along the way to a seaside cliff house.

★ **Mendocino Headlands State Park**   *surrounding town on S,W,N sides*   937-5397
This park was created to protect the meadows, wave-carved bluffs and natural bridges of the promontory that juts into the Pacific around town. Below the bluffs on the southeast side of town, the picturesque sandy beach at the mouth of the Big River is also included. Scenic hiking trails, view overlooks, picnic sites, and restrooms are well-located. Heeser Drive is a paved scenic loop that follows the blufftop to an access for public fishing and the beach on the west side of the promontory.

★ **Old Masonic Hall Sculpture**   *downtown on Lansing St.*
Don't miss the intriguing rooftop of this old building. The whimsical sculpture of Father Time braiding a maiden's hair captures the artistic and romantic spirit of Mendocino in a century-old piece of whitewashed redwood.

★ **Russian Gulch State Park**   *1 mi. N off CA 1*   937-5804
One of the West's most outstanding coastal parks includes a picturesque sandy beach where a shallow creek empties into the ocean. Beyond, dramatic wave-sculpted headlands reveal coves, tide pools, and a partially collapsed blowhole to hikers and beachcombers. In the canyon near the mouth of the creek are about thirty shady campsites. A waterfall in a fern-edged grotto is the highlight of an easy 3.5 mile trail through dense forests along the creek.

★ **Sportfishing**   *9 mi. N on CA 1 - Noyo*
Sportfishing is the major year-round attraction of the tiny village of Noyo situated near the mouth of the Noyo River. Coastal rocks and beaches, the jetty and wharves, and oceangoing party boats are all popular with fishermen, especially during the summer and fall salmon runs. Complete information on fishing charters and equipment rentals can be obtained at the Mendocino Coast Chamber of Commerce.

★ **Van Damme State Park**   *2.5 mi. S off CA 1*   *937-5804*
On scenic Little River, this splendid park has about eighty shady campsites inland from
the highway. Nearby is a sandy beach for sunbathing. The ocean is reasonably safe but
inevitably cold for swimming and skindiving. Shore fishing is popular. Delightful hiking
trails provide access to ocean views, a sword fern canyon, and an ancient pygmy forest of
stunted conifers.

Warm Water Features

★   **Caspar Tubbs**   *5 mi. N off CA 1 - Caspar*   *964-6668*
In a rustic natural setting on the grounds of the McCornack Center for the Healing Arts,
hot tubs in enclosures open to the sky may be rented by the hour. Each private enclosure
includes a whirlpool, sauna, sundeck, shower, and dressing room. Massage is also
available by appointment.

★   **Sweetwater Gardens**   *downtown at 955 Ukiah St.*   *937-4140*
Guests can rent a private room with a hot tub, sauna, and tiled bath; a small private tub;
or large communal hot tubs by the hour in this serene and artistic new facility adjoining
a fine organic restaurant. Massage is also available by appointment.

Wineries

In the latest decade, vineyards and wineries have become as important as long-
established apple orchards in the pretty little Anderson Valley inland from the Mendocino
coast. Three small, family-owned wineries are now clustered along CA 128 near the tiny
village of Philo.

★   **Edmeades**   *30 mi. SE on CA 128*   *895-3232*
One of the area's earliest wineries dates from 1971. Visitors may sample the full range of
premium wines in a rustic little hilltop tasting room. Tasting and sales 10-6. (11-5
Oct.-May.)

★   **Husch**   *29 mi. SE on CA 128*   *895-3216*
This attractive little winery was founded in 1971. A wooden cabin has been made into a
pleasant tasting room where all of the premium wines may be sampled. Tree-shaded
picnic tables are nearby. Tasting and sales 10-6.

★   **Navarro Winery**   *30 mi. SE on CA 128*   *895-3686*
The valley's youngest major winery was founded in 1975. A distinctive new woodcrafted
building used for tasting the full line of premium wines also provides picture window
views of the vineyards. An adjoining outdoor deck with umbrella-shaded picnic tables
overlooks the lovely scene. Tasting and sales 10-5.

SHOPPING

Mendocino has an enchanting little business district where strollers and shoppers are
rewarded with intriguing buildings and nineteenth century architectural embellishments
at every turn. Shops are clustered along one side of Main Street. Remarkably, the other
side of this street is a broad, grassy meadow with unobstructed views extending to
magnificent seascapes. The many galleries in town let visitors see how resident artists
have translated such scenes into oils, watercolors, photography, and other media.
Numerous specialty shops also reflect the deeply intertwined involvement of local
merchants and artisans with the natural beauty of the captivating surroundings.

Food Specialties

★ **Brings Pastries**   *downtown at 10540 Lansing St.*   *937-4188*
A delicious selection of European and American pastries and breads is served in a town-
view coffee room, on an outdoor deck, or to go.

★ **The Cheese Shop**   *downtown at 45050 Little Lake St.*   *937-0104*
In addition to a fine variety of imported and domestic cheeses, there are all kinds of
gourmet food specialties like pates, baguettes, and homemade jellies and jams. Some
items are displayed for tastes, too. Another section of the store has the area's best
selection of premium California wines, especially Mendocino County labels.

★ **Chocolate Moosse**   *downtown at 390 Kasten St.*   *937-4323*
Outstanding desserts are the specialty at the Blue Heron Inn. This charming little
Mendocino-style coffee shop is more than the sum of irresistible delicacies, knotty pine
floors, whitewashed wainscoting, brick fireplace, pegged chairs, and handcrafted solid
pine tables furnished with art-object sugar servers and fresh flowers.

Mendocino Bakery   *downtown at 10485 Lansing St.*   *937-0836*
Breads are the specialty. Pastries and pizza are also served to go, or at tables.
★ **Mendocino Ice Cream Co.**   *downtown at 45090 Main St.*   *937-5884*
Homemade ice cream is the feature of a little ice cream parlor where the acclaimed Black Forest ice cream is especially rich.
★ **Mendocino Jams and Jellies**   *downtown on Main St.*   *937-5266*
Outstanding raspberry jam is a highlight among delicious jams, jellies, and chutneys made locally and sold in this attractive new takeout shop. Tastes are offered.
Specialty Shops
★ **Book Loft**   *downtown at 522 Main St.*   *937-0890*
This small shop upstairs above Alphonso's Merchantile emphasizes paperbacks. Sitting in the chair positioned to overlook a picture window view of the rugged coast while listening to classical music and browsing through books can be an unforgettable experience.
Gallery Bookshop   *downtown at 319 Kasten St.*   *937-5796*
An excellent selection of hardcovers and paperbacks has been ingeniously packed into one tiny bookstore.
★ **Gallery Fair**   *downtown at Kasten/Ukiah Sts.*   *937-5121*
Museum-quality wall hangings, sculpture, and unique art objects of wood by local and regional artists are beautifully displayed in this large two-level gallery.
★ **Mendocino Art Center**   *downtown at 45200 Little Lake St.*   *937-5818*
The heart of the local art renaissance is a handsome little visual and performing arts complex. Visitors can watch painters, sculptors, potters, and other artisans at work in on-site studios. In addition, the public is invited to art fairs, wine tastings, afternoon concerts, plays, and other periodic events that take place here.
★ **Other Galleries**   *downtown*
Many fine galleries are concentrated within four blocks to the south and east of the Art Center. Excellent locally produced paintings, graphics, sculpture, ceramics, textiles, and jewelry are beautifully displayed.

NIGHTLIFE

A wide range of plays, concerts, and other productions are offered throughout the year, and distinctive gallery showings are a special feature on most weekend evenings. Several captivating lounges provide the right setting for a romantic interlude or a quiet drink. This is all in sharp contrast with the rowdy goings-on in a nearby roadhouse saloon where loud live music attracts drinkers, dancers, and people-watchers from miles around.
★ **Caspar Inn**   *4.5 mi. N off CA 1 - Caspar*   *964-5565*
Live music and a big dance floor make this sprawling, funky old-time tavern the action spot in the area on weekends. It's a popular place to shoot pool, throw darts and drink beer anytime.
★ **Heritage House**   *5 mi. S on CA 1*   *937-5885*
The genteel Apple Lounge near the resort's dining room offers plush sofas and armchairs in an intimate firelit room. The picture window views of verdant landscaping and rugged coastal headlands are inspiring.
★ **MacCallum House**   *downtown at 45020 Albion St.*   *937-5763*
The Grey Whale Bar is a romantic little drawing room with plush sofas, a fireplace, and lush plants. Drinks are also served on an intimate enclosed porch. A fine restaurant adjoins.
★ **Mendocino Hotel**   *downtown at 45080 Main St.*   *937-0511*
The opulent Victorian-style lounge has all kinds of overstuffed furniture for comfortably relaxing over a quiet drink amidst polished hardwoods and stained glass decor. The adjoining enclosed garden patio is also beautifully detailed.
★ **Mendocino Performing Arts Company**   *downtown at 45200 Little Lake St.*   *937-4477*
The Helen Schoeni Theatre is an intimate showplace where a variety of plays and concerts are performed throughout the year.
★ **Seagull Cellar Bar**   *downtown at the corner of Lansing & Ukiah Sts.*   *937-5204*
Live entertainment is featured several nights a week in an upstairs bar that is a classic Mendocino-style gathering place. Comfortable armchairs overlook a wall of windows, spectacular raised-relief wood murals, and several large, fanciful paintings. Drinks can also be enjoyed outdoors on a tiny redwood viewdeck.

RESTAURANTS

Some of the best restaurants in the West are located in and near town. In recent years, Mendocino has become a major source of New California cuisine, where seasonally fresh local ingredients are skillfully prepared in exciting new ways. Authentic Victorian surroundings and dramatic seascape views are also part of the allure of many fine local dining rooms.

★ **Albion River Inn Restaurant**   *6.8 mi. S on CA 1 - Albion*   *937-4044*
L-D.   *Moderate*
This relative newcomer to the area offers a fascinating assortment of fresh seafood and other specialties handled with a flair in the New California cuisine style. Fresh roses and ultra-modern candles adorn each table in a contemporary dining room warmed by a great brick fireplace. The sweeping picture window view of the outlet of Albion River and the ocean far below is awesome. Many local wines are available by the glass.

Brannon's Whale Watch Restaurant   *downtown at 45040 Main St.*   *937-4197*
B-L-D.   *Moderate*
A contemporary American menu is offered in a casual upstairs dining room with a fine ocean and town view, and a Franklin fireplace. Fresh flowers and raspberry jam pots decorate well-spaced tables. A sunny ocean view deck is also used when weather permits.

★ **Cafe Beaujolais**   *downtown at 961 Ukiah St.*   *937-5614*
B-L-D. No D on Tues.-Thurs. & fall-winter.   *Expensive*
Outstanding New California cuisine is served in the crowded and lively ambiance of a homey old Victorian building. Fresh, locally grown produce is given a wonderfully disciplined light touch for all meals. Breakfasts are especially renowned.

★ **Egghead Omelettes**   *10 mi. N on CA 1 at 326 N. Main St. - Ft. Bragg*   *964-5005*
B-L.   *Moderate*
Toast from homemade bread, fine jam in pots, and real maple syrup provide evidence of the fact that breakfast is treated seriously here. Specialty omelets are served all day in a pleasant little dining room.

Heritage House   *5 mi. S on CA 1*   *937-5885*
B-D. Closed Dec.-Jan.   *Expensive*
Meals are served to the public as well as guests in this prestigious and historic inn. The large, formally elegant dining room provides panoramic views of the spectacular coast.

★ **The Ledford House**   *3.5 mi. S on CA 1 - Little River*   *937-0282*
D only. Closed Sun. in winter.   *Expensive*
A short, interesting menu features California cuisine. Emphasis is on seasonally fresh, locally grown ingredients, and all baking is done on the premises. A rustic Civil War-era farmhouse overlooking the sea retains its historic charm with plush antique furnishings and a cozy fireplace.

★ **Little River Cafe**   *3 mi. S on CA 1 - Little River*   *937-0404*
D only. Closed Mon.-Wed.   *Expensive*
Hidden away in the back of the Little River Post Office is a posh, tiny haven of delicious New California cuisine. Nearly all of the prepared-to-order foods served during the two nightly seatings are homemade or home-grown.

Little River Inn   *3 mi. S on CA 1 - Little River*   *937-5942*
B-L-D. Closed last 3 wks. in Jan.   *Expensive*
Fresh breads, soups, and desserts made in the inn's country kitchen enhance seafood and steak specialties. The spacious, casually elegant dining room is the focal point of a nineteenth century mansion surrounded by gardens on a knoll overlooking the ocean.

★ **MacCallum House**   *downtown at 45020 Albion St.*   *937-5763*
D only. Closed Mon.   *Expensive*
Well-regarded Continental cuisine is served in the romantic atmosphere of a stately Victorian mansion. An old cobblestone fireplace is the showpiece of the beautifully furnished, intimate dining room. Lunch on the porch accompanied by bay and ocean views is also very popular.

★ **Main Street Deli**   *downtown at 45040 Main St.*   *937-5031*
B-L-D.   *Moderate*
Several kinds of big, delectable croissants are a specialty of this new deli/restaurant. Good light fare is served in a casual, modern dining room with some ocean view tables.

Mendocino Hotel   *downtown at 45080 Main St.*   *937-0511*
B-L-D.   *Expensive*
Steak and seafood are featured, and baked goods are made on the premises. The large dining room in this century-old hotel is decorated in lavish Victorian style. An adjoining glassed-in section with a proliferation of plants is a delightful place for breakfast.

★ **New Boonville Restaurant**   *38 mi. SE via CA 1 & CA 128 - Boonville*   *895-3478*
L-D.   *Expensive*
New California cuisine is showcased in a limited bill of fare featuring gourmet preparations of home-grown produce. The dining room of an old two-story hotel has been handsomely restored and updated with woodcrafted tables and benches, quality prints, and a lovely garden view.

Noyo River Inn   *9 mi. N at 19130 S. Harbor Dr. - Noyo*   *964-6341*
L-D.   *Moderate*
Local seafood and prime rib are always featured in this casually elegant dining room that overlooks picturesque Noyo Harbor. Occasional live entertainment is offered in the adjoining lounge.

The Restaurant   *10 mi. N at 418 N. Main St. - Ft. Bragg*   *964-9800*
L-D. Closed Wed.   *Moderate*
A distinctive contemporary menu is featured in this well-regarded newer restaurant. Unusual paintings and memorabilia personalize the dining rooms.

★ **The Sea Gull**   *downtown at Lansing & Ukiah Sts.*   *937-5204*
B-L-D.   *Moderate*
Fresh food prepared simply and well has made this a favorite for breakfast, when giant cinnamon rolls and homemade pastries draw enthusiastic crowds. The same attention is given to other meals. The interior is classic Mendocino. Handcrafted woods, fresh flowers, greenery, stained glass, and art objects abound.

★ **The Wellspring Restaurant**   *downtown at 955 Ukiah St.*   *937-4567*
L-D. Closed Tues. in winter.   *Moderate*
Delicious homemade rolls and pastries complement fresh seafood and gourmet vegetarian specialties. Artistry and craftsmanship blend smoothly in a charming Mendocino-style dining room embellished with intriguing wall hangings extending to a lofty ceiling, an intimate balcony dining area, abundant greenery, and an occasional vocalist.

The Wharf   *9 mi. N off CA 1 at 780 N. Harbor Dr. - Noyo*   *964-4283*
L-D.   *Moderate*
Fresh seafood is conventionally prepared in this very large and popular fishhouse. A panoramic window view of the tiny fishing village and harbor is the real feature.

LODGING

The creative spirit of Mendocino's artistic residents is evident in the many winsome accommodations available for visitors. Almost no conventional motels or large hotels despoil the setting. Instead, romantic little inns all along the coast reflect the area's Yankee Victorian heritage and magnificent surroundings in wonderfully personal ways. There are no bargains in summer. However, from fall through spring, non-weekend rates are often reduced at least 15% below those shown.

Albion River Inn   *6.8 mi. S at 3790 N. CA 1 - Albion*   *937-4044*
On a high bluff overlooking the ocean at the mouth of Albion Harbor is a small rustic motel adjacent to a well-regarded view restaurant.
    "Sea Cliff" — 2 BR, kit. with ocean view, free-standing fireplace in BR,
               grand ocean view in LR, pvt. balc. over ocean,   2 Q beds...$75
   ocean view room —   Q bed...$50
   regular room —   Q bed...$45

★ **Big River Lodge**   *1 mi. SE via CA 1 on Comptche-Ukiah Rd.*   *937-5615*
A two-story motel has been wonderfully transformed into a bed-and-breakfast inn. Some of the rooms have fine ocean and town views across spacious landscaped grounds. All units are graciously decorated with local art and antiques, and have cable color TV and a wood-burning fireplace. Bicycles are available free to guests. A Continental breakfast and a decanter of local wine are complimentary.
   #22 — expansive suite, fine shoreline views,   K bed..$135

#24 — excellent shoreline/town views,	K bed...$92
#25,#23 — fine ocean/town views,	Q bed...$92
regular room — some ocean/town views,	Q bed...$92

★ **Glendeven**   *2.4 mi. S at 8221 N. CA 1 - Little River*   *937-0083*

This is an elegant, beautifully furnished Victorian guest house overlooking headland meadows near the bay at Little River. A complimentary breakfast is served in the morning in a charming garden-view sitting room, and wine is offered by the fire in the evening.

"Eastlin" — pvt. bath & entrance, parlor stove, bay view, rosewood	Q bed...$80
"Garret" — top fl., pvt. bath, bay view, windows on 3 sides, Louis XV	Q bed...$70
regular room — shared bath,	D bed...$60

★ **Harbor House**   *16 mi. S on CA 1 - Elk*   *877-3203*

The blufftop setting provides sensational views of the rugged coastline. Far below is a small private beach. The stately Edwardian main house is a marvel of hand-fitted virgin redwood from the nearby Albion forests. Each luxuriously furnished room has a private bath and a fireplace or Franklin stove. Modified American plan rates include a gourmet breakfast and dinner in an elegant, intimate dining room. The inn is closed from Thanksgiving thru Christmas.

"Harbor" — top fl., brick fireplace, pvt. coast view, windows on 3 sides,	D & Q beds...$150
#1 — cabin, Franklin stove, fine pvt. coast views,	K bed..$130
#2 — cabin, Franklin stove, fine pvt. coast views, 4-poster	Q bed...$130
regular room — cabin,	Q bed...$100

★ **Harbor Lite Lodge**   *9 mi. N on CA 1 at 120 N. Harbor Dr. - Noyo*   *964-0221*

The best views of Noyo Harbor and the tiny fishing village are enjoyed by guests in this contemporary motel on the bluff at the north end of the harbor bridge. There is a trail to the beach, and a sauna. Each room has a phone and cable color TV.

#303 — end, pvt. balc., fine harbor/village view,	K bed...$56
#216,#214 — pvt. balc., fine harbor/ocean view,	2 Q beds...$48
regular room —	Q bed...$44

★ **Heritage House**   *5 mi. S off CA 1*   *937-5885*

Probably the most famous inn along California's north coast is this luxurious complex of buildings scattered over spacious landscaped grounds on a hillside above one of the most picturesque ocean coves anywhere. Each of the spacious rooms is decorated differently with furnishings that include many valuable antiques. Modified American plan rates include breakfast and dinner in the opulent ocean-view dining room. Closed Dec.-Jan.

"Meadow 1" — half of duplex, close to cove, awesome view,	K bed...$165
"Vista 3" — end, wood-burning iron fireplace, grand pvt. views,	2 D beds...$185
"Vista 1" — brick fireplace, shared view deck, fine views,	K bed...$165
regular room — some have ocean view,	D bed...$95

Hill House Inn   *.3 mi. N on Pallette Dr.*   *937-0554*

This recently constructed motel is a careful replication of a sprawling Victorian inn furnished in period decor. Each room has a phone and cable color TV, and some have ocean views. A complimentary Continental breakfast is served.

#201 — corner, fine view across town, fireplace,	K bed...$105
regular room —	2 D or K bed...$56

★ **Joshua Grindle Inn**   *downtown at 44800 Little Lake St.*   *937-4143*

All of the rooms in this beautifully restored century-old home have private baths and carefully selected antique furnishings. Breakfast is included.

"Master" — fireplace,	Q bed...$65
"Joshua Grindle","Nautical" — views over town to ocean,	Q bed...$60
regular room —	Q bed...$54

Little River Inn   *3 mi. S on CA 1 - Little River*   *937-5942*

The area's only 9-hole golf course is a feature of this long-established resort on expansive, landscaped grounds near the ocean, and there is a charming restaurant and lounge. Rooms vary from early California to contemporary decor, and many have ocean views.

#41 — end, pvt. balc., great semi-pvt. view,	K bed...$64
#17,#14 — ends of single-level bldg., fireplace,	K bed...$76
regular room — in the older main bldg.,	Q bed...$64

★ **MacCallum House**   *downtown at 740 Albion St.*   937-0289

One of Mendocino's earliest bed-and-breakfast inns occupies a century-old mansion that may be the most photographed place in town. Outstanding antique and handcrafted furnishings are used throughout the main building and surrounding structures. Most bathrooms are shared. A complimentary Continental breakfast is served in the lovely firelit dining room.

#14 "Watertower" — split level, Franklin fireplace, pvt. bath, ocean view,	Q bed...$85
#16 "Upper Barn Suite" — pvt. flowered deck, big tiled shower, stone fireplace, ocean view,	2 D beds...$115
#19 "Barn Apartment" — big stone fireplace in BR, kit. with massive redwood counter tops, tiled tub with shower,	2 D beds...$95
#7 "Greenhouse" — Franklin fireplace,	Q bed...$95
regular room — shared bath,	D bed...$45

Mendocino Hotel   *downtown at 45080 Main St.*   937-0511

Perhaps the most visible symbol of the town's Yankee heritage is this century-old three-story hotel. There is a kind of movie-set pizzazz to the completely rebuilt lobby, dining, and lounge areas that have been lavishly redecorated in Victorian style. Most of the guest rooms are small, individually decorated, and share bathrooms. A Continental breakfast is included.

#24 — pvt. bath, pvt. balc., ocean view,	Q bed..$165
regular room — pvt. bath,	Q bed...$70
regular room — shared bath,	D bed...$45

Mendocino Village Inn   *downtown at 44860 Main St.*   937-0246

A century-old mansion, thoughtfully preserved and reoutfitted with some period furnishings, is now a bed-and-breakfast inn. A full complimentary breakfast is brought to the room.

#4 — fireplace, corner, windows on 2 sides, pvt. bath, color TV, 4-poster	Q bed...$75
#8 — fireplace, parlor, pvt. bath, windows on 2 sides, color TV,	Q bed...$75
#5 — fireplace, corner windows/hill views, shower,	D bed...$56
"B" — attic, shared bath, view of hills,	D bed...$42
regular room "A" — attic, shared bath, partial ocean view,	D bed...$38

★ **1021 Main St.**   *downtown at 1021 Main St.*   937-5150

Craftsmanship, creative furnishings, and views are beautifully combined in this tiny, uniquely furnished bed-and-breakfast inn. A sunken living room has the West's most remarkable fireplace — "Hot Lips." An outdoor hot tub affords guests a stunning ocean view, and a private path leads to a picturesque sandy beach. A full complimentary breakfast is served to the room, downstairs, or on a lovely ocean view deck.

"Zen House" — pvt. bath with sunken tub, antique fireplace, refr., pvt. deck with awesome ocean & river view,	Q bed...$110
"The Attic" — tiny room reached by stepladder, shared bath, superb pvt. ocean view through leaded glass window, low mirrored ceiling, skylight over	K bed...$45
regular room — pot-bellied stove, shared bath,	T & D beds...$60

Sea Rock Motel   *.4 mi. N at 11101 N. Lansing St.*   937-5517

There is a good view of a beach and cove bordered by Mendocino Headlands from this small cottage colony. All of the comfortably furnished units have private baths and cable color TV.

#12 — Franklin fireplace, ocean view,	Q bed...$59
#2 — some view,	Q bed...$49
regular room —	D or Q bed...$49

★ **Whitegate Inn**   *downtown at 499 Howard St.*   937-4892

A century-old residence has been converted into a handsome bed-and-breakfast inn. Each room is furnished with antiques and has a sitting area. Breakfast is complimentary, as is wine served in the early evening.

"Cypress Room" — lg., Franklin fireplace, pvt. bath, some ocean view,	Q bed...$70
regular room "The Blue Room" — spacious, shared bath,	T & Q beds...$53

CAMPGROUNDS
Several of the West's most outstanding campgrounds are near town. The two best are in luxuriant forests along creeks in little sheltered canyons an easy stroll from picturesque ocean beaches.

★ **Paul M. Dimmick Wayside** *19 mi. SE: 11 mi. S on CA 1 & 8 mi. E on CA 128 937-5804*
The state operates this campground along a tranquil stretch of the gentle little Navarro River where it winds through a luxuriant evergreen forest. Hiking is popular, as are swimming, canoeing, and fishing when conditions are right in the tiny river. Flush toilets, but no showers or hookups, are available. Each of the tree-shaded, well-spaced sites has a picnic table and a fire area. base rate...$5

★ **Russian Gulch State Park** *2 mi. N on CA 1* *937-5804*
This state park facility has a splendid location by a small creek in a protected canyon just inland from a sandy ocean beach. Features include marked nature trails, a fern-lined path to a waterfall, an ocean cove, a blowhole, tidepools, and a pygmy forest. Surf fishing, sun bathing, scuba diving, beachcombing, and hiking are popular. Flush toilets and hot showers are available, but there are no hookups. Each tree-shaded, well-spaced site has a picnic table and a fire ring. base rate...$5

★ **Van Damme State Park** *2.7 mi. S on CA 1* *937-5804*
Just inland from a magnificent sandy cove at the mouth of Little River, this superb state park facility is naturally landscaped with coastal redwoods shading rhododendrons and miles of lush green ferns lining both sides of Little River. Scuba diving, ocean fishing, sunbathing, and hiking are popular. There are flush toilets and hot showers, but no hookups. Each tree-shaded well-spaced site has a picnic table and grill. base rate...$5

OTHER INFORMATION
Area Code: *707*

Mendocino Coast C. of C. *9 mi. N on CA 1 at 332 N. Main St. - Ft. Bragg* *964-3153*

Monterey, California

Elevation:

40 feet

Population (1980):

27,558

Population (1970):

26,302

Location:

130 mi. SE
of San Francisco

Monterey is a magical medley of superlative history and geography. Located by Monterey Bay in what has been called one of the most beautiful natural amphitheaters in the world, this seaport has played a major role in the development of the West for more than two centuries. It is now a renowned destination with a superabundance of lovingly preserved historic landmarks and sophisticated contemporary amenities that also benefits from an unusually temperate climate. Because snow and frost are rare, lush vegetation and outdoor activities are enjoyed year-round. Emerald-green flower-strewn landscapes in spring, and warm, rainless weather in summer and fall are especially delightful. At these times, and on weekends throughout the year, Monterey hosts capacity crowds. Beaches, wharfs, marinas, the cannery district, historic buildings, parks, and other leisure-oriented facilities have been provided over the years along the entire waterfront and downtown.

In 1602, Sebastian Viscaino became the first white man to set foot in the area. He dubbed it Monterey after the count who was then viceroy of New Spain. It wasn't until 1770, however, that settlement began. In that year, Gaspar de Portola established the first of Spain's four California presidios and Father Junipero Serra dedicated the second mission in Alta California. (He relocated it to the present site near the Carmel River a year later.) Monterey was California's capital under Spain until 1822, when it became the Mexican regional capital. So it remained until 1846 when the United States annexed California. Many buildings dating from those momentous times remain downtown as tangible reminders of Monterey's importance in the early settlement of the West. After California became a state in 1850, the town became a whaling, fishing, and canning center. It wasn't until after World War II that its destiny as one of the West's most playful towns was fulfilled.

Today, Cannery Row and Fisherman's Wharf are ingenious transformations from an earlier hard-working era into vibrant and colorful leisure complexes. Downtown, carefully restored remnants of the past blend into an increasingly appealing melange of shops and galleries. Gourmet and view restaurants are numerous, and nightlife is as diverse and exuberant as anywhere in the West. Accommodations of all kinds are abundant. In fact, Monterey's two major man-made landmarks are strikingly contemporary high-rise hotels in the heart of downtown.

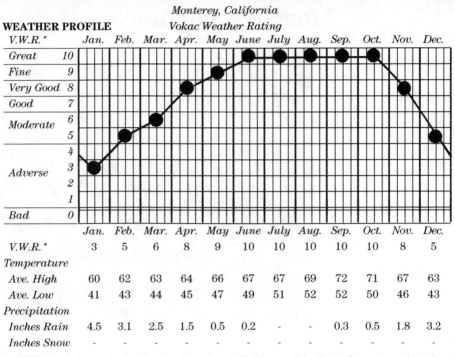

WEATHER PROFILE		Monterey, California Vokac Weather Rating											
V.W.R.*		Jan.	Feb.	Mar.	Apr.	May	June	July	Aug.	Sep.	Oct.	Nov.	Dec.
Great	10												
Fine	9												
Very Good	8												
Good	7												
Moderate	6												
	5												
	4												
Adverse	3												
	2												
	1												
Bad	0												

	Jan.	Feb.	Mar.	Apr.	May	June	July	Aug.	Sep.	Oct.	Nov.	Dec.
V.W.R.*	3	5	6	8	9	10	10	10	10	10	8	5
Temperature												
Ave. High	60	62	63	64	66	67	67	69	72	71	67	63
Ave. Low	41	43	44	45	47	49	51	52	52	50	46	43
Precipitation												
Inches Rain	4.5	3.1	2.5	1.5	0.5	0.2	-	-	0.3	0.5	1.8	3.2
Inches Snow	-	-	-	-	-	-	-	-	-	-	-	-

V.W.R. = Vokac Weather Rating: probability of mild (warm & dry) weather on any given day.

Forecast

		Temperatures		
Month	V.W.R.*	Daytime	Evening	Precipitation
January	3 Adverse	cool	cool	frequent rainstorms
February	5 Moderate	cool	cool	occasional rainstorms
March	6 Moderate	cool	cool	occasional rainstorms
April	8 Very Good	cool	cool	infrequent rainstorms
May	9 Fine	warm	cool	infrequent showers
June	10 Great	warm	cool	negligible
July	10 Great	warm	cool	none
August	10 Great	warm	cool	none
September	10 Great	warm	cool	negligible
October	10 Great	warm	cool	infrequent showers
November	8 Very Good	warm	cool	infrequent rainstorms
December	5 Moderate	cool	cool	occasional rainstorms

Summary

Monterey is beautifully located along Monterey Bay on the northeastern corner of the Monterey Peninsula which it shares with Pacific Grove and Carmel. One of the West's most desirable climates is nearly ideal for comfortably enjoying outdoor recreation. Even in **winter**, there is no really bad weather. Days and evenings are cool, but usually frost-free. Occasional Pacific rainstorms during this season contribute well over half of the average annual precipitation. **Spring** marks the beginning of consistently mild weather for enjoying almost any outdoor activity. Warm days, cool evenings, and infrequent showers may be marred for some by sea breezes and coastal fogs that are also common during this season. **Summer** is splendid, with warm days and cool nights. There is almost no rainfall, but coastal fog is routine. **Fall** is a delightful extension of summer with an added attraction. The year's highest temperatures normally occur at this time. Ideal conditions usually continue until after Thanksgiving when the rainy season begins again in earnest.

ATTRACTIONS & DIVERSIONS

Allen Knight Maritime Museum   *downtown at 550 Calle Principal*   375-2553
The fishing and whaling era in Monterey is portrayed through a comprehensive collection of pictures, paintings, shop models, and maritime artifacts.

★ **Bicycling**
There are several exclusive bike paths and many scenic routes on the Monterey Peninsula. Rentals and information are offered at:

> **Freewheeling Cycles**   *downtown at 188 Webster St.*   373-3855
> **Joselyn's Bicycles**   *1 mi. NW at 638 Lighthouse Av.*   649-8520
> **Boat Rentals**

★   **Monterey Bay Yacht Center**   *downtown at Wharf #2*   375-2002
Sailboats can be rented, and boating instruction is available here year-round.

★ **California's First Theater**   *downtown at Pacific/Scott Sts.*   375-4916
Completed in 1847 as a boarding house and saloon, the building was loaned to some American soldiers who, for the first time in California, charged admission for their theatrical performances. Today, Victorian melodramas are performed here year-round.

★ **Cannery Row**   *starts .5 mi. NW along Cannery Row*
Hulking cannery buildings and overpasses across Cannery Row still capture some of the flavor of the past. But, the canneries haven't been the same since sardines mysteriously vanished from Monterey Bay around 1950. The noise and the smell described in John Steinbeck's *Cannery Row* are gone — replaced by an imaginative assortment of shops and restaurants that have brought bright lights, the sound of music, and the smell of good food to ingeniously renovated old buildings and elaborate new structures. For a quiet, authentic reminder of the earlier era, peer into the windows of the weathered clapboard building in the 800 block of Cannery Row that was Steinbeck's friend "Doc" Rickett's Pacific Biological Laboratory.

★ **Colton Hall**   *downtown at 522 Pacific St.*
This classic revival building of stone and adobe mortar was built as a town hall and school in 1848. It was the first American public building in California, and the state's first constitution was written here in 1849. The handsomely restored building is located in the civic center next to Friendly Plaza.

★ **The Custom House**   *downtown near Fisherman's Wharf*
This is the oldest government building in California. The northern portion of the carefully restored adobe dates from 1827. There are some interesting exhibits and a wall-enclosed garden.

★ **Fisherman's Wharf**   *downtown at the N end of Olivier St.*
The original commerical fishing activities that operated from this wharf have long since stopped. But the wharf is still here and the buildings have evolved into a colorful potpourri of shops, restaurants, and open-air fish markets for swarms of visitors drawn by the bracing nautical atmosphere. In addition to panoramic marine views, the wharf affords visitors close-up glimpses of the bay's most antic residents — harbor seals and sea otters. It is also the peninsula's major terminus for both sportfishing and sightseeing boats.

Golf

★   **Old Del Monte Golf Course**   *1.5 mi. E at 1300 Sylvan Rd.*   373-2436
This beautifully landscaped, moderately hilly 18-hole golf course is open to the public year-round, and offers all necessary facilities and rentals.

Horseback Riding

Jack's Peak Stables   *3 mi. SE at 550 Aquajito Rd.*   375-4232
Horses can be rented for rides along beautiful forest trails in the pine-covered hills south of town.

Jack's Peak Regional Park   *5 mi. SE via Fremont St. & Aquajito Rd.*   424-1971
Panoramic views of the peninsula are the feature of this large park covering the high forested hills south of town. A mile-long hiking trail provides a scenic loop to the top of the peak from the parking lot, which is also near picturesque sites for a picnic in the pines.

★ **Lake El Estero Park**   *.3 mi. E on 3rd St.*
This large landscaped park next to downtown has a small lake with boat rentals, walkways, and picnic areas. The most distinctive feature, however, is Dennis the Menace

Playground where Hank Ketcham, creator of "Dennis the Menace," aided in the development of a variety of free-form "hands-on" pieces of play equipment. Narrow tunnels, balanced roundabouts, swinging bridges, giant slides, and other unusual devices attract children of all ages.

★ **Larkin House**   *downtown at Calle Principal/Jefferson St.*   *649-2836*
Built in the 1830s with a combination of Spanish-colonial and New England architectural features, this house became an architectural prototype widely copied in Monterey and throughout California. The carefully restored home of the first and only U.S. consul to Mexico in Monterey showcases outstanding antiques and furnishings. The interior can only be viewed on guided tours.

★ **Library**   *downtown at 625 Pacific St.*   *646-3930*
The Monterey Public Library completed a major expansion and renovation in 1984. The large, distinctive library is now carpeted, and features a well-lighted reading area with comfortable armchairs near picture windows.

★ **Monterey Bay Aquarium**   *1.2 mi. NW at Cannery Row/David Av.*   *649-6466*
After seven years of planning and construction, the West Coast's newest aquarium opened in late 1984 in a completely remodeled cannery. Visitors are given a unique and exciting view of the native inhabitants of Monterey Bay — sea otters, octopuses, salmon, sharks and several hundred other species of flora and fauna in a naturalistic setting. In addition to nearly one hundred close-up viewing tanks, and two giant tanks, the complex includes a restaurant and bookshop.

★ **Monterey State Historical Park**   *downtown at 210 Olivier St.*   *649-2836*
The impressive history and architectural heritage of Monterey is carefully preserved on a seven acre site near Fisherman's Wharf, and in several downtown buildings.

★ **Moped Rental**
   Olivercycle & Sons   *1.5 mi. E at 205 Ramona Av.*   *373-2696*
Motorized bicycles provide an exhilarating and relatively effortless way to tour the picturesque peninsula. Rentals can be arranged here by the hour or longer.

"Path of History"   *throughout downtown*
A faint red dashed line in the street is a long route which goes by almost every old house in town. Each is marked with a plaque explaining its history and architecture.

Presidio of Monterey   *.5 mi. N off Pacific St.*   *242-8414*
This is now the home of the U.S. Army Language School. A brochure and map are available for exploring ten historic sites on Presidio Hill. The Presidio Museum displays historical artifacts from the Indian, Spanish, Mexican, and American eras.

Royal Presidio Chapel   *.4 mi. SE at Church St.*
The only one of California's four presidio chapels still standing has been in continuous use since 1795. Its Spanish-baroque facade is still intact.

★ **Sportfishing**   *downtown on Fisherman's Wharf*
Several sportfishing boats leave daily year-round for deep sea fishing, and salmon fishing in season. Winter whale watching excursions and sightseeing cruises are also featured. The following operators, all located on Fisherman's Wharf, offer these services and all necessary equipment.
   Chris' Fishing Trips   *375-5951*
   Monterey Fishing Trips   *372-3501*
   Randy's Fishing Trips   *372-7440*
   Sam's Fishing Fleet, Inc.   *372-0577*

★ **Stevenson House**   *downtown at 530 Houston St.*   *649-2836*
Robert Louis Stevenson boarded at what was then the French Hotel in the fall of 1879. Many of his possessions are displayed in the adobe. The interior may only be seen on guided tours.

SHOPPING
All three specialty shopping districts in Monterey — the Cannery area, Fisherman's Wharf, and downtown — are within a mile of each other. Collectively, these photogenic settings include a remarkable array of distinctive stores housed in artistically converted historic buildings. Monterey is one of the few towns where strolling and shopping are enjoyed as much in the evening as during the day.

Food Specialties

Bagel Bakery   *.6 mi. NW at 210 Lighthouse Av.*   649-1714
Several different kinds of tasty bagels are produced in this popular bakery four times daily. A few self-service coffee tables adjoin the carryout line.

Bargetto Winery   *1 mi. NW at 702 Cannery Row*   373-4053
A good selection of wine-related items are sold in this tasting room on Cannery Row. The nearby winery's sun-sweetened fruit wines are notable.

California Seasons   *1 mi. NW at 379 Cannery Row*   372-5868
Monterey Jack cheese is the specialty. Free samples are offered, and the cheese can be purchased here, or shipped in gift boxes.

Carousel Candies   *downtown at 241 Alvarado Mall*   373-4129
This small shop makes chocolates, fudges, and brittles in many styles on the premises.

★ **Creme de la Creme Pastry**   *.8 mi. NW at 360 McClellan Av.*   373-3556
Delicious pastries can be purchased to go, or to enjoy with coffee at the few attractively furnished tables. Everything made here is fresh, from scratch, and sensational.

★ **The Giant Artichoke**   *16 mi. N on CA 1 - Castroville*   633-3204
The french-fried artichoke hearts served here are a tantalizing tribute to the "Artichoke Capital of the World." The large market/restaurant also has an outstanding display of seasonally available local and California produce, plus several sizes of marinated or water-packed artichoke hearts and other gourmet groceries.

La Maison du Croissant   *downtown at 271 Bonifacio Pl.*   646-1620
Various French croissants are baked here fresh daily, along with selected other French pastries. There are a few coffee tables at this primarily takeout bakery.

★ **Monterey Wine Market**   *1 mi. NW at 711 Cannery Row*   375-6551
This is an excellent place to learn more about local wines, since Monterey County wineries are showcased in several dozen wines offered for tasting daily by the glass. Light lunches are also served in this cheerful shop in a converted cannery.

★ **Oscar Hossenfellder's**   *1 mi. NW at 640 Wave St. in Cannery Row*   649-1899
Fine homemade ice cream, and several different outstanding pies (including a truly towering lemon meringue pie), are specialties among light fare served to go, or in a unique dining area next to a full-sized, hard-working 1905 carousel in the cavernous interior of the ingeniously converted Edgewater Packing Company.

Viennese Bakery Restaurant   *downtown at 469 Alvarado St.*   375-4789
A large assortment of conventional pastries, coffee cakes, and desserts are available to go or as an accompaniment to short orders served in an adjoining plain, popular coffee shop.

Specialty Shops

The Book Tree   *downtown at 118 Webster St.*   373-0228
A surprisingly large number of well-organized books are packed into this tiny shop.

★ **Monterey Peninsula Museum of Art**   *downtown at 559 Pacific St.*   372-7591
Permanent and changing displays of regional art are exhibited and sold, along with folk and Oriental art, and photography. Closed Mon.

NIGHTLIFE

The quality and diversity of nightlife is part of the great charm of this lively, romantic town. Lounges and nightclubs range from elegant bay view rooms to funky, cavernous dancehalls, while live music includes everything from easy-listening sounds to hard rock. There are also fine showplaces for live theater and movies. Most of the action is conveniently in or near the Cannery area and Fisherman's Wharf.

Boiler Room   *1 mi. NW at 625 Cannery Row*   373-1449
Dancing to live rock music is the main event every night in this big lounge with two full bars on the third floor of Cannery Row Square overlooking Monterey Bay.

★ **California's First Theater**   *downtown at Scott/Pacific Sts.*   375-4916
This is the home of the oldest little theater group in existence still producing authentic melodramas of the 19th century. Performances are staged year-round in a small facility where tables and chairs and bench seating furnish the right setting for this kind of entertainment.

The Club   *downtown at Del Monte Av./Alvarado St.*   646-9244
Attractions range from live rock music through comedy to male burlesque at different times during the week in this big modern nightclub.

Cuckoo's Nest   *downtown at 180 Franklin St.*   *373-4566*
Live music and dancing are featured nightly in this large contemporary lounge.

★ **Doc Rickett's Lab**   *1 mi. NW at 95 Prescott Av. in Cannery Row*   *649-4241*
Live country/western music and Monterey's biggest dance floor attract foot stompin'
crowds every night to the big casual downstairs saloon.

★ **Doubletree Inn**   *downtown at Pacific St./Del Monte Av.*   *649-4511*
The Brasstree, a large and classy lounge atop the hotel, features a beautiful wharf and
harbor view, plus live music for listening or dancing nightly.

★ **Dream Theater**   *1 mi. NW at Lighthouse/Prescott Avs. in Cannery Row*   *372-1331*
This "contemporary movie palace" is surprisingly comfortable and accommodating. In
addition to screening first-run films, the theater is outfitted with three types of seating —
spacious contour, rockers, and love seats for couples.

★ **First National Fog Bank Saloon** *1 mi. NW at 638 Wave St. in Cannery Row* *373-5754*
Live jazz music happens most nights in a cozy and comfortable lounge that is a local
favorite.

Flora's   *1 mi. NW at Prescott Av./Wave St. in Cannery Row*   *375-1921*
Decorated in the Victorian rococo style of a bordello described in Steinbeck's *Cannery
Row*, this flamboyant little lounge features a singer on weekends.

Kalissa's   *1 mi. NW at 851 Cannery Row*   *372-8512*
Impromptu live music is offered most nights along with a dozen coffees, plus beer, wine,
and light meals. The tiny, cosmopolitan cabaret also features flamenco music and belly
dancers at certain times each month. Closed Sun.

★ **Mark Thomas' Outrigger**   *1 mi. NW at 700 Cannery Row*   *372-8543*
Dancing to live music over the water at Cannery Row is offered most nights in the large
main lounge. A dramatic fireplace-lit extension provides both unique bay views and a
romantic setting for enjoying the exotic drinks featured here.

The Old Monterey Music Hall   *downtown at 425 Washington St.*   *373-8770*
This is a recently opened showplace for the latest "in" sound. Many fine stained glass pieces
are suspended over the big dance floor in a cavernous room with a raised stage and
multilevel seating.

The Rogue   *downtown at Wharf #2*   *372-4586*
Casual live music for easy listening or dancing is featured several nights each week, along
with romantic harbor views from a lounge built over the bay on the newer wharf.

★ **Sly McFly's Refueling Station**   *1 mi. NW at 700 Cannery Row*   *649-8050*
The atmosphere is unique. After all, how many "ladies rooms" are entered through the
door of a 1930s sedan? Replicas of antique race cars are imaginatively used throughout.

★ **Wharf Theater**   *downtown on Fisherman's Wharf*   *372-2882*
Good live theater is featured most evenings year-round on the second floor of a skillfully
converted old building near the end of the wharf.

RESTAURANTS

The town's rich heritage, its location near an abundance of choice produce, and growing
demand for memorable dining experiences have produced a bumper crop of illustrious
restaurants in Monterey. Visitors have their choice of gourmet cuisines, and dining room
views which range from intimate close-ups of the waterfront to panoramic overviews of
the magnificent bay.

Captain's Galley   *1 mi. NW at 711 Cannery Row*   *649-8676*
L-D. B also on Sat. & Sun.   *Moderate*
Omelets and seafood are served in a casual restaurant with a view of Cannery Row and
the bay.

Chart House   *1 mi. NW at 444 Cannery Row*   *372-3362*
D only.   *Moderate*
Steaks and seafoods are emphasized in this impressive representative of a stylish
restaurant chain. The contemporary wood-toned dining room over the bay has a fine
waterfront view.

★ **Clock Garden**   *downtown at 565 Abrego St.*   *375-6100*
L-D.   *Moderate*
Monterey's most enduring theme restaurant is still a popular destination for casual
Continental dining and homemade baked goods. An old adobe carriage house was
ingeniously converted into a contemporary restaurant decorated with a colorful clock
and bottle collection. A charming, walled garden patio is used for alfresco dining.

★ **Domenico's**   *downtown at 50 Fisherman's Wharf*   *372-3655*
L-D.   *Expensive*
Fresh fish and meats grilled on an open hearth over mesquite wood, plus homemade pasta and ice cream, distinguish this admirable source of New California cuisine. Guests overlook the inner harbor from an elegant contemporary dining room with a European flair.

The Doubletree Inn of Monterey   *downtown at 2 Portola Plaza*   *649-4511*
D only.   *Expensive*
Peter B's on the Alley is the showplace among dining facilities in this newer landmark hotel. Contemporary American dishes are presented in a luxurious and tranquil dining room away from the hotel hubbub.

★ **Fresh Cream**   *1 mi. NW at 807 Cannery Row*   *375-9798*
D only. Closed Mon.-Tues.   *Expensive*
Acclaimed French cuisine and intimate Continental atmosphere blend beautifully in a hidden-away little upstairs restaurant. A short list of entrees changes daily according to the freshest ingredients available.

Gallatin's   *downtown at 500 Hartnell St.*   *373-3737*
L-D.   *Expensive*
International cuisine is given a California touch in a newly remodeled historic adobe. There is live entertainment in the lounge.

★ **Gregory's Stonehouse**   *5 mi. SE on CA 68 at 2999 Monterey/Salinas Hwy.*   *373-3175*
L-D. No D on Mon. Closed Tues.   *Expensive*
Outstanding Continental cuisine is described on a short blackboard menu which changes according to the freshest seasonally available ingredients. An old stone house has been transformed into an intimate and elegant art deco haven with charming garden views and a fireplace. An adjoining landscaped patio and a cozy bar are also popular.

★ **Hammerheads**   *downtown at 414 Calle Principal*   *373-3116*
L-D. No L on Sat. & Sun.   *Expensive*
Nearly a dozen kinds of duck dishes, steaks cooked over oak wood and an enticing chocolate bar are among the specialties of this exciting new source of New California cuisine. The luxurious post-modern decor is a far cry from the building's firehouse origin.

Kathy's on the Korner   *downtown at 702 Cass St.*   *373-1712*
B-L. Closed Sun.   *Moderate*
Homemade foods, including delicious fruit muffins, are emphasized in this cheerful new coffee shop.

★ **Mario's Continental Restaurant**   *1 mi. NW at 710 Cannery Row*   *373-4492*
D only.   *Expensive*
Delicious Continental cuisine is served in elegant dining rooms.

Mark Thomas' Outrigger   *1 mi. NW at 700 Cannery Row*   *372-8543*
L-D.   *Moderate*
The Polynesian food and decor are all right, but the main attraction is the over-the-water location and dramatic bay views. A romantic little firelit lounge adjoins, and live entertainment and dancing are offered in the main lounge.

Mike's Seafood Restaurant   *downtown at 25 Fisherman's Wharf*   *372-6153*
L-D.   *Moderate*
This big relaxed restaurant sports one of the last of the old-fashioned, remarkably long menus that were once standard in seafood houses. For example, crab is prepared eight different ways. A fireplace and bay views enliven the dining room.

Old Fisherman's Grotto   *downtown at 39 Fisherman's Wharf*   *375-4604*
L-D.   *Moderate*
Well-made Monterey clam chowder is the highlight of this long-established seafood house, along with Monterey Bay prawns. The large casual dining room has a bay view.

★ **Perry House**   *downtown at Scott/Van Buren Sts.*   *372-7455*
L-D. Closed Tues.   *Expensive*
Regional California dishes and wines are served amidst Victorian elegance in a beautifully restored historic house with a panoramic view of Monterey and the bay.

★ **The Point Restaurant**   *downtown at 100 Pacific St.*   *373-1644*
L-D.   *Expensive*
A bonanza of dramatically displayed fresh pastas and exotic vegetables, and a high-tech frozen yogurt dessert island, hint that this rousing new restaurant may be the birthplace of a new generation of salad bars. Mesquite-broiled seafood and steaks are appropriate accompaniments. The expansive grey-and-purple-toned dining room that surrounds the raised salad and dessert island is a study in plush contemporary decor and careful detailing. Window walls on three sides give diners a close-up of Fisherman's Wharf and the bay.

Rocklands   *downtown at 375 Alvarado St.*   *649-3462*
L-D. Closed Sun.   *Moderate*
Lean California cuisine is combined with impressive contemporary art and background music in a newer restaurant with an appealing post-modern style.

The Rogue   *downtown at Wharf #2*   *372-4586*
L-D.   *Expensive*
Fresh seafood and choice beef are accompanied by panoramic harbor views in a large, nautically-themed bayside dining room. Formal service and linened table settings contrast with decor dominated by a fully outfitted fishing boat — complete with fish, crew, and sea gulls.

Sancho Panza   *downtown at 590 Calle Principal*   *375-0095*
L-D.   *Low*
Mexican and early California-style dishes are served in a historic adobe, and on a charming patio.

Sandbar and Grill   *downtown on Wharf #2*   *373-2818*
L-D.   *Moderate*
Fresh seafoods highlight a contemporary American menu in this new bar and grill with a boat's-eye view of the harbor and Fisherman's Wharf. Natural wood tones, plush blue seating, a classy island bar, and a piano accompaniment with dinner also contribute to the convivial atmosphere.

★ **Sardine Factory**   *1 mi. NW at 701 Wave St. in Cannery Row*   *373-3775*
L-D.   *Very Expensive*
This large, celebrated restaurant serves gourmet Continental cuisine and their own pastries and ice cream in an elegant historic setting. The Captain's Room recalls the plush ambiance of the height of the Victorian era. The Conservatory Room is a striking glass-domed space with the feeling of an elegant garden. There is also a sophisticated lounge.

Sierra's Landing   *downtown at Pacific/Scott Sts.*   *646-9744*
L-D.   *Moderate*
Homestyle Southern Italian meals are offered in an attractive California mission-style restaurant or on a delightful outdoor patio overlooking Fisherman's Wharf and the bay.

★ **Triples**   *downtown at 220 Olivier St.*   *372-4744*
L-D.   *Expensive*
Continental and French cuisine is served in an elegant new dining room fashioned out of a carefully converted old cottage.

★ **Whaling Station Inn**   *1 mi. NW at 763 Wave St. in Cannery Row*   *373-3778*
D only.   *Expensive*
In this large and very popular showcase of New California cuisine, an oak pit broiler is used to prepare fresh fish and choice steaks. Gourmet entrees are accompanied by exciting treatments of the finest seasonal produce and the peninsula's first all-California wine list. Much polished wood, greenery, and stained glass complement the Victorian decor.

The Wharfside Restaurant   *downtown at 60 Fisherman's Wharf*   *375-3956*
L-D.   *Moderate*
A contemporary seafood menu is supported by a half dozen varieties of ravioli that guests may select, along with more ordinary fare, from a classy update of a salad bar. Nicely appointed dining rooms occupy two levels in this large new restaurant. The wharf and bay views from upstairs are excellent.

LODGING

Monterey has a remarkable diversity of accommodations. Visitors can select from luxurious resorts, convention hotels, country-style inns, or an abundance of motels. Bargains are extremely scarce on weekends and during summer. On holiday and special-event weekends, some places even raise their rates well above the summer rates shown. Prices are typically reduced at least 30% below those listed on non-weekends from late fall through spring, especially by many of the motels along Fremont Street starting about a mile southeast of downtown, and on Munras Avenue starting just south of downtown.

Colton Inn - Travelodge *downtown at 707 Pacific St.* 649-6500
This newer motor lodge has a convenient downtown location, and a sauna. Each nicely furnished room has cable color TV and a phone.
   #201 — end, top fl., (duraflame log) fireplace, shared creekside balc., K bed...$64
   regular room — 2 Q or K bed...$64

★ **Doubletree Inn of Monterey** *downtown at 2 Portola Plaza* 649-4511
This newer landmark hotel between downtown and Fisherman's Wharf has a round outdoor pool, whirlpool, and (fee) tennis courts, plus impressive convention, restaurant, lounge, and shopping facilities. Each well-furnished room has a phone and cable color TV with (fee) movies.
   6th fl. — in-bath steambath, panoramic bay/town views, K bed...$132
   regular room — K bed...$94

El Castell Motel *2 mi. E at 2102 Fremont St.* 372-8176
A large indoor pool is the notable attraction of this well-maintained older motel. Each room has a phone and cable color TV with movies.
   regular room — K bed...$46

El Dorado Motel *.3 mi. S at 900 Munras Av.* 373-2921
This convenient, contemporary little motel is beautifully furnished. Each room has a phone and cable color TV with movies. A Continental breakfast is complimentary.
   #14 — end, top fl., (duraflame log) fireplace, some bay view, Q bed...$58
   regular room — Q bed...$48

Fireside Lodge *1 mi. E at 1131 10th St.* 373-4172
Raised gas-log fireplaces enhance each of the spacious, nicely furnished rooms in this contemporary motel, along with cable color TV, phones, and cooktop/refrigerator consoles. A hot tub is in the patio.
   top floor room — vaulted ceiling, K bed...$80
   regular room — Q bed...$70

★ **Holiday Inn** *2.5 mi. E at 2600 Sand Dunes Dr.* 394-3321
The Monterey Peninsula's only full-service beachfront hotel also has a large outdoor pool, plus a bay view-oriented restaurant and lounge. Bayside rooms offer floor-to-ceiling window views of Monterey across the water. Each spacious, well-furnished room has a phone and cable color TV with movies.
   #470,#370,#270 (in Bldg. E) — pvt. balc., superb bay view, K bed..$122
   regular room — 2 D beds...$100

★ **Hyatt Del Monte** *1 mi. SE at 1 Old Golf Course Rd.* 372-7171
The peninsula's largest lodging facility is a well-landscaped contemporary resort hotel. Twenty-one oak-shaded acres contain two outdoor swimming pools, a whirlpool, parcourse, and (for a fee) a beautiful 18-hole golf course and six tennis courts (two lighted). Elaborate convention, restaurant, lounge, entertainment, and some shopping facilities are also available. Each attractively furnished room has a phone and cable color TV with (fee) movies.
   view room — some overlook golf course/hills, K bed...$125
   regular room — some have open beam ceiling, K bed...$105

★ **The Jabberwalk** *1 mi. NW at 598 Laine St.* 372-4777
A convent above Cannery Row has been charmingly transformed into an antique-filled bed-and-breakfast inn. There are many extras, like goose down pillows and comforters, fresh flowers, a complimentary breakfast, and evening hors d'oeuvres and aperitifs.
   "Borogrove" — spacious, shower, windows on 3 sides, gas fireplace,
         superb bay view, K bed...$125
   regular room — shared bath, Q bed...$75

★ **The Mariposa**   *.6 mi. S at 1386 Munras Av.*   *649-1414*
Opened in 1984, this elegant motor inn has an outdoor pool, whirlpool, and covered garage. But, the real feature is the guest rooms. Each is spacious, beautifully decorated with some ultra-modern flourishes, and has cable color TV and a phone.

    #321,#223, "Spa Suites" — gas fireplace, in-room raised whirlpool, refr.,
                               double shower,   K bed...$100
    regular room —   Q bed...$72

★ **Monterey Sheraton Hotel**   *downtown at Del Monte Av./Calle Principal*   *649-4234*
The peninsula's newest and tallest hotel opened in 1984. At a time when most towns are losing their landmark hotels, Monterey now has two major full-service downtown hotels. Amenities at the Sheraton include an outdoor pool, whirlpool, and saunas, plus convention, restaurant, and lounge facilities and security parking. Each spacious room has a phone and color TV.

    regular room — pool view,   2 D or K bed...$110

Motel 6   *2 mi. E at 2124 Fremont St.*   *373-3500*
The **bargain** motel chain is represented by an extremely popular facility on motel row.

    regular room — pay TV,   D bed...$22

★ **Munras Lodge**   *.3 mi. S at 1010 Munras Av.*   *646-9696*
This plush ultra-modern motel has a whirlpool and sauna. Each spacious, well-furnished unit has a raised gas-burning fireplace, cable color TV, and a phone.

    #31 — top fl., corner, wet bar, pvt. balc., harbor/palm view,   K bed...$85
    #37 — corner, top fl., pvt. view,   K bed...$80
    regular room —   2 Q or K bed...$55

★ **Old Monterey Inn**   *.5 mi. SW at 500 Martin St.*   *375-8284*
A historic mansion built in 1920 has been converted into a gracious bed-and-breakfast inn in a lovely park-like setting. All rooms have private baths, and there are many charming extras — oversized beds, goose-down comforters, complimentary breakfast, and evening wine and cheese.

    "Library" — lg. windows on 3 sides, stone fireplace, pvt. tub/shower,   K bed...$135
    "Rookery" — cozy, fireplace, skylight, pvt. shower, pvt. view,   Q bed...$120
    regular room "Heatherwood" —   K bed...$100

Park Crest Motel - Best Western   *.4 mi. S at 1100 Munras Av.*   *372-4576*
Attractive landscaping and excellent furnishings give distinction to this small contemporary motel with an outdoor pool. Each room has cable color TV and a phone.

    #41 — end, top fl., Monterey pines view,   K bed...$68
    #34 — end, top fl., magnolia/park/ocean view,   K bed...$68
    regular room —   K bed...$60

The Pelican Inn   *.5 mi. S at Munras Av./Cass St.*   *375-2679*
An outdoor pool is a feature of this small, recently upgraded motel. Each of the cozy, nicely furnished rooms has a phone and color TV.

    #103,#109,#204 — raised fireplace, refr.,   Q bed...$70
    regular room —   Q bed...$50

Rancho Monterey Motel   *.5 mi. S at 1200 Munras Av.*   *372-5821*
This small single-level motel has nicely landscaped grounds and an outdoor pool with a slide. Each room has cable color TV and a phone.

    regular room —   Q bed...$45

★ **The Spindrift Inn - Best Western**   *1 mi. NW at 652 Cannery Row*   *646-8900*
The only bayfront lodging in the midst of Cannery Row opened in late 1984. It is a luxurious, European-style motor inn offering complimentary valet parking, Continental breakfast in the morning, and wine and cheese in the afternoon. Each beautifully decorated unit has a fireplace, refrigerator, phone, and remote-controlled cable color TV.

    oceanside room — fine bay view,   Q or K bed...$169
    regular room — overlooks Cannery Row,   Q or K bed...$129

★ **West Wind Lodge**   *.3 mi. S at 1046 Munras Av.*   *373-1337*
An attractive enclosed pool is the center of interest, and there is also a sauna in this stylish newer motel. Each well-furnished room has a phone and cable color TV with movies.

    "executive unit" (several) — spacious, gas fireplace, refr.,   K bed...$90
    regular room —   Q bed...$55

CAMPGROUNDS
Surprisingly, the only complete campground near town is far inland from the beach.

Laguna Seca Recreation Area   *7 mi. SE via CA 68*   *422-6138*
This large, county operated campground near a small reservoir has boat rentals, and features boating and fishing. Flush toilets, hot showers, and hookups are available. Each of the sites has a picnic table, fire ring and grill.   base rate...$9.50

SPECIAL EVENTS
Adobe Tour   *downtown*   *late April*
Attention is focused on historic buildings not normally open to the public during this one-day tour sponsored by the Monterey History and Art Association.

Monterey County Fair   *Fairgrounds*   *August*
Of special interest is the variety and quality of produce displayed and offered for sale in various forms in this major mid-summer event.

★ **Monterey Jazz Festival**   *Fairgrounds*   *mid-September*
The Monterey County Fairground is jammed for three days in September with jazz buffs listening to "living legends" and stars of tomorrow. Reservations should be made well in advance for this renowned event.

★ **Wine Festival**   *in town*   *late November*
Many of the nation's finest wineries are represented at a prestigious series of tastings, banquets, and seminars in praise of the grape.

OTHER INFORMATION
Area Code: *408*
Zip Code: *93940*
Monterey Peninsula Chamber of Commerce *downtown at 380 Alvarado St. 649-1770*

Nevada City, California

Elevation:

2,535 feet

Population (1980):

2,431

Population (1970):

2,314

Location:

148 mi. NE
of San Francisco

Nevada City is the picturesque essence of the Mother Lode country. Handsome Victorian homes and businesses line narrow streets that wind through steep forested foothills of the Sierra Nevada. A relatively mild, but damp, four season climate supports a luxuriant combination of broadleaf and pine trees that contribute to the town's distinctive appearance. Brilliant displays of fall colors and pleasant temperatures make fall the most appealing season. Yet the town is usually only crowded on weekends. Winters are cool and very wet. Snowfall is relatively light, so there are no major winter sports complexes in the area. Summer is the busiest season, when visitors explore both the historic town and nearby forests, lakes, rivers, and mountains on uniformly hot sunny days.

Miners founded the town in 1849 with a few tents and log cabins along Deer Creek. Placer gold was abundant, and even richer gravels were soon discovered in an ancient stream bed. By the end of 1850, several thousand people called the newly named town of "Nevada" home. (Fourteen years later the town's name was stolen when the State of Nevada was admitted to the Union. Begrudgingly, residents added the word "City" after "Nevada" to distinguish their town from the new state.) It became the seat of newly formed Nevada County in 1851. By 1856 it was California's third largest city with nearly ten thousand residents. After a disastrous fire that year, more substantial businesses were constructed of brick — with iron doors and shutters — and two fire companies were organized. A few years later, miners began to leave in great numbers for the new silver region in Nevada as the local gold placers and gravels began to play out. Thanks in part to its increasingly prosperous metal foundry, the town survived, albeit at a substantially reduced pace.

One of the West's most unspoiled Victorian business districts, still illuminated by gas lamps, is the priceless legacy of Nevada City's brief boom era. Impressive public buildings, historic theaters and churches, and a fine museum are all within an easy stroll of the heart of town. Other carefully restored and maintained brick and wood structures in the historic district house a growing number of specialty shops featuring Mother Lode artifacts, some good restaurants, and a captivating assortment of atmospheric theaters, bars, and saloons. There are surprisingly few places to stay, but the oldest operating hotel west of the Rockies is still the liveliest landmark in town.

Nevada City, California
Vokac Weather Rating

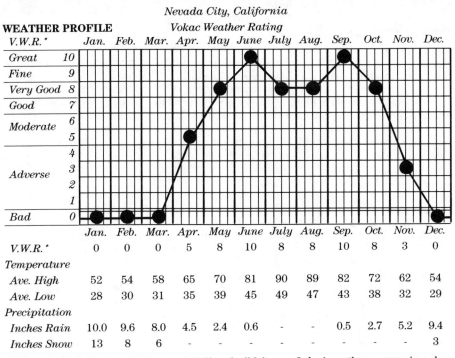

V.W.R. *		Jan.	Feb.	Mar.	Apr.	May	June	July	Aug.	Sep.	Oct.	Nov.	Dec.
V.W.R. *		0	0	0	5	8	10	8	8	10	8	3	0
Temperature													
Ave. High		52	54	58	65	70	81	90	89	82	72	62	54
Ave. Low		28	30	31	35	39	45	49	47	43	38	32	29
Precipitation													
Inches Rain		10.0	9.6	8.0	4.5	2.4	0.6	-	-	0.5	2.7	5.2	9.4
Inches Snow		13	8	6	-	-	-	-	-	-	-	-	3

*V.W.R. = Vokac Weather Rating: probability of mild (warm & dry) weather on any given day.

Forecast

Month	V.W.R. *		Temperatures Daytime	Evening	Precipitation
January	0	Bad	cool	chilly	frequent snowstorms/downpours
February	0	Bad	cool	chilly	frequent downpours/snow flurries
March	0	Bad	cool	chilly	frequent downpours/snow flurries
April	5	Moderate	warm	cool	occasional downpours
May	8	Very Good	warm	cool	infrequent rainstorms
June	10	Great	warm	cool	infrequent showers
July	8	Very Good	hot	warm	none
August	8	Very Good	hot	warm	none
September	10	Great	warm	cool	infrequent showers
October	8	Very Good	warm	cool	infrequent downpours
November	3	Adverse	cool	chilly	occasional downpours
December	0	Bad	cool	chilly	frequent downpours/snow flurries

Summary

Attractively situated in the Sierra foothills near the northern end of the Gold Camp country, Nevada City has a true four season climate. Almost all of the bad weather is concentrated into the **winter** months, when cool days and chilly evenings are coupled with frequent snowfalls and heavy rainstorms that preclude most outdoor activities. During **spring**, temperatures increase rapidly. Unfortunately, the enjoyment of normally warm days is diminished by rainstorms that persist through much of the season. **Summer** is relatively pleasant. Days are typically hot and sunny, evenings are warm, and there is almost no rainfall to keep people indoors. Early **fall** offers faultless weather until heavy rainstorms begin again in earnest after Halloween. This is unquestionably the most delightful time of year, because the surrounding countryside is ablaze with one of the West's most spectacular fall foliage displays. As an added attraction, it is also harvest time in the many nearby apple orchards.

ATTRACTIONS & DIVERSIONS

★ **The American Victorian Museum**   *downtown at 325 Spring St.*   *265-5804*
The museum occupies the historic Miners Foundry (1856), a group of stone, brick and frame buildings in which the Pelton Wheel (a key link between the water wheel and modern power generation) was first manufactured in 1878. Machine parts for mining operations were also made here, along with architectural iron used throughout the world. The museum is the only one in America devoted exclusively to displaying artifacts from the Victorian period (1840-1900). The complex also includes a popular theater, an unusual weekend restaurant and lounge, and a radio station. Closed Tues.-Thurs.

★ **Covered Bridge**   *14 mi. W in Bridgeport*
Built in 1862, the longest single-span wood covered bridge in America extends 225 feet across the South Yuba River at Bridgeport.

★ **Empire Mine St. Hist. Park**   *5 mi. S at 10791 E. Empire St. - Grass Valley*   *273-8522*
One of California's oldest and richest gold mines is also one of the deepest (9,000 feet) in the world. The grounds include a visitor center, mining exhibits, and the baronial Bourn Mansion. This former residence of the mine owner has been carefully restored and refurbished, as have the formal gardens surrounding the mansion. Guided tours are offered daily, except in winter.

Firehouse No. 1   *downtown at 214 Main St.*   *265-9941*
The Nevada County Historical Society now operates a museum in the photogenic 1861 structure. Pioneer implements and garb are exhibited.

Library   *downtown at 211 N. Pine St.*   *265-4606*
The Nevada City Public Library has served the area since just after the turn of the century from this substantial building. The unspoiled old-fashioned interior is distinguished by polished wood trim. Browsers are tempted to linger in a couple of fine old wooden rocking chairs.

★ **Malakoff Diggins State Historic Park**   *15 mi. NE off CA 49*   *265-2740*
Here was the world's largest hydraulic gold mine. The Malakoff Pit is an awesome testament to the destructive power of water under high pressure. It is a vast hole nearly 600 feet deep, 3,000 feet wide, and 7,000 feet long with a shallow lake at the bottom. Hydraulic mining was profitable, but it wrecked havoc with the environment. After a ten year legal battle, it was finally outlawed in California in 1884. Several interesting buildings still stand in the ghost town of North Bloomfield near the pit, including a former dance hall that is now a Park Museum with hydraulic mining exhibits. Nearby is the giant monitor nozzle that controlled the flow of water against the slopes. Wet winter weather closes the dirt access roads.

★ **North Star Mining Museum**   *4.5 mi. SW on Allison Ranch Rd. - Grass Valley*   *273-9853*
A giant thirty-foot Pelton waterwheel displayed here was the largest of its type in the world when it was installed in 1895. The massive old powerhouse now also houses a substantial collection of artifacts depicting the history and methods of California gold mining. Closed November-April except weekends.

Pioneer Park   *.5 mi. E on Nimrod St.*
A public outdoor swimming pool, tennis courts, playing fields, and shaded picnic tables are provided in this town park nestled in a fold of the hills.

Warm Water Feature
    Misty Mountain Tubs & Things   *downtown at 110 S. Pine St.*   *265-3149*
A Gold Camp update of the Saturday night bath furnishes private rooms with whirlpool tubs that can be rented by the hour. A sauna and a juice bar are other features. Massage can be arranged by reservation.

Winery
★   **Nevada City Winery**   *downtown at 321 Spring St.*   *265-9463*
This small new premium winery in the historic foundry complex is a delightful first for the area. The tasting room is dramatically, and aromatically, perched at the top of the wine storage and aging area. Tasting and sales 1-5.

SHOPPING
One of the West's most picturesque downtowns is a beguiling place to shop and stroll. The entire area is on the National Register of Historic Districts. Rows of pre-Civil War brick buildings line steep, narrow streets distinguished by wrought-iron gas lanterns and wooden street signs. Numerous specialty shops emphasize collectibles in arts, crafts, and artifacts related to the Mother Lode country.

Food Specialties
Apple Annie's   *6.5 mi. S via CA 49 at 13895 CA 174*   *273-9266*
Cider and homemade apple pie are served along with soups and sandwiches in a tiny roadside cafe, and at picnic tables in the orchard when weather permits. Fresh produce is sold in the adjoining market, including apples from their orchards harvested from September thru November.

★ **Friar Tuck's Wine Shop**   *downtown at 111 N. Pine St.*   *265-9093*
A fine assortment of premium California wines is attractively displayed. Several reasonably priced tastes are offered each day at an inviting wine bar. Closed Mon.

★ **Happy Apple Kitchen**   *11 mi. S via CA 49 on CA 174*   *273-2822*
Apples are showcased year-round in an imaginative variety of delectable homemade foods like apple/cream cheese muffins, apple milkshakes, and old-fashioned or French apple pie. These specialties are served with sandwiches and light lunches in a little dining room or on an adjoining covered porch. An adjacent fresh produce stand is only open during the summer, but apples from the orchard are sold a short distance down the road during the fall harvest.

Lily's Coffee House   *downtown at 315 Spring St.*   *265-3168*
All kinds of coffees, espressos, and other drinks are served with pastries (made in the area) and premium ice cream in an old house that is now a rustic haven of tranquility with fresh flowers, hanging plants, and classical background music.

★ **The Pastry Mill**   *.8 mi. S at 104 Argall Way*   *265-6330*
This plain little bakery offers a delicious assortment of donuts, pastries, cakes, and cookies to go, or with coffee at one of a few tables. Closed Sun.

Tad's Apple-a-day Farm   *2 mi. S via CA 49 at 10451 Pittsburg Rd.*   *273-6832*
Seven varieties of apples are harvested from September to December and sold with cold and delicious fresh-pressed cider at a photogenic little hillside farm.

Specialty Shops
★ **Alpha**   *downtown at 210 Broad St.*   *265-4503*
For more than a century, this large handsome store has been serving residents' houseware and hardware needs. It is still a great place to check out the latest in gold panning equipment, or at least to absorb the evolving spirit of the gold camps.

Grimblefinger   *downtown at 242 Commercial St.*   *265-5592*
Books and periodicals are offered, along with a gallery of prints and posters, in an inviting store next to a coffee house.

NIGHTLIFE
An outstanding assortment of theaters and bars offering live entertainment, drinking and dancing is clustered in the historic district at the heart of town. Many of these places are "living showcases" of authentic architecture and decor of the Victorian period.

★ **American Victorian Museum**   *downtown at 325 Spring St.*   *265-5804*
Live entertainment — plays, concerts, and more — take place most weekends in "the great stone hall." This cavernous brick and stone room was once the heart of a century-old iron foundry.

Cirino's   *downtown at 309 Broad St.*   *265-2246*
Live music and dancing are featured most nights. This comfortable new lounge gives patrons a choice of sofas, tables and chairs, or padded bar stools by a handsome hardwood back bar.

Coach House   *.9 mi. S at 754 Zion St.*   *265-5614*
Live country/western music is played nightly for dancing in a big, casual ranch-style lounge with comfortable armchairs. Closed Sun.

Deer Creek Bar   *downtown at 101 Broad St.*   *265-5808*
Music with a driving beat lures an energetic crowd of drinkers and dancers into a casual downstairs bar. An adjoining deck overhangs Deer Creek.

★ **Framastanyl's**   *downtown at 235 Commercial St.*   *265-9292*
Dancing to live music is offered most nights. This popular contemporary saloon has a firelit conversation area, some stained glass, a distinctive bar with padded-backed stools, abundant greenery, and a padded booth area that serves as a Mexican cafe during the day. A pleasant wood-decked courtyard is used when weather permits.

★ **McGees**   *downtown at 315 Broad St.*   *265-3205*
Occasional live entertainment enlivens a stylish brick-and-wood saloon with many plush sofas, numerous paintings, and a handsome bar.

★ **National Hotel**   *downtown at 211 Broad St.*   *265-4551*
An old upright piano is played frequently in the hotel's splendid Victorian saloon with its magnificent polished hardwood bar, period pictures, and ornate fixtures.

★ **Nevada Theater**   *downtown at 401 Broad St.*   *265-6161*
California's oldest theater building (1865) has been carefully restored. It serves once again as the community's cultural center. Musical and dramatic productions and special concerts are regularly scheduled and enthusiastically supported.

RESTAURANTS
Most of the good restaurants are concentrated in the historic district, and contribute to its charm with appropriately Victorian decor. American fare prevails, with a few notable exceptions.

Alvaro's Deer Creek Cafe   *downtown at 101 Broad St.*   *265-5808*
L-D.   *Moderate*
Authentically prepared South American dishes are an appealing surprise on a menu dominated by conventional Mexican fare. The new owners have refurnished the creekside location in plain Mexican-style decor.

The Apple Fare   *downtown at 203A York St.*   *265-5458*
B-L.   *Moderate*
Several good homemade pies are the specialty served with light meals in this cheerful, modest cafe.

Coach House   *.9 mi. S at 754 Zion St.*   *265-5614*
L-D.   *Moderate*
Steaks highlight hearty American dishes served in a large casual dining room next to a big lounge with Western music for dancing.

Creeky Cafe   *downtown at 300 Commercial St.*   *265-6951*
L-D.   *Moderate*
International dishes are served in an attractive brick-walled dining room, or on an intimate creekside patio when weather permits.

Friar Tuck's   *downtown at 111 N. Pine St.*   *265-2262*
D only. Closed Mon.   *Moderate*
Swiss and French fondue dinners are the specialty. Steaks, seafood, and chicken are also offered in a historic building refitted in brick-and-wood wine-cellar decor. The charming little front room bar has a good street view and an occasional vocalist.

★ **Jack's**   *downtown at 101 Sacramento St.*   *265-3405*
D only. Closed Sun.-Tues.   *Expensive*
Gourmet international cuisine is skillfully prepared from the freshest available ingredients. Five course dinners are presented at tables set with crystal, china, and silver in an elegant little dining room in an upstairs hideaway. Reservations are necessary.

National Hotel   *downtown at 211 Broad St.*   *265-4551*
B-L-D.   *Moderate*
American fare is served in the authentically Victorian dining room of Nevada City's landmark hotel. Bentwood chairs grace tables set with fresh flowers and kerosene lamps in a large room distinguished by polished wainscoting on high walls accented by ornately framed old pictures.

Rainbow Mountain Inn   *downtown at 238 Commercial St.*   *265-9939*
L only.   *Low*
Fresh coffees and all kinds of teas are served with a variety of omelets, homemade soups, and desserts in a casual little coffee shop next to an inviting bookstore.

Selaya's   *downtown at 320 Broad St.*   *265-5697*
D only. Closed Mon.   *Moderate*
Continental specialties are offered in a well-regarded Victorian-style dining room.

LODGING

Accommodations are surprisingly limited, considering the town's appeal. Visitors interested in staying in town should make reservations well in advance during the summer and fall, and on weekends throughout the year. Winter and spring rates are usually at least 15% less than those shown. A few more lodgings are available in nearby Grass Valley.

Airway Motel   *.3 mi. N at 575 E. Broad St.*   *265-2233*
This small, old **bargain** motel with an outdoor pool is a pleasant walk from the historic district. Each of the modest rooms has cable color TV, and units #7 thru #10 are backed by a tiny stream.

    regular room —   D bed...$22

Gold Country Inn - Best Western   *2.5 mi. S via CA 49 at 11972 Sutton Way*   *273-1393*
This contemporary motel by the freeway has an outdoor pool and whirlpool. The spacious rooms all have color TV and a phone.

    regular room —   Q bed...$38

Holiday Lodge   *3.5 mi. S at 1221 E. Main St.*   *273-4406*
An outdoor pool (enclosed in winter), a whirlpool, and sauna are features of this modern motel. Each room has cable color TV with movies, and a phone.

    regular room —   K bed...$34

★ **National Hotel**   *downtown at 211 Broad St.*   *265-4551*
Nevada City's three-story landmark, first opened in 1854, is the oldest continuously operated hotel in the state. Glimmerings of Victorian splendor flourish in the antique-filled public rooms. Modern amenities include an outdoor swimming pool, and private baths in most of the guest rooms. Rooms with shared baths are a **bargain**.

    #41 — top fl. corner, pvt. tiny balc., B/W TV, pvt. bath, town/mt. views,   Q bed...$38
    #20 — suite, corner, public balc., pvt. bath, some view, 4-poster   D bed...$64
    #34 — parlor suite, public balc., sitting room, B/W TV, pvt. bath, antique   K bed...$64
    regular room — pvt. bath,   D bed...$34
    regular room — shared bath,   D bed...$24

Northern Queen Motel   *.5 mi. S at 400 Railroad Av.*   *265-5824*
An outdoor pool and whirlpool distinguish this modern **bargain** motel. Each room has a color TV, a phone, and a refrigerator.

    deluxe room —   K waterbed...$34
    regular room —   Q bed...$27

Piety Hill Inn   *.4 mi. S at 523 Sacramento St.*   *265-2245*
A tiny old auto court built around a handsome chestnut tree has been ingeniously remodeled into a fashionable motor inn. Each artistically furnished room has a color TV and a private bath.

    #4 — spacious, captivating painting of 3 ladies,   K bed...$45
    regular room —   K bed...$35

★ **Red Castle Inn**   *.3 mi. E at 109 Prospect Av.*   *265-5135*
A Victorian mansion built in 1860 in carpenter gothic style on a hill overlooking downtown is now the area's favorite bed-and-breakfast inn. Rooms have been faithfully restored and furnished in Victorian antiques. Most have private baths. A complimentary Continental breakfast is served.

    Parlor Suite West — 1 BR, sitting room, wood-burning stove, pvt. bath,   D bed...$65
    regular room — shared bath,   D bed...$45

CAMPGROUNDS

There are many campgrounds in the area. The best are by wooded streams or reservoirs offering a good variety of water recreation.

Greenhorn Park   *11 mi. SE via CA 20, Brunswick Rd. & CA 174*   272-6100
This privately operated campground is on a gentle slope by Rollins Lake. Boat rentals, a ramp, and a dock are provided, and swimming, fishing, and boating are popular on the small reservoir. Pit toilets, cold showers, and hookups are provided. Each site has a view of the lake and a picnic table. Some are shaded, and there is a separate tenting area.
base rate...$6

★ **Oregon Creek**   *17 mi. NW via CA 49*   273-1371
This small Tahoe National Forest campground is beautifully sited by the Middle Yuba River. Swimming, fishing, and gold panning are popular in the little river, and there are hiking trails nearby. Flush toilets are provided, but no showers or hookups. Each of the tree-shaded well-spaced sites has a picnic table.   base rate...$4

★ **Scotts Flat Lake Recreation Area** *9 mi. E via CA 20 & Scotts Flat Rd.*   265-5302
A large private campground in a pine forest near a small reservoir has a sandy beach, boat rentals, and a (fee) dock and ramp. Boating, water-skiing, fishing, swimming, and hiking are popular. Flush toilets and hot showers, but no hookups, are available. Each site has a picnic table and a fire area. Some are pine-shaded with lake views.   base rate...$7.50

South Yuba Campground   *10 mi. NE on N. Bloomfield Rd.*   985-4474
The Bureau of Land Management operates this small campground in a rustic setting amidst pine and oak by the South Yuba River. Fishing, swimming, and gold panning are popular diversions, and a scenic trail through a rugged river canyon begins here. Only pit toilets have been provided. There are no showers or hookups. Each of the tree-shaded, well-spaced sites has a picnic table and fire area.   no fee

SPECIAL EVENTS

★ **Fall Color Spectacular**   *in/around town*   *October - November*
When the sugar maples are ablaze, along with aspen groves, orchards, and a host of other deciduous trees that lend brilliance to the countryside, Nevada City becomes one of the West's most colorful destinations.

★ **Victorian Christmas**   *downtown*   *Wednesdays in December*
Each year, on the four Wednesday nights preceding Christmas, the town celebrates its heritage with special food, music, and entertainment under the picturesque gaslights downtown.

OTHER INFORMATION

Area Code: *916*
Zip Code: *95959*
Nevada City Chamber of Commerce   *downtown at 132 Main St.*   265-2692
Tahoe National Forest Supervisor's Office *downtown at CA 1/Coyote St.*   265-4531

Ojai, California

Elevation:

746 feet

Population (1980):

6,816

Population (1970):

5,591

Location:

80 mi. NW
of Los Angeles

Ojai is the West's Eden. In fact, when the novel about "Shangri-La" was made into a movie, overview scenes were filmed here. Fruit and nut orchards fill the narrow little valley flanked by towering Coast Range mountains a dozen miles inland from the ocean. The climate is almost as exceptional as the setting. While every season is appealing, spring and fall are the most notable. Ideal weather accompanies the beauty and fragrance of citrus blossom-time in the spring, and the fruit and nut harvest in the fall. With nearby ocean beaches, a large man-made lake, and several hot springs, all kinds of water sports are extremely popular, especially on weekends throughout the year. Surrounding mountains attract hikers, backpackers, horseback riders, and campers. Scenic golf courses, tennis complexes, and other outdoor diversions are enjoyed year-round along with shopping in town.

The Chumash Indians settled in the valley and named it Ojai, which means "The Nest," long before Spaniards ventured along the nearby coast. Sequentially, Indians, Spanish, Mexicans, and Americans laid claim to this favored land. Since early in the twentieth century, the town has gradually evolved as both a secluded artists' colony and a serene resort. It was still a dusty little Western town by World War I, when a wealthy benefactor, Edward D. Libbey, began to translate his idea of simulating the architecture of southern Spain into an arcade, post office, and other downtown buildings. Much of the town's distinctive Spanish-style charm is a result of his legacy.

Today, the picturesque and compact downtown area lends itself to relaxing strolls and unusual shopping excursions. It is an appealing combination of inspired architecture, interesting specialty shops, and luxuriant vegetation. Numerous sophisticated studios and galleries display local arts and crafts. Ojai is an early source of New California cuisine. One of the nation's first restaurants to feature this style, which emphasizes innovative dishes skillfully prepared with fresh local ingredients, has become a valley landmark. Several other similarly oriented gourmet restaurants have been added in recent years. Nightlife is scarce in town and limited throughout the area, but it is available in places as diverse as plush resorts and funky roadhouses. Accommodations are also relatively scarce and sprinkled along the approaches to town. The best of these facilities lend graceful elegance to the quiet grandeur of the area.

WEATHER PROFILE — Vokac Weather Rating

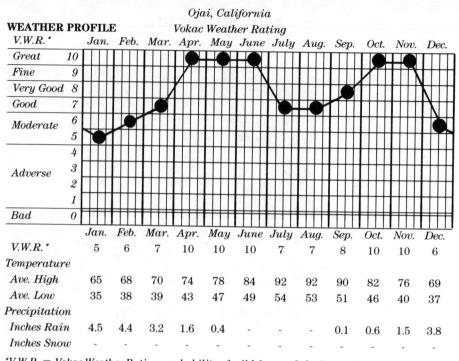

V.W.R.*	Jan.	Feb.	Mar.	Apr.	May	June	July	Aug.	Sep.	Oct.	Nov.	Dec.
V.W.R.*	5	6	7	10	10	10	7	7	8	10	10	6
Temperature												
Ave. High	65	68	70	74	78	84	92	92	90	82	76	69
Ave. Low	35	38	39	43	47	49	54	53	51	46	40	37
Precipitation												
Inches Rain	4.5	4.4	3.2	1.6	0.4	-	-	-	0.1	0.6	1.5	3.8
Inches Snow	-	-	-	-	-	-	-	-	-	-	-	-

*V.W.R. = Vokac Weather Rating: probability of mild (warm & dry) weather on any given day.

Forecast

Month	V.W.R.*	Temperatures Daytime	Temperatures Evening	Precipitation
January	5 Moderate	warm	cool	infrequent downpours
February	6 Moderate	warm	cool	infrequent downpours
March	7 Good	warm	cool	infrequent downpours
April	10 Great	warm	cool	infrequent downpours
May	10 Great	warm	cool	negligible
June	10 Great	hot	warm	none
July	7 Good	hot	warm	none
August	7 Good	hot	warm	none
September	8 Very Good	hot	warm	none
October	10 Great	warm	cool	infrequent rainstorms
November	10 Great	warm	cool	infrequent downpours
December	6 Moderate	warm	cool	infrequent downpours

Summary

Ojai is a New World Shangri-La, with a climate to match. Even during the **winter**, warm days are the rule. Heavy rainstorms only infrequently hinder outdoor activity, while nurturing a superabundance of lush vegetation. **Spring** is outstanding. Warm days, cool evenings, and little or no rainfall are ideal for outdoor activities. The delicate beauty and fragrance of millions of citrus and other blossoms is an unforgettable highlight of the little valley in this season. Surprisingly, **summer** is less usable because of uniformly hot, sunny days. There is normally no rainfall to relieve the heat or deter any outdoor plans. **Fall**, like spring, is extraordinary. Comfortably warm days, cool nights, and infrequent rainfalls are normal through Thanksgiving. It is a perfect time to explore the surrounding orchards while savoring the bounty of the fruit and nut harvest.

ATTRACTIONS & DIVERSIONS

★ **Bicycling**

Open Spaces *.5 mi. E at 996 E. Ojai Av.* 646-5205

Miles of flower-bordered paved byways provide access to all sections of the relatively flat little Shangri-La valley brimming with its subtropical orchards, luxurious gardens and grand old California live oaks sheltered by towering mountains. A good selection of bicycles can be rented by the hour or longer, and free maps are available at this open-air shop behind a gas station. Closed Sun.

Golf

★ **Ojai Valley Inn Golf Course** *1 mi. W off CA 150 on Country Club Dr.* 646-5511

Nationally known, this relatively level, spectacularly beautiful 18-hole golf course is open to the public year-round, along with a pro shop, putting green, club and cart rentals, and a fine view restaurant and lounge.

★ **Soule Park Golf Course** *.8 mi. E at 1033 Ojai Av.* 646-5633

This attractive county owned 18-hole championship course is open to the public year-round with all necessary rentals and facilities.

★ **Horseback Riding**

Chorro Grande Pack Station *25 mi. N on CA 150 at 22050 Maricopa Hwy.* 646-6606

Guided day, overnight, or extended horseback trips can be arranged into the high country wilderness of Los Padres National Forest.

Ojai Valley Inn Riding Stables *2 mi. W via CA 150 on Hermosa Rd.* 646-2837

Horses may be rented here by the hour for guided rides along oak-shaded byways around town.

Lake Casitas Recreation Area *6.4 mi. SW on CA 150* 649-2233

The site of the 1984 Olympic canoeing and rowing events is a many-armed freshwater reservoir surrounded by rolling grass-covered hills dotted with large oak trees. Its previous claim to fame has been as the source of state record bass and catfish. Scenic picnic sites plus many hundreds of campsites for tents and trailers overlook the lake. Because it is a domestic water supply, swimming, water-skiing, canoes, kayaks, and most inflatables are not allowed. Certain boats can be launched or rented, but only for fishing or sightseeing.

★ **Libbey Park** *downtown at Ojai Av./Signal St.*

Noble oaks and giant old sycamores preside over lawns and gardens, a fountain court, picnic and play areas, eight tennis courts, and the famed music bowl in a lovely little park in the heart of town.

★ **Library** *downtown at 111 E. Ojai Av.* 646-1639

The Ojai Library is in a distinctive little Spanish-style building. A working fireplace and comfortable sofas grace the periodical reading room. An adjacent walled, oak-shaded patio is a tiny haven of tranquility with year-round flowers maintained by the Garden Club.

★ **The Loop** *for 10 mi. E of downtown*

This ten-mile scenic drive suitable for either car or bicycle showcases the lush valley. It is an especially memorable tour when citrus groves fill the valley with an intoxicating fragrance during spring blossom-time. Miles of intriguing stone walls that line part of the road were built by Chinese labor during the 19th century. Drive east on Ojai Avenue 3.2 miles, then left on Reeves Road, McAndrew Road, and Thatcher Road.

★ **Los Padres National Forest** *N of town* 646-8293

This giant forest almost reaches the coast twenty miles west of town, and it includes all of the mountains towering above town to the north. The highest peaks reach pine-covered elevations nearly 9,000 feet above sea level. Some of the few remaining giant California condors are protected in the Sespe Condor Sanctuary a few miles east of town. The mountainous San Rafael Wilderness, Southern California's largest, is northwest of town. Hikers especially enjoy the rugged scenery and natural swimming holes on Matilija Creek north of town and along Sespe Creek to the east. Horseback riding, hunting, backpacking, fishing, and camping are also popular.

Valley of "Shangri-La"   *3.5 mi. E on CA 150*
The panorama representing Shangri-La that was seen by Ronald Colman years ago in the movie "Lost Horizons" is still magnificent from a small parking area near the top of the hill.

Warm Water Features

★ **Matilija Hot Springs**   *6 mi. NW via CA 33*   646-7667
Hidden away in a tiny scenic canyon, these hot springs were first developed as a health center and vacation resort in 1871. A large outdoor swimming pool is open during the summer, and an inviting picnic area overlooks a boulder-strewn creek. Meals are served in a rustic, cheerful dining room. In a nearby health studio are several small private hot mineral pools, some with whirlpool features, that may be rented by the hour. Massage can be arranged by appointment.

★ **Wheeler Hot Springs**   *7.7 mi. NW via CA 33*   646-8131
This century-old spa reopened in 1982. Redwood tubs can be rented in private rooms with skylights, both hot and cold mineral baths, and taped music. Massage is available by appointment.

SHOPPING
Ojai has one of the most compact and charming downtowns in the West. A cluster of Spanish-style buildings, many with graceful archways and landscaped courtyards, house a full range of quality stores including a notable assortment of art galleries and antique shops.

Food Specialties

★ **Bill Baker's Ojai Bakery**   *downtown at 457 E. Ojai Av.*   646-1558
A full line of breads, rolls, donuts, and pastries are displayed in this long-established bakery. A few coffee tables are available, as well as takeout service.

★ **Friend's Ranch**   *5 mi. NW on CA 33 at 15150 Maricopa Hwy.*   646-2871
Some of the finest local citrus, avocados, and nuts are sold at this roadside packing plant. Delicious fresh-squeezed orange juice is always available. Gift packs described in a free catalog will be shipped anywhere in the nation.

Good Taste   *downtown at 206 N. Signal St.*   646-2723
Gourmet deli items like homemade pates, quiches, and desserts, plus international cheeses, wines, coffees, etc., are packaged to go. They may also be enjoyed on a flower-strewn little deck or in a casual little dining room.

★ **Ojai Ice Cream & Candy Shoppe**   *downtown at 210 E. Ojai Av.*   646-6075
Many flavors of outstanding homemade ice cream and sherbets, plus homemade chocolates, are displayed in this tantalizing little takeout shop. The kiwi sherbet is a particularly innovative use of one of the locally grown exotic fruits.

★ **Ojai Liquors**   *.3 mi. W at 301 W. Ojai Av.*   646-5855
An excellent selection of premium California wines is nicely displayed and stored. Periodic evening tastings are featured. International beers and liquors are also well represented in this modern store.

Rancho Arnaz   *6.5 mi. SW on CA 33 - Oak View*   649-2776
From September to early November, you can pick your own apples. Several different kinds are grown. The ranch market also sells them packaged to go, plus cold cider, other seasonal fruits, nuts, and honey.

★ **Rancho Shangri-La**   *5.4 mi. E on CA 150 at 9340 Ojai Rd.*   646-1392
Fresh walnuts, shelled or in the shell, may be purchased starting in October at a roadside stand or at the farm. You can pick your own during the harvest (October-November) if you wish.

★ **Village Pastry**   *downtown at 217 E. Matilija St.*   646-2232
Delicious pastries, donuts, specialties like scones, and assorted breads are featured in this big cheerful bakery with several coffee tables.

Specialty Shops

★ **Bart's Corner**   *.3 mi. W at 302 W. Matilija St.*   646-3755
In this remarkable outdoor bookstore, thousands of used books are shelved around a giant oak tree that shades customers as they browse or read while drinking tea or juice. Flowers and gifts are also available. After hours, customers may select books from shelves that line the sidewalk, and pay for them by tossing coins through the gate.

★ **Beatrice Wood Studio**   *5 mi. E at 8560 CA 150*   *646-3381*
A magical setting in the hills above town complements the museum-quality pottery in this studio/gallery. The ceramist is renowned for the lustrous sheens that she has developed. Her exotic and erotic primitives are unforgettable.

★ **The Pottery**   *4 mi. E at 971 McAndrew Rd.*   *646-3393*
Quality dishes and vessels of all sorts are attractively displayed in an intriguing porcelain-stoneware studio/gallery. Closed Mon.

★ **Rain's**   *downtown at 218 E. Ojai Av.*   *646-1441*
The centerpiece for the captivating Ojai arcade is this long-established specialty department store, where everyday merchandise is displayed with a genuine flair.

★ **Running Ridge Gallery**   *downtown at 310 E. Ojai Av.*   *646-1525*
A contemporary collection of multimedia works by famous artists is beautifully showcased. An adjacent store bearing the same name features original-design clothing.

★ **Ruth H. Johnson Stoneware**   *4 mi. SW at 335 Encino Dr. - Oak View*   *649-9787*
Fanciful stoneware birds and beasts created by an award-winning potter are displayed in her studio/home. Both indoor and outdoor sculptures are for sale.

NIGHTLIFE
The tranquil little valley has a surprising diversity of possibilities for an evening's entertainment, ranging from the plush and peaceful comfort of a lush lounge in a sophisticated resort to the rowdy and rustic vitality of a ramshackle roadhouse.

The Art Center   *downtown at 113 S. Montgomery St.*   *646-0117*
Musicals, dramatic productions, dance performances, and lectures are presented in a small theater in the community art center on Fri., Sat., and Sun.

Deer Lodge   *2.5 mi. NW at 2259 Maricopa Hwy.*   *646-3813*
This rustic roadside tavern is an old-fashioned Western classic. Crowd-pleasing features include six kinds of tap beer (including Anchor Steam), several pool tables, darts, a patio, and short order home-cooked meals served all day.

Flaming Duck   *.3 mi. E at 815 E. Ojai Av.*   *646-7227*
Live country music is frequently played for dancing in a big, plain Western-style saloon.

★ **Ojai Valley Inn**   *1 mi. W off CA 150*   *646-5511*
There is usually live entertainment and dancing on weekends in the resort's comfortable lounge with picture window panoramas of the lush valley. The view from the adjoining terrace is even better.

The Wheel   *7.7 mi. N on CA 33 at 16816 Maricopa Hwy.*   *646-4069*
Live music draws crowds on weekends to a funky, lively old roadhouse with a much-used free-standing stone fireplace and some comfortable booths.

RESTAURANTS
Several gourmet restaurants have opened here in recent years, overseen by innovative chefs who take maximum advantage of the year-round availability of top quality, locally grown fruits and vegetables. As a result, the Ojai area has become a significant source of New California cuisine.

Antonio's   *downtown at 106 S. Montgomery St.*   *646-6353*
L-D.   *Low*
Authentic California-style Mexican food and atmosphere prevail. Don't be put off by the abundance of plastic and paper. The patio is pleasant and the food is good.

Flaming Duck   *.3 mi. E at 815 E. Ojai Av.*   *646-7227*
B-L-D. No D on Mon.   *Moderate*
A variety of breakfast omelets and good homemade biscuits are features in a casual Western-style restaurant with a conventional American menu.

★ **Gaslight**   *5 mi. SW on CA 33 at 11432 N. Ventura Av.*   *646-5990*
D only. Closed Mon.   *Moderate*
Several kinds of delicious veal dishes, Old World specialties, and al dente vegetables are highlights of this attractive dinner house. There is also a dining patio, and the lounge offers entertainment and dancing on weekends.

Landucci's   *downtown at 206 N. Signal St.*   *646-8829*
L-D. No L on Sun. Closed Mon.-Tues.   Moderate
Italian specialties are served in a contemporary dining room that adjoins an intimate
ultra-modern lounge with a fascinating slate mural and overstuffed armchairs.
★ **L'Auberge**   *.3 mi. W at 314 El Paseo Rd.*   *646-2288*
D only. Brunch on Sat. & Sun. Closed Tues.   Expensive
French-provincial cuisine emphasizing fresh ingredients is served in a lovely old home
that has been converted into a restaurant. In addition to a casually elegant dining room
with a cozy fireplace, there is a wonderfully tranquil garden porch.

★ **The Nest**   *downtown at 118 S. Montgomery St.*   *646-5256*
L-D. Brunch on Sat. & Sun. Closed Mon.   Moderate
The innovative soups, salads, sandwiches, and pastries made here fresh daily are classic
presentations of New California cuisine. This highly regarded restaurant is Ojai's most
sophisticated luncheon place. A first-rate gourmet deli recently opened in a front room.

Ojai Valley Inn   *1 mi. W off CA 150 on Country Club Dr.*   *646-5511*
B-L-D.   Expensive
Each of the resort's three large dining rooms offers distinctive views and classic American
food served in comfortable surroundings. Daily buffet lunches on the terrace are
outstanding because of the luxuriant vegetation and mountain-rimmed backdrop.

★ **The Ranch House**   *3 mi. W on S. Lomita Av.*   *646-2360*
D only. Sun. brunch. Closed Mon.-Tues.   Expensive
The valley's most famous restaurant was one of the West's first to feature New California
cuisine. Long before the regional style was widely known, the owner was creating unusual
gourmet dishes enhanced by locally grown herbs and vegetables, distinctive homemade
breads, and premium California wines. Picture windows in the informally elegant,
contemporary dining room overlook flower and herb gardens. Outside, tables shaded by
noble oaks are set under heat lamps for year-round enjoyment of the gardens, pools, and
fountains. Live chamber music is offered on Wednesday and Thursday evenings, and on
Sunday afternoons in spring and summer.

LODGING

Accommodations in Ojai are notably scarce, and there are no bargains on weekends.
Visitors interested in staying in one of the town's few good lodgings should have
reservations in advance on weekends year-round. Most places reduce their prices by at
least 15% during the week.

Capri Motel   *.8 mi. E at 1180 E. Ojai Av.*   *646-4305*
A large, scenic outdoor pool and whirlpool are features of this modern motel. Each
spacious room has a phone, cable color TV, and a private patio or balcony.
    #210,#209 — balc. with floor/ceiling view to mts.,   K bed...$45
    regular room —   2 D or K bed...$45
Casa Ojai - Best Western   *1 mi. E at 1302 E. Ojai Av.*   *646-8175*
There is a large outdoor pool and a whirlpool in this modern motel. A Continental
breakfast is complimentary. Each well-furnished room has a phone and cable color TV.
    regular room —   Q bed...$60
El Camino Lodge   *.3 mi. W at 406 W. Ojai Av.*   *646-4341*
This modern motel is the most convenient to downtown, and has an outdoor pool. Each
room has a phone and cable color TV.
    regular room —   2 D or K bed...$45
Los Padres Inn   *.8 mi. E at 1208 E. Ojai Av.*   *646-4365*
Set back from the highway, this contemporary Spanish-style motel has a large outdoor
pool and whirlpool. Each of the spacious well-furnished rooms has cable color TV and a
phone.
    deluxe room — newer, refr.,   2 Q beds...$52
    regular room —   2 Q or K bed...$52
The Oaks at Ojai   *downtown at 122 E. Ojai Av.*   *646-5573*
An old hotel and cottages have been converted into a popular health spa on beautifully
landscaped grounds. Guests are served three skillfully prepared low calorie meals daily

and given an opportunity to participate in all kinds of exercise, health, and self-awareness programs. Massage, facials, and other health and beauty services are available, plus an outdoor swimming pool, whirlpools, and saunas. Each room has a cable color TV and a phone.

cottage — spacious,	2 D beds...$180
regular room — in lodge,	2 D beds...$150

★ **Ojai Valley Inn**   *1 mi. SW off CA 150 on Country Club Dr.*   646-5511

For many years, this has been the premier resort of Ojai Valley. Year-round facilities on the spectacularly landscaped grounds of the renowned hideaway include a beautifully sited large outdoor pool, plus (for a fee) an 18-hole golf course, putting green, lighted tennis courts, and horseback riding, as well as several dining rooms, a lounge, and shops. Spacious modern rooms, each with a phone and cable color TV, are in several levels of a mountain view complex near the main building, and in luxuriously furnished older bungalows with patios. Rates are American plan, with breakfast and dinner included.

deluxe room — mt. or valley view, refr.,	*Q bed...$175*
regular room —	*2 T or D bed...$125*

★ **Roseholm Inn**   *5 mi. S at 51 Sulphur Mountain Rd.*   649-4014

A pink mansion built during the 1920s on a bluff near town became one of the West's most magnificent bed-and-breakfast country inns in 1984. Meticulously landscaped grounds include a large whirlpool, steamroom, and wine cellar. Each room has a lavish private bath and is beautifully decorated and furnished with antiques. Attention to details is reflected in luxurious towels and soaps, hand-painted rose tiles, and much more. Guests are greeted with fresh flowers, seasonal fruit, and premium champagne. A gourmet breakfast, and appetizers and wine, are complimentary, as are homemade desserts in the evening.

"Paradise" — top floor suite, fireplace, whirlpool, pvt. balcony,	Q bed...$295
"Masquerade" — suite, fireplace, whirlpool,	Q bed...$245
regular room "Tiffany" — whirlpool,	D bed...$185

CAMPGROUNDS

There are several campgrounds in the area. The best provide a choice of either a large and complete facility by a reservoir, or a smaller rustic campground by a cool mountain stream.

Lake Casitas Recreation Area   *6.4 mi. SW on CA 150*   649-2233

The municipal water district operates an enormous campground located on two miles of landscaped slopes by Lake Casitas. Rentals/dock/ramps are available for fishing boats. Most other kinds of boats, water-skiing and swimming are not allowed. The reservoir holds state records for bass and channel catfish. Flush toilets, (fee) hot showers, and hookups are available. Each of the closely spaced sites has a picnic table and a fire area. Most have a view of the scenic reservoir.   base rate...$7

Wheeler Gorge   *9 mi. N: 1 mi. W on CA 150 & 8 mi. N on CA 33*   646-4348

The U.S. Forest Service has provided a picturesque campground in Los Padres National Forest by a stream deep in a narrow rugged canyon. Fishing, swimming, and hiking are popular. There are flush toilets, but no showers or hookups. Each site has a picnic table and a fire area.   base rate...$6

SPECIAL EVENTS

★ **Ojai Music Festival**   *downtown in Libbey Park*   *first weekend in June*

The area's most famous annual event takes place in a tree-shaded outdoor amphitheater where classical and jazz concerts are performed before large and enthusiastic audiences.

★ **Ojai Tennis Tournament**   *downtown in Libbey Park*   *late April*

Since the nineteenth century, amateurs have been competing in this oldest invitational tournament of its kind in the U.S.

OTHER INFORMATION

Area Code: *805*
Zip Code: *93023*
Los Padres Nat. For. - Ojai Ranger Office   *.8 mi. E at 1190 E. Ojai Av.*   646-8293
Ojai Chamber of Commerce   *downtown at 338 E. Ojai Av.*   646-3000

Pacific Grove, California

Elevation:

50 feet

Population (1980):

15,755

Population (1970):

13,505

Location:

132 mi. SE
of San Francisco

Pacific Grove is a seaside haven of tranquility. Situated along a strikingly beautiful coastline where the waters of the Pacific Ocean and Monterey Bay converge, the town has been evolving as a refined refuge for nearly a century. Lovingly maintained Victorian homes and businesses predominate amid landscapes of mature trees and colorful gardens. Complementing the peaceful setting is a temperate year-round climate that is one of the West's finest. Spectacular displays of flowers and lush green hues in spring are especially memorable. Summer and fall are the busiest seasons, when warm, rainless days assure comfortable enjoyment of all area attractions. Carefully tended shoreline parks with delightful gardens, sandy beaches, coves, and winding paths frame the entire ocean and bayside perimeters of town. Strolling, bicycling, beachcombing, sunbathing, scuba diving, sailing, and fishing are popular activities. Inland, browsing the wonderfully old-fashioned business district, or exploring quiet neighborhoods, a notable small museum, or a historic lighthouse are other favorite pastimes. Nearby, outstanding facilities for golf and tennis draw players to some of the prettiest sites anywhere.

Methodists founded the town in 1875 when they started using the area as a summer retreat. Strict ordinances regulating dancing, drinking, swimming, and even profanity lasted until quite recently. In fact, it wasn't until 1969 that Pacific Grove residents voted to permit the sale of alcohol in what had been California's last "dry" town. The legacy of the austere early settlers was the creation of a genteel haven amidst extravagent surroundings.

Today, well-groomed Victorian houses and shops on quiet tree-shaded streets lend distinction to the town. This is especially evident downtown, where the charming appearance and feeling of a Northeastern village center before the turn of the century has been wonderfully retained. Some sophisticated galleries and specialty shops are features of the classic district. While there is little "action" to disturb tranquil evenings, well-regarded live theater is available, and two plush bayside cocktail lounges frame unforgettable seascapes through their picture windows. Accommodations range from some of the West's finest Victorian inns to comfortable motels. Several lodgings are clustered in a shady forest that is the famed winter home of millions of monarch butterflies. Others overlook the bay or ocean.

Pacific Grove, California

WEATHER PROFILE   *Vokac Weather Rating*

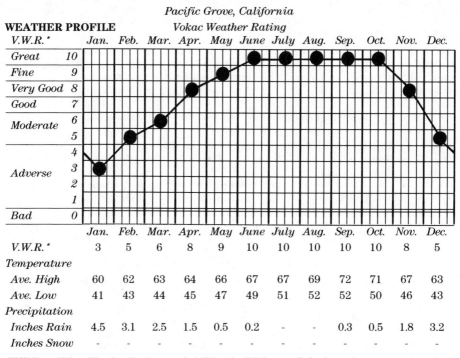

V.W.R.*	Jan.	Feb.	Mar.	Apr.	May	June	July	Aug.	Sep.	Oct.	Nov.	Dec.
V.W.R.*	3	5	6	8	9	10	10	10	10	10	8	5
Temperature												
Ave. High	60	62	63	64	66	67	67	69	72	71	67	63
Ave. Low	41	43	44	45	47	49	51	52	52	50	46	43
Precipitation												
Inches Rain	4.5	3.1	2.5	1.5	0.5	0.2	-	-	0.3	0.5	1.8	3.2
Inches Snow	-	-	-	-	-	-	-	-	-	-	-	-

V.W.R. = Vokac Weather Rating: probability of mild (warm & dry) weather on any given day.

Forecast

Month	V.W.R.*		Temperatures		Precipitation
			Daytime	Evening	
January	3	Adverse	cool	cool	frequent rainstorms
February	5	Moderate	cool	cool	occasional rainstorms
March	6	Moderate	cool	cool	occasional rainstorms
April	8	Very Good	cool	cool	infrequent rainstorms
May	9	Fine	warm	cool	infrequent showers
June	10	Great	warm	cool	negligible
July	10	Great	warm	cool	none
August	10	Great	warm	cool	none
September	10	Great	warm	cool	negligible
October	10	Great	warm	cool	infrequent showers
November	8	Very Good	warm	cool	infrequent rainstorms
December	5	Moderate	cool	cool	occasional rainstorms

Summary

Pacific Grove occupies the picturesque northwestern tip of the Monterey Peninsula, and shares one of the West's most desirable climates with Monterey and Carmel. Mild conditions prevail except during **winter**, when cool, frost-free weather is the norm, along with occasional rainstorms which contribute well over half of the average annual precipitation. In **spring**, shower activity diminishes, fog and sea breezes become more common, and an unbroken stretch of comfortably warm days and cool evenings begins. There are two fascinating natural phenomena that occur during these seasons. Monarch butterflies by the millions return to their favorite trees on the west side of town for the winter, and the slopes along the bayfront parks become flamboyant masses of vivid purple as carpets of tiny iceplants salute spring. **Summer** is remarkable. Warm days, cool nights, and no rainfall are perfect (occasionally marred by fogs) for comfortably enjoying this scenic seaside hideaway. **Fall** extends summer weather, and even improves it with the year's highest temperatures normally occurring at this time. Ideal conditions prevail until after Thanksgiving, when the rainy season begins again in earnest.

ATTRACTIONS & DIVERSIONS

★ **Butterfly Trees**   *.5 mi. W around Lighthouse Av. & Seventeen Mile Dr.*
Pacific Grove is known as "Butterfly Town, U.S.A." because of the annual migration of hundreds of thousands of monarch butterflies to selected groves of trees (especially west of Seventeen Mile Drive and south of Lighthouse Avenue) between October and March.

Golf

★   **Pacific Grove Municipal Golf Course**   *1.2 mi. NW at 77 Asilomar Blvd.*   375-3456
With nicely maintained, relatively level fairways carved out of low sand dunes near the ocean, this public 18-hole golf course is one of the most popular on the peninsula. Facilities include a pro shop, practice range, club and cart rentals, and a restaurant.

Library   *downtown at Central & Fountain Avs.*   373-0603
The Pacific Grove Library is a modern building with high arched windows. The inviting periodical reading area has armchairs and numerous wall hangings. Closed Sun.

★ **Lover's Point**   *.3 mi. N at the bay end of 17th St.*
A small bayside park combines sandy coves, dramatic rock formations, Monterey cypress, and colorful landscaping into one of the peninsula's most romantic and photogenic highlights.

★ **"The Magic Carpet of Mesembryanthemum"**   *N along the bay*
This fanciful tongue-twister is the name for masses of ice plants that drape a stretch of Monterey Bay shoreline northwest of Lover's Point. From April through August, a solid lavender-pink carpet of tiny flowers provides a brilliant accompaniment to green grass and shrubs above the rockbound bay.

★ **Pacific Grove Museum of Natural History** *downtown at Forest/Central Avs.* 372-4212
Once singled out as the highest rated museum of its size in the United States, this free facility has a notable exhibit concerning the monarch butterfly. Also, a relief map of the peninsula and bay graphically depicts the great chasm of Monterey Bay, which plummets within a few miles from shore to 8,400 feet below sea level — far deeper than the Grand Canyon. Closed Mon.

★ **Point Pinos Lighthouse**   *1.2 mi. W on Ocean View Blvd.*
The oldest continuously operating lighthouse on the Pacific Coast has stood at the entrance to Monterey Harbor since 1855. It is open to the public only on Saturdays and Sundays between 1 and 4 p.m.

★ **Shoreline Parks**   *N & W along Ocean View Blvd. and Sunset Dr.*
One of the West's most picturesque coastline drives winds for four miles along a variously flower-bordered, rockbound, and sandy shoreline. The road is a boundary between the residential portions of town and a continuous series of seaside parks. Along Monterey Bay, beautifully landscaped parks provide access to numerous sandy beaches tucked into coves along the rocky headlands. Sunbathing, strolling, and picnicking are popular, and scuba diving is ideal when the bay is calm and clear. During the summer, glass-bottom boats take visitors out to marine gardens just offshore. On the ocean side, the rugged, rocky shoreline is flanked by low grassy sand dunes stopped short by a pine forest that never quite reaches the sea.

Warm Water Feature
    Different Soaks   *1 mi. S at 1157 Forest Av.*   646-8293
Hot tubs with whirlpool jets are the main attraction in private rooms with redwood decks, garden settings, showers, music, and a phone for ordering soft drinks. There is also a sauna. Tubs can be rented by the hour during the day or evening.

Windsurfing
    The Wind Center   *1 mi. S at 1012 Olmstead Av.*   375-0100
Windsurfing equipment rentals and lessons are offered to anyone interested in participating in this increasingly popular sport on Monterey Bay.

SHOPPING

Remarkably tidy Victorian structures dominate a compact central business district with a full range of distinctive shops. All of the colorful buildings are extensively landscaped and convenient to free parking areas.

Food Specialties

Bagel Bakery   *1 mi. S at 1180 C Forest Av.*   649-6272
A variety of good, locally produced bagels are served with coffee or to go.

★ **Cloris' Croissants**   *.7 mi. E at 125 Ocean View Blvd.*   372-3046
Awesome plain and filled croissants are made fresh daily in an exhibition kitchen, and served to go or with beverages and preserves at tables in this luscious new shop.

★ **Liquor Barn**   *1 mi. S at 1170 Forest Av.*   646-8571
An outstanding selection of local and other California premium wines is sold at a worthwhile discount in a converted grocery store.

Scotch Bakery   *downtown at 545 Lighthouse Av.*   375-3569
This place has been serving the area with a full line of baked goods and some specialties like scones for more than fifty years. Closed Sun.-Mon.

Specialty Shops

★ **American Tin Cannery**   *.7 mi. E at 125 Ocean View Blvd.*
A cavernous old tin can manufacturing plant near Cannery Row has been ingeniously transformed. The original high ceilings and banks of skylights now impart a bright and spacious feeling to a series of specialty shops and restaurants amidst attractive fountains and plants.

★ **Bookworks**   *downtown at 667 Lighthouse Av.*   372-2242
One of the peninsula's most complete and well-organized bookstores also has a large selection of magazines and newspapers. A coffee bar features espresso and other hot beverages, plus croissants, bagels, and desserts from local sources in an atmosphere of classical music and all-you-can-read.

★ **Holman's Department Store**   *downtown at 542 Lighthouse Av.*   372-7131
This delightful, family-owned department store has been providing old-fashioned service and quality in a downtown landmark for more than a half century. The top floor restaurant/deck has a superb view of town and Monterey Bay.

★ **Pacific Grove Art Center**   *downtown at 568 Lighthouse Av.*   375-2208
A handsome building in the heart of town is now a lively art center. Displays of locally created arts and crafts in a variety of media are nicely showcased. A new exhibit with a reception is featured every five weeks. Closed Sun.-Mon.

★ **Vintage House**   *downtown at 213 Forest Av.*   649-6091
This new store is a one-stop shopping center for contemporary gourmet provisions — wines, cheese, chocolates, preserves, pates, and more. There are also a few small tables where you can enjoy a cup of first-rate freshly brewed coffee.

NIGHTLIFE

Pacific Grove is still a haven of tranquility after dark, as it has been for over a century. While most of the action is in Monterey, there are a few genteel places to enjoy live entertainment, a quiet drink, or good live theater in town.

★ **The California Repertory Theater**   *.7 mi. E at 125 Ocean View Blvd.*   372-4373
A full range of professional theater is presented throughout the year in a small, comfortable playhouse in the newly transformed American Tin Cannery Complex.

★ **Old Bath House**   *.3 mi. N at 620 Ocean View Blvd.*   375-5195
A historic bayside bathhouse has become an acclaimed restaurant and a lounge with plush romantic decor, a splendid Victorian back bar, and a memorable view of Monterey Bay.

★ **The Tinnery**   *.3 mi. N at 631 Ocean View Blvd.*   646-1040
Easy listening live music is featured nightly in this restaurant's elegant and ultra-contemporary lounge. The panoramic view of the landscaped coastline at Lover's Point is unforgettable.

RESTAURANTS

Several gourmet dining rooms have been added in recent years to a large assortment of restaurants serving primarily American dishes in pleasant surroundings. Several have fine bay views.

★ **First Watch**   *.7 mi. E at 125 Ocean View Blvd.*   372-1125
B-L.   *Moderate*
Unusual egg dishes, many omelets, and pancakes are featured in cheerful rooms with comfortable booths and tables set with fresh flowers and jam pots. A small courtyard is used for alfresco dining in good weather.

★ **La Maisonette**   *downtown at 218 17th St.*   *372-4481*
L-D. No D on Mon.-Wed. Closed Sun.   Moderate
A charming little French bistro is operating out of a recently converted Victorian cottage.
Gourmet crepes and other French specialties are served in casual country-cottage
atmosphere, and in a tiny courtyard.

Monarch Restaurant   *downtown at 162 Fountain Av.*   *373-7911*
B-L-D. Closed Sun.   *Moderate*
Homemade desserts and biscuits, and a variety of breakfast omelets, are specialties in this
popular and unassuming coffee shop.

★ **Old Bath House Restaurant**   *.3 mi. N at 620 Ocean View Blvd.*   *375-5195*
D only. Sun. brunch.   *Expensive*
Continental cuisine is featured, along with homemade desserts. A magnificent view of
Monterey Bay is complemented by romantic, informally elegant atmosphere in an
ingeniously converted Victorian bathhouse.

Old European Restaurant   *downtown at 663 Lighthouse Av.*   *375-1743*
D only. Closed Mon.   *Expensive*
European specialties are served amidst pleasant Old World atmosphere.

Pasta Mia   *downtown at 481 Lighthouse Av.*   *375-7709*
D only.   *Moderate*
Tempting Italian dishes like shrimp in champagne and cream sauce, homemade dessert
pastries, and gelato are served in cozy, casual dining rooms in a converted cottage.

★ **Pheasant's Eye**   *.6 mi. E at 159 Central Av.*   *372-7009*
D only. Closed Sun.-Mon.   *Expensive*
The gourmet menu changes weekly depending on the best seasonally available meats and
produce. An old cottage has been artistically transformed into an elegant ultra-nouveau
restaurant where careful attention is paid to every detail of the decor as well as the New
California-style food.

Pierre's   *1.5 mi. W at 1996 Sunset Dr.*   *372-2221*
B-L-D. No. D on Mon. Closed Tues.   *Low*
Homemade pastry such as scones, biscuits, and pies, plus french-fried artichoke heart
appetizers (in season), highlight an informal Continental menu offered in a motel's casual
dining room.

Solarium Coffee Shop   *downtown at 542 Lighthouse Av.*   *372-7131*
L only. Closed Sun.-Mon.   *Low*
Light American fare is served, but the real crowd-pleaser is the outstanding panoramic
view of Monterey Bay and Pacific Grove from this large pleasant dining room atop
Holman's Department Store.

Tillie Gort's   *.6 mi. E at 111 Central Av.*   *373-0335*
L-D. Closed Sun.   *Moderate*
This natural food restaurant, coffee house, and art gallery does interesting things with
homemade soups and baked goods. Rustic barnwood decor, far-out graphics painted on
the ceiling, lacquered wood tables, and artifacts everywhere suggest the enduring
Bohemian spirit of the place.

The Tinnery   *.3 mi. N at 631 Ocean View Blvd.*   *646-1040*
B-L-D.   *Moderate*
The menu offers a variety of international dishes, but the highlight of this plush
contemporary restaurant is an expansive window-wall view of Lover's Point Park and
Monterey Bay.

LODGING
Accommodations honor the natural beauty and serene Victorian spirit of Pacific Grove in
facilities ranging from stylish contemporary motels to lovingly restored Victorian guest
homes. None of the major motel or hotel chains are present. All of the lodgings are
relatively small, except the specialized Asilomar Conference Center. Bargain rooms are
nonexistent, and vacancies are unusual on any weekend and throughout summer. From
late fall through spring, non-weekend rates are often reduced at least 25% below those
shown.

Andril Fireplace Cottages   *1.1 mi. W at 569 Asilomar Blvd.*   *375-0994*
These units are in the pines a short walk from an ocean beach. Each of the newer cottages has a wood-burning fireplace and full kitchen, plus cable color TV and a phone.

regular room —	Q bed...$54

★ **Beachcomber Inn**   *1.5 mi. SW at 1966 Sunset Dr.*   *373-4769*
This modern motel is near ocean beaches and sand dunes. There is a pool and a sauna, and complimentary bicycles are a popular feature. Each room has cable color TV with movies, and a phone.

#24 — end, top (2nd) fl., pvt. patio, refr., view to ocean,	K bed...$69
regular room —	Q bed...$53

Borg's Motel   *.3 mi. N at 635 Ocean View Blvd.*   *375-4206*
This is one of the Monterey Peninsula's few waterfront motels. Some rooms have views across a street to a lovely park by Monterey Bay. Each modestly furnished room has cable color TV and a phone.

#50 — spacious, corner of top (2nd) fl., bay view windows on 2 sides,	Q bed...$68
regular room —	Q bed...$45

Butterfly Grove Inn   *.8 mi. NW at 1073 Lighthouse Av.*   *373-4921*
The adjacent woods are home to vast numbers of monarch butterflies from October to March each year. An outdoor pool and whirlpool are available to guests. Each room has cable color TV and a phone.

regular room —	Q bed...$40

★ **Butterfly Trees Lodge - Best Western** *1 mi. NW at 1150 Lighthouse Av.*   *372-0503*
An outdoor pool and whirlpool, plus a sauna, are features of this completely remodeled motel a short walk from the ocean. A Continental breakfast and wine and cheese are complimentary. Each beautifully decorated new unit has a phone and cable color TV.

#216,#218,#115,#117 — 1 BR, kit. with microwave, fireplace,	
balc., ocean view,	K bed...$120
#204 — fireplace, balc., ocean view,	Q bed...$76
#206,#216 — fireplace, balc., ocean view,	K bed...$84
regular room —	Q bed...$58

Centrella Hotel   *downtown at 612 Central Av.*   *372-3372*
Recently, a century-old building was meticulously restored and upgraded into a large bed-and-breakfast inn. Plush period furnishings and pastel colors are used in each individually decorated room. A complimentary Continental breakfast is served in the morning, and sherry in the evening.

"Vera Franklin Suite" — pvt. bath, wet bar, color TV, some bay view,	Q bed...$115
regular room #24 — shares bath with one other room,	Q bed...$60

★ **Gosby House Inn**   *downtown at 643 Lighthouse Av.*   *375-1287*
An authentic Victorian mansion in the heart of town now serves as a bed-and-breakfast inn tastefully furnished with original antiques. A Continental breakfast is included, as is late afternoon tea or sherry. Bicycles are available for the asking.

#11 — fireplace, pvt. bath,	Q bed..$110
#17 — pvt. bath, window seat,	Q bed...$97
regular room — small, pvt. bath,	D bed...$65

★ **Green Gables Inn**   *.5 mi. E at 104 5th St.*   *375-2095*
The bay is less than one hundred feet from a magnificent turn-of-the-century mansion that is now a bed-and-breakfast inn. Elegant period furnishings are used throughout. A complimentary breakfast is served in the dining room each morning, and wine is offered in the parlour each afternoon.

"Lacey Suite" — parlor with a fireplace, pvt. bath,	Q bed...$125
"Gable" — shared bath, ocean view windows,	Q bed...$90
"Balcony" — shared bath, balc., view to ocean,	Q bed...$90
regular room "Garrett" — shared bath, ocean view,	D bed...$70

Larchwood Inn   *1.2 mi. SW at 740 Crocker Av.*   *373-1114*
This newer motel is in a woodsy setting near Asilomar State Beach. Each of the spacious units has a duraflame log fireplace, color TV, and a phone.

#121 — top fl., corner windows, pine view,	Q bed...$40
regular room —	Q bed...$40

Olympia Motor Lodge   *1 mi. NW at 1140 Lighthouse Av.*   *373-2777*

There is an outdoor pool in this contemporary wood-toned motel. Some of the spacious units have an almost Oriental simplicity, and balconies with distant ocean views. Each has cable color TV and a phone.

#7A — corner, pitched roof, 2 decks, pvt. view to waves,	K bed...$68
#8B — corner, pitched roof, view to waves, kitchenette,	Q bed...$68
regular room —	Q bed...$38

Pacific Gardens Inn   *1.2 mi. W at 700 Asilomar Blvd.*   *646-9414*

This is a small, new motel in the pines a short walk from an ocean beach. There is a whirlpool. Each of the well-furnished rooms has a pressed-log fireplace, cable color TV and a phone.

regular room —	K bed...$70
regular room —	Q bed...$65

★ **Seven Gables Inn**   *.3 mi. NE at 555 Ocean View Blvd.*   *372-4341*

Monterey Bay is across the street from this handsomely restored Victorian mansion. Each room has a private bath and is lavishly decorated with an eclectic collection of mostly antique furnishings. A generous Continental breakfast is included.

"W side of 2nd fl." — fine bay views, refr.,	Q bed...$100
"NE side of 2nd fl." — fine bay views,	Q bed...$100
regular room —	D bed...$75

The Wilkie's Motel   *.8 mi. NW at 1038 Lighthouse Av.*   *372-5960*

Most of the rooms in this attractively furnished modern motel have cable color TV and a phone.

#12 — end of top fl., corner windows, bay/pines view,	K bed...$58
regular room —	Q bed...$50

CAMPGROUNDS

No campground on the peninsula accommodates both tents and RVs, but there are two complete campgrounds within a half hour's drive inland.

Laguna Seca Recreation Area   *10 mi. SE past Monterey via CA 68*   *422-6138*

This large Monterey County campground near a small reservoir has boat rentals and ramps, and features boating and fishing. Flush toilets, hot showers, and hookups are available. Each of the sites has a picnic table, fire ring, and grill.   base rate...$9.50

Saddle Mountain Recreation Park   *9 mi. SE via Carmel Valley Rd.*   *624-1617*

This privately operated campground has a (fee) pool and a rec room. Flush toilets, hot showers, and hookups are available. Each site has a picnic table and fire area.

base rate...$10

SPECIAL EVENTS

Good Old Days Celebration   *several locations in town*   *late April*

A classic Victorian homes tour is featured, along with an arts and crafts fair, a parade, and entertainment.

★ **Feast of Lanterns**   *shoreline parks*   *last week of July*

A lantern-lit procession along the shore accompanied by fireworks is the highlight of a unique celebration that also includes street dancing, sporting events, live entertainment, and a barbecue.

★ **Butterfly Festival**   *downtown*   *October*

A parade where no commercial aspects are allowed, plus a carnival and bazaar, celebrate the arrival of hundreds of thousands of beautiful monarch butterflies that annually migrate hundreds of miles to their winter destination — groves of trees on the west side of town.

OTHER INFORMATION

Area Code: *408*

Zip Code: *93950*

Pacific Grove Chamber of Commerce   *downtown at Forest & Central Avs.*   *373-3304*

Palm Springs, California

Elevation:

448 feet

Population (1980):

32,271

Population (1970):

20,936

Location:

107 mi. E
of Los Angeles

Palm Springs is America's desert showplace. A striking patchwork of sleek, low-profile buildings and lush manicured landscapes is interspersed with barren rock and sand along the base of one of southern California's highest mountains. The precipitous bulk of this towering peak and its dazzling mantle of winter snow provides a remarkable contrast to the flat desert floor. It even affects the climate by throwing a shadow over the town while the rest of the desert to the east continues to bake in the afternoon sun. Spring and fall are appealing seasons, but Palm Springs is the only great town where the best weather occurs in winter. Then, while the rest of the nation copes with snow or rain, a variety of special events are celebrated during warm sunny days enhanced by the intoxicating aroma of citrus and other fragrant vegetation. The desert offers memorable natural beauty in and around town — as undulating sand dunes; endless beaches without water; barren rock and boulder gardens; and as America's most phenomenal natural oases in desert canyons where thousands of native palms provide an exotic backdrop to streams, pools, and falls along the lower reaches of the San Jacinto Mountains. Nearby, irrigation has transformed hostile flatlands into mind-boggling numbers of golf courses, tennis courts, swimming pools, parks, and gardens. These facilities attract capacity crowds in winter, and (thanks to centralized air conditioning) even attract bargain seekers during the area's long, relentlessly scorching summers.

By the late nineteenth century, U.S. government maps identified the tiny settlement in this area as "Palm Springs," recognizing both the hot springs and palm trees nearby. Around the turn of the century, the government granted many even-numbered sections along the base of the mountains to descendants of Cahuilla Indians who preceded the earliest white settlers to the area. Odd-numbered sections had been given earlier to the Southern Pacific Railway as incentive for developing a transcontinental railroad. Growth was slow until effective air conditioning made the desert livable year-round in the 1950s. Also in that decade, celebrity golf tournaments and other star-studded events began to confirm Palm Spring's destiny as the center of America's desert playground.

Today, stylish contemporary businesses along and near Palm Canyon Drive showcase the town's vitality, wealth, and an increasingly cosmopolitan flair. This beautifully landscaped area has some of the most elaborate specialty shops, galleries, restaurants, and entertainment places that money can buy. Among the abundant lodgings in the area, a growing array of opulent resort hotels with lavish facilities are within an easy stroll of the heart of town.

WEATHER PROFILE

Palm Springs, California
Vokac Weather Rating

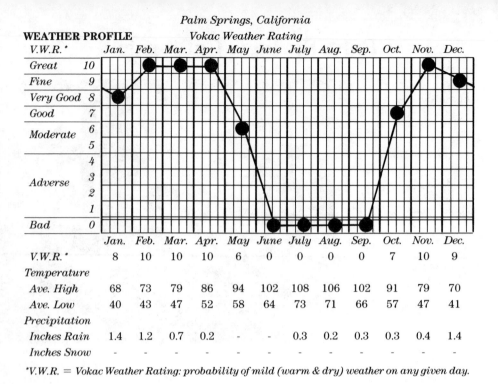

V.W.R.*		Jan.	Feb.	Mar.	Apr.	May	June	July	Aug.	Sep.	Oct.	Nov.	Dec.
Great	10												
Fine	9												
Very Good	8												
Good	7												
Moderate	6 5												
	4												
Adverse	3 2												
	1												
Bad	0												

	Jan.	Feb.	Mar.	Apr.	May	June	July	Aug.	Sep.	Oct.	Nov.	Dec.
V.W.R.*	8	10	10	10	6	0	0	0	0	7	10	9
Temperature												
Ave. High	68	73	79	86	94	102	108	106	102	91	79	70
Ave. Low	40	43	47	52	58	64	73	71	66	57	47	41
Precipitation												
Inches Rain	1.4	1.2	0.7	0.2	-	-	0.3	0.2	0.3	0.3	0.4	1.4
Inches Snow	-	-	-	-	-	-	-	-	-	-	-	-

*V.W.R. = Vokac Weather Rating: probability of mild (warm & dry) weather on any given day.

Forecast

Month	V.W.R.*		Temperatures		Precipitation
			Daytime	Evening	
January	8	Very Good	warm	cool	infrequent downpours
February	10	Great	warm	cool	infrequent downpours
March	10	Great	warm	cool	infrequent rainstorms
April	10	Great	hot	warm	negligible
May	6	Moderate	hot	warm	none
June	0	Bad	torrid	hot	none
July	0	Bad	torrid	hot	negligible
August	0	Bad	torrid	hot	negligible
September	0	Bad	torrid	hot	negligible
October	7	Good	hot	warm	negligible
November	10	Great	warm	cool	negligible
December	9	Fine	warm	cool	infrequent downpours

Summary

Only four hundred feet above sea level at the base of mountains that tower almost two miles above town, Palm Springs has one of the West's most awesome locations and its most distinctive climate. The outlook for comfortable **winter** weather is better here than anywhere in the West. With warm days and cool nights, sportswear and swimsuits are the rule in this desert playground. Rainfalls are scarce but heavy. Early **spring** is the most desirable season, when warm dry weather perfectly showcases the phenomenon of the desert in spectacular bloom. Later in the season, daytime temperatures become too hot to comfortably enjoy outdoor activities. **Summer** is unusable because of consistently sweltering heat (even during the evenings) and almost no rainfall to even temporarily relieve the oppressive temperatures. In **fall**, however, temperatures decline rapidly and are ideal again before Thanksgiving. Warm days, cool evenings, and rare, unpredictable downpours continue through the season.

ATTRACTIONS & DIVERSIONS

★ **Aerial Tramway**　　*6 mi. NW via CA 111 & Tramway Rd.*　　*325-1391*
One of the world's most spectacular aerial rides transports passengers almost 6,000 feet up from the desert (the Valley Station is 2,643 feet above sea level in Chino Canyon) to the Mountain Station (8,516 feet above sea level on San Jacinto Mountain). Two eighty-passenger gondolas make the 2.5 mile trip in about twenty minutes several times daily. Both stations have observation decks and picnic areas, plus a snack shop and lounge. The Mountain Station also has a restaurant. In the Mt. San Jacinto Wilderness State Park at the top of the tramway, hiking, backpacking, and wilderness camping are popular in summer. There is no extra charge for taking gear on the tram. In winter, cross-country skiing offers a startling contrast to warm weather sports in the desert below. Equipment can be rented at the Nordic Ski Center on the mountain.

Balloon Flights
Scenic balloon flights are a recent recreational innovation that offers an exciting new perspective on the desert and mountains. Passenger flights can be arranged at:
　　Desert Balloon Charters　　*14 mi. SE - Palm Desert*　　*346-8575*
　　Sunrise Balloons　　*14 mi. SE - Palm Desert*　　*346-7591*

★ **Bicycling**
Bicycle trails are scenic, flat, relatively safe (and occasionally separated), and well-marked by blue and white signs on more than thirty miles of streets in town. A bikeway map is available from the Convention & Visitors Bureau or the Leisure Services Department at City Hall. Bike rentals are available at:
　　Burnett's Bicycle Barn　　*1 mi. E at 429 S. Sunrise Way at Ramon Rd.*　　*325-7844*
　　Mac's Bike Rentals　　*2 mi. SE at 700 E. Palm Canyon Dr.*　　*327-5721*

★ **Golf**
Palm Springs is the "Winter Golfing Capital of the World." There are more than forty courses, including many of championship quality, within a fifteen mile radius of town. Several are open to the public, and others offer outside guest privileges. Collectively, they provide a wonderful variety of conditions and scenery for everyone interested in pursuing small white balls around picturesque oases. Additional information can be obtained at the Convention & Visitors Bureau, or at one of the nation's most beautiful and complete public 18-hole courses, the:
　　Palm Springs Golf Course　　*5 mi. SE via CA 111 & Golf Club Dr.*　　*328-1005*

Horseback Riding
★ **Smoke Tree Stables**　　*3 mi. SE at 2500 Toledo Av.*　　*327-1372*
Horses of all types may be rented hourly with or without guides for rides on miles of safe desert trails up into the scenic Palm Canyon areas.

Libraries
★ **Palm Springs Library Center**　　*1 mi. E at Sunrise Way/Baristo Rd.*　　*323-8291*
This large, contemporary building houses a comprehensive collection of books and audio-visual material. The periodical section is a fine place to relax in upholstered chairs near window walls overlooking a garden patio.
　　Wellwood Murray Mem. Library *downtown at 100 S. Palm Canyon Dr.*　　*323-8296*
This small library occupies a charming older building that is a well-liked retreat with comfortable chairs for reading or playing chess or checkers. Closed Sat.-Sun.

Living Desert Reserve　　*14 mi. SE at 47900 Portola Av. - Palm Desert*　　*346-5694*
Almost two square miles have been set aside to preserve and depict several types of American deserts. In addition to botanical gardens, there is a visitor center with regional geological exhibits, an unusual "after-sundown" exhibit of live desert mammals and reptiles, an aviary, and several miles of self-guided trails. Picnic facilities are attractively located. Closed mid-June thru Aug.

★ **Moorten Botanical Garden**　　*1.4 mi. S at 1701 S. Palm Canyon Dr.*　　*327-6555*
In this four acre arboretum, nearly two thousand varieties of desert plants from throughout the world have been arranged according to geographic regions. The gardens have been a landmark since 1938, and are also a sanctuary for birds and wildlife.

★ **Moped Rentals**
    Mopeds & Things   *6.4 mi. S at 68950 CA 111 - Cathedral City*   *324-1557*
Motorized bicycles are a relatively effortless and exhilarating way to enjoy scenic routes in town and to tour nearby desert byways. Moped rentals can be arranged by the day or longer here. Closed Sun.

★ **Palm Canyon**   *6 mi. S on Palm Canyon Dr.*
The nation's largest stand of native Washingtonia palms lines this steep, narrow canyon for several miles. Hundreds of the giant fan palms can be seen from the rim parking lot at the end of the road. Hiking trails lead down to the canyon floor, where a stream meanders among palms estimated to be up to 2,000 years old. Nearby Andreas and Murray Canyons also have picturesque palm groves and streams with deep pools and waterfalls that are especially delightful in late winter and spring when they're filled with snow runoff. All canyons remain in a relatively natural condition as part of a reservation belonging to a tiny group of Indians, who may be among the world's wealthiest. The tribe charges an entrance fee to hike in or to drive to parking areas at the base of the canyons.

★ **Palm Springs Desert Museum**   *downtown at 101 Museum Dr.*   *325-9186*
This strikingly handsome two-story cultural arts center was opened in 1976 on a twenty acre site against the San Jacinto Mountains. Five permanent collections and changing exhibits are displayed in several galleries. A 450-seat theater is used for lectures and concerts. Dancing fountains and sunken sculpture gardens embellish the beautifully landscaped grounds.

★ **Palms-to-Pines Highway**   *for 130 miles W of town*
A dramatically scenic highway climbs thousands of feet from desert date palm groves to pine forests and summer home areas high in the San Jacinto Mountains during a 130-mile loop drive. Take CA 111 south to Palm Desert; CA 74 west into the mountains; CA 243 through the pines to Idyllwild; and return via I-10 and CA 111.

Ruth Hardy Park   *.5 mi. NE at Tamarisk Rd./Caballeros Av.*
Tennis courts, elaborate play equipment, and shaded picnic tables with splendid mountain views are features of this large park with well-maintained lawns and gardens.

Salton Sea   *41 mi. SE on CA 111*
Sprawled for twenty-five miles along the lowest portion of the desert basin (235 feet below sea level) is a vast salty lake formed accidentally in 1905-1907 by Colorado River water that broke through irrigation canals. Water level is currently rising and raising havoc with shoreline facilities, but motor boating, water-skiing, and fishing are popular from fall through spring. The Salton Sea State Recreation Area also offers camping and picnic sites.

★ **Sightseeing**   *downtown*
The Sun Special Bus Line provides convenient access around town aboard colorful two-level buses with fine visibility from topless upstairs seats.

Warm Water Features
★   **Palm Springs Swim Center**   *1 mi. SE at Sunrise Way/Cerritos Dr.*   *323-8278*
An Olympic-sized fifty meter (fee) swimming pool with high diving boards is usually open to the public. A nicely landscaped half acre lawn and deck surround the pool and provide good mountain views.

★   **The Spa Hotel**   *downtown at 100 N. Indian Av.*   *325-1461*
The public is invited (for a fee) to enjoy natural hot mineral waters at the Spa Hotel in indoor and outdoor pools and Roman tubs with whirlpool action. Massage, steam, gym, and related facilities are also lavishly available.

SHOPPING
Palm Springs has one of the West's most well-developed and photogenic downtowns. Architectural controls have resulted in human-scale buildings and luxuriant landscaping accented by garden courtyards, fountains and sculptures. Off-street parking is plentiful and there are no parking meters. Although the main thoroughfare, Palm Canyon Drive, is a one-way street with heavy traffic flowing south, strolling and sightseeing are as popular as shopping. More than 1,200 large palm trees, illuminated nightly with individual spotlights, complement an abundance of major department and chain stores, distinctive specialty shops, galleries, entertainment places, and restaurants along this bustling thoroughfare.

Food Specialties

★ **Cinema Sweets Desertery**   *downtown at 130 E. Andreas Rd.*   *325-5900*
Fresh homemade ice cream plus gelato and homemade cookies and desserts are served in an inviting little coffee shop.

★ **Croissant Connection**   *downtown at 198 S. Palm Canyon Dr.*   *320-9666*
Fine croissants and Danish pastries are offered to go or with light food in this stylish new cafe.

★ **Desert Garden Date Shop**   *downtown at 282 N. Palm Canyon Dr.*   *325-6661*
This is Palm Springs' original date shop. Free samples of the major date varieties are frequently offered. Date shakes, made with fresh dates and ice cream, are the specialty. Arrangements can be made to have dates in gift packs shipped anywhere in the world.

★ **Gaston's Patisserie**   *.3 mi. E at 777 E. Tahquitz-McCallum Way*   *320-7750*
Fine Continental pastries and breads are the attraction in this new little carryout shop adjoining one of the town's best restaurants.

★ **Gourmet Gallery Ltd.**   *downtown at 255 S. Palm Canyon Dr.*   *322-0083*
An outstanding selection of gourmet pates, cheeses, meats, pastas, coffees, teas and more is displayed in this tantalizing new shop.

★ **Grandma's Fudge Shop**   *downtown at 130 N. Palm Canyon Dr.*   *325-9869*
Preparation of the fine variety of homemade fudge, nut brittles, cookies, and candies sold here may be watched through display windows.

Haagen-Dazs Ice Cream Shoppe   *downtown at 139 E. Arenas Rd.*   *325-8484*
A good selection of the chain's premium ice cream is sold in all kinds of fountain treats in this bright little shop.

★ **Indian Wells Date Garden**   *14 mi. SE at 74774 CA 111 - Indian Wells*   *323-3305*
This long-established date shop is located amidst forty acres of Medjool and Deglet Noir dates, and citrus orchards. Date or orange shakes are a delicious specialty that can be enjoyed at outdoor garden tables. Dates, fresh citrus, and dried fruit are sold in gift packs that will be shipped anywhere. The above specialties, plus gelato, are also available at the downtown store at 364 N. Palm Canyon Drive.

★ **Liquor Barn**   *downtown at 350 S. Palm Canyon Dr.*   *325-6073*
Safeway has converted an old grocery store into a cavernous showroom for beer, liquor and a fine assortment of premium California and other wine. Everything is sold at discount prices.

★ **Morrow's**   *downtown at 222 N. Palm Canyon Dr.*   *320-9268*
Quality nuts, candies, Continental pastries, and gelato served in freshly made Danish cones make this classy, brassy new store an easy winner.

Nicolino's Italian Bakery   *downtown at 311 E. Arenas*   *323-2885*
Authentic Italian breads, rolls, and pastries like cannolis and fig cookies are made here from scratch daily.

The Royal Bagel   *6.4 mi. SE at 68950 CA 111 - Cathedral City*   *328-7742*
At least a dozen varieties of well-made bagels are featured in this popular little takeout shop. Closed Mon.

★ **Shield's Date Gardens**   *18 mi. SE at 80225 CA 111 - Indio*   *347-0996*
One of the world's largest date shops serves date shakes, and sells a wide selection of quality dates and fresh citrus to go or in gift packs to be shipped anywhere. The picturesque grounds around this venerable roadside landmark include a variety of mature date and citrus trees. The historic film "Romance and the Sex Life of the Date" is shown continuously.

Swensen's Ice Cream Factory   *downtown at 204 N. Palm Canyon Dr.*   *325-7073*
The popular chain is represented here with quality ice cream served in many flavors and styles in a pleasant coffee shop atmosphere.

Vienna Cafe & Chocolates   *downtown at 120 E. Tahquitz-McCallum Way*   *320-0517*
Homemade chocolates and a variety of specialty truffles are sold to eat here with light foods, packaged to go, or in gift boxes.

Specialty Shops

★ **Alan Ladd Hardware & Gifts**   *.4 mi. S at 500 S. Palm Canyon Dr.*   *325-1265*
This large, gleaming showcase of all that makes a house a home has become a Palm Springs tradition since its founding years ago by the Ladd family of film fame.

Bookland   *downtown at 102 N. Palm Canyon Dr.*   *325-1020*
This popular, long-established shop has packed a good selection of best sellers, general and regional interest books, and magazines into a cheerful little store on the main street.
Crown Books   *downtown at 368 S. Palm Canyon Dr.*   *320-0038*
Every book in this well-organized newer outlet of a bookstore chain is discounted.
★ **Karen Asher Galleries, Ltd.**   *downtown at 265 S. Palm Canyon Dr. (E-1)*   *320-3333*
Fantasy plant and animal sculptures are showcased in a fascinating display. Sizes range from tiny to gigantic and materials vary from metal, wood, or rock through soft fabric to high-tech fiber optics.
★ **Nelson Rockfeller Collection**   *.3 mi. E at 707 Tahquitz-McCallum Way*   *320-9554*
Exclusive fine art objects from life-sized bronzes to wall hangings, and from primitive to modern, are beautifully displayed.
★ **Other Galleries**
Almost forty art galleries in the Palm Springs area offer quality work in all media. Most are located downtown on Palm Canyon Drive. The Chamber of Commerce has free copies of "The Desert Arts Calendar" with a guide describing the collections in most of the area's galleries.

NIGHTLIFE
A while ago, Palm Springs was famous for its many piano bars. It still is, but the town now also offers most of the evening diversions of major cities — with admissions and cover charges to match. The concentration of elaborate nightclubs and lounges (many clustered downtown) featuring ultra-modern light-and-sound systems and high-tech decor is one of the largest in the West. As a counterpoint to these frenetic new night spots, relaxed opulence and easy listening music are the hallmarks of many of the tony resort lounges scattered throughout the area.
★ **Brandy's**   *downtown at 238 N. Palm Canyon Dr.*   *327-1311*
An ultra-modern lounge with cushy booths and stools offers live music most nights and a "light show" dance floor. Pool, backgammon, and other games are also available.
★ **Canyon Hotel**   *3 mi. S at 2850 S. Palm Canyon Dr.*   *323-5656*
This celebrated resort includes Raffles, a big well-furnished lounge with live music for dancing every night except Sunday.
★ **Cecil's West Disco**   *3 mi. SE at 1775 E. Palm Canyon Dr.*   *320-4204*
This large and dazzling disco showplace "gets it on" with heavy sounds-and-lights every night. Next door, Continental food is served in a glitzy room dominated by disco dance floor decor.
★ **Doubles**   *.3 mi. SW at 701 W. Baristo Rd.*   *323-3100*
A window wall view of luxuriant landscapes is a daytime feature, while live music for dancing is offered most nights in the plush contemporary lounge.
★ **Hilton Riviera**   *1.5 mi. N at Indian Av./Vista Chino*   *327-8311*
A Las Vegas-style extravaganza is staged nightly in the cavernous showroom of this resort hotel, except on Monday when a big band plays for dancing.
★ **L.N.O. Pompeii**   *5 mi. SE at E. Palm Canyon Dr./Golf Club Dr.*   *328-5800*
The desert's most fantastic new fun center for adults features a "working" volcano by the entrance. Patrons can dance to a super high-tech sound-and-light show, watch the antics of a full-sized, fully automated robot band, or relax and enjoy a spectacular view of town and the mountains through a window wall beyond the dance floor. A sleek contemporary restaurant adjoins. The early acclaim for this huge and innovative new complex is well deserved.
★ **Saturday's**   *downtown at 265 N. Palm Canyon Dr.*   *320-0101*
A high-tech lighted dance floor and loud and lively music draw crowds to this lounge/dining room most nights. There is a separate bar with interesting ceiling fans, and an outdoor dining/drinking area. Large drinks are a specialty.
Sheraton Plaza   *downtown at 400 E. Tahquitz-McCallum Way*   *320-6868*
The first major new downtown hotel in years includes Harvey's Piano Lounge, a plush, comfortable hideaway with musical entertainment.
Valley Players Guild Theater   *downtown at 135 E. Tahquitz-McCallum Way*   *324-4353*
Live theater is presented here on weekends throughout the year.

★ **Zelda's**   *downtown at 169 N. Indian Av.*   325-2375
Here is a glittering landmark of space-age decor. Lots of flashing lights, chrome, and high-tech furnishings give pizzazz to the bars, dance floor, and lounge overlooking a center mall. Dancing to disco or the latest in live sounds is the main event nightly.

RESTAURANTS
The Palm Springs area has a remarkable number of restaurants. Many feature expensively decorated "theme" dining rooms. A few offer first-rate meals. Almost all of the area's gourmet restaurants have been added during the booming development of recent years. Unfortunately, prices have also accelerated rapidly, and are now generally higher than in any other great town. Notable dining rooms in the major resort hotels are mentioned in the "lodging" section.

The Adriatic   *9 mi. SE at 71877 CA 111 - Rancho Mirage*   346-0252
D only.   *Expensive*
Yugoslavian and Mediterranean dishes are featured in a pleasant restaurant with an Eastern European flair.

Aerial Tramway   *6 mi. NW via CA 111 & Tramway Dr.*   325-1391
L-D.   *Moderate*
A popular ride-'n-dine special couples a conventional buffet dinner with a spectacular view from a restaurant high on Mt. San Jacinto.

Banducci's   *1 mi. S at 1260 S. Palm Canyon Dr.*   325-2537
D only.   *Moderate*
Authentic Italian fare is served in a long-established restaurant with a popular dining porch by the main thoroughfare.

Billy Reed's   *1.6 mi. N at 1800 N. Palm Canyon Dr.*   325-1946
B-L-D.   *Moderate*
This huge coffee shop/restaurant/lounge complex is a favorite for hearty American fare and their own baked goods served amid a profusion of old-time bric-a-brac and plants.

Bit Of Country   *downtown at 418 S. Indian Av.*   325-5154
B-L.   *Moderate*
Homestyle cooking is the specialty of this well-liked, unassuming coffee shop.

Cafe Croissant   *downtown at 370 N. Palm Canyon Dr.*   320-8989
B-L-D.   *Moderate*
Freshly prepared baked goods are featured on a short menu in a congested little French-style sidewalk cafe.

★ **Cattails**   *6 mi. SE at 68369 CA 111 - Cathedral City*   324-8263
D only.   *Very Expensive*
A blackboard identifies half a dozen gourmet Continental entrees nightly in this romantic hideaway. The dining room is a study in contemporary elegance where pastel colors and soft fabrics complement beautifully appointed, well-spaced tables.

Chart House   *7 mi. SE at 69924 CA 111 - Rancho Mirage*   324-5613
D only.   *Moderate*
Fresh seafood, steaks, and an impressive salad bar are accompanied by strikingly handsome free-form architecture and decor in one of the best dining rooms representing a restaurant chain in the desert.

Chateau Grand Cru   *downtown at 333 N. Palm Canyon Dr.*   320-1157
L-D. Closed Tues.   *Very Expensive*
Continental specialties are served amid contemporary decor, or on an appealing patio on the main street. Several premium wines are poured by the glass daily. Both a wine bar and extensive wine storage have been built into the dining area.

Dar Maghreb *9.2 mi. SE via CA 111 at 42300 Bob Hope Dr. - Rancho Mirage* 568-9486
D only.   *Very Expensive*
Traditional multi-course Moroccan feasts are served by a lavishly costumed staff amid extravagant Near Eastern atmosphere. Fanciful dining areas with low sofas and deep cushions overlook dramatically lighted gardens.

★ **David's Desert Greenhouse**   *11 mi. S at 73725 El Paseo - Palm Desert*   568-0300
L-D.   *Expensive*
Lamb is the highlight among American dishes skillfully prepared with a light touch. Plush booths and elegant table settings distinguish this sleek new addition to desert dining.

Don the Beachcomber   *1 mi. N at 1101 N. Palm Canyon Dr.*   *325-2061*
D only. Sun. brunch.   *Moderate*
Polynesian-style dishes are featured along with evocations of South Seas decor in this
large and enduring link in a well-known restaurant chain.

★ **Doubles at the Tennis Club**   *.3 mi. SW at 701 W. Baristo Rd.*   *323-3100*
L-D.   *Expensive*
Delicious Continental favorites are served amid quintessential Palm Springs decor.
Window walls frame views of the luxuriant greenery of town one way, and stark desert
vegetation is spotlighted on a mountain slope the other way. The large, split-level dining
room is accented by a unique side-by-side rock wall fireplace-and-waterfall. A plush view
lounge adjoins.

Fairchild's   *3 mi. SE at 1005 S. El Cielo Rd.*   *327-3518*
B-L-D.   *Expensive*
Continental specialties are featured in a large and luxurious bistro-style dining room at
Bel Air Greens. A lovely mountain-view dining terrace separates the restaurant from the
golf course.

★ **Gaston's**   *.3 mi. E at 777 Tahquitz-McCallum Way*   *320-7750*
L-D.   *Very Expensive*
Acclaimed French cuisine is presented in a plush and pretty, contemporary dining room
that is one of the desert's finest. Next door, a sleek, comfortable bistro/bar provides grand
piano music.

Hamburger Hamlet   *downtown at 105 N. Palm Canyon Dr.*   *325-2321*
L-D.   *Moderate*
American fast foods are treated with distinction in the desert's representative of a
popular coffee shop/restaurant chain.

Iron Gate Restaurant   *12.5 mi. SE at 45406 CA 74 - Palm Desert*   *346-4453*
L-D.   *Moderate*
Prime rib is a specialty served in candlelit dining rooms, or by a fountain in an intimate
landscaped courtyard. The lounge has live entertainment and dancing.

La Cave   *7 mi. SE at 70064 CA 111 - Rancho Mirage*   *324-4673*
D only. Closed Mon.   *Very Expensive*
French cuisine is served in a formally elegant downstairs dining room in one of the West's
most expensive restaurants. Background music is played on a grand piano nightly.

La Grillade   *9.2 mi. SE at 42250 Bob Hope Dr. - Rancho Mirage*   *568-6800*
D only.   *Expensive*
Steaks and other meats are given a French accent by way of California in this strikingly
handsome new dining room.

Las Casuelas Terraza   *downtown at 222 S. Palm Canyon Dr.*   *325-2794*
L-D.   *Moderate*
The newest addition to a notable local restaurant chain offers a variety of conventional
Mexican dishes amidst decor themed to a 19th century colonial hotel with several
elaborately furnished dining rooms. Sidewalk patios combine alfresco dining with people-
watching. Elsewhere, a lounge features large margaritas, twirling fans, and hanging
plants.

Le Cafe de Paris   *10 mi. S at 72820 El Paseo - Palm Desert*   *346-7356*
L-D.   *Expensive*
French cuisine is the specialty in this tastefully decorated dining room.

Le Paon   *13 mi. SE at 45640 CA 74 - Palm Desert*   *568-3651*
D only.   *Very Expensive*
French cuisine is served amid candlelit elegance or on a heated patio.

★ **Le Vallauris**   *downtown at 325 W. Tahquitz-McCallum Way*   *325-5050*
L-D. Sun. brunch. Closed Mon.   *Very Expensive*
French nouvelle cuisine is served amid congested, formal elegance in an attractively
restored house. The intimate, shady patio is a local favorite for lunch. A comfortable piano
lounge adjoins.

L.N.O. Pompeii   *5 mi. SE at E. Palm Canyon & Golf Club Drs.*   *328-5800*
D only. Closed Mon.   *Expensive*
New California cuisine is a highlight of a large, contemporary dining room with a window
wall view of town and the mountains from well-spaced, nicely appointed tables.

★ **Louise's Pantry**   *downtown at 124 S. Palm Canyon Dr.*   *325-5124*
B-L-D.   *Low*
Homemade pies and pastries have been the specialties here for many years. The tiny old-fashioned coffee shop is so popular that people are usually lined up on the sidewalk waiting to get in.

Medium Rare   *7 mi. SE at 70064 CA 111 - Rancho Mirage*   *328-6563*
L-D.   *Moderate*
Prime rib is the specialty among American and Continental dishes served in several dining rooms where comfortable armchairs and well-padded booths set the tone.

★ **Melvyn's Restaurant**   *.4 mi. S at 200 W. Ramon Rd.*   *325-2323*
L-D. Sat.-Sun. brunch.   *Expensive*
Highly regarded Continental cuisine and tableside cooking are featured in a handsomely appointed dining room and on a glass-enclosed patio of the beautifully restored old Ingleside Inn. Live entertainment is offered in an intimate and comfortable piano lounge nightly.

Nate's Deli   *downtown at 283 N. Palm Canyon Dr.*   *325-3506*
B-L-D.   *Low*
New York-style deli specialties have dominated a very long menu offered to patrons seated in the many booths of this casual deli/restaurant since 1948.

Old World Restaurant   *downtown at 262 S. Palm Canyon Dr.*   *325-5502*
B-L-D.   *Moderate*
Soups, salads, sandwiches, and other casual American fare, plus rich desserts, are served in a stylish coffee shop comfortably furnished with armchairs. There is also a sidewalk cafe on the main street, and a lounge.

Perrina's   *downtown at 340 N. Palm Canyon Dr.*   *325-6544*
D only.   *Expensive*
Italian cuisine is served in dark-toned, heavily-linened atmosphere in this restaurant/piano bar.

Raphael's   *.5 mi. S at 691 S. Palm Canyon Dr.*   *320-8221*
D only.   *Moderate*
Gourmet Italian dishes are offered in a darkly handsome room with comfortable booths, fresh flowers, and crisp linen.

Riccio's   *2 mi. N at 2155 N. Palm Canyon Dr.*   *325-2369*
D only.   *Expensive*
Classic Italian specialties are presented in a lively and congested dining room. A baby grand piano bar adjoins.

Sorrentino's   *1 mi. N at 1032 N. Palm Canyon Dr.*   *325-2944*
D only. Closed June-Sept.   *Moderate*
This popular seafood house features inviting Mediterranean decor and a lounge with live entertainment.

Tennison's   *1.6 mi. N at 1700 N. Indian Av.*   *320-9998*
L-D.   *Expensive*
The innovative theme of this new restaurant is to reproduce classic recipes from famous regional American restaurants. An informal contemporary dining room adjoins a lounge offering live entertainment for dancing nightly.

Tony Rama's Place   *downtown at 450 S. Palm Canyon Dr.*   *320-4297*
L-D.   *Moderate*
Barbecued baby back ribs and a loaf of onion rings are the specialty on a limited American menu. This is one of the few places in town that serves past midnight every night. A piano lounge adjoins.

★ **Wally's Desert Turtle**   *9 mi. SE at 71755 CA 111 - Rancho Mirage*   *568-9321*
L-D.   *Very Expensive*
Gourmet Continental cuisine is formally presented in the desert's definitive showcase of contemporary opulence. Careful attention was paid to every detail in the large multilevel dining room, on the delightful patio, and in the luxurious lounge with a grand piano bar.

The Wilde Goose   *5.8 mi. SE at 67938 CA 111 - Cathedral City*   *328-5775*
D only. Sun. brunch. Closed Mon.   *Expensive*
Continental cuisine is given a contemporary styling in this well-regarded new dining room.

LODGING

America's foremost desert destination has an appropriately outstanding assortment of accommodations. Major resort hotels are the area's most spectacular landmarks. Each is architecturally distinctive, elaborately landscaped, and includes a range of recreation, entertainment, drinking, and lodging facilities. More than 150 lodgings dot the area, but during the winter season there are usually few vacancies and almost no bargains in town. From June through September, however, remarkable discounts of 50% or more from the winter rates shown below are normally available. Even the major resorts that stay open reduce their prices by as much as fifty percent.

Biltmore Hotel　　*2 mi. SE at 1000 E. Palm Canyon Dr.*　　　　　　*323-1811*
Public rooms, cottages and bungalows occupy twelve acres of landscaped grounds. This older resort has a large landscaped pool and whirlpool with mountain views, plus tennis courts. The *1000 East* is an attractive dining room with a garden view, and there is a lounge and coffee shop. Each room has a phone and cable color TV.

　　#15,#12,#10,#8,#6 — spacious, sunken tile bath/spa,　　　　　　K　bed...$110
　　regular room —　　　　　　　　　　　　　　　　　　　　　　Q　bed...$90

★ **Canyon Hotel**　　*3 mi. S at 2850 S. Palm Canyon Dr.*　　　　　　*320-6841*
Palm Springs' most complete resort is the only one with a private 18-hole championship golf course. There are also three swimming pools, three whirlpools, ten (fee) tennis courts (several night-lighted), and a health club on beautifully landscaped grounds. *Perry's* Restaurant offers elegant formal dining. *Bogie's* is a relaxed, atmospheric restaurant and lounge; *Raffles* features exotic atmosphere for live entertainment and dancing; and the *Greenhouse* is a bright, plant-filled lounge. Each spacious, well-furnished room has a phone and cable color TV. The resort is closed during the summer.

　　suite — separate BR with wet bar,　　　　　　　　　　　K　bed...$225
　　regular room —　　　　　　　　　　　　　　　　　　　　K　bed...$165

Casa de Camero　　*1.5 mi. N at 1480 N. Indian Av.*　　　　　　*320-1678*
This tiny single-level motel has a large outdoor pool with a fine mountain view. Each of the small, plain rooms has cable TV.

　　regular room —　　　　　　　　　　　　　　　　　　　　D　bed...$33

Casa Del Camino　　*1.4 mi. N at 1447 N. Palm Canyon Dr.*　　　　*325-9018*
This unassuming little motel has an outdoor pool and whirlpool. Each room has a cable TV.

　　regular room —　　　　　　　　　　　　　　　　　　　　K　bed...$40
　　regular room —　　　　　　　　　　　　　　　　　　　　Q　bed...$33

★ **Gene Autry Hotel**　　*4 mi. SE at 4200 E. Palm Canyon Dr.*　　　　*328-1171*
One of the area's long-established large resort hotels is on nicely landscaped grounds with three outdoor pools and whirlpools, lighted (fee) tennis courts, plus a dining room and a lounge with entertainment. Each room has a phone and cable color TV.

　　suite —　　　　　　　　　　　　　　　　　　　　　　　K　bed...$150
　　regular room —　　　　　　　　　　　　　　　　　　　　K　bed...$70

Hilton Riviera Hotel　　*1.5 mi. N at 1600 N. Indian Av.*　　　　*327-8311*
Palm Springs' largest resort hotel features a Las Vegas-style convention facility and showroom. The twenty-one landscaped acres also include an Olympic-sized outdoor pool; whirlpool; fifteen lighted (fee) tennis courts; plus a restaurant and lounge. Each room has a phone and cable color TV.

　　suite —　　　　　　　　　　　　　　　　　　　　　　　K　bed...$225
　　regular room —　　　　　　　　　　　　　　　　　　　　K　bed...$95

Hotel 6 Palms　　*1.6 mi. SE at 595 E. Palm Canyon Dr.*　　　　*327-2044*
The Motel 6 economy chain is represented by a large, renamed motel (the word "motel" is not used in Palm Springs) that is the best **bargain** in town. Typically reserved months in advance in winter, it is conveniently located and has a landscaped outdoor pool. Each room has a (pay) TV.

　　regular room —　　　　　　　　　　　　　　　　　　　　D　bed...$22

★ **Ingleside Inn**　　*.4 mi. S at 200 W. Ramon Rd.*　　　　　　*325-0046*
This handsomely restored small hotel is wonderfully overgrown with bouganvilla and flowering trees. There is a small outdoor pool and a whirlpool in a garden. *Melvyn's*

Restaurant and the *Casa Blanca* Lounge are among the best in town. Each room is individually furnished with antiques, and has a phone, cable color TV, a refrigerator, plus an in-bath steam bath and whirlpool.

suite — fireplace, sitting area,	Q bed...$195
Penthouse #4 — end unit, pvt. mt. view,	Q bed...$105
regular room —	Q bed...$85

International Hotel Resort   *2.5 mi. SE at 1800 E. Palm Canyon Dr.*   *323-1711*
A landscaped courtyard with a big outdoor pool and two whirlpools is surrounded on all sides by three floors of rooms in this large, modern resort hotel. Saunas and (fee) massage are also available, along with a restaurant, lounge, and coffee shop. Each room has a phone, cable color TV, private balcony or patio, and a refrigerator.

view room (several) — spacious, top fl., north side,	2 Q or K bed...$115
regular room —	Q bed...$95

★ **La Mancha**   *1 mi. NE at 444 N. Av. Caballeros*   *323-1775*
The premiere of a new generation of ultra-plush "personal" resorts is this Spanish-style villa complex. Amenities include a beautifully landscaped outdoor pool and whirlpool, plus a sauna, gym, and tennis courts. Bikes and motorbikes are available. Each spacious, luxuriously furnished suite has a phone, cable color TV, fully equipped kitchen, living room and dining room, and a private patio.

"Studio Villa" — pvt. outdoor whirlpool, wet bar, gas barbecue,	K bed...$160
"Estate Villa" — 1 BR, pvt. walled yard with sm. pool, wet bar, gas BBQ,	K bed...$250
regular room —	K bed...$90

★ **La Quinta**   *19 mi. SE via CA 111 at 49499 Eisenhower Dr. - La Quinta*   *564-4111*
The most celebrated old resort in the desert retains all of its unique charm. Remote and serene, the sprawling oasis includes two large outdoor pools; whirlpools; and (for a fee) an 18-hole championship golf course; a putting green; many tennis courts (some lighted); and rental bicycles. Acres of date groves are nearby, and lovely formal gardens and citrus trees surround gracious public rooms, including an elegant dining room and a lounge with live entertainment and dancing. Each beautifully furnished adobe bungalow unit has a phone and color TV.

suite —	Q bed...$200
regular room —	Q bed...$110

★ **Marriott's Rancho las Palmas**   *9 mi. S at 41000 Bob Hope Dr.-Rancho Mirage* *568-2727*
The current state of the art in luxury desert resorts, this large California-style hotel has two big outdoor pools and whirlpools in a flower-filled garden setting, saunas, a game room, and (for a fee) a spectacular 27-hole golf course with small lakes, a putting green, twenty-five tennis courts (eight lighted), and rental bicycles. The multilevel *Cabrillo* dining room serves gourmet dinners amid elegant early-California decor. In the *Fountain Court*, all meals are served in a delightful tropical courtyard setting. The *Sunrise Terrace* offers patio dining and fine mountain views. *Miguel's* is a comfortable lounge with live entertainment and dancing. Each of the spacious, well-furnished guest rooms has a phone, cable color TV, refrigerator, and a patio or balcony.

suite — 1 BR, mt. view,	K bed...$300
regular room — mt. or garden view,	K bed...$160

Mira Loma Hotel   *1.4 mi. N at 1420 N. Indian Av.*   *320-1178*
This small, single-level older motel has a large outdoor pool. In February and March, citrus trees surrounding the pool and guest rooms have an intoxicating fragrance. Each room has a phone, cable color TV, and a refrigerator.

regular room — poolside,	Q bed...$56
regular room — small,	D bed...$31

Monte Vista Hotel   *.3 mi. N at 414 N. Palm Canyon Dr.*   *325-5641*
This nicely landscaped older motel features a large outdoor pool and whirlpool, plus many mature citrus trees. Each room has a cable color TV.

regular room —	2 T or D bed...$33

Mountain View Inn   *downtown at 200 S. Cahuilla Rd.*   *325-5281*
An outdoor pool and a whirlpool are enhanced by a garden setting in this older single-level motel. Bicycles are furnished. Each of the well-maintained rooms has a cable color TV and kitchenette.

#11 — end unit, fireplace, pvt. patio,	2 T beds...$55
regular room —	2 T beds...$35

★ **Royce Resort Hotel**   *6.5 mi. SE at 34567 Cathedral Canyon Dr.*   *321-9000*
This large new all-suite hotel offers lighted tennis courts, an outdoor pool, (a fee for) an 18-hole golf course, plus a daily complimentary Continental breakfast and a cocktail party. *Arthur's* features an exhibition mesquite broiler and serves all meals. Each nicely furnished unit has a living room/dining room, complete kitchen and bedroom, plus a phone, cable color TV with movies, and a balcony.
    regular suite — 1 BR,   K bed...$150
Sandstone Inn   *2 mi. N at 2385 N. Indian Av.*   *325-7191*
A large outdoor pool is the center of attention in this tiny, single-level older motel. Each modest room has a cable TV and refrigerator.
    regular room —   D bed...$33

★ **Sheraton Oasis Hotel**   *downtown at 155 S. Belardo Rd.*   *325-1301*
This large modern resort hotel has one of the best locations downtown. The nearby mountains provide a towering backdrop to luxuriant landscaping in garden courtyards containing two outdoor pools and a whirlpool. *Hank's Cafe American* is an exotic dining room reminiscent of Casablanca. Live entertainment and dancing are available in the comfortable lounge. Each spacious well-furnished unit has a phone, cable color TV, and a private balcony or patio.
    #375,#373,#371,#369 — top floor, mt. view,   K bed..,$110
    #374,#368 — mt. view,   K bed...$110
    regular room — in older annex,   Q bed...$50

★ **Sheraton Plaza**   *downtown at 400 E. Tahquitz-McCallum Way*   *320-6868*
The newest downtown resort hotel is a showcase of contemporary architecture and decor. A flower-filled interior courtyard has a large outdoor pool, two whirlpools, and a sea of deck chairs with splendid mountain views. There is a fully equipped spa with a sauna, plus (for a fee) massage and other services, and six lighted tennis courts. The *Tapestry* offers French cuisine in an elegant ultra-modern setting. The *Terrace* is a glass-enclosed dining room serving all meals. *Harvey's Bar* is a comfortable, plush lounge with entertainment. Each spacious, beautifully furnished room has a phone, cable color TV, and a balcony or patio.
    #340,#345,#366,#367 — fine mt. views,   K bed...$195
    #339,#346,#365 — 1 BR suites, fine mt. views,   K bed...$220
    regular room —   K bed...$135

★ **Spa Hotel**   *downtown at 100 N. Indian Av.*   *325-1461*
Palm Springs' only mineral springs facility is a big modern hotel in the heart of town. A large outdoor pool, a hot mineral whirlpool, and still pools (all with mountain views) are free to guests. In addition, (for a fee) there are lighted tennis courts and a lavish health spa with mineral springs whirlpools, steam baths, massage, and gym. All meals are served in the old-fashioned, casually elegant *Agua Room,* and there is live entertainment for dancing. Each of the newly remodeled, nicely furnished rooms has a phone, cable color TV, and a private patio or balcony. The best views are on the upper floors on the west side above the pool.
    suite — 1 BR, bar/kit./living room, window wall view of mt.,   K bed...$290
    regular room — window-wall view,   2 D beds...$120

★ **Sundance Villas**   *2.5 mi. NW at 378 W. Cabrillo Rd.*   *325-3888*
Here is a quintessential example of personalized luxury in the Palm Springs life style. All of the units share a beautifully landscaped outdoor pool, whirlpool, sauna, and a lighted tennis court. But the real attraction is the spacious, sybaritic two- or three-bedroom villas. Each has a private outdoor pool or whirlpool or both in an enclosed yard, plus a fireplace, wet bar and stocked liquor cabinet, kitchen, phone, and cable color TV. A jug of fresh orange juice, fruit, and pastries are provided on arrival, and a bottle of wine is presented each day, in addition to other pleasant surprises.
    Villa — 3 BR,   2 Q & K beds...$295
    regular suite — 2 BR villa,   Q & K beds...$275

CAMPGROUNDS

There are several relatively elaborate recreation vehicle and trailer parks around town. However, there are no campgrounds that provide tent sites anywhere in the area.

SPECIAL EVENTS

★ **Palm Springs Mounted Police Rodeo**   *downtown & stadium*   *late January*
One of the West's few mid-winter rodeos is a major two-day competition, preceded by the largest equestrian parade in California.

★ **National Date Festival**   *22 mi. SE at Indio Fairgrounds*   *mid-February*
The Arabian Nights (and days) atmosphere at the fairgrounds in Indio — "The Date Capital of the World" — is the right setting for this unique and popular ten-day celebration that includes parades, cultural exhibits, and live entertainment — even camel races.

OTHER INFORMATION

Area Code: *619*
Zip Code: *92262*
Palm Springs Chamber of Commerce   *downtown at 190 W. Amado Rd.*   *325-1577*
Convention & Visitor Bureau *2 mi. E at the Airport*   *327-8411*

St. Helena, California

Elevation:

256 feet

Population (1980):

4,898

Population (1970):

3,173

Location:

65 mi. N
of San Francisco

St. Helena is the heart of America's most illustrious wine-producing valley. In every direction beyond the compact town, a sea of vineyards splashes against steep-sided oak-covered mountains that frame the flat valley floor. An appealing blend of bucolic charm and urbane diversions is complemented by a temperate climate. The excellent weather of spring is usually perfect for viewing the greening of endless vineyards and for savoring wineries' new releases. Idyllic weather returns again in the fall, and coincides with the harvest and crush. Especially during this season, visitors arrive in overwhelming numbers to experience the beauty of grapes on the vine, to observe the harvest, and to taste new premium wines. Crowds also fill the handsome little valley to capacity during the hot, sunny days of summer. Hiking, bicycling, ballooning, and boating are enjoyed, but the most popular activities are associated with the grape. In winter, the disadvantages of cool wet days are offset by the leisurely pace and absence of crowds throughout the area.

The town was founded in 1853 by an Englishman, J.H. Still, who opened a general store and offered free land for potential businesses. Within a few years, St. Helena was flourishing as a farming and milling center. Shortly after the Civil War, grape growing and wine production began near town. A combination of talented wine makers and ideal conditions soon established Napa Valley as the center of California's premium wine production. It is still the nation's most renowned wine making region.

Today, a wonderful diversity of landmark wineries may be visited in beautifully maintained Victorian mansions and in distinctive contemporary structures on the approaches to town. St. Helena retains much of the charm of a Victorian farming village in spite of rapid growth in recent years. The unspoiled heart of the compact business district features romantic settings for picnics in delightful little parks with noble shade trees, plus many carefully restored historic buildings housing specialty and gourmet shops. One of the West's newest major concentrations of gourmet restaurants is another attraction downtown . After dark, entertainment is scarce. Instead, lounges offer atmospheric, quiet surroundings well suited to conversation. Several also feature a variety of local wines by the glass. Lodgings are in surprisingly short supply. However, this is one of the West's centers of stylish bed-and-breakfast inns, and there are three outstanding contemporary motor lodges in the vicinity.

WEATHER PROFILE
Vokac Weather Rating

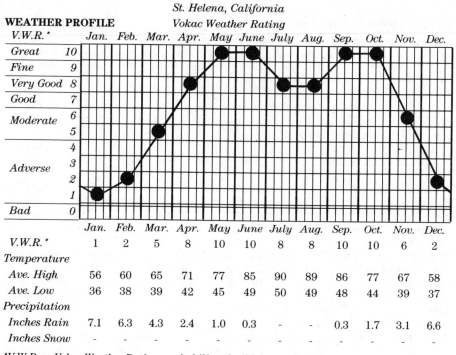

V.W.R.*		Jan.	Feb.	Mar.	Apr.	May	June	July	Aug.	Sep.	Oct.	Nov.	Dec.
Great	10												
Fine	9												
Very Good	8												
Good	7												
Moderate	6												
	5												
	4												
Adverse	3												
	2												
	1												
Bad	0												

	Jan.	Feb.	Mar.	Apr.	May	June	July	Aug.	Sep.	Oct.	Nov.	Dec.
V.W.R.*	1	2	5	8	10	10	8	8	10	10	6	2
Temperature												
Ave. High	56	60	65	71	77	85	90	89	86	77	67	58
Ave. Low	36	38	39	42	45	49	50	49	48	44	39	37
Precipitation												
Inches Rain	7.1	6.3	4.3	2.4	1.0	0.3	-	-	0.3	1.7	3.1	6.6
Inches Snow	-	-	-	-	-	-	-	-	-	-	-	-

*V.W.R. = Vokac Weather Rating: probability of mild (warm & dry) weather on any given day.

Forecast

Month	V.W.R.*		Temperatures		Precipitation
			Daytime	Evening	
January	1	Adverse	cool	chilly	frequent downpours
February	2	Adverse	cool	chilly	frequent downpours
March	5	Moderate	warm	cool	occasional downpours
April	8	Very Good	warm	cool	infrequent downpours
May	10	Great	warm	cool	infrequent rainstorms
June	10	Great	hot	warm	negligible
July	8	Very Good	hot	warm	none
August	8	Very Good	hot	warm	none
September	10	Great	hot	warm	negligible
October	10	Great	warm	cool	infrequent rainstorms
November	6	Moderate	warm	cool	infrequent downpours
December	2	Adverse	cool	chilly	frequent downpours

Summary

St. Helena is the heart of Napa Valley, where weather is moderated by marine air pouring through a gap in the Coast Range at the Golden Gate and spreading northward beyond San Francisco Bay. As a result, there is almost no snow. Instead, **winter** is cool and damp with frequent heavy rainfalls providing well over half the year's normal precipitation. **Spring** is delightful. Warm days, cool evenings, plus fewer and lighter rainfalls contribute to easy enjoyment of the luxuriant green valley. **Summer** days are usually hot and sunny and evenings are warm. There is no precipitation to disrupt outdoor activities. **Fall** signals the return of excellent weather. Warm days, cool evenings, and light rainfalls assure final vine ripening prior to the normally bountiful grape harvest and add to the visitors' pleasure in sampling the fruits of this labor.

ATTRACTIONS & DIVERSIONS

Bale Grist Mill State Historical Park   *3.2 mi. N on CA 29*   942-4575
Built in 1846, this picturesque mill provided flour for upper Napa Valley farmers until 1879. It was acquired by the State in 1974, and is now being meticulously reconstructed. Shady picnic sites have been provided nearby, overlooking a creek.

★ **Ballooning**
Fine weather and lovely countryside make the Napa Valley a natural for hot-air balloon flights. Several companies now offer guests a unique vantage point to both the sights and sounds of the area, including:
   Napa Valley Balloons   253-2224
   Silverado Balloon Co.   *1 mi. NW at 1970 Dean York Lane*   963-5515

★ **Bicycling**
   St. Helena Cyclery   *downtown at 1156 Main St.*   963-7736
The relatively flat terrain, fine wine country scenery and attractions, and good weather are all reasons for the enormous popularity of bicycle touring in Napa Valley. Rentals by the hour and longer can be arranged here.

★ **Bothe-Napa Valley State Park**   *4.8 mi. N on CA 29*   942-4575
Marked hiking trails in this 1,800 acre park pass through some of the most easterly stands of Coast redwoods as well as a luxuriant forest of oak and madrone. Wildflower displays are particularly beautiful in spring. An outdoor swimming pool is open to the public in summer. Tree-shaded picnic tables and creekside campsites are available year-round.

★ **Library**   *downtown at 1492 Library Lane*   963-5244
The St. Helena Public Library occupies an architecturally unusual newer building. Attractively furnished reading areas with upholstered armchairs and cushioned window wells have picture window views of adjacent vineyards. The Napa Valley Wine Library is also here. Closed Sun.-Mon.

Lyman Park   *downtown on Main St.*
This pretty little tree-shaded park near the heart of town is a perfect spot for a picnic.

★ **Silverado Museum**   *downtown at 1490 Library Lane*   963-3757
One of the world's largest collections of Robert Lewis Stevenson memorabilia is displayed in a new extension of the St. Helena Public Library. Closed Mon.

★ **Wineries**
St. Helena, the heart of the world famous Napa Valley wine district, is surrounded by more than one hundred wineries and about 24,000 acres of premium vineyards. Below is a cross-section of large, well-known wineries that encourage visitors to drop in for tours, tastes and sales. Many smaller premium wineries throughout the valley offer personalized tours and tasting by appointment. The Chamber of Commerce and bookstores have detailed guides and maps.

★   **Beaulieu**   *4 mi. SE on CA 29*   963-2411
Founded in 1900 by Georges de Latour, this became one of California's grand old family wineries. It is still a landmark, although now owned by a conglomerate. A handsome wood-crafted visitor center at one side of the winery is the beginning point for tours, and where selected wines may be tasted. Tasting, tours, and sales 10-4 daily.

★   **Beringer**   *.6 mi. N on CA 29*   963-7115
This winery has been in continuous operation since it was founded in 1876. An impressive seventeen-room Rhine House mansion was built by the Beringer brothers in 1883 as a tribute to their homeland. Inside is one of the most gracious tasting centers anywhere. Tasting, tours, and sales 9-4:45 daily.

★   **Christian Brothers**   *1 mi. N on CA 29*   963-2719
The monumental Greystone Cellar dates from 1888 when it was the largest stone cellar in the world. There is a popular, friendly tour of this aging cellar, which is part of the largest winery operation in Napa Valley. The building also houses some of Brother Timothy's vast corkscrew collection. Most of a long list of wines is available for sampling. Tasting, tours, and sales 10:30-4 daily.

★ **Domaine Chandon**   *10 mi SE off CA 29*   *944-2280*
A heroically scaled, strikingly modern winery was built by Moet-Hennessy of France to make sparkling wines from California grapes in the traditional manner of French champagne production. There is a fee for tasting the premium red or white styles of sparkling wines indoors or, weather permitting, on a lovely garden terrace adjoining the spectacular restaurant/tasting complex. Tasting (for a fee), tours, and sales 11-6 daily. (Closed Mon.-Tues. from Oct. thru May.)

★ **Inglenook**   *4.5 mi. SE off CA 29*   *963-7184*
The heart of this historic winery is a stately 1880s-vintage stone building that houses a museum, and a tasting room offering a broad sampling of wines made here. The winery is now part of a conglomerate. Tasting, tours, and sales 10-5 daily.

★ **Louis M. Martini**   *1.1 mi. SE on CA 29*   *963-2736*
Founded in 1933, this remains a family operation all the way. The winery has perhaps the most generous attitude about tasting in the Napa Valley with the complete roster of Martini wines available for sampling. Tasting, tours, and sales 10-4 daily.

★ **Robert Mondavi Winery**   *5.5 mi. SE on CA 29*   *963-9611*
Many of California's state-of-the-art advances in premium wine making originated in this mission-style complex founded in 1966. The spacious lawn at the junction of the two wings of the building is the site of acclaimed summer concerts, plus art shows and special tastings. Limited selections are available for tasting only to those who take the tour. Tasting, tours, and sales 9-5 daily (10-4:30 daily Oct. thru Mar.).

★ **Yountville**   *9 mi. SE off CA 29*
This town was a bustling village by 1855. It hasn't grown much since, but it is now the site of some of the region's finest shops and restaurants. The town park on the north side has pleasant, tree-shaded picnic spots.

SHOPPING
St. Helena has a compact downtown where handsome Victorian buildings house a small but growing number of specialty and gourmet shops, in addition to the kinds of stores that have served an agricultural economy for more than a century. Today, utility wires are underground, downtown streets are tree-shaded, and there are still no parking meters or traffic lights.

Food Specialties
The Bottle Shop   *downtown at 1321 Main St.*   *963-3092*
The area's original wine store has been impressively updated. Premium Napa Valley wines are beautifully displayed in a chilled back room.

★ **Chutney Kitchen**   *9.5 mi. SE off CA 29 in Vintage 1870 - Yountville*   *944-2788*
A variety of outstanding locally-made chutneys are displayed for tasting and purchase at a tiny carryout.

The Cook's Corner   *9.5 mi. SE off CA 29 in Vintage 1870 - Yountville*   *944-8100*
Local products are emphasized in an excellent assortment of specialty foods, including mustards, olives, breads, cheeses, pates, sausages, and much more. The selection of gourmet cookware is equally impressive.

The Croissant Place   *9.5 mi. SE at 6528 Washington St. - Yountville*   *944-8096*
This bright little carryout shop offers several kinds of croissants made here daily, plus gelato. An adjoining tree-shaded courtyard has several picnic tables.

★ **Ernie's Wine Warehouse**   *1.4 mi. S at 699 S. CA 29*   *963-7888*
A mind-boggling array of California wines is sold, including those sold inexpensively under a private label. Small premium wineries are a specialty, and there is a good selection of wines from around the world. Two or more evening tastings are held each month, and the public is invited.

★ **Fantasie au Chocolat**   *9.5 mi. SE off CA 29 - Yountville*   *944-8096*
Beautifully displayed in this chocoholic's downfall is an awesome selection of hand-dipped chocolate truffles, molded dark chocolates, and freshly baked pastries and cakes. Coffee is also available.

★ **Groezinger Wine Co.**　　*9.5 mi. SE off CA 29 in Vintage 1870 - Yountville*　　*944-2331*
Well over one hundred California wineries' bottlings are conveniently displayed in a refurbished, massive old stables. There is also a tasting bar.

Napa Valley Connection　　*downtown at 1201 Main St.*　　　*963-1111*
This big, handsome culinary emporium features numerous pates and cheeses among selected gourmet provisions, and premium wines, plus a notable assortment of cookware and recipe books.

★ **Napa Valley Olive Oil Mfg. Co.**　　*.5 mi. SE at 835 McCorkle Av.*　　*963-4173*
Fine olive oil has been produced here for nearly a century. All kinds of quality cheeses, ripe olives, sausages, and other California gourmet groceries are also sold at surprisingly low prices in this unabashedly old-fashioned store.

★ **The Nuttery**　　*2.4 mi. N at 3111 N. CA 29*　　　*963-9217*
A new shop in the Cement Works features one of the largest assortments of nuts in the West. Several kinds are usually displayed for tasting. Gift packs will be mailed anywhere.

★ **Oakville Grocery Co.**　　*6 mi. SE on CA 29 - Oakville*　　　*944-8802*
This little roadside grocery store has become renowned for the most tantalizing selection of sophisticated international gourmet foods to be found in any store this size.

★ **The Original Court of Two Sisters** *9.5 mi. SE in Vintage 1870 - Yountville*　*944-2138*
Splendid Continental pastries are served with coffee at a few marble-topped tables set with fresh flowers indoors, on a scenic patio, or to go.

★ **V. Sattui Winery**　　*1.5 mi. S off CA 29 on White Lane*　　　*963-7774*
This winery's bottlings are available for tasting and sale here only. There is also an outstanding selection of cheeses, plus pates, sausages, specialty breads, and other gourmet items. Inviting picnic grounds are adjacent.

★ **The Wineworks**　　*2.4 mi. N at 3111 N. CA 29*　　　*963-9484*
Napa Valley and other California premium wines are the highlight of an expansive new shop in the Cement Works. About a dozen wines are featured daily by the taste or glass. In addition, gourmet cheeses, pates, smoked meats, local chantrelles, and other provisions are beautifully displayed in this inspired showcase of the area's culinary endowments.

★ **The Wurst Place**　　*9.5 mi. SE off CA 29 in Vintage 1870 - Yountville*　　*944-2224*
One of Northern California's largest assortments of sausages is displayed here. Many are homemade and excellent. Seasonally available exotic fresh mushroom varieties are also featured. Closed Mon.

Specialty Shops

★ **Cement Works**　　*2.4 mi. N at 3111 N. CA 29*　　　*963-1261*
An abandoned cement works has become the valley's newest complex of fine shops. Quality arts and crafts, gift items, gourmet foods, premium wines, and distinctive restaurants and lounges are housed in stylish wood-toned buildings on well-landscaped grounds. Acres of tree-shaded picnic sites are nearby.

★ **Freemark Abbey Complex**　　*2.1 mi. N at 3020 N. CA 29*　　　*963-7211*
The Hurd Beeswax Candle Factory is the highlight of a shopping complex in a converted stone winery that includes a big gourmet-and-gift shop (with a fine selection of books of regional interest and wine accessories) plus the large Abbey Restaurant.

★ **Vintage 1870**　　*9.5 mi. SE off CA 29 - Yountville*　　　*944-2451*
A fascinating complex of quality specialty shops occupies a massive brick and timber complex that was the valley's second oldest winery — Groezinger's. There are many delightful touches — large sculptures, a gazebo, colorful garden areas, and so on.

NIGHTLIFE
After dark, peace and quiet prevail. Still, there are a few enticing places to go for a nightcap.

★ **Fox & Hound**　　*2.4 mi. N on CA 29*　　　*963-0256*
As many as ten beers (including Anchor Steam and Henry Weinhard's Private Reserve) are on tap, along with champagne, in a detailed reproduction of a traditional English pub. There is also live music several nights each week, plus darts and comfortably upholstered armchairs, in this novel addition to the Cement Works.

★ **Hotel St. Helena**   *downtown at 1309 Main St.*   *963-9023*
Sixteen different types of wine by the glass are offered for tasting daily in the hotel's comfortable little lounge. Plush furnishings include pillow sofas and overstuffed bar stools. An extensive California wine list is complemented by a variety of beers, appetizers, and desserts. Closed Mon.-Tues.

Mama Nino's   *9.1 mi. SE off CA 29 at 6772 Washington St. - Yountville*   *944-2112*
In this pleasant and popular lounge are a cheery fireplace and chrome-and-wood armchairs. The wine list is limited to Napa and Sonoma wineries, and several wines by the glass are featured. Closed Wed.

Pastime Club   *downtown at 1351 Main St.*   *963-4045*
This stylish "locals" bar in a nicely refurbished old building with an interesting rock wall interior and comfortable furnishings is a good place for a quiet nightcap.

★ **St. George**   *.3 mi. S at 1050 Charter Oak Av.*   *963-7938*
Adjoining a distinguished restaurant is an enchanting lounge filled with authentic baroque antiques including a carved, polished hardwood-and-brass bar, an ornate working fireplace, and towering walls graced with pictures of colossal nudes in rococo gold leaf frames. It is a memorable place for drinks and conversation.

RESTAURANTS

Nowhere is the change from farming village to urbane community more apparent than in the sophisticated restaurants which have opened in the St. Helena area in recent years. Some of the West's finest dining rooms are now in or near town. Almost all of the best restaurants have notable wine lists with an appropriately chauvinistic emphasis on California wineries.

★ **Auberge du Soleil**   *5 mi. SE at 180 Rutherford Hill Rd.*   *963-1211*
L-D. Closed Wed.   *Very Expensive*
Prix fixe meals are stylish presentations of nouvelle cuisine in the valley's most monumental landmark restaurant. An imposing chateau-style structure provides sublime views of the vineyards from a hillside on which it was recently constructed. Cocktails or wine are particularly memorable when savored on the deck by the plush lounge.

★ **Chutney Kitchen**   *9.5 mi. SE off CA 29 in Vintage 1870 - Yountville*   *944-2788*
L only.   *Moderate*
This long-time favorite luncheon spot offers excellent homemade soups, sandwiches, fresh salads and their own delicious chutneys. Fresh flowers and linen grace the tables in this bustling corner of a converted winery building. Alfresco lunches are served on a vine-covered patio overlooking a vineyard during spring and summer.

★ **The Diner**   *9.6 mi. SE off CA 29 at 6476 Washington St. - Yountville*   *944-2626*
B-L-D. No D on Tues. & Wed. Closed Mon.   *Moderate*
Fresh ingredients and homestyle cooking are at their best in this simple, friendly, old-fashioned diner. Breakfasts are remarkably good, and evening Mexican dinners in "El Diner" are also well-liked.

★ **Domaine Chandon**   *10 mi. SE off CA 29 on California Dr.*   *944-2467*
L-D. No D on Mon.-Tues.   *Very Expensive*
The French have produced an outstanding showplace for their sparkling wines made here. The restaurant is a modern architectural tour de force of wood, glass, and concrete surrounded by charming pastoral scenery. Gourmet lunches are served on a flower-strewn outdoor patio during the warm months. Disciplined French haute cuisine, including grand pastries, is served in dining rooms that are usually fully reserved well in advance.

★ **French Laundry**   *9.2 mi. SE at 6440 Washington St. - Yountville*   *944-2380*
D only. Closed Mon.-Tues.   *Very Expensive*
Memorable country-style French cuisine prepared with only the freshest ingredients is served to one seating of guests each evening. A stone and redwood building that was a French laundry at the turn of the century has no signs identifying it as a restaurant, and it is not listed in the yellow pages. Nevertheless, it is a real "find." The vineyard view from the casually elegant upstairs dining room is especially pleasant in summer, while the fireplace downstairs has a warm, romantic appeal in winter.

★ **La Belle Helene**   *downtown at 1345 Railroad Av.*   *963-1234*
L-D. Closed Tues.   *Expensive*
Highly regarded French haute cuisine and splendid homemade baked goods are accompanied by casually elegant atmosphere and classical background music in a charming enhancement of a Victorian stone building. Lunch and wines-by-the-glass are served in the adjoining Cafe des Arts.

La Crepe Cafe   *9 mi. SE at 6783 Washington St. - Yountville*   *944-2550*
B-L-D. Closed Wed.   *Moderate*
Crepes are the only dishes served, but they are delicious in this bright, tiny cafe. There are a few additional tables on the patio.

Le Chardonnay   *9.5 mi. SE at 6534 Washington St. - Yountville*   *944-2521*
L-D. Closed Mon.   *Expensive*
Robust French cuisine is served in a fashionable room with a canopied ceiling and arched windows. Fresh flowers, crystal, and fine china lend elegance to each table.

Le Rhone   *downtown at 1234 Main St.*   *963-0240*
D only. Closed Mon.-Tues.   *Very Expensive*
Classic French cuisine and homemade desserts are served prix fixe in this new restaurant. The intimate, country-elegant dining room is entered through a courtyard.

★ **Mama Nino's**   *9.1 mi. SE at 6772 Washington St. - Yountville*   *944-2112*
D only. Closed Wed.   *Moderate*
Fresh homemade pasta is the specialty on an appealing Italian menu. Dining rooms are outfitted with fresh flowers and plants amidst wood-and-chrome decor. Patio dining is popular during the warm months. A cheerful fireplace lounge adjoins.

★ **Meadowwood**   *2 mi. E at 900 Meadowwood Lane*   *963-3646*
D only. Sun. brunch. Closed Mon.-Tues.   *Expensive*
New California cuisine is wonderfully enshrined here. The freshest ingredients are skillfully used in exciting new entrees. A feeling of quiet country elegance in the dining room is complemented by picture window views through nearby oaks to a golf course and heavily wooded hills. A redwood deck is used for alfresco dining when weather permits.

★ **Miramonte**   *downtown at 1327 Railroad Av.*   *963-3970*
D only. Closed Mon.-Tues.   *Very Expensive*
Renowned nouvelle cuisine is the attraction in a picturesque old hotel that has been restored with a dining room decorated in the style of a baronial hunting lodge — complete with a large working fireplace. The menu is constantly changing according to the freshest available ingredients. Prix fixe five-course meals are delicious and artful presentations.

★ **Mustards Grill**   *7.5 mi. S on CA 29*   *944-2424*
L-D.   *Moderate*
The creative New California cuisine prepared in this contemporary dinner house is already a smash hit, even though this is one of the area's youngest restaurants. Mesquite-broiled and brick oven-smoked meats are flavorful hallmarks of the new style here. Support dishes are given a wonderfully light touch, and many wines are available by the glass. A profusion of crisp white linen complements wood-tones and prints in the dining room and the whitewashed openness of a cool, screened porch.

★ **Palmer's**   *downtown at 1313 Main St.*   *963-1788*
B-L-D. Only brunch on Sun. Closed Mon.   *Moderate*
Delectable homemade pastries are featured at all meals, along with carefully prepared light fare. Selected wines are poured by the taste or the glass. The quality of the food compensates for the relaxed, place-your-own-order setting of this simply furnished little cafe.

★ **Rose et le Favour**   *downtown at 1420 Main St.*   *963-1681*
D only. Closed Mon.-Tues.   *Very Expensive*
There is only one seating each evening at the seven tables in this opulent newer restaurant where a prix fixe multi-course dinner of fearlessly eclectic New California cuisine is served. Every dish is prepared with skill and imagination from the freshest and choicest ingredients. The intimate dining room is lavishly furnished with flowers and paintings, and each table is meticulously appointed with starched white linen and expensive china.

★ **St. George**   *.3 mi. S on Main St. at 1050 Charter Oak*   *963-7930*
L-D.   *Moderate*
Distinguished Italian cuisine is served amid museum-quality baroque decor — antique
marble busts, brass chandeliers, polished woodwork, jumbo mirrors, and monumental
nude paintings in a sumptuous, high-ceilinged dining room. Lunch is served on a tree-
studded, walled, brick terrace during the summer. The firelit lounge is also furnished with
baroque antiques.

Spring Street Restaurant   *downtown at 1245 Spring St.*   *963-5578*
L only. Closed Sat.-Sun.   *Moderate*
Soups, salads, sandwiches and desserts are popular in a pleasant dining room or on the
porch of a converted house.

Washington Street Restaurant   *9.4 mi. SE off CA 29 - Yountville*   *944-2406*
L-D. No. L on Mon. & Tues.   *Moderate*
Casual Continental cuisine is served in spacious, firelit surroundings in a restored old
brick mansion with splendid views of adjacent vineyards. Wood trim and brass distinguish
the adjoining lounge.

LODGING

In recent years, St. Helena has become one of the country inn capitals of the West. These
bed-and-breakfast lodgings have restored some of the area's finest residences into
distinctive showplaces filled with authentic Victorian charm. Visitors can also select from
a few motels, including four with remarkably plush furnishings. The town carefully
protects its distinction of having no large-scale accommodations. Unfortunately, there are
no bargain rooms in the area, although rates are often reduced by 20% and more on
weekdays during winter and spring.

★ **Bordeaux House**   *9.3 mi. SE off CA 29 at 6600 Webber - Yountville*   *944-2855*
This modernistic little brick inn has rooms stylishly decorated with Continental-
contemporary furnishings and private, sunken baths. Each of the rooms has a fireplace
and some have a private balcony. Complimentary Continental breakfasts and an evening
glass of wine are offered.

"Chablis" — end, top (2nd) fl., tree view from pvt. balc.,	Q bed...$120
"Sherry" — end, some view,	Q bed...$115
regular room —	2 raised T beds...$100

Chalet Bernensis   *1.2 mi. S at 2257 S. CA 29*   *963-4423*
An impressive century-old Victorian mansion with landscaped gardens has been
converted into a bed-and-breakfast inn. All rooms are furnished with antiques, and share
a bath. In an adjacent water tower replica, each room has antique furnishings, a private
bath, and a gas fireplace. A Continental breakfast is included, and sherry is served in the
sitting room.

#9 "Water Tower" — top fl., pvt. bath, gas fireplace, some view,	Q bed...$74
#3 — corner, windows on 2 sides, shared bath, view	
past giant camellia bush,	D bed...$58
regular room — small, shared bath,	D bed...$50

Cinnamon Bear   *downtown at 1407 Kearney St.*   *963-4653*
Each of the rooms in this large, homey old bed-and-breakfast residence has a private
bathroom, some Victorian furnishings, and teddy bears. A complimentary country-style
breakfast is served on the porch in warm weather.

downstairs room — lg., footed tub with shower,	Q bed...$78
regular room —	Q bed...$78

Creekside Inn   *.3 mi. S at 945 Main St.*   *963-7244*
A pleasant, newer home adjacent to a creek now serves as a bed-and-breakfast inn with
several nicely furnished rooms. A complimentary Continental breakfast is served. Baths
are shared.

queen bed room — lg., windows on 3 sides,	Q bed...$65
regular room — corner, windows on 2 sides,	D bed...$65

El Bonita Motel   *.8 mi. S at 195 Main St.*   *963-3216*
A landscaped outdoor pool is an attraction of this small, nicely maintained modern motel.
Each room has a phone and cable color TV.
　　#23 — spacious, in quiet back section, refr.,   K bed...$58
　　regular room —   D bed...$35
★ **Harvest Inn**   *1.1 mi. S at 1 Main St.*   *963-9463*
Situated in a twenty acre working vineyard amid carefully tended gardens with a large
outdoor pool and a whirlpool is an imposing, newer Tudor-style motor inn lavishly
furnished with antiques and quality reproductions. Each spacious, beautifully appointed
room has a refrigerator, cable color TV, and a phone.
　　#30 "Knight of Nights" — grandiose suite, grand curved staircase,
　　　　　　　　wet bar, refr., in-room whirlpool, 2 fireplaces,
　　　　　　　　balc., pvt. vineyard view,   K bed...$300
　　#32 "Lord of the Manor" — grandiose suite, wet bar, refr.,
　　　　　　　　in-room whirlpool, 2 fireplaces,
　　　　　　　　balc., pvt. vineyard views,   K bed...$310
　　#23 "Vin Rose" — wet bar, raised stone fireplace, balc., vineyard view,   K bed...$140
　　#1 "Gamay" — wet bar, raised stone fireplace,   K bed...$135
　　regular room —   Q or K bed...$85
Hotel St. Helena   *downtown at 1309 Main St.*   *963-4388*
This century-old hotel was recently reopened after being completely refurbished. Most of
the lushly carpeted rooms have Victorian accents and private baths. A Continental
breakfast and glass of wine are complimentary.
　　"North Wing" room — pvt. bath,   Q bed...$65
　　regular room — shared bath,   Q bed...$50
★ **Magnolia Hotel**   *9.5 mi. SE off CA 29 at 6529 Yount - Yountville*   *944-2056*
In the 1960s, this century-old three-story inn was completely renovated with period
furnishings, and a private bath was added to each room. There is a whirlpool in an
enclosed redwood patio, and a large pool in a garden area. Complimentary full breakfasts
are served in the dining room.
　　"Magnolia" — spacious, fireplace, view windows, balc.,   K bed...$145
　　"Cabernet" — spacious, view windows on 2 sides, window seat,   K bed...$115
　　"Chardonnay" — intimate, view windows,   Q bed...$90
　　regular room — small,   D bed...$75
★ **Meadowwood**   *2 mi. E at 900 Meadowwood Lane*   *963-3646*
Tennis, an outdoor pool, whirlpool, a Parcours circuit, and (for a fee) golf, plus a
Continental breakfast and the morning paper are all part of the daily fare in this great
place to "get away" amidst majestic oaks in a secluded canyon.
　　"suite" — fireplace, wet bar, deck, pvt. views,   K bed...$140
　　regular room "studio" — pvt. views, wet bar, deck,   K bed...$115
★ **Napa Valley Lodge - Best Western**   *9 mi. SE on Madison St. - Yountville*   *944-2468*
This newer, tastefully furnished motel is the largest accommodation in the area. A large
swimming pool and a whirlpool are immediately adjacent to vineyards. Each room has a
cable color TV and a phone.
　　#15 — spacious, end, refr., gas fireplace, vineyard view,   K bed...$88
　　regular room — many have a vineyard view,   K bed...$78
★ **Wine Country Inn**   *2 mi. N at 1152 Lodi Lane*   *963-7077*
Hidden away on a slope above a vineyard, this bed-and-breakfast motor inn, constructed
in 1975, offers individually decorated rooms with antique furnishings, good vineyard
views, and private baths. Many of the spacious, well-furnished units have fireplaces. A
complimentary Continental breakfast is served.
　　#24 — lg. suite, Franklin fireplace, pvt. balc.,
　　　　　　　panoramic vineyard view, canopied   Q bed...$120
　　#26 — lg. suite, fireplace, pvt. deck, vineyard view,   Q bed...$100
　　regular room —   D bed...$80

CAMPGROUNDS

The area's best campground with complete facilities is by a picturesque creek near town. Several additional campgrounds are a half hour drive east at a reservoir (Lake Berryessa) with complete camping and lakeside recreation facilities.

★ **Bothe-Napa Valley State Park**   *4.8 mi. N on CA 29*   *942-4575*

This large state operated facility is in a luxuriant forest of oaks and pines close to town. Fishing in tiny Ritchie Creek, a beautifully sited outdoor swimming pool (in summer), plus hiking and marked nature trails are attractions. Flush toilets and hot showers are available, but there are no hookups. All of the well-spaced sites are shaded by large broadleaf trees. Each site has a picnic table, grill/fire pit, and a wooden storage locker. There are a few walk-in tent sites.   base rate...$6

Spanish Flat Resort   *22 mi. E via CA 128 & Knoxville Rd.*   *966-2101*

This large, privately operated campground is located on an oak-and-grass-covered slope by Lake Berryessa. Boat rentals, plus a ramp and dock, are provided. The big reservoir is used for boating, water-skiing, fishing, and swimming. Flush toilets, hot showers, and hookups are available. Each site has a picnic table, fire ring, and grill. Some sites are shaded and have lake views.   base rate...$7

OTHER INFORMATION

Area Code: *707*
Zip Code: *94574*

St. Helena Chamber of Commerce   *downtown at 1508 Main St.*   *963-4456*

San Luis Obispo, California

Elevation:

230 feet

Population (1980):

34,252

Population (1970):

28,036

Location:

195 mi. NW
of Los Angeles

San Luis Obispo is a classic California town. It is an architectural showcase for a multicultural heritage that includes a centuries-old Spanish mission in the heart of town surrounded by an engaging mixture of Victorian and modern structures. Geographically, it is at the center of a picturesque valley bordered by Coast Range mountains only a few miles from the ocean. Vast sand dunes, miles of hard sand beaches, secluded ocean coves, large scenic reservoirs, picturesque hot springs, and a mountain wilderness are among noteworthy features within a short drive. The area also benefits from one of the nation's finest year-round climates. Crowds are heaviest on weekends in every season and daily throughout summer. For some, the best season is spring, after winter rains have restored lush green hues to countrysides accented by masses of wildflowers. Fall is also favored, because warm sunny days linger until very late in the year.

Father Junipero Serra correctly sensed the site's desirability and established Mission San Luis Obispo de Tolosa here in 1772 as the fifth in the chain of California's missions. During the next century, Spaniards and Indians were joined by an admixture of Mexican farmers, Portuguese fishermen, Chinese railroad builders, Japanese vegetable growers, and Swiss dairymen, among others. Architectural contributions of these early pioneers are still evident downtown. American settlers from the East and Midwest began arriving in large numbers before the turn of the century. They built substantial businesses and homes similar to the ones they had left back home. A surprising number of Victorian remnants still serve their original purpose. Many others have been creatively adapted to contemporary uses.

The town's economic vitality and diversity is apparent in one of the West's most handsome business districts. Its centerpiece is a beautifully preserved old adobe mission that overlooks a sunny plaza and lush greenery along the banks of San Luis Creek. Footpaths, bridges, and attractive landscaping have turned this small meandering stream into a unique feature lined by inviting restaurants, galleries, and specialty shops. Areawide, restaurants and nightlife are relatively abundant and surprisingly conventional. A short but growing list of places offer gourmet food, or music and dancing in distinctive surroundings. Accommodations are plentiful both in town and along nearby beaches. As added attractions, the nation's first motel is still operating in San Luis Obispo, as is the most unusual motel anywhere.

WEATHER PROFILE
Vokac Weather Rating

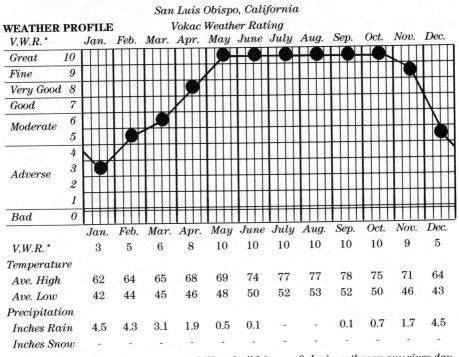

V.W.R.*	Jan.	Feb.	Mar.	Apr.	May	June	July	Aug.	Sep.	Oct.	Nov.	Dec.
Great 10												
Fine 9												
Very Good 8												
Good 7												
Moderate 6 / 5												
4												
Adverse 3 / 2												
1												
Bad 0												

	Jan.	Feb.	Mar.	Apr.	May	June	July	Aug.	Sep.	Oct.	Nov.	Dec.
V.W.R.*	3	5	6	8	10	10	10	10	10	10	9	5
Temperature												
Ave. High	62	64	65	68	69	74	77	77	78	75	71	64
Ave. Low	42	44	45	46	48	50	52	53	52	50	46	43
Precipitation												
Inches Rain	4.5	4.3	3.1	1.9	0.5	0.1	-	-	0.1	0.7	1.7	4.5
Inches Snow	-	-	-	-	-	-	-	-	-	-	-	-

*V.W.R. = Vokac Weather Rating: probability of mild (warm & dry) weather on any given day.

Forecast

		Temperatures		
Month	V.W.R.*	Daytime	Evening	Precipitation
January	3 Adverse	cool	cool	frequent rainstorms
February	5 Moderate	cool	cool	frequent rainstorms
March	6 Moderate	warm	cool	occasional rainstorms
April	8 Very Good	warm	cool	occasional rainstorms
May	10 Great	warm	cool	negligible
June	10 Great	warm	cool	none
July	10 Great	warm	cool	none
August	10 Great	warm	warm	none
September	10 Great	warm	warm	none
October	10 Great	warm	cool	infrequent showers
November	9 Fine	warm	cool	infrequent rainstorms
December	5 Moderate	cool	cool	occasional downpours

Summary

San Luis Obispo, with a mountain-sheltered location near the ocean, is just far enough inland to escape much of the winter fog of coastal areas and the extreme heat of summer common to most interior locations. The temperate climate is one of the town's most appealing features, and one of the best in the West. **Winter** is cool, with no frost of any consequence, and wet, with frequent rainstorms contributing well over half of the annual precipitation. **Spring**, while often breezy, usually offers warm days, cool evenings, and diminishing rainfalls. There is an exhilarating allure about this season, when the senses are rewarded by lavish displays of lovely and aromatic new blooms, including certain flowering trees that lend to the pervasive fragrance of the lush green scene. **Summer** is remarkable. Consistently warm weather and no rainfall assure comfortable enjoyment of all outdoor activities. Warm sunny days continue through late **fall**, until the rainy season begins again in earnest after Thanksgiving.

ATTRACTIONS & DIVERSIONS

★ **Avila Beach** . *10 mi. SW via US 101 on San Luis Bay Dr.*
This raffish little town is unique along the central coast for its combination of a south-facing shoreline and a sheltered harbor. Fine sunbathing and ocean swimming can be enjoyed along a safe beach where the water occasionally gets above 70°F in summer. Facilities include a plain little beachfront park with picnic tables and fire rings. Nearby are a fishing pier, launching ramp, and charter boats and gear rental concessions for sportfishing (Port San Luis Sportfishing — 595-7200). Horseback riding can be arranged a short distance inland (Avila Livery Stable — 595-7144). Pirate's Cove (accessible from a dirt parking area .3 miles south of the oil tank farm overlooking town) is a remote, sheltered shoreline that has been unofficially adopted as a very popular swimming-suits-optional beach.

★ **Bicycling**
An extensive bike path system in and around town is identified on a map available at the Chamber of Commerce. Bikes can be rented at:

Bicycle Bill's	*downtown at 445 Higuera St.*	*544-6083*
Mountain Air Bikes	*downtown at 695 Higuera St.*	*544-2453*

Cal Poly *1 mi. N on California Blvd.* *544-6084*
California State Polytechnic University is the fifth oldest unit (1901) of the California state university system. It occupies more than 5,000 acres of rolling hills at the base of the Santa Lucia Mountains at the northern edge of town. About 15,000 full time students use the attractive campus, distinguished by tropical and subtropical landscaping and a number of impressive new buildings. The schools of agriculture and architecture are among the nation's largest. A schedule of intercollegiate athletics, music, theater, art and craft productions, and special events is available at the University Union.

Cuesta Ridge Road *6 mi. N off US 101*
A spectacularly scenic drive begins just south of the Cuesta Grade Summit of US 101 at a dirt turnout space for trucks. A poorly paved, narrow road rewards courageous drivers with awesome panoramas as it winds upward for 2.5 miles. Just below the TV transmitters at the top of Cuesta Ridge are a dirt parking lot, rugged picnic sites (no tables), and hiking trails with ocean views. The Cuesta Grade Botannical Area, an interesting dwarf pine forest of the rare Santa Lucia fir, is half a mile beyond.

Golf

Morro Bay Golf Course *12 mi. NW in Morro Bay State Park* *772-4341*
This 18-hole course on a landscaped slope overlooking Morro Bay is open to the public with all necessary services and rentals.

★ **San Luis Bay Inn Golf Course** *10 mi. SW off US 101 - Avila Beach* *595-2307*
The resort's challenging 18-hole course is beautifully sited along a creek near the ocean. A driving range, club and cart rentals, and food and beverage service are open to the public as well as guests.

Sea Pines Golf Club *12 mi. NW via Los Osos Rd. at 250 Howard Av.* *528-1788*
The public is invited to use this pretty little 9-hole course overlooking Morro Bay and the ocean. A driving range, food and beverages, and all necessary services and rentals are provided.

Library *downtown at 888 Morro St.* *549-5991*
The San Luis Obispo City Library is a big, conventional facility with a good selection of newspapers and periodicals, and a few armchairs in the reading area. Closed Sun.

★ **Lopez Lake Recreation Area** *18 mi. SE via CA 227 & Lopez Canyon Rd.* *489-2095*
Open year-round, this picturesque 956-acre reservoir with twenty-two miles of shoreline offers a remarkable diversity of recreation possibilities. Segregated campsites for tents and trailers are attractively located on oak-studded, grassy slopes near the lake. A food and supplies store, picnic areas, barbecue facilities, restrooms, playgrounds, a museum, and horseback riding are also available. For offbeat excitement, the Mustang Water Slide is the area's best onshore feature, with two 600-foot water slides and four hot whirlpools. The main attraction, however, is the lake, with designated swimming areas, good trout and bass fishing, a marina with a paved boat launch, and boat rentals. (Call 489-1006 for reservations of motor boats, sailboats, kayaks, jet skis, bumper, or paddle boats.) Sailing is also very popular, and this is one of the best freshwater wind surfing sites in the West.

★ **Mission San Luis Obispo de Tolosa**   *downtown at Chorro/Monterey Sts.*   *543-6850*
The "Prince of Missions" is the fifth of the California missions, founded in 1772 by Father Junipero Serra. It was built of adobe brick by the Chumash Indians with walls up to five feet thick. Completed in 1794, this mission was the first with a tiled roof in California. The restored building still serves as a parish church and also includes an eight-room museum and gardens. The adjacent beautifully landscaped plaza, recreated in 1971, is still the town's focal point and the center of many community events throughout the year.

★ **Montana de Oro State Park**   *17 mi. W via Los Osos Valley Rd.*   *543-2161*
Hiking in rugged hills and headlands above unspoiled sandy beaches and secluded coves is the major attraction in this largely undeveloped park where wildlife and spring wildflowers abound. Beachcombing, clamming, skin diving, and shore fishing are other possibilities. A boat launch, campsites, and picnic tables are provided.

Morro Bay Embarcadero   *12 mi. NW via CA 1 — Morro Bay*
A tourist attraction with a lively nautical atmosphere has developed along the little bay, with many family-oriented gift shops and restaurants. In the midst of this is a tiny park that features a giant outdoor chess board with two-to-three foot tall pieces, available free to the public by reservation through the Morro Bay Parks and Recreation Department (772-2214 ext. 226). Charter boat operators such as Virg's Deep Sea Fishing (772-2216) are readily available for ocean fishing year-round, and for whale watching tours during the annual winter migration of the great grey whales (January thru March).

★ **Morro Bay State Park**   *11 mi. W via CA 1 & State Park Rd. - Morro Bay*   *772-2560*
Facilities in this outstanding marine area include a large campground, shady picnic sites, a scenic golf course, nature walks and hiking trails, a museum, plus boat and bicycle rentals. Pismo clamming and fishing, good surfing, skin diving, and cold water swimming are also enjoyed. Remote sand dunes and beaches on the peninsula between the ocean and bay are well worth the walk, or boat trip. To get to Sand Spit Wild Area, take Los Osos Valley Road and Pecho Valley Road to the first dirt road to the west.

Morro Rock   *12 mi. W via CA 1 - Morro Bay*
A solid rock monolith, Morro Rock, juts 576 feet above Morro Bay. Unfortunately, the natural grandeur of this geological phenomenon is marred by the adjacent giant Morro Bay Power Plant and its three towering 450-foot stacks. Several larger but less precipitous morros create a dramatic "backbone" down the middle of the Los Osos Valley that extends back to San Luis Obispo and beyond.

Path of History   *downtown*
A two-mile self-guided tour past many nicely maintained and restored Victorian homes and businesses is made easy by a green line painted on downtown streets. The Chamber of Commerce has a nineteen-stop brochure that identifies some of the best of these nostalgic remnants.

★ **Pismo State Beach**   *13 mi. S off CA 1*   *489-2684*
Auto driving on the beach is permitted for eight miles south of Pismo Beach. This is one of the few places in California where you can experience smooth, hard beach sand under your wheels. Renting a three-wheeled sand vehicle is an exhilarating way to explore the miles of dunes that lie just beyond the beach at Pismo Dunes State Vehicular Recreation Area. (Call the Sand Center, 489-6014, in Oceano for reservations.) There are plenty of places for sunbathing and picnicking, and you can easily get away from the crowds in the fenced dunes area reserved for hikers. The casual carnival atmosphere in this sand-lovers' paradise entices fun-lovers of all ages to try Pismo clamming, swimming, surfing, fishing, or even horseback riding on the beach by renting a horse at the Livery Stable in Oceano (489-8100).

Santa Lucia Wilderness   *9 mi. NE via US 101*   *543-4244*
The crest of the Santa Lucia Range with peaks towering 3,000 feet above the nearby ocean lies just east of town. It has been designated as a wilderness area in the Los Padres National Forest, with an area about fifteen miles long and two miles wide. Backpacking, camping, hiking, and hunting are popular.

Warm Water Features
  Avila Hot Springs   *8 mi. S at US 101/Avila Rd.*   *595-2359*
This venerable family-oriented hot springs spa has a 50' x 100' warm swimming pool and large hot tub outdoors. These and indoor private hot mineral baths and massage facilities are open year-round.

★ **Mustang Water Slide** *18 mi. SE via CA 227 & Lopez Canyon Rd.* 489-8898
In Lopez Lake Recreation Area, visitors are treated to the excitement of two 600-foot
curving warm water slides and four hot mineral whirlpools on an oak-studded hillside
above the lake.

★ **Sycamore Mineral Springs** *9 mi. SW via US 101 on Avila Beach Rd.* 595-7302
Open twenty-four hours every day, this unique facility rents redwood hot tubs by the hour
in seductive natural settings on a steep oak-covered hillside. The ones named "Shangri-La"
and "Rendezvous" are in especially remote sylvan settings. An adjoining motel has hot
mineral whirlpools on private, oak-shaded decks next to the bedrooms.

Wineries
Many good wineries have been developed within an hour's drive to the north around Paso
Robles and to the south near Solvang. Complete information and a map of all central
coast wineries can be obtained at the Chamber of Commerce. In recent years, a major
newly-recognized wine growing district has been established within a few miles of town to
the southeast in Edna Valley. Several wineries have opened, with more on the way.
Currently, the most impressive facility is:

★ **Corbett Canyon Vineyards** *8 mi. SE at 2195 Corbett Canyon Rd.* 544-5800
This largest of the southcentral coast wineries only dates back to the late 1970s. After a
recent ownership change, it is now producing a limited variety of premium wines with
grapes from regional vineyards. The knowledgable staff is friendly and generous with
tastes. Shaded picnic tables occupy alcoves of the big Spanish-style building overlooking
much of the Edna Valley. Tasting, tours, and sales 10-4:30 daily.

SHOPPING
Downtown is a fascinating blend of preservation and progress, with many early buildings
still serving their original commercial purposes, while several large older buildings have
been ingeniously converted into appealing mini-malls. An unusual variety of both shops
and merchandise is complemented by luxuriant rows of trees, an abundance of flowers,
and street furniture. A landscaped stream provides a wonderfully strollable center of
attention for this vital district.

Food Specialties
★ **The Bakery Cafe on the Creek** *downtown at 1040 Broad St.* 549-0551
An array of splendid croissants is displayed in one of the West's most outstanding new
bakeries. Other delicious baked goods and light meals are also served to go, inside, or on
a tranquil deck over a landscaped creek.

★ **Boston Bagel Co.** *downtown at 1127 Broad St.* 541-5134
Outstanding bagels (as many as two dozen varieties), including some delicious specialties
like whole wheat apple walnut bagels, are served with a choice of toppings and coffee at
a few tables, or to go.

California Gold Rush *downtown at 778 Higuera St.* 544-4663
Popular Bernardoz ice cream, made nearby, can be enjoyed on a sunny deck overlooking
the creek behind the Network. Fresh-baked hot soft pretzels are another feature. Closed
Sun.

★ **Cattaneo Bros.** *1 mi. S at 769 Caudill St.* 543-7188
Some of the best beef jerky in the West is made here in all styles (thin cut, thick cut, hand
cut, peppered, etc.). It can be purchased here, and it is shipped to customers nationwide.
Closed Sat.-Sun.

Cowboy Cookie N' Grub Co. *downtown at 1035 Chorro St.* 543-2096
Tempting cookies, brownies, quiches, and muffins are available in this little carryout.
Closed Sun.

Delite Bakery *downtown at 723 Higuera St.* 543-5842
This enduring bakery offers an impressive assortment of old-fashioned breads, pastries,
and donuts, mostly to go.

★ **Eclair Bakery** *11 mi. S via US 101 at 221 Pomeroy - Pismo Beach* 773-4145
In this delightful newer European-style bakery/deli, first-class pastries are served in a
comfortable seating area, or to go. Closed Mon.-Tues.

★ **Gelare Ice Cream Italiano** *downtown at 570 Higuera St.* 544-1925
A fine selection of rich Italian-style ice cream is made in this little shop in the Creamery
complex.

A Gourmet Touch   *downtown at 600 Marsh St.*   549-9111
Gourmet pastas, pates, desserts, and specialty foods are packaged to go in a classy new shop.

Haagen-Dazs   *downtown at 949 Higuera St.*   544-3060
A bright little representative of the premium ice cream chain offers a variety of flavors made from natural ingredients and sold in all kinds of ice cream treats.

★ **Old Country Deli**   *downtown at 600 Marsh St.*   541-2968
The showcases in this new deli are packed with home-cured ham, sausage, jerky and other meats, plus cheeses, gourmet foods and local wines. Ribs are barbecued over oak wood in front of the store every Saturday. Closed Sun.

★ **Old West Cinnamon Rolls And . . .**   *11 mi. S at 861 Dolliver - Pismo Beach*   773-1428
This tiny takeout bakery specializes in excellent cinnamon rolls, and also has coffee and a few other breads and pastries.

★ **Rocky Mountain Chocolate Factory**   *downtown at 848 Higuera St.*   541-2221
Fresh-made chocolate specialties, hand-dipped fruits, truffles, fudge and other gourmet confections are sold in this snazzy new representative of a Durango candy chain.

★ **San Luis Sourdough Co.**   *downtown at 781 Higuera St.*   546-9609
Delicious sourdough-based baked goods, plus fine traditional breads and croissants, are displayed in this outstanding new carryout bakery. Samples are offered. Closed Sun.

★ **Wine Street Wines**   *downtown at 774F Higuera St.*   543-0203
Many styles of regional and other California premium wines are attractively displayed and well stored in this downstairs shop in the Network. Closed Sun.

Specialty Shops

Art Center Art Association Gallery   *downtown at 1010 Broad St.*   543-8562
Local artists are featured in a variety of media, with emphasis on paintings and sculpture.

Bookland   *downtown at 787 Higuera St.*   544-0150
This shop offers a large selection of hardcover and paperback books.

The Creamery   *downtown at 570 Higuera St.*
An old turn-of-the-century creamery has been transformed into a lively little complex of specialty shops, galleries, and restaurants.

★ **Mission News**   *downtown at 1030 Chorro St.*   543-3169
A surprisingly large number of magazines and newspapers, plus paperback books, are well organized in this bright little shop.

★ **The Network**   *downtown at 774 Higuera St.*
An old department store was carefully converted into an appealing two-level arcade of boutiques and restaurants with a choice of creekside or wine cellar dining.

Norwood Books   *downtown at 942 Chorro St.*   543-4391
This shop carries a full line of books, including many of local and regional interest.

NIGHTLIFE

A variety of noteworthy bars and lounges throughout the area feature live entertainment and dancing. Several of the best are concentrated downtown. Most are associated with major restaurants.

Dark Room   *downtown at 1037 Monterey St.*   543-5131
This small hideaway is often crowded because of its good reputation for folk and acoustic rock music. Light meals are also served. Closed Sun.

★ **J.P. Andrews Saloon**   *downtown at Monterey & Osos Sts.*   541-1888
Live easy listening music is offered most nights in a historic building that has been remodeled into an upbeat, updated saloon trimmed with abundant greenery, brass, and wood. Fresh pasta and seasonally available fresh fish are served for lunch and dinner. Closed Sun.

★ **Madonna Inn**   *1 mi. W at 100 Madonna Rd.*   543-3000
An old-fashioned orchestra plays big band sounds for dancing most nights in a large one-of-a-kind lounge in the West's most flamboyant motel.

★ **F. McLintock's Saloon**   *downtown at 686 Higuera St.*   541-0686
This comfortable Old Western-style saloon is loaded with period paintings and paraphenalia. Live entertainment is offered on weekends, along with casual meals. Closed Sun.

Motel Inn   *1 mi. E at 2223 Monterey St.*   *543-4000*
Popular groups play music for dancing nightly in the Branding Iron Lounge, a showplace of "early modern" decor in the world's first motel.

★ **Olde Port Inn**   *12 mi. S via US 101 - Avila Beach*   *595-2515*
Well-known names occasionally provide the live music for dancing in a casual nautical lounge with picture window views of the waterfront. A popular seafood restaurant shares the building on Avila Bay pier.

Tortilla Flats   *downtown at 1051 Nipomo*   *544-7575*
Live entertainment and dancing are offered most nights in a large Mexican cantina-style lounge next to a dining room featuring Mexican dishes.

RESTAURANTS
Conventional dining places are abundant. Several distinctive restaurants have opened in and around town in recent years. Many of the best are themed to the historical merits of the area.

Apple Farm   *.9 mi. E at 2015 Monterey St.*   *544-6100*
B-L-D.   *Low*
This large, country-charming family restaurant serves homestyle American fare like hot apple dumplings, cornbread and pies, and there is a salad bar.

Assembly Line   *downtown at 970 Higuera St.*   *544-6193*
L-D. No L on Sun.   *Moderate*
An elaborate soup and salad bar is the highlight, supported by beef ribs and chicken dishes. The pleasant dining room is well outfitted with booths and plants.

★ **The Bakery Cafe on the Creek**   *downtown at 1040 Broad St.*   *549-0551*
B-L.   *Moderate*
More than a dozen kinds of huge, delicious croissants plus other fine pastries and desserts complement light fare including nicely prepared omelets and specialties like walnut chicken salad. Pastries, cheeses and pate plates are served in the afternoon, and box lunches can be packaged to go. The balcony over the landscaped creek is downtown's most picture-perfect dining place.

Cafe Roma   *.5 mi. SE at 1819 Osos St.*   *541-6800*
L-D. Closed Sun.-Mon.   *Moderate*
Homemade pasta and other Italian fare are offered in a well-regarded, congested trattoria.

Chocolate Soup   *downtown at 980 Morro St.*   *543-7229*
L-D. Closed Sun.   *Low*
A nightly special, crepes, a salad bar, and homemade soups (including "chocolate soup"), breads, and desserts are served to patrons in high-gloss blue booths.

Cigar Factory   *downtown at 726 Higuera St.*   *543-6900*
D only.   *Moderate*
Contemporary American fare is served in an old cigar factory that was recycled as one of the area's first theme restaurants. A popular Victorian-style bar downstairs features live music nightly.

Del Monte Cafe   *.5 mi. SE at 1901 Santa Barbara St.*   *541-1901*
B-L. D on Thurs. & Fri.   *Moderate*
All-American fare is served in a skillfully converted historic cottage.

★ **Dorn's Original Breakers**   *12 mi. NW at 801 Market Av. - Morro Bay*   *772-4415*
B-L-D.   *Moderate*
Fresh seafood is carefully prepared in this big casual restaurant on a bluff above the Embarcadero. Breakfasts are especially noteworthy, with a variety of crepe-style omelets, homemade muffins, pancakes, waffles, and more. The area's best views of Morro Rock and Morro Bay are another feature of this long-popular restaurant.

1865   *.8 mi. E at 1865 Monterey St.*   *544-1865*
L-D.   *Moderate*
Prime rib is the specialty of this large, contemporary restaurant. Loft dining is a feature, and the decor is accented by lots of natural wood beams, hanging plants, and tapestries. The comfortable lounge offers live music by popular groups most nights.

★ **Golden China Restaurant**   *downtown at 675 Higuera St.*   *543-7354*
L-D.   *Moderate*
Mandarin and Szechwan dishes, including fresh seasonal specialties like asparagus cooked several ways, are skillfully prepared with light vegetable oil. Tables set with crisp white linen, and high walls with large raised-relief murals, set the tone for this casual and popular new restaurant.

Louisa's Place   *downtown at 964 Higuera St.*   *541-0227*
B-L-D. No D on Sat. & Sun.   *Moderate*
Good, all-American dishes are served in plain, friendly atmosphere in this old-fashioned cafe. Breakfasts are particularly popular.

Madonna Inn   *1 mi. W at 100 Madona Rd.*   *543-3000*
B-L-D.   *Expensive*
The fairly ambitious menu and elaborate homemade pastries might go unnoticed by first-timers. In a remarkable motel that is a paean to pink, both the coffee shop and dining room are flamboyant fairy tales that have added new dimensions to interior decor. Even the restrooms are so unique that women occasionally sneak into the men's room when the coast is clear just to see the incomparable fixtures.

★ **F. McLintock's**   *9 mi. S via US 101 at 750 Mattie Rd.*   *773-2488*
L-D.   *Moderate*
A historic roadhouse restaurant was restyled awhile ago. Western atmosphere is now matched by very complete Western meals highlighting central California's gourmet specialty, oak-pit barbecued steaks and ribs. Live country/western music is featured nightly in the adjoining saloon.

F. McLintock's Saloon   *downtown at 686 Higuera St.*   *541-0686*
B-L-D. Closed Sun.   *Moderate*
Beef is the specialty on a casual all-American menu that also includes buffalo burgers. Both food and drinks are served in a comfortable reproduction of a Western-style saloon dining room.

Michael's   *downtown at 785 Higuera St.*   *544-4040*
B-L.   *Moderate*
This New York-style deli cafe serves delicious breads and pastries from the splendid sourdough bread bakery next door.

Old Custom House   *10 mi. SW at 324 Front St. - Avila Beach*   *595-9972*
B-L-D.   *Moderate*
Highly regarded breakfasts include a dozen specialty omelets, or create-your-own from a dozen ingredients. Although it looks like a tiny beachfront cafe, there is also a heated garden patio in the back.

Plessa's Tavern   *11 mi. S via US 101 at 891 Price St. - Pismo Beach*   *773-2060*
L-D. Closed Tues.   *Moderate*
Since 1921, this seafood house has specialized in baked clams on the half shell au gratin. The old-fashioned dish is still worth a detour.

San Luis Bay Inn   *10 mi. SW via US 101 - Avila Beach*   *595-2333*
B-L-D.   *Expensive*
A centerpiece for the resort is a large, casually elegant bay-view dining room featuring Continental specialties and tableside cooking. An adjacent lounge offers live entertainment and dancing.

Sebastian's   *downtown at Monterey/Chorro Sts.*   *544-5666*
L-D.   *Moderate*
Steak and seafood are served in a nicely furnished dining room or on a terrace overlooking the Mission. There is also a comfortable lounge with easy listening music most evenings.

Spike's Place   *downtown at 570 Higuera St.*   *544-7157*
L-D.   *Low*
Potato skins are served a dozen ways here, along with fresh deep-fried artichokes and other veggies, and unusual desserts. Alcoholic fruit-flavored shakes are another of the eclectic enticements offered amidst wood and greenery indoors or on a back deck.

The Spindle   *downtown at 778 Higuera St.*   *543-5555*
L only.   *Moderate*
Casual foods, beer, and wine are especially enjoyable on the deck of San Luis's original creekside cafe behind the Network. Live music on Friday and Saturday afternoons is another alfresco attraction.

★ **This Old House**   *3 mi. NW at 740 W. Foothill Blvd.*   *543-2690*
D only.   *Moderate*
Crowds love the smells and flavors that oak-pit barbecue cooking gives to the very complete steak and ribs dinners served in this big comfortable steak house. Rustic ranch decor is well brought off in several dining rooms and in a wood-toned firelit lounge.

★ **Wine Street Inn**   *downtown at 774 Higuera St.*   *543-4488*
L-D. No L on Sun.   *Moderate*
Delicious fondues are the specialty, and chicken and seafood dishes are also served in a dining room uniquely situated in the middle of a shop with one of the best California wine selections in the state. By advance arrangement, these wines may be enjoyed in the restaurant.

LODGING

San Luis Obispo gave the world the word "motel" more than half a century ago. Today, most of the major motel chains have joined the "historic" Motel Inn in town to share the growing demand for overnight accommodations in this area. A small but increasing number of really distinctive lodging places reflects the town's expanding role as a vacation destination. Most of the area's lodgings are concentrated on Monterey Street east of downtown. While there are few bargains in summer and on most weekends, rates are usually reduced at least 20% apart from those times.

Heritage Inn   *.3 mi. N at 978 Olive St.*   *544-7440*
The first bed-and-breakfast facility in town is located in a newly restored, antique-filled Victorian inn. Guests enjoy Continental breakfasts and complimentary wine, fresh flowers, and a delightful parlour with a fireplace. Clubfoot tubs are down the hall, and bikes are available.

Del's Room — gas fireplace, shared bath,		Q bed...$68
regular room — pvt. bath,		D bed...$68

Homestead Motel   *.3 mi. N at 920 Olive St.*   *543-7700*
An outdoor pool is a feature in this modern single-level motel. Each room has a phone and cable color TV with movies.

#25 — spacious, pvt. view of trees over a creek,		2 T & K beds...$65
#22,#23 — spacious, some view above creek,		2 T & Q beds...$60
regular room —		D bed...$45

★ **Kon Tiki**   *10.7 mi. S via CA 1 at 1621 Price St. - Pismo Beach*   *773-4833*
A large outdoor view pool and whirlpool, plus easy access to the beach, are features along with a restaurant and lounge in this large modern four-story motor hotel on a bluff by the ocean. Each room has a phone, cable color TV, and a private balcony.

#401,#402 — free-standing fireplace, pvt. ocean view balc.,		K bed...$62
regular room — many have an ocean view,		K bed...$52

★ **Madonna Inn**   *1 mi. W at 100 Madonna Rd.*   *543-3000*
San Luis Obispo's most fantastic lodging is unique in all of the West. For more than a quarter of a century, this place has been delighting travelers with its outrageous flamboyance. The more recently completed guest rooms are so popular that they must be reserved well in advance. Each room has a phone and cable color TV.

#137 — rock ceilings, walls, floors & rock waterfall in bathroom,		K bed...$105
#130 — lush greens, natural rock walls, huge fireplace,		K bed...$105
#143 — massive rocks everywhere, even in the bathroom,		K bed...$95
#146 — subdued pink & grey decor, massive rock fireplace,		K bed...$105
#128 — lg., contemporary room in blue tones,		K bed...$62
#125 — spacious, contemporary decor, muted shades of blue,		D & K beds...$70
regular room —		Q bed...$62

Motel Inn   *1 mi. E at 2223 Monterey St.*   *543-4000*
The world's first motel is a curiously contemporary "antiquity" that has been refurbished through the years. Attractively landscaped grounds include a variety of mature citrus trees and banana palms, and a large outdoor pool, plus a dining room and lounge. Most of the rooms are in quiet, single-level buildings, and have phones and cable color TV.
> "A1", "L5" — lg., nicely furnished,   K bed...$39
> regular room —   D bed...$35

Motel 6   *2 mi. SW by US 101 at 1433 Calle Joaquin*   *544-8400*
The **bargain** motel chain is represented by a modest, modern facility close to the freeway with an outdoor pool.
> regular room —   D bed...$22

★ **San Luis Bay Inn** *10 mi. SW via US 101 and Avila Rd. - Avila Beach*   *595-2333*
This self-contained resort overlooking a bay offers a splendid (fee) 18-hole golf course, plus lighted tennis courts, a large outdoor pool, and other resort amenities including a well-regarded dining room and lounge. Each spacious room has a phone, cable color TV, and a private balcony.
> ocean view room —   Q or K bed...$108
> regular room — a few have ocean view,   Q bed...$88

★ **Sea Crest** *10.3 mi. S via US 101 at 2241 Price St. - Pismo Beach*   *773-4608*
This large, modern motel has a beautifully sited big outdoor pool, whirlpool, and private access to the beach. Each room has a phone, cable color TV and an ocean view.
> #229,#259 — spacious, pvt. balc., great ocean view,   round K bed...$62
> regular room — many have an ocean view,   K bed...$58

★ **Shore Cliff Lodge - Best Western**   *10 mi. S at 2555 Price St. - Pismo Beach*   *773-4671*
A large outdoor pool, sauna, whirlpool, and two lighted tennis courts are on a bluff above the ocean, and there is a stairway to the beach on the well-landscaped grounds of this large contemporary motor hotel. An ocean view dining room and a lounge are also provided. Each spacious well-furnished room has a phone, cable color TV, and a private patio or balcony.
> #304,#306 — top fl., floor-to-ceiling whitewater view,   K bed...$66
> regular room — many have ocean view,   K bed...$62

Sunbeam Motel   *.6 mi. E at 1656 Monterey St.*   *543-8141*
This small, older motel is a rustic **bargain**. Each modest room has a cable color TV.
> regular room —   D bed...$25

The Sycamore Hotel   *9 mi. S via US 101 on Avila Beach Rd.*   *595-7302*
On the grounds of Sycamore Mineral Springs is a modest little motel with only one amenity — most of the simply furnished rooms have a private whirlpool on an enclosed tree-view deck.
> "Ultra" — spacious, tranquil, oak branches view from pvt. whirlpool,   Q bed...$55
> spa room — whirlpool in room or on pvt. deck,   Q bed...$55
> regular room — no whirlpool,   Q bed...$40

Villa San Luis Motel   *.8 mi. E at 1670 Monterey St.*   *543-8071*
An outdoor pool is a feature of this small motel. Each of the rooms has a phone and cable color TV with movies.
> regular room —   Q bed...$38

CAMPGROUNDS
Several nearby campgrounds showcase the town's remarkable variety of water-oriented features. Campers can select sites next to the ocean, Morro Bay, Lopez Lake, or Avila Hot Springs pool.

Avila Hot Springs Spa & RV Park   *8 mi. S on US 101*   *595-2359*
A big outdoor hot springs pool is the attraction at this privately operated campground. Swimming, hot mineral baths, and massage are offered (for a fee). Flush toilets, hot showers, and hookups are available. Each of the closely spaced sites has a picnic table and grill. There is a separate grassy tenting area.   base rate...$10

★ **Lopez Lake Recreation Area**   *18 mi. SE via Orcutt Rd. & Lopez Dr.*   *489-2095*
This huge park is one of the most outstanding county operated recreation facilities anywhere. Located on gentle, grassy oak-dotted slopes by a large picturesque reservoir, it features rentals/docks/ramps for boating, sailing, water-skiing, fishing, lake swimming, a (fee) water slide and whirlpool complex, horse riding trails, and hiking trails. The enormous campground has flush toilets, hot showers, and hookups. Each well-spaced, oak-shaded site has a picnic table and fire area. Many have a fine view of the lake.
base rate...$8

★ **Montana de Oro State Park**   *16 mi. W via Los Osos Valley*   *528-0513*
A state operated campground is beautifully situated near unspoiled ocean beaches and coves in a remote section of the park. Beachcombing, fishing, skin diving, swimming, clamming, and hiking are popular. Only pit toilets are available. There are no showers, hookups or drinking water. Each of the sites has a picnic table and a fire area.
base rate...$3

★ **Morro Bay State Park**   *12 mi. NW via CA 1 & South Bay Blvd.*   *489-2784*
This large state operated park is adjacent to Morro Bay. Boat rentals; a (fee) dock and ramp; saltwater swimming, boating, and fishing; bicycle rentals; a museum; a (fee) golf course and driving range; hiking trails; and a remote sand dune area across the bay are features. Flush toilets, hot showers, and hookups are available. Each site has a picnic table and fire area.
base rate...$6

SPECIAL EVENTS

★ **Poly Royal** *California Polytechnic State University*   *last weekend in April*
An unusual two-day "country fair on a college campus" is hosted by the students of Cal Poly. Features include a rodeo, a tractor pull and other sporting events, live theater and dance, a carnival, educational exhibits, plus a delicious array of international and all-American foods prepared with locally-grown produce.

★ **La Fiesta de San Luis Obispo**   *downtown*   *third weekend in May*
In celebration of the town's Spanish heritage, there are three gala days of parades, dances, barbecues, a Spanish market place, and live music by costumed participants.

★ **Mozart Festival**   *Cal Poly campus and the Mission*   *first weekend in August*
Guest musicians from all over the country join local talent for six days of indoor and outdoor concerts — including recitals, orchestra concerts, choral music, and chamber music.

OTHER INFORMATION
Area Code: *805*
Zip Code: *93401*
San Luis Obispo Chamber of Commerce   *downtown at 1039 Chorro St.*   *543-1323*

Solvang, California

Elevation:

480 feet

Population (1980):

3,091

Population (1970):

2,004

Location:

130 mi. NW
of Los Angeles

Solvang is the Danish capital of America. All of the sights, sounds, and delicious aromas of an authentic Danish village are present here in the heart of the lovely Santa Ynez Valley. All around, lush pasturelands accented by noble oak trees dominate the landscape. A massive ridge of Coast Range mountains towers to the south, and the ocean is only a few miles away. The peaceful setting is also favored by one of the West's most delightful climates. Mild daytime temperatures and cool evenings prevail year-round. Since most outdoor activities are enjoyable in every season, Solvang is thronged with visitors on weekends throughout the year. Shopping and strolling in town, bicycling and wine touring in the valley, hiking and camping in the Coast Range, plus sailing and fishing in southern California's largest lake, are popular leisure time pursuits. During the summer, the nearby ocean warms sufficiently that it can be comfortably used for swimming and surfing off the fine state park beaches near town.

There has been a settlement on this site since 1804, when the Spanish built Mission Santa Ines with the Chumash Indians. For more than a century, however, little development occurred. Early in the twentieth century, a group of Danes established a school and village next to the mission as a place where immigrants from Denmark could be educated. After World War II, visitors started to discover this unique cultural enclave as a source of Scandinavian specialties. As a result, merchants and homeowners were encouraged to further emphasize their heritage with more consistently "Danish" architecture to replace the earlier Spanish and Yankee styles.

Careful attention is still paid to nostalgic Old World details as new structures are added. This is especially apparent in the unique central business district, which is a recreated corner of Denmark. Creaking windmills, steep tiled and thatched roofs, cobblestone courtyards, gas street lamps, traditional guard booths, and other fanciful embellishments are everywhere. Significantly, descendants of the Danish-Americans who started all this still preside in a large and growing number of Scandinavian import shops, gourmet food stores, bakeries, and restaurants. After dark, peace and quiet reign. Good live theater during the summer festival is the most noteworthy evening diversion in town. Several places nearby offer drinking and entertainment with distinctive Old Western atmosphere. Both the architecture and plush contemporary appointments of lodging places in town also reflect the Danish heritage. Little touches like complimentary Continental breakfasts further distinguish these inns and display the friendly spirit of the townsfolk. Most of the best lodgings are an easy stroll from the heart of town.

Solvang, California

WEATHER PROFILE   *Vokac Weather Rating*

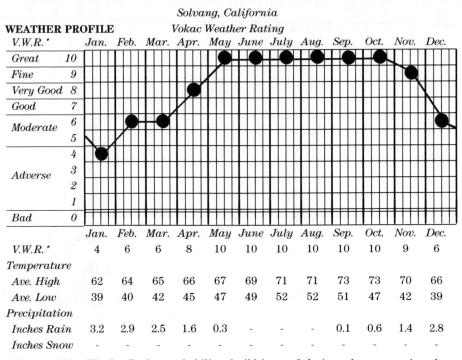

V.W.R.*		Jan.	Feb.	Mar.	Apr.	May	June	July	Aug.	Sep.	Oct.	Nov.	Dec.
Great	10												
Fine	9												
Very Good	8												
Good	7												
Moderate	6												
	5												
	4												
Adverse	3												
	2												
	1												
Bad	0												

	Jan.	Feb.	Mar.	Apr.	May	June	July	Aug.	Sep.	Oct.	Nov.	Dec.
V.W.R.*	4	6	6	8	10	10	10	10	10	10	9	6
Temperature												
Ave. High	62	64	65	66	67	69	71	71	73	73	70	66
Ave. Low	39	40	42	45	47	49	52	52	51	47	42	39
Precipitation												
Inches Rain	3.2	2.9	2.5	1.6	0.3	-	-	-	0.1	0.6	1.4	2.8
Inches Snow	-	-	-	-	-	-	-	-	-	-	-	-

V.W.R. = Vokac Weather Rating: probability of mild (warm & dry) weather on any given day.

Forecast

Month	V.W.R.*		Temperatures Daytime	Evening	Precipitation
January	4	Adverse	cool	cool	occasional rainstorms
February	6	Moderate	cool	cool	occasional rainstorms
March	6	Moderate	warm	cool	occasional rainstorms
April	8	Very Good	warm	cool	infrequent rainstorms
May	10	Great	warm	cool	negligible
June	10	Great	warm	cool	none
July	10	Great	warm	cool	none
August	10	Great	warm	cool	none
September	10	Great	warm	cool	none
October	10	Great	warm	cool	infrequent showers
November	9	Fine	warm	cool	infrequent rainstorms
December	6	Moderate	warm	cool	occasional rainstorms

Summary

Solvang has a beautifully pastoral location in a broad luxuriant valley flanked on the south by the Coast Range. With the ocean only a few miles away, the town also benefits from one of the West's most desirable climates. The only season when light sportswear might be unsuitable is **winter**, which is usually cool. Snow and frost are rare, but occasional rainstorms sweeping in from the Pacific provide more than half of the annual precipitation. Rainfall diminishes rapidly in **spring**, which is the beginning of many months of warm days and cool evenings. This is the best time for exploring the countryside while it is emerald green from earlier rains. **Summer** is ideal, with warm sunny days, cool evenings, and no rain. As an added attraction, ocean water temperatures along the beaches a few miles to the south are comfortably warm for swimming and other water sports during the season. Excellent weather usually continues through **fall**, with more warm days and cool evenings. Occasional rainstorms are routine after Thanksgiving.

ATTRACTIONS & DIVERSIONS

Bethania Lutheran Church *downtown at 603 Atterdag Rd.* 688-4637
This church typifies Danish provincial architecture. It's worth a quiet visit to see the model of a full-rigged ship hanging from the ceiling in accordance with Scandinavian seafaring tradition.

★ **Bicycling**
    Dr. J's Bicycles *downtown at 1661-B Fir Av.* 688-6263
The less-traveled highways and byways throughout the pastoral Santa Ynez Valley provide unlimited opportunities for leisurely bicycling. Bicycles can be rented here by the hour or longer.

★ **El Capitan State Park** *26 mi. SE on US 101* 968-0019
Sunbathing, surfing, and warm ocean swimming (in summer only); pier fishing (which doesn't require a license); boating and sailing (there is a boat hoist); and camping are enjoyed. A usually uncrowded swimming-suits-optional beach is within a mile south along the coast. To reach it, look for parked cars just off the highway by the railroad tracks, and carefully follow the gully trails down the bluff.

Horseback Riding
★   **Circle Bar B Ranch** *25 mi. SE via CA 246, US 101 & Refugio Canyon* 968-5929
The Reagan ranch shares boundaries with this guest ranch where the owner has turned Secret Service agents into occasional cowboys. It is the only rental stables for many miles where horses tailored to each rider's ability can be reserved for unescorted trail rides. Waterfalls and natural swimming holes up nearby canyons provide idyllic destinations.

★ **Lake Cachuma Recreation Area** *11 mi. SE via CA 246 & CA 154* 688-4658
The largest freshwater reservoir in southern California provides excellent fishing, boating and sailing opportunities. Motorboat and sailboat rentals are available (phone: 688-4040). Swimming is not permitted in the lake, but there is an outdoor pool at the recreation center, plus a roller skating rink and miniature golf. Picnic tables and barbecue grills are attractively sited under big oak trees and there is a large campground. Horses may be rented for guided trail rides near the entrance to the dam (phone: 668-3018).

★ **Mission Santa Ines** *just E of downtown at 1760 Mission Dr.* 688-4815
Established in 1804, this "hidden gem" was the nineteenth in the chain of twenty-one California missions. Skillfully restored, the large adobe building is used as a church. The grounds also include a picturesque arched colonnade and a garden.

★ **Nojoqui Falls County Park** *6.5 mi. S on Alisal Rd.* 688-4217
An impressive natural waterfall is reached by a well-worn trail through a serene forest of oak and sycamore. This county park is a great place for picnics during the winter and spring — the waterfall dries up during the summer! There are also some campsites.

★ **Refugio Beach State Park** *22 mi. SE on US 101* 968-0019
A sandy beach in a sheltered cove is backed by an attractively landscaped state park. Conditions are excellent for warm ocean swimming, surfing, and scuba diving during the summer. Surf fishing, camping, and a play area are enjoyed all year.

Sightseeing *downtown at Alisal Rd./Copenhagen Dr.*
Guides in Scandinavian attire take visitors on tours of the village in a colorful red trolley pulled by Clydesdale horses.

Warm Water Feature
    Las Cruces Hot Springs *10.5 mi. SW via CA 246 & US 101*
A naturalized pool dug out of a hillside overflows with hot mineral water from an adjoining spring. It's not deep enough for a swim, but the ooze on the bottom is soothing, and the lush green surroundings can be delightfully tranquil. From the small parking area on the east sides of US 101 at CA 1, it's a pleasant .7 mile hike.

★ **Wineries**
Solvang is the center of the largest concentration of premium wineries in southern California. The Santa Ynez Valley is well on its way to becoming a famous wine-producing district. The premium wineries identified below are perhaps the most readily accessible. However, visitors can, by calling ahead, also enjoy the leisurely pursuit of fine wine discoveries in several other young wineries in vineyards near town. The Chamber of Commerce has maps and details about all wineries in the area.

★ **The Firestone Vineyard** *11 mi. N via US 101 & Zaca Station Rd.* *688-3940*
Established in 1972, the massive winery is housed in a dramatically contemporary wooden structure on a blufftop promontory. A unique view of both the flourishing vineyards below and of barrels aging wine is provided from different sets of windows in the tasting room. Several estate-bottled wines are offered. Tasting, sales, and tours 10-4. Closed Sun.

★ **Rancho Sisquoc Winery** *27 mi. N via Foxen Canyon Rd.* *937-3616*
This small redwood and stone winery was bonded in 1977. Located at the picturesque headquarters of a large, diversified ranch in the pastoral Sisquoc River Valley, the winery uses only a small percentage of grapes produced in the vineyard. Premium varietal wines are sold exclusively at the winery. Large trees shade a secluded picnic area near a tasting room where the entire line is offered. Tasting and sales 10-4 daily.

★ **Santa Ynez Valley Winery** *3.5 mi. SE at 365 Refugio Rd.* *688-8381*
Since it opened in 1976, this has become one of the valley's best known wineries. While the specialty is primarily white wine, a notable blanc de cabernet is also produced. A pleasant view deck with picnic tables adjoins a tasting room where the entire line of premium wines is offered. Tasting, sales and tours 10-4 daily.

★ **Vintage House** *downtown on Mission Dr./Atterdag Rd.* *688-7585*
The downtown tasting room for the Ballard Canyon Winery is a new facility that generously offers tastes of the winery's entire line of premium wines. Appetizers may be purchased to enjoy with wine in a pleasant, flower-strewn patio. Tasting and sales daily.

★ **Zaca Mesa Winery** *15 mi. N via Ballard Canyon/Foxen Canyon Rds.* *688-3310*
The original 1978 cellar of this young winery has already been expanded into a larger barn-like building where several premium wines are produced. A limited number are offered for tasting. Shaded picnic sites occupy a nearby slope. Tasting, sales, and tours 10-4 daily.

SHOPPING
Downtown Solvang is a pleasure for drivers and pedestrians. All of the town's attractions are within comfortable walking distance of five large free parking lots that even include public toilets. On-street parking is also free. The entire downtown area has a Danish motif brimming with little architectural surprises. Cobblestone sidewalks beneath old-fashioned gas lamps, fanciful gables, wood-shingled and copper-tiled rooftops, creaking windmills, hand-carved benches, fountains, and statues abound. So do ersatz thatched rooftops, stork nests and birds, and colorful royal guard boxes. Collectively, these embellishments provide a unique pedestrian-scaled showcase for the West's most remarkable collection of Scandinavian import shops, restaurants, and bakeries.

Food Specialties
★ **Bakeries** *all over downtown*
Tempting aromas drift from bakeries scattered throughout downtown Solvang. Here is the largest concentration of European specialty bakeries in the West. Each is marked by a guild sign showing a kringle — a pretzel-shaped pastry — with a crown. Sampling baked goods to "discover" the best in town is a delight of any visit. Most of the bakeries are open every day, and also serve outstanding Danish coffee in casual dining areas near tantalizing display counters.

Copenhagen Cellars *downtown at 448 Alisal Rd.* *688-4218*
Local premium wines are displayed along with an international wine assortment in this cheerful little shop. Wine tastes are offered in tiny plastic cups.

The Great Danish Cone Company *downtown at 441 Alisal Rd.* *688-1718*
This popular little ice cream takeout features delicious, freshly-made Danish cones.

★ **Halversen's Solvang Sausage & Deli** *downtown at 476 1st St.* *688-4044*
Excellent European and Danish-style sausages are made and sold here, along with home-smoked Black Forest ham.

★ **H & P's Vinhus Ltd.** *downtown at 440 Alisal Rd.* *688-7117*
Many international cheeses are displayed, and some tastes are offered. A fine assortment of premium wines and gourmet foods is also featured.

★ **Jim Garrahy's Fudge Kitchens**   *downtown at 1696 Copenhagen Dr.*   *688-7048*
Solvang may well be the fudge capital of the West. Visitors to this shop and several others in the downtown area can watch it being made, taste free samples, make a purchase, or arrange for shipment anywhere of excellent prepackaged or custom packed fudges.

★ **The Little Mermaid**   *downtown at 1546 Mission Dr.*   *688-6141*
Aebleskiver is the most popular and distinctively Scandinavian pastry in Solvang. Pancake-like batter is cooked in special pans which turn out little round treats described as the Danish version of a donut. They are the specialty of this Danish restaurant, where visitors can watch them being made in an exhibition kitchen in a front dining room.

Pretzel N Cheese Inc.   *downtown at Alisal Rd./Copenhagen Dr.*   *688-0980*
Fresh hot pretzels are made all day and served with a notable cheddar cheese spread in this little carryout shop.

★ **The Solvang Bakery**   *downtown at 1682 Copenhagen Dr.*   *688-5713*
This bakery displays the full line of fine European specialty pastries and breads sold in numerous bakeries downtown. A colorful coffee room in back and handsome show windows and glass cases brimming with tantalizing baked goods suggest why Solvang's bakeries are renowned.

NIGHTLIFE
Fine live theater in summer and a few restaurant lounges provide the only nightlife in town. However, there are a couple of notably atmospheric saloons nearby.

Belle Terrasse Pub   *downtown at 1564 Copenhagen Dr.*   *688-2762*
Live music is provided most nights in an intimate pub setting next to a popular restaurant.

★ **Cold Spring Tavern**   *21 mi. S via CA 154 at 5995 Stagecoach Rd.*   *967-0066*
Live music for dancing is featured most nights at this authentic, unspoiled old stagecoach stop high in the mountains south of town. The rustic Old West atmosphere in the firelit bar is unforgettable.

★ **Solvang Theaterfest**   *downtown at 420 2nd St.*   *922-8313*
One of the oldest repertory theaters on the West Coast presents a mixture of dramas and musicals in an appealing, half-timbered open air theater. The season runs from early July to late September.

The Valhalla Lounge   *downtown at 400 Alisal Rd.*   *688-8000*
Live music for dancing is featured most nights in a casual lounge with a stone fireplace in the new Sheraton Royal Scandinavian Inn.

Zaca Creek Saloon   *5.5 mi. NW at 1297 N. US 101 - Buellton*   *688-2412*
Live entertainment and dancing draws crowds from miles around on weekends to this big, comfortable Western-style saloon. The adjoining steak house is also popular.

RESTAURANTS
Most of the restaurants in town feature Scandinavian dishes. A few take pride in authentic Old World specialties. Several fine restaurants tucked away in the surrounding countryside reflect a surprisingly long tradition of thoroughly Yankee charm.

★ **Ballard Store**   *4 mi. N via Alamo Rd. at 2449 Baseline Av.*   *688-5319*
D only. Closed Mon.-Tues.   *Moderate*
This is the premier restaurant of the Santa Ynez Valley. Classic Continental cuisine is featured. Only the highest quality meats and the freshest vegetables are prepared along with homemade sauces, soups, bread, and desserts. Reservations are essential, often many days in advance. The recently enlarged dining rooms still convey the Yankee charm of what once was a country general store. Delicious appetizers and desserts, plus wines by the glass, are served in a stylish little wine bar between the casually posh dining rooms.

Belgian Cafe   *downtown at 475 1st St.*   *688-6316*
B-L.   *Moderate*
Assorted fresh-baked Belgian waffles and crepes are served by costumed waitresses in a cheerful little coffee shop, or in an umbrella-shaded garden courtyard that is usually jammed on sunny days.

Belle Terrasse   *downtown at 1564 Copenhagen Dr.*   *688-2762*
L-D.   *Expensive*
Northern Italian specialties with a "light touch" are served in several casually elegant small
dining areas in a handsome newer restaurant.

★ **Cold Spring Tavern**   *21 mi. S via CA 154 at 5995 Stagecoach Rd.*   *967-0066*
L-D.   *Moderate*
Hearty American fare, including wild game, is skillfully prepared and accompanied by
delicious homemade bread. All of the charm of a bygone era is present in this historic
stagecoach stop. The buildings have a ramshackle authenticity unmatched in southern
California. The tiny firelit bar is particularly romantic.

Danish Inn Restaurant   *downtown at 1547 Mission Dr.*   *688-4813*
L-D.   *Expensive*
This large restaurant produces the most celebrated of Solvang's Danish smorgasbords, in
addition to an extensive assortment of Danish/Continental dishes. Comfortable
armchairs, crisp linens, and fireplaces enhance the informally plush Old World
atmosphere of the dining room and a small lounge.

The Little Mermaid   *downtown at 1546 Mission Dr.*   *688-6141*
B-L-D.   *Low*
Authentic aebleskiver with homemade raspberry jam and Danish sausage, the best dishes
here, are served all day in casual, Danish-style dining rooms. The pleasant little restaurant
also has Danish beer on tap.

Mattei's Tavern   *6 mi. N on CA 154 - Los Olivos*   *688-4820*
D only.   *Moderate*
In continuous operation since 1886, this valley landmark is now operated as a restaurant
by the Charthouse chain. Good steaks, plus seafood and a salad bar, are offered in
carefully restored Old Western dining rooms. An authentic saloon and parlor with
working fireplaces contribute to the warmly nostalgic atmosphere.

Mollekroen   *downtown at 435 Alisal Rd.*   *688-4555*
L-D.   *Low*
Well-prepared Danish specialties and a bountiful smorgasbord attract enthusiastic
crowds to this casual and congested upstairs restaurant. Downstairs, a lounge provides
live entertainment on weekends.

The Mustard Seed   *downtown at 1655 Mission Dr.*   *688-1318*
B-L. Closed Mon.   *Moderate*
Omelets and some homemade pastries are served in a bright little coffee shop, and on a
pleasant patio overlooking the main street and town park.

Pea Soup Andersen's   *4 mi. W at US 101 - Buellton*   *688-5581*
B-L-D.   *Moderate*
Since it opened in 1924, this place has evolved into a huge family-oriented tourist stop.
Their famous split pea soup is still a crowd-pleaser. Free cheese samples and wine tastes
are offered in a complex of shops adjoining the dining rooms.

Yorick's   *downtown at 443 2nd St.*   *688-4822*
B-L.   *Moderate*
In this colorful newer sidewalk cafe, fresh croissants and muffins accompany light fare
served indoors or out, and several premium wines are poured by the glass.

Zaca Creek Restaurant   *5.5 mi. NW at 1297 N. US 101*   *688-2412*
D only.   *Moderate*
Oak-pit broiled steaks are the specialty on a contemporary American menu. This large
newer restaurant gets a warm country feeling from natural wood decor and a lot of
plants. The comfortable adjacent lounge features music and dancing on weekends.

LODGING

Motor lodges in more-or-less Danish architectural styles have proliferated throughout the
downtown area. Most are well-furnished and offer complimentary Continental
breakfasts. From spring through fall and on weekends year-round, it is not uncommon for
every room in town to be full. Rates are usually reduced at least 10% in winter and from
Sunday thru Thursday except in summer.

★ **The Alisal Ranch**   *2.6 mi. S on Alisal Rd.*   688-6411
One of the most luxurious guest ranches in California is in a pretty little canyon near town. Beautifully maintained single-story bungalows are set amidst flowers, oaks, and sycamores in the rolling green foothills of the Santa Ynez Mountains. Facilities (available to guests only) include tennis courts, a picturesque 18-hole golf course, stables for guided horseback rides, the resort's own tiny lake for sailing and fishing, a large landscaped pool, plus a fine dining room and lounge. Each spacious, beautifully decorated room has a wood-burning fireplace. Rates are for two people on a modified American plan — breakfast and dinner included.

    regular room — studio,   2 T or K bed...$176

★ **Chimney Sweep Inn**   *downtown at 1554 Copenhagen Dr.*   688-2111
This newer Danish contemporary motor inn is backed by an intimate flower-filled garden with a secluded whirlpool. A complimentary Continental breakfast is offered. Each spacious, lavishly furnished unit has a phone and cable color TV.

    #2 "The Dawn Treader" — 2-story cottage, kit., patio with
                       pvt. whirlpool, 2 fireplaces,   K bed...$175
    #1 "The Tree House" — 2-story cottage, kit., pvt. tree branch
                      balc., fireplace, pvt. patio with stream,   K bed...$175
    #50,#49 — split-level suite,   raised K bed...$85
    regular room —   Q bed...$48

★ **The Danish Lodge - Best Western**   *downtown at 1455 Mission Dr.*   688-2018
A whirlpool overlooking an oak grove and a small outdoor pool are features of this large new motor inn, along with a sauna and a charming oak view dining room (serving breakfast only). Each spacious, well-furnished room has a phone and cable color TV with movies.

    deluxe room — E side of 2nd fl. has pvt. balc. with oak views,   K bed...$72
    regular room —   K bed...$62

Meadowlark Motel   *2 mi. E on CA 246 at 2644 Mission Dr.*   688-4631
This modern single-level motel is in a rural setting with a small outdoor pool. Each large, quiet room has cable color TV.

    regular room —   Q bed...$36

Motel 6   *4 mi. W at 333 McMurry Rd. - Buellton*   688-3293
The **bargain** motel chain has a modest, modern facility with an outdoor pool adjacent to the freeway in nearby Buellton.

    regular room —   D bed...$22

San Marcos Motel   *4 mi. W at 536 Av. of Flags - Buellton*   688-5511
This small single-level motel is part of a little motel row that serves as a spillover when in-town Solvang's lodgings are full. An outdoor pool and color TV are available.

    regular room —   K bed...$46
    regular room —   D bed...$38

Sheraton Royal Scandinavian Inn   *downtown at 400 Alisal Rd.*   688-8000
Solvang's largest motor hotel opened in 1984 near the heart of town on a bluff overlooking the Santa Ynez river valley. The conventional facility includes an outdoor pool and whirlpool, a sauna, plus an instantly-Old-World restaurant and lounge. Each spacious, well-furnished room has a phone and cable color TV.

    large room —   K bed...$76
    regular room —   Q bed...$61

Solvang Gaard Lodge   *downtown at 293 Alisal Rd.*   688-4404
This small single-level motel is the only real **bargain** in town, and it is conveniently located on the quiet side of downtown. Each large, well-maintained room has a cable color TV.

    regular room —   Q bed...$25

★ **Svensgaard's Lodge**   *downtown at 1711 Mission Dr.*   688-3277
An outdoor pool and whirlpool are located in a courtyard of this Danish-style motel in the heart of town. Each unit has a phone, cable color TV, and a refrigerator. A free Continental breakfast is served.

    #40,#59 — suite, spacious, fine village/mt. view, gas fireplace, kit.,   K bed...$70
    #24 — spacious, gas fireplace, wet bar,   K bed...$50
    regular room —   Q bed...$40

Viking Motel   *downtown at 1506 Mission Dr.*   *688-4827*
This tiny, no-frills, single-level motel is convenient to everything in town. Each unit has a cable color TV.
    regular room —   K bed...$48
    regular room —   Q bed...$38

CAMPGROUNDS
Three of the West's finest California-subtropical campgrounds have choice oceanfront locations less than a half hour drive from town. Even nearer inland, southern California's largest reservoir is the site of a huge and popular campground.

★ **El Capitan State Beach**   *25 mi. SE via CA 246 & US 101*   *968-1411*
This large, state operated campground occupies a picturesque area by a sandy ocean beach. Sunbathing, swimming (in summer), fishing, and hiking are favorite pastimes. There are flush toilets and hot showers, but no hookups. Each site has a picnic table, fire ring, and grill.   base rate...$8

★ **Gaviota State Beach**   *13.6 mi. SW via CA 246 & US 101*   *968-0019*
A lovely sheltered cove by a sandy ocean beach provides an idyllic site for this state operated campground. Sunbathing; swimming, surfing, and skin diving (in summer); fishing; and boat rentals/hoist are features. Flush toilets and hot showers, but no hookups, are available. Park officials advise bringing drinking water. Each of the sites has a picnic table, fire ring, and grill.   base rate...$8

Lake Cachuma Recreation Area   *11 mi. SE via CA 246 & CA 154*   *963-7108*
An enormous county operated campground is attractively sited on oak-shaded slopes above Lake Cachuma. Lake swimming is not allowed in southern California's largest reservoir, but fishing, boat rentals/ramps, an outdoor pool, and horseback riding rentals are popular. Flush toilets, hot showers, and hookups are available. Each site has a picnic table and a fire area.   base rate...$6

★ **Refugio State Beach**   *22 mi. SE via CA 246 & US 101*   *968-1350*
This state operated campground is in a beautifully landscaped sheltered cove by a sandy ocean beach. Sunbathing; swimming, surfing, and skin diving in summer; and fishing are popular. Flush toilets and hot showers, but no hookups, are available. Each site has a picnic table, fire ring, and grill.   base rate...$8

SPECIAL EVENT
★ **Danish Days Festival**   *throughout town*   *third weekend in September*
Residents wear Danish costumes and celebrate their heritage in the town's biggest event. Highlights include parades, a feast and ball, theatrical productions and other live entertainment.

OTHER INFORMATION
Area Code: *805*
Zip Code: *93463*
Solvang Chamber of Commerce   *downtown at 1623 Mission Dr.*   *688-3317*

Sonoma, California

Elevation:

81 feet

Population (1980):

6,054

Population (1970):

4,259

Location:

47 mi. NE
of San Francisco

Sonoma is the treasury of northern California history. For more than 160 years, the heart of town has been a large, beautifully landscaped plaza. It is still almost completely surrounded by nineteenth century buildings. Beyond, gentle grass-and-oak-covered hills define the southern end of "The Valley of the Moon" a few miles north of San Francisco Bay. Majestic rows of eucalyptus shade the orchards and vineyards that fill the valley around town. Sonoma also benefits from a temperate climate. Spring is the finest season when blossoms everywhere accent emerald green landscapes, vintners are pouring their new releases, and crowds are usually light. The town is filled with visitors throughout summer and fall when dry sunny days are popular for winery touring, for picnics and hiking in the hills, or for bicycling, golf, or tennis in the valley. Since the area's finest attractions are all indoors — in historic buildings, distinctive shops, or wineries — even winter appeals to visitors willing to accept cool damp weather in exchange for a slower pace and absence of crowds.

Sonoma, "the birthplace of California viticulture," was founded in 1823 by the Franciscan fathers as the twenty-first of their El Camino Real chain of missions. It was also the last and most northerly of these historic Spanish settlements. California's first vineyards were planted here by the padres in 1824 so wines for sacramental purposes would be available. Within a decade, Sonoma's Mexican commander, Mariano Guadalupe Vallejo, planted other grape varieties for table wines. Mexican control ended when the short-lived California Republic was born in Sonoma with the raising of the Bear Flag on the plaza in 1846. Four years later, California became an American state. During the Civil War, Sonoma once again made viticultural history when America's first big experimental vineyard was established by a Hungarian nobleman, Count Agoston Haraszthy, at Buena Vista.

The wine industry remains the key to the town's prosperity. Vineyards dating from those momentous times endure as charming reminders of a rich heritage. Downtown, the spacious plaza is a continuing delight for strollers and picnickers. It provides a picturesque counterpoint to historic structures all around which now house an outstanding array of specialty shops, gourmet food stores and restaurants, and atmospheric bars and lounges. Accommodations are surprisingly scarce in the valley. All of the best are in restorations of historic structures. Several are luxuriously furnished and within a stroll of the plaza.

Sonoma, California

WEATHER PROFILE — *Vokac Weather Rating*

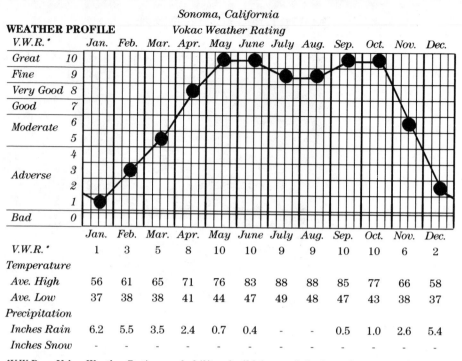

V.W.R.*		Jan.	Feb.	Mar.	Apr.	May	June	July	Aug.	Sep.	Oct.	Nov.	Dec.
Great	10												
Fine	9												
Very Good	8												
Good	7												
Moderate	6 / 5												
	4												
Adverse	3 / 2												
	1												
Bad	0												

	Jan.	Feb.	Mar.	Apr.	May	June	July	Aug.	Sep.	Oct.	Nov.	Dec.
V.W.R.*	1	3	5	8	10	10	9	9	10	10	6	2
Temperature												
Ave. High	56	61	65	71	76	83	88	88	85	77	66	58
Ave. Low	37	38	38	41	44	47	49	48	47	43	38	37
Precipitation												
Inches Rain	6.2	5.5	3.5	2.4	0.7	0.4	-	-	0.5	1.0	2.6	5.4
Inches Snow	-	-	-	-	-	-	-	-	-	-	-	-

*V.W.R. = Vokac Weather Rating: probability of mild (warm & dry) weather on any given day.

Forecast

Month	V.W.R.*		Temperatures Daytime	Evening	Precipitation
January	1	Adverse	cool	chilly	frequent downpours
February	3	Adverse	cool	chilly	frequent downpours
March	5	Moderate	warm	cool	occasional downpours
April	8	Very Good	warm	cool	infrequent rainstorms
May	10	Great	warm	cool	infrequent showers
June	10	Great	hot	warm	negligible
July	9	Fine	hot	warm	none
August	9	Fine	hot	warm	none
September	10	Great	hot	warm	negligible
October	10	Great	warm	cool	infrequent rainstorms
November	6	Moderate	warm	cool	occasional rainstorms
December	2	Adverse	cool	chilly	frequent downpours

Summary

Located near the southern end of the Valley of the Moon, Sonoma is only a few miles north of San Francisco Bay. Marine air pouring through the Coast Range gap at the Golden Gate is a major influence. While there is normally almost no snow, **winter** is cool and very wet, with frequent downpours providing well over half the year's normal precipitation. **Spring** is the beginning of a long period of comfortable weather. Warm days, cool evenings, and fewer and lighter rainfalls encourage casual enjoyment of the verdant countryside. **Summer** days are typically fairly hot, evenings are warm, and there is remarkably little precipitation. **Fall** is outstanding. Warm days, cool evenings, and infrequent rainfalls assure the final ripening of grapes. The weather is perfect for observing the transformation of grapes into wine, and for savoring the fruits of this labor.

ATTRACTIONS & DIVERSIONS

Ballooning
    Airborn of Sonoma County   *528-8133*
A champagne flight in a hot-air balloon is a unique way to achieve a serene perspective on the sights and sounds of the "Valley of the Moon."

Bear Flag Monument   *NE corner of plaza*
A heroic bronze figure holding a Bear Flag marks the site where thirty American horsemen rode into Sonoma, captured General Vallejo without a struggle, and proclaimed the "California Republic" on June 14, 1846.

Bicycling
★   **Sonoma Wheels Bicycle Shop**   *downtown at 523 Broadway*   *935-1366*
All kinds of bicycles may be rented here by the hour or day to tour the pastoral countryside. A short and scenic separated bikeway on the north side of town supplements well-marked highways and byways in the relatively level Valley of the Moon.

Blue Wing Inn   *just off NE corner of plaza on Spain St.*
Built in 1840 by General Vallejo for travelers, this partially-restored structure is probably Sonoma's oldest remaining building. While much of it is now occupied by shops, its ancient register includes such famous names as John C. Fremont, U.S. Grant, and Kit Carson.

Golf
    Sonoma National Golf Club   *3.3 mi. NW at 17700 Arnold Dr.*   *996-0300*
This attractive 18-hole championship course on the gentle west slope of the Valley of the Moon is open to the public year-round. Facilities include club and cart rentals, plus a clubhouse, driving range, and restaurant.

★ **Jack London State Historic Park**   *9 mi. NW via CA 12*   *938-5216*
The park is part of the famed author's "Beauty Ranch" where he resided from 1905 until his death in 1916. The "House of Happy Walls," a large fieldstone structure built in 1919 by his widow, has an excellent collection of his memorabilia, and is the park interpretive center. A half-mile trail leads through woods to the ruins of the ill-fated "Wolf House." Stark walls and massive chimneys of native volcanic stone are all that remain of the imposing structure that was destroyed by fire shortly before the Londons could move in. The author's grave is nearby. A three-mile trail to the summit of Sonoma Mountain offers impressive views of the Valley of the Moon.

Library   *.8 mi. W at 755 W. Napa*   *996-5217*
The Sonoma Regional Library occupies a large, contemporary building. Many upholstered armchairs draw browsers to a well-lighted periodical reading area.

★ **The Plaza**   *downtown*
This National Historic Landmark is a delight to visitors and residents alike. Surrounding the old City Hall are well-landscaped, expansive lawns with paths, monuments, ponds and shade trees ideally suited to picnickers and strollers.

★ **Sonoma State Historic Park**   *N side of plaza*   *928-1578*
A number of major historic structures have been restored downtown. Casa Grande, the adobe home of General Vallejo, was built in 1836 and destroyed by fire in 1867. Only the Indian servants' wing remains. The Mission San Francisco de Solano was the last (1823) of California's twenty-one missions built by Father Junipero Serra. The chapel no longer serves a religious purpose, but it is nicely preserved. Other rooms in the long adobe structure house a large collection of historic relics. The Sonoma Barracks, erected in 1836 of redwood timbers and adobe brick, housed General Vallejo's troops when he was the last Mexican governor of California. The building has been restored to resemble its original appearance, right down to the dusty rear courtyard.

★ **Spring Lake County Park**   *17 mi. NW via CA 12 & Montgomery St.*   *539-8092*
A small reservoir in a lovely rural setting has been ingeniously converted into a superb water recreation facility by the county and local water district. Well-landscaped, tree-shaded grounds include an expansive swimming lagoon with a sandy beach. On the lake itself, boating (electric motors only), rental boats, a ramp and dock, and fishing are available. Hiking trails, bicycle paths, picnic tables and a campground are other attractions.

★ **Vallejo Home ("Lachryma Montis")**   *.5 mi. NW on 3rd St. W*
This stately Carpenter Gothic home of General Mariano Vallejo was built in 1852. "Lachryma Montis," as it was called; the adjoining Swiss chalet; and several outbuildings are now state-owned museums housing his momentoes. The carefully maintained grounds reflect Vallejo's fascination with horticulture. A giant old pommelo tree in front of the chalet is spectacular early in the year when the huge grapefruit-like fruit is ripe.

Warm Water Features
  Agua Caliente Springs *2.8 mi. W via CA 12 at 17350 Vailetti Dr.*   996-6822
A large warm mineral springs pool, open to the public, is the centerpiece of a historic facility that includes picnic tables under shade trees on an adjoining lawn area. Closed Tues.-Wed.

  Morton's Warm Springs *11.5 mi. NW via CA 12 at 1651 Warm Spgs. Rd.*   833-5511
A large outdoor pool in a scenic location is open to the public daily in summer. Many picnic tables are located on an adjoining tree-shaded lawn. Closed Mon.

Wineries
Sonoma is the birthplace of America's premium wine industry. Grapes were first grown here in 1823 to make wine for sacramental purposes. Soon, secular wines were also being produced. After the Civil War, Sonoma became the state's largest wine producer. This area remains one of California's most illustrious producers of premium wine. For detailed information and a map of all wineries in the area, contact the Chamber of Commerce, or any bookstore.

★ **Buena Vista Winery**   *1 mi. E at 18000 Old Winery Rd.*   938-1266
Founded in 1857 by Count Agoston Haraszthy, this is the oldest winery in the valley and a state historic landmark. A self-guided tour of the 1857 cellar and wine caves dug into the hillside is a must. Shaded picnic grounds in front of the ivy-covered old stone building are set amidst ancient eucalyptus by a creek. Tasting, tours, and sales 10-5.

★ **Chateau St. Jean**   *11 mi. NW at 8555 CA 12*   833-4134
This young winery (1974) is one of the outstanding producers of premium wine in the nation. Visitors are free to enjoy informative self-guided tours of the impressive new wine production and storage complex. Nearby, a splendid old Mediterranean-style chateau includes a wood-paneled room where selected tastes are offered. The attractively landscaped grounds include romantic, shady picnic areas. Tasting, tours, and sales 10-4:30.

★ **Hacienda Wine Cellars**   *1 mi. E at 1000 Vineyard Lane*   938-3220
This small winery, occupying a Spanish colonial-style building on part of the original Buena Vista estate, concentrates on a limited selection of premium wines. An informative display of premium grapevine varieties is adjacent to the tasting room entrance. Nearby, a spacious picnic area offers charming tree-shaded or sunny views of the vineyards and valley. Tasting and sales 9-5.

★ **Kenwood Vineyards**   *10 mi. N at 9592 CA 12*   833-5891
A rustic redwood building is used to house a congenial tasting room with stained glass windows and a ceiling of grape stakes. Tastes of all varieties are offered. This outstanding little winery set in old-fashioned wood barns has been notably successful in recent years in developing premium quality wines. Tasting and sales 10-4:30.

★ **St. Francis Vineyards**   *11 mi. NW at 8450 CA 12*   833-4666
The plush new tasting room of this young (1979) premium winery has a fireplace and picture window views of surrounding vineyards. Several picnic tables are on a pleasant adjoining patio. Tasting, tours and sales 10-4:30.

★ **Sebastiani Vineyards**   *.4 mi. E at 389 4th St. E*   938-5532
The largest wine maker in the valley, this historic landmark is still a family operation. Many wines are produced and most are generously available for tasting. The cellars include a fascinating collection of carved casks. Tasting, tours and sales 10-5.

SHOPPING
A unique, vital central business district completely surrounds the large plaza that has been the heart of town for more than one hundred and fifty years. Picturesque nineteenth century facades invite closer inspection of a fascinating collection of specialty and gourmet shops, dining and drinking places, and secret courtyards like Place des Pyrenees and El Paseo de Sonoma with their clusters of unusual boutiques around cobblestone walkways and secret gardens.

Food Specialties

The Cherry Tree   *4 mi. S on CA 12 & CA 121 at 1901 Fremont Dr.*   *938-3480*
Fruit spreads and a variety of natural juices like cherry cider are featured in this enduring roadside shop.

★ **Fantasie au Chocolat**   *N side of plaza at 40 W. Spain St.*   *938-2020*
An irresistible selection of chocolate candies, pastries, and cookies is displayed and sold. The new shop has a pleasant seating area where coffee and a variety of other beverages are served with the delicious chocolates.

Home Grown Bagels *near SW corner of plaza at 122 W. Napa*   *996-0166*
The various well-made bagels produced here daily can be enjoyed at a few plain tables with coffee or taken out.

★ **Moosetta's**   *2 mi. W at 18976 CA 12*   *996-1313*
Excellent piroshki — pastry dough filled with meat or vegetables, plus casseroles and small sweet pastries are displayed and sold in this unusual little carryout shop. Closed Sun.-Mon.

★ **Simmons Pharmacy**   *S side of plaza at 29 E. Napa St.*   *996-3696*
An authentic solid marble soda fountain is the highlight of this quintessential village pharmacy. Visitors have enjoyed ice cream, sundaes, phosphates, and cold lemonade here for almost eighty years.

★ **Sonoma Cheese Factory**   *N side of plaza at 2 W. Spain St.*   *938-8200*
Visitors can watch superb Sonoma Jack cheese being made. It and more than one hundred other cheeses can be purchased to eat indoors in the deli or on an enclosed patio, to go, or for shipment. Other local gourmet deli specialties along with wines, and a wine-by-the-glass bar, are also available. Unfortunately, only one cheese is offered for samples each day.

★ **Sonoma Creamery**   *NE corner of plaza at 400 1st St. E*   *938-2938*
In a converted creamery building, a full range of locally made ice cream treats is served at the counter or at tables set amidst plant-laden decor accented by a weeping rock wall. The adjacent deli features a good assortment of cheeses, meats, sandwiches, and wines.

★ **Sonoma French Bakery**   *NE side of plaza at 468 1st St. E*   *996-2691*
Here is a gastronomic shrine for all lovers of genuine sourdough French bread. Since the 1950s, this enormously popular bread has been captivating all who discover it. Other breads, pastries, and cookies are also sold in a disarmingly plain little carryout bakery. Closed Mon.-Tues.

★ **Sonoma Sausage Co.**   *W side of plaza at 453 1st St. W*   *938-8200*
Dozens of different kinds of top-quality sausage plus smoked meats are produced locally and sold in this handsomely restored historic building.

Sonoma Wine Shop   *E side of plaza at 412 1st St. E*   *996-1230*
Local California wineries are well represented in this small shop, and there is a full line of wine accessories. Several local wines are usually available for tasting at the wine bar in the back room.

★ **Vella Cheese Co.**   *.3 mi. NE at 315 2nd St. E*   *938-3232*
The fresh jack, cheddar, and other cheeses made here are good, and reasonably priced. Tastes of any of the cheeses are provided..

Specialty Shops

★ **Arts Guild of Sonoma**   *E side of plaza at 460 1st St. E*   *996-3115*
Guild members' works in a variety of media are beautifully displayed in a well-lighted little gallery.

Bookends Book Store   *.3 mi. W at 201 W. Napa*   *938-5926*
A large selection of books includes many of local and regional interest. There is also a good selection of topographic and other maps, and magazines.

NIGHTLIFE

There are several distinctive places to enjoy a drink on the plaza. Most of the rest of the action is in a string of tiny villages a few miles northwest in the Valley of the Moon.

Gino's of Sonoma   *E side of plaza at 420 1st St. E*   *996-4466*
This friendly "locals" bar has a wood-toned interior accented by plants, stained glass lamps, and a view of the plaza.

Little Switzerland   *2 mi. NW at Grove & Riverside Dr. - El Verano*   *938-9990*
A live band plays polka and waltz music for dancing and listening on Friday through Sunday nights in a turn-of-the-century roadhouse tavern with Old World decor and a patio. European and American food is also served. Closed Mon.-Thurs.

London Lodge   *8 mi. NW at 13740 Arnold Dr. - Glen Ellen*   *996-3100*
Visitors can relax in hardwood armchairs in a saloon from the Jack London era that still sports a polished wood floor, a handsome old bar, and brick walls adorned by nostalgic pictures. A popular restaurant is in the next room.

★ **Marioni's**   *N side of plaza at 8 W. Spain St.*   *996-6866*
The intimate lounge area fronting on the plaza with a raised adobe fireplace and director chairs is a fine place for a quiet drink. A contemporary bar adjoining the restaurant inside is also popular.

★ **Sonoma Hotel**   *NW corner of plaza at 110 W. Spain St.*   *996-2996*
A good place for a quiet drink is the beautifully restored saloon in this historic hotel. Polished wood floors and hardwood trim are enlivened with stained glass, shiny brass, fine period paintings, a handsome hardwood front and back bar, and fresh flowers on antique tables.

RESTAURANTS

In recent years, Sonoma has enjoyed a starring role in the dramatic expansion of fine dining in the wine country. Several excellent restaurants have opened which, along with established favorites, inevitably feature local seasonally-fresh ingredients and first-class regional wines. With an emphasis on creative New California cuisine, Sonoma is becoming one of the gourmet dining capitals of the West. Surprisingly reasonable prices are an added feature.

★ **Au Relais**   *.3 mi. S at 691 Broadway*   *996-1030*
L-D. No D on Thurs.   *Expensive*
Country French cuisine is served in a charming cottage filled with stained glass, polished hardwoods, prints, and plants. This long-established restaurant also has a pleasant brick patio for alfresco dining, and a cozy lounge.

★ **Bistro Parisien**   *SE corner of plaza at 101 E. Napa St.*   *996-3866*
L-D. Closed Mon.-Tues.   *Moderate*
Gourmet game dishes highlight a Continental bill of fare. The emphasis is on skillfully prepared fresh ingredients and herbs in this new, romantic little restaurant.

Capri   *9 mi. N at 9900 CA 12 - Kenwood*   *833-6326*
D only. Sun. brunch. Closed Mon.   *Moderate*
Hearty Continental dinners are served in a casual new restaurant accented by crisp linens.

★ **Depot Hotel**   *.3 mi. N at 241 1st St. W*   *938-2980*
L-D.   *Expensive*
Five-course dinners vary according to availability of seasonally fresh ingredients in this restaurant tucked away in a historic little hotel building. Place settings of linens, crystal and china add to the refined ambiance. On warm summer evenings, romantic candlelit tables can be reserved around a landscaped outdoor pool.

★ **Garden Court Cafe**   *6.5 mi. N at 13875 CA 12 - Glen Ellen*   *935-1565*
B-L.   *Moderate*
A limited menu of all-American dishes is carefully prepared from scratch and served in a cheerful little roadside cafe where fresh flowers and jam pots grace each table.

★ **Glen Ellen Inn**   *8 mi. NW at 13670 Arnold Dr. - Glen Ellen*   *938-3478*
L-D. No D on Sun. Closed Mon.-Tues.   *Moderate*
Almost everything is fresh, homemade, and very good, including distinctive omelets served all day and delicious dessert pastries. The limited selection of well-prepared items in this casual little restaurant reflects the new owner's concern for quality.

La Casa   *near NE corner of plaza at 121 E. Spain St.*   *996-3406*
L-D.   *Low*
An extensive menu of well-prepared traditional Mexican specialties is served amidst colorful Mexican furnishings. An inviting cantina is in the next room.

London Lodge   *8 mi. NW at 13740 Arnold Dr. - Glen Ellen*   *996-3100*
L-D. Closed Tues.-Wed.   *Moderate*
Hearty American and Italian fare is served in a well-furnished large dining room or on a
deck overlooking picturesque Sonoma Creek. Next door, a nostalgic bar has pictures and
furnishings that capture the flavor of Jack London's era.

Marioni's   *N side of plaza at 8 W. Spain St.*   *996-6866*
L-D. Closed Mon.   *Moderate*
Steak and seafood are served amidst colorful contemporary Southwestern decor. A tiled
courtyard with an adobe fireplace that fronts on the plaza is especially charming, and the
decor and multilevel dining areas inside are striking.

Pasta Nostra   *near SE corner of plaza at 139 E. Napa St.*   *938-4166*
L-D. No L on Tues.-Thurs.   *Moderate*
Freshly made pasta and sauces plus veal and chicken dishes are featured in a colorful,
congested trattoria.

Peterberry's   *near SE corner of plaza at 140 E. Napa St.*   *996-5559*
L-D.   *Moderate*
Coffees and espresso are served with a variety of locally-made pastries and light fare. This
casual new coffee house offers dining in several cozy areas, and some tables by picture
windows overlooking the street.

★ **Pilou Restaurant**   *E side of plaza at 464 1st St. E*   *996-2757*
L-D. B also on Sat. & Sun. Closed Mon.   *Moderate*
Hidden away in a cobblestone courtyard, this lovely little restaurant is a notable addition
to gourmet dining in Sonoma. Fresh local produce is used extensively and creatively in
French and New California cuisine.

Sharl's   *near SW corner of plaza at 136 W. Napa St.*   *996-5155*
L-D. Closed Tues.   *Expensive*
This newer restaurant serves Continental cuisine in an expansive dining room enhanced
by skylights, a fireplace, plants and fresh flowers, and posh table settings. A shaded patio
is also used in summer. An adjacent sunken bar offers comfortable armchairs and slick,
modern decor.

★ **Sonoma Hotel**   *NW corner of plaza at 110 W. Spain St.*   *996-2996*
L-D. Closed Wed.-Thurs.   *Moderate*
Fresh and homemade ingredients are skillfully used to prepare a limited number of
creative New California dishes offered on a menu that changes weekly. A century-old
hotel has been carefully restored to its former status as a Victorian landmark with an
artistically refurbished dining room and saloon, and a tranquil garden patio.

Sonoma Mission Inn   *2.5 mi. W at 18170 CA 12*   *996-1041*
D only. Sun. brunch. Closed Mon.   *Very Expensive*
Continental dishes are served in a casually elegant dining room of the stylishly restored
Sonoma Mission Inn, and on an adjoining scenic poolside patio.

★ **Willabe's**   *near SE corner of plaza at 133 E. Napa St.*   *996-4663*
L-D. Closed Tues.   *Moderate*
Fresh seafoods and New California specialties are prepared on a mesquite charcoal grill
and served with homemade pastas in this well-regarded new restaurant. Diners can
choose between a casually elegant firelit room or a tranquil tree-shaded fountain court.

LODGING

Accommodations in and around Sonoma are relatively scarce and expensive. There is
only one bargain motel in the area. Visitors interested in staying in any of the noted
lodgings should make reservations well in advance from spring through fall. Rates are
often reduced by at least 20% during the winter, except on weekends.

★ **Beltane Ranch**   *8 mi. NW at 11775 CA 12*   *996-6501*
An authentic Victorian-era ranch offers fine pastoral views of the Valley of the Moon from
porches that surround second floor rooms in an unspoiled building that now serves as a
bed-and-breakfast country inn. Period antiques, ceiling fans, and private baths are
featured in each room. A Continental breakfast of home-grown food is complimentary.

"Fireplace Room" — sitting room with a view, iron fireplace,   K bed...$70
regular room —   D bed...$70

Chalet Bed and Breakfast   *1.2 mi. W at 18935 5th St. W*   *996-0190*
Cows graze on the hillside next to a quaint old chalet that has been made into a bed-and-breakfast country inn. Features include a hot tub with a tranquil pastoral view, an upstairs sitting room warmed by a pot-bellied stove, and peacocks strolling among citrus trees on lush grounds. A real country breakfast is complimentary.
"New Cottage" — spacious, pvt. bath, fireplace, refr., view on 3 sides,   D bed...$85
regular room — shared bath,   D bed...$65

London Lodge   *8 mi. NW at 13740 Arnold Dr. - Glen Ellen*   *938-8510*
An outdoor pool and a scenic location by Sonoma Creek are features of this modern motel. Each room has cable TV and a phone.
#34,#23 — end unit, large,   K bed...$45
regular room —   2 Q or K bed...$45

★ **Sonoma Hotel**   *NW corner of plaza at 110 W. Spain St.*   *996-2996*
This three-floor, century-old landmark was recently thoroughly renovated. Each room is furnished with authentic Victorian antiques. A Continental breakfast is included.
#1 — spacious, corner overlooking the plaza, bathtub,   brass D bed...$56
#3 "Vallejo Room" — spacious, clawfoot bathtub, carved rosewood   D bed...$68
#4 — good view, unique armoire, clawfoot tub,   small D bed...$56
regular room — shared bath,   2 T or D bed...$45

Sonoma Mission Inn   *2.5 mi. W at 18170 CA 12*   *996-1041*
An aging three-story landmark was recently transformed into an exclusive hotel. Monochromatic earth tones and natural fabrics are used throughout to create understated contemporary elegance. Lighted tennis courts, an Olympic-sized outdoor pool, and (for a fee) a complete health spa, plus a restaurant and lounge are provided. Private baths, color TV, phones, and canopy beds are featured in all of the small, beautifully decorated rooms and in larger suites. A Continental breakfast is offered.
deluxe room — rounded room, pvt. sundeck,   K bed..$155
regular room —   2 T or Q bed...$115

Thistle Dew Inn   *near NW corner of plaza at 171 W. Spain St.*   *938-2909*
This new bed-and-breakfast inn offers turn-of-the-century ambiance in two ingeniously converted older buildings close to everything. A complimentary buffet-style Continental breakfast is served in the morning, and sherry is offered each evening by the fireplace.
#4 "Back House" — spacious, pvt. bath,   Q bed...$85
regular room — shared bath,   Q bed...$60

★ **Victorian Garden Inn**   *.3 mi. SE at 316 E. Napa St.*   *996-5339*
A new bed-and-breakfast inn occupies a historic farmhouse and water tower in a picturesque garden. A small stream runs through the property, and there is a large outdoor pool. A Continental breakfast and afternoon wine or sherry are complimentary.
"Woodcutters Cottage" — spacious, vaulted ceiling, pvt. entrance,
                    big bath, fireplace, by stream,   Q bed...$110
"Tower" — pvt. entrance & bath, by stream,   D bed...$79
regular room — in main house, shared bath,   Q bed...$69

Vineyard View Village   *4.5 mi. S on CA 121 at 23000 Arnold Dr.*   *938-2350*
This single-level older motel is the only **bargain** for many miles. Each small, modest room has color TV.
regular room —   Q bed...$27
regular room —   D bed...$25

CAMPGROUNDS

There are two notable campgrounds within easy driving distance of town, providing a choice between rustic facilities in a scenic canyon or complete facilities near a picturesque little reservoir.

★ **Spring Lake County Park**   *19 mi. NW via CA 12*   539-8092

Sonoma County and a local water district operate this campground by a lovely little reservoir with a swimming lagoon, a sandy beach, rental boats, a ramp and dock, boating (no motors allowed), fishing, and hiking and bicycle paths. Flush toilets and hot showers are available, but there are no hookups. Each site has a picnic table and a fire area.

base rate...$6

Sugarloaf Ridge State Park *14.5 mi. NE via CA 12 & Adobe Canyon Rd.*   833-5712

This state operated campground is in a secluded oak-shaded canyon. Fishing in a tiny stream and hiking and riding trails are attractions. Only pit toilets are available — no showers or hookups. Sites have picnic tables.

base rate...$6

SPECIAL EVENTS

★ **Valley of the Moon Vintage Festival**   *on the plaza*   *late September*

A weekend of parades, pageants, art shows, dances, music, and entertainment coincides with the annual grape harvest for the year's biggest and liveliest event. Light-hearted homage is paid to the valley's most famous product in the blessing of the grape, grape stomping, and wine tasting parties.

OTHER INFORMATION

Area Code: *707*

Sonoma Valley Chamber of Commerce *on the plaza at 453 1st St. E*   996-1033

Sonora, California

Elevation:

1,825 feet

Population (1980):

3,247

Population (1970):

3,100

Location:

132 mi. E
of San Francisco

Sonora is the robust "Queen of the Mother Lode." Well-tended Victorian homes and businesses still lend a gold camp flavor to this thriving hub in the foothills of the High Sierras. With a relatively mild four season climate, little snow falls in town during the winter. But, not far away, there is plenty in the higher mountains for every kind of snow sport. The best weather usually occurs during late spring and early fall. Crowds are only noticeable in summer, when long, hot days create great demand for the remarkable assortment of lakes, reservoirs, and rivers in oak-and-grass-covered foothills and pine-forested mountains surrounding town. Swimming, boating, sailing, fishing, river running, and gold panning lead a long list of outdoor recreation opportunities. The most popular year-round attraction, however, is the historic town itself and other nearby well-preserved Mother Lode towns.

Mexican miners established an encampment here in 1848 and named it the "Sonoran Camp." A short time later, when gold was discovered, Americans quickly supplanted Mexican and Chilean miners in the area. When California became a state in 1850, Sonora was named the Tuolumne County seat. After a disastrous fire in 1852, the town was rebuilt more substantially with stone, brick, adobe, and iron. The big Bonanza Mine, located just north of downtown, was perhaps the richest pocket mine in the Mother Lode. The high school now stands on land that gave up some of the largest pure nuggets ever found in this part of the state. The mines played out many decades ago, but Sonora continued to grow as a commercial center because of its convenient location. Recently, it has also become a leisure destination because of an increasing awareness of the area's historic significance and recreation opportunities.

Sonora stretches across several hills that are lightly forested with a pleasing combination of broadleaf and pine trees. A little creek is showcased in a minipark where it runs through the business district. Many notable Victorian buildings remain. Some still serve their original purpose as churches, public buildings, saloons, or stores. Others have been carefully transformed into specialty shops, galleries, and restaurants. Several distinctive Western-style entertainment spots are clustered in the heart of town. The collection of Victorian homes surrounding the business district is one of the best in the Mother Lode country. Lodgings are not abundant. There are several conventional motels. However, the most noteworthy accommodations are in historic hotels in the area, including a refurbished landmark downtown and several handsome restorations with atmospheric gold camp furnishings.

Sonora, California

Vokac Weather Rating

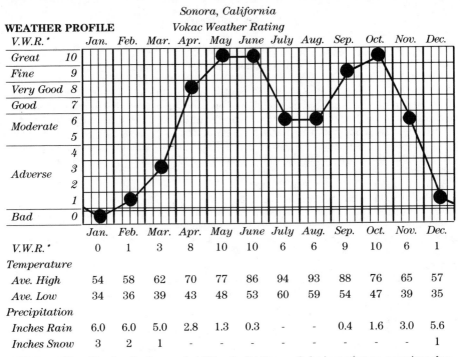

V.W.R. *		Jan.	Feb.	Mar.	Apr.	May	June	July	Aug.	Sep.	Oct.	Nov.	Dec.
Great	10												
Fine	9												
Very Good	8												
Good	7												
Moderate	6												
	5												
	4												
Adverse	3												
	2												
	1												
Bad	0												

	Jan.	Feb.	Mar.	Apr.	May	June	July	Aug.	Sep.	Oct.	Nov.	Dec.
V.W.R. *	0	1	3	8	10	10	6	6	9	10	6	1
Temperature												
Ave. High	54	58	62	70	77	86	94	93	88	76	65	57
Ave. Low	34	36	39	43	48	53	60	59	54	47	39	35
Precipitation												
Inches Rain	6.0	6.0	5.0	2.8	1.3	0.3	-	-	0.4	1.6	3.0	5.6
Inches Snow	3	2	1	-	-	-	-	-	-	-	-	1

*V.W.R. = Vokac Weather Rating: probability of mild (warm & dry) weather on any given day.

Forecast

Month	V.W.R. *		Temperatures		Precipitation
			Daytime	Evening	
January	0	Bad	cool	chilly	frequent downpours/snow flurries
February	1	Adverse	cool	chilly	frequent downpours/snow flurries
March	3	Adverse	cool	cool	occasional downpours
April	8	Very Good	warm	cool	infrequent downpours
May	10	Great	warm	cool	infrequent rainstorms
June	10	Great	hot	warm	negligible
July	6	Moderate	hot	warm	none
August	6	Moderate	hot	warm	none
September	9	Fine	hot	warm	negligible
October	10	Great	warm	cool	infrequent rainstorms
November	6	Moderate	warm	cool	infrequent downpours
December	1	Adverse	cool	chilly	occasional downpours

Summary

Sonora is located in the scenic Sierra foothills near the southern end of the Gold Camp country. The area has a relatively mild four season climate. All of the nominally bad weather is concentrated in **winter**. Heavy frosts and cold days are rare, but typically cool days and chilly evenings are frequently accompanied by heavy rains and some snow flurries which provide more than half the year's total precipitation. **Spring** is the most pleasant season. It becomes increasingly delightful each month, as days grow warmer and there are fewer and lighter rainstorms. **Summer** days are hot, evenings are warm, and there is usually no rainfall. While these conditions reduce the comfortable enjoyment of some attractions, they are perfect for river running, swimming, and other popular water sports available in abundance in surrounding lakes and rivers. **Fall** offers some great weather. Warm days, cool evenings, and infrequent rainstorms last into November, when the rainy season normally begins again in earnest.

ATTRACTIONS & DIVERSIONS

★ **Columbia State Historic Park**   *4 mi. N off CA 49 on Parrotts Ferry Rd.*   *532-4301*
Part of the old business district in Columbia is being faithfully restored to its appearance in gold rush days. For a few years during the 1850s, thousands of people lived here while fabulously rich placer mines were yielding $87 million in gold. The state has already restored several buildings that may be viewed on a self-guided walking tour including: the firehouse (and an 1852 two-cylinder fire engine); an 1860 two-story brick schoolhouse; St. Anne's Church (1856); the Wells Fargo Express office (1858), now a museum; the Fallon House Theater (1860); and the City Hotel (1857). A tour of a gold mine, stagecoach rides, and gold panning are some of the unusual activities offered during the summer and on most weekends year-round.

★ **Don Pedro Lake**   *15 mi. S on CA 49*   *989-2383*
The Mother Lode country's largest water body is a twenty-six-mile-long reservoir with a shoreline of 160 miles reaching into scenic woodland foothills. Houseboats and fishing boats can be rented at either of two full service marinas. Sailing is also popular. Swimming coves are numerous, and a large sandy beach area has been provided. Picnic and camping areas are located at several scenic sites near the lake.

Flying
   Columbia Aviation   *4 mi. N via CA 49, Parrotts Ferry & Airport Rds.*   *533-1900*
Scenic flights over the southern Mother Lode country or above Yosemite Valley can be reserved for any day except Monday.

★ **Gold Panning**
There is still enough gold left in the once-fabulously-rich placer deposits of nearby streams to provide an occasional thrill for latter-day argonauts. You can learn to pan, dredge, and separate gold at "Gold Mining Adventures" (928-4342) in Columbia State Park where you only pay if you get some gold while you learn. Then, buy a pan and hike upstream from the Camp Mine Road on the Stanislaus River.

★ **Jamestown**   *3.5 mi. SW via CA 49*
A narrow main street lined with two-story balconied buildings is the highlight of this tiny Victorian relic. The picturesque town has been used as the setting for several classic Hollywood westerns. A few shops and several restaurants and bars are well worth visiting.

Library   *.3 mi. S at 465 S. Washington St.*   *533-5707*
The Tuolumne County Library is a modest facility in a refurbished older building with a nicely displayed selection of magazines and newspapers.

Moaning Cave   *14 mi. NW at 5150 Moaning Cave Rd.*   *736-2708*
Discovered around 1850, this is California's largest public cavern. A guided tour descends a 100-foot spiral staircase into a gigantic chamber with impressive formations.

★ **Railtown 1897 State Historic Park**   *3.5 mi. SW off CA 49 - Jamestown*   *984-3953*
Since 1982, the state has operated steam-powered passenger trains over a historic twelve-mile route through oak-studded hill country each weekend in summer. The old roundhouse and shop complex is open to the public daily.

★ **River Running**
Sonora is between two of the most famous whitewater streams in the West — the Stanislaus and the Tuolumne Rivers. Some of the best rapids are now submerged beneath the waters of huge downstream reservoirs. However, exciting one or two day raft trips can still be enjoyed further upstream on the remaining scenic portions of the rivers. Several guide services operate between April and November. Among the most popular are:
   OARS, Inc.   *16 mi. NW on CA 49 near Angels Camp*   *736-2924*
   Zephyr River Expeditions   *5 mi. N via CA 49 at 10620 N. Airport Rd.*   *532-6249*

★ **St. James Episcopal Church**   *downtown at Washington & Snell Sts.*   *532-7644*
This picturesque Episcopal church, built in 1859 on a rise at the north end of downtown, may be California's oldest. Many consider it the most beautiful frame building in the Mother Lode. A Victorian mansion across the street is also notable.

Tuolumne County Museum   *downtown at 158 W. Bradford St.*   *532-4212*
Gold camp photographs and memorabilia are displayed, along with an authentically furnished jail cell in a building that housed the local jail well over a century ago.

Warm Water Feature
   Sierra Hot Tub   *1.5 mi. SE on CA 108 at 1255 Mono Way*   *532-1522*
Private hot tub enclosures, indoors or outdoors under oak trees, are rented by the hour until late each evening. Guests may bring in their choice of beverages.

★ **Water Features**
A remarkable number of lakes, streams, and reservoirs are within an hour's drive of town. During the uniformly sunny and hot months of summer, Sierra waters are a compelling attraction for swimmers, as well as fishermen, water-skiers, sailers, river runners, and all others who enjoy cool, clear water recreation. Public parks with sandy beaches and private coves abound on Don Pedro, New Melones, McClure, Woodward, Modesto, Turlock and other nearby man-made lakes. There are also excellent swimming holes and sandy beaches on the Stanilaus and Tuolumne Rivers and other nearby rivers flowing through the Sierra foothills.

★ **Weird Wanda's**   *3.6 mi. SW off CA 49 at 10365 9th St. - Jamestown*   *984-4149*
This unique store easily lives up to its name with bizarre displays of coyote claws; rare bird pelts, wings, and feathers; demonic masks; and other strange stuff for sale.

Wineries
   Shenandoah Vineyards *4 mi. N at 2260B Parrotts Ferry Rd. - Columbia* *532-3771*
In the Columbia Tasting Room, visitors may sample and buy the full line of premium wines made at a small family winery in Plymouth, sixty miles north on CA 49. Tasting and sales 10-5 daily.

★   **Stevenot Winery**   *21 mi. N on Sheep Ranch Rd. — 2 mi. N of Murphys*   *728-3436*
The small winery and vineyards are tucked away at the bottom of a deep gorge. Modern, quality equipment is housed in a restored 110-year-old hay barn. Zinfandel is the Mother Lode's most famous contribution to wine, and visitors may sample a notable example here, along with other premium varietals in a recently opened, atmospheric tasting room. The little valley is ideal for a pastoral picnic. Tasting, tours, and sales 10-4 daily.

Winter Sports
   Dodge Ridge Ski Area   *33 mi. NE off CA 108 on Dodge Ridge Rd.*   *965-3474*
With a vertical drop of approximately 1,000 feet, the longest run is 4,250 feet. A triple and five double chairlifts serve the area. Concessions include ski rentals and school, a cafeteria, and a bar. Open daily from mid-November to mid-April.

★   **Leland Meadows Resort**   *30 mi. NE off CA 108 - Pinecrest*   *965-3745*
This is a popular snow play area. Features include a tobogganing hill where toboggans, saucers, or inner tubes can be rented — or bring your own. There is also a cross-country ski area with designated trails. Lessons can be arranged. Hourly or daily snowmobile rentals and sleigh rides are also available. Open daily from December to April.

★   **Yosemite National Park**   *52 mi. SE via CA 49 and CA 120*   *372-4605*
Well over two million people visit this world famous national park each year. Its magnificent waterfalls and sheer granite domes are unsurpassed. Giant sequoia groves, vast high country wilderness areas, snowfields, and crystal-clear lakes and streams with sandy beaches are some of the attractions that have won the acclaim of increasing hordes of recreation enthusiasts since before the turn of the century.

SHOPPING
Sonora's business district is a distinctive combination of historic and new buildings that exists in spite of a string of shopping centers along highways near town. The narrow main business thorofare — Washington Street — is a delight for strollers as well as shoppers. A barber shop with a much-used pot-bellied stove, an unspoiled old-time grocery store with a wooden floor and a beer bar, and a sporting goods store serving tap beer over a well-worn back bar illustrate the amiable authenticity of this still-vital commercial district.

Food Specialties
★ **Country Kitchen Gourmet** *3.5 mi. SW at 18231 Main St. - Jamestown* *984-3326*
Assorted delicious croissants are made here daily and given a tempting display near the front of the new store. Other fine homemade baked goods are also served to go, or in a casual cafe with coffee. A good selection of gourmet foods and a dozen different fudges are also available.

★ **Hershey Chocolate Plant**   *35 mi. SW on Albers Rd. — Oakdale*   *847-0381*
Sprawling aromatically on wide-open farmlands just south of Oakdale is a giant factory
that supplies the entire West with Hershey chocolate. Half-hour guided tours pass mind-
boggling, fully automated facilities used for making Hershey candies. Each visitor is given
a Hershey milk chocolate bar at the end of the tour. Closed Sat.-Sun.

Penny Candy & Ice Cream Parlour   *downtown at 24 S. Washington St.*   *533-4747*
Big Olaf homemade cones are filled with a variety of ice creams. Many other ice cream
treats, candies, and fountain treats like cherry cokes are served in this cheerful,
refurbished soda fountain and confectionary.

Riverbank Cheese Co.   *39 mi. SW at 6603 2nd St. - Riverbank*   *869-4533*
Several cheeses are made here, including Teleme — a delicious creamy jack cheese first
made by Greek-Americans. Visitors can purchase cheese to go or in gift packs in this
modern little factory. Tours and samples are available on request.

★ **Sonka's Apple Ranch**   *8 mi. SE via Tuolumne Rd. at 19200 Cherokee Rd.*   *928-4689*
Magnificent mile-high apple pie and other outstanding homemade apple pies, pastries
and preserves, plus many varieties of apples (in season) are sold at this old-fashioned
roadside farm.

Stanislaus Cheese Co.   *39 mi. SW at 3141 Sierra Av. - Riverbank*   *869-2558*
Greek, Italian, and American cheeses, including Teleme, a delicious soft creamy Jack
cheese, are made and sold in this casual little old-fashioned cheese factory, to go, or in gift
packs. Tours and samples are available upon request.

Specialty Shops

★ **Antiques**
The area is still a bonanza for antique hunters. A list of the many shops that feature
Mother Lode memorabilia and antiques can be obtained at the Chamber of Commerce.

Charley's Washington Hall Books   *downtown at 77 N. Washington St.*   *532-6242*
An amazing jumble of books and magazines is crammed into this tiny shop.

Heritage Books and Coffee Mill   *downtown at 52 S. Washington St.*   *532-6261*
Books about the region are featured, and there is a casual coffee and pastry bar in the
back. Closed Sun.

NIGHTLIFE
The Old West lives on in several remarkably authentic saloons in the historic downtown
sections of Sonora, Murphys, Jamestown, and Columbia.

Fallon House Theatre   *4 mi. N at Broadway/Washington Sts. - Columbia*   *532-4644*
Musicals, comedies, and dramas are staged here from June thru August. Closed Mon.

★ **Gunn House**   *downtown at 286 S. Washington St.*   *532-3421*
Hidden away in the back of the historic inn is a romantic and intimate bar with an
impressive stone fireplace, plush Victorian furnishings and an ornate hardwood back bar.

★ **Hotel Willow**   *3.5 mi. SW at Main & Willow Sts. - Jamestown*   *984-4388*
The building was recently authentically restored as a restaurant and saloon. One of the
most picturesque barrooms in the Mother Lode country includes an outstanding back bar
and front bar that gold miners bellied up to well over a century ago, an ornate working
Franklin stove, well-worn floorboards, hardwood bar stools, and period pictures.

★ **The Murphys Hotel Saloon**   *18 mi. N on Main St. - Murphys*   *728-3444*
This classic saloon in a landmark hotel that has operated since 1856 is a Mother Lode
favorite. Natives and visitors alike flock in on weekends for live music and to enjoy
authentic gold camp atmosphere enhanced by a pot-bellied stove, a beautiful old back
bar, and hardwood armchairs.

The 90s   *downtown at 131 S. Washington St.*   *532-9963*
Poker, Lo-Ball, and pool attract players into a casual, comfortable saloon dominated by
one of the most splendid back bars anywhere.

Rawhide Saloon   *3.5 mi. SW on CA 49 - Jamestown*   *984-5113*
Live music and the area's largest dance floor (wall-to-wall slick concrete) draw throngs on
weekends. A large fireplace and several pool tables are other attractions of this rustic and
rowdy roadhouse.

★ **St. Charles Saloon**   *4 mi. N at 22801 Main St. - Columbia*   *533-4656*
This authentically restored old saloon is a fine place to drop in for a drink, to shoot pool, or to just relax in a wooden armchair and contemplate the handsome old back bar, the pot-bellied stove, or the well-worn hardwood floor.

Sonora Inn   *downtown at 160 S. Washington St.*   *532-7468*
Live music and dancing are featured on weekends in a comfortably updated lounge in Sonora's landmark hotel.

RESTAURANTS
Most of the area's best restaurants are located in the historic downtown sections of Sonora and the tiny nearby gold rush towns. Hearty American fare is emphasized, with a few cosmopolitan exceptions.

Bonavia's Yosemite Inn   *9 mi. SW on CA 108 at Yosemite Jct.*   *984-5847*
D only.   *Moderate*
Abundant American meals that include a relish plate, soup, salad, entree, beverage, and dessert are served in the casual dining room of a big modern roadhouse. In the next room is a relaxed firelit bar.

★ **City Hotel**   *4 mi. N via Parrotts Ferry Rd. on Main St. - Columbia*   *532-1479*
L-D. Closed Mon.   *Expensive*
Outstanding French cuisine is skillfully prepared from seasonally fresh ingredients and presented amid beautifully restored Victorian elegance in one of the most significant heirlooms of the gold rush days. A classic old-time saloon adjoins.

The Eproson House Restaurant   *12 mi. E on CA 108 - Twain Harte*   *586-5600*
B-L-D.   *Moderate*
American specialties are featured. A polished knotty pine interior and old-fashioned table settings give the dining room a feeling of country charm. Live entertainment and dancing are offered most nights in the lounge.

Europa Coffee Shop   *downtown at 275 S. Washington St.*   *532-9957*
B-L-D.   *Low*
A large selection of basic American dishes including homemade pies, plus a few Greek pastries, are prepared simply and served twenty-four hours every day in a homespun, old-fashioned coffee shop that hasn't changed much in more than forty years.

★ **Good Heavens - a Restaurant**   *downtown at 51 N. Washington St.*   *532-3663*
L only. Closed Mon.   *Moderate*
Unusual soups, sandwiches, and desserts offered on a short menu and on a frequently changing chalkboard are delicious. The warmly nostalgic atmosphere in this little lunch place is just right for a recently restored historic building on main street.

★ **Hotel Leger**   *37 mi. N on CA 49 - Mokelumne Hill*   *286-1401*
B-L-D.   *Moderate*
Splendid French cuisine is served amid Victorian elegance in the beautifully restored dining rooms of a 130-year-old gold rush hotel.

★ **Hotel Willow Restaurant**   *3.4 mi. SW on Main St. - Jamestown*   *984-4388*
L-D. No L on Sat.   *Moderate*
Carefully prepared Continental cuisine is served in two romantic dining rooms that genuinely display their Victorian origins in polished wainscoting, wooden booths, dark bentwood chairs, crisp linen, fresh flowers, and candlelight. The outstanding saloon in the next room reflects the same concern for details.

★ **Il Rifugio**   *18 mi. N on Main St. - Murphys*   *728-3964*
D only. Closed Tues.-Wed.   *Moderate*
First-rate Northern Italian cuisine is the specialty in a sophisticated newer restaurant with intimate country decor.

Jamestown Hotel   *3.5 mi. SW off CA 49 - Jamestown*   *984-3902*
L-D.   *Moderate*
Nicely prepared international specialties are served in a dining room furnished in updated period decor. Victorian-style reproductions are also used in an adjoining bar and in the small upstairs guest rooms of this recently renovated hotel.

Kinland Cove Restaurant　　*2.5 mi. E at CA 108/Tuolumne Rd.*　　　*532-0193*
L-D. No L on Sat. Closed Mon.　　　　*Moderate*
A fish market out in front sells seasonally fresh fish and shellfish which are also the specialties served in the nautical dining room or on an outside viewdeck. The modern bar in the next room is a tribute to ballooning.

The Kitchen　　*3.5 mi. SW off CA 49 on Main St. - Jamestown*　　　*984-3573*
B-L.　　　　　　*Low*
American favorites are given an honest down-home treatment in this humble, popular little cafe.

The Miners Shack　　*downtown at 157 S. Washington St.*　　　*532-5252*
B-L.　　　　　*Low*
Many omelets are offered all day as the feature among all-American short order foods served in this plain little cafe.

Murphys Hotel　　*18 mi. N on Main St. - Murphys*　　　*728-3444*
B-L-D.　　　　*Moderate*
Steaks and other American dishes (like liver and onions) are emphasized in the remodeled dining room of a restored pre-Civil War hotel.

National Hotel　　*3.4 mi. SW off CA 49 - Jamestown*　　　*984-3446*
L-D. Closed Tues.　　　*Moderate*
American and Italian dishes are served amid mining camp decor in the large dining room of a carefully restored pre-Civil War hotel, or in a tranquil vine-covered courtyard when weather permits. An authentic little gold camp saloon is next door.

Ozzie's　　*1.4 mi. SE on CA 108 at 1183 E. Mono Way*　　　*532-6623*
L-D. No L on Sat. Closed Sun.　　　*Moderate*
In this new restaurant, Continental specialties are served in a pleasant dining room with a European feeling.

★ **The Smoke Cafe**　　*3.4 mi. SW off CA 49 - Jamestown*　　　*984-3733*
D only. Closed Mon.　　　*Low*
Specialties from all regions of Mexico are carefully prepared and enthusiastically enjoyed by patrons in a spiffy update of a Victorian dining room and a charming adjoining bar in a historic building.

Villa d'Oro　*12 mi. NE at 23036 Joaquin Gulley Rd. - Twain Harte*　　*526-2182*
D only. Sun. brunch.　　　*Moderate*
Family-style Italian dinners include antipasto, soup, entree, and dessert. Veal dishes are emphasized in the casual, comfortably furnished split-level dining room.

LODGING

There aren't many places to stay in the Sonora area. But, visitors do have a real choice between authentically furnished historic hotels and modern motels with contemporary amenities. Rates are usually at least 10% lower than those shown during the fall-to-spring off-season, except on weekends.

City Hotel　　*4 mi N via Parrotts Ferry Rd. on Main St. - Columbia*　　*532-1479*
Built in the midst of the gold rush, this small two-story brick hotel remains a landmark of that era. Several years ago the building was completely restored. It once again serves as a gracious Victorian hotel with one of the West's finest dining rooms and an atmospheric Old West saloon. Each bedroom has a toilet and marble sink, and there is a hall shower. A complimentary breakfast is offered.

"Balcony Suite" — corner, above bar, main st. view,　　　　D bed...$60
#9 — end, quiet, 2 lg. windows with pvt. hill view,　　　　D bed...$53
regular room —　　　　　　　　　　　　　　　　　　　D bed...$53

★ **Gunn House**　　*downtown at 286 S. Washington St.*　　　*532-3421*
Many additions have been made to the original two-story adobe built in 1851, including a large landscaped oval pool and a plush intimate bar. Each room is furnished with some gold rush era antiques — plus an unobtrusive phone, cable TV, and a bathroom.

#18,#22 — corner, windows on 2 sides, balc. walkway,　　　Q bed...$41
regular room —　　　　　　　　　　　　　　　　　　　D bed...$36

★ **Hotel Leger**   *37 mi. N on CA 49 - Mokelumne Hill*   286-1401
This restored Mother Lode landmark now features a large outdoor pool tucked away in
back and surrounded by luxuriant vegetation, and an excellent restaurant and saloon.
Each room has period furnishings.

#2 — pvt. bath, fireplace, corner windows above main st.,		D bed...$57
#3 — shared bath, fireplace,		D bed...$47
regular room — shared bath,		D bed...$37

★ **Jameson's**   *9.3 mi. E via CA 108 at 22157 Feather River Dr.*   532-1248
A modern wood-trimmed home in a near-wilderness shaded by majestic oak and pine
trees has recently become a tranquil bed-and-breakfast inn. Small waterfalls flow under
the house which was built on top of enormous boulders. A complimentary Continental
breakfast always includes fresh Irish soda bread or scones. Each room shares a bath and
is beautifully furnished.

"Bridal Suite" — spacious, exotic Arabian Nights decor,		Q bed...$60
"Charmaine" — French decor, overlooks a waterfall,		Q bed...$45
regular room —		D or Q bed...$45

Mountain View Motel   *2 mi. SE on CA 108 at 1642 Mono Way*   532-4961
This plain, older single-level motel is a **bargain**. There is a heated pool, and each room has
a color TV.

regular room —		Q bed...$29

Rail Fence Motel   *5 mi. E at 19950 CA 108*   532-9191
In a country setting, this modern little motel has a pool and a hot tub. A Continental
breakfast is offered. Each room has a color TV.

regular room —		Q bed...$33

Royal Hotel   *3.5 mi. SW off CA 49 on Main St. - Jamestown*   984-5271
This newly restored little 1920s hotel in the heart of Jamestown features plush blue carpet
and attractive wallpaper, updated furnishings, plus some private bathrooms. A
Continental breakfast is complimentary.

"Royal Room" — pvt. bath, corner, balc. above main st., town view windows,		Q bed...$49
regular room — pvt. bath,		D bed...$43
regular room — shared bath,		D bed...$35

★ **Sonora Inn**   *downtown at 160 S. Washington St.*   532-7468
In an era when downtown hotels are being converted or replaced, this big old landmark
has been restored and now serves as the county's only full service hotel. Amenities include
an outdoor pool, an indoor whirlpool, and a large, nicely refurbished restaurant and
lounge. A modern motel section is across a street by a creek. Each room has a phone, color
TV, and bathroom.

#31,#32 — in newer motel section, creek view/sound,		K bed...$42
#201 — corner, spacious, in hotel, overlooking main street,		K bed...$42
regular room — in hotel, small,		D bed...$34

Sonora Towne House I & II   *downtown at 350 S. Washington St.*   532-3633
Sonora's largest accommodation is a modern motel complex with two outdoor pools and
a hot tub. Each nicely furnished room has a phone and cable color TV.

regular room —		K bed...$47
regular room —		D bed...$43

CAMPGROUNDS
There are several campgrounds in the area. Outstanding water-oriented campgrounds
have been provided on nearby Don Pedro Reservoir.

★ **Flaming Meadows**   *25 mi. S via CA 108 & La Grange Rd.*   852-2396
The Don Pedro Recreation Area operates a spacious campground on grassy oak-and-
pine-shaded slopes near the dam on Don Pedro reservoir. An unusually attractive sandy
beach and swimming lagoon, boating (plus rentals, ramp, and dock), houseboating,
sailing, water-skiing, and fishing attract campers to this end of the big, popular lake. Flush
toilets, hot showers, and hookups are available. Each tree-shaded site has a picnic table
and fire area.   base rate...$7

★ **Mocassin Point**   *15 mi. S on CA 49 at Jacksonville Rd.*   *852-2396*
The Don Pedro Recreation Area operates this sprawling campground on grassy oak-and-pine-shaded slopes above scenic Don Pedro Reservoir. Boating (plus rentals, ramp and dock), water-skiing, sailing, houseboating, swimming, and fishing are enjoyed on the big lake, and there are hiking trails on the adjoining oak-and-pine-studded hills. Flush toilets, hot showers, and hookups are available. Each well-spaced, tree-shaded site has a lake view, picnic table, raised fireplace, grill, and food storage box.   base rate...$7

SPECIAL EVENT

Mother Lode Round-up   *fairgrounds*   *early May*
The Sheriff's Posse sponsors a colorful weekend of Western festivities, including a parade, rodeo, and live entertainment to celebrate Mother's Day.

OTHER INFORMATION

Area Code: *209*
Zip Code: *95370*

Tuolumne County C. of C. *downtown at Stockton & S. Green Sts.*   *532-4212*
Stanislaus Natl. Forest-Supervisor's Office *1.5 mi. E at 19777 Greenley Rd.* *532-3671*

South Lake Tahoe, California

Elevation:

6,260 feet

Population (1980):

20,681

Population (1970):

12,921

Location:

192 mi. NE
of San Francisco

South Lake Tahoe is where the action is in the High Sierras. This sprawling boom town is ideally situated in a lush pine forest along the southern shore of one of the world's most beautiful high mountain lakes. Magnificent surroundings are perfectly complemented by the right weather during two notable seasons. Warm, sunny days with very little chance of rain attract teeming hordes of visitors to the Lake Tahoe area every summer. In town, there are long sandy beaches for swimming and sunbathing. Several marinas offer outstanding sportfishing, boating, water-skiing, and sailing, plus a remarkable variety of sightseeing cruises. State parks, national forests, and a wilderness area provide a diversity of other outdoor recreation opportunities in inspiring lake shore and mountain settings. Scenic golf and tennis facilities, miles of separated bicycle paths, and an aerial tramway ride are among diversions in town that compete with a cluster of lavish casinos just across the Nevada state line. Winter usually provides enormous snowfalls well-suited to downhill and cross-country skiing and a wealth of other snow sports. The base of the nation's largest alpine skiing complex is in town. The wide-angle view of the lake and Sierras from the top of the lifts is spellbinding in winter or summer.

Development occurred slowly along the south shore after the first settlement in the late nineteenth century. During the 1950s, construction of major casinos at the stateline signaled the beginning of year-round action, and development of an enormous skiing complex soon established the town as a winter sports capital. More than two-thirds of the total population surrounding the lake now lives in South Lake Tahoe.

Fortunately, much of the sylvan beauty of the setting has been retained. Towering pines are still abundant, even along the business strip. There is no traditional heart of town where business and government are focused. Instead, a tight cluster of high-rise casinos on the Nevada side of the state line anchors an awesome proliferation of visitor-related facilities at the town's eastern extremity. As a result, the hustle and bustle of around-the-clock gambling and big-name entertainment are only a stroll away from the relative tranquility of one of the West's largest and most sophisticated concentrations of lodgings. Restaurants are also abundant. A small but increasing number offer gourmet cuisine or spectacular views. Shops are surprisingly ordinary and scattered, but there are some good sources of outdoor recreation equipment.

WEATHER PROFILE — Vokac Weather Rating

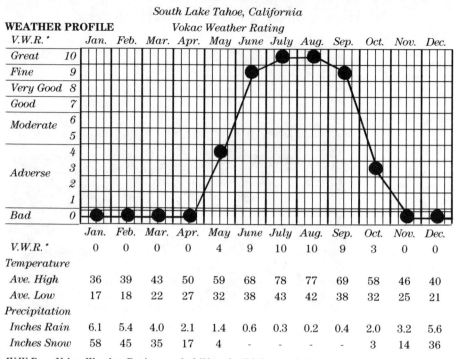

V.W.R.*	Jan.	Feb.	Mar.	Apr.	May	June	July	Aug.	Sep.	Oct.	Nov.	Dec.
Great 10												
Fine 9												
Very Good 8												
Good 7												
Moderate 6 / 5												
4												
Adverse 3 / 2												
1												
Bad 0												

	Jan.	Feb.	Mar.	Apr.	May	June	July	Aug.	Sep.	Oct.	Nov.	Dec.
V.W.R.*	0	0	0	0	4	9	10	10	9	3	0	0
Temperature												
Ave. High	36	39	43	50	59	68	78	77	69	58	46	40
Ave. Low	17	18	22	27	32	38	43	42	38	32	25	21
Precipitation												
Inches Rain	6.1	5.4	4.0	2.1	1.4	0.6	0.3	0.2	0.4	2.0	3.2	5.6
Inches Snow	58	45	35	17	4	-	-	-	-	3	14	36

*V.W.R. = Vokac Weather Rating: probability of mild (warm & dry) weather on any given day.

Forecast

Month	V.W.R.*	Temperatures Daytime	Evening	Precipitation
January	0 Bad	chilly	cold	frequent snowstorms
February	0 Bad	chilly	cold	frequent snowstorms
March	0 Bad	chilly	cold	occasional snowstorms
April	0 Bad	cool	chilly	occasional snowstorms
May	4 Adverse	cool	chilly	infrequent rainstorms/snow flurries
June	9 Fine	warm	cool	infrequent rainstorms
July	10 Great	warm	cool	negligible
August	10 Great	warm	cool	none
September	9 Fine	warm	cool	negligible
October	3 Adverse	cool	chilly	infrequent downpours/snow flurries
November	0 Bad	chilly	chilly	occasional snowstorms
December	0 Bad	chilly	cold	occasional snowstorms

Summary

Well over a mile high on the southern shore of one of the world's most beautiful big alpine lakes, South Lake Tahoe has a classic two season climate. **Winter** is chilly, snowy, and ideal for all winter sports. In fact, snowfalls are usually heavier than in any other great town except Tahoe City, which shares the same winter wonderland. **Spring** is a continuation of winter until May, when there is a short muddy transition with cool breezy days and occasional snowfalls through Memorial Day. All of the best weather is concentrated into **summer**. In this splendid season, warm sunny days, cool evenings, and inconsequential rainfall assure hassle-free comfort while exploring America's most renowned lake-and-mountain playground. With the arrival of **fall**, the weather quickly becomes unusable. Temperatures cool rapidly; and unpredictable, increasingly heavy rainfalls are replaced by snowstorms that normally provide the base for outstanding skiing after Thanksgiving.

ATTRACTIONS & DIVERSIONS

Aerial Tramway

★ **Heavenly Valley Ski Area**   *2 mi. S via Ski Run Blvd. on Saddle Rd.*   *544-6263*
An enclosed gondola lifts passengers more than 2,000 feet above the lake via a spectacular aerial tramway. The views of the lake and mountains are magnificent. Indoor and outdoor dining with a panoramic backdrop is featured at the Top of the Tram Restaurant.

★ **Bicycling**
There are several miles of exclusive bike paths in and near town over relatively flat, safe, and scenic terrain. The best segment is almost four miles of paved trail through a pine forest near south shore beaches. There are several bike rental shops. Among these are:

    Anderson's Bike & Skate Rental   *6 mi. SW at 645 CA 89*   *541-0500*
    Sierra Cycle Works   *1.7 mi. SW at 3430 US 50*   *541-7505*
    Tahoe Bike Shop   *4 mi. SW at 2277 US 50*   *544-8060*

★ **Boat Rentals**
Every kind of boating imaginable can be enjoyed on more than two hundred square miles of crystal-clear water. Visitors can rent an extraordinary assortment of craft — fishing boats, ski or cruising boats, sailboats, catamarans, canoes, or windsurf boards — by the hour or longer at several marina facilities, including:

    Jet and Sail Rentals   *1 mi. SW at foot of Ski Run Blvd.*   *544-7240*
    Richardson's Marina   *8 mi. W via CA 89 at 1900 Jameson Beach Rd.*   *541-1777*
    Ski Run Marina (para-sailing, too)   *1 mi. SW at foot of Ski Run Blvd.*   *544-0200*
    Timber Cove Marina   *1.7 mi. SW at 3411 US 50*   *544-2942*
    Windsurf, Tahoe   *1 mi. SW at foot of Ski Run Blvd.*   *541-2915*
    Zephyr Cove Sailing Center   *4 mi. N on US 50 - Zephyr Cove*   *(702)588-3369*

Boat Rides

★ **Lake Tahoe Cruises**   *1 mi. SW at foot of Ski Run Blvd.*   *541-4652*
Large modern sightseeing boats with glass bottom windows cruise four times daily, including a dinner-dance cruise, to Emerald Bay.

★ **Miss Tahoe Cruises**   *downtown at 828 Park Av.*   *541-3364*
This big modern vessel has a glass bottom window. There are daily trips to Emerald Bay and a sunset dinner-dance cruise each evening. The ship operates year-round.

★ **M.S. Dixie**   *4 mi. N off US 50 on Zephyr Av.*   *(702)588-3508*
A paddlewheeler with a 350-passenger capacity offers live music for dancing in the cocktail lounge, and steak dinners for evening cruises to Emerald Bay. The glass-bottom view is popular on morning and afternoon trips daily from May thru October.

★ **Sierra Sail Charters**   *2 mi. SW at 3411 US 50*   *541-3043*
Parasail rides are offered here, as well as sailing excursions, sightseeing tours, and a complete water-ski school.

★ **Woodwind**   *4 mi. N off US 50 on Zephyr Av.*   *(702)588-3000*
Sailing excursions are scheduled four times daily to Emerald Bay aboard a large trimaran with glass bottom windows. A sunset cruise features complimentary champagne.

★ **Desolation Wilderness**   *12 mi. W off CA 89*   *544-6420*
In mountains that reach nearly 10,000 feet above sea level, approximately eighty named lakes lie amid a "desolation" of huge boulders and glacier-polished granite slopes nearly devoid of trees. There are also clear streams, vast pine forests, and fields of wildflowers accessed by more than fifty miles of trails. Summer backpacking and camping are so popular that a campsite reservation system is in effect from mid-June to Labor Day. Horses and guides are available nearby for overnight, and longer, pack trips into the wilderness. Information and permits are available at the Eldorado National Forest Visitor Center.

★ **D.H. Bliss State Park**   *15 mi. NW on CA 89*   *525-7277*
The park offers excellent hiking trails and swimming off one of the lake's largest beaches. A large forested campground is situated by the lake just north of Emerald Bay.

★ **Eldorado Beach**   *2 mi. SW at US 50 & Harrison Av.*   *544-3317*
This half-mile long sandy beach is a favorite place for sunbathing and swimming with splendid views of the magnificent mountain-rimmed lake.

★ **Eldorado National Forest Visitor Center**   *8 mi. W on CA 89*   *544-6420*
The U.S. Forest Service operates the world's largest underground stream profile chamber here, giving visitors an opportunity to look through glass windows directly into Taylor Creek to watch trout pass. Also in summer months, self-guided trails, guided nature walks, and boat trips originate from here. In winter, guided cross-country ski tours are featured. This is the best place to get information about the Eldorado National Forest and the Desolation Wilderness Area.

★ **Emerald Bay State Park**   *11 mi. NW on CA 89*   *541-3030*
The most famous landmark of Lake Tahoe is Emerald Bay, which includes the lake's only island — Fannette. Cut into mountain slopes high above the water, the road around the bay provides panoramic views that are unforgettable. A mile-long footpath from Inspiration Point leads steeply down to the shore, where Vikingsholm, a thirty-eight room mansion, can be toured during the summer. It was built in 1929 as a summer residence patterned after a Viking's castle. At the head of the bay is a parking area for the short hike up to Eagle Falls. Scenic picnic sites are nearby. On the bay's east side is a large sylvan campground, with fishing, boating, and a swimming beach nearby.
   Golf
★   **Edgewood Tahoe Golf Course**   *.3 mi. N on Loop Rd.*   *(702)588-3566*
Between the lake and the casino district, this scenic and relatively level 18-hole championship golf course is open to the public with all facilities, rentals, and services.
★   **Lake Tahoe Country Club**   *8 mi. S on US 50*   *577-0788*
A relatively flat and well-tended 18-hole championship golf course on the Truckee River is open to the public with complete facilities, rentals, and services.
★ **Horseback Riding**
Quiet, wooded trails are found throughout the Tahoe basin. Several riding stables are located near town. All offer horse rentals by the hour, half day, or day. Most also provide guides for riders on breakfast, dinner, or moonlight rides, and for fishing or pack trips.
   Camp Richardson's Corral   *8 mi. W on CA 89*   *541-3113*
   Cascade Stables   *11 mi. NW via CA 89 on Cascade Rd.*   *541-2055*
   Stateline Stable (guide optional)   *downtown at US 50 & Park Av.*   *541-0962*
   Zephyr Cove Stables (guide optional)   *4 mi. N on US 50*   *(702)588-6136*
★ **Lake Tahoe**   *the northern border of town*
Straddling the California/Nevada state line 6,229 feet above sea level is a mountain-rimmed lake that is one of nature's grandest achievements. The water is said to be so pure that a white dinner plate can be seen at a depth of almost two hundred feet. Lake Tahoe is the largest deep alpine lake on the continent. In fact, with its twenty-two mile length, twelve mile width, and maximum depth of 1,645 feet, the lake's volume would cover the entire state of California with more than a foot of pure water. But statistics can't do justice to this serious contender for the world's most beautiful water body. It's also one of the most usable, with a remarkable assortment of watercraft available for rent, charter, or tours, plus a proliferation of onshore recreation facilities to better enjoy the forests, sandy beaches, dramatic bouldered coves, and the river, streams, and mountains that surround the lake. A seventy-two mile highway loop around the lake is immodestly described by the South Lake Tahoe Visitor's Bureau as "The Most Beautiful Drive in America" on their map and guide describing eighteen points of interest along the route.

★ **Lake Tahoe State Park**   *starts 13 mi. NE via US 50 on NV 28*   *(702)588-4180*
Several miles of the lake's northeastern shoreline are included in this large Nevada park. Pine-shaded picnic grounds near picturesque granite boulders and sandy beaches are popular, along with fishing and boating — launching facilities are provided.

★ **Library**   *2 mi. SW at 1000 Rufus Allen Blvd.*   *541-4416*
The El Dorado County Library is in a large contemporary building with picture window views through a pine forest to the lake. The well-furnished facility includes an inviting periodical reading area with fabric-backed armchairs and sofas.

★ **Mopeds**
An exhilarating, relatively effortless way to enjoy the scenic roads around the lake is on a moped. Hourly and longer rentals can be arranged at several shops in town, including:

Country Moped, Inc.	*5 mi. SW at 800 CA 89*	*544-3500*
The Moped Place	*2 mi. SW at US 50 & Harrison Av.*	*544-7160*
Tahoe Rent-a-Car	*downtown at Park & Cedar Sts.*	*544-4500*

★ **Nude Beaches**   *starting 17 mi. NE via US 50 & NV 28*
More than two miles of the lake's remote northeastern shoreline is a popular swimming-suits-optional area. Picturesque granite boulders and numerous tiny sandy beaches are backed by steep forested hills. Park off the road wherever there are clusters of cars. Sandy trails lead down to the beach from these informal parking areas.

★ **Regan Beach**   *2.5 mi. SW at the foot of Sacramento Av.*   *541-2900*
A grassy area above this sandy beach is a favorite for sunbathing and sightseeing.

South Lake Tahoe Recreation Center *2 mi. SW at 1180 Rufus Allen Blvd.*   *541-4611*
A large heated swimming pool (enclosed in winter) is open to the public year-round. This impressive contemporary center includes a gymnasium, game room, and exercise room.

Warm Water Features

★   **Nephele Restaurant**   *1 mi. SW at 1169 Ski Run Blvd.*   *544-8130*
Hot tubs with whirlpool jets can be rented hourly in attractively furnished private rooms with stereo music and towels. Cocktail service is on-call. Each of the roofless rooms has a fine pine-top view.

★   **Shingle Creek Hot Tubs**   *1 mi. SW at 1142 Ski Run Blvd.*   *544-5400*
Patrons can select any of six nicely decorated private outside enclosures, each with a pine-top view, hot tub with therapy jets, piped-in stereo music, and towels. Cocktails may be ordered through room service.

Winter Sports

★   **Hansen's Resort**   *1.5 mi. S at 1360 Ski Run Blvd.*   *544-3361*
A toboggan and saucer hill with banked turns and packed runs is open daily in winter with a mechanical lift to return toboggans to the top of the hill. All equipment can be rented.

★   **Heavenly Valley**   *2 mi. S via Ski Run Blvd. on Saddle Rd.*   *541-1330*
America's largest ski area sprawls into two states and covers more than twenty square miles of varying terrain with runs up to seven miles long. Spellbinding views of both Lake Tahoe and the Carson Valley are accessed by sixteen chairlifts (including two triple chairs) and a gondola. The vertical drop is more than 4,000 feet. Both day and night skiing are available on well-groomed slopes designed for every range of ability. Helicopter skiing can be arranged, and excellent cross-country trails are nearby. The aerial tramway also operates during summer months to a scenic observation platform and restaurant.

★   **Skiing**
Three downhill ski areas surround town, and twenty-two are within a fifty mile radius. Four cross-country skiing centers are located near the south shore. The remarkable number and quality of facilities is closely correlated to the breathtakingly beautiful and endlessly varied terrain. Ski rental equipment and lessons for both downhill and cross-country skiing are available at most of the major ski areas. In addition, almost a dozen places in town sell and rent all kinds of skiing equipment, and have maps and information on all areas.

★   **Sleigh Rides**   *downtown near the High Sierra Hotel*   *541-2953*
During the winter months, visitors can bundle up for a forty minute horse-drawn sleigh ride to a high plateau for a panoramic lake view.

★   **Tahoe Paradise Winter Sports**   *9 mi. S on US 50*   *577-2121*
Snowmobiles can be rented for use on an area that is groomed daily. An ice-skating rink and complete skate rentals are also available.

SHOPPING
South Lake Tahoe has no central business district or conventional downtown. Instead, a full range of shops are strung out along a five-mile strip between the "Y" (intersection of US 50 and CA 89) and the state line where huge hotel/casinos in Nevada border the largest concentration of businesses in South Lake Tahoe. Because the skyscraper hotels are the area's dominant visual reference, the state line area is referred to as "downtown."

Food Specialties

★ **The Cork & More**   *1 mi. SW at 1140 Ski Run Blvd.*   *544-5253*
Wine tastings are featured daily from an impressive selection of all-California wines.
Gourmet foods and deli items are also sold.

Cream Puff Bakery   *3.9 mi. SW at US 50/Sierra Blvd.*   *544-2141*
Pastries, cakes, cookies, and breads, plus some fine European specialties, are displayed in
this takeout bakery located in the Swiss Village Shopping Center.

★ **Dart Discount Liquors**   *.4 mi. N at US 50/NV 19*   *(702)588-5187*
More than 700 wine labels, plus hundreds of liquors, are deeply discounted in this big,
modern store.

Dunk-N-Spice Donuts   *4 mi. SW at 2122 US 50*   *541-9805*
A distinctive assortment of delicious donuts is displayed in this independently-owned
little carryout.

The Good Omen   *5 mi. SW on US 50*   *541-1258*
Tucked away in a shopping center is a small store with more than one hundred cheeses,
smoked meats and sausages, other gourmet foods, and a good selection of beer and wine.

Specialty Shops

Hot Gossip   *1 mi. SW via US 50 at 1007 Ski Run Blvd.*   *541-4823*
This tiny shop caters to a variety of needs with an eclectic mixture of magazines, flowers,
and assorted coffees and pastries that can be enjoyed at a few tables.

Sierra Bookshop   *5 mi. SW on US 50 at 1068 Emerald Bay Blvd.*   *541-6464*
A large selection of casually-arranged books and topographic maps are for sale in this
shopping center store.

NIGHTLIFE

The third largest and most compact cluster of casinos in the West (after Reno and Las
Vegas) is only a stroll from dozens of motels in town. As a result, there is non-stop
gambling action, and more "name" entertainment year-round in major showrooms than
in any other great town. Also, drinking and dancing places are notably diverse, ranging
from elegant to rustic and from rowdy to relatively serene.

★ **Caeser's Tahoe**   *downtown on US 50 at Stateline*   *(702)588-3515*
This huge hotel/casino, clone of the Las Vegas operation, has a prodigious assortment of
extravagant facilities offering live entertainment, dancing, and non-stop gambling.

★ **Christiania Inn**   *2 mi. SW via Ski Run Blvd. on Saddle Av.*   *544-7337*
A charming little inn at the Heavenly Valley Ski Area offers a perfect place for a peaceful
respite from the casino action. Several intimate areas have been created in a multilevel
lounge with a handsome stone fireplace, an intriguing wine cellar window wall, and a posh
assortment of sofas and easy chairs.

★ **Harrah's Tahoe**   *downtown on US 50 at Stateline*   *(702)588-6606*
The superstar of Tahoe resort casinos has an outstanding array of entertainment
facilities, in addition to a cavernous high-tech gambling casino. The South Shore Room is
a first-class, big-name dinner theater. The Stateline Cabaret features top-name lounge
acts nightly. Above it all, the Summit Lounge offers live background music and
breathtaking panoramas of the lake and mountains from the contemporary opulence of
an 18th floor hideaway that is an unforgettable setting for a romantic interlude.

★ **Harvey's Resort Hotel**   *downtown on US 50 at Stateline*   *(702)588-2411*
This large hotel/casino offers non-stop gambling on the ground floor. On the top floor
(11th), the Top of the Wheel features cocktails, dining, and dancing nightly, plus good
views of Lake Tahoe. Exotic Polynesian drinks and decor are offered in the
adjacent Tiki Lounge.

★ **High Sierra Hotel/Casino**   *downtown on US 50 at Stateline*   *(702)588-6211*
In addition to a recently improved name (it was once the Tahoe Sahara), this high-rise
hotel/casino has an impressive variety of entertainment facilities as well as non-stop
gambling. The High Sierra Theater showcases well-known performers year-round in a big
theater/restaurant. The Pine Cone Lounge offers name acts nightly. The Brass Spittoon
features casual live music for dancing and listening.

RESTAURANTS

Most of the proliferation of restaurants in and near town feature hearty American fare. Gourmet cuisine is surprisingly scarce, but several fine restaurants have opened in recent years. Many of the better dining rooms provide stylish high-country decor, and several have splendid views of Lake Tahoe.

Caesar's Tahoe   *downtown on US 50 at Stateline*   *(702)588-3515*
Within the extravagant hotel/casino complex are several major specialty restaurants. The *Edgewood (D only-Very Expensive)* features gourmet dining and plush decor. Polynesian dishes are served amidst waterfalls in a tropical setting in *Paradise Cove (D only-Expensive)*. The sumptuous *Evergreen* buffet *(B-L-D-Low)* is a bargain. The most innovative restaurant is the posh *Alpine Cafe (L only-Expensive)* located in a fanciful boulder-strewn corner of a bright and airy room that also includes a large lagoon-style swimming pool with an impressive swim-under waterfall.

The Chart House   *1.5 mi. NE on NV 19*   *(702)588-6276*
D only.   *Moderate*
This representative of a first-rate restaurant chain features prime rib and steaks accompanied by a salad bar. But, the main attraction is an awe-inspiring view of Lake Tahoe from the big contemporary dining room high on a hill east of town. The view from the lounge is also impressive.

The Cheesecake Factory   *1.8 mi. SW at 3330 US 50*   *544-7893*
L only. Closed Sat.-Sun.   *Moderate*
Well-regarded cheesecake is served along with other homemade desserts and luncheon fare in a tiny coffee shop or on a small deck outside.

★ **Chez Villaret**   *6 mi. SW at 636 CA 89*   *541-7868*
D only.   *Expensive*
Nouvelle French cuisine is skillfully prepared and served in a cozy, congested French provincial dinner house.

★ **Christiania Inn**   *2 mi. S via Ski Run Blvd. on Saddle Rd.*   *546-7337*
D only.   *Expensive*
Skillfully prepared Continental cuisine is complemented by romantic contemporary furnishings including a picture window view of a wine cellar and a great stone fireplace. There is also an outstanding lounge.

The Cook Book   *5.5 mi. W at 787 CA 89*   *541-8400*
B-L-D.   *Moderate*
Homemade breads and pastries are the recently-added specialty that has given new life to a long-popular roadside restaurant where an elaborate menu of uninspired omelets is featured in pleasant, country-charming dining rooms.

★ **Crystal Cafe**   *1 mi. SW at US 50/Ski Run Blvd.*   *544-2429*
B-L-D.   *Moderate*
Delicious four-egg omelets and other fine dishes are carefully prepared from scratch in a stylish little restaurant recently opened in a remote corner of a shopping center. It's well worth finding, especially for breakfast.

The Dory's Oar   *2 mi. SW at 1041 Fremont Av.*   *541-6603*
D only.   *Moderate*
Live Maine lobsters, soft shell Maryland crabs, blue point oysters, and steamed clams are flown in fresh from the East Coast. New England-style cooking reigns amid casual Cape Cod decor.

The Driftwood Cafe   *downtown at 4115 Laurel Av.*   *544-6545*
B-L.   *Moderate*
Some unusual specialties like cashew waffles highlight the light fare offered in this pleasant little cafe where breakfast is served all day.

Frank's Restaurant   *6 mi. SW at 1207 CA 89*   *544-3434*
B-L.   *Moderate*
A huge menu describes all kinds of waffles, hot cakes, and omelets, plus delicious homemade biscuits and pies. Here is a classic, old-fashioned all-American roadside coffee shop.

The Fresh Ketch *5.5 mi. SW via Tahoe Keys Blvd. to 2435 Venice Dr. E.*   *541-5683*
L-D.   *Moderate*
Fresh seafood is emphasized in this large new restaurant with several casually elegant
rooms overlooking Tahoe Keys Marina and the lake. A scenic and handsome lounge
features fifty kinds of beer, plus several premium wines by the glass.

The Greenhouse   *downtown at 4140 Cedar Av.*   *541-6278*
D only.   *Expensive*
Gourmet Continental specialties are served in a firelit environment of hanging plants and
stained glass. A copper-top bar lends interest to the cozy lounge.

★ **Harrah's Tahoe**   *downtown on US 50 at Stateline*   *(702)588-6611*
Lake Tahoe's most distinguished hotel/casino has eight restaurants. Three are especially
notable. The *Summit (D only-Very Expensive)* presents Continental cuisine in a formal,
opulent setting with a magnificent 18th floor view of Lake Tahoe and the high Sierra. The
Forest (B-L-D-Moderate) features the finest buffet on the lake amidst unusually
innovative decor in an 18th floor dining room with mountain and lake views. The *South
Shore Room (D only-Very Expensive)* combines dinner with exclusively "big name"
entertainment in a grandiose showroom.

Harvey's Resort Hotel   *downtown on US 50 at Stateline*   *(702)588-2411*
Three specialty restaurants highlight the area's oldest major hotel/casino. The *Top of the
Wheel (D only-Expensive)* offers Polynesian and American dishes with a panoramic lake
view. The *Sage Room Steak House (D only-Expensive)* features beef in an atmosphere of
Western elegance. The *El Dorado* buffet *(B-L-D-Low)* displays a tempting array of
American specialties and desserts in a large, pleasant dining room.

Heavenly Valley Ski Resort   *2 mi. SW via Ski Run Blvd. on Saddle Rd.*   *544-6263*
L-D.   *Moderate*
A spectacular aerial tram ride takes diners more than 2,000 feet above Lake Tahoe. At the
top, a broad selection of American fare is served with a truly breathtaking view from
indoors or on the deck.

Heidi's   *1.6 mi. SW at 3485 US 50*   *544-8113*
B-L.   *Moderate*
Plain hearty breakfasts of all kinds are served in a big, casual wood-trimmed coffee shop.

High Sierra Hotel/Casino   *downtown on US 50 at Stateline*   *(702)588-6211*
Several restaurants are located in this enormous hotel/casino. The *House of Lords (D
only-Very Expensive)* is darkly elegant. The *Bonanza* buffet *(B-L-D-Low)* provides an
abundance of food in a plain setting. The *High Sierra Theatre (D only-Very Expensive)*
combines elaborate meals with name entertainment in a mammoth showroom.

Little Switzerland   *9 mi. SW on US 50 - Tahoe Paradise*   *577-5646*
B-L-D.   *Moderate*
Breakfast omelets, rosti potatoes (fried, with swiss cheese, bacon, and onions) and
blueberry muffins are among the specialties of this casual, old country-style restaurant.

Nephele's   *1 mi. SW at 1169 Ski Run Blvd.*   *544-8130*
D only.   *Moderate*
International cuisine is the highlight of an intimate contemporary dining room that is a
delightful blend of wood tones and stained glass.

Red Hut Cafe   *3.5 mi. SW at 2723 US 50*   *541-9024*
B-L.   *Low*
Outstanding waffles and the best prices in town on an assortment of omelets and other
breakfast specialties account for the enduring popularity of this rustic little roadside cafe.

Station House Inn   *downtown at 901 Park Av.*   *542-1101*
B-L-D.   *Moderate*
This motor hotel features a good selection of all-American specialties in a handsome
contemporary restaurant. The bar spills out onto a well-landscaped wood deck with a
mountain and pool view.

Swiss Chalet   *3.9 mi. SW at US 50 & Sierra Blvd.*   *544-3304*
D only.   *Moderate*
European specialties, fondues, and homemade pastries complement Old World decor in
this large and long-established dinner house.

Tep's Villa Roma   *3.8 mi. SW at US 50 S. Reno Av.*   *541-8227*
D only.   *Moderate*
The longest Italian menu on the lake and a large help-yourself antipasto bar are featured in a casual, congested dining room.

LODGING

South Lake Tahoe boasts one of the West's greatest concentrations of accommodations. There are more than 7,000 rooms in lakefront or forest locations to suit every taste and budget. In addition, there are more than 1,700 rooms in the four casino/hotel towers clustered at the state line. (These rooms are not included in this listing. While the entertainment and dining facilities in the big hotels are notable, accommodations in the hotel towers are both more expensive and more remote from the lake and forest than are the first-class lodgings in town.) During the summer, bargains are almost non-existent and reservations should be made in advance, especially on weekends. However, most places offer discounts from October to May of at least 10% on Friday and Saturday and 30% or more on weekdays.

Chateau L'Amour   *1.1 mi. SW at 3620 US 50*   *544-6969*
Hedonism hit the high country when a modern little motel was converted into a complex of uninhibited romper rooms for adults only. Guests have a choice of bright reds, blues, or browns as the color scheme for flamboyant furnishings that include cable color TV with X-rated movies, mirrored walls and ceilings, and carpeted floors and walls.

#9 "Honeymoon Suite" — red decor, in-room big heart-shaped whirlpool, champagne,	8′ round K	waterbed...$95
#10 — blue decor, in-room whirlpool,	8′ round K	waterbed...$85
regular room — in-room whirlpool,	K	waterbed...$80
regular room —	K	waterbed...$60

★ **Christiania Inn**   *2 mi. S at Heavenly Valley Ski Area*   *544-7337*
Overlooking the base of Heavenly Valley Ski Area, this classic little bed-and-breakfast inn offers beautifully furnished units with private baths, cable color TV, and dramatic ski slope views. A Continental breakfast and decanter of brandy are complimentary. Because of the ideal location in ski season, winter rates are substantially higher than the prices quoted.

#4 suite — spacious, split level, wet bar, fireplace, high window wall with slope view,	round K bed...$120
suite — spacious, wet bar, fireplace, in-bath steam bath,	K bed...$120
regular room — spacious,	Q bed...$60

★ **Fantasy II**   *downtown at 924 Park Av.*   *544-6767*
This modern motel has a small outdoor pool. It is near the beach and the casinos. The real distinction, though, is the decor — intended exclusively for adults interested in accommodations unlike anything back home. Rooms are decorated in flamboyant reds, browns, or blues with carpet and mirrors everywhere — even on the walls and ceiling. Each room has X-rated movies on adult closed-circuit color TV, a phone, and a stereo radio.

#127 — spacious, in-room heart-shaped whirlpool,	K bed...$96
regular room — in-room heart-shaped whirlpool,	Q bed...$88
regular room —	Q bed...$72

Frontier Lodge   *.5 mi. SW at 3880 Pioneer Trail*   *541-6226*
This big modern motel has a large outdoor pool and a redwood hot tub in the pines. Each spacious room has cable color TV and a phone.

regular room —	Q bed...$38

Hansen's Resort   *2 mi. SW at 1360 Ski Run Blvd.*   *544-3361*
Adjacent to a toboggan lift in a quiet forested location is a rustic motel and several cabins.

Cabin #6 — 2 BR, LR with fireplace, kit.,	2 D & Q beds...$80
regular room — in motel,	Q bed...$40

Holiday Lodge   *downtown at 4095 Laurel St.*   *544-4101*
Near the casinos and a short stroll from the beach, this big modern motel has large indoor and outdoor pools, a whirlpool, and saunas. Each room has a phone and cable color TV.

regular room —	K bed...$59

★ **Inn by the Lake**   *1.8 mi. SW at 3300 US 50*   *542-0330*
The lake and a fine public beach are across the highway from this contemporary motel
which has a large outdoor pool, two whirlpools, and a sauna. Each nicely furnished room
has a phone, cable color TV with movies, and a balcony or patio.
    deluxe room — lake view, wet bar, refr.,   K bed...$80
    regular room —   Q bed...$70

★ **Lakeland Village**   *1.2 mi. SW at 3535 US 50*   *541-7711*
Nestled among nineteen acres of pines is a large condo complex adjoining Lake Tahoe on
a thousand feet of private sandy beach that is ideal for swimming and sunning. A fishing
pier, rental boats, two landscaped outdoor pools, a whirlpool, saunas, and two tennis
courts are also available to guests. Each unit has a phone, cable color TV, a kitchen,
fireplace, and a private balcony. Unfortunately, only units with three or more bedrooms
have lakefront views.
    Townhouse — 1 BR, two-level,   Q bed...$115
    regular unit — studio, hideabed,   Q bed...$69

Motel 6   *4 mi. SW at 2375 US 50*   *541-6272*
The West's biggest **bargain** chain of motels is represented by a very large facility with an
outdoor pool, and (fee) TV.
    regular room —   D bed...$22

★ **Pacifica Lodge**   *downtown at 931 Park Av.*   *544-4131*
In addition to a convenient location near both the beach and casinos, this modern motel
has a large outdoor pool and an enclosed whirlpool. Each room has a phone and cable
color TV. Coffee and donuts are brought to the rooms daily. The real attraction, however,
is the assortment of stylishly decorated, feature-filled adult rooms.
    #117 "Queen of Hearts" — spacious, wet bar, fireplace, raised in-room
                            heart-shaped whirlpool,   K waterbed...$75
    #118 "Captain's Quarters" — spacious, nautical decor, wet bar, fireplace, raised
                            in-room heart-shaped whirlpool,   K waterbed...$75
    #311,#312 — spacious, nautical or Egyptian decor, raised in-room
                            heart-shaped whirlpool, wet bar, pine view from K bed...$70
    #508,#511,#517 — spacious, blue, red, or orange tones, raised
                            stone fireplace, pvt. balc.,   K bed...$60
    regular room —   K bed...$47

Play Chalet Motel   *1 mi. SW at 1200 Ski Run Blvd.*   *544-4661*
A recently refurbished motel a few blocks from the ski slopes has a large outdoor hot tub
in the pines. Each of the spacious rooms has a cable color TV.
    special room — raised heart-shaped in-room whirlpool,   Q bed...$60
    regular room —   Q bed...$50

★ **Royal Valhalla Motor Lodge**   *.3 mi. W at 4401 Lake Shore Dr.*   *564-2233*
This contemporary lakefront motel has guest privileges at a splendid private beach across
the street. There is also a large outdoor pool. Each spacious room has a private balcony
(most overlook the lake), cable color TV, and a phone.
    lakefront room — view overlooks the lake,   Q bed...$63
    regular room —   Q bed...$48

Ski Inn   *1 mi. SW at 3641 US 50 & Ski Run Blvd.*   *544-2016*
An outdoor pool and hot tub are available in a motel that is only a block from the beach.
Each room has cable color TV.
    #23 — cabin, fireplace, kit., in-room raised whirlpool,   Q waterbed...$65
    #29 — fireplace, kit.,   K bed...$55
    regular room —   D bed...$38

Tahoe Hacienda   *1 mi. SW at 3820 US 50*   *541-3805*
A large outdoor oval-shaped pool and a whirlpool are features of this pine-shaded single-
level motel. Each room has a phone and cable color TV.
    #5,#6 — spacious, fireplace,   K waterbed...$75
    #29,#30 — spacious, in-room heart-shaped whirlpool, **refr.**, Q bed...$95
    #32 — spacious, blue decor, in-room whirlpool, refr.,   Q waterbed...$95
    regular room —   K bed...$58

★ **Tahoe Marina Inn**   *1.8 mi. SW at US 50 & Bal Bijou Rd.*   *541-2180*
This contemporary condominium resort includes five hundred feet of private sandy beach, a large outdoor pool with a fabulous lakeside view, and a sauna. Each of the spacious, beautifully furnished units in the motor inn or adjacent condos has a phone, cable color TV with movies, and a lakeside balcony or deck.
   #318,#315,#212,#114 — inn room, corner, fine lake views, kit.,   2 Q beds...$84
   #230,#234 — condo, fine lake views, fireplace, kit.,   2 T & Q beds...$94
   regular room — inn room,   Q bed...$77
★ **Tahoe Seasons Resort**   *2 mi. SW at Keller & Saddle Rds.*   *541-6700*
Near the aerial tramway at Heavenly Valley, this large resort opened in 1984 with an outdoor pool, whirlpool, two tennis courts, paddleball courts, and an exercise room. A garage, restaurant and lounge are also available. Each room has an in-room whirlpool, a gas fireplace, cable color TV, and a phone.
   suite — top floor, wet bar, balc., slope view,   Q bed..$110
   regular room — mountain view,   Q bed...$90
★ **Timber Cove Lodge-Best Western**   *1.7 mi. SW at US 50 & Bal Bijou Rd.*   *541-6722*
This large contemporary motor hotel is on attractively landscaped lakefront grounds and six hundred feet of private sandy beach next to one of the best public beaches on the lake. In addition to fine lake swimming, there is a fishing pier, a marina with boat rentals, a large outdoor pool and two whirlpools, plus an attractive fireplace lobby/lounge and dining room. Each spacious, well-furnished room has cable color TV and a phone.
   #512,#508,#504,#269,#245,#221 — end rooms, fine lakefront view.
                      semi-pvt. balc.,   K bed...$65
   regular room —   2 D or K bed...$65
Villa Montreux   *1 mi. SW at 971 Ski Run Blvd.*   *544-3224*
A half block from the beach in a quiet location, this modern motel has a large outdoor pool. Each room has a phone and cable color TV with movies.
   regular room —   Q bed...$37
   regular room —   D bed...$35

CAMPGROUNDS

Numerous campgrounds are located on or near the south shore of Lake Tahoe. The best provide complete camping and recreation facilities in luxuriant pine forests by beaches along the majestic lake.
★ **Camp Richardson**   *8 mi. W via US 50 & CA 89*   *541-0708*
This huge campground is located in a pine forest next to a fine beach along Lake Tahoe. Sunbathing, swimming, boating (plus a ramp and dock), water-skiing, fishing, bicycle trails (plus rentals), and tennis courts are among the attractions and diversions. Flush toilets, hot showers, and hookups are available. Each pine-shaded site has a picnic table and fire area. Some have a lake view.   base rate...$7
★ **El Dorado Recreation Area**   *2 mi. W on US 50*   *544-3317*
Across the highway from one of the lake's finest sandy beaches is a large municipal campground. Sunbathing, swimming, boating (plus a ramp and dock), water-skiing, and fishing are very popular. A large municipal (fee) indoor/outdoor pool is adjacent. Flush toilets, hot showers, and hookups are available. Each of the pine-shaded sites has a picnic table and a raised fire grill.   base rate...$7
★ **Emerald Bay State Park**   *11 mi. W via US 50 & CA 89*   *541-3030*
On a peninsula between the south shore of picturesque Emerald Bay and Lake Tahoe is a large state operated campground. Sunbathing, swimming, boating (plus a dock), fishing, and hiking are popular activities. Flush toilets and hot showers, but no hookups, are available. Each pine-shaded site has a picnic table and fire area.   base rate...$7
Nevada Beach Campground   *2.6 mi. N via US 50 & Elks Point Rd.*   *544-6420*
This national forest campground by Lake Tahoe is just inside Nevada. Activities include swimming, sunbathing, boating, and fishing. Flush toilets are available, but there are no showers or hookups. Each site has a picnic table and a fire area.   base rate...$5

SPECIAL EVENTS

South Lake Tahoe Winter Carnival   *in town*   *1st week of January*
This week-long event features races, games, contests, and live entertainment in a mid-winter celebration of ice and snow.

Tahoe Wild West Week   *in town*   *3rd week in June*
A draft horse pulling contest, buffalo chip throwing contest, cowboy polo, mudbath tug-of-war, haystack scramble, Wild West show, parade, and chili cook-off are some of the events in this wild and woolly week-long celebration.

OTHER INFORMATION

Area Code: *916*
Zip Code: *95705*

South Lake Tahoe Chamber of Commerce	*2 mi. SW on US 50*	*541-5255*
Eldorado National Forest Visitor Center	*8 mi. W at 870 CA 89*	*544-6420*

Tahoe City, California

Elevation:

6,253 feet

Population (1980):

1,840

Population (1970):

1,400

Location:

200 mi. NE
of San Francisco

Tahoe City is the outdoor recreation hub of the Sierra high country. It is situated in a luxuriant pine forest along the northern shore of one of the world's most beautiful high mountain lakes. Two seasons perfectly complement this splendid natural environment. Summer usually provides warm sunny days that are ideal for enjoying both Lake Tahoe, the Sierra's greatest natural attraction, and the Truckee River which flows out of the lake through town. Some of the finest sections of the lakeshore, river, and nearby mountains have been set aside for public use in an outstanding assortment of parks, forests, and wilderness areas. In town, splendid beaches attract swimmers and sunbathers; marinas offer cruises, sailing, boating, water-skiing, and fishing; and guides and equipment are available for river running. Bicycle paths, hiking trails, campgrounds, golf, and tennis facilities are also enjoyed by capacity crowds all summer. In winter, snowfalls are usually enormous. Downhill and cross-country skiing and a full range of other snow sports attract throngs to a remarkable number of major facilities in the mountains around town.

Summer resorts began to develop along the north shore of Lake Tahoe during the 1870s. In part because of its unique location at the only river outlet of the lake, Tahoe City became the terminus for a small railroad that served the lake near the turn of the century. Growth was slow until the late 1950s when major ski areas and casinos turned the Tahoe basin into a year-round attraction. Since that time, Tahoe City has become the hub for eight ski areas within a dozen miles. It is also a tranquil alternative to several substantial casinos that have opened in the Crystal Bay area fifteen miles eastward on the Nevada side of the northern lake shore. With so much to do nearby, the north shore's first downtown finally began to develop in a picturesque location near the lake in the heart of Tahoe City between the Truckee River and Tahoe State Recreation Area.

Today, this is the best defined business district on the entire lake. Several distinctive shopping complexes share a wood-toned "Tahoe style" of architecture that blends nicely with the luxuriant pine forest along the lake shore. Excellent sportswear and sporting goods stores are numerous, and there are several unusual specialty shops and galleries. Downtown is also the core of one of the West's noteworthy concentrations of gourmet restaurants. After dark, several places offer live entertainment, but nightlife is primarily oriented toward comfortable lake view lounges. Major gambling action and "name" entertainment are only a short drive away in Nevada. Lodgings are surprisingly scarce in town, but there are some luxuriously furnished lakeview units, in addition to several motels.

Tahoe City, California

WEATHER PROFILE Vokac Weather Rating

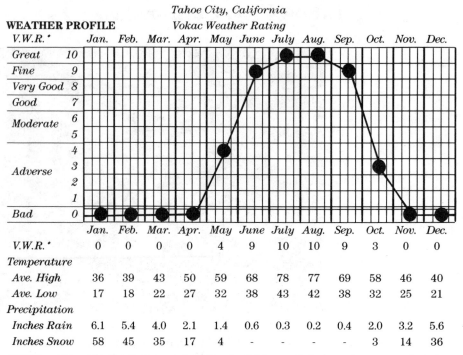

V.W.R.*		Jan.	Feb.	Mar.	Apr.	May	June	July	Aug.	Sep.	Oct.	Nov.	Dec.
Great	10							●	●				
Fine	9						●			●			
Very Good	8												
Good	7												
Moderate	6												
	5												
	4					●							
Adverse	3										●		
	2												
	1												
Bad	0	●	●	●	●							●	●

	Jan.	Feb.	Mar.	Apr.	May	June	July	Aug.	Sep.	Oct.	Nov.	Dec.
V.W.R.*	0	0	0	0	4	9	10	10	9	3	0	0
Temperature												
Ave. High	36	39	43	50	59	68	78	77	69	58	46	40
Ave. Low	17	18	22	27	32	38	43	42	38	32	25	21
Precipitation												
Inches Rain	6.1	5.4	4.0	2.1	1.4	0.6	0.3	0.2	0.4	2.0	3.2	5.6
Inches Snow	58	45	35	17	4	-	-	-	-	3	14	36

*V.W.R. = Vokac Weather Rating: probability of mild (warm & dry) weather on any given day.

Forecast

Month	V.W.R.*		Temperatures		Precipitation
			Daytime	Evening	
January	0	Bad	chilly	cold	frequent snowstorms
February	0	Bad	chilly	cold	frequent snowstorms
March	0	Bad	chilly	cold	occasional snowstorms
April	0	Bad	cool	chilly	occasional snowstorms
May	4	Adverse	cool	chilly	infrequent rainstorms/snow flurries
June	9	Fine	warm	cool	infrequent rainstorms
July	10	Great	warm	cool	negligible
August	10	Great	warm	cool	none
September	9	Fine	warm	cool	negligible
October	3	Adverse	cool	chilly	infrequent downpours/snow flurries
November	0	Bad	chilly	chilly	occasional snowstorms
December	0	Bad	chilly	cold	occasional snowstorms

Summary

On the northern shore of one of the world's most beautiful big alpine lakes at an elevation well over a mile high, Tahoe City has a climate with two remarkable seasons. **Winter** is one—cold, snowy, and perfect for almost all winter sports. Snowstorms during this season are frequent and among the heaviest in the West, which normally assures many months of quality skiing. **Spring** is a continuation of winter until May, when a short, sloppy transition gives way to mild weather after Memorial Day. **Summer** is the other outstanding season. Warm sunny days, cool evenings, and little or no rainfall are a perfect accompaniment to unlimited water and mountain sports. **Fall** is another brief transitional season. Shortly after Labor Day the area's outdoor attractions become relatively unusable as temperatures cool rapidly, and infrequent rainfalls are replaced by snowstorms that normally provide the base for outstanding skiing after Thanksgiving.

ATTRACTIONS & DIVERSIONS

Aerial Tramway
★ **Squaw Valley Tram** *8.5 mi. NW via CA 89 & Squaw Valley Rd.* 583-6985
Visitors are whisked 2,000 feet up from the valley floor to the top of one of the nearby ridges where the High Sierra provide a memorable backdrop to lunch on an outdoor view deck.

Alpine Slide
★ **Boreal Alpine Slide** *24 mi. NW via CA 89 & I-80 - Boreal exit* 426-3666
A scenic chairlift ride up a mountain is followed by more than a half mile of exciting curves and straight-aways on an alpine slide where the speed of the sled is controlled by the rider.

★ ### Bicycling
There are several miles of separated bike paths in and around town that are relatively flat, safe and scenic. Bicycles can be rented by the hour or longer at:
Basecamp's Bike Shop *downtown at 255 N. Lake Blvd.* 583-9530
Olympic Bicycle Shop *downtown at 620 N. Lake Blvd.* 583-6415

★ ### Boat Rentals
Every kind of boating imaginable is enjoyed on Lake Tahoe. Several places rent watercraft, including fishing, pleasure, ski and sail boats, canoes, kayaks or jet skis. Following are some of the more convenient:
Come Ski With Me *downtown at Tahoe Marina Lodge* 583-6292
High Sierra Boat Rental *6 mi. S at 5180 CA 89 - Homewood* 525-5589
Obexer's *6 mi. S at 5355 CA 80 - Homewood* 525-7962
Sierra Surfing (windsurfing) *downtown at 255 N. Lake Blvd.* 583-7139
Tahoe Water Adventures *downtown at 120 Grove St.* 583-3225

Boat Rides
★ **North Tahoe Cruises** *downtown at 700 N. Lake Blvd.* 583-0141
Sightseeing cruises along the north shore of Lake Tahoe aboard the fifty-passenger "Sunrunner" are offered daily. A complete cocktail and snack bar is on board.

★ ### Chimney Beach *21 mi. E off NV 28*
Swimming suits are optional at secluded, sandy beaches scattered along a shoreline of dramatic granite outcroppings. Visitors can park on dirt turnouts by the road starting 2.3 miles south of the car entrance to Sand Harbor on the lake's northeast side.

Fanny Bridge *downtown on CA 89 just S of CA 28*
Everyone looks off this bridge over the Truckee River to see big rainbow trout waiting below to snap up food that's tossed down to them. Nearby are the Lake Tahoe outlet gates which are used to control the flow of water into the Truckee River — the lake's only outlet.

Flying
★ **Cal-Vada Aircraft Inc.** *6 mi. S at 5180 CA 89 - Homewood* 525-7143
Chartered scenic sea plane rides are one unusual and exciting way to view the lake and mountains.

Gatekeeper's Cabin Museum *downtown at Truckee River outlet*
The North Lake Tahoe Historical Society has restored the cabin once used by the person who controlled the flow of water out of Lake Tahoe. It now contains historic Tahoe photos and relics. Adjacent lakeside picnic tables are beautifully located.

Golf Courses
★ **Incline Golf Course** *15 mi. NE via CA 28 at 955 Fairway Dr.* (702)832-1141
This beautifully landscaped 18-hole championship golf course was designed by Robert Trent Jones. It is open to the public and offers all facilities and services.
Tahoe City Golf Course *downtown at 215 N. Lake Blvd.* 583-1516
Conveniently located downtown, this relatively level pine-studded 9-hole golf course is open to the public. There is also a putting green, bar, and restaurant.

★ ### Hiking
Basecamp *downtown at 255 N. Lake Blvd.* 583-5306
The U.S. Forest Service and the State Parks Department maintain miles of scenic hiking trails near town. Maps, information, and backpack and tent rentals are available here.

★ **Horseback Riding**
Several stables in the area rent horses by the hour or longer for guided trail rides. Pack trips can also be arranged. The nearest stables are:

Alpine Meadows Stables   *5 mi. NW via CA 89 on Alpine Meadows Rd.*   *583-3905*
Squaw Valley Stables   *8 mi NW via CA 89 at 1525 Squaw Valley Rd.*   *583-0419*

★ **Lake Tahoe**   *the eastern border of town*
One of the world's most beautiful lakes straddles the California/Nevada border 6,229 feet above sea level. This water wonderland is twenty-two miles long, twelve miles wide, and as much as 1,645 feet deep. In spite of massive development along the shoreline, it is said that the lake is still so clear that a white dinner plate can be seen at a depth of almost two hundred feet. A splendid assortment of recreation facilities contributes to the appeal of forests, streams, river, sandy beaches, and dramatic bouldered coves that surround the mountain-rimmed lake. Even though the maximum water temperature normally only reaches 68°F, swimming is popular on warm summer days. A seventy-two-mile highway loop around the lake is immodestly described as "The Most Beautiful Drive in America." Visitors can judge for themselves using a free map and guide describing eighteen points of interest along the route — available at the Chamber of Commerce.

★ **Library**   *downtown at 740 N. Lake Blvd.*   *583-3382*
The Placer County Branch Library is in a contemporary building with a large working fireplace and comfortable reading chairs near lake-view windows. When the weather is pleasant, outdoor lake-view seating is also provided.

★ **River Running**
The Truckee River offers some small rapids and scenic calm stretches through a beautiful pine forest for almost four miles below the Lake Tahoe outlet in town. You can do-it-yourself with rental equipment and transportation provided by Truckee River Raft Rentals, or leave everything to Mountain Air Sports for a two-hour float.

Mountain Air Sports   *.3 mi. W at 255 CA 89*   *583-5606*
Truckee River Raft Rentals   *.3 mi. W at 185 CA 89*   *583-9724*

★ **Sportfishing**
Trout and kokanee salmon fishing can be excellent on Lake Tahoe and the Truckee River. Professional guides have charter sportfishing boats and the latest in fishing equipment to improve visitors' luck year-round.

Hooker for Hire   *downtown*   *525-5654*
King Fish Guide Service   *downtown*   *583-0350*
Mickey's Guide Service   *downtown*   *583-4602*

★ **Sugar Pine Point State Park**   *10 mi. S on CA 89*   *525-7982*
In a dense forest of sugar pines, this very popular park offers delightful beaches for swimming and sunbathing, plus picnic sites, hiking trails, and camping in summer. The imposing Ehrman Mansion, the former vacation residence of a wealthy San Francisco family, is now an interpretive center and museum with Tahoe memorabilia. In winter, cross-country skiing, snowshoeing, and winter camping attract visitors.

★ **Tahoe City Public Beach**   *downtown*
Adjacent to the business district is a photogenic, pine-shaded sandy beach where swimming and sunbathing are enormously popular in summer.

★ **Tahoe State Recreation Area**   *.3 mi. N on CA 28*   *583-3074*
The little beach is nearly always crowded in summer, as is the adjacent campground because of the pine-forested lakefront location adjacent to the north end of the business district.

Winter Sports
★ **Skiing**
With eight downhill ski areas within a dozen miles of town, this is one of the most thoroughly developed ski regions in the world. In addition, cross-country ski touring centers are numerous. The attraction is the awesome snowpack each winter and breathtakingly beautiful mountain and lake scenery. Ski equipment rentals, sales, maps and information can be obtained at any of the ski areas or from several sporting goods stores downtown.

Sleigh Rides
    Squaw Valley Stables   *8 mi. NW via CA 89 at 1525 Squaw Valley Rd.*   *583-0419*
Sleigh rides can be arranged here any day in winter.

★   **Snowmobiles**
    Tahoe City Recreation Area   *downtown at 251 N. Lake Blvd.*   *583-1516*
In winter, the downtown golf course becomes part of a recreation area where snowmobiles can be rented by the hour or half hour.

★   **Snow Play Area**
    Granlibakken   *1.5 mi. SW via CA 89 on Tonopah Dr.*   *583-4242*
A rope tow and poma lift take beginner skiers up a gentle slope at the oldest established ski resort by Lake Tahoe. Sled runs, and rentals, are also provided.

★   **Squaw Valley Ski Area**   *8 mi. NW off CA 89 on Squaw Valley Rd.*   *583-5585*
The site of the 1960 Winter Olympics is the largest downhill ski area in north Tahoe. This world-class complex has an outstanding variety of downhill slopes. The vertical drop of 2,700 feet is served by twenty-five lifts, including an aerial tram, gondola, and three triple chairs. There is also a major cross-country ski center. All rentals and services are provided along with restaurants, bars, and lodging at the base. A major new alpine village is under construction and a plush resort hotel opened in 1983.

★   **Tahoe Nordic Ski Area**   *2.5 mi. NE via CA 28 at 925 Country Club Dr.*   *583-9858*
More than twenty miles of groomed trails provide spectacular views of Lake Tahoe from pine-forested slopes and brilliant meadows. Rentals, lessons, guided tours (both day and moonlight), and a day lodge are at the area.

SHOPPING
Several architecturally distinctive shopping complexes built in recent years have given the town an unusual lakefront business district. Excellent sporting goods stores and several fine art galleries are especially worth discovering.

Food Specialties
The Cork & More   *downtown at 760 N. Lake Blvd.*   *583-2675*
An impressive collection of California premium wines is complemented by regular wine tastings and gourmet deli items in an upstairs shop at the Boatworks Mall.

★ **Gourmet Chalet**   *downtown at 521 N. Lake Blvd.*   *583-2292*
A large selection of well-stored wines, plus a variety of cheeses, coffees, teas, and other gourmet items are sold. An adjoining deli/sandwich shop also offers wine by the glass.

Pennypacker's   *downtown at 760 N. Lake Blvd.*   *583-1315*
An inviting assortment of cookies and candies are made here.

Tahoe City Bakery   *downtown at 954 N. Lake Blvd.*   *583-3068*
A traditional line of pastries and breads is served to go, or at a few coffee tables.

Specialty Shops
★ **The Boatworks Shopping Mall**   *downtown at 760 N. Lake Blvd.*   *583-1488*
A two-level, enclosed structure of natural wood design by the lake features dozens of shops, several restaurants, and fine lake and mountain views.

★ **Cobblestone Antiques**   *downtown at 475 N. Lake Blvd.*   *583-9143*
A fascinating collection of pre-electric slot machines is displayed. They are for sale to residents of the thirty-four states where it is legal to have one of these antiques in your home. Beautifully restored antique pot-bellied stoves are another specialty.

★ **The Cobblestone Center**   *downtown at 475 N. Lake Blvd.*
This small shopping complex sports a Tyrolean motif, complete with a clock tower.It has several interesting specialty shops.

The Roundhouse   *downtown next to the Boatworks*
A refurbished turn-of-the-century roundhouse by the lake is now an enclosed shopping mall with specialty shops and restaurants.

NIGHTLIFE
Entertainment in Tahoe City is sedate when compared to the action at the nearby state line. In town the best places for a quiet drink or live entertainment also feature tranquil views of Lake Tahoe. Meanwhile, only a dozen miles away, elaborate casinos on the Nevada side of the north shore offer non-stop gambling and all kinds of live entertainment in cavernous showrooms and glitzy lounges.

★ **Cloud's Cal-Neva**   *11 mi. NE on CA 28 - Crystal Bay*   *(702)832-4000*
This big, modern Las Vegas-style casino offers a variety of live entertainment in the
showroom and lounge, and provides constant gambling action.
Crystal Bay Club   *11 mi. NE on CA 28 - Crystal Bay*   *(702)831-0512*
A variety of live entertainment is offered nightly in the lounge of this casino.
★ **Gatsby's**   *downtown at 850 N. Lake Blvd.*   *583-5131*
A sleek new lounge in the Lighthouse Center offers live entertainment on weekends and
a view of the lake. The room is comfortably outfitted with sofas and armchairs and a
dramatic fireplace. Light meals are also served.
★ **Hyatt Lake Tahoe**   *15 mi. NE via CA 29 - Incline Village*   *(702)831-1111*
The north shore's largest hotel and casino occasionally features "big name" entertainment
in a large and luxurious showroom.
★ **Jake's on the Lake**   *downtown at 780 N. Lake Blvd.*   *583-0188*
Great views both inside and out on the deck are the main attraction of this contemporary
bar/restaurant. It's a popular place to relax over a drink and watch the boats come and
go at the docks below.
Nevada Lodge   *11 mi. NE on CA 29 - Crystal Bay*   *(702)831-0660*
The large casino and nightly live entertainment in the theater/restaurant attract crowds
to this modern facility.
★ **Ric's Lounge**   *downtown at 395 N. Lake Blvd.*   *583-1835*
Pool tables, shuffleboard, and a darts room fit comfortably into a handsome new wood-
toned bar with lots of plants and stained glass.
Sunnyside Resort   *2.7 mi. S on CA 89 at 1850 W. Lake Blvd.*   *583-4226*
Live entertainment and dancing are offered every weekend in a big, casual lounge with a
lake view.
Tahoe House Lounge   *.8 mi. S on CA 89 at 625 W. Lake Blvd.*   *583-1377*
An iron fireplace and an unusual tree trunk view are part of the decor in a cozy lounge
well outfitted with sofas and armchairs.
Victoria Station   *downtown at 425 N. Lake Blvd.*   *583-6939*
Live entertainment and dancing are offered most weekends in a big casual bar. One area
has plush sofas, and an enclosed porch offers views of the lake across the highway. A large
contemporary railroad-theme restaurant adjoins.

RESTAURANTS
In recent years, Tahoe City has become the center of a major concentration of fine
restaurants. Several feature both gourmet cuisine and wonderful views of the lake and
mountains. Rustic Tahoe-style natural wood decor predominates, but formally elegant
dining is also available.
Bacchi's Inn   *2 mi. NE at 2905 Lake Forest Rd.*   *583-3324*
D only.   *Moderate*
Italian family-style dinners, including appetizers, soup, salad, entrees, and pasta have
been served in this big old-fashioned restaurant for more than fifty years.
★ **Bon Vivant**   *8 mi. NE on CA 29 at 7046 N. Lake Blvd.*   *546-5903*
D only. Closed Mon. in fall & spring.   *Expensive*
Highly regarded French cuisine is featured in a gracious old lakeside building. A massive
flagstone fireplace houses a Franklin fireplace in winter and a tiny recirculating waterfall
in summer. Many of the beautifully appointed, closely spaced tables have good views of
Lake Tahoe. A lakeside deck is also used in summer.
The Bridge Tender   *downtown on CA 89 at 30 W. Lake Blvd.*   *583-3342*
L-D.   *Moderate*
Casual fare is served amidst classic Tahoe decor — rough beams, wood floors, a rock wall,
an iron fireplace, and lots of plants. The adjoining patio has a delightful view of the
Truckee River and Fanny Bridge.
Cafe Cobblestone   *downtown at 475 N. Lake Blvd.*   *583-2111*
B-L-D.   *Moderate*
A contemporary cafe menu is offered in a new restaurant with a Bavarian flair. Both the
dining room and an inviting outdoor patio have lake views across the highway.

★ **Captain Jon's**   *8.2 mi. NE on CA 28 at 7220 N. Lake Blvd.*   *546-4819*
L-D. Closed Mon. in winter.   *Expensive*
Unusual seafood dishes highlight Continental specialties served in intimate, plush dining areas. A spectacular view lounge was recently added over the lake.

Carnelian House   *5.2 mi. NE on CA 28 at 5000 N. Lake Blvd.*   *546-5954*
D only. Closed Mon.   *Moderate*
Continental dishes are accompanied by lake views from every table in a large, dark-toned dinner house. A grand piano, fireplace, and lakeside views distinguish the adjoining lounge.

Chart House   *downtown at 700 N. Lake Blvd.*   *583-0233*
D only.   *Moderate*
Steaks and prime rib are specialties in a large, attractively furnished dining room with a shoreline view of the marina, lake, and mountains. A big, comfortable lounge shares space in a historic roundhouse.

★ **The Christy Hill Inn**   *8 mi. NW via CA 89 at 1650 Squaw Valley Rd.*   *583-8551*
B-L-D. Closed Tues.   *Moderate*
Exciting New California cuisine skillfully prepared with the freshest available ingredients is the highlight of an informally elegant firelit dining room overlooking Squaw Valley.

Clementine's   *3 mi. S on CA 89 at 2255 W. Lake Blvd.*   *583-3134*
D only. Sun. brunch.   *Low*
Hearty homestyle specialties are offered in a casual and popular old landmark with three stone fireplaces, rustic beam ceilings, and knotty-pine walls. There are also patios for outdoor dining in summer, and a bar with a fireplace.

★ **The Creekside**   *9 mi. NW via CA 89 at the W end of Squaw Valley Rd.*   *583-1501*
D only.   *Moderate*
In the Olympic Village Inn, New California cuisine is presented in an intimate, opulent dining room. This strikingly contemporary showplace also has picture window views of the new resort's distinctive water gardens and famed ski mountains.

★ **Fire Sign Cafe**   *2.5 mi. S at 1785 W. Lake Blvd.*   *583-0871*
B-L.   *Moderate*
Delicious fresh baked breads, pastries, and desserts complement light, homestyle meals served amidst antique furnishings in a fireside atmosphere.

Honkers Bar & Grill   *downtown at 640 N. Lake Blvd.*   *583-5700*
L-D.   *Moderate*
Marinated rabbit and roast duckling with blueberries are among the distinctive dishes listed on a contemporary menu. Fresh flowers, crisp linens, and armchairs enhance the cheerful, congested dining room. Lake Tahoe can be viewed through the trees from the dining room, bar, or deck of this well-liked new restaurant.

Jake's on the Lake   *downtown at 780 N. Lake Blvd.*   *583-0188*
L (summer only)-D.   *Moderate*
American dishes accompany a splendid lakefront view from contemporary wood-toned dining rooms. The stylish bar also has a terrific view.

Lakehouse Omelette Co.   *downtown at 600 N. Lake Blvd.*   *583-2225*
B-L.   *Moderate*
All kinds of omelets are offered in an upstairs dining room with a fine lakefront view.

La Vieille Maison   *16 mi. N on CA 267 at E. River - Truckee*   *587-2421*
D only. Closed Mon.-Tues.   *Very Expensive*
Robust French cuisine with a garlic accent is presented fixe prix amidst charming, intimate atmosphere.

★ **Le Petit Pier**   *8.2 mi. NE on CA 288 at 7252 N. Lake Blvd.*   *546-4464*
D only. Closed Tues.   *Expensive*
Acclaimed French cuisine is served in the congested elegance of a French provincial-style dinner house. Window tables in tiny indoor rooms or on a heated deck have splendid lakefront views.

★ **Marina Creperie**   *downtown at 780 N. Lake Blvd.*   *583-0051*
B-L-D.   Moderate
Highlights include a limited selection of carefully prepared crepes (the Sunrise Crepe is superb), sauces and soups, and delicious homemade pastries. The casual dining room overlooks the marina through giant portholes. An inviting wood deck is used for outdoor summer dining.

Offshore Bar & Grill   *downtown at 550 N. Lake Blvd.*   *583-4550*
L-D.   Moderate
A varied menu of American fare is offered amid pleasant nautical atmosphere in an upstairs dining room with fine lake views shared by a bar and a cozy dining deck.

Pfeifer House   *.8 mi. W at 760 River Rd.*   *583-3102*
D only. Closed Tues.   Moderate
Middle European specialties are the feature of this inviting alpine-style dinner house.

★ **Ric's Restaurant**   *downtown at 395 N. Lake Blvd.*   *583-1835*
L-D. Closed Sun.   Moderate
Delicious seafoods are complemented by homemade soups, sauces, and salad dressings and given a creative light touch in a tiny, tucked-away dining room with informally elegant, modern decor.

River Ranch   *4 mi. NW on CA 89*   *583-4264*
D only.   Moderate
A good selection of American entrees is served in several small, well-furnished dining rooms with a two-sided fireplace and river and forest views. The pine-shaded terrace overlooking rapids of the Truckee River is used for luncheon barbecues. A circular lounge has live entertainment most nights, and great river views.

★ **Rosie's Cafe**   *downtown at 571 N. Lake Blvd.*   *583-8504*
B-L-D. No D on Mon. & Tues. in winter.   Moderate
Delicious breakfasts are served with freshly made bagels or sopaipillas. Attention to details and skillful cooking make lunch or dinner special, too. The dining room/bar is a study in casual "old Tahoe" decor, with wooden floorboards, a big, brick see-through fireplace, many hanging plants, some etchings over the bar, and honey and blackberry jam dishes gracing simple table settings. Several tables are also used on the porch when weather permits.

Swiss Lakewood Lodge   *6 mi. S on CA 89 at 5055 W. Lake Blvd.*   *525-5211*
D only. Closed Mon.   Expensive
Gourmet Continental and Swiss specialties are served in an attractive dining room.

Tahoe House   *.8 mi. S at 625 W. Lake Blvd.*   *583-1377*
D only. Closed Mon.   Moderate
Swiss and Continental specialties are featured. A natural stone fireplace and stained glass lend distinction to comfortably furnished dining rooms. An intimate fireside lounge adjoins.

★ **Water Wheel**   *downtown at 115 W. Lake Blvd.*   *583-4404*
D only. Closed Mon.   Moderate
Carefully prepared Szechwan dishes are presented at tables set with crisp linens in an intimate firelit dining room that incorporates both Oriental and Western touches. A picturesque riverside deck is also used when weather permits.

★ **Wolfdale's**   *6.2 mi. S on CA 89 at 5335 W. Lake Blvd.*   *525-7833*
D only. Closed Mon.-Tues.   Moderate
The international menu changes daily, depending on what's freshest. Everything is prepared from scratch and all pastries and breads are homemade. The country decor in the intimate dining room is eclectic and sophisticated.

LODGING

There aren't a lot of accommodations in town, but they are distinctive. Several large hotel/casinos are on the Nevada side of the state line starting twelve miles northeast, and numerous motels are concentrated along CA 28 in Tahoe Vista and Kings Beach between seven and twelve miles northeast of town. Bargains and vacancies are scarce during summer, but rates are usually at least 20% less in spring and fall.

★ **Fantasy Inn III**   *downtown at 790 N. Lake Blvd.*   *583-8578*
The indulgent decor of this modern motel is remarkably popular with adult visitors interested in something truly different than they have back home. Rooms in bold red, brown, or blue decor are outfitted with closed-circuit TV and X-rated movies, phones, stereo radios, and carpet and mirrors everywhere — even on the walls and ceiling.
#32 "Blue Suite" — in-room heart-shaped whirlpool, heart-shaped   waterbed...$90
deluxe room — in-room raised whirlpool,   K waterbed...$84
regular room —   K waterbed...$70

Lake Pines Motel   *1.8 mi. NE at 2815 Lake Forest Rd.*   *583-3209*
Bargain housekeeping and sleeping cottages are available in a quiet forested setting two blocks from a beach. Each of the modest, nicely maintained little units has cable color TV.
regular room — cottage,   2 T or D bed...$25

Mayfield House   *downtown at 236 Grove St.*   *583-1001*
A charming older home has been attractively converted into a bed-and-breakfast inn a block from the downtown beach. Each room is beautifully furnished and shares a bath. A Continental breakfast and afternoon wine are complimentary.
"Mayfield" — spacious,   K bed...$75
"Julia" — spacious,   K bed...$65
·regular room —   Q bed...$55

★ **Olympic Village Inn**   *9 mi. NW via CA 89 at W end of Squaw Valley Rd.*   *583-1501*
A large new resort hotel was recently completed as the first phase for a whole new alpine village at the base of the ski lifts. Amenities in the spectacular showplace include an unusual "water garden" with hot tubs nestled amidst wildflowers by a meandering stream. A waterfall tumbles from fanciful boulders into a large outdoor pool. Horseback riding and tennis are offered (for a fee). Inside, an enormous lobby-and-more is distinguished by state-of-the-art decor. The lounge and the intimate, ultra-toney dining room are perfect for a luxurious mountain resort. Each beautifully furnished one-bedroom suite has a phone, cable color TV, kitchenette with a microwave oven, and a private garden/ mountain view balcony. Winter rates are approximately twice the quoted summer rates.
regular room — 1 BR suite,   Q bed...$95

★ **Peppertree Inn**   *downtown at 645 N. Lake Blvd.*   *583-3711*
This modern seven-floor motor lodge offers good lake views from upper floors. The public beach is across the highway. There is an outdoor pool (covered in winter). Each spacious room has a phone and color TV.
#701,#704,#705 — lake view beyond public walkway,   Q bed...$47
regular room —   Q bed...$47

River Ranch   *4 mi. NW on CA 89 at Alpine Meadows Rd.*   *583-4264*
A scenic restaurant, lounge, and dining terrace by the Truckee River are features of this refurbished lodge. Each room is nicely furnished with some antiques, a phone, and cable color TV with movies.
#26 — spacious, corner, fine river view windows, 2 pvt. balcs.,   K bed...$55
#23 — spacious, corner, fine river view windows, 2 pvt. decks,   Q bed...$55
#1,#2 — next to river rapids,   Q bed...$55
regular room —   Q bed...$55

Tahoe City Travelodge   *downtown at 455 N. Lake Blvd.*   *583-3766*
Only steps away from the beach and golf course in the center of town is a modern motel with a heated pool. Each spacious room has a cable color TV and phone.
#224,#217 — pvt. view of golf course,   Q bed...$67
regular room —   Q bed...$64

★ **Tahoe Marina Lodge**   *downtown at 270 N. Lake Blvd.*   *583-2365*
This contemporary Western-style condominium lodge is perfectly sited by Lake Tahoe and the Truckee River outlet. Well-landscaped grounds include a peaceful private sandy beach, a pier, tennis courts, and a large scenic outdoor pool. Each well-furnished unit has a cable color TV, phone, kitchen, private deck and/or patio, and a native-stone fireplace.
#37 thru #40 — 2 BR, pvt. beachfront view, 2 T beds in loft,   Q bed...$120
#1 — 1 BR, fine lake view,   Q bed...$85
regular room — 1 BR, garden view,   Q bed...$85

Tamarack Lodge Motel   *1.2 mi. NE on CA 28 at 2311 N. Lake Blvd.*   *583-3350*
Off the highway in the pines a stroll from the beach is an older one-level **bargain** motel
with a newer two-story addition. Each unit has a knotty-pine interior and cable B/W TV.
#32 — spacious, kit., partial lake view,   K bed...$34
regular room — older motel room,   Q bed...$24

CAMPGROUNDS

One picturesque campground by Lake Tahoe is a stroll from downtown. Two other
lakeside campgrounds are only a few miles from town.

★ **Lake Forest Campground**   *3 mi. NE via CA 28 on Edgewater Dr.*   *583-5544*
This small campground has a pine-shaded site by Lake Tahoe. Swimming, sunbathing,
boating, fishing, hiking, and bicycling are popular activities. Flush toilets, showers, and
hookups are available. Each site has a picnic table and a fire area.   base rate...$5

★ **Sugar Pine Point State Park**   *10 mi. S on CA 89*   *525-7982*
The State of California operates this large campground in a spectacularly scenic, pine-
forested location by Lake Tahoe. A sandy beach for swimming and sunbathing, boat dock,
hiking trails, tennis courts, and the Ehrman Mansion Visitor Center are features. Flush
toilets, hot showers, and hookups are available. Each pine-shaded site has a picnic table
and fire area.   base rate...$7

★ **Tahoe State Recreation Area**   *.3 mi. NE on CA 28*   *583-3074*
This state operated campground has an ideal location by the lake on the north side of
town. Swimming, boating, pier fishing, and bicycling on nearby paths are popular
activities. Flush toilets and hot showers are available, but there are no hookups. Each
pine-shaded site has a picnic table, fire ring, raised grill, and a storage cabinet. Some sites
also have a view of the lake.   base rate...$7

SPECIAL EVENT

Oktoberfest   *downtown*   *4th weekend in October*
Fall colors coincide with a fun-filled Oktoberfest — complete with a "battle of the bands"
music festival, dancing, food and drink.

OTHER INFORMATION

Area Code: *916*
Zip Code: *95730*
North Lake Tahoe Chamber of Commerce *downtown at 950 N. Lake Blvd.*   *583-2371*
U.S. Forest Service   *2 mi. S on CA 89 at William Kent Campground*   *583-3642*

Aspen, Colorado

Elevation:

7,907 feet

Population (1980):

3,678

Population (1970):

2,437

Location:

160 mi. SW
of Denver

Aspen is the heart of the Colorado Rockies. Romantic, festive, and historically aware, it is a year-round celebration of urbane and earthly pleasures. The town is located in a high, mountain-rimmed valley where long cold winters usually produce enough powder snow to delight hordes of winter sports enthusiasts from around the world. Flanked by several mountains covered with a phenomenal assortment of ski slopes, including one that ends abruptly downtown, Aspen is America's preeminent ski town. All of the fine weather for the year is concentrated in summer, and the town again hosts crowds of visitors. Pine-forested mountains, rivers, and streams extending in every direction easily accommodate all who pursue the physical pleasure of outdoor activities in natural settings. In town, well-tended parks, golf courses, tennis and swimming complexes, and miles of bicycle paths compete with a splendid array of shops and the famed summer music festival for the attention of visitors. Spring and fall, between the popular seasons, offer uncrowded tranquility. For those lucky enough to witness mountain slopes ablaze with brilliant yellow and red aspen leaves, fall can be unforgettable.

In 1879, prospectors found silver on the slopes of Aspen Mountain. Within a decade, the town boasted 15,000 inhabitants. Silver mines which dotted the mountain worked fabulously rich veins. One mine produced a single nugget of nearly pure silver that weighed almost one ton. In 1893, the government repealed the Sherman Act, and silver was no longer the support of American currency. Suddenly, the mining town lost its market. Mines and shops closed, banks failed, and the population collapsed. There were only about 700 residents in the late 1930s when a modest ski area was established in town on the advice of a Swiss mountain expert. When the Aspen Institute for Humanistic Studies was founded in 1949 by a Chicago industrialist committed to the arts, the basis for the second boom was in place. Just as Aspen had been in the forefront of the silver mining era, so it became a leader in a new era oriented toward physical and intellectual pleasure.

Today, the town is alive with the sound of music all summer, thanks to the renowned music festival. Mill structures and tailings have been replaced by condominiums and ski slopes, and landmarks from the Victorian era have been carefully preserved and recycled for contemporary uses. Pedestrian malls, fountains, parks, and landscaping have been added, and overhead utility wires are being removed. These developments have been complemented by a proliferation of inviting shops and galleries, as well as one of the West's most bedazzling concentrations of gourmet restaurants and plush nightlife. Numerous contemporary accommodations ranging from plain to opulent are within strolling distance of the heart of town.

Aspen, Colorado

WEATHER PROFILE — *Vokac Weather Rating*

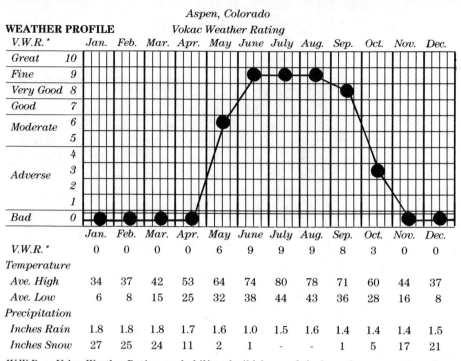

V.W.R.*		Jan.	Feb.	Mar.	Apr.	May	June	July	Aug.	Sep.	Oct.	Nov.	Dec.
Great	10												
Fine	9												
Very Good	8												
Good	7												
Moderate	6												
	5												
	4												
Adverse	3												
	2												
	1												
Bad	0												

	Jan.	Feb.	Mar.	Apr.	May	June	July	Aug.	Sep.	Oct.	Nov.	Dec.
V.W.R.*	0	0	0	0	6	9	9	9	8	3	0	0
Temperature												
Ave. High	34	37	42	53	64	74	80	78	71	60	44	37
Ave. Low	6	8	15	25	32	38	44	43	36	28	16	8
Precipitation												
Inches Rain	1.8	1.8	1.8	1.7	1.6	1.0	1.5	1.6	1.4	1.4	1.4	1.5
Inches Snow	27	25	24	11	2	1	-	-	1	5	17	21

*V.W.R. = Vokac Weather Rating: probability of mild (warm & dry) weather on any given day.

Forecast

Month	V.W.R.*		Temperatures		Precipitation
			Daytime	Evening	
January	0	Bad	chilly	frigid	frequent snowstorms
February	0	Bad	chilly	frigid	occasional snowstorms
March	0	Bad	chilly	cold	occasional snowstorms
April	0	Bad	cool	chilly	frequent snow flurries/showers
May	6	Moderate	cool	chilly	occasional showers/snow flurries
June	9	Fine	warm	cool	infrequent rainstorms
July	9	Fine	warm	cool	frequent showers
August	9	Fine	warm	cool	frequent showers
September	8	Very Good	warm	cool	occasional showers
October	3	Adverse	cool	chilly	occasional showers/snow flurries
November	0	Bad	chilly	cold	infrequent snowstorms
December	0	Bad	chilly	frigid	frequent snowstorms

Summary

Spectacularly located in a beautiful valley high in the central Colorado Rockies, Aspen normally has a long **winter**. Daytime temperatures are chilly, it is extremely cold by evening, and there are frequent snowstorms. These conditions generate the legendary deep powder snow that attracts properly-dressed winter enthusiasts from all over the world to the renowned skiing complexes in town and nearby. **Spring** is an extension of winter, with excellent skiing into April. As the season progresses, snowstorms are gradually replaced by showers that turn snow to slush and then mud, as the ground thaws. In **summer**, the alpine grandeur around town can be comfortably explored during warm days and cool evenings which are frequently disrupted by minor thundershowers. The brisk sunny days of early **fall** normally accompany wonderful displays of color in surrounding aspen forests. After Halloween, heavy snowstorms once again transform the area into a winter wonderland.

ATTRACTIONS & DIVERSIONS

Aerial Tramway

★ **Sky Ride at Aspen Highlands** *1.5 mi. W via CO 82 & Maroon Cr. Rd.* *925-5300*
A smooth chairlift ride to the top of a nearby mountain offers magnificent high country panoramas all summer.

Aspen Center for Env. Studies *.4 mi. N at 100 E. Puppy Smith Rd.* *925-5756*
Historic photographic exhibits and a library on current environmental concerns plus a gift shop are open to the public in a barn studio next to tranquil little Hallam Lake. Resident naturalists hold classes and guide hikes. Closed Sat.-Sun.

★ **Bicycling**
Miles of paved separated bikeways, and secondary roads in and around town, offer rewarding scenic jaunts. Several places rent bicycles, including:

Aspen Sports	*downtown at 408 E. Cooper Av.*	*925-6331*
Hub of Aspen	*downtown at 315 E. Hyman Av.*	*925-7970*
Sabbatini's	*downtown at 434 E. Cooper Av.*	*920-1180*
Sherpa Sports	*downtown at 720 E. Durant Av.*	*925-1977*

★ **Carriage Rides** *downtown on Hyman Av. next to Aspen Drug*
Antique horse-drawn carriages take passengers around town and through neighborhoods of beautifully restored Victorian homes every day in summer.

Climbing

★ **Rocky Mountain Climbing School** *downtown at 300 S. Mill St.* *925-2849*
Technical climbing gear and information, plus instruction in rope handling, belaying, descending techniques and safety are provided. Beginners are given a chance to put climbing fundamentals to use on some of the faces and peaks near town.

★ **Flying** *4 mi. W on CO 82 at Aspen Airport*
The West's most remarkable assortment of commercial flying machines offers thrilling overviews of the magnificent central Rockies. Adventurous visitors can reserve experiences ranging from a sublime champagne flight in a balloon to a thrilling barnstorming cruise in a two-seater biplane. All flights leave from the Aspen Airport. For information, contact:

Aspen Barnstorming Co.	(biplane)	*925-3331*
Gliders of Aspen Inc.	(glider)	*925-3418*
Murnane Aviation	(scenic)	*925-5589*
Tailwinds, Ltd.	(scenic)	*925-7510*
Unicorn Balloon Company	(balloon)	*925-5752*

★ **The Fountain** *downtown at Hyman Av./Mill St.*
It looks just like an iron grate sunk into a street when it's not operating. But when it is, the row of dancing water spouts of this computer-programmed fountain delight everyone. Many first-timers (and others) feel compelled to dash through. Only the spry stay dry.

Golf

★ **Aspen Championship Golf Course** *1 mi. W at 22475 CO 82* *925-2145*
This spectacularly scenic, relatively level 18-hole golf course is open to the public. Facilities include a pro shop, driving range, club and cart rentals, restaurant and lounge.

★ **The Grottos** *6 mi. SE on CO 82*
Natural pools have been carved in the boulder-strewn bed of the Roaring Fork River. Sunbathers and swimmers flock here on hot summer days. The pine-studded rock garden is also popular for picnics, hiking and boulder hopping. Paths extend to the river from a parking area at the end of a dirt road on the south side of the highway near the Weller Campground.

★ **Horseback Riding**
Several stables surrounded by miles of alpine trails rent horses by the hour, half day or full day. They will also arrange extended pack trips like the fabulous two-day trip to Crested Butte at the height of fall colors. Breakfast or dinner rides, and hayrides with entertainment, can also be arranged. For information and reservations, contact:

Heatherbed Stables	*3 mi. SW via CO 82 at 1679 Maroon Cr. Rd.*	*925-6987*
Pomegranite Stables	*2 mi. W on CO 82*	*925-2700*
Red Mountain Horse Center	*1 mi. N at 1428 Red Mt. Rd.*	*925-9287*
T-Lazy-7 Ranch	*4.8 mi. SW at 3129 Maroon Creek Rd.*	*925-7040*

★ **Independence Pass**   *35 mi. SE on CO 82*
The scenic eastern route into town taken by early silver prospectors is now a paved, frighteningly narrow highway that crosses the Continental Divide at 12,095 feet. Literally breathtaking panoramas abound. The road is only open from June through October.

★ **Jeep Tours**
Guided half day or full day trips provide access to old mining ghost towns and magnificent scenery on the high mountains around town throughout summer and fall. Arrangements can be made at:

Roaring Fork Jeep Rentals (daily rental) *4 mi. W at 20292 CO 82-Airport* 925-8574
Snowmass Jeep Tours   *12 mi. W at 45 Village Sq. - Snowmass*   923-4544

★ **Library**   *downtown at 120 E. Main St.*   925-7124
The Pitkin County Library includes a large, well-furnished periodical reading area with a mountain view. A special music room is equipped with headsets and a notable collection of records and tapes from earlier Music Festival performances.

★ **Marble Quarry**   *60 mi. SW via CO 82, CO 133, and a dirt road*
Marble used in the Lincoln Memorial and the Tomb of the Unknown Soldier in Washington, D.C. was quarried above the near-ghost-town of Marble. The awesome quarry is well worth the steep hike up several miles of jeep trail. The highway from Aspen to Marble via the Roaring Fork, Crystal and East River Valleys is one of the most spectacular in the West. Halfway along the Crystal River in the tiny town of Redstone, the landmark Redstone Inn has recently been restored. The large, authentically refurbished restaurant and lounge are handsome reflections of an illustrious Victorian heritage.

★ **Maroon Bells**   *10 mi. S off CO 82*
These two deep purple bell-shaped peaks (both over 14,000 feet high) are probably the most photographed mountains in Colorado. There are scenic hiking trails around a small foreground lake and delightful picnic sites. The road is closed in winter. From mid-July to Labor Day, no private vehicles are allowed, but buses leave from Aspen Highlands Ski Area many times daily. (Call 925-2020 for more information.)

★ **River Running**
Several services specialize in half day, full day, or overnight rafting trips down the Roaring Fork River near town, and on the nearby Colorado and Arkansas Rivers, from June through August. All equipment and meals are provided for scenic, fishing, or whitewater trips. For more information contact:

Aspen Watersports Center   *downtown at 611 E. Durant Av.*   925-8299
Aspen Whitewater Adventures   *downtown at 403 S. Galena St.*   925-5730
Blazing Paddles   *downtown at Mill St./Hyman Av.*   925-5652
River Rats Inc.   *downtown at S. Mill St./Cooper Av.*   925-7648

Warm Water Features

★   **Conundrum Hot Springs**   *6.5 mi. to trailhead via CO 82 & Castle Cr. Rd.*
Idyllic rock pools overflowing with natural hot mineral water are surrounded by solemn grandeur 11,200 feet above sea level. Swimming suits are optional in these blissful bathtubs reached by a steep, well-marked trail that parallels Conundrum Creek for eight miles. The trailhead is at the end of about two miles of a rough dirt side road that crosses Castle Creek to the right off of Castle Creek Road about five miles from town.

★   **Glenwood Hot Springs**   *43 mi. NW via CO 82 - Glenwood Springs*   945-7131
The world's largest outdoor hot springs pool (more than 400 feet long) is backed by an authentic Gay 90s spa lodge. An adjoining hot water soaking pool is outfitted with some unusual jet chairs, and a looping tubular water slide was recently added above a grassy slope by the main pool. Visitors are also drawn to a small adjoining health center where hot mineral water and steam emerge into vapor caves in a cliff behind the building. The eerie tranquility of these natural steam baths has made them one of the West's most durable and different attractions.

Winter Sports

★   **Aspen Highlands**   *3 mi. W via CO 82 & Maroon Cr. Rd.*   925-5300
The vertical rise is 3,800 feet and the longest run is 3.5 miles. Elevation at the top is 11,800 feet. There are eight chairlifts. All facilities, services and rentals are available at the base for downhill skiing. There are a few bars and restaurants at the base and three lodges within walking distance. The ski season extends from late November to mid-April .

★ **Aspen Mountain**　　*downtown at S end of Monarch St.*　　925-1220
The vertical rise is 3,370 feet and the longest run is more than three miles. Elevation at the top is 11,212 feet. There are seven chairlifts. All facilities, services and rentals are available at the base in town for downhill skiing. More bars, restaurants and lodging facilities are within walking distance of these lifts than any ski area in the West. The ski season is late November to mid-April .

★ **Buttermilk**　　*2.2 mi. W via CO 82 & Buttermilk West Rd.*　　925-1220
The vertical rise is 2,000 feet and the longest run is two miles. Elevation at the top is 9,840 feet. There are six chairlifts. All essential services, facilities and rentals are available at the base for downhill skiing. A restaurant and bar are at the base, and a motor hotel is within walking distance. The ski season is early December to early April.

Dog Sled Trips
　Krabloonik Husky Kennels　　*10 mi. SW via CO 82*　　923-3953
Thrilling half day and full day dog sled trips along spectacular mountain trails can be reserved from December through April.

Ice-Skating
　Aspen Ice Garden　　*.3 mi. W at 233 W. Hyman Av.*　　925-7485
Public skating hours are scheduled throughout the year (except August). Skates can be rented in this large, beautifully maintained indoor rink.

★ **Sleigh Rides**
Scenic sleigh rides along byways near town can be arranged at:
　Snowmass Stables　　*12 mi. W via CO 82 & Brush Cr. Rd.*　　923-3075
　T-Lazy-7 Ranch　　*4.8 mi. SW via CO 82 at 3129 Maroon Cr. Rd.*　　925-7040

★ **Snowmass**　　*12 mi. W via CO 82 & Brush Cr. Rd.*　　923-2085
The vertical rise is 3,600 feet and the longest run is 3.5 miles. Elevation at the top is 11,808 feet. There are thirteen chairlifts, including two triples. All services, facilities and rentals are available at the base for both downhill and cross-country skiing. There are about fifty miles of cross-country ski trails. Nearly a dozen restaurants and a similar number of bars are concentrated at the base, and almost two dozen lodging facilities (primarily condominiums) are within walking distance. The ski season is late November to mid-April.

★ **Snowmobiles**
　T-Lazy-7 Ranch　　*4.8 mi. SW via CO 82 at 3129 Maroon Cr. Rd.*　　925-4614
Snowmobiles can be rented by the hour or longer any day in winter for exploring the winter wonderland along Castle Creek.

★ **White River National Forest**　　*around town*　　925-3445
This giant forest includes much of northcentral Colorado's finest mountain country. Features include the world-renowned winter sports areas at Aspen and Vail. There are portions of seven wilderness areas, including the magnificent Maroon Bells-Snowmass Wilderness between Aspen and Crested Butte. Several large man-made lakes, including Ruedi Reservoir, offer a variety of water sports. A good system of highways and dirt roads, and hundreds of miles of trails, access limitless opportunities for hiking, backpacking, horseback riding, pack trips, mountain climbing, hunting, fishing, boating, camping and winter sports.

SHOPPING
Downtown Aspen is one of the West's great human-scale enclaves. Several streets have been converted into beautifully landscaped pedestrian malls paved with bricks from old mining structures and accented by sculptures, fountains — even a grass-lined stream. Handsome century-old buildings now house an outstanding assortment of galleries, distinctive shops, restaurants and bars. Civic vigilance and architectural control assure that all new buildings complement the town's proud Victorian heritage. The listings which follow are only highlights among scores of fine shops that await your discovery.

Food Specialties
★ **Aspen Fudgeworks**　　*downtown at 418 E. Hyman Av.*　　920-1197
Distinctive fudges and chocolates are all made on the premises of this beautiful new shop, and samples are offered. Premium ice creams and nuts are also carried.

★ **Bristol Bay Fudge Co.**　　*downtown at 205 S. Mill St.*　　925-6179
Fudge, and chocolates in many unique shapes, are made in this modern store. Samples are offered.

★ **Cookie Munchers Cafe**   *downtown at 500 E. Cooper Av.*   *925-1591*
Gelato ice cream is made on the premises in several flavors, along with cookies.
Sandwiches are also served in a sidewalk patio, or to go.

Delice Pastry Shop Inc.   *downtown at 315 E. Hyman Av.*   *925-7244*
French pastries are featured, along with hot and cold lunches, in an attractive bakery/
coffee shop.

★ **Fry by Night Doughnuts**   *downtown at 308 S. Hunter St.*   *925-6960*
Many kinds of delicious donuts are displayed in this appealing little shop, and coffee is
available.

★ **Great Western Spirit Co.**   *.3 mi. N at 300 Puppy Smith Rd.*   *925-8200*
An outstanding collection of premium California and foreign wines is displayed in an
enophile's dream where bottles are perfectly stored in a separate temperature-controlled
room. There is an instant wine-chilling machine. A good assortment of beers and liquors
is also sold.

Haagen-Daz   *downtown at 404 E. Hyman Av.*   *925-3137*
The popular premium ice cream chain has a convenient outlet near the heart of town.

★ **Le Gourmet Aspen**   *downtown at 710 E. Durant Av.*   *925-7756*
A remarkable assortment of gourmet foods from all over the world is well organized in this
handsome new shop.

★ **Les Chefs D'Aspen**   *downtown at 405 S. Hunter St.*   *925-6217*
This is a complete shop for gourmet cooks. The finest cookware and specialty foods are
displayed, and classes are given in an intimate demonstration kitchen.

Little Cliff's Bakery   *downtown at 121 S. Galena St.*   *925-3722*
A full line of pastries, breads (even English muffins) and dessert specialties made on the
premises are sold to go, or they may be enjoyed at picnic tables in front of this small
bakery. Closed Sun.-Mon.

★ **Of Grape and Grain**   *downtown at 434 E. Cooper Av.*   *925-8600*
In this complete liquor store, a fine display of premium California wines is a highlight.

★ **Pour la France**   *downtown at Main/Mill Sts.*   *920-1151*
Fresh baked croissants, pastries, breads and cakes are served with light meals and
classical music in a handsome new shop, on a sidewalk cafe, or to take out. (This is the best
of several shops in a local chain.)

★ **Rocky Mountain Chocolate Factory** *downtown at 523 E. Cooper Av.*   *925-5112*
Seasonal fresh fruits dipped in chocolate and delicious fudges made on the premises are
tantalizingly displayed. Samples are offered.

Specialty Shops

★ **Aspen Center for the Visual Arts**   *.4 mi. N at 590 N. Mill St.*   *925-8050*
The site of the town's century-old hydroelectric plant for the early silver mines has been
thoughtfully renovated. Artistic expressions through the ages and among all cultures are
examined in exhibitions of painting, sculpture, photography, film and video, and other
media. Local and international artists are featured in lectures, symposia, workshops,
exhibits, and special events. The complex also includes a growing sculpture garden, a
small art library and a sales desk. Closed Mon.

★ **Aspen Mountain Jewelers**   *downtown at 520 E. Durant Av.*   *920-1211*
Gold-plated and pine cone jewelry are displayed and sold in a shop that will also do
custom jewelry from anything that's grown around Aspen.

Aspen Unlimited   *downtown at 615 E. Cooper Av.*   *925-2488*
Works of Aspen and Colorado craftsmen are featured, including aspenwood candles,
Colorado gold jewelry, aspen leaf jewelry, stained glass, and more.

★ **The Country Flower**   *downtown at 422 E. Hyman Av.*   *925-6522*
Museum-quality pieces of stained glass, both antique and new, are beautifully exhibited in
this eye-catching new shop.

★ **Explore Booksellers**   *downtown at 221 E. Main St.*   *925-5336*
This complete bookstore in a restored Victorian house is a great place to browse and select
books from an extensive, attractively displayed collection. Comfortable chairs and free
coffee or tea are provided. Classical records and tapes are also sold, including works by
artists performing at the Music Festival.

★ **Unicorn Books**   *downtown at 413 E. Cooper Av.*   *925-7500*
A large and well-organized selection of books and records is offered, along with maps, magazines, and an art gallery. Cheerful, modernistic decor is complemented by soothing background music and some seating.

NIGHTLIFE

A major source of Aspen's charm is the town's wonderfully varied and lively assortment of after-dark facilities. Just about any ambiance is present for a night on the town.

★ **Andres**   *downtown at 312 S. Galena St.*   *925-6200*
The third floor nightclub is a fabulously imaginative blending of Victorian and high-tech decor. Don't miss the dance floor surrounded on three sides by a phantasmagoria of lights-and-mirrors, disco decor, and state-of-the-art sound system. Large retractable skylights provide a star-studded contrast. Seating is posh, padded and inevitably heavily used. The neo-Victorian first floor bar features live entertainment and dancing on weekends, while the opulent second floor (when opened) is ideal for intimate conversation. A good restaurant completes the complex.

Cooper Street Pier   *downtown at 508 E. Cooper Av.*   *925-7758*
This very popular two-level bar has a fine view of the passing street scene and of Aspen Mountain. Shuffleboard, pool tables, and electronic games contribute to a lively atmosphere. Light meals are served.

E'wus Paradise   *downtown at 450 S. Galena St.*   *925-9157*
Live rock sounds are featured most evenings in this big multilevel cellar nightclub. Chinese meals are served earlier.

★ **The Jerome Bar**   *downtown at Mill/Main Sts.*   *925-3241*
In the Jerome Hotel is the oldest bar in town — built in 1889. It is as popular as it was when it was a favorite watering hole for the miners. The flavor hasn't changed much either, with polished hardwood, inlaid floors, stamped tin ceiling and well-worn comfortable furniture.

★ **Little Nell's**   *downtown at 611 E. Durant Av.*   *925-3636*
This quintessential apres-ski bar at the base of Aspen Mountain has a sundeck with picnic tables overlooking the slopes that may be the town's favorite hangout. There is late evening entertainment and dancing indoors under a unique lighting system.

Paddy Bugatti's   *downtown at Galena/Dean Sts.*   *925-2717*
A casual little cellar lounge in the Continental Inn offers diverse listening music nightly. Hotel guests can swim up. A dining room adjoins.

★ **Paragon**   *downtown at 419 E. Hyman Av.*   *925-7499*
Live entertainment and dancing are offered most nights in an elegant Victorian-style lounge. One room displays a fabulous collection of locally crafted stained glass. Elsewhere, patrons luxuriate on plush Victorian furniture in several intimate nooks of a room distinguished by heroic nude paintings and a polished hardwood bar. Light breakfasts and lunches are also featured. A delightful sidewalk dining/drinking area on the mall is particularly inviting on summer evenings when artists with the Music Festival are playing classical pieces nearby.

★ **Red Onion Bar**   *downtown at 420 E. Cooper Av.*   *925-6853*
In operation for nearly a century, this authentically rustic hangout is still a good place for a beer and casual meals.

★ **The Spinnaker Lounge**   *downtown at 600 S. Spring St.*   *925-7627*
Live entertainment is offered nightly amidst contemporary opulence in the Woodstone Inn. From plush armchairs and padded barstools with arms, there is a fine view of Aspen Mountain. The decor is a pleasing blend of polished light woods, shiny brass trim, stained and antiqued glass, luxuriant plants and a rock wall. Hotel guests can use a swim-up bar with water stools. Downstairs is an attractive seafood restaurant.

★ **The Tippler**   *downtown at 535 E. Durant Av.*   *925-3151*
Above the Copper Kettle Restaurant is an "in" place for apres-ski conversations with a raw bar serving oysters and shrimp. Live entertainment and dancing are featured nightly amid Victorian atmosphere graced by Tiffany lamps and a copper dance floor.

★ **Ute City Banque Bar**   *downtown at Galena St./Hyman Av.*   *925-4373*
Soft music, small tables and stylish decor are ideal for casual conversation in this intimate, extremely popular bar. Picture windows overlook the bustling street scene at the center of town. Much of the decor in the bar and adjoining dining rooms is original from the bank that was here in Victorian times.

★ **Wheeler Opera House**   *downtown at 328 E. Hopkins Av.*   *925-2050*
The town's cultural landmark has just been completely renovated. It now serves as a showplace for performances of all kinds year-round.

RESTAURANTS
Aspen has one of the West's most cosmopolitan collections of fine dining rooms. Among nearly one hundred restaurants, quality and charm are abundantly available in a delightful diversity of settings.

★ **Abetone Ristorante**   *downtown at 620 E. Hyman Av.*   *925-9022*
D only. Closed Mon.   *Expensive*
Classic Northern Italian cuisine and fresh seafood flown in from the New England coast and Europe are featured. The decor is intimate and elegant. An interior garden mall has several umbrella-shaded tables. A sleek, plush bar adjoins.

The Anchorage   *downtown at 600 S. Spring St.*   *925-6602*
L-D.   *Moderate*
Fish specialties, including a fresh catch of the day, are served in a casual contemporary downstairs restaurant in the Woodstone Inn.

★ **Andres**   *downtown at 312 S. Galena St.*   *925-6200*
B-L-D. No B on Tues.-Thurs.   *Moderate*
Contemporary American fare is served at all meals in summer. Continental dishes are offered during the ski season. The beautifully decorated historic Victorian building also houses sensational lounges.

★ **Arthur's Chinese Restaurant**   *.3 mi. W at 132 W. Main St.*   *925-7931*
D only.   *Expensive*
An extensive selection of gourmet Szechwan and Mandarin cuisine is served amidst lavish Victorian furnishings in several rooms of a large restaurant fashioned from a historic home. Outdoor view dining is offered in summer, and there is a darkly handsome bar.

★ **The Arya**   *downtown at 701 S. Mill St.*   *925-6266*
L-D.   *Moderate*
Gourmet specialties of six different countries are served in elegantly appointed, individually decorated intimate rooms, or in a main dining room enhanced by a tall rock fireplace in the Aspen Inn. Flaming desserts are a specialty. Lunches are served by the poolside.

Aspen Meadows Restaurant   *1.2 mi. W at 845 Meadows Rd.*   *925-3426*
D only. Closed Wed.   *Expensive*
Artistically prepared Nouvelle cuisine is featured, and there is music with dinner in this tranquil dining room.

Aspen Mine Co.   *downtown at 426 E. Hyman Av.*   *925-7766*
B-L-D.   *Moderate*
American fare is served in a casual, long-established Victorian-style restaurant with lots of stained glass. There is also a charming patio on the mall and live entertainment on weekends.

Charlemagne   *.5 mi. W at 400 W. Main St.*   *925-5200*
L-D.   *Expensive*
French country cuisine is offered in an elaborately furnished newer restaurant located in a converted Victorian house.

Chart House   *downtown at Monarch St./Durant Av.*   *925-3525*
D only. Closed Sun.   *Moderate*
Steak, seafood and a salad bar are the mainstays in this large, plant-filled, rustic-wood representative of a quality restaurant chain. An attractive lounge adjoins.

Chez Grandmere   *12 mi. W via CO 82 & Brush Cr. Rd. - in Snowmass Mall*   *923-2570*
D only. Closed Sun.   *Very Expensive*
Continental cuisine is featured on a fixed price menu. There is only one seating nightly in the casually elegant dining room. By reservation only.

Colucci's   *1.6 mi. W at 22475 CO 82*   *925-4742*
B-L-D.   Moderate
Northern Italian specialties highlight a Continental menu in this stylish new restaurant at
the Red Roof Inn. Elegant, contemporary decor is complemented by a mountain view that
includes majestic Pyramid Peak. Meals are also served outdoors on a view deck, weather
permitting. A handsome bar adjoins.

★ **Copper Kettle**   *downtown at 535 E. Dean St.*   *925-3151*
D only. Closed Mon.-Tues.   *Expensive*
Exotic fare from a different region of the world is spotlighted each evening, accompanied
by homemade pastry, relishes and jams. The atmosphere is elegant, and there is an
outstanding lounge.

Country Road Ltd.   *downtown at Mill/Main Sts.*   *925-6556*
L-D.   *Moderate*
Fresh fish is flown in daily and you can pick your own lobster from the tank in this
attractively furnished downstairs restaurant. Upstairs is an old-fashioned bar.

★ **Crystal Palace**   *downtown at 300 E. Hyman Av.*   *925-1455*
D only. Closed Sun.-Mon.   *Very Expensive*
An outstanding original revue is performed by the waiters and waitresses following a
gourmet dinner in one of the nation's finest theater/restaurants. A magnificent collection
of stained glass enhances the elegant dining-and-entertainment showplace.

★ **The Diner**   *downtown at 611 E. Durant Av.*   *925-1236*
B-L.   *Moderate*
The fifties live on. Cherry cokes and Philly sandwiches are balanced by giant homemade
muffins and desserts as East meets West in this classy updated diner. When the
equipment works, fifties music can be selected on table-top juke boxes at each booth. An
outdoor patio with umbrella-shaded tables adjoins.

Eastern Wind   *downtown at 520 E. Cooper Av.*   *925-5160*
L-D.   *Moderate*
Fine Mandarin and Szechwan cuisine is served in a large, modestly furnished restaurant.
The few booths in the front room are best because they have a good view of the street
scene and ski slopes.

Freddie's Mainstreet Cafe   *downtown at 600 E. Main St.*   *925-5283*
B-L. Closed Sat.-Sun.   *Moderate*
French toast is a highlight among freshly made American specialties. So is the cheddar
cheese and apple pie in this plain, pleasant little cafe.

★ **The Golden Horn**   *downtown at Cooper Av./Mill St.*   *925-3373*
D only. Closed Wed.   *Expensive*
Continental and Swiss specialties are served in refined, quiet atmosphere. Veal prepared
in a variety of ways and game in season are highlights. A large fireplace conversation pit
serves as a perfect summer location for a classical string quartet moonlighting from the
Music Festival.

★ **Grand Finale**   *downtown at 300 E. Hyman Av.*   *920-1488*
D only. Closed Sun.-Mon.   *Very Expensive*
A sparkling musical revue follows a gourmet dinner in this sleek New York-style theater
where black and white set the tone. There is one seating at 8:00 p.m. by reservation only.

The Greenhouse Restaurant   *downtown at 315 E. Hyman Av.*   *925-6328*
L-D.   *Moderate*
Italian and French dishes are served in a small, informally elegant downstairs restaurant
accented by plants and artwork. A tiny courtyard is used for dining in good weather.

Guido's   *downtown at 403 S. Galena St.*   *925-7222*
L-D.   *Moderate*
Swiss and European foods and fondues are offered in a dining room decorated in casual
country style. A flowery patio on the mall is popular for lunch.

The Home Plate   *downtown at 333 E. Durant Av.*   *925-1986*
D only. Closed Sun.   *Moderate*
Hearty home-cooked fare, a reasonably priced short American menu, and pleasant
fireside atmosphere are features. This dining room in the Mountain Chalet Lodge is very
popular, especially with families.

Hotel Jerome Restaurant   *downtown at 330 E. Main St.*   *925-3241*
B-L.   *Moderate*
Good breakfasts and classical music (occasionally provided by music students from the
Festival) distinguish a Victorian dining room decorated with a fine collection of paintings,
stained glass, and many plants. Lunch is served here, in the nostalgic old bar, or on a
poolside patio.

★ **Krabloonik Restaurant**   *10 mi. SW off CO 82*   *923-3953*
D only. Closed in spring & fall.   *Expensive*
Innovative cuisine includes wild game when available on a menu that changes nightly. The
unusual restaurant is in a rustic setting at the Krabloonik Kennels.

★ **La Cocina**   *downtown at 308 E. Hopkins Av.*   *925-9714*
D only.   *Low*
A well-trained staff prepares delicious Santa Fe-style New Mexican food like blue corn
tortillas and posole in this large, highly regarded restaurant. A monumental copper wall
hanging distinguishes the back room, and a garden patio is used in good weather.

★ **Maurice's**   *.3 mi. SE at 700 Ute Av.*   *925-7822*
D only. Closed Sun.-Mon.   *Expensive*
Gourmet French cuisine from skillfully prepared fresh ingredients is presented in an
intimate, elegant dining room with a large two-sided stone fireplace. Meals are served in
this long-popular restaurant in the Aspen Alps by reservation only.

Paddy Bugatti's   *downtown at Galena/Dean Sts.*   *925-2717*
D only. Closed Tues.   *Expensive*
Italian specialties include homemade pastas in this casual downstairs dining room in the
Continental Inn. A popular lounge adjoins.

Paragon   *downtown at 419 E. Hyman Av.*   *925-7499*
B-L.   *Moderate*
Good light meals provide an excuse for enjoying the sidewalk cafe in front of this Victorian
dining/drinking establishment. The view of the Fountain and activity on the Hyman Street
Mall is exceptional.

★ **Parlour Car**   *.7 mi. W at 615 W. Hopkins Av.*   *925-3810*
D only.   *Very Expensive*
Classic French cuisine from a fixed price menu that changes weekly is formally presented
in romantic splendor. An authentically restored turn-of-the-century railway car has been
subdivided into six opulent private dining rooms.

Pine Creek Cookhouse   *13 mi. SW via Castle Creek Rd. - Ashcroft*   *925-1971*
L-D. Closed Mon.   *Moderate*
International favorites are prepared in an attractive little restaurant in a picturesque
ghost town. Reservations and menu selections for dinner are required at least one day in
advance.

Pinocchio's   *downtown at 517 E. Cooper Av.*   *925-7601*
L-D. No L on Tues.   *Moderate*
Pizza and Italian pasta dinners with hearth bread are emphasized in a casual bentwood
and plants setting.

Poppie's Bistro Cafe   *1 mi. W at 834 W. Hallam St.*   *925-2333*
L-D. No L on Sat. & Sun.   *Expensive*
Gourmet country cuisine is presented in darkly handsome bistro-style dining areas of a
converted Victorian home. Live music is usually provided by a classical guitarist or by
music students in summer.

★ **The Ritz**   *downtown at 205 S. Mill St.*   *925-1212*
L-D.   *Expensive*
New American cuisine has found a stylish home in this elegant new restaurant. Super-
plush art deco decor, mountain-view picture windows, a rooftop viewdeck and a sleek
lounge, waiters and waitresses in black-and-white tuxedos, and music of the 1930s
contribute to the charm.

Skiers Chalet   *downtown at 710 S. Aspen St.*   *925-3381*
L-D.   *Moderate*
Steaks have been the specialty for decades at this casual, reasonably-priced restaurant
next to the No. 1 chairlift on Aspen Mountain.

Szechwan Garden   *downtown at 533 E. Hopkins Av.*   *920-1303*
L-D.   *Moderate*
Szechwan specialties are emphasized in this large new Chinese restaurant where full linen service enhances inviting contemporary decor.

★ **Ute City Banque**   *downtown at Galena St./Hyman Av.*   *925-4373*
L-D.   *Expensive*
Gourmet Continental cuisine is served in an elegant bistro fashioned from the paneled interior of a Victorian bank. Both the dining room and the adjoining bar are deservedly acclaimed.

★ **Wienerstube Restaurant**   *downtown at 519 E. Cooper Av.*   *925-3357*
B-L. Closed Mon.   *Moderate*
Delicious homemade pastries complement European and American specialties in a plant/flower-filled dining room. Patio dining and a lounge are also available along with takeout service for the pastries.

LODGING

Accommodations are abundant and remarkably diverse. Most of the better facilities are within walking distance of the ski slopes and/or downtown. Winter is the "high" season, with rates usually at least 100% higher than the summer rates quoted below. Spring and fall rates are often at least 10% below summer rates. There are few bargains in town in summer, and none in winter. Reservations are advised during both the summer and winter seasons. As much as a one week minimum stay may be required in winter.

Alpine Lodge   *.7 mi. E at 1240 E. CO 82*   *925-7351*
This rustic older lodge has **bargain** units and cabins, plus a hot tub, on attractively landscaped grounds.

cabin — kitchenette,	D bed...$35
regular room — pvt. bath,	D bed...$30
regular room — shared bath,	D bed...$25

Aspen Silverglo Condominiums   *.4 mi. SE at 940 E. Waters Av.*   *925-8450*
An outdoor pool and sauna are features of a recently refurbished older condominium complex. Each unit has a phone and color TV.

deluxe apartment — 1 BR, fireplace, kit.,	D or K bed...$53
regular apartment — studio, fireplace, kitchenette,	Q bed...$43
regular room —	2 D beds...$32

★ **Aspen Ski Lodge**   *downtown at 101 W. Main St.*   *925-3434*
One of the area's newest and most luxurious motor lodges has a heated year-round outdoor pool and whirlpool, plus complimentary membership at the Aspen Health Club for tennis and racquetball. A Continental breakfast and afternoon wine and cheese are also complimentary. Each of the beautifully appointed units has a phone, cable color TV with movies, and a refrigerator.

#28 — fireplace, skylighted whirlpool, pvt. deck, Aspen Mt. view from	K bed...$139
#2 — see-through mirrored fireplace, whirlpool,	K bed...$129
#27 — fireplace, skylighted whirlpool,	K bed...$129
#11 — fireplace, skylighted bath, pvt. deck,	K bed...$95
regular room —	Q bed...$69

★ **Aspen Square**   *downtown at 617 E. Cooper Av.*   *925-1000*
A large outdoor year-round heated pool with a fine Aspen Mountain view, plus a whirlpool, saunas, and underground parking are some of the amenities in this big condo complex. Best of all, it is perfectly sited in the heart of town near the slopes. Each of the luxuriously furnished apartments has a fully equipped kitchen, a wood-burning fireplace, phone, cable color TV, and a private balcony.

#418,#417,#416,#415,#413,#412 — studios, superb views of Aspen Mt.,	Q bed...$70
regular room — studio,	Q bed...$70

Bell Mountain Lodge   *downtown at 720 E. Cooper Av.*   *925-3675*
This older **bargain** motel with a landscaped outdoor pool is near both downtown and the slopes. Each modest room has a color TV.

#208 — view from bed of Aspen Mt. beyond balc./corridor,	Q bed...$32
regular room — in back, some mountain view,	T & D beds...$32
regular room — small,	D bed...$30

★ **Boomerang Lodge**   *.6 mi. W at 500 W. Hopkins Av.*   925-3416
There is a small year-round heated outdoor pool plus a whirlpool and sauna in this attractive motor lodge. Each of the well-furnished units has a phone, cable color TV, and a private balcony or patio.

#22 — studio, spacious, kit., fireplace, many mt. view windows,	Q & 2 T beds...$95
#7,#8 — kitchenette, corner fireplace, many mt. view windows,	Q & D beds...$83
#34 — kiva fireplace, view,	Q bed...$62
regular room —	Q bed...$59

Continental Inn   *downtown at 515 S. Galena St.*   925-1150
Aspen's largest hotel has an unusual indoor/outdoor pool with a swim-up bar, plus a whirlpool, saunas, a sundeck overlooking adjacent Aspen Mountain, plus a restaurant and lounge. Each of the conventional units has a phone and cable color TV.

fireplace room — fireplace,	K bed...$68
regular room —	2 D or K bed...$68

Cortina Lodge   *downtown at 230 E. Main St.*   925-2787
This ramshackle older motel is a conveniently located **bargain.** Most of the no-frills rooms have a color TV.

regular room —	D bed...$28

★ **Durant Condominiums**   *downtown at 718 S. Galena St.*   925-7910
There are some fine views from these condominium apartments at the base of Aspen Mountain, plus an outdoor pool and whirlpool. Each luxury unit has a phone, cable color TV with movies, a living room, and kitchen.

suite — 1 BR, ski slope view, fireplace,	K bed...$84
regular room — 1 BR, garden level,	Q bed...$78

★ **The Gant**   *.3 mi. E at 610 West End St.*   925-5000
One of Aspen's largest and most complete condominium complexes offers contemporary Western architecture complemented by two large scenic outdoor pools, three whirlpools, two saunas, and (for a fee) five tennis courts. Each well-furnished unit has a phone, cable color TV, wood-burning fireplace, kitchen, and a balcony.

regular room — 1 BR,	Q bed...$100

★ **Heatherbed Lodge**   *3 mi. SW on Maroon Cr. Rd.*   925-7077
On Maroon Creek across the highway from the base of Aspen Highlands Ski Area, this motor lodge has a picturesque outdoor pool and deck above the creek and a sauna.

#207 — spacious,	2 T & K beds...$46
studio — kitchenette,	2 T & Q beds...$48
regular room —	2 T or D bed...$44

★ **Holiday Inn of Aspen**   *2.2 mi. W at 21646 CO 82*   925-1500
Next to the lifts at the base of Buttermilk Mountain is a large, handsome motor hotel. Full service facilities include a big outdoor pool with a mountain view, a whirlpool, saunas, plus a restaurant and lounge. Each of the units has a phone and cable color TV.

"King Leisure Suite" (several) — mt. view, balc.,	K bed...$60
regular room —	Q bed...$50

★ **The Hotel Jerome**   *downtown at 330 E. Main St.*   925-1040
Aspen's only remaining hotel built during the silver boom days is still a local landmark. There is a large heated outdoor pool, and the Victorian era lingers in the nostalgic atmosphere of the lobby, restaurant and bar.

"PC" — parlour, some Victorian furnishings, fine town views,	D bed...$50
#233 — parlour, fine view east to mts.,	D bed...$50
#398 — fine south view to mts.,	D bed...$40
regular room —	D bed...$36

Limelight Lodge   *downtown at 228 E. Cooper Av.*   925-3025
Large and small year-round heated outdoor pools and a whirlpool (plus a sauna in winter) are features of this modern motel. A complimentary Continental breakfast is available. Each room has a phone and cable color TV with movies, and most have a refrigerator.

#130,#120 — great view of Independence Pass & Aspen Mt.,	K bed...$58
#133 — fine (not pvt.) view of Aspen Mt. across park,	2 Q beds..$58
regular room —	Q or K bed...$58

★ **Maroon Creek Lodge**   *2.9 mi. SW on Maroon Creek Rd.*   *925-3491*
Next to the base and lifts at Aspen Highlands, this small contemporary motor lodge has a landscaped outdoor view pool, and a sauna. Each spacious apartment has a phone and cable color TV.

    #1 — single level, kitchen, ski in/out, good slope view,   K bed...$60
    regular room —   Q bed...$48

★ **Molly Gibson Lodge**   *downtown at 120 W. Hopkins Av.*   *925-2580*
This splendid little contemporary bed-and-breakfast motor lodge features a year-round outdoor heated pool in a lovely garden patio, complimentary membership in the Aspen Racquet Club, Continental breakfast, and a (weekly) wine tasting party in the posh fireside lounge. Each nicely furnished unit has a phone and cable color TV with movies, and most have a refrigerator.

    #7 — 1 BR, Q sofabed in LR, kitchenette, fine Aspen Mt. view,   Q bed...$99
    #16 — deluxe room, refrigerator, fine view of Aspen Mt.,   Q bed...$89
    regular room —   Q bed...$59

Pomegranate Inn   *1.8 mi. W at 22094 CO 82*   *925-2700*
This contemporary motor hotel has a heated year-round outdoor pool and whirlpool with a fine mountain view, sauna, (fee) horseback riding, plus an attractive dining room and lounge. Each room has a phone and cable color TV.

    #311,#312 — raised stone fireplace, balcony, pool/mt. view,   K bed...$75
    regular room —   Q bed...$50

★ **Red Roof at Aspen**   *1.6 mi. W at 22475 CO 82*   *925-9308*
On the Aspen Golf Course is a luxurious new motor hotel with a very large outdoor pool and whirlpool with outstanding mountain views, saunas, and a nicely decorated view restaurant and lounge. Each well-furnished unit has a phone, cable color TV, a wet bar/refrigerator and a private balcony.

    #132,#130,#120,#118 — fireplace, fine mt. view,   K bed...$59
    regular room — fine mt. view,   K bed...$59

★ **St. Moritz Lodge**   *.4 mi. W at 334 W. Hyman Av.*   *925-3220*
An outdoor pool, whirlpool, saunas and bicycles are amenities of this European-style motor lodge. A complimentary Continental breakfast is available. Each spacious unit has a phone and cable color TV with movies.

    apartment — 1 BR, fireplace, kit., sundeck,   D bed...$85
    regular room —   D bed...$50

Skiers Chalet   *downtown at 710 S. Aspen St.*   *925-2904*
Next to a chairlift on Aspen Mountain, this modest little motor inn has a heated year-round outdoor pool. Each unit has a color TV and refrigerator.

    #25,#20 — corner, fine view of slopes,   2 D beds...$45
    #22 — corner, fine view of town,   2 D beds...$45
    regular room —   2 D beds...$35

Tipple Inn   *downtown at 747 S. Galena St.*   *925-6580*
Next to the Little Nel chairlift, this tiny modern apartment complex has a gourmet restaurant and fine lounge, plus a whirlpool in the building. Each apartment has a phone, cable color TV and a kitchen.

    #5,#8 — studio, metal fireplace, balcony, fine view of slopes,   Q bed...$72
    regular room — studio,   Q bed...$62

Tipple Lodge   *downtown at 747 S. Galena St.*   *925-1116*
Next to the Little Nell chairlift is a small modern motor lodge. A complimentary Continental breakfast is offered in winter. Each unit has a phone and cable color TV.

    studio — fireplace, kit.,   Q bed...$68
    regular room —   Q bed...$40

Tyrolean Lodge   *.3 mi. W at 200 W. Main St.*   *925-4595*
This no-frills motel has units with a phone, cable color TV, and a small kitchen.

    regular room —   D bed...$34

Ullr Lodge   *.6 mi. W at 520 W. Main St.*   *925-7696*
This pleasant little European-style motor lodge has an outdoor pool, whirlpool, sauna, and a game room. Breakfast is complimentary.

    apartment — 1 BR, phone, cable color TV, kit.,   Q bed...$60
    regular room —   2 T or K bed...$37

★ **The Woodstone**   *downtown at 709 E. Durant Av.*   *925-6760*
Near both the Little Nell lift and the heart of town, this large contemporary complex includes a big scenic indoor/outdoor pool with an unusual swim-up bar, a whirlpool, saunas, covered parking, and an attractive restaurant and lounge. A complimentary Continental breakfast is offered in winter. Each well-furnished unit has a phone, cable color TV with movies, a refrigerator, and a balcony.

    suite — 1 BR, fireplace,   K bed...$75
    regular room —   Q bed...$60

CAMPGROUNDS

Several scenic primitive campgrounds are located near town by streams or small lakes high in the magnificent central Colorado Rockies. The nearest complete facility is a conventional campground by the highway a half hour drive from town.

Aspen-Basalt KOA Campground   *20 mi. W on Hwy. 82*   *927-3532*
The nearest campground with flush toilets is this large, private facility. Amenities include a small outdoor pool, therapy pool, rec room, and an outdoor game area. Flush toilets, hot showers, and hookups are available. Each of the closely spaced sites has a picnic table and fire ring. There are some shade trees and a separated tent area with small grassy sites.
    base rate...$9.50

Difficult   *4.5 mi. SE: 4 mi. SE on CO 82 & .5 mi. SE on FR 15108*   *925-3445*
This White River National Forest campground is on a pine-shaded flat by the scenic Roaring Fork River. Fishing and hiking are popular. Pit toilets are available. There are no showers or hookups. Each shady, well-spaced tent-or-RV site has a picnic table, fire area, and grill.   base rate...$5

★ **Maroon Lake**   *12.6 mi. SW: 1.6 mi. W on CO 82 & 11 mi. SW on FR 125*   *925-3445*
This White River National Forest campground is in a spectacular pine-and-aspen forested valley near a photogenic little lake high in the Rockies. Fishing in Maroon Lake is popular and there are marked nature trails. Pit toilets are available. There are no showers or hookups. Each grassy site has a picnic table, fire area, and grill.   base rate...$5

SPECIAL EVENTS

★ **Winterskol**   *in town and on the ski slopes*   *mid-January*
Parades, parties and madcap events highlight a winter carnival that is enthusiastically enjoyed by residents and visitors alike.

Aspen/Snowmass International Wine Classic   *in town & Snowmass*   *mid-June*
Three days of wine tasting, lectures and panel discussions feature premium wines provided by dozens of major vintners. A sparkling and dessert wine extravaganza climaxes the event.

★ **Aspen Music Festival**   *the music tent & throughout town*   *late June-late Aug.*
More than 100 events are scheduled during this renowned festival, including full symphony concerts, chamber music, jazz ensembles, choral and operatic workshops, solo recitals, and student concerts.

Ballet/Aspen   *Aspen High School*   *early July-mid-August*
One of America's largest dance companies and acclaimed guest stars perform Wednesday through Saturday each week.

OTHER INFORMATION

Area Code: *303*
Zip Code: *81611*

Aspen Chamber of Commerce   *downtown at 303 E. Main St.*   *925-1940*
White River National Forest   *.8 mi. W at 806 W. Hallam St.*   *920-1664*

Breckenridge, Colorado

Elevation:

9,535 feet

Population (1980):

818

Population (1970):

548

Location:

79 mi. W
of Denver

Breckenridge is a reborn Old Western boom town. This time, growth is based on breathtaking surroundings rather than mineral deposits. The town lies in a broad pine-forested valley surrounded by the central Colorado Rockies, including some of the nation's highest peaks. Almost 9,600 feet above sea level, it is one of the highest towns on the continent. Winters are long and cold, yet Breckenridge has recently become a snow sports capital with huge downhill and cross-country skiing complexes that attract enthusiastic crowds to slopes that rise abruptly from downtown. All of the year's good weather occurs in summer, when visitors return to explore magnificent snow-capped peaks, and pine-forested valleys with rushing streams and clear, cold lakes. Hiking, backpacking, mountain climbing, horseback riding, jeep touring, fishing, and boating are popular. New golf courses, tennis complexes, bicycle paths, and other recreation facilities like an alpine slide have recently been provided in town. Visitors are scarce between seasons. While there isn't much to do, the serene grandeur of the setting can be memorable in the crisp thin air of spring or fall.

In 1859, gold was discovered in the Blue River. By the following year, Breckenridge was a sprawling boom town and the county seat. Within four years, the easily panned and sluiced stream gold was gone. In the late 1870s, more sophisticated mining methods created an even bigger boom period. At the turn of the century, the gold boat dredge, an Australian import formerly used to clear seaport channels, began to spew huge piles of boulders dug from the fragile stream channel. The dredging finally ended during World War II, leaving huge piles of boulders for miles along the stream and a town that was forgotten. In 1961 the Breckenridge ski area opened. The transformation since then is even more remarkable than the one that originally despoiled the area after the turn of the century.

While many of the rock piles remain, the stream is becoming a delightful series of small lakes, waterfalls, and rapids bordered by paths and surrounded by handsome new buildings and park spaces. The adjoining downtown area is a cleaned-up mixture of the few remaining carefully restored Victorian landmarks with a much larger array of new Victorian-style structures. A rapidly growing number of fine art galleries and specialty shops, plus excellent restaurants and bars, now occupy colorful buildings on well-landscaped streets. At the base of chairlifts a short walk from the heart of town, two high-rise condominium hotels offer luxurious facilities appropriate to a contemporary world-class ski resort.

Breckenridge, Colorado

WEATHER PROFILE — *Vokac Weather Rating*

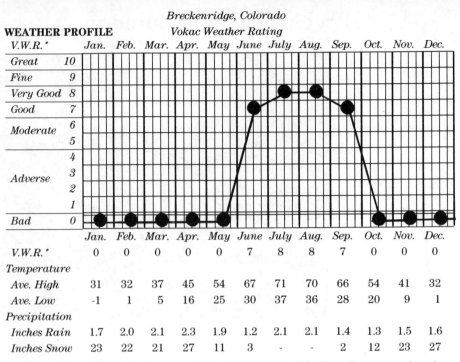

V.W.R. *		Jan.	Feb.	Mar.	Apr.	May	June	July	Aug.	Sep.	Oct.	Nov.	Dec.
Great	10												
Fine	9												
Very Good	8												
Good	7												
Moderate	6 / 5												
Adverse	4 / 3 / 2 / 1												
Bad	0												

	Jan.	Feb.	Mar.	Apr.	May	June	July	Aug.	Sep.	Oct.	Nov.	Dec.
V.W.R. *	0	0	0	0	0	7	8	8	7	0	0	0
Temperature												
Ave. High	31	32	37	45	54	67	71	70	66	54	41	32
Ave. Low	-1	1	5	16	25	30	37	36	28	20	9	1
Precipitation												
Inches Rain	1.7	2.0	2.1	2.3	1.9	1.2	2.1	2.1	1.4	1.3	1.5	1.6
Inches Snow	23	22	21	27	11	3	-	-	2	12	23	27

*V.W.R. = Vokac Weather Rating: probability of mild (warm & dry) weather on any given day.

Forecast

Month	V.W.R. *		Temperatures Daytime	Evening	Precipitation
January	0	Bad	cold	frigid	occasional snowstorms
February	0	Bad	cold	frigid	frequent snowstorms
March	0	Bad	chilly	frigid	frequent snowstorms
April	0	Bad	chilly	cold	frequent snowstorms
May	0	Bad	cool	chilly	occasional snow flurries
June	7	Good	warm	chilly	occasional showers/snow flurries
July	8	Very Good	warm	cool	frequent showers
August	8	Very Good	warm	cool	frequent showers
September	7	Good	warm	chilly	infrequent snow flurries/showers
October	0	Bad	cool	chilly	infrequent snowstorms
November	0	Bad	chilly	cold	infrequent snowstorms
December	0	Bad	cold	frigid	occasional snowstorms

Summary

Breckenridge is almost two miles above sea level in a broad mountain-rimmed valley in the central Colorado Rockies. It is the highest of the great towns. Not surprisingly, it also has the shortest period of comfortably usable weather. **Winter** is intense, with cold days and frigid evenings. Abundant powder snow from numerous storms, however, attracts properly-dressed skiers to a superb complex of in-town skiing facilities. Freezing temperatures, snowstorms, and fine skiing conditions continue through most of **spring**. Almost all of the year's good weather normally occurs in **summer**. Long warm days and cool evenings are briefly but frequently disrupted by thundershowers. The magnificent high country can normally be comfortably explored until Labor Day. In **fall**, temperatures plummet and unpredictable snowstorms become heavier. As one result, Breckenridge usually has some of the West's earliest good skiing conditions—as much as two months before winter officially begins.

ATTRACTIONS & DIVERSIONS

★ **Alpine Slide**   *1 mi. W on Ski Hill Rd.*   *453-2918*

A scenic chairlift operates from mid-June to late September, taking riders to the top of dual alpine slide tracks. The panoramic view of the Colorado Rockies is impressive. The rider has full control of the speed of the wheeled sled as it travels down the half-mile-long fiberglass track.

★ **Arapahoe National Forest**   *around town*   *668-3314*

This vast forest includes some of the highest peaks in the Rocky Mountains. The continent's highest paved road provides breathtaking views from the summit of 14,260-foot Mount Evans. A good system of dirt roads access numerous ghost towns, occasionally using abandoned narrow-gauge railroad right of ways. There are two wilderness areas and hundreds of miles of hiking trails. Dillon Reservoir and several others are popular boating facilities. Outstanding recreation opportunities include camping, hiking, backpacking, horseback riding, mountain climbing, boating, and fishing, plus an endless variety of snow sports in several major winter sports areas.

★ **Bicycling**

    The Knorr House   *downtown at 303 S. Main St.*   *453-2631*

There are several miles of separated scenic bikeways in and near town, and numerous worthwhile short trips on the broad, gently sloping valley floor. Hearty bikers able to pedal at a base elevation nearly two miles high can rent bicycles and gear and get maps and information at this shop.

★ **Dillon Reservoir**   *6 mi. N on CO 9*

Majestic peaks provide a scenic backdrop for a relatively large (five square miles) man-made lake with about twenty-five miles of shoreline. It is always too cold for swimming at 8,800 feet above sea level, but power and sail boating (rentals are available at the Dillon Yacht Basin - 468-2936) and fishing are very popular. The shoreline is studded with pine-shaded picnic and camp sites.

Golf

★   **Breckenridge Golf Course**   *4 mi. N off CO 9*

The area's first scenic 18-hole championship golf course was designed by Jack Nicklaus on a relatively flat site on the broad valley floor. When open to the public in 1985, it will include a pro shop, club and cart rentals, restaurant and bar.

★ **Horseback Riding**

Horses are rented by the hour or by the day for rides on forested paths around town. Breakfast rides, steak fries, fishing, and pack trips can also be arranged at:

    Breckenridge Inn Stables (guided or unguided) *.3 mi. S on CO 9*   *453-2333*
    Breckenridge Stables (guided)   *downtown at 505 S. Columbine Rd.*   *453-1460*

★ **Jeep Tours**

One-to-four hour driver-guided tours of ghost towns and breathtaking scenery above timberline can be reserved at:.

    Going Places   *downtown at 555 S. Columbine Rd.*   *453-6464*
    Tiger Run   *4 mi. N on CO 9*   *453-2231*

★ **Moped Rentals**

    Going Places   *downtown at 555 S. Columbine Rd.*   *453-6464*

Motor bikes can be rented any day in summer for two hours or more. They offer an exhilarating and relatively effortless way to explore ghost towns and other lures of the area's back roads.

Winter Sports

★   **Breckenridge Ski Area**   *downtown via Village Rd.*   *453-2368*

The vertical rise is 2,300 feet and the longest run is more than 2.5 miles. Elevation at the top is 11,840 feet. There are eleven chairlifts including a triple and a quadruple. All facilities, services, and rentals are available at three complete base areas in town for both downhill and cross-country skiing. Some bars, restaurants, and lodging facilities are within walking distance of the bases, and an excellent selection is nearby downtown. The ski season is late November to mid-April.

★ **Ski Touring**

Breckenridge Edsbyn Nordic Ski Center   *1 mi. W off Ski Hill Rd.*   *453-6855*
More than twelve miles of groomed and marked trails are maintained at the base of Peak 8. The spacious new facility offers a complete cross-country ski shop with rentals and lessons, lunches, a fireplace, and sun decks.

★ **Sleigh Rides**

All Seasons Sleigh Rides   *.5 mi. SW at 649 Village Rd.*   *453-6000*
Scenic sleigh rides can be arranged any day in winter at Beaver Run.

★ **Snowmobile Tours**

Experienced guides and appropriate suits and boots are furnished for exhilarating snowmobile tours in the Arapahoe National Forest by:

Going Places   *downtown at 555 S. Columbine Rd.*   *453-6464*
Summit Motor Sports   *6 mi. N at 16135 CO 9*   *453-0353*
Tiger Run   *4 mi. N on CO 9*   *453-2231*

SHOPPING

Main Street is the heart of a delightfully human-scaled downtown. While cleaned-up, pastel-toned new buildings greatly outnumber authentic Victorian landmarks, all blend harmoniously. A proliferation of distinctive galleries and specialty shops has occurred in recent years.

Food Specialties

Bailey's Wine and Cheese Shop   *downtown at 203 S. Main St.*   *453-2043*
A good selection of domestic and imported wines and beers, plus cheeses, meats, gourmet foods, and sandwiches make this a popular place to put together a picnic.

Blue River Diggings   *downtown at 200 W. Washington St.*   *453-1357*
Fresh baked pastries, donuts, bread, and bagels, plus pita bread sandwiches, are offered by this carryout bakery.

★ **Breckenridge Cookie Co.**   *downtown at 100 S. Main St.*   *453-0504*
Delicious cookies, plus hot pretzels and ice creams, are displayed in this attractive little carryout shop.

★ **The Golden Butterhorn Bake Shoppe**   *9 mi. NW at 408 Main St. - Frisco*   *668-3997*
An assortment of outstanding pastries and breads are featured to go or with coffee at a few tables in this irresistible new bakery.

★ **The Ice Cream Parlor**   *downtown at 325 S. Main St.*   *453-6969*
Otherwise known as "The Sweet Surrender," this colorful shop serves delicious homemade ice cream amidst detailed Victorian ice cream parlor atmosphere, or on a funky wooden deck with a mountain view. Soups, sandwiches and other light foods are also served.

★ **Rocky Mountain Chocolate Factory**   *downtown at 222 S. Main St.*   *453-2094*
Fudge is made here on marble slabs and sold with fine chocolates from Durango in a beautifully furnished shop.

Specialty Shops

★ **The Bay Street Company**   *downtown at 232 S. Main St.*   *453-6303*
Here is a remarkable, eclectic collection of gifts and accessories assembled from all over the world.

★ **Breckenridge Galleries Inc.**   *downtown at 121 S. Main St.*   *453-2592*
This fine arts gallery is an artistic showcase for painting and sculpture of the Southwest.

Great Northern Book & Poster Co.   *downtown at 555 S. Columbine Rd.*   *453-2444*
This small bookstore has a good selection of Colorado books and maps, plus magazines and posters.

NIGHTLIFE

In a very few years, Breckenridge has accumulated an excellent assortment of places to enjoy music, dancing, live theater, or a quiet drink in distinctive surroundings.

The Backstage Theatre   *downtown at 355 Village Rd.*   *453-0199*
A new theater has been donated for winter and summer stagings of mysteries, musicals, comedies, and special events featuring visiting artists and a local repertory company. Reservations are recommended.

★ **Briar Rose**   *downtown at 109 E. Lincoln St.*   *453-9948*
A splendid old-time bar filled with wild animal trophies and nude paintings adjoins an acclaimed restaurant.

★ **Flipside**   *downtown at 255 Village Rd.*   453-6600
High-tech disco dancing is available most nights in a large contemporary lounge that is comfortably furnished with plush sofas and overstuffed armchairs.

★ **The Mogul**   *downtown at 109 S. Main St.*   453-0999
Live music and dancing are offered most nights in this handsome cellar lounge. All of the walls are lined by comfortable sofa-pillow seating.

★ **Shamus O'Toole's Roadhouse Saloon** *downtown at 115 S. Ridge St.*   453-2004
Live entertainment and dancing are part of the action, along with pool, darts, foosball, shuffleboard, and electronic games in this rowdy and popular saloon.

★ **Tiffany's**   *.5 mi. SW at 649 Village Rd.*   453-6000
In the Beaver Run complex, there is disco dancing nightly in a dramatic high-tech and wood-toned lounge with comfortable armchair seating throughout.

★ **Tillie's**   *downtown at 213 S. Ridge St.*   453-0669
This local favorite features a splendid Victorian interior with an elegant teak back bar and a marble bartop. The highlight is an eight-foot square stained glass piece set in the pressed tin ceiling. A small front patio and a back mountain view deck are also used for drinks and light meals.

RESTAURANTS
A surprising number of notable restaurants have opened in recent years. Gourmet meals served in unusually appealing dining rooms have become one of the town's most admirable attributes.

Adams Street Cafe   *downtown at Main/Adams Sts.*   453-6805
L-D. Closed Sun.-Wed.   *Expensive*
Continental fare and fresh pastry desserts are offered in an intimate upstairs dining room. A mountain view deck is used on nice days. A cozy bar and patio are downstairs.

★ **Blue Front Cafe**   *downtown near Park Av./Four O'Clock Rd.*   453-1357
B-L-D.   *Moderate*
A delicious assortment of light contemporary fare is served in a stylish new dining room with a large fireplace and a sleek modern bar.

★ **The Blue Spruce Inn**   *9 mi. N at 120 W. Main St. - Frisco*   668-5243
D only.   *Expensive*
Steaks are featured on a Continental menu enhanced by homemade breads, pastries, and ice cream. Informal Western decor prevails in this well-regarded restaurant.
Upstairs is a cozy firelit dining room and a tiny bar.

★ **Briar Rose**   *downtown at 109 E. Lincoln St.*   453-9948
D only.   *Moderate*
Wild game dishes are given gourmet attention in season. Colorado beef and prime rib are also highlighted in a charming Old West-style dining room on the site of a Victorian boarding house. A fascinating bar adjoins.

The Gold Pan Restaurant   *downtown at 103 N. Main St.*   453-9075
B-L-D.   *Low*
This is a place for good early breakfasts like honeywheat pancakes, omelets, and Mexican specialties. The rustic little coffee shop adjoins a funky bar.

Horseshoe II Restaurant   *downtown at 115 S. Main St.*   453-9804
B-L-D.   *Moderate*
American-style breakfast specialties are featured, and light meals are served all day. There is a full bar in the rustic little dining room. An attractive courtyard deck is also used, weather permitting.

★ **La France Restaurant**   *13 mi. N at Buffalo/Chief Colorow - Dillon*   468-6111
D only. Sun. brunch.   *Moderate*
Both the gourmet French dishes and the decor of this firelit dining room reflect the thoroughly Gaullic personality of the owner/chef.

McCarthy's   *downtown at 208 N. Main St.*   453-0063
D only. Closed Sun.   *Moderate*
A Continental menu includes some unusual specialties like apricot pork chops. The pleasant wood-toned dining room is in a converted century-old building. A small comfortable bar is downstairs.

Ninety-Six Hundred Feet Club *downtown at 450 S. Columbine* *453-6223*
L-D. *Moderate*
Exhibition outdoor grilling enlivens an unusual log cabin-style dining room and a delightful umbrella-shaded deck by Maggie Pond. An atmospheric bar in the dining room is outfitted with wood stump barstools.

★ **The St. Bernard Inn** *downtown at 103 S. Main St.* *453-2572*
D only. Closed Mon. *Expensive*
Northern Italian cuisine with fresh homemade breads and pastas is featured in a handsome candlelit dining room restored to its original Victorian decor. An atmospheric bar adjoins.

★ **The Terrace** *downtown at 109 S. Main St.* *453-0986*
L-D. No D on Sun. *Expensive*
Continental specialties with an emphasis on fresh fish are served in an elegant contemporary dining room and on a rooftop terrace with a panoramic view over town to the mountains.

The Village Pub *downtown at 555 S. Columbine Rd.* *453-0369*
L-D. *Moderate*
Steak, seafood and chicken dishes with some innovations are offered by the waterfall adjoining beautiful Maggie Pond in the Bell Tower Mall. There is a splendid mountain view from the dining room, terrace and lounge.

Weber's Restaurant *downtown at 200 N. Main St.* *453-9464*
D only. Closed Mon.-Tues. *Moderate*
Hearty German and American meals include homemade soups, breads, and dessert pastries in a cozy, casually elegant Victorian setting.

The Whale's Tale *downtown at 323 S. Main St.* *453-2221*
L-D. *Moderate*
Fresh fish and seafood specialties are accompanied by a salad bar and a bustling nautical atmosphere. A deck fronting on main street is used in summer. There is a popular adjoining bar and an outdoor seating area for cocktails.

LODGING

Most of the accommodations in town are modern and relatively lavish condominium rentals. Bargains are scarce in town, but plentiful in older motels in Frisco (9 mi. NW on CO 9). Rates are usually at least 50% higher than those shown during the winter ski season and 10% lower in spring and fall. Several major condominium management companies handle many of the best units around town, including the river-fronting "Tannenbaum" and "Powderhorn" complexes, and "The Village" on Maggie Pond by the Peak 9 chairlift. Among the largest are:

Resort Rentals Inc. *downtown at 301 S. Main St.* *321-2246*
SCI Management Inc. *downtown at 120 S. Main St.* *453-2288*

A & B Court *9 mi. NW via CO 9 at 310 Main St. - Frisco* *668-3587*
This old log cabin-style **bargain** motel has a color TV in each of the modest rooms.
regular room — D bed...$25

Angler's Inn *9 mi. NW via CO 9 at 211 Main St. - Frisco* *668-5666*
In this small **bargain** motel, each room has a cable color TV.
regular room — D bed...$21

★ **Beaver Run** *.5 mi. W at 649 Village Rd.* *453-6000*
Adjacent to one of the main chairlifts in town, this lavish new eight-story complex is one of Colorado's largest and finest condominium resort hotels. State-of-the-art facilities include a large indoor/outdoor pool, view whirlpools, steambaths, saunas, a tennis court, a health club, exercise room, restaurants, lounges, specialty shops, and indoor parking. Each spacious and beautifully decorated unit has a phone and cable color TV with movies.
#839 — 1 BR, kit., fireplace, mt. view, Q bed...$85
#207,#107 — 1 BR, kit., fireplace, ski slope/mt. view, Q bed...$85
#840 — 2 BR, kit., fireplace, mt. view, 2 T & Q beds...$115
regular room — hotel room, Q bed...$65

Breckenridge Inn & Resort *downtown at 600 S. Ridge St.* 453-2333
A big outdoor pool with a splendid mountain view sundeck, tennis courts, and (for a fee) horseback riding are features of this older motor lodge. Each room has a phone and cable color TV.

regular room — 2 D beds...$35

Fireside Inn *downtown at 212 Wellington St.* 453-6456
A Western-style bed-and-breakfast inn in a conveniently located house has **bargain** rooms and a hot tub. A Continental breakfast is complimentary and other meals may be purchased by guests. Each room has a private bath.

"Brandywine" — spacious, pvt. bath & stairs to hot tub, Q bed...$48

regular room — D bed...$28

Mt. Royal Motel *9 mi. NW via CO 9 at 117 Main St. - Frisco* 668-5222
This older single-level **bargain** motel has rooms with cable color TV.

regular room — Q & D beds...$22

Sky-vue Motel *9 mi. NW via CO 9 at 305 S. 2nd Av. - Frisco* 668-3311
A large indoor pool is the main attraction of this newly refurbished single-level **bargain** motel. Each room has cable TV with movies.

regular room — 2 D or Q bed...$30

Snowshoe Motel *9 mi. NW via CO 9 at 521 Main St. - Frisco* 668-3444
This **bargain** motel has a phone and cable color TV with movies in each unit.

"The Suite" — whirlpool, kit., Q waterbed...$45

regular room — Q bed...$28

Summit Inn *3.5 mi. N on CO 9* 453-2900
This single-level, modern motel is a no-frills **bargain**.

regular room — 2 D beds...$25

Tannhauser *downtown at 420 S. Main St.* 453-2136
In addition to saunas and a rec room, this small condominium apartment complex has privileges (for a fee) at a local club with all recreation facilities. Each unit has two bedrooms, a full kitchen, and a living room with a raised flagstone wood-burning fireplace, plus a semi-private deck and cable color TV.

"3B1","2B1" — top fl., windows on 2 sides, fine mt. view, 2 T & D beds...$50

"3A6","2A6" — top fl., fine ski slope & mt. views, 2 T & 2 D beds...$50

regular room — 2 BR, 2 T & D beds...$50

★ **The Village at Breckenridge** *downtown at Village Dr./Park Av.* 453-6153
The best location in town is occupied by a large, seven-level condominium complex. By Blue River and the base of the Breckenridge Ski Area, the contemporary condo/hotel is also an easy stroll from anywhere downtown. Amenities include restaurants, bars, a live theater/cinema, shops and (for a fee) horseback riding and health club facilities, plus (in winter) a chairlift and ice-skating. Each well-appointed unit has a phone, cable color TV with movies, kitchen, wood-burning fireplace, and a private balcony.

"Bldg. A, 5th & 4th fl., SW corner" — 1 BR, splendid pond/slope/mt. view, Q bed...$60

"Bldg. B, 7th,6th,5th fl., SW corner" — 1 BR, slope/mt. view, Q bed...$60

regular unit — 1 BR, Q bed...$60

CAMPGROUNDS
The nearest scenic campgrounds are several miles north by Dillon Reservoir. These relatively primitive sites in pine-forested settings backed by spectacular peaks are only popular for a couple of summer months because of the usually cold nights at this high elevation.

Peak One *7 mi. NW on CO 9* 668-5404
This White River National Forest campground is in a pine forest near a large scenic reservoir. Activities include boating and fishing on Dillon Lake. Boat ramps and nature trails have been provided. There are flush and pit toilets, but no showers or hookups. Each pine-shaded site has a picnic table, fire ring, and grill. A separate tents-only area is available. base rate...$5

SPECIAL EVENTS

★ **Ullr Fest**   *in town and on the ski slopes*   *end of January*
The Norse God of Winter reigns over a week-long winter carnival. Events include a downtown parade and bonfire, a torchlight parade, fireworks on the mountain, ice-skating demonstrations, races, broomball tournaments, and a grand ball.

Breckenridge Music Institute   *downtown*   *July - early August*
Professional musicians present performances ranging from full orchestra concerts to solo recitals, and there are a series of workshops during this six week festival.

★ **Gathering at the Great Divide**   *downtown*   *Labor Day Weekend*
This arts and crafts festival includes exhibitions around town, a fine arts competition, an old-time fiddlers contest, and a historic house and cemetery tour.

OTHER INFORMATION

Area Code: *303*
Zip Code: *80424*
Breckenridge Resort Chamber *downtown at 201 W. Washington St.*   *453-2918*
Arapahoe National Forest Visitor Center *9 mi. N at 101 W. Main - Frisco*   *668-3314*

Crested Butte, Colorado

Elevation:

8,885 feet

Population (1980):

959

Population (1970):

372

Location:

232 mi. SW
of Denver

Crested Butte is a treasure trove of the real Old West. The little cluster of wood-sided buildings seems even smaller against the side of a broad sage-and-grass-covered valley surrounded by majestic peaks of the central Colorado Rockies. Almost 9,000 feet above sea level, it is one of the nation's highest communities. Winters are long and cold, but an abundance of powder snow attracts increasing numbers of visitors to a major ski area nearby on the slopes of the town's handsome namesake. Snow-capped peaks, forests, streams, and lakes around town are especially popular in summer, when the weather is suitable for hiking, backpacking, mountain climbing, horseback riding, fishing, and river running, plus such unusual "contemporary" diversions as jeep touring, fat-tire bicycling, hot-air ballooning, and hang gliding.

Miners started looking for gold and silver in the area in the 1870s. Crested Butte was incorporated in 1880, the same year that the Denver and Rio Grande laid their narrow-gauge railroad up from Gunnison. The town served as a supply center for outlying mining camps, but the discovery of coal in the late 1880s actually sustained it. The last coal mine closed in 1952, and Crested Butte languished briefly. Development of a major ski area on Mt. Crested Butte during the 1960s began the fulfillment of the area's year-round recreation potential. Energetic new residents restored old buildings for homes and businesses again. New construction was carefully blended with historic buildings under the watchful eyes of an architectural review board. In 1974 the entire town was designated a National Historic District in recognition of its remarkable preservation and unusual heritage as an Old Western working-class town. Ironically, Crested Butte's new status as a major recreation destination may be as brief as its original role as a supply center for the short-lived gold and silver mines. In 1977, one of the world's largest deposits of molybdenum (a space-age mineral used to alloy steel) was discovered on a mountain overlooking town. If a mine is developed to full potential on that site, the little town's newfound greatness may end as the tranquil splendor of the area is displaced by heavy industry.

For now, the village delights all who discover it. The compact historic business district boasts a number of fine restaurants and fascinating bars, and a small but growing number of art galleries and specialty shops. Accommodations in town are scarce, rustic, and within an easy stroll of all of the Victorian relics on the likeable main street. There are plenty of contemporary lodgings three miles east at the base of the ski area.

WEATHER PROFILE
Vokac Weather Rating

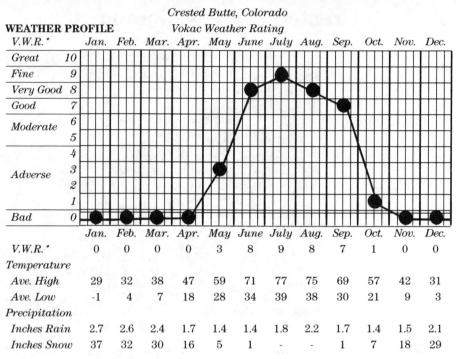

V.W.R.*		Jan.	Feb.	Mar.	Apr.	May	June	July	Aug.	Sep.	Oct.	Nov.	Dec.
Great	10												
Fine	9												
Very Good	8												
Good	7												
Moderate	6												
	5												
	4												
Adverse	3												
	2												
	1												
Bad	0												

	Jan.	Feb.	Mar.	Apr.	May	June	July	Aug.	Sep.	Oct.	Nov.	Dec.
V.W.R.*	0	0	0	0	3	8	9	8	7	1	0	0
Temperature												
Ave. High	29	32	38	47	59	71	77	75	69	57	42	31
Ave. Low	-1	4	7	18	28	34	39	38	30	21	9	3
Precipitation												
Inches Rain	2.7	2.6	2.4	1.7	1.4	1.4	1.8	2.2	1.7	1.4	1.5	2.1
Inches Snow	37	32	30	16	5	1	-	-	1	7	18	29

*V.W.R. = Vokac Weather Rating: probability of mild (warm & dry) weather on any given day.

Forecast

Temperatures

Month	V.W.R.*		Daytime	Evening	Precipitation
January	0	Bad	cold	frigid	occasional snowstorms
February	0	Bad	cold	frigid	occasional snowstorms
March	0	Bad	chilly	frigid	occasional snowstorms
April	0	Bad	chilly	cold	occasional snowstorms
May	3	Adverse	cool	chilly	occasional showers/snow flurries
June	8	Very Good	warm	cool	infrequent rainstorms
July	9	Fine	warm	cool	occasional showers
August	8	Very Good	warm	cool	frequent showers
September	7	Good	warm	chilly	occasional showers
October	1	Adverse	cool	chilly	infrequent snow flurries
November	0	Bad	chilly	cold	infrequent snowstorms
December	0	Bad	cold	frigid	occasional snowstorms

Summary

Many of the spectacular peaks of the central Colorado Rockies are visible from tiny Crested Butte, which is tucked against the side of a sagebrush-covered high country basin. Because cold air from the surrounding mountains settles into the lowest portions of this basin, **winter** nights are extremely cold, and daytime high temperatures normally are below freezing. These conditions, plus occasional heavy snowstorms, assure many months of excellent skiing at the major complex nearby. Winter sports continue well into **spring**. Snow flurries and freezing temperatures usually end after Memorial Day. The spring runoff is replaced by wildflower fields and mild **summer** weather. Warm days and cool evenings are ideal for exploring the splendid alpine countryside, except during brief but persistent thundershowers. Around the beginning of **fall**, temperatures plummet and snowstorms soon transform the landscape into a winter wonderland. But, during a brief transition, panoramas of aspen-covered slopes ablaze with color beneath peaks mantled by dazzling new snow are the year's most inspiring natural highlights.

ATTRACTIONS & DIVERSIONS

Backpacking
    The Alpineer   *.3 mi. E at 419 6th St.*   *349-5210*
Backpacks, camping and mountaineering gear are rented and sold, and backcountry tours can be arranged by these outdoor specialists.

Bicycling
    Bicycles, etc.   *downtown at 311 5th St.*   *349-6286*
There are no exclusive bikeways, and the highways and rugged dirt byways around town go up and down a lot of steep hills. Nevertheless, the scenery is breathtaking — a feeling enhanced by reduced oxygen in this high country. Thick-framed, fat-tire bikes that are perfect for touring the demanding countryside can be rented here. Information, maps, and sightseeing tours are also available.

★ **Curecanti National Recreation Area**   *37 mi. SW via CO 135 on US 50*   *641-2337*
In a vast sage-and-pine-covered rangeland basin, three man-made lakes on the Gunnison River have been set aside as a major water recreation site. Fishing, boating (and boat rentals), water-skiing, swimming, and camping are popular in summer. Blue Mesa Lake, a twenty-mile-long reservoir, is Colorado's largest lake (when filled to capacity) and the area's primary focus of water sports. Scenic two-hour boat trips are the distinctive feature of Morrow Point, a reservoir deep within a canyon of the Gunnison. Private boats must be hand-carried to Morrow Point Lake, and to Crystal Lake, a small, fiord-like reservoir.

Golf
★   **Skyland Resort and Country Club**   *2 mi. SE on CO 135*   *349-6129*
A spectacular, mountain-rimmed 18-hole championship golf course designed by Robert Trent Jones, Jr., opened to the public in 1984 with a pro shop, club and cart rentals, plus a restaurant and bar.

★ **Gunnison National Forest**   *around town*   *349-5213*
There are more than two dozen peaks over 12,000 feet high in this vast Rocky Mountain highland. Features include a fine winter sports area on the slopes of Crested Butte. Portions of four wilderness areas include the magnificent Maroon Bells-Snowmass wilderness that occupies most of the area between Crested Butte and Aspen. Throughout the forest, a good system of dirt roads and hundreds of miles of trails provide access to hiking, backpacking, mountain climbing, horseback riding, hunting, fishing and most winter sports.

★ **Historic District**   *on/near Elk Av.*
A delightful conglomeration of restored century-old clapboard structures, plus more recent add-ons and similarly-designed newer buildings, has been designated as a National Historic District. Attractions include the Old Town Hall (1883), a picturesque building on Elk Avenue that was used by the Town Trustees and the Fire Department. It is now a theater and art gallery, but it is still used for town council meetings. Totem Pole Park (3rd St./Maroon Av.) was created to surround an impressive totem pole made with chain saws in 1974. An authentic two-story outhouse is in the alley off Maroon Avenue between 3rd and 4th Streets. The upper level is offset from the lower level so that it could be used simultaneously by persons on each floor — believe it or not. A walking tour map and information can be obtained from the Chamber of Commerce.

★ **Horseback Riding**
A horse can provide access to remote wilderness areas via hundreds of miles of forest trails. Two stables offering rentals and trail rides are:
    Cement Creek Ranch   *12 mi. S via CO 135 on Cement Cr. Rd.*   *349-5541*
    Just Horsin' Around   *downtown at 29 Whiterock Av.*   *349-6821*

★ **Jeep Rentals and Tours**
    Crested Butte Lodge   *3 mi. NE at 21 Emmons Rd.*   *349-7555*
A four-wheel drive jeep provides a relatively easy and fast way to explore the rugged countryside around town. Daily or weekly jeep rentals, or tours of various lengths, can be arranged here.

★ **Lake Irwin**   *10 mi. W via dirt road - near Kebler Pass*
Nearly two miles high in the mountains west of town is a small clear lake popular for fishing and small boats (no motors). Hiking trails circle the lake, which features picturesque boulder formations, pine-shaded campgrounds, and picnic facilities.

River Running
The Gunnison River offers rafters fairly easy runs and good scenery in summer, especially along The Palisades south of Almont. Float fishing is best starting in July — after the heavy spring runoff. More whitewater is available on the Taylor River above Almont. Arrangements can be made for a variety of floats at:

Avalanche Outfitters, Inc.	*17 mi. S on CO 135 - Almont*	*641-1009*
Sawtooth Mountain Outfitters	*28 mi. S on CO 135 - Gunnison*	*641-5077*

Warm Water Feature
★ **The Four Seasons**   *downtown at Elk Av./1st St.*   *349-7331*
A funky old log building just off the main street has been made into an updated Old West bathhouse. A large communal hot water whirlpool set in natural rock, an adjoining cold pool, a sauna, and redwood decks are open every afternoon and evening. Visitors pay a single fee for all facilities, shower, soap and towels. Massage is also available. A rustic bed-and-breakfast boarding house adjoins.

Winter Sports
★ **Crested Butte Mountain Resort**   *3 mi. NE via Gothic County Rd.*   *349-2333*
The vertical rise is 2,150 feet and the longest run is almost two miles. Elevation at the top is 11,250 feet. There are seven chairlifts (including an enclosed cabin). All facilities, services, and rentals are available at the base for both downhill and cross-country skiing. Numerous restaurants, bars and lodgings are at the base. The ski season is early December to mid-April.

   Ice-Skating   *3 mi. NE via Gothic County Rd.*   *349-2333*
Ice-skating may be enjoyed daily in winter (weather and rink conditions permitting) on a picturesque outdoor rink at the base of the ski area.

★ **Sleigh Rides**   *3 mi. NE on Gothic County Rd.*   *349-2211*
During the winter, guests snuggle under wool blankets on a horse-drawn sled while they ride through a starlit night over snow-covered hills. In a large tent by the Slate River, everyone warms up around a wood stove and drinks spiced apple cider and hot chocolate while being entertained with folk songs.

SHOPPING
Crested Butte has a compact downtown distinguished both by its historic continuity and its delightfully human scale. A small but growing number of galleries and specialty shops are concentrated on and near Elk Avenue (the main street).

Food Specialties
Acme Liquor Store   *.3 mi. E at 603 6th St.*   *349-5709*
Premium domestic and imported wines, plus liquors, are displayed in an authentic old-time setting.

★ **The Bakery Cafe**   *downtown at 302 Elk Av.*   *349-7280*
Outstanding (and huge) croissants, strudels and other pastries, cakes and breads can be taken out, or enjoyed with coffee and light meals in this esteemed bakery's pleasant indoor or patio dining areas.

Specialty Shops
Cole's Crafts, Inc.   *6 mi. SE on CO 135*   *349-5138*
Hand-turned aspenwood vases and vessels are displayed and sold in an authentic old one-room schoolhouse furnished to look as it did decades ago.

★ **The Crested Butte Hardware Store**   *downtown at 331 Elk Av.*   *349-5582*
One of the last of the old-timers, this fascinating bit of pure Western Americana has been in continuous operation at this location for a century. The unspoiled interior casually displays what is perhaps the world's largest trophy elk-head. Nearby, a wonderfully embellished turn-of-the-century pot-bellied stove is still a gathering spot for locals.

Paragon Gallery   *downtown at 132 Elk Av.*   *349-6484*
In the century-old Town Hall is an art gallery run by, and displaying the works of, local artists.

Silent Pictures   *.3 mi. E at 429 6th St.*   *349-6208*
This design studio and fine arts gallery features original work, especially in stained glass.

Susan H. Anderton Gallery   *downtown at 331 Elk Av.*   *349-5289*
Fine art in a variety of media by local artists is attractively displayed.

Zacchariah Zypp & Co.　　*downtown at 301 Elk Av.*　　　　*349-5913*
Aspen leaves and pine cones are made into silver and gold art objects in this old-time store. The large selection of hand-wrought and cast jewelry was producod here by gold and silversmiths.

NIGHTLIFE
Downtown is as lively as ever, with an old-fashioned movie house and a live theater that offers plays most of the year, plus an outstanding collection of unspoiled old-time bars. Contemporary Western-style lounges are featured at the nearby ski area.

Crested Butte Mountain Theatre　　*downtown at 132 Elk Av.*　　*349-5685*
For about a decade, good live theater has been offered in a large upstairs room of the Old Town Hall. All kinds of productions, including serious dramas, are staged during the summer and winter seasons.

Eldorado Cafe　　*downtown at 215 Elk Av.*　　　　*349-5737*
There is live music most nights, and an adjoining sundeck overlooking downtown is a favorite place for afternoon drinks. Lunch and dinner are also served in this inviting second floor cafe/bar.

Forest Queen　　*downtown at 129 Elk Av.*　　　　*349-5336*
A friendly "locals" bar with a genuine old-time feeling and a fine back bar is located in the Forest Queen Hotel — one of the town's oldest buildings.

The Grubstake　　*downtown at 229 Elk Av.*　　　　*349-9982*
Recently, one of the area's favorite watering holes was carefully renovated. It now claims the state's largest collection of spirits — all proudly displayed behind the bar. A good restaurant adjoins.

★ **Kochevar's**　　*downtown at 127 Elk Av.*　　　　*349-6745*
Periodic live entertainment is a feature in an authentic workingman's saloon that was reopened recently after being closed for more than sixty years. Basically unchanged from its pre-Prohibition era origins, the comfortably-worn atmosphere is enhanced by a pot-bellied stove, an old juke box, and trophy game animals in a room with a high polished-wood ceiling, wainscoting, and uneven old floorboards.

Princess Theatre　　*downtown at 218 Elk Av.*　　　　*349-5119*
Current films are screened in a tiny old movie theater that exudes an honest nostalgic charm. The oleo curtain is a knockout.

Rafters　　*3 mi. NE via Gothic County Rd.*　　　　*349-2249*
Live country bands entertain nightly for dancing at the base of the lifts in Ski Area Central. Lunch and dinner are also served, emphasizing gourmet hamburgers and special buffets.

Talk of the Town　　*downtown at 230 Elk Av.*　　　　*349-6809*
Occasional live entertainment is offered in a skillfully modernized bar/dining room with casual American fare. A marvelous mounted moose presides.

★ **The Wooden Nickel**　　*downtown at 222 Elk Av.*　　　　*349-9983*
The town's oldest saloon continues to attract crowds with its big fireplace, conversation pit, comfortably padded booths, and handsome wood-and-mirror back bar. An eclectic menu offers dishes ranging from hamburgers and beer-batter onion rings to steamed clams.

RESTAURANTS
Crested Butte has a surprising concentration of good restaurants for a town of its size. All of the best occupy carefully restored old buildings downtown where gourmet dining blends easily with authentic Victorian atmosphere. Several restaurants are closed during the off-seasons (spring and fall).

The Alpenhof　　*3 mi. NE at 621 Gothic Rd.*　　　　*349-5692*
L-D. Closed Sun.　　　　　　　　*Moderate*
Austrian and German dishes are served amidst Old World decor in this small, pleasant restaurant near the slopes.

The Artichoke　　*3 mi. NE at 433 Emmons Rd.*　　　　*349-5400*
D only. B-L-D in winter.　　　　　*Moderate*
Steaks and a salad bar are dinner features in a contemporary restaurant with a sundeck overlooking the base of the ski area.

Bacchanale   *downtown at 208 Elk Av.*   *349-5257*
D only.   *Moderate*
Italian cuisine and fine desserts are specialties of this small, well-furnished restaurant and bar.

The Forest Queen   *downtown at 129 Elk Av.*   *349-5336*
B-D. No D on Sun. & Mon.   *Moderate*
Traditional American foods including homemade desserts are offered in a relaxed and distinctive century-old hotel.

The Gourmet Noodle   *downtown at Elk Av./2nd St.*   *349-7401*
L-D. Closed Mon.-Tues.   *Moderate*
Everything is homemade and there is an emphasis on Italian dishes in this casual, colorful restaurant.

The Grubstake   *downtown at 229 Elk Av.*   *349-6107*
L-D. No L on Sat. & Sun.   *Moderate*
Prime rib and other American dishes are noted on a short blackboard list in an easygoing little restaurant next to a popular bar.

Jeremiah's   *3 mi. NE at 21 Emmons Rd.*   *349-5349*
B-D.   *Moderate*
Prime rib is the specialty on a varied menu, and homemade baked goods lend support. The recently remodeled contemporary dining room is in the Crested Butte Lodge at the base of the ski runs. In summer, guests also dine outdoors. The bar offers periodic live entertainment.

★ **Le Bosquet Restaurant**   *downtown at 201 Elk Av.*   *349-5808*
L-D.   *Moderate*
French gourmet cuisine and homemade desserts are presented in an informally elegant dining room. There is also a handsome bar, and a delightful creekside view patio.

★ **Penelope's**   *downtown at 120 Elk Av.*   *349-5178*
D only. Brunch on Sat. & Sun.   *Moderate*
Fine Continental cuisine and homemade baked goods are offered in a luxuriant greenhouse-style dining room amidst casually elegant Victorian decor, or outdoors near the creek in summer. An antique-laden bar adjoins.

★ **The Slogar**   *downtown at 517 2nd St.*   *349-5765*
D only.   *Expensive*
A short list of skillfully prepared Continental cuisine and homemade desserts is identified on a blackboard menu. The dining room is in a historic house that has been lovingly restored to genuine Victorian splendor. Cocktails are served in an elegant parlor.

Soupcon   *downtown at 127 Elk Av.*   *349-5448*
D only.   *Expensive*
Continental cuisine is served in the rustic, congested atmosphere of a tiny old log cabin on the alley behind the Silver Queen Hotel.

The Vineyard   *downtown at 313 3rd St.*   *349-5820*
D only.   *Moderate*
Continental fondues and dinner crepes are featured in this informal little restaurant located in a century-old building.

LODGING

Accommodations are relatively scarce, rustic, and inexpensive in town. At the nearby ski area, lodgings are readily available, recently constructed, and range in decor from plain to elegant. Most of the better lodgings are only open during summer and winter. Winter is the "high" season when rates are usually slightly higher in town and 50-100% higher at the ski area than the quoted summer rates.

★ **Crested Butte Lodge**   *3 mi. NE at 21 Emmons Rd.*   *349-7555*
Near the Mt. Crested Butte Ski Area slopes, this modern motor lodge has a large indoor pool, whirlpools and saunas, plus a restaurant and lounge. Each of the units has a phone and cable color TV.

"suite" — 1 BR, wet bar, refr., fireplace,   Q bed...$60
regular room —   Q or K bed...$40

★ **Crested Mountain Condominiums**   *3 mi. NE at 21 Emmons Rd.*   *349-7555*
This luxurious condominium building is directly on the slope by the lifts at the heart of Mt. Crested Butte Ski Area. Guests have privileges at the nearby Crested Butte Lodge for use of a large indoor pool, whirlpools and saunas. Each of the handsomely furnished two or three bedroom apartments has a phone, cable color TV, living room, fireplace, kitchen, private balcony, washer/dryer, and a private in-bath whirlpool.

#A2,#B2,#C2,#D2,#E2,#F2,#G2 — 2 BR, on ski slope, grand privateviews
of the mountain   2 T & Q beds...$80
regular apartment — 2 BR,   2 T & Q beds...$80

Elk Mountain Lodge   *downtown at 2nd St./Gothic Av.*   *349-5114*
An old miners' boarding hotel has been renovated and expanded, but it's still a **bargain** for people willing to go down the hall to a shared bath. There is a whirlpool. Each of the plain little rooms has cable color TV.

regular room — with private bath,   2 D beds...$38
regular room — shared bath,   D bed...$26

The Forest Queen   *downtown at 129 Elk Av.*   *349-5336*
Rustic, well-worn accommodations are a **bargain** in this historic century-old building in the heart of town. A good restaurant and bar are downstairs.

#1 — corner, main street & creek view, private bath,   D bed...$30
#6 — creek sounds, shared bath,   D bed...$25
regular room — shared bath,   D bed...$25

★ **Gateway**   *2.8 mi. NE via Gothic County Rd. on Snowmass Rd.*   *349-7555*
This handsome new condominium complex is directly adjacent to the slope and lifts just east of the heart of the ski area. Amenities include a sauna and an outdoor whirlpool with a spectacular mountain view, plus a covered garage. Guests have privileges at the nearby Crested Butte Lodge's indoor pool, whirlpools, and sauna. Each luxuriously appointed apartment has a phone, cable color TV, living room, fireplace, kitchen, washer/dryer, balcony, and an in-bath whirlpool.

#102 thru #105 — 2 BR, grand view of Crested Butte/town,   Q bed...$70
#101 — 1 BR, ski out the door to the chairlift,   Q bed...$55
#301 - 1 BR, great view of Crested Butte,   Q bed...$55
regular apartment — 1 BR,   Q bed...$55

Irwin Lodge   *12 mi. W via part-dirt road*   *349-5140*
An imposing cedar lodge furnished in Victorian decor overlooks beautiful Lake Irwin, and provides accommodations for a retreat-like experience in a splendid mountain environment. No phones or television are present, but the dining room serves ample family-style meals to guests, and there is a well-stocked bar. Various alpine recreation opportunities are available during both the summer and winter seasons. American plan rates include breakfast, lunch, and dinner.

regular room —   D bed...$147

Ore Bucket Lodge   *.5 mi. NE at 621 Maroon Av.*   *349-5519*
Between downtown and the ski area is a newer, no-frills **bargain** motel. Each plain room has a private bath.

regular room —   D bed...$24

Rozman's   *.3 mi. SE on CO 135*   *349-6669*
Surprisingly, this modest little facility is the only conventional motel in town. There is a restaurant. Each room has a phone and cable color TV.

regular room —   D bed...$35

★ **Three Seasons Condominiums**   *3.5 mi. NE at 701 Gothic Rd.*   *349-6126*
The ski area's biggest condo/lodge features a central enclosed courtyard with a large heated pool. Other amenities include a whirlpool, sauna, and game room, plus a restaurant and bar. Each attractively furnished unit has a phone, cable color TV, kitchen, moss rock fireplace, and a private balcony.

#343,#243 — 1 BR, corner windows, mt. view,   Q bed...$55
regular room — 1 BR,   Q bed...$55

CAMPGROUNDS

There are few campgrounds in the area and they are relatively primitive. The best are located in pine forests by a crystal clear lake or stream surrounded by splendid peaks of the central Colorado Rockies.

Cement Creek *11 mi. SE: 7 mi. S via CO 135 & 4 mi. E on For. Rd. 740*   *349-5213*
This small Gunnison National Forest campground is located in pines by Cement Creek. Features include fishing and hiking. There are pit toilets, but no showers or hookups. Each widely-spaced, shaded site has a picnic table and fire ring/grill. A few sites are by the creek.   base rate...no fee

Lake Irwin *10 mi. W: 7.3 mi. W on Cty. Rd. 2 & 3 mi. N on For. Rd. 826*   *641-0471*
The picturesque shoreline of a little mountain lake is an ideal location for this small Gunnison National Forest campground. Features include boating (no motors) and fishing in Lake Irwin, and hiking trails. Pit toilets are available. There are no showers, drinking water, or hookups. Each shady site has a picnic table.   base rate...$5

SPECIAL EVENTS

Festival of the Arts   *downtown on Elk Av.*   *early August*
The finest local and regional arts and crafts are displayed on the main street. Live music and dance performances add to the festive weekend.

★ **Aerial Weekend**   *in town and nearby*   *mid-August*
A colorful collection of hot-air balloons, hang gliders, glider planes, sky divers, aerobatic pilots, and helicopters fill the sky around town. Visitors share music and refreshments with participants from all over the West for one uplifting weekend.

OTHER INFORMATION

Area Code: *303*
Zip Code: *81224*
Crested Butte-Mt. Crested Butte C. of C. *downtown at 405 2nd St.*   *349-6438*
Gunnison Natl. Forest-Ranger's Office *downtown at 108 Gothic Av.*   *349-5213*

Durango, Colorado

Elevation:

6,512 feet

Population (1980):

11,426

Population (1970):

10,333

Location:

335 mi. SW
of Denver

Durango is the recreation center of the southern Rocky Mountains. It occupies scenic pinon pine-and-juniper-covered benchlands along the Animas River. A few miles to the north is a natural gateway to the spectacular San Juan Mountains, with several of the nation's highest peaks. Nearby to the south are mesas and plateaus of the vast Southwestern desert. Durango enjoys a four season climate and a longer period of comfortable weather than any other great town in Colorado. The best weather occurs in late spring and in summer, which is easily the most popular season for pursuing outdoor recreation opportunities. A few miles northeast, Vallecito Reservoir accommodates all kinds of water sports on a big fiord-like lake surrounded by a luxuriant pine forest. The San Juan Mountains offer excellent hiking, backpacking, horseback riding, jeeping, and fishing. Nearby to the southwest in Mesa Verde National Park is the nation's finest concentration of Indian ruins. River running, bicycling, golf, tennis, and swimming are enjoyed in town, along with a series of attractive riverside parks. Winters are snowy enough that facilities for some winter sports have been provided in town, and a major ski area is in the nearby San Juans.

Extensive gold and silver ore discoveries after the Civil War prompted the Denver and Rio Grande Railroad to extend its line to this area. Because the valley's existing town (Animas City) refused to make certain concessions to the railroad, a new town (Durango) was surveyed in 1880 one and a half miles to the south. Narrow-gauge locomotives began to arrive in 1881. The new town quickly developed as the crossroads for the San Juan Basin, and eventually swallowed up Animas City. Unlike most Colorado mining towns, Durango never experienced a "bust" because it was always the region's commercial center.

The narrow-gauge railroad that created the town is still running today. Durango's Old West charm is uniquely enhanced by the dramatic presence of this splendid relic — the area's major attraction. A remarkable number of century-old buildings have been beautifully preserved and restored. Downtown, the well-landscaped main street is lined for blocks with massive brick Victorians and carefully integrated newer structures. These buildings house a notable array of art galleries and specialty shops displaying Southwestern arts and crafts. Here also are some good restaurants, and one of the West's most outstanding collections of saloons, live theaters, and hotels that perpetuate the spirit of the Old West. Accommodations are plentiful. Many plain, modern motels line the approaches to town. Nearby, resorts and dude ranches offer luxurious facilities in awesome wilderness settings.

Durango, Colorado

WEATHER PROFILE — *Vokac Weather Rating*

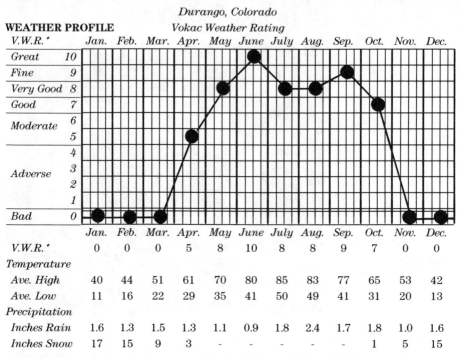

V.W.R. *		Jan.	Feb.	Mar.	Apr.	May	June	July	Aug.	Sep.	Oct.	Nov.	Dec.
Great	10						●						
Fine	9									●			
Very Good	8					●		●	●				
Good	7										●		
Moderate	6												
	5				●								
	4												
Adverse	3												
	2												
	1												
Bad	0	●	●	●								●	●

	Jan.	Feb.	Mar.	Apr.	May	June	July	Aug.	Sep.	Oct.	Nov.	Dec.
V.W.R. *	0	0	0	5	8	10	8	8	9	7	0	0
Temperature												
Ave. High	40	44	51	61	70	80	85	83	77	65	53	42
Ave. Low	11	16	22	29	35	41	50	49	41	31	20	13
Precipitation												
Inches Rain	1.6	1.3	1.5	1.3	1.1	0.9	1.8	2.4	1.7	1.8	1.0	1.6
Inches Snow	17	15	9	3	-	-	-	-	-	1	5	15

V.W.R. = Vokac Weather Rating: probability of mild (warm & dry) weather on any given day.

Forecast

Month	V.W.R. *		Temperatures		Precipitation
			Daytime	Evening	
January	0	Bad	chilly	cold	occasional snowstorms
February	0	Bad	chilly	cold	occasional snowstorms
March	0	Bad	cool	chilly	occasional snow flurries
April	5	Moderate	cool	chilly	occasional showers/snow flurries
May	8	Very Good	warm	cool	infrequent showers
June	10	Great	warm	cool	infrequent showers
July	8	Very Good	hot	warm	frequent showers
August	8	Very Good	hot	warm	frequent showers
September	9	Fine	warm	cool	occasional showers
October	7	Good	warm	chilly	infrequent rainstorms
November	0	Bad	cool	chilly	infrequent snow flurries
December	0	Bad	chilly	cold	infrequent snowstorms

Summary

Durango is dramatically sited along the sagebrush-and-pine-studded San Juan River valley at the southern gateway to the magnificent San Juan Mountains. The town enjoys four normal seasons and a longer period of comfortable weather than the other great towns of Colorado. **Winter** days are chilly and evenings are cold. Occasional snowfalls are sufficient to ensure excellent conditions at a nearby major ski area, and for all kinds of winter sports in and around town. In **spring** mild weather returns in May, with warm days, cool evenings, and infrequent showers. **Summer** is pleasant. Days are surprisingly hot and temperatures remain warm into the evening. The river and lakes in the area are especially appealing during this season. Brief frequent showers relieve the heat and bring out the aromatic tang of nearby pine forests. Early **fall** cold snaps develop brilliant color in the nearby stands of aspen. Days are normally warm and sunny enough to provide some of the best fall color touring in the West during September and October.

ATTRACTIONS & DIVERSIONS

★ **Alpine Slide**   *25 mi. N on US 550*   *247-9000*
A scenic chairlift operates daily in summer at the Purgatory Ski Area, taking riders to the top of dual alpine slide tracks. The panoramic view of the San Juans is as breathtaking as the ride down the nearly half-mile-long fiberglass course. The rider has full control of the speed of the sled in this exhilarating mountain sport.

★ **Backpacking Rentals**
Backpacks, topographic maps, camping, and (in winter) ski touring gear are rented and sold in:
    Hassle Free Sports   *1.5 mi. N at 2615 Main Av.*   *259-3874*
    Pine Needle Mountaineering   *downtown at 835 Main Av.*   *247-8728*

★ **Bicycling**
A lot of scenic, but hilly, highways and byways plus dirt roads and trails surrounding town can be accessed by "mountain bikes" (fat-tired multi-geared bicycles capable of taking anything the rider can). Bicycle rentals and information are available at:
    Purgatory Sports (mountain bikes)   *downtown at 528 Main Av.*   *259-1485*
    Spokes for Folks (10-speed bikes)   *downtown at 600 Main Av.*   *385-4917*

Boat Rentals
★   **Lake Haven Marina**   *18 mi. NE at 14452 County Rd. 501*   *884-2517*
Pleasure, fishing, water-skiing and sail boats can be rented by the hour or longer here on Vallecito Lake.

★ **Durango & Silverton Narrow-Gauge Railroad**   *downtown at 479 Main St.*   *247-2733*
America's last regularly scheduled narrow-gauge passenger train is now a National Historic Landmark. It has been in continuous service since 1882. Now running between Durango and Silverton, trains depart from the downtown depot each morning and return in the early evening daily from mid-May to late October. Original coal-fired steam engines and passenger coaches are used for the three-plus hour trip through continuously spectacular mountain scenery along the Las Animas River. Reservations should be made weeks in advance for this world famous trip in summer.

Golf
    Hillcrest Golf Club   *2 mi. E at 1565 County Rd. 238*   *247-1499*
This 18-hole golf course with panoramic mountain views is open to the public. All golfing facilities and services are provided.

★ **Horseback Riding**
Scenic trail rides, breakfast rides, and overnight or longer pack trips can be arranged at:
    Bar D Riding Stables   *8625 County Rd. 250*   *247-5755*
    Bear Ranch   *20 mi. N at 42570 US 550*   *240-0111*

★ **Jeep Tours and Rentals**
Jeeps may be rented by the day or longer during summer. Half or all day tours can also be reserved to explore the fascinating ghost towns, mining relics, and scenic attractions surrounding town from:
    Durango Rent-a-Jeep (rentals)   *3 mi. N at 3600 Main Av.*   *259-1252*
    Purgatory Hi Country Jeep Tours (tours)   *downtown at 528 Main Av.*   *259-1486*
Library   *downtown at 1188 E. Second Av.*   *247-2492*
The Durango Public Library has a notable collection of Southwestern literature. There are also a good set of local topographic maps and a comfortable periodical reading area. Closed Sun. in summer.

★ **Mesa Verde National Park**   *36 mi. W via US 160 and park rd.*   *529-4465*
The only national park dedicated to the works of man features the world's most extensive cliff dwelling ruins. The large plateau, towering up to 2,000 feet above surrounding valleys, was the home of the Anasazi Indians (the old ones) who suddenly and mysteriously left the area about 1300 A.D. Well-preserved evidence of their architectural skills may be viewed from two self-guided loop drives, each six miles long. Several ruins are open to the public via ranger-guided trips. In addition to walking and bus tours, there is a visitor center and a museum. Restaurants, lodging, and camping facilities are provided in the park which is open year-round.

★ **Million Dollar Highway**   *for approx. 70 mi. N on US 550 - to Ouray*
One of the nation's most sensational mountain highways extends from Durango to Ouray. When the original wagon toll road was improved sixty years ago for auto travel, a particularly difficult section cost more than a million dollars — hence the name. Now an all-weather paved highway filled with breathtaking vistas, it is still not for the faint-hearted.

Riverfront Parks
Memorial Park (Third Av./32nd St.) and Schneider Park (Roosa Av. just W of downtown) are landscaped, tree-shaded areas along the scenic Animas River with fishing access, picnic tables, barbecue facilities and playgrounds.

★ **River Running**
Professional river guides arrange scenic and whitewater river trips in rafts, canoes and kayaks on the Animas River (in town) and others nearby during the summer. Half day, full day, overnight, or extended trips with everything provided can be reserved at:

Animas River Trips *.5 mi. N at Main Av./15th St.*		259-3493
Colorado River Tours		259-0708
Hassle Free Sports (rents inflatable boats and equipment)		259-3874
Rocky Mountain Outpost		259-4783
Wild Goose River Adventures		259-4453

★ **San Juan National Forest**   *starts 5 mi. N of town*   247-4874
Several peaks are more than 14,000 feet high in this huge forest. Features include a major winter sports area at Purgatory, and almost the entire route of the narrow-gauge railroad between Durango and Silverton. There are portions of three wilderness areas, including the state's largest. The Weminuche Wilderness has more than 250 miles of trails accessing scores of peaks over 13,000 feet high. Picturesque Vallecito Reservoir and others offer a full range of water sports. A good system of roads and trails through lush pine forests provides access to mining relics, waterfalls, streams and lakes. Camping, hiking, backpacking, horseback riding and pack trips, mountain climbing, fishing, hunting (for both big game and upland game birds), water sports, and (in winter) a full range of snow sports are among recreation possibilities.

★ **Silverton**   *50 mi. N on US 550*
Hard rock mining has been the major source of income here for more than a century. Located on the wide floor of the Animas River valley more than 9,000 feet above sea level, the tiny community is surrounded by towering peaks of the San Juan Range. Access to the area is via the dramatic "Million Dollar Highway" or the narrow-gauge railroad from Durango. Numerous well-preserved Victorian buildings house mining memorabilia, while several restaurants and saloons proudly display nostalgic reminders of the early boom times.

★ **Vallecito Lake**   *18 mi. NE via Florida Rd.*
The state's most beautiful large reservoir offers excellent fishing, boating and water-skiing, plus hiking and horseback riding opportunities in the surrounding luxuriant pine forest and beyond in the Weminuche Wilderness. A variety of sail and motor boats can be rented at several boat docks. Numerous rustic lodges, campgrounds, restaurants, and bars line the twenty-two-mile shoreline.

Warm Water Feature
Municipal Swimming Pool   *1.4 mi. N at 2400 Main Av.*   247-9876
A very large outdoor pool is open to the public daily during the summer months.

Winter Sports
Chapman Hill   *1 mi. NE at Riverview Dr./Florida Rd.*   247-5622
This little, in-town slope is open every day for downhill skiing, ski jumping, tubing, and ice-skating from December into March.

★   **Purgatory Ski Area**   *25 mi. N on US 550*   684-9868
The vertical rise is 1,600 feet and the longest run is about two miles. Elevation at the top is 10,550 feet. There are five chairlifts. All facilities, services and rentals are available at the base for both downhill and cross-country skiing. A bar and restaurant are located at the base. Several others, and some lodgings, are nearby. The ski season is late November to mid-April.

★ **Snow Cat Tours** *2.8 mi. N at 3473 W. Second Av.* *247-9000*
Half and full day tours through the magnificent San Juan Mountains in a completely enclosed snow cat begin at the top of the scenic chairlift at Purgatory Ski Area.

★ **Snowmobile Rentals**
Guided tours, or daily or weekly snowmobile rentals, for exploring the backcountry can be arranged at several shops, including:
Durango Snowmobile Rentals Inc. *8 mi. N at 31420 US 550* *247-3055*
Garlick's Getaways, Inc. *1 mi. S on US 160* *247-8411*
Ted's Rentals and Sales *2.2 mi. N at 3001 Main Av.* *247-2930*

SHOPPING
Durango's century-old business district is centered along Main Avenue, a landscaped thoroughfare of beautifully preserved Victorians and newer turn-of-the-century-style buildings. A distinguished array of galleries and specialty shops, and one of the West's most substantial concentrations of Old West saloons, restaurants, and hotels, are all within an easy stroll of the narrow-gauge railroad depot at the south end of Main Avenue.

Food Specialties
Dagwood's Bakery Deli *downtown at 801 Main Av.* *247-0017*
Fine homemade pastries, donuts, and breads are the highlights of this large new deli/cafe. Closed Sun.

Daylight Donut Shop *.5 mi. N at 1480 E. Second Av.* *247-3943*
Pine cones and fruit pies are specialties among an appetizing mixture of donuts. All are served to go or to enjoy in a small coffee shop. Closed Sun.

★ **Fudgeworks of Durango** *downtown at 600 Main Av.* *259-0318*
A delicious variety of creamy fudges are made here. Samples are offered, and boxed candy will be shipped anywhere.

★ **Honeyville** *10 mi. N at 33633 US 550* *247-1474*
You can watch the bees make honey in glass hives. Colorado wildflower honey is a specialty, along with eight flavors of creamed honey, honey candy, and a variety of delicious jams and relishes all made with honey. Gift items will be shipped anywhere.

★ **Liquor World** *downtown at 695 Camino del Rio* *259-0144*
A fine selection of well-stored California and other premium wines is offered at reasonable prices. Good assortments of beers and liquors are also sold in the large store.

★ **Rocky Mountain Chocolate Factory** *downtown at 519 Main Av.* *259-1408*
All chocolates are hand-dipped and homemade, and you can watch fudge being made the old-fashioned way in the candy factory that is the source of chocolates distributed to stores throughout the West. Samples are offered.

★ **Stone House Bakery** *downtown at 140 E. 12th St.* *247-3435*
Fine European pastries and freshly made bagels and breads are the features of this little bakery with carryout or coffee table service.

Swensen's Ice Cream Factory *downtown at 106 E. 5th St.* *259-1902*
Many flavors made on the premises are served in a variety of fountain treats in a cheerful ice cream parlor, or to go.

Specialty Shops
★ **Appaloosa Trading Co.** *downtown at 131 E. 8th St.* *259-1994*
This tiny new shop smells appealingly of fine leather goods made on the premises. Many unusual pottery items and belt buckles are also displayed, and custom orders in leather are accepted.

Avalanche Bookstore *downtown at 835 Main Av.* *247-4520*
This full line shop has a good collection of Southwestern Americana, including all kinds of local maps about topography, jeep and hiking trails, gold prospecting sites, and more.

The Book Shop *downtown at 928 Main Av.* *247-1438*
A two-level store with a good selection of general interest books has a well-worn sofa for browsers on the balcony level.

★ **Durango Sheepskin Co.** *10 mi. N via US 550 at 8340 County Rd. 203*   385-4649
The factory showroom displays an outstanding line of sheepskin products, ranging from coats, vests and hats to belts, purses, wallets — even bikinis and wall hangings. You can also watch them make the handcrafted sheepskin and leather products.

★ **Durango Threadworks** *1.2 mi. S off US 550 at 98 Everett St.*   247-9468
Lightweight daypacks, backpacks, fanny packs, wallets, and totes are designed and manufactured here in a facility that includes a factory outlet.

★ **The Earthen Vessel**   *downtown at 835 Main Av.*   247-1281
A notable variety of hand-thrown stoneware dishes and vessels is artistically displayed amidst barnwood decor.

★ **Gallerie Marguerite**   *downtown at 144 E. 8th St.*   259-2377
Fine Southwestern art is collectively showcased in this handsome contemporary gallery. Even everyday objects like bathtubs serve as distinctive plant holders.

★ **The Greenery of Durango**   *downtown at 780 Main Av.*   259-0663
A large historic building has been ingeniously converted into a "contemporary happening" for adults. Classical music complements a spacious interior accented by a colorful profusion of plants and flowers displayed for sale. In this unusual environment, visitors can browse splendid collections of regional and general interest books, scan a sea of magazines, leaf through material in an "adults only" room, shop for gourmet foods, or peruse elaborate displays of arts and crafts.

★ **Main Mall**   *downtown at 835 Main Av.*
This modern enclosed shopping mall in the heart of town is a beautifully updated reflection of the Victorian architecture of adjacent buildings. Two levels of specialty shops surround a spacious atrium.

O'Farrell Hat Company   *downtown at Second Av./6th St.*   259-2517
Skilled craftsmen can be watched making Western and traditional hats on turn-of-the-century equipment.

★ **Piedra's Gallery**   *downtown at 1021 Main Av.*   247-9395
Multimedia works of local and regional artists and craftsmen are showcased in a stylish gallery.

★ **Toh-Atin Trading Co.**   *downtown at 150 W. 7th St.*   247-8277
Indian arts and crafts primarily from the Southwest are beautifully exhibited in this outstanding new shop.

Waldenbooks   *downtown at 104 E. 5th St.*   247-3838
A good assortment of books and magazines is displayed in a bright and modern shop.

NIGHTLIFE
One of the West's most convivial concentrations of after-dark facilities captures the spirit of the Old West in the Victorian heart of town. Some saloons feature romantic atmosphere and museum-quality memorabilia, while others offer live entertainment and dancing amidst cleverly updated Western decor. Classic melodramas, musicals, and chuck wagon dinner shows also compete for attention on summer evenings.

Abbey Theatre   *downtown at 152 E. 6th St.*   247-2626
All kinds of live theatrical productions are staged year-round. The handsome little theater is outfitted with tables and chairs so patrons can enjoy drinks with the performances.

Bar D Chuckwagon   *8.5 mi. NE via US 550 on Trimble Lane*   247-5753
Traditional Western-style chuckwagon dinners are served to a large crowd outdoors each evening from May into September. A Western stage show of songs, stories and comedy follows.

Clancy's Pub   *downtown at 128 E. 6th St.*   247-9083
Occasionally, vocalists and instrumental artists provide entertainment in this cozy cellar pub. Adult cabaret entertainment is offered most late evenings in July and August.

Cowboy Bar-B-Que   *12 mi. NE at 11920 County Rd. 240*   249-4948
An open-pit barbecue is used to prepare sirloin steak dinners served outdoors and followed by a Western music show each evening from June to early September. Closed Mon.

★ **Crystal Tavern**   *downtown at 809 Main Av.*   *247-1530*
Live entertainment and dancing are featured in one of the most beautifully restored
bars in the West. A splendid back bar is the centerpiece of a darkly handsome room
framed in mirrors and polished hardwoods housed in a landmark building.

★ **The Diamond Belle**   *downtown at 699 Main Av.*   *247-4431*
The barroom doors have swung for almost a century in this authentically baroque
Victorian saloon in the Strater Hotel. The peerless decor is usually enlivened by a really
good ragtime pianist.

★ **Diamond Circle Theatre**   *downtown at 699 Main Av.*   *247-4431*
The town's oldest live theater is a charming showcase for turn-of-the-century Western
vaudeville in the Strater Hotel. Well-attended shows are presented nightly throughout
summer. Closed Sun.

★ **Farquahrts**   *downtown at 725 Main Av.*   *247-5440*
Live entertainment and dancing are offered every night except Sunday in a popular
food and drink facility imbued with a casual gusto.

The Gold Slipper   *downtown at 645 Main Av.*   *247-9936*
Occasional live entertainment and dancing are offered in an old, locally popular
saloon with a handsome back bar and comfortable chairs.

★ **The Nest**   *downtown at 658 Main Av.*   *247-8502*
This cozy little second-story bar above the Lost Pelican Restaurant has a good view of
Main Avenue. Comfortably posh Victorian-style furnishings provide a romantic setting
for enjoying a quiet conversation or the upright piano that is played most nights.

★ **Olde Tymer's Cafe**   *downtown at 1000 Main Av.*   *259-2990*
One of Durango's oldest buildings now houses a well-liked bar and grill. Wine by the glass
and light American fare are features in a showplace of Durango-style decor with a
stamped metal ceiling, brick and stone walls, polished wood balcony, padded booths, and
a flower-strewn back patio.

★ **The Quiet Lady Tavern**   *downtown at 1 Depot Place*   *247-2018*
Piano music enlivens this plush Victorian-style lounge on weekends. Patrons relax in
overstuffed armchairs and sofas surrounded by a paneled library, well-lighted dart
boards, and some first-rate nude paintings and stained glass pieces.

Sixth St. Parlour   *downtown at 110 W. Sixth St.*   *259-2888*
Live music is usually available for dancing, and light meals are served in a refurbished
building with a distinctive stone wall and abundant greenery.

★ **The Solid Muldoon**   *downtown at 561 Main Av.*   *247-9151*
Here is a quintessential example of nineteenth century saloon opulence. A magnificent
hardwood back bar and resplendent stained and cut glass pieces accentuate the
luxurious setting. Plush Victorian parlour furniture is used throughout.

★ **Sundance Saloon**   *downtown at 601 E. Second Av.*   *247-8821*
Country and western music reigns in this big frontier-style dancehall. Stained glass
over the back bar highlights Durango's famed train, and a trophy moose oversees the
action from a giant flagstone fireplace.

RESTAURANTS
An abundance of restaurants offer hearty American fare. Most of the better dining
rooms reflect the town's Victorian heritage and some provide views of the surrounding
mountains.

The Assay Office   *2.5 mi. N at 3206 Main Av.*   *247-1316*
D only. Sun. brunch.   *Moderate*
A short American menu is offered in a post-modern dining room featuring free-form
redwood walls, well-done paintings and stained glass, and comfortable booths. A
cheerful plant-filled greenhouse room with mountain views is in the back and an
intimate bar is downstairs.

★ **The Atrium**   *1 mi. W at 21382 US 160*   *385-4834*
B-L-D.   *Moderate*
New American cuisine is carefully executed in this stylish new restaurant. The dining
rooms are a sophisticated blend of blue-hued accents, skylights, and luxuriant
greenery. The circular back room is a tour de force of plush contemporary table
settings and padded private booths.

★ **Durango Diner**   *downtown at 957 Main Av.*   *247-9889*
B-L-D. No D on Sun.   *Low*
Delicious breakfasts are highlighted by big fluffy homemade biscuits or outstanding cinnamon rolls baked here each morning and served with well-made crepe-style omelets. Complete, remarkably inexpensive dinners are another feature of this unspoiled all-American cafe.

Edelweiss Restaurant   *3.8 mi. N at 689 County Rd. 203*   *247-5685*
B-D.   *Moderate*
Home-cooked German dinners and desserts are served amid quiet European atmosphere. German entertainment is offered on weekends and there is a piano bar.

Katie O'Brien's   *downtown at 152 E. 6th St.*   *247-9083*
D only.   *Moderate*
Steaks and seafood are offered with a salad bar in a pleasant Victorian setting. A cozy pub is downstairs.

★ **L'Entrepont**   *.8 mi. N at 1769 Main Av.*   *247-3751*
L-D. No L on Sat. & Sun. Closed Mon.   *Very Expensive*
Magnificent French cuisine with creole/Caribbean accents is beautifully presented in one of the West's foremost culinary shrines. Elegant table settings complement understated contemporary decor in a converted church.

Lost Pelican   *downtown at 658 Main Av.*   *247-8502*
D only.   *Moderate*
Quality seafood is the specialty of a pleasant little dining room with a salad bar. A charming Victorian-style lounge is upstairs.

★ **New York Bakery**   *downtown at 750 Main Av.*   *259-1007*
B-L-D.   *Moderate*
Delicious homemade pastries, omelets and towering French toast are breakfast specialties available in a location that has featured food service for more than a century. All baked goods are also available to go. International dishes are served by lantern light at night in a pleasant little dining room backed by tantalizing cases of desserts made on the premises.

Ore House   *downtown at 147 E. 6th St.*   *247-5707*
D only.   *Moderate*
Steaks are emphasized among American dishes and there is a salad bar in this bustling Western-style restaurant. Wine-by-the-glass is an attraction of the popular adjoining bar.

Oscar's   *downtown at 18 Town Plaza*   *247-0526*
B-L. Closed Sun.   *Low*
Big fluffy biscuits complement specialty omelets and other carefully made breakfast fare served in this plain modern cafe tucked away in a nondescript shopping center.

Palace Restaurant   *downtown at S end of Main Av.*   *247-2018*
B-L-D.   *Moderate*
Nicely prepared American dishes are served amid Victorian-themed decor brightened by many stained glass pieces. The adjoining lounge features elegant Victorian atmosphere.

Southwest Coffeehouse   *downtown at 747 Main Av.*   *259-2996*
B-L-D.   *Moderate*
Various coffees and teas are served along with light meals and occasional entertainment in the dining room, or in an enclosed sidewalk cafe.

Strater Hotel   *downtown at 699 Main Av.*   *247-4431*
L-D. No L on Sat. & Sun.   *Moderate*
The Columbian Room offers some Continental dishes amidst casually elegant Victorian atmosphere. Elsewhere in Durango's landmark hotel are a family restaurant, an acclaimed melodrama theater, and a grand saloon.

Tamarron   *18 mi. N on US 550*   *247-8801*
D only.   *Expensive*
Le Canyon, the famed resort's gourmet dining room, features Continental specialties in an opulent contemporary setting with panoramic mountain views. A coffee shop and a handsome view lounge are also available.

LODGING

Accommodations in Durango are plentiful, plain and conveniently concentrated along Main Avenue north of downtown. A few distinctive facilities capture the town's Victorian spirit or the grandeur of the surroundings. Rates are generally at least 25% less than those quoted apart from summer and the Christmas holidays.

Adobe Inn   *1.3 mi. N at 2178 Main Av.*   *247-2743*
This small modern motel has an indoor pool and sauna. Each room has a phone and cable color TV with movies.
   regular room —   Q bed...$52

Bear Paw Lodge   *20 mi. NE at 18011 County Rd. 501*   *884-2508*
A group of cabins are nestled in a lush blue spruce forest within a mile of Vallecito Lake. Each fully carpeted unit has a kitchen, a bath, and a wood-burning fireplace.
   regular room — 1 BR duplex cabin,   D bed...$39

Brookside Court   *1.4 mi. N at 2300 Main Av.*   *259-9960*
This older single-level motel is a **bargain.** Each room has a B/W or color TV.
   regular room —   D bed...$28

★ **Cascade Village**   *26 mi. N on US 550*   *259-3500*
One mile north of the base of the Purgatory Ski Area is a new condominium resort with an indoor pool, whirlpool, saunas, tennis courts, a view restaurant and lounge, and underground parking. Each well-furnished unit has a fireplace, kitchen, phone, and cable color TV with movies. Rates double during the ski season.
   "Forester" — 2 BR, wet bar, in-bath view whirlpool,   Q & K beds...$79
   regular room — 1 BR,   Q bed...$56

Edelweiss Motel   *3.8 mi. N via US 550 at 689 County Rd. 203*   *247-5685*
A whirlpool and sauna, plus a good restaurant and lounge, are amenities in this small motel. Each room has a phone and cable color TV.
   regular room —   Q bed...$32

End 0 Day Motel   *1 mi. SE at 350 E. Eighth Av.*   *247-1722*
Bargain units are the feature of this small, older, single-level motel. Each room has a phone and cable color TV with movies.
   regular room —   D bed...$26

★ **General Palmer House**   *downtown at 567 Main Av.*   *247-4747*
This authentically restored 1890 hotel is near the narrow-gauge railroad depot in the heart of town. The lobby, restaurant and lounge are outfitted with charming relics and replicas of Victorian fixtures. Each room has a phone and cable color TV.
   #203 — spacious, main street view,   Q bed...$55
   regular room —   D bed...$50

Gypsy Motel   *3 mi. N at 3701 Main Av.*   *247-9950*
This tiny motel has some **bargain** rooms with cable color TV.
   regular room —   Q bed...$32
   regular room —   D bed...$28

Hermosa Court   *9 mi. N via US 550 at 7397 County Rd. 203*   *247-2413*
This older, single-level motel is a **bargain** with modest kitchenettes, but no TV or air conditioning.
   regular room —   D bed...$20

Iron Horse Resort   *5.2 mi. N on US 550*   *259-1010*
This large, conventional condominium complex has a big indoor view pool, saunas and a restaurant and lounge. Each unit has a phone, cable color TV, and a fireplace.
   #141 and all odd #'s thru #165 — fireplace in LR, loft with mt. view,   Q bed...$38
   regular room — as above, but no view,   Q bed...$38

Mountain Shadows - Best Western   *2.5 mi. N at 3255 Main Av.*   *247-5285*
This contemporary Western-style motel has a glass-domed indoor pool and whirlpool. Each of the rooms has a phone and cable color TV.
   regular room —   Q or K bed...$57

Redwood Lodge   *4 mi. N via US 550 at 763 County Rd. 203*   *257-3895*
This motel has some **bargain** units with cable color TV.
   regular room —   Q bed...$30

★ **Safari Lodge**   *22 mi. NE at 21730 County Rd. 501*   *884-2482*
Log cabins on the shore of Vallecito Lake by the mouth of Los Pinos River are available in a variety of sizes. Horses and boats may be rented here. Each unit has a kitchen.
large cabin — fireplace, lake view,   2 D beds...$44
regular room — lake view,   D bed...$32

Siesta Motel   *2.8 mi. N at 3475 Main Av.*   *247-0741*
This small **bargain** motel offers rooms with cable color TV and a refrigerator.
regular room —   D bed...$30

Sleepy Hollow Motel   *2.2 mi. N at 2970 Main Av.*   *247-1741*
Each of the spacious rooms has cable color TV in this small motel near the river.
#15 — pvt. balc., view across river & park to mts.,   Q bed...$42
#17,#16 — pvt. balc., river/mts. view,   2 Q beds...$48
regular room —   Q bed...$36

★ **Strater Hotel**   *downtown at 699 Main Av.*   *247-4431*
A magnificent century-old hotel is still the major landmark in the heart of town. On the first (of four) floors are restaurants, a saloon, a live theater and shops. Each carefully restored room is graced with authentic Victorian walnut antiques, plus modern conveniences (a phone, cable color TV and a bathroom).
#322 "the Bridal Suite" — corner, splendid downtown/mt. view,   D bed...$85
#422,#222 — corner rooms (above & below bridal suite), fine views,   2 D beds...$85
regular room —   D bed...$52

Sunset Motel   *1.5 mi. N at 2855 Main Av.*   *247-2653*
This motel has an outdoor pool and (in winter only) a whirlpool and sauna. Each room has a phone and cable color TV with movies.
regular room —   D bed...$34

★ **Tamarron Resort**   *18 mi. N on US 550*   *247-8801*
Tamarron is a large, renowned motor hotel and condominium complex with a fabulous array of recreation facilities, including a large indoor/outdoor pool with a slide, a whirlpool and a sauna. A fee is charged for an 18-hole golf course, indoor and outdoor tennis courts, bicycle rentals, horseback riding, the health club, and nearby jeep tours and river rafting. In the winter there is an ice-skating rink, tobogganing, plus (for a fee) beginner lifts. Plush view restaurants, a lounge, and shops are in the main building. Each spacious, nicely decorated unit has a phone, color TV and a kitchenette or kitchen.
#825 — 1 BR townhouse, kit., fireplace, bar,   Q bed...$121
"Loft Inn Suite"(several) — kitchenette, mt. view, balc.,   2 T & Q beds...$121
regular room — some have a kitchenette,   Q bed...$110

Vagabond Inn   *1.3 mi. N at 2180 Main Av.*   *247-9923*
Durango's first bed-and-breakfast inn is a skillfully transformed small motel. A large redwood hot tub, sauna and complimentary Continental breakfast are features. Each well-furnished room has cable color TV.
#201 "Honeymoon Suite" — corner, large, heart-shaped in-room tub,   Q bed...$95
#206 — corner, spacious, large raised fireplace,   2 Q beds...$79
regular room — small,   D bed...$37

Valley View Lodge   *8 mi. N via US 550 at 5802 County Rd. 203*   *247-3772*
This older, single-level **bargain** motel has cable color TV with movies in each of the modest rooms.
regular room —   2 D beds...$24

Vista Motel   *2.8 mi. N at 3537 Main Av.*   *247-1321*
This older motel is a **bargain.** Each simply furnished room has cable color TV.
regular room —   Q bed...$28

CAMPGROUNDS

As a result of Durango's spectacular location and pleasant summer weather, one of the West's finest assortments of scenic campgrounds is here. The most notable are a half hour from town by Vallecito Reservoir, where the sylvan beauty of a high mountain lake is coupled with a remarkable assortment of recreational amenities. Near town, several privately operated campgrounds provide complete facilities in attractive settings.

Jaycee Memorial Campground *.5 mi. NW via 9th St. & Av. del Sol*　　　*247-1977*
Near the rim of a bluff overlooking downtown is a small, casual campground with flush toilets, hot showers and hookups. Each site is shaded by pinon pines and has a picnic table, fire ring and grill. Several sites have fine town/valley views.　　base rate...$8

★ **Middle Mountain Campground**　　*29 mi. NE on Vallecito Reservoir*　　*884-2512*
This little San Juan National Forest campground is located in a lush pine forest by a beautiful reservoir high in the Colorado Rockies. Features include excellent fishing, boating, sailing and water-skiing on Vallecito Lake. Boat and horse rentals and launching facilities are nearby. Pit toilets are available, but there are no showers or hookups. Each shady site is nicely spaced and has a lake view plus a picnic table and fire area.　　base rate...$5

Safari-Lightner Creek Campground *4.5 mi. NW via US 160*　　　*247-5406*
This large private facility features fishing in tiny cottonwood-shaded Lightner Creek, an outdoor swimming pool, a rec room, and an outdoor game area. Flush toilets, hot showers and hookups are available. Each shady site has a picnic table and fire ring. Many sites are by the creek.　　base rate...$9

United Campgrounds of Durango *4.6 mi. N via US 550 on Cty. Rd. 789*　　*247-3853*
In the scenic Animas River valley is a large private campground with a heated outdoor pool with a slide, a rec room, and an outdoor game area. The narrow-gauge Durango-Silverton Railroad runs by the park. Flush toilets, hot showers, and hookups are available. Each of the treeless sites has a picnic table. A separate grassy area is designated for tents.　　base rate...$10

SPECIAL EVENTS

★ **Snowdown**　　*in town*　　　*end of January*
More than fifty events are featured during "Durango's winter celebration" including a snow sculpture contest, hotdog jumps, a torchlight parade, and fireworks.

★ **Navajo Trail Fiesta**　　*in town*　　　*early August*
A parade, rodeo, and horse racing are highlights of this popular weekend event.

La Plata County Fair　　*fairgrounds*　　　*mid-August*
A draft horse pulling contest is the memorable event in this traditional Western harvest fair.

Nightly Rodeo　　*fairgrounds*　　　*June - August*
All of the traditional events are presented at rodeos scheduled on Monday, Wednesday and Friday evenings throughout summer.

OTHER INFORMATION

Area Code: *303*
Zip Code: *81301*
Durango Chamber of Commerce　　*1.4 mi. N at 2301 Main Av.*　　*247-0312*
San Juan Nat. For.-Supervisor's Office *downtown at 701 Camino del Rio*　*259-0159*

Estes Park, Colorado

Elevation:

7,522 feet

Population (1980):

2,703

Population (1970):

1,616

Location:

63 mi. NW
of Denver

Estes Park is the West's all-American tourist town. One of the nation's most popular playgrounds lies among hills in a park-like little basin rimmed by the snow-capped peaks of the Front Range of the Colorado Rockies. In a lush pine forest 7,500 feet above sea level, winters are cold, but there are no major ski areas nearby. This may be because the heaviest snowfalls usually occur in spring. Good weather in summer normally fills the town to capacity with vacationers pursuing a wealth of outdoor recreation opportunities. Renowned Rocky Mountain National Park, adjacent to town on the west, has long been the area's major attraction with its abundance of towering peaks, scenic waterfalls, crystal-clear streams and lakes, and the nation's highest major highway. In and near town, golf, tennis, fishing and boating, plus some unusual facilities like an aerial tramway, bumper boats, giant slides, and a water tube cater to the playful moods of every member of the family. In early fall, crowds are gone and the scenery is at its most spellbinding on clear days when peaks are newly white with early snows, and aspen forests are ablaze with color.

Estes Park is the only great Colorado town to have been primarily a tourist destination from its beginnings more than a century ago. Named for Joel Estes who was the first settler in the flat grassy area (called a "park" in the nineteenth century), the town began to develop after a toll road into the area was opened to travel in 1874 and a hunting lodge was built by an English nobleman shortly afterward. Hunting and sightseeing continued to attract more visitors, and in 1909 the Stanley Hotel opened. This expansive wooden facility, built by one of the twins who became wealthy with the "Stanley Steamer," propelled Estes Park into world-class resort status. In 1915, the federal government set aside the area west of town as Rocky Mountain National Park. By 1920 the Fall River Road was completed through the park to Grand Lake. The narrow dirt road, and all of its sharp switchbacks, is still open in summer. However, it was supplanted years ago by the paved "Trail Ridge Road" which reaches 12,183 feet above sea level and is the park's most popular feature.

Downtown Estes Park is at the base of mountains where several highways converge. It is now a flamboyant jumble of gift shops, homemade candy and other carryout food stores, bars, cafes, and restaurants surrounded by an abundance of family-oriented attractions and accommodations. All of these facilities continue to reflect the town's unabashed desire to meet the needs of vacationing families in this ever-popular mountain playground.

WEATHER PROFILE   *Vokac Weather Rating*

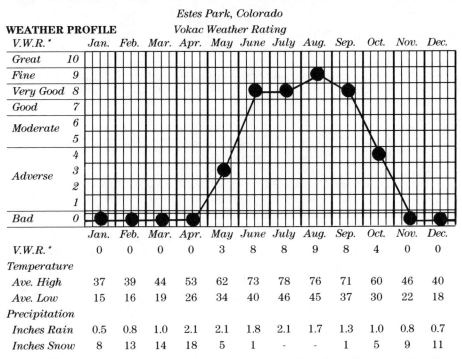

V.W.R.*	Jan.	Feb.	Mar.	Apr.	May	June	July	Aug.	Sep.	Oct.	Nov.	Dec.
V.W.R.*	0	0	0	0	3	8	8	9	8	4	0	0
Temperature												
Ave. High	37	39	44	53	62	73	78	76	71	60	46	40
Ave. Low	15	16	19	26	34	40	46	45	37	30	22	18
Precipitation												
Inches Rain	0.5	0.8	1.0	2.1	2.1	1.8	2.1	1.7	1.3	1.0	0.8	0.7
Inches Snow	8	13	14	18	5	1	-	-	1	5	9	11

V.W.R. = Vokac Weather Rating: probability of mild (warm & dry) weather on any given day.

Forecast

		Temperatures		
Month	V.W.R.*	Daytime	Evening	Precipitation
January	0 Bad	chilly	cold	infrequent snowstorms
February	0 Bad	chilly	cold	infrequent snowstorms
March	0 Bad	chilly	cold	infrequent snowstorms
April	0 Bad	cool	chilly	occasional snowstorms
May	3 Adverse	cool	chilly	occasional rainstorms
June	8 Very Good	warm	cool	occasional rainstorms
July	8 Very Good	warm	cool	frequent showers
August	9 Fine	warm	cool	occasional showers
September	8 Very Good	warm	cool	infrequent showers
October	4 Adverse	cool	chilly	infrequent showers/snow flurries
November	0 Bad	chilly	chilly	infrequent snowstorms
December	0 Bad	chilly	cold	infrequent snowstorms

Summary

Estes Park is attractively situated in a pine forest rimmed by snow-capped peaks at the eastern entrance to Rocky Mountain National Park. **Winter** is chilly, and evenings are cold. Snowstorms during this season are usually too infrequent and light to support winter sports complexes as elaborate as those in other great Colorado towns. Surprisingly, the year's heaviest snowfalls occur in early **spring**. Flurries continue through most of the season. **Summer** offers the year's best weather as an added incentive to experience this splendid sylvan playground. Long warm days, cool evenings, and brief frequent thundershowers can be expected. Light sportswear is appropriate until approximately the beginning of **fall**, when temperatures begin to drop precipitously. Chilly days and infrequent snowfalls usually mark the return of wintry weather before Thanksgiving.

ATTRACTIONS & DIVERSIONS

★ **Aerial Tramway** *.4 mi. SE at 420 E. Riverside Dr.* 586-3675
Two small, enclosed tram cars suspended from steel cables take visitors to the top of Prospect Mountain daily from mid-May to mid-September. In addition to a fine panoramic view of town and peaks of the Colorado Front Range, there are picnic areas and hiking trails.

★ **Bicycling**
The Cosmic Wheels Cyclery *.3 mi. S at 342 W. Riverside Dr.* 586-2975
Highways and byways around town cover many miles of relatively easy and scenic terrain. Bicycles can be rented by the hour or longer here.

Big Thompson Canyon *approx. 25 mi. E on US 34*
One of the main eastern approaches to town is via a steep-sided narrow canyon barely wide enough for a highway along the picturesque Big Thompson River. Delightful picnic, camping, and fishing sites line the route.

Boat Rentals
Lake Estes Marina *1.8 mi. E on US 34 at 1770 Big Thompson Av.* 586-9794
Sailboats, fishing boats, paddle boats and canoes can be rented here daily all summer for use on the little reservoir.

Fun City *.3 mi. SW on CO 36 at 375 Moraine Av.* 586-2070
A sixty-foot rug slide, bumper cars, two miniature golf courses and a video arcade are featured in a family fun center open every day in summer and on weekends in the fall.

Golf
Rocky Mountain Golf Course *1.4 mi. SE at 1080 S. CO 7* 586-4361
This 18-hole golf course with panoramic mountain views is open to the public. A driving range and putting green are available along with all golfing facilities and services.

★ **Horseback Riding**
Scenic trail rides, breakfast or dinner rides, and overnight or longer pack or fishing trips can be arranged at more than a dozen places in or near town, including:
Allenspark Livery (unguided rides, too) *17 mi. S on CO 7* 747-2552
Elkhorn Stables *.4 mi. W on US 34 at 650 Elkhorn Av.* 586-3191
National Park Village Stables *5 mi. W at 4600 W. US 34* 586-5269
Silver Lane Stables *.5 mi. E on US 34 at 621 Big Thompson Av.* 586-4695
Sombrero Ranch (unguided, too) *1.8 mi. E at 1895 US 34* 586-4577

Jeep Tours
★ **National Forest Tours** *.3 mi. W on US 34 at 481 Elkhorn Av.* 586-4237
Three-hour jeep tours culminate in an outstanding 360° view from the thirty-five foot observation tower atop Panorama Peak in Roosevelt National Forest. Tours leave twice daily all summer. There are also steak fry tours four nights each week that include dinner and a Western sing-along around a campfire.

★ **Library** *downtown at 225 E. Elkhorn Av.* 586-3180
The Estes Park Public Library has an inviting reading area with comfortable armchairs in front of a working fireplace, and an inviting periodical reading section. A series of special lectures and films are scheduled each summer for adults.

★ **Moped Rental**
Motor-driven bicycles provide a relatively effortless alternative to bicycles for touring scenic byways around town. Mopeds can be rented by the hour or longer at:
The Cosmic Wheels Cyclery *.3 mi. S at 342 W. Riverside Dr.* 586-2975
Mountain Moped *downtown at 354 E. Elkhorn Av.* 586-4375

Mountain Climbing
★ **Fantasy Ridge** *.3 mi. SW on CO 36 at 351 Moraine Av.* 586-5758
This school operates the only mountain climbing concession in Rocky Mountain National Park. Climbing techniques and mountain safety are taught, and guided climbs of Longs Peak are a highlight.

Museums
There are six museums in and around town. Collectively, they graphically depict homesteading, ranching and the evolution of tourism in the area. For locations and details, stop at the Chamber of Commerce.

Olympus Ride-a-Kart   *2.2 mi. E on US 34*   *586-3222*
Easy-to-drive go-carts operate on a well-paved track, and bumper boats provide an
exhilarating spin around a pond. There is also a miniature railway and an arcade. This
family fun center is open daily through summer.

★ **Rocky Mountain National Park**   *5 mi. W on US 34 or US 36*   *586-2371*
The renowned park contains one of the highest regions in the country along the
Continental Divide in the Front Range of the Rocky Mountains. Dominating the
spectacular skyline, Longs Peak (14,255 feet) towers above a profusion of steep-walled
canyons, waterfalls, lakes and cataracts. Dense forests blanket the lower slopes of
mountains that reach well above timberline. Hundreds of varieties of wildflowers
contribute ephemeral brilliance to upland meadows. Deer, elk, bighorn sheep, beaver and
other animals are numerous in this wildlife sanctuary. The awe-inspiring Trail Ridge Road
is the only paved highway across the park. At Fall River Pass, the Alpine Visitor Center
exhibits and describes the mountain tundra environment. Bear Lake, a photogenic little
jewel of glacial origin circled by a self-guided nature trail, is also a very popular trailhead.
Hidden Valley Ski Area is a winter destination.

★ **Roosevelt National Forest**   *N, E and S of town*   *586-3440*
Numerous tiny glaciers dot the highest peaks of this large forest. These, together with icy
lakes, streams, and waterfalls carved into flower-filled upland meadows, provide splendid
backcountry destinations accessed by hundreds of miles of trails. The Rawah Wilderness
and others offer true high country experiences away from vehicles. Camping, hiking,
backpacking, horseback riding and pack trips, mountain climbing, fishing, hunting and
winter sports are among recreation possibilities.

★ **Trail Ridge Road**   *for approx. 50 mi. SW to Grand Lake*
The highest continuous paved auto road in North America (a four-mile section is over
12,000 feet above sea level) offers breathtaking views of the Rocky Mountains and, far to
the east, the Great Plains. For more than eleven miles the road is above timberline. Grand
Lake (Colorado's biggest natural water body) is the scenic western terminus with a
lakeside resort village offering an assortment of restaurants, bars and lodging.

Warm Water Feature
   Water Tube Express   *1.2 mi. SW on CO 36*   *586-8729*
This tubular water slide is a wet-and-wild new roadside attraction for the entire family.

Winter Sports
   Hidden Valley   *10 mi. W via US 34*   *586-4887*
The vertical rise is 2,000 feet and the longest run is about two miles. Elevation at the top
is 11,400 feet. This facility — located in Rocky Mountain National Park — has no chairlifts,
only Pomalifts and T-bars. Essential facilities, services, and rentals are available at the
base for downhill skiing. A cafeteria is at the base, but no restaurants, bars, or lodging. The
ski season is early December to mid-April.

   Rocky Mountain Ski Tours   *downtown at 156 E. Elkhorn Av.*   *586-2114*
The town's only certified cross-country ski school provides instruction, guides tours, and
rents equipment.

SHOPPING
Estes Park's flamboyant little business district is concentrated along Elkhorn Avenue (US
34) near where the Fall and Big Thompson Rivers join. A colorful melange of building
styles is represented, each vying for attention. Collectively, the buildings and shops display
nearly a century of evolution in tourist-serving architecture and decor.

Food Specialties
The Big Cheese of Estes   *downtown at 213 W. Elkhorn Av.*   *586-4016*
Many varieties of cheese and a good selection of deli items are offered in this well-stocked
deli.

★ **Cookie Mugger**   *downtown at 157 W. Elkhorn Av.*
Freshly made cookies may be enjoyed with ice cream at a few tables, or to go.

Danish Cone Factory   *downtown at 191 W. Elkhorn Av.*   *586-8624*
Freshly baked Danish-style cones are a fine accompaniment to premium ice creams sold
at this carryout.

★ **Donut Haus**   *.3 mi. S at 342 Moraine Av.*   586-2988
This popular little carryout bakery offers a good assortment of donuts, pastries and cookies, plus selected breads.

★ **Fudgeworks of Estes**   *downtown at 102 E. Elkhorn Av.*   586-4207
Handmade chocolates include chocolate-dipped seasonal fresh fruits plus delicious homemade fudge. Samples are offered.

★ **Joy's Candy Box**   *downtown at 133 W. Elkhorn Av.*   586-5784
Homemade candies, fudge and taffy, fresh-made lemonade, and several flavors of homemade ice cream served in Danish cones are specialties in an inviting little carryout shop.

The Sundae Saloon   *downtown at 125 Moraine Av.*   586-3598
This gaudy ice cream parlor with old-timey decor offers a full range of fountain treats plus light lunches and desserts.

★ **The Taffy Shop**   *downtown at 121 W. Elkhorn Av.*   586-4548
Taffy is pulled on a machine by the front window and sold with a variety of other sweets made in this half-century-old shop. Gift boxes will be shipped anywhere.

Specialty Shops

Intrigue   *downtown at 112 E. Elkhorn Av.*   586-4217
Aspen leaf jewelry made in Estes Park is the specialty here. Select leaves from the Colorado mountains are handcrafted through a twenty-one step process that includes gold or silver plating.

MacDonald Book Shop   *downtown at 152 E. Elkhorn Av.*   586-3450
This store has a good selection of books, magazines, and newspapers, and an inviting fireplace for warmth and atmosphere.

★ **Ricker-Bartlett Pewter Casting Studio**   *2 mi. E at 2050 US 34*   586-2030
The largest pewter casting studio in the country features a new visitor center with an elaborate display of handcast pewter miniatures. Many pieces are available for purchase. Visitors may watch the artisans at work every day.

Thoughts and Things   *downtown at 403 W. Elkhorn Av.*   586-4290
This attractive store features a good book and magazine selection.

NIGHTLIFE
The emphasis is on Western-style family entertainment after dark. Wholesome melodramas, country music shows, rodeos, and chuck wagon dinner shows are staples of summer evenings. There are also a few bars offering live music for dancing.

Barleen Family Country Music Theatre   *1 mi. SE on CO 7*   586-5749
Three generations of the musical Barleen family perform in a family show filled with country music and comedy. There is comfortable theater seating, or table seating for patrons interested in an all-American dinner for a small additional charge. No alcoholic beverages are served. Shows are offered nightly in summer.

★ **Courtyard Tavern**   *downtown at 250 Virginia Dr.*   586-9564
Comfortably modish armchairs and sofas provide an inviting setting for a quiet conversation. An adjoining courtyard deck overlooks tiny waterfalls and ponds.

The Crags Lodge   *.6 mi. S at 300 Riverside Dr.*   586-6100
Melodramas are presented in the historic lodge's Balcony Theater nightly in summer.

The Stanley Hotel   *.6 mi. NE at 333 Wonderview Av.*   586-3371
Nightly entertainment and dancing are featured in the contemporized Dunraven Lounge of the turn-of-the-century landmark hotel. A full range of theatrical productions are offered Thursday through Sunday in the historic Stanley Hall Theater.

Gatsby's   *downtown at 120 W. Elkhorn Av.*   586-5855
This casual upstairs club is the place for live rock music most evenings.

Inn of Estes Park   *1.5 mi. E on US 34 at 1701 Big Thompson Av.*   586-5363
The Inn offers live entertainment and dancing most nights in the large, modern Big Thompson Lounge.

Lazy B Ranch Chuck Wagon   *3.5 mi. NE via US 34 on Dry Gulch Rd.*   586-5371
Family-oriented Western entertainment follows chuckwagon-style dinners served each evening in a vast enclosed pavilion that can be heated when necessary.

Lonigan's   *downtown at 110 W. Elkhorn Av.*   *586-4346*
An eclectic mix of (occasional) live entertainment, a fireplace conversation area, pool tables, and casual furnishing seems to work in this popular bar.

★ **Stanley Park Rodeo Grounds**   *1 mi. E on N. St. Vrain Av.*
Public rodeos, horse shows, special drills, and competitions lend credibility to the town's unabashed claim as the "Horse Capital of the Nation." Some kind of equestrian event is staged almost every night at the rodeo grounds.

RESTAURANTS
There are plenty of restaurants. Most feature reasonably-priced, hearty American fare in family-oriented, Western-style surroundings.

Black Canyon Restaurant   *.7 mi. N at 800 MacGregor Av.*   *586-4648*
D only.   *Moderate*
Carefully prepared American dishes and homemade desserts are served in a handsome turn-of-the-century hunting lodge with several dining areas and a rustic fireside lounge.

Crags Lodge   *.6 mi. S at 300 Riverside Dr.*   *586-6100*
D only. Closed Mon.   *Moderate*
American fare is served in a historic lodge with a window wall providing an outstanding town-and-mountains panorama from both the big dining room and the adjoining lounge.

The Dunraven Inn   *3.3 mi. SW at 2470 CO 66*   *586-6409*
D only.   *Moderate*
Italian cuisine is served in a casual fireside dining room. There is a cozy bar.

Fawnbrook Inn   *16 mi. S on CO 7 - Allenspark*   *747-2556*
L-D. Closed Mon.   *Moderate*
Old World specialties and homemade pastries are highlights in a historic log inn with a beautiful outdoor garden and a rustic bar.

The Gazebo   *downtown at 250 Virginia Dr.*   *586-9564*
L-D. Sun. brunch.   *Expensive*
Continental dishes are served in a colorful dining room with a mountain view, or on a cheerful deck overlooking water features and plants in a courtyard. A stylish lounge adjoins.

The Inn of Glen Haven   *7 mi. N at 7468 County Rd. 43*   *586-3897*
D only. Closed Wed. & Oct.-May.   *Moderate*
Homemade soups and baked goods complement Continental cuisine prepared with the freshest ingredients in this charming and intimate restaurant.

La Casa del Estorito   *downtown at 222 E. Elkhorn Av.*   *586-2807*
B-L-D.   *Low*
Mexican dishes and a few American specialties like cinnamon rolls and biscuits are featured in a pleasant little dining room.

★ **La Chaumiere**   *12 mi. SE on US 36 - Pinewood Springs*   *823-6521*
D only. Closed Mon.-Tues. & fall-spring.   *Moderate*
Expertly prepared French cuisine is offered on a fixed price menu that varies daily. Items from the on-premises smoke house and bakery are noteworthy, as are the extraordinary homemade ice creams. The distinctively embellished dining room has mountain-view picture windows.

L'Auberge Restaurant   *4.3 mi. W on US 34 at 3700 Fall River Rd.*   *586-5418*
D only. Closed Tues.   *Moderate*
Continental cuisine is served amidst Old World decor enhanced by a fireplace and mountain view at the Fawn Valley Inn. A pleasant deck over the Fall River is used when weather permits, and there is a comfortable firelit lounge.

Longs Peak Inn and Guest Ranch   *9 mi. S on CO 7*   *586-2110*
L-D. No D on Sun.   *Moderate*
American fare, with homemade bread and desserts, accompanies a fine view of Longs Peak at two dinner seatings (by reservation only) each evening.

National Park Village North   *5 mi. W on US 34*   *586-3183*
B-L-D. Closed Sept.-May.   *Moderate*
The huge cinnamon rolls made here are delicious. These and other pastries justify a stop at this cavernous tourist-family emporium where a dining room with pseudo-covered-wagon booths and other simulated Old Western decor overlooks an endless sea of trinkets. Occasional buffet dinners are all-American extravaganzas adorned with ice sculptures worthy of the feast.

Nicky's   *2 mi. W on US 34 at 1350 Fall River Rd.*   *586-2123*
D only.   *Moderate*
Steaks and prime rib cooked with rock salt are featured in an ornate, firelit dining room. Several of the elaborately furnished tables are by streamside windows. An adjacent lounge offers entertainment and dancing.

Old Church Restaurant   *downtown at 157 W. Elkhorn Av.*   *no phone*
B-L-D.   *Moderate*
Good American and German dishes are often accompanied by a guitarist at lunchtime in a pleasant new dining room in the Old Church Shopping Complex.

The Old Plantation   *downtown at 128 E. Elkhorn Av.*   *586-2800*
L-D. Closed Nov-May.   *Low*
Bountiful American fare has been served for more than a half century amidst Old South-style decor in this casual family restaurant.

The Other Side Restaurant   *1.5 mi. SW on CO 36 at 900 Moraine Av.*   *586-2171*
B-L-D.   *Moderate*
American fare is featured in a bright and cheerful dining room with a view across a small lake.

P.S. Flowers   *downtown at 247 W. Elkhorn Av.*   *586-5735*
L-D.   *Moderate*
American dishes are served in an Old World pub setting, and on an umbrella-shaded sidewalk cafe located in a mall courtyard.

The Stanley Hotel   *.6 mi. NE at 333 Wonderview Av.*   *586-3371*
B-L-D.   *Expensive*
American and Continental specialties are presented in the large and stately MacGregor Room of this renowned historic landmark. A spectacular mountain view through enormous picture windows is a highlight. A lounge with live entertainment and a live theater are nearby.

LODGING

A multitude of places provide lodgings in and around town, especially along US 34 east and west of downtown. Accommodations range from tiny motels to elaborate dude ranches and historic hotels. While many close in winter, those that stay open usually discount the summer prices shown below by 20% and more. Only a few bargains are available during the summer season when reservations are appropriate.

Brynwood   *1.1 mi. SW on CO 36 at 710 Moraine Av.*   *586-4484*
In this little cottage complex on the Big Thompson River, each unit has a phone and cable color TV with movies.

   #26 — 2 BR, spacious, kitchen, riverside sun deck, fireplace,   2 D & Q beds...$65
   regular room —   Q bed...$35

Caribou Chalet   *1.5 mi. E on US 34 at 1450 Big Thompson Av.*   *586-2358*
A large outdoor pool with a slide, and a whirlpool, are features of this modern motel. Each room has a phone and cable color TV.

   #28,#27,#29 — pvt. balc., fine mt. view through pines from   Q bed...$42
   regular room —   Q bed...$40

★ **Crags Lodge**   *.6 mi. S at 300 Riverside Dr.*   *586-6100*
This historic seventy-year-old lodge has a scenic outdoor pool, an old-fashioned window wall dining room and lounge with an outstanding town and mountain view, and a live theater. Each room has cable color TV.

   #320 — cheerful, modern, fine town/mt. view from   Q bed...$40
   #216 — old-fashioned decor, fine view from   D bed...$37
   regular room — some have northern (mt.) view,   D bed...$34

★ **Deer Crest Chalets**   *1.8 mi. W on US 34 at 1400 Fall River Rd.*   *586-2324*
This contemporary motel overlooks the Fall River and has a scenic outdoor pool and whirlpool. Each beautifully furnished unit has a phone, cable color TV with movies, and a refrigerator.

#12 — kitchenette, fireplace, by creek,	Q bed...$65
#209,#207 — over creek,	Q bed...$44
regular room —	Q bed...$44

Elkhorn Lodge   *.5 mi. W on US 34 at 600 W. Elkhorn Av.*   *586-4416*
Estes Park's oldest accommodation is a large wood-sided building on the National Register of Historic Places. The rustic **bargain** includes a large heated outdoor pool, fishing on the Fall River where it runs through the property, and (for a fee) horseback riding. Closed Dec.-Apr.

cabin —	D bed...$35
regular room — in the old lodge,	D bed...$30

Fall River Motor Inn *2.3 mi. W on US 34 at 1660 Fall River Rd.*   *586-4118*
Fall River is only a step away from this newer motel. Knotty pine decor is used throughout. Each attractive unit has a cable color TV with movies, a private terrace and a fireplace.

#1,#5 — pvt. streamside deck, kit.,	Q bed...$54
#3,#4 — deck by stream, refr.,	Q bed...$46
regular room —	D bed...$43

★ **Fawn Valley Inn**   *4.3 mi. W on US 34 at 2760 Fall River Rd.*   *586-2388*
This luxurious condominium complex in a lush pine forest on Fall River has a large picturesque outdoor pool and a notable restaurant and lounge. Either well-furnished apartments or **bargain** motel units are available with a phone and cable color TV.

"Edelweiss" — 1 BR, corner fireplace, kit., balc. by river,	2 T & Q beds...$56
"Ponderosa" — balc., sylvan view,	Q bed...$36
regular room —	Q bed...$29

Four Winds Motor Lodge *1 mi. E on US 34 at 1120 Big Thompson Av.*   *586-3313*
This modern single-level motel has a large scenic outdoor pool and a whirlpool. Each room has a phone and cable color TV with movies.

#40,#39 — large brick fireplace, refr., fine mt. view,	D & Q beds...$48
regular room —	D bed...$37

Glacier Lodge   *2.9 mi. SW at 2166 CO 66*   *586-4401*
A modern cottage complex on the Big Thompson River has a scenic outdoor pool. Most of the units have kitchens and fireplaces.

"Vista" & "River" — 1 BR cottages, porch by river, kit., fireplace,	D bed...$52
"Wilderness" — cottage by river, large porch,	D bed...$42
regular room — deck by river,	D bed...$42

Idlewilde by the River   *3.1 mi. SW at 2282 CO 66*   *586-3864*
This small cottage colony in the pines on the Big Thompson River has a hot tub, and each knotty pine unit has a kitchen and a screened porch.

"Ataloa" — next to river,	D bed...$43
regular cabin —	D bed...$43

The Inn at Estes Park   *1.7 mi. E on US 34 at 1701 Big Thompson Av.*   *586-5363*
This motel has a large hexagonal indoor pool and saunas, plus a restaurant, and a lounge with live entertainment. Each unit has a phone and cable color TV.

#272 — corner, spacious, mt. view,	K bed...$40
#270 — spacious, pvt. balc., mt. view,	K bed...$40
regular room —	K bed...$40

★ **Lake Estes Resort - Best Western** *1.7 mi. E at 1650 Big Thompson Av.*   *586-3386*
This modern, single-level motor hotel has a large outdoor pool with a water slide, whirlpool and sauna, plus a restaurant and lounge. Each well-furnished unit has a phone and cable color TV with movies.

#48 — end unit, windows on 3 sides with pvt. lake/Longs Peak views,	K bed...$59
#8 — fireplace, refr. & wet bar in LR,	K bed...$76
#6 "Bridal Suite" — fireplace, refr. & wet bar in LR,	K waterbed...$85
regular room —	Q bed...$53

Mountain Eight Inn   *1 mi. E on US 34 at 1220 Big Thompson Av.*   *586-4421*
This contemporary **bargain** motel has a large outdoor view pool with a water slide. Each
room has a TV.

#204,#104,#103 — pleasant rooms,	K bed...$31
#210 — mt. views from picture windows on 2 sides,	2 D beds...$45
#115 — mt. view from windows on 3 sides,	2 D beds...$40
regular room —	Q bed...$30
regular room —	D bed...$28

★ **Nicky's**   *2 mi. W on US 34 at 1360 Fall River Rd.*   *586-5376*
This modern motor lodge in a dense pine forest on the Fall River has a large scenic
outdoor pool with a slide and two tennis courts, plus a restaurant and lounge by the river.
Each room has a phone and cable color TV.

#22 — spacious, by river, rock fireplace,	K bed...$55
regular room —	K bed...$50

★ **Ponderosa Lodge**   *2.7 mi. W on US 34 at 1820 Fall River Rd.*   *586-4233*
The river is directly adjacent to this attractive new wood-toned motel. Each well-
furnished unit has a cable color TV and a semi-private balcony overlooking the river.

#2,#3,#7,#8 — fireplace,	Q bed...$42
#16,#6,#13,#1 — corner, windows on 2 sides, kit., fireplace,	Q bed...$50
regular room —	Q bed...$42

River View Pines   *1.6 mi. W on US 34 at 1250 Fall River Rd.*   *586-3627*
This small, modern motel is next to Fall River. Each room has cable color TV.

#34 — spacious, pvt. deck,	2 D beds...$36
#28 — spacious, pvt. balc.,	2 D beds...$36
regular room —	2 D beds...$36

Rockmount Cottages   *2.4 mi. SW at 1852 CO 66*   *586-4168*
All of these newly decorated cottages by the Big Thompson River have kitchens and
knotty pine walls, and most have stone fireplaces.

#12 "Columbine" — 1 BR, beautifully secluded, stone fireplace,	T & D beds...$52
regular room — no fireplace,	D bed...$46

The Stanley Hotel   *.6 mi. NE at 333 Wonderview Av.*   *586-3371*
The area's major landmark is listed on the National Register of Historic Places. The stately
old wood-sided hotel is currently undergoing renovation. Amenities include a large scenic
outdoor pool, a handsome view dining room, a lounge, and a live theater. Many of the
rooms have been refurbished.

#417,#415 — fine mountain views,	D bed...$65
#432,#430 — fine lake views,	D bed...$65
regular room —	D or Q bed...$55

Trails West   *2.4 mi. W on US 34 at 1710 Fall River Rd.*   *586-4629*
In the pines along Fall River is a cottage colony featuring a scenic hot tub and deck. Each
carpeted unit has a cable color TV and a fireplace.

#3 — 1 BR, kit., deck framed around a tree,	Q bed...$45
#16,#15 — kit., deck,	2 D or Q bed...$55
regular unit — deck,	Q bed...$39

Tyrol Motel   *1.2 mi. E on US 34 at 1240 Big Thompson Av.*   *586-3382*
An outdoor pool, whirlpool, and a sauna are features in this contemporary motel. Each
room has a phone and cable color TV.

#405 — spacious, fine views from 2 sides, refr.,	2 Q beds..$65
#404,#401 — spacious, good views,	Q bed...$42
regular room —	Q bed...$42

CAMPGROUNDS

Many campgrounds are located around town. The most scenic are by streams or lakes in
the dense pine forests at the base of the towering Front Range. Near town, several
privately operated campgrounds provide complete facilities in more prosaic locations.

Glacier Basin   *9 mi. SW via CO 66 on Bear Lake Rd.*   *586-2371*
This large Rocky Mountain National Park campground is located near scenic Glacier Creek. Features include fishing plus horseback and hiking trails. There are flush toilets, but no showers or hookups. Each of the shady sites has a picnic table and fire grill.
                                                                                base rate...$6

KOA - Estes Park   *2 mi. E on US 34*   *586-2888*
The nearest campground to town is a private facility with a mountain view beyond the highway. Horseback riding rentals are adjacent. Flush toilets, hot showers and hookups are available. Each of the small, terraced sites has a picnic table and fire grill. Some are pine-shaded.   base rate...$9

Mary's Lake Campground   *4 mi. S via CO 7 on Peak View Dr.*   *586-4411*
A tiny fishing lake is a feature of this large, privately owned campground and trailer park in a quiet mountain view area. Flush toilets, hot showers and hookups are available. Each treeless site has a picnic table and a fire ring. There is a separate tenting area.
                                                                                base rate...$8

National Park Resort   *4 mi. W on US 34*   *586-4563*
This large, privately operated facility is in a pine forest near the Fall River entrance to Rocky Mountain National Park. Flush toilets, hot showers (fee), and hookups are available. Each shady site has a picnic table and fire ring.   base rate...$9

SPECIAL EVENT
★ **International Aspenfest**   *in and around town*   *last half of September*
This celebration of the aspens turning color includes an elaborate Scottish Highland Festival, folk dancing, an arts and crafts show, magic performances, live entertainment and street dances. A World Champion Elk "Marble" Shoot and bus trips into the National Park to hear Elk bugling are the most unusual events.

OTHER INFORMATION
Area Code: *303*
Zip Code: *80517*
Estes Park C. of C.   *.4 mi. NE on US 34 at 500 Big Thompson Ave.*   *586-4431*
Rocky Mountain Natl. Park - Headquarters *2 mi. SW off CO 66*   *586-2371*
Roosevelt Natl. Forest - Ranger Station *.6 mi. SE at 161 2nd St.*   *586-3440*

Steamboat Springs, Colorado

Elevation:

6,695 feet

Population (1980):

5,098

Population (1970):

2,340

Location:

160 mi. NW
of Denver

Steamboat Springs is an exciting blend of the Old and New West. Surrounded by lush rangeland, the town lies in a broad upland valley flanked on the east by the northern Colorado Rockies. Winters are long, cold, and snowy, to the delight of hordes of visitors enjoying outstanding downhill and cross-country skiing complexes nearby and the famed ski jump in town. The weather is uniformly fine throughout summer, which is the other busy season. The pine-forested mountains just east of town have an assortment of lakes and streams, and are in demand for hiking, backpacking, horseback riding, hunting, and fishing. A large nearby reservoir offers boating and fishing; and scenic golf courses, tennis courts, and miles of bicycle paths have been provided in the area. The most popular in-town attraction is a splendid Olympic-sized pool and water slide complex warmed by local hot springs and open all year. Several parks and recreation features have been developed along the banks of the Yampa River in town. On warm summer days, floating on the river is a favorite pastime.

It was the agricultural potential of the lush Yampa River Valley that first attracted homesteaders to this area in the 1870s. The town's name was derived from the chugging sound made by hot springs next to the river in those days. Ranching prospered, and by 1900 the little town was incorporated. It became the county seat of Routt County in 1911. Thanks to a Norwegian, the town was introduced to skiing and ski jumping on a slope next to downtown in 1913. It was already internationally known by the 1930s. Growth was slow, however, until the 1970s when development of a vast skiing complex at the nearby base of Mt. Werner really confirmed the town's reputation as "Ski Town, U.S.A."

Booming development at the mountain has brought additional vitality to the town's handsome little business district which remains the vital core for the area. Many new structures share downtown with solid turn-of-the-century buildings that have been carefully restored. A few galleries and specialty shops have joined an already outstanding cluster of Western ware stores. Distinctive restaurants and bars are also proliferating, often with plush Western decor appreciated as much by farmers and ranchers as by sportsmen and apres-skiers. Most of the area's luxurious lodgings have been built recently at the base of Mt. Werner, while a number of good conventional accommodations are downtown and nearby.

Steamboat Springs, Colorado

WEATHER PROFILE — Vokac Weather Rating

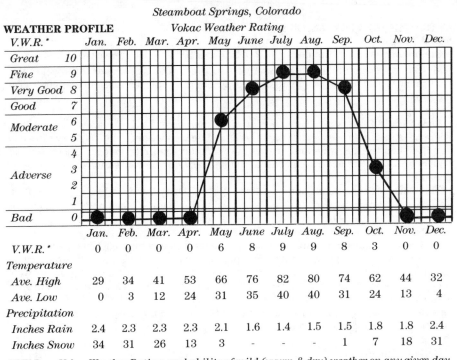

V.W.R.*	Jan.	Feb.	Mar.	Apr.	May	June	July	Aug.	Sep.	Oct.	Nov.	Dec.
V.W.R.*	0	0	0	0	6	8	9	9	8	3	0	0
Temperature												
Ave. High	29	34	41	53	66	76	82	80	74	62	44	32
Ave. Low	0	3	12	24	31	35	40	40	31	24	13	4
Precipitation												
Inches Rain	2.4	2.3	2.3	2.3	2.1	1.6	1.4	1.5	1.5	1.8	1.8	2.4
Inches Snow	34	31	26	13	3	-	-	-	1	7	18	31

*V.W.R. = Vokac Weather Rating: probability of mild (warm & dry) weather on any given day.

Forecast

Month	V.W.R.*		Temperatures Daytime	Evening	Precipitation
January	0	Bad	cold	frigid	frequent snowstorms
February	0	Bad	chilly	frigid	frequent snowstorms
March	0	Bad	chilly	cold	frequent snowstorms
April	0	Bad	cool	chilly	occasional snow flurries
May	6	Moderate	warm	chilly	occasional rainstorms/snow flurries
June	8	Very Good	warm	cool	infrequent rainstorms
July	9	Fine	warm	cool	occasional showers
August	9	Fine	warm	cool	occasional showers
September	8	Very Good	warm	cool	occasional showers
October	3	Adverse	cool	chilly	occasional snow flurries/rainstorms
November	0	Bad	chilly	cold	occasional snowstorms
December	0	Bad	cold	frigid	frequent snowstorms

Summary

Steamboat Springs is located by the Yampa River in a broad valley along the western flank of the northern Colorado Rockies. In this picturesque setting, **winter** evenings are extremely cold and daytime high temperatures are usually below freezing. However, because the area also gets frequent heavy snowstorms, it is one of the West's finest and most popular winter recreation areas highlighted by a splendid skiing complex only two miles from downtown. Good skiing continues into **spring**. There is a brief muddy transition when the snow cover melts, and snow flurries are replaced by showers. **Summer** weather is fine for every kind of outdoor activity, with warm days, cool evenings, and occasional brief showers. Mild conditions end abruptly in early **fall**, when freezing temperatures turn aspen-forested hills to gold, and cooler days and snow flurries foreshadow the return of winter weather before Thanksgiving.

ATTRACTIONS & DIVERSIONS
Aerial Tramway
★　**Steamboat Ski Area Gondola**　　*3.2 mi. SE via US 40 & Mt. Werner Rd.*　　*879-0740*
A six-passenger gondola takes passengers to the top of Mt. Werner for spectacular panoramic views from mid-June to Labor Day. There are picnic sites and hiking trails at the top.

Bicycling
★　**Sore Saddle Cyclery**　　*downtown at 1136 Yampa Av.*　　*879-1675*
There are some scenic separated bikeways in and near town, and relatively easy rides can be enjoyed on the highways and byways in the picturesque Yampa River Valley. Rentals, repairs and sales are available at this architecturally unique bike shop.

Boating
　　The Dock at Steamboat Lake　　*26 mi. N via County Road 129*　　*879-7019*
Sailboats (catamarans, etc.), fishing boats, ski boats, paddle boats and canoes can be rented for three hours or longer any day in summer.

★　**City Park**　　*.3 mi. N at Lincoln Av./13th St.*
Four distinctive natural hot springs features are identified in this delightful town park by the Yampa River. The grassy banks are a popular take-out point for river runners who have navigated the easy waters of the Yampa through town. Tables and fire grills are well-sited for memorable picnics while enjoying the river, springs and mountain backdrop.

★　**Fish Creek Falls**　　*4 mi. E via Fish Creek Falls Rd.*
This 283-foot waterfall is especially impressive during the heavy spring runoff. Picnic facilities and hiking trails are provided.

★　**Flying**
　　Balloon The Rockies　　*879-7313*
Luxurious champagne flights by balloon over the Yampa Valley, or longer Continental Divide crossings, are available by reservation.
　　Steamboat Aviation　　*3 mi. NW via US 40 on County Rd. 129 - Airport*　　*879-1204*
Scenic flights over any of the nearby high country can be reserved here.

★　**Horseback Riding**
Hourly rentals for scenic rides, plus breakfast and dinner rides, and overnight or longer pack trips can be arranged at several stables, including:
　　All Seasons Ranch　　*6 mi. E via US 40 at 41090 County Rd. 80*　　*879-7295*
　　Elk River Guest Ranch　　*22 mi. NE via County Rd. 129 - Clark*　　*879-2606*
　　Vista Verde Guest Ranch　　*25 mi. N via County Rd. 129 - Clark*　　*879-3858*
Jeep Tours
　　Colorado Adventures, Inc.　　*downtown at 703 Lincoln Av.*　　*879-2039*
Jeep tour guides take visitors into the remote high country for close-up views of mountains, waterfalls and mineral springs in the area. Various trips (up to four hours) can be reserved here.

★　**Library**　　*.3 mi. N at 1289 Lincoln Av.*　　*879-0240*
The Bud Werner Memorial Library has an inviting periodical reading area with a sofa near picture windows in a modern A-frame building. A "Western room" downstairs has a good selection of books about the region and a pleasant work area.

★　**Llama Trekking**　　*18 mi. N via County Rd. 129 - Clark*　　*879-1780*
For an unusual experience, let a llama carry your lunch up to a lake in the Mt. Zirkel Wilderness. Hassle-free hikes into the high country with these appealing pack animals start from the Home Ranch, by reservation.

★　**River Running**
Professional river guides lead scenic, whitewater, and fishing trips of one or more days in rubber rafts, McKenzie boats, and kayaks. The Yampa and nearby rivers are in demand from May to September. For reservations and details, contact:
　　Adventure Bound, Inc.　　*879-1100*
　　Alpine River Expeditions　　*879-5541*
　　Mother Goose Sportyak Trips (one-person boats)　　*879-7427*

★ **Routt National Forest**   *N, E, and SW of town*   879-1722
This large forest includes numerous remote hot springs, several major lakes and reservoirs, and the Mt. Zirkel Wilderness area with 200 miles of trails and more than seventy lakes. The Steamboat Ski Area is a renowned winter destination. Camping, hiking, horseback riding and pack trips, fishing, hunting and winter sports are seasonally popular.

★ **Steamboat State Park**   *25 mi. N on County Rd. 129*
Steamboat Lake, a sprawling 1,100-acre reservoir in the midst of an expansive rangeland basin, is the focus of activities in the park. Picnicking along the shore and camping nearby are popular, as are fishing, boating (rentals are available), water-skiing and swimming (on the warmest days).

Warm Water Feature
★   **Steamboat Springs Recreation Center**   *.3 mi. SE at 136 Lincoln Av.*   879-1828
An Olympic-sized outdoor pool, a soaking pool, an exhilarating 350-foot hydro-tube slide, and saunas are highlights of a superb warm mineral springs complex.

Winter Sports
★   **Cross-Country Touring and Instruction**
Several places provide instruction, guided tours, and rental equipment, including:
    Mountain Craft   879-2368
    Scandinavian Lodge   879-0517
    Ski Valley Lodge   879-5158
★   **Howelsen Hill Area**   *downtown via 5th St. on River Rd.*   879-4300
World records have been set here on a long-established ski jumping facility overlooking downtown. Skiing and ice-skating are also popular. Tennis courts, sports fields, and rodeo grounds at the base are heavily used in summer.

★   **Sleigh Rides**
An old-fashioned sleigh ride can be arranged at:
    Vista Verde Guest Ranch   *25 mi. N via County Rd. 129 - Clark*   879-3858
★   **Snowmobiling**
    Glen Eden Guest Ranch   *20 mi. N at 54737 County Rd. 129 - Clark*   879-3906
Guided snowmobile tours can be reserved here.

★   **Steamboat Ski Area**   *3.2 mi. SE via US 40 & Mt. Werner Rd.*   879-6111
The vertical rise is 3,600 feet and the longest run is 2.5 miles. Elevation at the top is 10,500 feet. There are chairlifts, including five triple chairs and a six-passenger gondola. All facilities, services and rentals are available at the base for both downhill and cross-country skiing. More than a dozen restaurants, a similar number of bars, and about two dozen lodging facilities are within walking distance of the lifts. The ski season is late November to mid-April.

SHOPPING
Lincoln Avenue between the Courthouse and the Library has been the commercial heart of the area for decades. A pleasing combination of old and new Western-style buildings houses an increasing number of galleries and specialty shops, as well as a long-established assortment of Western ware stores, bars, and restaurants. A smaller concentration of distinctive shops has been growing in recent years at the ski area three miles south.

Food Specialties
Blackbird Bakery   *1.2 mi. NW on US 40*   879-4342
A full line of quality baked goods made here fresh daily is served to go, or with coffee at a few tables. A smaller outlet downtown gets their baked goods from here.

★ **The Bottleneck**   *downtown at 734 Lincoln Av.*   879-1255
An outstanding selection of California and European wines is well stored and beautifully displayed in this Rocky Mountain enophile's haven. There's even a quick-chilling machine. Beers and liquors are also well represented.

Candy Mountain Sweet Stuff   *3.2 mi. SE at 1910 Mt. Werner Rd.*   879-0703
An impressive selection of tasty muffins, pastries and pies are served to go or in a cozy coffee shop.

Haagen Dazs   *downtown at 845 Lincoln Av.*   *879-7424*
Premium ice creams are featured in this bright new representative of the quality ice cream chain.

The In-Season Bakery-Cafe   *downtown on 11th St. near Oak Av.*   *879-1840*
Good French pastries, breads, and desserts are sold in a handsome newer bakery with carryout service and a pleasant creek view dining area featuring light meals.

★ **Steamboat Seafood Co.**   *1.4 mi. SE via US 40 on Anglers Dr.*   *879-3504*
Fresh seafoods are only one of the features of this remarkable market. Freshly squeezed juices are also available, along with enticing displays of gourmet pastas, produce and pates.

★ **Toot Sweet**   *downtown at 803 Lincoln Av.*   *879-8668*
Outstanding homemade ice creams in a variety of flavors are used in all kinds of delicious creations served in a delightful contemporary parlor. Chocolates from the Rocky Mountain Chocolate Factory in Durango are also sold. Samples are offered.

Specialty Shops

★ **Boggs Hardware**   *downtown at 730 Lincoln Av.*   *879-0764*
A classic Western combination of a historic general store and a modern home specialty shop make this place a shopping/browsing experience.

★ **F. M. Light & Sons**   *downtown at 830 Lincoln Av.*   *879-1822*
Established near the turn of the century, this emporium has become an outstanding source of Western ware, including the largest selection of boots and hats in western Colorado.

Steamboat Art Company   *downtown at 810 Lincoln Av.*   *879-3383*
This large gallery features arts and crafts in a variety of media by local and regional artists.

NIGHTLIFE
Several distinctive bars have live entertainment and dancing on weekends, both downtown and at the ski area. A number of places provide plush furnishings or view decks for quiet conversations. Live theater is also offered in summer.

★ **Brandywine**   *downtown at 57 8th St.*   *879-9939*
A proliferation of Victorian artifacts, stained glass, and lush greenery complement the elegant parlour furniture in this plush Old Western-style lounge.

★ **The Cameo**   *downtown at 600 Lincoln Av.*   *879-4421*
Occasional live entertainment supplements shuffleboard, bumper pool, and bowling in a casual old-time bar with comfortable booths and a pleasant outdoor deck. Light meals are served all day.

Faces   *3 mi. SE at 2305 Village Inn Court*   *879-9862*
Live music for dancing is played most nights in this contemporary Western lounge in the Steamboat Village Plaza.

★ **Old West Steakhouse**   *downtown at 1104 Lincoln Av.*   *879-1441*
Piano entertainment occasionally enlivens a charming upstairs lounge with an all-sofa room, and a unique two-tiered, wine-barrel-booths room. A family-oriented steak house is downstairs.

★ **The Sheraton at Steamboat**   *3.2 mi. SE at 2200 Village Inn Court*   *879-2220*
Well-known performers occasionally provide the live entertainment for dancing. The resort's sleek, modern lounge also has splendid picture window views of the base of the ski slopes.

★ **Shortbranch Saloon**   *downtown at 741 Lincoln Av.*   *879-3555*
Live entertainment is featured amidst Victorian-style atmosphere that includes some game trophies and a very long bar.

★ **The Tugboat**   *3.2 mi. SE at 1860 Mt. Werner Rd.*   *879-9990*
This casual saloon is a local favorite with live entertainment most nights in a room loaded with trophy heads and bric-a-brac. There is also a pool table and a shady view deck where light meals are served, weather permitting.

RESTAURANTS

Area restaurants reflect the town's comfortable blend of the Old West and the New West in both food styles and decor.

Brandywine　*downtown at 57 8th St.*　　　879-9939
D only. Sun. brunch.　　　*Moderate*
Contemporary American fare is served in a resplendent Victorian setting of antique furniture, stained glass, and hanging plants. A classy, romantic lounge adjoins.

★ **Cipriani's**　*3.5 mi. SE on Mt. Werner Rd.*　　879-2220
D only.　　　*Moderate*
Gourmet Italian dinners with homemade baked goods, pastry and pasta are featured. The intimate dining room is a beautiful example of contemporary elegance.

The Clocktower Restaurant　*3.2 mi. SE at 1724 Mt. Werner Rd.*　879-3220
L-D.　　　*Moderate*
Steak and hickory-smoked barbecue specialties are served in rustic Western atmosphere with a panoramic view of the ski area. Live entertainment and dancing are offered in the bar.

★ **The Gallery**　*5 mi. SE at 33607 Storm Meadows Dr.*　　879-0239
L-D.　　　*Moderate*
Continental gourmet specialties are served in an expansive contemporary dining room with a window wall view of the ski area and Yampa Valley. A cozy fireplace lounge and view deck adjoin.

Giovanni's　*downtown at 912 Lincoln Av.*　　　879-5016
D only.　　　*Moderate*
Italian cuisine is served nightly in an intimate, attractively furnished dining room that has another identity during the day.

★ **Good Taste Crepe Shoppe**　*downtown at 442 Lincoln Av.*　　879-4106
B-L-D.　　　*Moderate*
Many kinds of delicious omelets, crepes, and waffles are featured in a cozy little upstairs cafe.

Mattie Silks　*3.3 mi. SE on Ski Time Square*　　879-2441
D only.　　　*Expensive*
Continental specialties are served in a congested, casually elegant little dining room next to a classy Old West-style bar.

Pine Grove Restaurant　*1.5 mi. SE via US 40 at 1465 Pine Grove Rd.*　879-1190
D only.　　　*Moderate*
Steaks are the specialty, along with homemade bread, rolls, and desserts. There is also a salad bar. A large, handsomely converted old barn is filled with Western relics in several dining rooms and in a saloon.

Remington's　*3.2 mi. SE at 2200 Village Inn Court*　　879-2220
B-L-D.　　　*Moderate*
In the Sheraton at Steamboat, American dishes (notably buffalo steak) are served in this elegant contemporary dining room overlooking the slopes. A lounge with live entertainment and dancing adjoins.

The Sidestep　*downtown at 738 Lincoln Av.*　　　879-9933
B-L-D.　　　*Low*
Good American and Mexican fare distinguish a bustling little dining room that also sports the town's tiniest bar.

★ **Soupcon**　*downtown at 912 Lincoln Av.*　　　879-5016
L only. Closed Sun.　　　*Moderate*
Delicious home-cooking lends appeal to a variety of soups and muffins in this pleasant little dining room.

★ **Steamboat Juice Company**　*1.4 mi. SE via US 40 on Anglers Dr.*　879-6858
B-L-D. No D on Mon.　　　*Moderate*
Outstanding country breakfasts are a specialty, including fresh-squeezed juices and homemade pastries. Fresh seafood is featured for dinner. The finest natural ingredients are used in this well-liked restaurant with a cheerful plant-filled solarium dining room, and a stylish contemporary bar.

LODGING

Accommodations are plentiful, and range from rustic little motels to opulent resort hotels. Most are along Lincoln Avenue (US 40) in and near downtown, and at the base of nearby Mt. Werner. Rates are generally nearly 100% more than the summer rates quoted for the best facilities by the ski slopes during the height of the winter season (around the Christmas holidays) and at least 50% more during the remainder of the skiing season, even in town. Spring and fall rates are usually at least 10% less than in summer.

Anchor Motel *downtown at 24 5th St.* 879-0675
This small **bargain** motel near the heart of town has a quiet location near the river. Each room has a cable color TV.

    regular room — D bed...$22

★ **Bear Claw** *3.5 mi. SE via Mt. Werner Rd. on Ski Trail Lane* 879-6100
Steamboat's premier location is on the main slope atop the beginners run uphill from the gondola. This luxurious contemporary condominium complex has a large outdoor heated pool, whirlpool, sauna, and game room. Each spacious, beautifully furnished unit has a color TV, phone, wood-burning fireplace with adjoining Jenn-air grill, fully equipped kitchen, and a private balcony.

    #205,#515,#415 — 2 BR, splendid pvt. view of the slopes, 2 T & Q beds...$115
    regular room — 1 BR, Q bed...$83

★ **Bronze Tree** *4 mi. SE via US 40 on Storm Meadows Dr.* 879-1035
This striking new curvilinear condominium complex is within walking or skiing distance of the slopes and the ski village. The building has an indoor pool, whirlpool, and sauna. Guests have free access to Steamboat Athletic Club facilities (elsewhere in Storm Meadows Resort complex), and (for a fee) massage, racquetball and two indoor tennis courts. Each lavishly contemporary unit has a phone, cable color TV with movies, kitchen, raised flagstone fireplace, window walls, and a huge view balcony.

    #604,#605,#606,#504,#505,#506 — 2 BR, superb slope/village views, 3 Q beds...$88
    regular unit — 2 BR, 3 Q beds...$88

Dream Island Motel *.3 mi. NW at 1401 Lincoln Av.* 879-0261
Just beyond the lovely town park is an older single-level motel that is a no-frills **bargain**.

    regular room — 2 D or Q bed...$26

Harbor Hotel *downtown at 703 Lincoln Av.* 879-1522
In the heart of town, this recently remodeled hotel has some modest **bargain** rooms, plus a restaurant and bar. Each simply furnished room has a private bath.

    regular room — phone, cable color TV, D bed...$36
    regular room — older section of hotel, small, D bed...$26

Nite's Rest Motel *downtown at 601 Lincoln Av.* 879-1212
This **bargain** motel near the heart of town offers a phone and color TV in each of the modest rooms.

    regular room — D or Q bed...$26

Ptarmigan Inn - Best Western *3.2 mi. SE at 2304 Apres Ski Way* 879-1730
This large motor hotel at the base of Mt. Werner near the gondola lift has a large outdoor pool (heated year-round), a sauna, and a casual restaurant and lounge. Each spacious room has a phone and cable color TV. Most have balconies.

    "3rd or 4th floor on slope side" — fine ski slope view, Q or K bed...$38
    regular room — Q bed...$38

Rabbit Ears Motel *.3 mi. SE at 201 Lincoln Av.* 879-1150
Directly across from the town's outstanding hot springs pool complex is a modern motel with several newer units in a quiet location by the Yampa River. All rooms have a phone and cable color TV with movies.

    #201,#122 — spacious, on river, pvt. balc., 2 Q beds...$38
    regular room — older section, D bed...$32

Rainbow Cottages *downtown at 702 Oak St.* 879-1834
This small older **bargain** motel in a quiet location by the heart of town has plain rooms with cable color TV.

    regular room — D bed...$24

★ **Ramada Inn**   *1.5 mi. SE via US 40 at 1000 Ramada Dr.*   *879-2900*
The lodging chain has a large five-floor motor hotel on a hill overlooking town with a big indoor pool, whirlpool, saunas, game room, and two outdoor tennis courts, plus a restaurant and lounge. Each nicely furnished room has a phone and cable color TV. Suites with kitchenettes and gas fireplaces are available.

#417,#416 — good town/mt. views, in-bath steambath/whirlpool,	K bed...$56
#411,#410 — good town/mt. views, in-bath steambath/whirlpool,	2 Q beds...$56
regular room —	Q bed...$44

★ **Sheraton at Steamboat**   *3.2 mi. SE at 2200 Village Inn Court*   *879-2220*
The area's largest and most complete resort is an eight-story hotel with an outstanding location at the base of the slopes by the gondola. The luxurious, modern complex has two year-round heated pools, saunas, whirlpools, plus (for a fee) a nearby 18-hole Robert Trent Jones golf course and several tennis courts (four lighted). There are several distinctive restaurants and lounges. Each spacious, beautifully furnished unit has a phone, color TV, and a private balcony.

#609 — 1 BR, corner windows, circular fireplace, kit., slope view,	2 Q beds...$115
#506,#406 — corner windows, splendid slope view,	2 Q beds...$75
regular room —	Q bed...$50

Springs Motor Lodge   *downtown at 917 Lincoln Av.*   *879-1400*
Here is a European-style **bargain** hotel in the heart of town. Each simply furnished room has a phone, B/W TV, and private sink and toilet (bath is shared with one other room).

#33,#34 — corner rooms, views of ski jumps & Howelsen Hill,	D bed...$20
regular room —	D bed...$20

Steamboat Motor Inn   *downtown at 1122 Lincoln Av.*   *879-1050*
This modern motel has an outdoor pool and a sauna. Each room has a phone and cable color TV with movies.

regular room —	Q bed...$34

★ **Storm Meadows Resort**   *4 mi. SE via US 40 at 2135 Burgess Creek Rd.*   *879-1035*
In the winter, guests ski or walk to the lifts. There are mountain slope views year-round. Amenities in the nearby athletic club include a large outdoor pool, whirlpool, sauna, steambath, exercise room and (for a fee) massage, racquetball, and four tennis courts (two indoors), plus a fine restaurant and lounge. Each spacious, well-furnished modern condominium or townhouse apartment has a phone, cable color TV with movies, kitchen, moss rock fireplace, and private deck or patio.

#50,#40 (East Bldg.) — 1 BR, splendid pvt. slope/mt. views,	2 T & sofa Q beds...$59
#60 (East Bldg.) — 2 BR, as above,	2 T & sofa Q beds...$79
regular room — 1 BR,	2 T & sofa Q beds...$59

Super 8 Motel   *3 mi. SE on US 40 at 3195 S. Lincoln Av.*   *879-5230*
The thrifty motel chain recently added a high-country example of the state of the art in modern **bargain** motels. There is a sauna, and each room has a phone and color TV.

regular room —	D bed...$28

★ **Thunderhead Lodge**   *3.5 mi. SE at 35215 Mt. Werner Rd.*   *879-2220*
Adjacent to the slopes of Mt. Werner, this newly remodeled motor lodge has a large outdoor pool, whirlpool, and sauna, plus a fine restaurant. Each attractively furnished unit has a phone, color TV, and balcony.

apartment — 1 BR, fireplace, kit., some have slope view,	2 Q beds...$80
regular room — studio, fireplace, kitchenette, some have slope view,	2 Q beds...$60

CAMPGROUNDS
Several nearby campgrounds have primitive facilities on a lake or stream. However, the best is convenient to town in a shady location by the river, and it has complete facilities.

Fish Creek Campground   *1.5 mi. E on US 40*   *879-5476*
The nearest campground is a privately operated facility that offers fishing in the nearby river and a rec room. Flush toilets, hot showers, and hookups are available. Most of the grassy sites have picnic tables and grills. The few sites by the stream are also tree-shaded. There is a separate tenting area.   base rate...$9

★ **Ski Town Campground**   *2 mi. W on US 40*   *879-0273*
This large privately owned facility has a picturesque site by the Yampa River. Features include fishing in the river and (fee) float trips, an outdoor whirlpool, and a small rec room. Flush toilets, hot showers and hookups are available. Each of the grassy sites includes a picnic table and fire ring. The separate tenting area, on an island in the river, has several grassy cottonwood-shaded riverside sites.   base rate...$9

SPECIAL EVENTS

★ **Winter Carnival**   *in and around town*   *mid-February*
One of the oldest winter carnivals in the U.S. is highlighted by ski jumping events on a hill across the river from downtown, and cutter races in the streets.

The Way It Wuz Days   *in and around town*   *mid-June to mid-September*
Western-style events are scheduled throughout the summer, including a chili jamboree, mountain man rendezvous, boat race, bluegrass festival, and more.

★ **Cowboys Roundup Rodeo**   *in town*   *July 4*
A Rocky Mountain Oyster Fry is an unusual highlight of this annual four-day celebration that also includes a parade, outdoor concerts, dances, fireworks and a top-notch rodeo.

OTHER INFORMATION

Area Code: *303*
Zip Code: *80477*
Steamboat Springs Chamber/Resort Assoc. *.3 mi. N at 1201 Lincoln Av.*   *879-0880*
Routt Nat. Forest-Supervisor's Office   *downtown at 401 Lincoln Av.*   *879-1722*

Telluride, Colorado

Elevation:

8,750 feet

Population (1980):

1,047

Population (1970):

553

Location:

336 mi. SW
of Denver

Telluride is a matchless Victorian relic with a silver-lined past and a solid gold future. This irrepressible village has a startlingly beautiful site. Some of the nation's highest peaks tower majestically above pine-covered slopes that rise precipitously from the level floor of a narrow little valley almost 9,000 feet above sea level. Within earshot, the state's highest waterfall tumbles into the canyon and becomes a major stream that flows along the town's south side. Here in one of the West's most isolated locations, the heavy snowfall of long cold winters has been turned into "white gold" with the recent development of major skiing facilities in town. Summer has traditionally been the busiest season, when good weather invites unlimited recreational enjoyment of breathtaking mountains, dramatic canyons, and clear cold streams and lakes in the vast surrounding forests. Many summer visitors remain in town for a succession of popular festivals devoted to everything from wine or films to bluegrass or jazz music. Fall is a quiet, uncrowded time, and unforgettably beautiful when the aspen forests on nearby slopes put on their brief annual display of color beneath peaks newly white with the season's first snows.

Telluride was founded as a gold and silver mining camp in the 1870s. It boomed and prospered with sturdy brick buildings and an impressive array of businesses. There were 5,000 residents around 1900, and the town earned a wild and woolly reputation for its gaming and sporting house district. But, mining activity declined dramatically after the Depression. Only about 500 residents remained by the end of the 1960s, and most buildings were boarded up. In 1972, the Telluride Ski Area opened with five chairlifts, and the "white gold" boom began.

Since then, the last mine has closed and the skiing complex has become one of the largest and most exalted in the West. With strict planning and architectural controls, residents have preserved and enhanced the flavor of Telluride's flamboyant past, while accommodating growth generated by increasingly renowned winter and summer attractions. Today, the whole town is a nationally registered historic landmark. A growing number of galleries and specialty shops are helping to revitalize the charming little business district. Several fascinating bars recall the splendor of the first boom, and some distinctive restaurants are available. Accommodations are relatively limited, and there are no conventional motels. Instead, lodgings include converted boarding houses and several luxurious little condominium hotels. All are concentrated within an easy stroll of the heart of town.

Telluride, Colorado

WEATHER PROFILE — *Vokac Weather Rating*

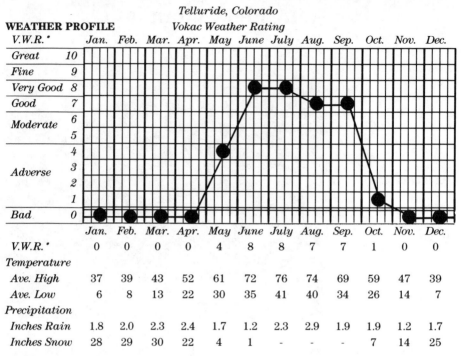

V.W.R.*		Jan.	Feb.	Mar.	Apr.	May	June	July	Aug.	Sep.	Oct.	Nov.	Dec.
Great	10												
Fine	9												
Very Good	8												
Good	7												
Moderate	6												
	5												
	4												
Adverse	3												
	2												
	1												
Bad	0												

	Jan.	Feb.	Mar.	Apr.	May	June	July	Aug.	Sep.	Oct.	Nov.	Dec.
V.W.R.*	0	0	0	0	4	8	8	7	7	1	0	0
Temperature												
Ave. High	37	39	43	52	61	72	76	74	69	59	47	39
Ave. Low	6	8	13	22	30	35	41	40	34	26	14	7
Precipitation												
Inches Rain	1.8	2.0	2.3	2.4	1.7	1.2	2.3	2.9	1.9	1.9	1.2	1.7
Inches Snow	28	29	30	22	4	1	-	-	-	7	14	25

*V.W.R. = Vokac Weather Rating: probability of mild (warm & dry) weather on any given day.

Forecast

Month	V.W.R.*		Temperatures Daytime	Evening	Precipitation
January	0	Bad	chilly	frigid	occasional snowstorms
February	0	Bad	chilly	frigid	occasional snowstorms
March	0	Bad	chilly	cold	frequent snowstorms
April	0	Bad	cool	chilly	frequent snowstorms
May	4	Adverse	cool	chilly	occasional showers/snow flurries
June	8	Very Good	warm	cool	infrequent showers
July	8	Very Good	warm	cool	frequent showers
August	7	Good	warm	cool	frequent showers
September	7	Good	warm	cool	occasional showers
October	1	Adverse	cool	chilly	occasional snow flurries/showers
November	0	Bad	chilly	cold	infrequent snowstorms
December	0	Bad	chilly	frigid	occasional snowstorms

Summary

Tucked away near the head of a glacier-carved valley high in the remote San Juan Mountains, Telluride has one of the most magnificent locations in the world. **Winter** is long, with chilly days, extremely cold nights, and occasional snowstorms that provide plenty of snow for the well-groomed slopes of the major in-town ski area. Mild **spring** weather usually begins after Memorial Day, because winter's freezing temperatures and snowfalls linger through May. **Summer** offers very good conditions for enjoying outdoor festivals in town, and for exploring the awesome high country. Days are warm and evenings are cool, but there are persistent brief thundershowers. **Fall** is heralded by glorious displays of color in the surrounding aspen forests. Soon, increasingly heavy snowfalls prepare the slopes overlooking town for another ski season, which generally begins in November.

ATTRACTIONS & DIVERSIONS

Bicycling
Telluride Sports   *downtown at 226 W. Colorado Av.*   728-3501
A variety of bicycles can be rented here by the hour or longer to explore the picturesque, relatively flat valley, or to get into the breathtaking high country.

★ **Bridal Veil Falls**   *2 mi. E on CO 145*
Colorado's highest waterfall tumbles more than 400 feet down mist-shrouded cliffs at the end of a box canyon visible from downtown. The precariously perched hydroelectric plant atop the falls, built by one of the big mining companies in 1904, is now a National Historic Landmark.

★ **Historic District**   *downtown on/near Colorado Av.*
A substantial concentration of Victorian buildings earned a National Historic Landmark designation for the entire town. Among the most notable are the San Miguel County Courthouse on Colorado Avenue, constructed in 1887 of brick. Next door, the "Galloping Goose" is one of several unique railway buses built during the Depression to try to keep the railroad alive between Telluride and Durango. Unfortunately, the attempt failed and the bizarre passenger service stopped operating in 1952. "The Cribs" on Pacific Street are remnants of a once-bawdy gambling and red-light district. The tiny Town Jail on Spruce Street is now the San Miguel County Library. The San Miguel County Museum (1893) was a miners' hospital until 1963. It now houses a collection of Old West memorabilia on display from May through October. A walking tour map and information can be obtained from the Chamber of Commerce.

Horseback Riding
Bear Creek Livery Stables   *.4 mi. SW on Mahoney Dr.*   728-3896
In addition to guided trail rides of various durations, hay rides and chuckwagon dinners are offered, and pack trips can be arranged by advance reservation.

★ **Jeep Rentals**
Telluride Outfitters   *downtown at 231 W. Colorado Av.*   728-3687
Jeeps can be rented by the half day or longer to explore the many fascinating ghost towns and scenic attractions surrounding town.

Trout Lake   *14 mi. SW via CO 145*
This small lake is the largest in the area and offers boating and fishing amidst spectacular high country scenery. Picturesque picnic sites and a primitive campground are nearby.

★ **Uncompahgre National Forest**   *around town*
Several peaks are over 14,000 feet high in this vast forest. Features include a superb winter sports complex at Telluride, and one of the West's most photographed peaks, Mt. Sneffels, is a few miles north of town. All of the highest mountains are in federally designated primitive areas, accessible only by miles of hiking trails. Paved roads and rugged dirt roads pass ghost towns, old mines, streams, waterfalls and a few small lakes, all backed by a magnificent skyline far above dense pine forests. Camping, hiking, backpacking, horseback riding, pack trips, mountain climbing, fishing, hunting and snow sports are all seasonally popular.

Winter Sports
Sleigh Rides
Bear Creek Livery Stables   *.4 mi. SW on Mahoney Dr.*   728-3896
Sleigh rides can be arranged here throughout the skiing season.

★ **Telluride Ski Resort**   *.4 mi. SW off CO 145 on Mahoney Dr.*   728-3856
The vertical rise is 3,105 feet and the longest run is almost three miles. The "Plunge" off the north face into town is one of the West's truly legendary expert slopes. Elevation at the top is 11,840 feet. There are six chairlifts. All facilities, services and rentals are at the base (in town) for both downhill and cross-country skiing. A few bars, restaurants, and lodgings are concentrated at the base, and many more are within walking distance downtown. The ski season is mid-December to early April.

SHOPPING
The picturesque downtown area is concentrated along and near Colorado Avenue within three blocks of the County Courthouse.

Food Specialties

★ **Baked in Telluride**   *downtown at 127 S. Fir St.*   728-9902
This full service bakery offers outstanding pastries, several kinds of bagels, and many breads (like delicious sprouted whole wheat). Sandwiches and light meals are also served at the few tables.

★ **Belmont Liquor & Wine Shop**   *downtown at 122 E. Colorado Av.*   728-3329
A good selection of premium wine is given a balcony showcase in a historic store that also features liquor and beer.

★ **Monika's Gourmet Carryout**   *downtown at 219 E. Colorado Av.*   728-3305
Fine French-style pastries and gourmet provisions (pates, cheeses, truffles, pasta salads, desserts, etc.) are tantalizingly displayed in an inviting new shop. Custom-made picnics are a specialty.

Telluride Liquors   *downtown at 219 W. Colorado Av.*   728-3380
A quick-chilling machine for wines is an attraction in this well-stocked little store.

Specialty Shops

★ **Between the Covers**   *downtown at 224 W. Colorado Av.*   728-4504
An eclectic book collection includes a fine selection of regional interest books neatly displayed amidst charming Telluride atmosphere. Magazines, topographic maps, records and tapes, and posters are also stocked.

Telluride Art Gallery   *downtown at 120 N. Fir St.*   728-3974
Originals displayed here in a variety of media are illustrative of the high quality of locally-produced artistic efforts.

21st Century Fox   *downtown at 210 W. Colorado Av.*   728-3414
Fine art is nicely showcased in a handsome contemporary add-on to a historic building.

NIGHTLIFE

Telluride has tamed down from its lusty early days of gambling and red-light districts. But, downtown still provides one of the West's finest collections of distinctive saloons, and it plays host to a surprising variety of motion picture, live theater, and musical events.

★ **Floradora Saloon**   *downtown at 103 W. Colorado Av.*   728-9937
This renowned bar exudes a scruffy, old-time authenticity that appeals to both locals and visiting fun-lovers alike.

Fly Me to the Moon Saloon   *downtown at 132 E. Columbia Av.*   728-3443
Disco dancing, foosball, shuffleboard and pool enliven this comfortable cellar bar.

★ **Last Dollar Saloon**   *downtown at 100 W. Colorado Av.*   728-9922
Comfortable armchairs overlook dart boards, a pool table, and a raised stone fireplace in this popular saloon.

★ **The Senate**   *downtown at 123 S. Spruce St.*   728-3683
Telluride's most outstanding Victorian bar is filled with a memorable collection of Western antiques. A fine restaurant shares the historic building.

★ **Sheridan Bar**   *downtown at 231 W. Colorado Av.*   728-4351
Authentic turn-of-the-century surroundings still prevail in Telluride's oldest (1895) continuous drinking establishment. A splendid back bar is accompanied by polished, wood-backed bar stools and chairs.

★ **Sheridan Opera House**   *downtown at 110 N. Oak St.*   728-3642
The home of the annual film festival is also a plush showplace for live concerts, current movies, and live theatrical productions. The beautifully restored little 1913 theater sports a horseshoe-shaped balcony and a theater bar that is open on show nights.

Trinity Tavern   *downtown at 200 W. Colorado Av.*   728-3323
Live entertainment ranging from poetry readings to bluegrass music is performed in a large bar with comfortable armchairs.

RESTAURANTS

All of the notable dining places in the area are clustered downtown. A small but growing number serve gourmet meals in unusual surroundings.

Cimarron   *downtown at 150 W. San Juan Av.*   728-3377
D only.   *Moderate*
Contemporary American dishes with a Hawaiian slant are featured in a winsome, personalized dining room decorated with memorabilia of a legendary surfer — the owner.

★ **Excelsior**   *downtown at 200 W. Colorado Av.*   *728-4250*
L-D.   *Moderate*
Classical music accompanies fondues, homemade soups and salads, and other light fare. The delicious homemade pastries are outstanding. An ingeniously restored historic building has dining on two levels, plus the best view in town of the main street and mountains through extra-high windows.

Floradora   *downtown at 103 W. Colorado Av.*   *728-9937*
L-D.   *Moderate*
Gourmet burgers and a soup-and-salad bar are offered in charming turn-of-the-century atmosphere next to a renowned saloon.

★ **Flour Garden**   *downtown at 138 E. Colorado Av.*   *728-3502*
B-L.   *Moderate*
Popular breakfast items include a selection of fine omelets and pancakes served in a tiny rustic coffee shop with a stamped tin ceiling, or on a scenic outdoor patio.

★ **Julian's**   *downtown at 233 W. Colorado Av.*   *728-3839*
B-L-D. No D on Tues. & Wed.   *Moderate*
Northern Italian cuisine is featured amidst Victorian elegance in the authentically restored main dining room of the landmark New Sheridan Hotel. Lunch is served, weather permitting, on a delightful patio with a fine view of the main street and mountains.

Powder House   *downtown at 226 W. Colorado Av.*   *728-3622*
D only. Closed Apr.-May & mid-Nov.-early Dec.   *Moderate*
Contemporary Continental dishes plus a salad and seafood bar are specialties. The dining rooms and lounge are themed to casual Victorian decor.

★ **The Senate**   *downtown at 123 S. Spruce St.*   *728-3683*
D only.   *Moderate*
An international menu, including homemade baked goods and special desserts, is offered amidst antique-filled Old Western surroundings. The adjoining bar is also an authentic Victorian showcase.

The Silver Glade   *downtown at 115 W. Colorado Av.*   *728-4943*
D only. Closed Mon.   *Moderate*
Fresh seafood is carefully prepared on a mesquite grill. The plush restaurant, opened in 1984, is already one of Telluride's favorite dining establishments.

Sofio's   *downtown at 110 E. Colorado Av.*   *728-4882*
B-D. No D on Sun.   *Moderate*
Traditional Mexican-style cooking plus American breakfast specialties are featured in this pleasant, modern little restaurant.

LODGING
Most of the best accommodations reflect Telluride's Victorian spirit — whether through skillful restorations or careful derivatives. There is no motel row, and there are no big, full service facilities in the area. Instead, each of the lodges, inns, and motels displays the human scale and the architectural craftsmanship that were the bases for the entire town being placed on the National Register of Historic Places. Bargains are scarce during the summer, and non-existent during festivals and the winter skiing season when rates are normally at least 30% higher than those shown.

★ **Coronet Creek**   *.3 mi. W at 105 S. Davis St.*   *728-3970*
This recently-built little condominium complex offers choice mountain views and fine stained glass windows. It is only a block from the ski lifts and a short stroll from downtown. Each unit features superb wood craftsmanship, fine contemporary furnishings, a complete modern kitchen, and cable color TV.

#303 — 3 BR, corner, iron fireplace, in-bath whirlpool/		
steambath, ski run/mt. views,	2 D & Q	waterbeds...$88
#302 — 2 BR, in-bath whirlpool, fine mt. view,	2 Q	beds...$82
#304 — 2 BR, in-bath whirlpool, fine mt. view,	2 T & D & Q	beds...$82
#102 — 1 BR, in-bath steam bath, pvt. creekside view,	K	bed...$55
regular room — 1 BR,	Q	bed...$55

The Dahl Haus   *downtown at 122 S. Oak St.*   *728-4158*
An 1890s boarding house has been refurbished as a bed-and-breakfast inn. Antique furnishings and **bargain** prices during the summer make up for the bath at the end of the hall in the old building. A Continental breakfast is included.

new condo rooms — pvt. bath,	Q bed...$40
regular room — in old bldg., shared bath,	D bed...$25

Johnstone Inn   *downtown at 403 W. Colorado Av.*   *728-3316*
This carefully restored Victorian dwelling is now a **bargain** bed-and-breakfast inn. A Continental breakfast is complimentary. Most rooms share a bath.

#2 — pvt. bath,	D bed...$35
regular room — shared bath,	D bed...$30

★ **Manitou Hotel**   *downtown at 333 S. Fir St.*   *728-4401*
Here is a great escape for romantics. A little contemporary wood-trimmed lodge by the river offers memorable views of the mountains and a feeling of tranquility in an out-of-the-way location. Each comfortably furnished unit has a refrigerator.

#5,#6 — 2-level, spacious, pvt. super view balcony, in-room tub across from free-standing metal fireplace, loft with great mt. view,	2 D beds...$52
#7 — as above, but kitchenette instead of fireplace,	2 D beds...$52
regular room — view,	D bed...$37

★ **Manitou Riverhouse**   *downtown at 333 S. Fir St.*   *728-4311*
The only facility right on the San Miguel River is also adjacent to the mountain. You can ski down to your door, and both lifts and downtown are within walking distance. A large redwood hot tub is positioned by the stream. Each spacious, contemporary unit is beautifully furnished and includes a refrigerator and cable color TV.

#117 — 1 BR condo, end, pvt. balc., kit., fireplace, fine town view,	K bed...$70
#119 — 1 BR condo, end, kit., great town/creek view, balc.,	Q bed...$70
#102 — in-bath whirlpool,	Q bed...$45
#104,#106 — on the river, pvt. balc.,	Q bed...$45
regular room — pvt. balc.,	Q bed...$45

★ **New Sheridan Hotel**   *downtown at 231 W. Colorado Av.*   *728-4354*
One of the Old West's great Victorian landmarks is this brick three-story hotel. Facilities include a fine restaurant, bar, and theater that were skillfully renovated a few years ago. Each room has a phone and cable color TV. Many rooms sharing a bath are **bargains**.

#30 — large, pvt. bath, corner windows, main st./mt. view,	T & Q beds...$50
#23 — pvt. bath, corner, only 1 window but fine mt. view,	Q bed...$45
regular room — shared bath,	Q bed...$30

Victorian Inn   *downtown at 401 W. Pacific Av.*   *728-3684*
This small, newer motel has a whirlpool and sauna. Each of the attractively furnished units is spacious. Refrigerators are available.

regular room —	Q bed...$38

CAMPGROUNDS
Campgrounds are surprisingly scarce, primitive, and beautifully sited.

Matterhorn   *10 mi. SW on CO 145*   *327-4261*
This small Uncompahgre National Forest campground has a scenic location high in the San Juan Mountains. Picturesque Trout Lake is nearby. Fishing and hiking are popular. There are pit toilets — no showers or hookups. Each of the sites has a picnic table and a fire ring.   base rate...$5

Telluride Town Park Campground   *.4 mi. E via Colorado Av.*   *no phone*
Telluride operates a casual little campground by a stream near downtown. The tree-shaded location, surrounded by majestic peaks, is awesome. There are flush toilets and (fee) showers, but no hookups. The sites have picnic tables and fire rings. base rate...$5

SPECIAL EVENTS

★ **Telluride Wine Festival**   *in town*   *mid-June*
Lovers, producers, distributors, and critics of wine are all treated to seminars on cooking with wine and wine production techniques, as well as bountiful wine tastings and gourmet dining.

★ **Telluride Music Festivals**   *festival grounds*   *late June to mid-August*
   Bluegrass & Country Music Festival   *late June*
   Rock and Roll Festival   *late July*
   Chamber Music Festival   *early August*
   Jazz Festival   *mid-August*

A remarkable number of celebrity performers are attracted to these popular three-day musical events in the "music festivals capital of Colorado."

★ **Telluride Film Festival**   *downtown*   *early September*

This has been called the smallest, most original and most stimulating of the major film festivals. International film personalities are honored each year and world premieres of significant films are screened.

OTHER INFORMATION
Area Code: *303*
Zip Code: *81435*
Telluride Chamber of Commerce   *downtown at 225 W. Colorado Av.*   *728-3614*

Vail, Colorado

Elevation:

8,200 feet

Population (1980):

2,261

Population (1970):

484

Location:

94 mi. W
of Denver

Vail is the West's foremost planned ski town. The illustrious young boomtown fills a narrow forested valley backed by spectacular peaks of the central Colorado Rockies. During long, cold, snowy winters, skiing reigns supreme on the state's largest single mountain complex, and the slopes above town are as popular as Vail itself. Summer weather is usually fine for enjoying a wealth of recreation opportunities in nearby deep forested canyons or on rocky, snow-capped mountains. In and around town are beautiful golf courses, tennis and swimming complexes, and miles of scenic bicycle and hiking paths. A lovely clear stream is enhanced by numerous small parks, walkways, and bridges as it rushes through the heart of town. Yet, for all of the summer attractions, crowds are much smaller than in winter. Fall can also be a rewarding time for those lucky enough to be here on clear crisp days when nearby aspen forests are ablaze with color.

Founded in 1962, Vail is the youngest of the great towns. In that single year, both the townsite and ski runs were completed. By the end of its first winter season, Vail Village was established among the top half dozen ski areas in the country. But the real growth began a decade later, during the same period as the much-publicized visits of President Gerald Ford. Celebrity status and the completion of the interstate highway from Denver generated exuberant growth. In the latest decade, skyscrapers were introduced in a more imposingly-scaled second village center (LionsHead) built a mile down the creek, and massive condominium complexes have nearly filled the valley for several miles along the new freeway.

While the original alpine-style architecture has been somewhat subordinated to more monumental, angular structures in newer areas, both of Vail's commercial centers are built around pedestrian-only cores as dictated by the earliest Master Plan. An abundance of artistic amenities — fountains, sculptures, flower-strewn walkways, courtyards, parks by the creek, and sidewalk cafes — has always been the town's most appealing asset. An inviting human scale is reinforced by a high-tech tram bus system in which continuous free service interconnects the two centers and outlying areas. Vail Village and LionsHead are also the two major bases for all ski runs on Vail Mountain. Together, they offer an outstanding proliferation of sophisticated galleries and specialty shops, and one of the West's most notable arrays of contemporary restaurants and lounges. Accommodations are abundant. Many are in opulent high-rise condominium hotels an easy stroll from both the slopes and the village centers.

Vail, Colorado

WEATHER PROFILE *Vokac Weather Rating*

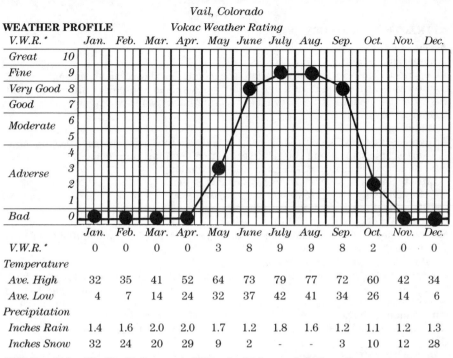

V.W.R.*		Jan.	Feb.	Mar.	Apr.	May	June	July	Aug.	Sep.	Oct.	Nov.	Dec.
V.W.R.*		0	0	0	0	3	8	9	9	8	2	0	0
Temperature													
Ave. High		32	35	41	52	64	73	79	77	72	60	42	34
Ave. Low		4	7	14	24	32	37	42	41	34	26	14	6
Precipitation													
Inches Rain		1.4	1.6	2.0	2.0	1.7	1.2	1.8	1.6	1.2	1.1	1.2	1.3
Inches Snow		32	24	20	29	9	2	-	-	3	10	12	28

*V.W.R. = Vokac Weather Rating: probability of mild (warm & dry) weather on any given day.

Forecast

Month	V.W.R.*		Temperatures Daytime	Evening	Precipitation
January	0	Bad	cold	frigid	frequent snowstorms
February	0	Bad	chilly	frigid	frequent snowstorms
March	0	Bad	chilly	cold	frequent snowstorms
April	0	Bad	cool	chilly	frequent snowstorms
May	3	Adverse	cool	chilly	occasional showers/snow flurries
June	8	Very Good	warm	cool	occasional showers
July	9	Fine	warm	cool	frequent showers
August	9	Fine	warm	cool	frequent showers
September	8	Very Good	warm	cool	occasional showers
October	2	Adverse	cool	chilly	occasional snow flurries/showers
November	0	Bad	chilly	cold	infrequent snowstorms
December	0	Bad	chilly	frigid	frequent snowstorms

Summary

Vail lies deep in a sylvan valley high in the central Colorado Rockies. In this picturesque setting, **winter** is long, with chilly days and bitter cold evenings. Frequent heavy snowstorms normally assure the special conditions that have made the in-town slopes and other winter sports facilities world famous. In **spring**, freezing temperatures and snowfalls extend the skiing season into April and linger through May. All of the year's fine weather is concentrated into **summer**. Warm days, cool evenings, and frequent light showers produce spectacular wildflower displays in the surrounding high country. **Fall** is a short transition season. Rapidly cooling temperatures and increasingly heavy snowstorms usually result in good skiing conditions on the carefully-manicured slopes above town in November.

ATTRACTIONS & DIVERSIONS

Aerial Tramway

★ **LionsHead Gondola**   *L.H. (LionsHead)*   *476-5601*

An enclosed gondola whisks visitors into the mountains above Vail for magnificent high country views throughout summer and on weekends in September after Labor Day. Hiking trails (including a "Berry Picker's Trail" back into town), picnic sites, and a restaurant are at the top.

★ **Bicycling**

An excellent system of separated bikeways in and near town contributes to the popularity of short scenic trips along the relatively flat valley floor. Bicycle rentals, maps and information are available at several locations, including:

Christy Sports   *V.V. (Vail Village) at 293 Bridge*   *476-2244*
Colorado Insight   *L.H. at 492 E. LionsHead Cir.*   *476-3689*
Village Inn Sports   *V.V. at 100 E. Meadow Dr.*   *476-4515*
Colorado Ski Museum   *V.V. at 15 Vail Rd.*   *476-1876*

Exhibits, photos and films illustrate the history of skiing in Colorado and of the people who made that history. Closed Sun.-Wed.

★ **Dillon Reservoir**   *28 mi. E via I-70*

Colorado Rocky Mountain high country provides a dramatic backdrop for a relatively large (five square miles) man-made lake with about twenty-five miles of shoreline. Fishing, power and sailboating (rentals — Dillon Yacht Basin: 468-2936) are very popular. There is no swimming, however, because the water 8,800 feet above sea level is always too cold. The shoreline is studded with pine-shaded, scenic picnic and camp sites.

Golf

Beaver Creek Golf Course   *9 mi. W via I-70*   *949-6400*

Only recently constructed, this beautiful 18-hole golf course designed by Robert Trent Jones, Jr. has already captured the public's fancy. Facilities include a pro shop, club and cart rentals, a restaurant, and a lounge.

Eagle-Vail Golf Club   *7 mi. W via I-70*   *949-5267*

This difficult, scenic 18-hole golf course is open to the public. There is a pro shop, driving range, practice putting green, club and cart rentals, restaurant and bar.

★ **Vail Golf Club**   *1 mi. E at 1778 Vail Valley Dr.*   *476-1330*

Gorgeous views of the towering Gore Range are reason enough for playing this 18 hole championship golf course. It is open to the public with a pro shop, club and cart rentals, clubhouse, restaurant and lounge.

★ **Horseback Riding**

Stables rent horses by the hour for guided or unguided scenic trail rides and/or chuck wagon cookouts. Pack trips into the wilderness can also be arranged.

Piney River Ranch (guided/unguided)   *14 mi. N on Red Sandstone Rd.*   *476-3941*
Spraddle Creek Ranch   (guided) *.5 mi. E at 100 N. Frontage Rd. E*   *476-6941*

Jeep Tours

Vail Guides, Inc.   *1 mi. NW at 1000 Lions Ridge Loop*   *476-5387*

Guided scenic and historical tours into the remote backcountry can be arranged here.

★ **Library**   *L.H. at 292 W. Meadow Dr.*   *476-7000*

The new Vail Public Library is the quintessential statement of library architecture and decor in the West. Between Vail Village and LionsHead, the expansive single-level building features enormous window walls providing delightful forest and mountain views. A working stone fireplace is surrounded by designer leather sofas and armchairs. The periodical area has plush overstuffed sofas and a pillow-and-carpet window alcove. A huge globe, high-tech music listening equipment, a gallery/special events room, and creekside patio are other amenities. Closed Sun.

River Running

Several river guide services feature half day, whole day, or overnight rafting trips on the upper Colorado River — especially through picturesque Glenwood Canyon — during the summer. All equipment and meals are provided for these whitewater trips. Contact:

Action Bound, Inc.   *2.5 mi. NW at 2211 N. Frontage Rd. W*   *476-4033*
Colorado River Runs (Vail Guides)   *1 mi. NW at 1000 Lions Ridge Loop*   *476-5387*
Vail Mountaineering (Timberline Tours)   *L.H. at 500 LionsHead Mall*   *476-1414*

Winter Sports

★ **Beaver Creek Ski Area**   *10 mi. W via I-70*   476-5601

The vertical rise is 3,280 feet. Elevation at the top is 11,380 feet. There are seven chairlifts, including four triples. All facilities, services and rentals are available at the base for both downhill and cross-country skiing. A few bars, restaurants, and condominiums are already at the base, and more are being added to this big new skiing resort complex. The skiing season is mid-December to mid-April.

★ **Cross-Country Skiing**

Cross-country skiing specialists provide lessons and guided tours. For information, contact:

Timberline Tours   *L.H. at 500 W. LionsHead Mall*   476-1414
Vail Associates, Inc.   *L.H. at 586 W. LionsHead Mall*   476-5601

★ **Ice-Skating**   *L.H. at John A. Dobson Arena on E. LionsHead Circle*   476-1560

The public can ice-skate during designated hours in this capacious, modern indoor arena throughout the year, or watch competitions, exhibitions and games in the comfortable grandstand.

Sleigh Rides

Sleigh Rides in Vail   *1 mi. E at 1178 Vail Valley Dr.*   476-6941

After-skiing and dinner sleigh rides are offered on the Vail Golf Course.

Snowmobile Tours

Piney River Ranch   *14 mi. N on Red Sandstone Rd.*   476-3941

Guided snowmobile tours can be arranged here with all equipment furnished.

★ **Vail Ski Area**   *Vail Village & LionsHead*   476-5601

The vertical rise is 3,050 feet and the longest run is 4.5 miles. Here is the largest single mountain skiing complex in the U.S. with ten square miles of skiing terrain. There are sixteen chairlifts (including three triples) and one six-passenger enclosed gondola. All facilities, services and rentals are available at the base in town for both downhill and cross-country skiing. More than sixty restaurants and bars and about thirty lodging facilities are within walking distance of the slopes. The skiing season is late November to mid-April.

★ **White River National Forest**   *around town*   827-5715

This giant forest comprises much of northcentral Colorado's finest mountain country. Features include world-renowned winter sports complexes at Vail and Aspen. There are portions of seven wilderness areas, many small lakes and several reservoirs. A good system of highways and dirt roads, plus hundreds of miles of trails, provides access to limitless opportunities for hiking, backpacking, horseback riding and pack trips, mountain climbing, hunting, fishing, boating, and all snow sports in season.

SHOPPING

Vail has a delightfully human scale in pedestrians-only centers along Gore Creek at Vail Village and LionsHead. Gardens, fountains, and the clear stream, backed by the magnificent Gore Range, complement picturesque buildings housing a cosmopolitan array of galleries, distinctive shops, restaurants, and bars. Vail Village is interconnected with the newer commercial area (a half mile west) called LionsHead by an outstanding free-and-frequent shuttle bus/tram system.

Food Specialties

Chocolate Mountain   *L.H. at 675 LionsHead Mall*   476-1033

Soft ice cream with high butterfat content and Swiss-style hard ice cream are featured in assorted fountain treats. Quality candies are also displayed in this modern little carryout with an attractive patio area.

Gourmet Cheese Shop   *V.V. at 225 Wall St.*   476-5800

Cheeses and gourmet foods from around the world are featured in an attractive little shop.

Laura's Fudge Shop   *V.V. at 143 E. Meadow Dr.*   476-0686

Chocolate candies and more than a dozen fudges are made (with whipping cream) on an exhibition marble slab. All candies will be shipped anywhere.

Le Petit Cafe   *L.H. in the Gondola Bldg.*   476-6150

Good croissants are the specialty, served in a bright little cafe/deli or on a patio with breakfast or lunch. A second cafe is in Vail Village.

★ **Tea Room Alpenrose**   *V.V. at 100 E. Meadow Dr.*   *476-3194*
Acclaimed European pastries, croissants, and cakes are sold to go, or with meals served all day in several charming dining areas and outdoor patios. Closed Mon.

★ **Vail Cookie Co.**   *L.H. at 520 E. LionsHead Cir.*   *476-4568*
A variety of delicious cookies made here are invitingly displayed in this popular little carryout. Gift boxes are also available.

★ **West Vail Liquor Mart**   *2.4 mi. W at 2151 N. Frontage Rd. W*   *476-2420*
In West Vail Mall, the area's largest liquor store features a notable array of California and other premium wines, as well as full lines of beer and liquor. Closed Sun.

Specialty Shops

★ **Cima Jewellers of Vail**   *V.V. at 122 E. Meadow Dr.*   *476-0578*
Gold-plated aspen leaves and pine cone art objects are showcased with fine jewelry in this refined shop.

★ **Columbine Creations**   *V.V. at 143 E. Meadow Dr.*   *476-1730*
Quality handcrafted art objects in many media, exclusively by Colorado artists, are displayed in a handsome modern store. Closed Sun.

★ **Confetti**   *V.V. at 143 E. Meadow Dr.*   *476-4238*
Skillful displays of specialty art objects from around the world share space with aspen leaf and pine cone jewelry and Nambe ware from the American West.

★ **Driscol Gallery**   *V.V. at E. Meadow Dr./Willow Bridge Rd.*   *476-5171*
An outstanding collection of Western fine art is the highlight of this tasteful gallery.

The Gaslight   *V.V. at 225 Wall St.*   *476-5853*
Colorado artist Michael Ricker's unique pewter pieces are featured, along with fine collector steins and other artworks from Europe and elsewhere.

Indian Paint Brush   *V.V. at 183 E. Gore Creek Dr.*   *476-4660*
Paintings and sculpture by Western artists, redwood burl coffee tables, and aspen leaf and pine cone jewelry are specialties.

★ **The Vail Gallery**   *V.V. at 122 E. Meadow Dr.*   *476-6737*
Western artists are emphasized in quality paintings, sculpture, stained glass and other media displayed in a beautifully designed gallery.

NIGHTLIFE

Sophisticated examples of both "New Western" and "Old World" decor are abundantly available in one of the West's most impressive concentrations of places to go for live entertainment, dancing, or quiet conversations.

Alfie Packer's   *L.H. at 536 LionsHead Mall*   *476-2121*
A big, sunny deck provides fine views of the creek, slopes, and gondola. The Western-themed bar is connected to a restaurant serving American fare for lunch and dinner.

Bart & Yeti's   *L.H. at 553 E. LionsHead Cir.*   *476-2754*
Drinks are served in a woodsy bar/dining area or on a terrace with an excellent view of the gondola and mountain. Light meals are available for lunch or dinner.

★ **Cyrano's**   *V.V. at 298 Hanson Ranch Rd.*   *476-5551*
Premium wine by the glass and other libations are served in a plush conversation area by a kiva fireplace, or out on a fireplace deck with an excellent ski slope view. A stained glass back bar and abundant greenery further enhance the intimate setting. A fine restaurant adjoins.

★ **Fondue Stube**   *V.V. at 13 Vail Rd.*   *476-5631*
A guitarist plays, and wines by the glass are among drinks served, to patrons relaxing in overstuffed sofas and armchairs gathered near a wood-burning fireplace in a plush Old Western-style parlor. First-rate fondues are also featured in this Holiday Inn showplace. Closed Sun.-Mon.

Hong Kong Cafe   *V.V. at 227 Wall St.*   *476-1818*
A wine machine dispenses premium wines by the glass in an inviting enclosed garden lounge above a new Oriental restaurant.

★ **Kelly's**   *V.V. at 20 Vail Rd.*   *476-4152*
In the Kiandra Lodge, live piano entertainment is a frequent feature of the intimate lounge. Outfitted with comfortable sofas and padded armchairs, the room also has a large brick fireplace and a picturesque view of the creek and ski slopes.

★ **Mickey's at the Lodge**   *V.V. at 174 E. Gore Creek Dr.*   476-5011
The comfortable, firelit hunting-lodge-style lounge in the Lodge at Vail has been popular since Vail was first developed. It is named after the acclaimed pianist who entertains nightly. Closed Sun.-Mon.

The Ore House   *V.V. at 228 Bridge St.*   476-5100
The atmosphere is still casual in this popular, newly-remodeled drinking and dining spot.

Rumours   *V.V. downstairs at 228 Bridge St.*   476-4814
Music, dancing and light meals are offered in a new, contemporary lounge.

★ **Shadows**   *L.H. at 715 W. LionsHead Cir.*   476-4444
Live music and dancing are featured nightly in one of Vail's most elegant nightclubs on the mezzanine level of Marriott's Mark Resort.

Sheika's   *V.V. at 220 E. Gore Creek Plaza*   476-1515
Live entertainment is occasionally featured in this casual downstairs lounge.

The Slope   *V.V. at 278 Hanson Ranch Rd.*   476-5296
There are cushioned, tiered rows of carpeted floor looking toward the stage in a newly remodeled nightclub offering live entertainment most nights.

RESTAURANTS

Among the more than seventy restaurants in Vail are some outstanding dining rooms. An increasing number feature gourmet cuisine. Several have succeeded in combining Old World ambiance with the trim natural materials and colors of the contemporary West. During spring and fall, many of the best restaurants are closed.

★ **Alain's**   *V.V. at 292 E. Meadow Dr.*   476-0152
D only.   *Expensive*
Provincial French cooking and flaming entrees and desserts are highlighted in informally elegant surroundings overlooking an atrium garden. There is also a plush contemporary lounge with a piano bar.

★ **Alfredo's**   *.8 mi. W of L.H. at 1000 S. Frontage Rd. W*   476-7111
D only.   *Expensive*
In the new Westin Hotel, the top-billed restaurant serves Northern Italian cuisine in an elegant contemporary dining room with a mountain view.

★ **Ambrosia**   *V.V. at 17 E. Meadow Dr.*   476-1964
D only.   *Expensive*
Continental gourmet specialties are served in refined elegance in one of the area's most distinguished restaurants.

Bully's III   *V.V. at 20 Vail Rd.*   476-4152
L-D.   *Moderate*
In the Kiandra Lodge, this English-style pub is a favorite for casual firelit dining and drinking with a fine creek view.

The Chart House   *L.H. at 610 W. LionsHead Cir.*   476-1525
D only.   *Moderate*
A contemporary American menu of steaks, prime rib, and seafood is accompanied by a large salad bar. The large wood-toned dining room accented by an abundance of pictures and windows is a representative of a fine California restaurant chain. Alfresco lunches are served on an umbrella-shaded deck.

★ **Cyrano's**   *V.V. at 298 Hanson Ranch Rd.*   476-5551
L-D.   *Expensive*
Continental specialties are given an exciting New Western slant in a romantic contemporary restaurant. The intimate wood-toned dining rooms have an abundance of stained glass and hanging greenery. An inviting deck and bar overlook the slopes.

D.J.'s   *L.H. at 616 W. LionsHead Cir.*   476-2336
B-L-D. No D on Sun. Closed Mon.   *Moderate*
Good omelets and crepes are served all day in a popular little cafe with counter stools built around an exhibition-cooking kitchen.

★ **The Fountain Cafe**   *V.V. at 223 E. Gore Creek Dr.*   476-5885
B-L-D.   *Expensive*
Well-made crepes of every type plus fine omelets and other light fare are served in a modest little glass-enclosed cafe or on a picturesque patio overlooking the delightful Children's Fountain and plaza.

Fulton Ironworks   *1 mi. NW at 1126 Lions Ridge Loop*   *476-9906*
D only.   *Moderate*
Unlimited soup, salad and wine are included with family-style dinners in a casual dining room tucked away in the Homestake Condominiums.

Gasthof Gramshammer   *V.V. at 231 E. Gore Creek Dr.*   *476-5626*
L-D.   *Expensive*
This long-established Austrian-style lodge includes Pepi's, where lunch and cocktails are served in a lively flower-strewn sidewalk cafe in the heart of the village. Austrian specialties are offered for dinner amidst colorful Old World decor. In the Antler's Room (used only in winter), gourmet wild game dishes (like antelope and elk) and tableside cooking are featured.

Guilino's   *L.H. at 531 LionsHead Mall*   *476-0337*
D only.   *Moderate*
Italian cuisine is accented by several kinds of milk-fed veal and fresh seafood specialties in an attractive European-style dining room.

KB Ranch Co. Restaurant   *L.H. at 660 LionsHead Pl.*   *476-1937*
D only. Closed Mon.   *Moderate*
Contemporary American fare, including a large salad bar, is offered in a casual dining room in the Lion Square Lodge. The main attraction is an intriguing view of the creek and the adjacent gondola lift.

Lancelot Inn   *V.V. at 201 E. Gore Creek Dr.*   *476-5828*
D only. Closed Sun.   *Moderate*
Vail's original prime rib house also offers steak and seafood. Wooden tables, gaslight candles, and knight's armor set the tone of a dining room that overlooks a landscaped stream. There is also a piano bar.

★ **La Tour**   *V.V. at 122 E. Meadow Dr.*   *476-4403*
L-D. Closed Mon.   *Expensive.*
Skillfully prepared gourmet French specialties are served in intimate elegance in a beautiful blue-hued dining room, and on a pleasant view patio.

★ **The Left Bank**   *V.V. at 183 E. Gore Creek Dr.*   *476-3936*
D only. Closed Wed.   *Expensive*
French gourmet specialties and magnificent homemade pastries and ice creams are presented in a large and gracious dining room in the Sitzmark Lodge.

The Louvers   *V.V. at 352 E. Meadow Dr.*   *476-0445*
L-D. No D on Sun. Closed Mon.   *Expensive*
In the Vail Athletic Club, Continental favorites are given an exciting New Western update in an opulent contemporary setting with velvet and chrome accents and good art displays. A cheerful creekside deck and a high-tech lounge are also popular.

Potato Patch Restaurant & Bar   *1 mi. NW at 950 Red Sandstone Dr.*   *476-1614*
L-D. No D on Sun.   *Expensive*
A limited Continental menu is featured along with a variety of homemade desserts. The striking contemporary decor of the dining room/lounge can't compete with the magnificent mountain view from the adjoining shaded deck.

★ **St. Moritz**   *V.V. at 242 E. Meadow Dr.*   *476-5176*
D only. Closed Sun.   *Expensive*
Continental cuisine is served in an intimate and elegant dining room in the Hotel Sonnenalp.

★ **Sweet Basil**   *V.V. at 193 E. Gore Creek Dr.*   *476-0125*
L-D.   *Expensive*
Creative Continental specialties and delicious homemade desserts are offered in a refreshingly contemporary setting, or on a lovely deck by a landscaped stream. There is a distinctive cozy lounge.

★ **Tea Room Alpenrose & Restaurant**   *V.V. at 100 E. Meadow Dr.*   *476-3194*
B-L-D. No D Sun. in summer. Closed Mon.   *Expensive*
Fine European pastries are a highlight in a large, well-regarded patisserie with four dining levels and two view patios. Continental cuisine is featured in the evening when a classical guitarist plays for guests seated in intimate contemporary dining areas.

Tyrolean Inn   *V.V. at 400 Meadow Dr.*   *476-2204*
D only. Closed Sun.   *Expensive*
Wild game, plus veal, lamb, and fowl are given gourmet treatment in an elegant alpine
setting in the Tyrolean Building. An umbrella-shaded view deck overlooks the creek and
Vail Mountain.

The Watch Hill Oyster Club   *V.V. at 223 E. Gore Creek Dr.*   *476-1761*
L-D.   *Moderate*
Live Maine lobster, fresh oysters on the half shell, and other seafoods are taken seriously
in a comfortable, woodsy restaurant with an oyster bar and a picture-perfect deck by a
landscaped creek.

Windows   *L.H. at 715 W. LionsHead Cir.*   *476-4444*
D only.   *Expensive*
A Continental menu is presented in this refined rooftop restaurant in the Marriott Mark
Resort. The dining room lives up to its name with a splendid view of Vail Mountain.

LODGING

Accommodations are abundant. Most of the best are in high-rise contemporary buildings
that are unusually well-furnished and within walking distance of one or another ski slope.
Winter is "the" season, with rates at least 100% higher than the quoted summer rates.
Several lodges reduce their rates by at least 20% below summer rates in spring and fall.
There are no conventional motels in town, and no real bargains. Reservations are advised
during the winter season when a one-week minimum stay is required at some places.

Christiania-at-Vail   *V.V. at 356 E. Hanson Ranch Rd.*   *476-5641*
This long-established, four-level lodge is located at the base of Vail Mountain. Bavarian
decor is featured, along with a heated outdoor pool, saunas, and a restaurant. A
Continental breakfast is offered in winter. Each unit has a phone and cable color TV.

3rd fl. apartment — 1 BR, fireplace, kit., balc., mt. view,	K bed...$130
regular room — in-bath whirlpool, steam bath, mt. view,	Q bed...$45

★ **Gasthof Gramshammer**   *V.V. at 231 E. Gore Creek Dr.*   *476-5626*
A small Tyrolean lodge in the heart of the village has a charming restaurant and lounge.
Guests also have golf and facility privileges at the Vail Athletic Club. Each well-furnished
unit has a phone and cable color TV.

#301,#401 — 1 BR, spacious, fireplace, pvt. balc., town/mt. view,	K bed...$95
#201 — balc., town view,	K bed...$55
#213, #216 — balc.,	2 D beds...$46
regular room —	2 D beds...$46

Golden Peak House   *V.V. at 278 Hanson Ranch Rd.*   *476-5667*
A superb location at the base of the main chairlifts by the heart of the village is this small
lodge's primary attraction. Each simply furnished unit has a phone and color TV.

"B" — 1 BR, fireplace, 2 balc., kit., super slope view,	Q bed...$60
#308,#204 — balc.,	D bed...$45
#304,#306 — kitchenette, balc.,	D bed...$60
regular room —	D bed...$45

★ **Holiday Inn at Vail**   *V.V. at 13 Vail Rd.*   *476-5631*
This big, modern hotel has a large scenic outdoor pool, whirlpool, saunas, game room,
restaurants, and a lounge. Each well-furnished room has a phone and cable color TV.
Many have a balcony and ski mountain view.

#302,#402,#202 — in-bath steambath, pvt. balc., view of Vail Mt.,	K bed...$80
regular room —	Q bed...$57

★ **Kiandra Lodge**   *V.V. at 20 Vail Rd.*   *476-5081*
Lawns and gardens along Gore Creek provide an appealing setting for a large, modern
four-story lodge with two outdoor pools, a whirlpool and saunas, plus fine restaurant and
lounge facilities. Each nicely furnished, spacious unit has a phone and cable color TV.

#8005 — studio, kit., balc., fireplace, mt. view,	Q bed...$80
deluxe room — in lodge, balc., Vail Mt. & creek view,	2 Q or K bed...$70
regular room — studio, fireplace, kit.,	2 D or Q bed...$70
regular room — in lodge,	Q bed...$60

Lifthouse Condominiums   *L.H. at 555 E. LionsHead Cir.*   *476-2281*
This four-level apartment complex next to the gondola has a whirlpool. Each unit has a phone, cable color TV, kitchen, fireplace and a private balcony.
    regular room — 1 BR, sofa/Q sleeper in LR,   Q bed...$50
★ **Lion Square Lodge**   *L.H. at 660 W. LionsHead Cir.*   *476-2281*
Bordering Gore Creek by the gondola is a large eight-story condominium hotel with a big scenic outdoor pool by the river, whirlpools, saunas, and a view restaurant and lounge. Each unit has a phone and cable color TV with movies.
    apartment — 1 BR, fireplace, kit., pvt. balc., Vail Mt./creek view,   2 Q beds...$98
    regular room — in hotel, some have Vail Mt./creek view,   2 Q beds...$65
The Lodge at LionsHead   *L.H. at 380 E. LionsHead Cir.*   *476-2700*
Gore Creek rushes past this large, modern lodge with a scenic outdoor pool and a sauna. Each unit has a phone, color TV and a balcony.
    #240,#230 — 1 BR, fireplace, kit., Vail Mt./creek view,   Q or K bed...$50
    #340,#330 — studio, kit., fireplace, Vail Mt./creek view,   D bed...$45
    regular studio — fireplace, kit.,   2 T or D bed...$45
★ **The Lodge at Vail**   *V.V. at 174 E. Gore Creek Dr.*   *476-5011*
Almost adjacent to the main ski lift in the heart of Vail Village is a large multilevel hotel. Amenities include a big outdoor pool, saunas, restaurant, lounge, and garage. Each well-decorated unit has a phone and cable color TV with movies.
    apartment — 1 BR, balc., fireplace, kit., many have Vail Mt. view,   2 D or K bed...$125
    regular room — balc., Vail Mt. view,   2 D or K bed...$69
★ **Manor Vail Lodge**   *V.V. at 595 E. Vail Valley Dr.*   *476-5651*
This large condominium complex is operated as a hotel near the main lifts. There are two outdoor pools, plus a whirlpool, saunas, steamroom, restaurant and lounge. Each unit has a phone and color TV.
    #386,#172 — studio, kit., fireplace, lg. pvt. balc., mt. view,   K bed...$60
    regular room —   D or Q bed...$52
★ **Marriott's Mark Resort**   *L.H. at 715 W. LionsHead Cir.*   *476-4444*
This large, modern seven-level hotel has a big outdoor pool, whirlpool, saunas, plus a health club with an exercise room and (for a fee) massage, four tennis courts, three racquetball courts, and a garage. There are good restaurants, including a rooftop view dining room, and lounge facilities. Each well-decorated room has a phone, cable color TV with movies, and a refrigerator.
    deluxe room — fireplace, Vail Mt. view,   2 Q or K bed...$85
    regular room —   2 Q or K bed...$75
Montaneros   *L.H. at 641 W. LionsHead Cir.*   *476-2491*
A large outdoor pool and whirlpool, plus covered parking, are features of this contemporary condominium motor inn. Each spacious unit has a phone, cable color TV, kitchen, fireplace, and a large private view balcony.
    regular room — 1 BR,   Q bed...$75
★ **Mountain Haus**   *V.V. at 292 E. Meadow Dr.*   *476-2434*
An outdoor pool, whirlpool, saunas, and a restaurant are features in this conveniently located, modern condominium lodge. Each well-furnished unit has a phone, cable TV, refrigerator and a balcony.
    apartment — 1 BR, kit., fireplace, pvt. view balc., Vail Mt. view,   Q or K bed...$100
    regular room — valley view,   Q bed...$55
Roost Lodge   *2 mi. W at 1783 N. Frontage Rd. W*   *476-5451*
By the freeway, this modest little motel has an enclosed heated pool and a sauna. Each room has a phone and cable color TV.
    deluxe room — spacious, newer,   Q bed...$42
    regular room —   D bed...$39
★ **Sonnenalp at Vail**   *V.V. at 242 E. Meadow Dr.*   *476-5656*
There is an international spirit in this Bavarian-style inn with a whirlpool and sauna, and a fine restaurant. Each beautifully appointed unit has a phone and cable color TV. A breakfast is served to guests.
    regular room — balc., Vail Mt. view,   K bed...$62

★ **Vail Athletic Club and Hotel**   *V.V. at 352 E. Meadow Dr.*   *476-0700*
Vail's combination hotel and athletic club has an indoor lap pool, whirlpool, saunas, plus
(for a fee) complete athletic club facilities and services, and a fine restaurant and lounge.
Spacious, luxuriously appointed units have a phone and cable color TV.

#314,#214 — mt. view,	K bed...$85
1 BR — kit., fireplace, balc., mt. view,	2 D beds...$190
studio — kit., fireplace, mt. view,	Murphy D bed...$105
regular room — some have mt. view,	2 D beds...$85

Vail Run Resort   *1 mi. NW of L.H. at 1000 Lions Ridge Loop*   *476-1500*
This large condominium/motor lodge has an outdoor pool, whirlpool, sauna, indoor (two)
and outdoor (one) tennis courts, game room, and garage parking. Each unit has a phone,
color TV, complete kitchen, and a flagstone fireplace.

apartment — 1 BR, balc.,	T & Q beds...$75
regular studio —	Murphy D bed...$65

★ **The Westin Hotel - Vail**   *.8 mi. W of L.H. at 1000 S. Frontage Rd. W*   *476-7111*
Vail's newest large resort hotel is the first built by the luxury-class hotel chain outside of
a major city. The four-level, alpine-style building overlooks a big outdoor heated pool and
a whirlpool by Gore Creek. Inside are saunas, a full-service athletic facility, an array of
stylish restaurants and lounges, and a (pay) garage. Each spacious, beautifully appointed
room has a phone and cable color TV with movies.

view room — mt./stream view,	2 D or K bed...$110
regular room —	2 D or K bed...$90

The Willows   *V.V. at 74 E. Willow Rd.*   *476-2231*
At the base of Vail Mountain is a one-bedroom condominium complex with a whirlpool
and sauna available during the day. Each attractively furnished unit has a phone, color
TV, corner fireplace, kitchen, and private balcony.

regular room — 1 BR, mt. view,	Q bed...$60

CAMPGROUNDS
Campgrounds are surprisingly scarce, but shady sites by a clear mountain stream are
available in campgrounds with either complete or primitive facilities a few miles from
town.

Cliffside Campground   *5.5 mi. W: 5 mi. W on I-70 & .5 mi. W on US 6*   *949-4207*
This large, privately owned facility is the nearest to town. Fishing is enjoyed in the nearby
Eagle River, and there are motorbike, bicycle and hiking trails in the area. Flush toilets, hot
showers, and hookups are available. Some sites are shaded, and each has a picnic table.
                                                                              base rate...$8

Gore Creek   *6.5 mi. E: 4 mi. E on I-70 & 2.5 mi. SE on Forest Rd.*   *827-5715*
The White River National Forest includes a campground in a scenic location high in the
mountains near Gore Creek. Fishing in the little stream and hiking are features. Only pit
toilets are available. There are no showers or hookups. Each shady site has a picnic table
and fire area.   base rate...$5

SPECIAL EVENTS
Vail America Days   *downtown*   *July 4th weekend*
A parade, bands and street dances, sports events, and fireworks are features of a lively
two-day celebration.

★ **Vail Institute for the Performing Arts** *theater & arena*   *mid-July to late August*
Theatrical and musical events are scheduled every weekend.

★ **Vailfest**   *in and around town*   *last weekend in September*
The brilliant colors of aspen leaves in the fall are celebrated with scenic tours, beer fests,
oom-pah-pah bands, and more.

OTHER INFORMATION
Area Code: *303*
Zip Code: *81657*
Vail Resort Association   *V.V. at 241 E. Meadow Dr.*   *476-1000*

Coeur D'Alene, Idaho

Elevation:

2,152 feet

Population (1980):

20,054

Population (1970):

16,228

Location:

312 mi. E
of Seattle

Coeur d'Alene is the hub of a Rocky Mountain water wonderland. Surrounded by magnificent lakes and rivers, it shares the northern shore of one of the world's most beautiful lakes with a luxuriant pine forest that extends to nearby mountains and beyond. The lovely setting also benefits from a relatively mild four season climate highlighted by warm comfortable weather from late spring through early "Indian summer" autumns. Summer is by far the busiest season when hot sunny days are ideally suited to every kind of water-oriented leisure activity. In town, one of the West's most desirable lakefront parks features colorful gardens, tree-shaded picnic sites, a scenic promenade by a long sandy beach, swimming areas, and a municipal pier for boats offering a variety of lake cruises. An elaborate new complex of water slides is also available in town, along with good facilities for golf and tennis. In winter, Coeur d'Alene Lake rarely freezes over. Most smaller lakes do, however, so ice-skating and ice fishing are enjoyed. There is enough snow in the nearby mountains to support modest downhill and cross-country ski areas and other winter sports.

Coeur d'Alene Lake, more than thirty miles long yet little more than two miles in width, has always been the key influence in the development of the area. In 1877, Gen. William Sherman chose the point of land where the Spokane River flows out of the northern side of the lake as the site of a military outpost. Construction began the next year, but the Indian Wars were over almost before the fort was fully active. Following the Spanish-American War, it was abandoned. (North Idaho College occupies the site today.) Meanwhile, the adjoining town prospered with the coming of the transcontinental railroad and the lumber industry. During a brief and colorful steamboating era, Coeur d'Alene was the northern terminus of the busiest little waterway west of the Mississippi River.

Forest products and transportation remain key industries, but steamboating has long since been replaced by pleasure boating as an important source of economic activity. With improvements to highways and outdoor sports equipment, the town is continuing to develop as a large and lively recreation destination. Distinctive restaurants, lodgings, and shops are beginning to share the special setting with an abundance of plain facilities that typified Coeur d'Alene until recently.

Coeur d'Alene, Idaho
Vokac Weather Rating

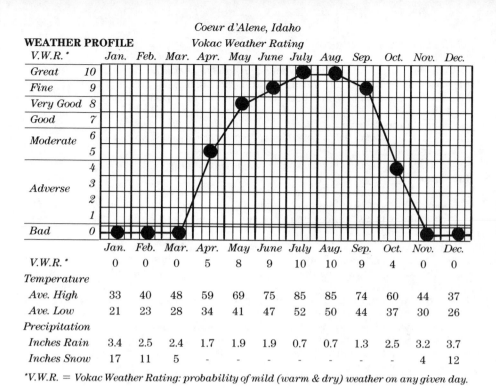

V.W.R.*		Jan.	Feb.	Mar.	Apr.	May	June	July	Aug.	Sep.	Oct.	Nov.	Dec.
Great	10												
Fine	9												
Very Good	8												
Good	7												
Moderate	6												
	5												
	4												
Adverse	3												
	2												
	1												
Bad	0												

	Jan.	Feb.	Mar.	Apr.	May	June	July	Aug.	Sep.	Oct.	Nov.	Dec.
V.W.R.*	0	0	0	5	8	9	10	10	9	4	0	0
Temperature												
Ave. High	33	40	48	59	69	75	85	85	74	60	44	37
Ave. Low	21	23	28	34	41	47	52	50	44	37	30	26
Precipitation												
Inches Rain	3.4	2.5	2.4	1.7	1.9	1.9	0.7	0.7	1.3	2.5	3.2	3.7
Inches Snow	17	11	5	-	-	-	-	-	-	-	4	12

V.W.R. = Vokac Weather Rating: probability of mild (warm & dry) weather on any given day.

Forecast

Month	V.W.R.*		Temperatures Daytime	Evening	Precipitation
January	0	Bad	chilly	cold	frequent snow flurries
February	0	Bad	chilly	cold	frequent snow flurries
March	0	Bad	chilly	chilly	frequent showers/snow flurries
April	5	Moderate	cool	chilly	occasional showers
May	8	Very Good	warm	cool	occasional showers
June	9	Fine	warm	cool	occasional showers
July	10	Great	hot	warm	infrequent showers
August	10	Great	hot	warm	infrequent showers
September	9	Fine	warm	cool	occasional showers
October	4	Adverse	cool	chilly	occasional rainstorms
November	0	Bad	chilly	chilly	frequent rainstorms/snow flurries
December	0	Bad	chilly	cold	frequent snow flurries

Summary

Coeur d'Alene is in a luxuriant pine forest on the north shore of a large, picturesque lake. The area boasts a classic four season climate. **Winter** days are short and chilly, evenings are cold, and snowfalls are frequent enough to support a wide range of winter sports nearby. **Spring** weather usually begins on schedule, and by April freezing temperatures are unlikely. Light sportswear is appropriate by May, with warm days, cool evenings, and occasional showers. **Summer** is ideal for every kind of outdoor activity. Long, relatively hot days, warm evenings, plus infrequent light showers are perfect weather conditions for this water wonderland. Early **fall** is pleasant. However, mild temperatures and occasional showers are replaced by chilly days, frequent rainstorms, and snow flurries after Halloween.

ATTRACTIONS & DIVERSIONS

★ **Bicycling**

    Wilderness Mountaineering   *downtown at 315 Sherman Av.*   *667-1342*

Bicycles may be rented for touring environs that include several miles of separated bikeways. Full lines of bicycling, backpacking, and skiing supplies are available.

Boat Rentals

★   **Coeur d'Alene Marina**   *.8 mi. SE at 1100 E. Lakeshore Dr.*   *667-9483*

Fishing boats, pontoon boats, ski boats and water skis can be rented here.

★   **North Shore Marina**   *downtown at foot of 3rd St.*   *664-9241*

Sailboats, fishing boats, and houseboats can be rented here.

Boat Rides

★   **Finney Transportation**   *downtown at City Park Dock*   *664-2827*

Six-hour scenic cruises of the entire length of the lake and part of the St. Joe River can be reserved aboard the "Dancewana" any Sunday, and most Wednesdays, in summer. Shorter lake cruises (2.5 hours) leave at noon on most weekdays.

★   **Mish-an-Nock Cruises, Inc.**   *downtown at City Park Dock*   *661-9241*

Two-hour scenic cruises are featured every day, and sunset dinner cruises can be reserved on certain Mondays in summer on a 110-foot long vessel with food and beverage service.

★ **City Park and Beach**   *W side of downtown*   *667-9533*

One of the West's most picturesque urban parks has a long sandy beach that fronts on Lake Coeur d'Alene. Lifeguards are stationed there in summer when lake swimming is popular. Independence Point features a delightfully landscaped stream and garden that also provides a photogenic lakeside viewpoint. Noble trees shade choice picnic sites and recreation facilities throughout the park.

★ **Coeur d'Alene National Forest**   *begins 3 mi. E*   *765-7223*

Recreation opportunities abound on mountains, lakes, and rivers in this lush pine forest. Boating, fishing, camping, hiking, backpacking, and hunting are popular. River running is good and relatively easy on the upper Coeur d'Alene River. A variety of snow and ice sports are enjoyed in winter.

Fishing Charters

★   **North Shore Marina**   *downtown at foot of 3rd St.*   *667-9241*

Chartered fishing boats (pontoon kayots) leave three times daily from mid-May to mid-November by reservation. All equipment is provided for catching kokanee (small "land locked" salmon) and cutthroat trout.

Flying

★   **Brooks Flying Service**   *downtown next to City Park dock*   *664-2842*

Scenic forty-minute flights aboard a five-passenger Cessna 185 float plane provide an eagle's eye view of the entire lake and surrounding forests and mountains. Longer flights and charters to remote fishing lakes can also be arranged.

★   **Henley Soaring**   *17 mi. N on US 95 - Athol*   *683-2581*

Complete facilities are available for scenic sailplane flights for one or two people. The unusual airport also provides a base for many antique and experimental aircraft on public display.

Golf

    Coeur d'Alene Golf Course   *2.5 mi. NW via US 95A at 2201 Fairway Dr.*   *765-0218*

In addition to a ponderosa pine-shaded 18-hole public course, a scenic driving range and putting greens, a pro shop, club and cart rentals, and a coffee shop are available.

★ **Hayden Lake**   *5 mi. N via US 95 & Hayden Av.*

Crystal clear water, small beaches, numerous coves, and timbered shores are features of a picturesque lake that is well-liked for a variety of summer and winter sports. Although only seven miles long and one to two miles wide, the lake has about forty miles of shoreline because of its irregular shape.

Horseback Riding

★   **Bobbitt Ranch**   *8 mi. SW via US 95 at 8225 W. Green Ferry Rd.*   *667-0168*

Horses can be rented here for unaccompanied as well as guided rides. Big game hunts can also be arranged.

★ **Lake Coeur d'Alene**   *adjacent to downtokwn on S side*
One of the loveliest lakes in the nation is more than thirty miles long, averages little more than two miles wide, and has 110 miles of shoreline. Surrounded by mountains and lush pine forests, it is a deservedly renowned destination. Lakeside recreation facilities in town and scattered down-lake provide a notable variety of boating, water-skiing, fishing, swimming, and camping opportunities in summer. A 109-mile scenic loop highway circles the lake and provides access to numerous recreation sites and viewpoints.

★ **Library**   *downtown at 703 Lakeside Av.*   667-4676
The Coeur d'Alene Public Library has an unusual home in a handsome old mansion. The newspaper/magazine reading area is a fine place to relax in a comfortably upholstered chair by an artistically tiled, working fireplace.

★ **Museum of North Idaho**   *downtown at 108 Northwest Blvd.*   664-3448
This contemporary museum features a notable steamboating exhibit from the days when Coeur d'Alene Lake was the steamboating capital of the West. Other exhibits depict the history of logging and Indians in the area. Closed Sun.-Mon.

St. Joe River   *38 mi. S via US 95 & ID 5*
The short stretch between Lake Chatcolet and Round Lake near the south end of Lake Coeur d'Alene is said to be the world's highest navigable river. The timbered, tranquil shoreline is lovely, and trout fishing is excellent.

Tubbs Hill   *.3 mi. S from foot of 4th St.*
This large, woodsy hill is next to the lake. From a free parking area downtown, hiking trails lead to numerous scenic vantage points overlooking town and the lake.

Warm Water Feature

★   **Wild Waters**   *1.5 mi. N at 2119 N. Government Way*   667-6491
Eleven water slides race down a sixty-foot high hill and end in two heated pools. There are plenty of loops, turns, rapids, and even a soothing stretch. One price includes all-day access and unlimited use of slides. A large lawn has been provided for picnicking and sunbathing. Other facilities include a snack shop and arcade. The park is open every day from June into September.

Winter Sports

   Silverhorn Ski Area   *38 mi. SE off I-90 - Kellogg*   786-9521
The vertical rise is 1,900 feet and the longest run is two miles. Elevation at the top is 6,000 feet. There is one chairlift. Essential facilities, services and rentals are available at the area for downhill skiing, but there are no restaurants or lodgings. The skiing season is mid-November to mid-April.

SHOPPING

Coeur d'Alene has a vital and attractive downtown in spite of a recent proliferation of shopping centers in outlying areas. It is beautifully located between the town's two major parks by the lake.

Food Specialties

★ **County Fair Homemade Pies**   *2 mi. N at 221 W. Appleway*   667-5545
Fine pies of all kinds are the highlight of this bakery/restaurant. Casual lunches and dinners are served amid family-fun decor in a large adjoining dining room.

★ **Mrs. Cavanaugh's Candies**   *downtown at 503 Sherman Av.*   667-2705
You can watch tantalizing filled chocolates being made here from the finest ingredients (no preservatives). These and other candies and ice cream are available to go.

Pines Bakery   *downtown at 409 Sherman Av.*   664-3420
Since 1920, the area's original bakery has done a fine job with cinnamon rolls and has a good selection of other pastries, donuts and breads.

★ **Rosauer's Supermarket**   *2 mi. N at US 95/Appleway*   667-5411
The state of the art in grocery stores has an excellent selection of gourmet meats and produce, a big in-store bakery, and well-stored premium wines, as well as the usual supermarket items. Everything in this large contemporary showplace is so clean, fresh, and attractively displayed that it's worth browsing even if you don't need anything.

★ **The Sugar Shack**   *1 mi. NW at 1522 Northwest Blvd.*   667-9119
An outstanding assortment of cookies, cakes, pastries and candies are made here fresh daily. An adjoining room features fascinating graphics and candy manufacturing machines and conveyor belts. Samples are available.

Specialty Shops

★ **The Bookseller**   *downtown at Sherman Av./5th St.*   664-8811
This attractive multilevel shop offers a broad selection of books and greeting cards. A quiet table has been provided for patrons to examine books, write cards, and enjoy classical music.

★ **The Gallery**   *downtown at 507 Sherman Av.*   667-2898
Fine arts in a variety of media are displayed in a stylish contemporary gallery featuring Northwestern artists. Other arts and crafts shops adjoin in Pioneer Plaza.

★ **The Wickiup**   *downtown at 211 Sherman Av.*   667-1956
This small shop offers a limited selection of quality Indian crafts and Western arts.

NIGHTLIFE
After-dark possibilities include summer theater and periodic concerts, in addition to live entertainment and dancing in several lounges. Decor ranges from elegant to roadhouse rustic. Some of the most comfortably furnished places take full advantage of the remarkable lakeside setting.

★ **Cloud 9**   *downtown at 115 S. 2nd St.*   664-9241
Live music is offered for listening or dancing on weekends in the posh, elevated cocktail lounge of the North Shore Hotel. During the rest of the week, outstanding panoramic views of the lake, marina, and park make this an ideal spot for a quiet conversation.

Club Car Lounge   *downtown at 407 Sherman Av.*   667-7314
Live country or easy listening music are featured most nights in this big casual saloon.

Coeur d'Alene Summer Theatre   *.6 mi. NE at 14th St. & Garden Av.*   667-1323
Several popular musical comedies are played in repertory from July into September in a little theater fashioned from an old residential neighborhood church. Closed Mon.

★ **Fore N Aft**   *downtown at 204 Sherman Av.*   667-9082
Live music and dancing are offered most nights, along with all kinds of specialty drinks. The unusual stone-walled lounge is outfitted with comfortable sofas, and there is a fireplace with a separate conversation pit.

★ **Mr. G's Cork & Cleaver**   *6 mi. N at Miles Av./Government Way*   772-2016
Country music usually fills the vast dance floor in this casual, cavernous roadhouse saloon adjoining a steakhouse.

Peabody's   *1.5 mi. E at 314 S. 24th St.*   667-9057
Dancing to live, mostly hard rock music happens nightly in this big popular saloon.

★ **Shore Lounge**   *downtown at 115 S. 2nd St.*   664-9241
Off the lobby of the North Shore Resort is a large, beautifully appointed lounge. Live entertainment and a high-tech dance floor with plenty of twinkling lights attract crowds most nights, with the help of a fine lake view, plus well-padded sofas and armchairs.

★ **Third Street Cantina**   *downtown at 201 N. 3rd St.*   664-0581
The lounge, adjoining one of the area's favorite restaurants, has unique neo-tropical decor plus comfortable velour armchairs and sofas. Fruit margaritas by the glass or pitcher are a highlight on a remarkable list of specialty drinks and imaginative appetizers.

RESTAURANTS
Hearty homestyle American cooking predominates and prices are surprisingly inexpensive, with few exceptions. Several of the better places also provide fine lake views.

Black Forest Restaurant   *.8 mi. E at 1613 Sherman Av.*   667-7758
B-L-D.   *Low*
Good American dishes are served in a plain coffee shop.

Cedars Floating Restaurant   *2 mi. W via US 95 on Blackwell Island*   664-2922
D only.   *Moderate*
Contemporary American fare and a salad bar are offered in a floating dining room with a fine lakeside view. The adjoining lounge shares both the view and the sway.

★ **Cloud 9**   *downtown at 115 S. 2nd St.*   664-9241
L-D.   *Moderate*
The area's most elegant restaurant is on the top floor of the North Shore Hotel. Continental specialties are prepared at tableside, and complemented by pastries baked on the premises. The fine food is upstaged, however, by the stunning panoramic view of the lake and mountains from window walls on three sides of the beautifully appointed dining room.

The Inn Trepid   *2 mi. SE on I-90*   *667-4818*
D only.   *Moderate*
Seafood, steak and chicken are served over the water of Coeur d'Alene Lake. The casual,
contemporary restaurant provides lakeside views from both the dining room and an
adjoining lounge.

★ **Le Croissant**   *downtown at 507 Sherman Av.*   *666-1594*
B-L-D.   *Moderate*
This refreshing new bakery/cafe offers a sophisticated assortment of delicious croissants,
French breads, and seasonal desserts. Distinctive sandwiches, homemade soups, and
specialty coffees and teas are also served amid well-executed gallery atmosphere that
complements an adjoining fine art store.

Mad Portagee Seafood   *downtown at 320 Sherman Av.*   *664-2318*
B-L-D. Closed Sun.   *Low*
Cinnamon rolls and special breakfast omelets are standouts. Seafood and steak are also
served in this pleasant plants-and-wood-trim coffee shop.

Muffins n' Cream   *downtown at 412 Sherman Av.*   *667-2774*
B-L.   *Low*
At least half a dozen different kinds of freshly made muffins are featured, along with
soups, sandwiches, and quality ice cream. Everything that is served in the plain little shop
is also available to go.

Pioneer Pies   *downtown at 501 Sherman Av.*   *667-9459*
B-L-D.   *Low*
Many kinds of pies are the specialty in a big, family-oriented restaurant with wood-and-
greens decor.

Rustler's Roost   *downtown at 612 Sherman Av.*   *664-5513*
B-L.   *Low*
Homestyle country breakfasts accompanied by large delicious biscuits are served all day
in this shaped-up, woodsy coffee shop.

★ **Third Street Cantina**   *downtown at 201 N. 3rd St.*   *664-0581*
L-D. No L on Sat. & Sun.   *Low*
The carefully prepared, mild Mexican-style dishes with a local flair are very popular.
Elaborate tropical decor predominates in four distinctive dining areas, but the fanciful
fabric cactus garden is the real show-stopper in this unique restaurant.

Village Pantry   *1 mi. N at 410 E. Harrison*   *667-5821*
B-L-D.   *Low*
Fine pancakes and good omelets are served along with a conventional assortment of
American fare in a big, modest, 1950s-style coffee shop.

LODGING
Accommodations in Coeur d'Alene are plentiful, plain, and remarkably reasonably priced.
Numerous bargain motels are conveniently concentrated along Sherman Avenue (US 95
Business Alternate) for more than a mile eastward from downtown. From fall through
spring, rates are often at least 30% less than those shown.

City Center Motel   *.8 mi. E at 1504 Lakeside Av.*   *664-4822*
This small, single-level motel is an older **bargain**. Each simply furnished room has cable
TV.
    regular room —   D bed...$14

Garden Motel   *1 mi. NW at 1808 Northwest Blvd.*   *664-2743*
A large indoor pool is a feature of this small, older **bargain** motel. Each spacious room has
a phone and a cable color TV.
    kitchenette unit —   Q bed...$33
    regular room —   Q bed...$25
    regular room —   D bed...$20

Kingsport Inn   *1.3 mi. E at 2100 Sherman Av.*   *664-8191*
An old, single-level motel has been refurbished and upgraded. There is an outdoor pool.
Each room has a phone and cable color TV.
    #19 - corner, sunken whirlpool in sep. room with pvt. window & skylight, Q bed...$83
    regular room —   D bed...$35

Motel 6   *2 mi. N at 416 Appleway*   765-6006
This large modern motel is a representative of a no-frills chain of **bargain** accommodations. There is an outdoor pool and (fee) TV.
regular room —   D bed...$22

Murphy's Landing   *downtown at 40 N. Shore Plaza*   664-9291
Bordering the splendid town park and beach, this older motor hotel has free use of pools and other facilities at the nearby North Shore Resort Hotel. There is a newly remodeled restaurant and coffee shop. Each room has a phone and color TV.
#43 — great park & beach view,   T & 2 D beds...$49
#53 "Honeymoon Suite" — fine views,   K bed...$50
regular room —   D bed...$39

★ **North Shore Resort Hotel - Best Western** *downtown at 115 S. 2nd St.*   664-9241
The area's finest and most complete facility is a large, modern motor hotel. A perfect site on the lake shore adjacent to downtown includes a marina with a variety of boat charters, cruises and rentals. An excellent public beach and park are less than a block away. A large indoor pool, wading pool, whirlpool, sauna, and bicycle rentals, plus delightful dining, drinking and dancing facilities are available. Each spacious well-furnished room has a phone and color TV, plus floor-to-ceiling view windows, and a private balcony.
#598,#498,#398 — corner, refr., lake/town view, windows on 2 sides,   K bed...$65
6th,5th,4th floors on lakeside — fine lake/mts./marina views,   Q bed...$49
regular room —   Q bed...$49

Travel's 9 Motel   *2 mi. N at 330 W. Appleway*   667-0546
A newer **bargain** motel by the freeway has a phone and color TV in each of the nicely furnished rooms.
regular room —   D bed...$26

CAMPGROUNDS
There are several campgrounds near town, but surprisingly few by Lake Coeur d'Alene. The best is a small lakeside campground with complete facilities and all kinds of water recreation.

KOA - Coeur d'Alene   *8.7 mi. E via I-90 (to exit 22) & US 97*   667-9307
This large, privately owned campground is near Coeur d'Alene Lake. Features include boating, lake/river fishing, boat rentals (with access to the lake by a short canal), small outdoor pool, outdoor games area, and a rec room. Flush toilets, hot showers, and hookups are available. Closely spaced sites have picnic tables, and grills are available. There is a separate grassy tenting area.   base rate...$8.50

Robin Hood Campground   *1 mi. NW on Northwest Blvd. at Lincoln Way*   664-2306
This privately owned campground and trailer park has flush toilets, hot showers, and hookups. Each of the small grassy sites is shaded and has a picnic table. There is a separate tenting area.   base rate...$8.50

★ **Squaw Bay Resort** *15.6 mi. SE: 8 mi. E on I-70 & 7.6 mi. S on US 97*   664-6782
This small, privately owned lakeside campground with swimming, boating, fishing, scuba diving, and water-skiing is beside a pretty cove by Lake Coeur d'Alene. A sandy beach, ramp, dock, plus all kinds of boat rentals are provided, and there is a rec room and snack pavilion. Flush toilets, hot showers, and hookups are available. Most sites have a picnic table. There are a few choice pine-shaded, grassy tent sites by the sandy beach.
base rate...$10.50

SPECIAL EVENT
Fourth of July Celebration   *downtown*   *July 4th weekend*
A fireworks display from mid-lake is the highlight of a celebration that also includes a parade and air shows.

OTHER INFORMATION
Area Code: *208*
Zip Code: *83814*
Coeur d'Alene Chamber of Commerce *downtown at 2nd St./Sherman Av.*   664-3194
Idaho Panhandle Nat. For.-Sup. Office *2 mi. NW at 1201 Ironwood Dr.*   765-7223

Ketchum, Idaho

Elevation:

5,817 feet

Population (1980):

2,200

Population (1970):

1,454

Location:

281 mi. NW
of Salt Lake City

Ketchum is the unheralded gateway to a vast mountain realm. Well over a mile high, this agreeable blend of the old and new West occupies an attractive little river valley at the base of a towering mountain. To the north, the jagged peaks of the Sawtooth Range accent an enormous expanse of wilderness with endless pine forests, crystal clear lakes, and cold rushing streams. The rugged surroundings are paired with fine weather in summer. Vacationers flock to the area's superb alpine recreation opportunities. There are also outstanding golf and tennis complexes, miles of bicycle paths, a hot springs pool in town, plus an adjoining world famous resort — Sun Valley. Heavy winter snows cause the gentle sagebrush-covered hills around town to resemble giant dollops of whipped cream. Western skiing was first popularized on these slopes. Eventually, facilities were expanded to include most of Bald Mountain, the landmark that rises abruptly from town. Visitors from all over the world flock to Ketchum and Sun Valley during winter, the area's most popular season.

Ketchum was founded in 1881 as the supply point and smelter for surrounding silver mines. Rail lines extended to the town in 1884, accelerating a boom that ended only a few years later when the price of silver collapsed. About that time, sheepmen (mostly Basques) began to funnel herds through town to summer pastures high in the surrounding mountains. By the 1920s Ketchum was the largest sheep and lamb shipping station in the nation. During the Depression, the sheep industry declined. Once again, the little town was saved because of its location by a new industry. In 1935, the Union Pacific Railroad bought a nearby ranch and established "Sun Valley." The new destination ski resort was soon famous. Wealthy vacationers from around the world debarked in Ketchum and, before journeying to the resort, visited saloon-casinos that established the town as the region's nightlife center. Gambling was banned in 1954, and Ketchum languished again. In 1965 the railroad company finally sold Sun Valley. The new owner soon began development of a much larger resort. Since then, Ketchum has attracted its own share of the new recreation boom because of its preeminent location at the base of the superb ski slopes on Bald Mountain, and as the main access to the new Sawtooth National Recreation Area.

The compact town center houses a fine assortment of art galleries, Western ware shops, and gourmet food stores. Excellent restaurants are numerous, and there are several deluxe contemporary lodgings. As an added attraction, convenient access between town and adjacent resort areas is provided by free Ketchum Area Rapid Transit buses.

WEATHER PROFILE

Ketchum, Idaho
Vokac Weather Rating

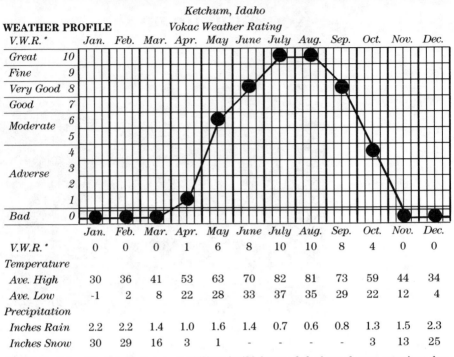

V.W.R.*	Jan.	Feb.	Mar.	Apr.	May	June	July	Aug.	Sep.	Oct.	Nov.	Dec.
V.W.R.*	0	0	0	1	6	8	10	10	8	4	0	0
Temperature												
Ave. High	30	36	41	53	63	70	82	81	73	59	44	34
Ave. Low	-1	2	8	22	28	33	37	35	29	22	12	4
Precipitation												
Inches Rain	2.2	2.2	1.4	1.0	1.6	1.4	0.7	0.6	0.8	1.3	1.5	2.3
Inches Snow	30	29	16	3	1	-	-	-	-	3	13	25

*V.W.R. = Vokac Weather Rating: probability of mild (warm & dry) weather on any given day.

Forecast

Month	V.W.R.*		Temperatures Daytime	Evening	Precipitation
January	0	Bad	cold	frigid	occasional snowstorms
February	0	Bad	chilly	frigid	occasional snowstorms
March	0	Bad	chilly	frigid	infrequent snowstorms
April	1	Adverse	cool	chilly	infrequent snow flurries/showers
May	6	Moderate	cool	chilly	occasional showers
June	8	Very Good	warm	cool	infrequent rainstorms
July	10	Great	warm	cool	infrequent showers
August	10	Great	warm	cool	infrequent showers
September	8	Very Good	warm	cool	infrequent showers
October	4	Adverse	cool	chilly	infrequent snow flurries/showers
November	0	Bad	chilly	cold	infrequent snowstorms
December	0	Bad	chilly	frigid	occasional snowstorms

Summary

Ketchum is located where sagebrush rangeland abuts the southern extremities of the majestic Sawtooth Mountains. By **winter**, the treeless hills just east of town around Sun Valley assume the appearance of a whimsical jumble of giant marshmallows. Chilly days, bitter cold nights, and occasional heavy snowstorms are the seasonal characteristics of this world-renowned winter wonderland. **Spring** is the least desirable season because freezing temperatures linger through May while daytime temperatures have long since become warm enough to turn snow to slush and snowstorms to rainshowers. **Summer** makes up for it with fields of wildflowers and great weather. Long warm days, cool evenings, and infrequent light showers are ideal for enjoying the splendid countryside. Freezing temperatures normally return even before **fall** officially begins. There is a relatively short transition to winter weather, which often arrives before Thanksgiving with heavy snowstorms.

ATTRACTIONS & DIVERSIONS

Bicycling

★ **The Elephant's Perch**   *downtown at Sun Valley Rd./225 East Av.*   726-3497
Secondary roads around town offer miles of scenic, relatively easy bicycling. An assortment of bicycles may be rented here, and repairs and sales are available. Topographic maps and a full line of camping equipment can also be rented, plus cross-country skiing equipment in winter.

★ **The Snug Co.**   *downtown at 680 Sun Valley Rd. E*   662-9300
Bicycle rentals, repairs and sales are available, along with other summer and winter sports equipment and clothing.

Boat Rentals

★ **Formula Sports**   *downtown at East Av./Sun Valley Rd.*   726-3194
River runners can rent Avon inflatable rafts and all accessories for private whitewater river expeditions in Idaho. Wind surfers can rent sailboards and accessories for use on nearby lakes and/or arrange for lessons.

Golf

Elkhorn Golf Course   *2.5 mi. E via Sun Valley/Dollar/Elkhorn Rds.*   622-5226
This sunny 18-hole course, designed by Robert Trent Jones on rolling wide-open rangeland, is open to the public with club and cart rentals and all necessary services.

★ **Sun Valley Golf Course**   *1.5 mi. NE via Sun Valley Rd.*   622-4111
Recently redesigned by Robert Trent Jones, Jr., this scenic and famous 18-hole course is open to the public with all services and rentals available.

Horseback Riding

Mystic Saddle Ranch   *52 mi. NW off ID 75 at Redfish Lake*   774-3591
At the Redfish Corrals, guided hourly, half day, and all day rides, as well as longer pack trips into the Sawtooth Range, can be reserved.

Sun Valley Horseman's Center   *1 mi. NE via Sun Valley Rd.*   662-4111
Group trail rides of one-to-two hours can be arranged.

Flying

Sun Valley Soaring   *11 mi. S via ID 75 at Hailey Airport*   788-3054
An exciting and effortless way to see this splendid high country is in a sailplane that can accommodate one or two persons plus the pilot. Rides and rentals can be reserved year-round.

Knob Hill Park   *downtown at N end of East Av.*
A short hike to the top of a rocky outcropping rewards the visitor with a panoramic view of town and Bald Mountain beyond a slope carpeted with a rainbow of wildflowers in summer.

★ **Library**   *downtown at 415 Spruce Av. N*   726-3493
The Ketchum Community Library houses the Hemingway Collection as a memorial to the one-time resident. The wood-toned contemporary building features comfortable leather chairs around a massive stone fireplace by the periodical display. A high ceiling and massive picture windows dramatize views of nearby mountains.

★ **River Running**   *73 mi. N on ID 75*
A six-hour scenic float trip down the headwaters of the Salmon River in the Sawtooth National Recreation Area is a wonderful way to experience the rugged grandeur of this mountain playground. Several river guide services feature this exhilarating run, plus other trips of up to six days. Lunch, all equipment, and transportation from Ketchum are provided by:

    Dave's Float Trips   726-3350
    Middle Fork River Co.   726-8888
    Sevy Guide Service   788-3440

★ **Sawtooth National Recreation Area**   *starts 8 mi. N of town*   726-8291
The rugged heart of an enormous system of national forests in central Idaho was made into a national recreation area a decade ago. The well-named granite spires of the Sawtooth Range provide an inspiring backdrop to the broad-meadowed valley through which the area's only highway passes. The Redfish Lake Visitor Center contains history,

geology, plants and wildlife exhibits. Self-guided trails and a variety of programs are offered. Picturesque Redfish Lake has boat rentals and cruises to the trail heads at the far end of the lake, fishing, and scenic beaches. Lodging and supplies are available nearby. One-day river runs can be arranged in rustic Stanley, a tiny social center for the wilderness that looks like a remarkably authentic Old West movie set. Beyond the tiny town, hundreds of miles of trails thread among high-country wooded valleys, peaks and gemlike lakes which provide splendid opportunities for hiking, mountain climbing, horseback riding, backpacking, camping, picnicking, fishing, boating and even cold water swimming. All facilities are usually open from mid-June to early September.

Warm Water Feature
Bald Mountain Hot Springs   *downtown at 151 S. Main St.*   726-9963
An outdoor Olympic-sized hot springs pool is open to the public daily from Memorial Day to Labor Day.

Winter Sports
★   **Ice-Skating**   *1.5 mi. NE via Sun Valley Rd.*   622-3888
At Sun Valley Lodge, year-round ice-skating is open to the public in three sessions daily on world-renowned, full-sized indoor and outdoor ice rinks.

★   **Sun Valley Ski Area**   *.5 mi. S at end of Ski Lift Rd.*   635-8261
Bald Mountain, with Ketchum along its base, is a world-class delight for skiers. It is so vast that there are four distinct ski areas accessed by lifts that begin on the south and west ends of Ketchum. The vertical rise is 3,400 feet and the longest run is three miles. Elevation at the top is 9,150 feet. There are twelve chairlifts, including seven triples. All facilities, services and rentals are available at the area for downhill and cross-country skiing. While dining, drinking, and lodging facilities are limited at the bases, they are abundant in town.The ski season is mid-December to mid-April. (The "Queen Mother of Western Skiing" is 1.5 miles east of town near Sun Valley Lodge. Skiing in the West became fashionable after the world's first chairlift began operation here nearly half a century ago. Today, Sun Valley's Dollar Mountain Ski Area and the adjacent, recently-added Elkhorn Ski Area provide four chairlifts to beginner and intermediate slopes with a vertical rise of about 700 feet.)

SHOPPING
In recent years, downtown (concentrated around the intersection of Main Street and Sun Valley Road) has become the site of numerous fine art galleries, specialty shops, and gourmet food stores. In addition, an impressive assortment of shops featuring sporting goods supports the town's increasingly important role as a year-round base camp for the Idaho Rockies.

Food Specialties
★ **Atkinson's**   *downtown at Leadville Av./4th St.*   726-5668
A fine selection of wine, cheeses, pates and other gourmet items are displayed in a modern, well-furnished market.

★ **Ketchum Coffee Grinder & Gallery** *downtown at 321 4th St. E*   726-8048
Gourmet coffees and teas, fine pastries from Lynndee's Bakery, plus unusual soups and sandwiches are served, along with wine or beer by the glass, in an attractive handcrafted shop.

★ **Ketchum Wine Market**   *downtown at 312 East Av. N*   726-8101
Wine (some by the glass), cheeses and pates are served on an inviting little patio.

Little Annie's   *downtown at 310 Leadville Av. N*   726-5484
Here is a popular little ice cream parlor where quality ice cream in a variety of flavors and styles is served at a few tables or to go.

★ **Lynndee's Bakery**   *downtown at 119½ Leadville Av. N*   726-8341
This tiny, acclaimed carryout bakery features a full line of breads and pastries. Specialties range from delicious sourdough cinnamon rolls and whole-grain bread to quiches and spinach pie.

★ **Pendl's**   *downtown at 940 Leadville Av. N*   726-8565
A full line of fine Viennese and American pastries, pies, and breads can be enjoyed in the tiny bakery with a variety of beverages, or taken out. Gift cannisters can be shipped anywhere. Closed Sun.

Specialty Shops

★ **Backwoods Mountain Sports**   *downtown at ID 75/Warm Springs Rd.*   *726-8818*
All kinds of backpacking and cross-country gear are sold or may be rented in this well-organized contemporary shop.

★ **Chapter One Book Store**   *downtown at 320½ East Av. N*   *726-5425*
This appealing shop has a surprisingly diverse collection of books and greeting cards. Attractive displays spill into several small rooms, and chairs have thoughtfully been provided for browsers.

★ **Gallery Square**   *downtown at Leadville Av./4th St.*
The Sun Valley Center Gallery, Trails West Gallery, and Wood River Gallery are all included in one notable complex. Classic and contemporary Western fine arts and crafts are well represented. There are frequent gallery shows.

★ **Sheepskin Coat Factory**   *downtown at 525 4th St. E*   *726-3588*
The sheepskin clothing sold here was designed and handmade in Ketchum. Visitors can watch the manufacturing process.

NIGHTLIFE

From its boisterous beginnings a century ago, Ketchum has always been "where the action is." There is still an appealing frontier feeling in some of the well-worn watering holes downtown. But the rustic edge is now balanced by contemporary sophistication in several notable lounges. In addition, theaters and concert halls provide a proper setting for staged and musical events scheduled throughout the year.

Cedars Yacht Club   *downtown at 231 Main St. N*   *726-5233*
A large fireplace is visible from two sides of an intimate lounge outfitted with comfortable sofas, armchairs, and padded barstools. A steak house adjoins.

The Ore House   *1.5 mi. NE via Sun Valley Rd. in Sun Valley Mall*   *622-4363*
Live entertainment is offered most nights in a large, comfortably furnished Western-style lounge, while an adjoining restaurant offers contemporary American dishes indoors or on a pleasant view deck.

River Street Retreat   *downtown at 120 River St. E*   *726-9502*
This rustic little bar has a rare wine collection, and rotating wine tastings are listed on a blackboard.

★ **Silver Creek Saloon**   *downtown at 271 Main St. N*   *726-3314*
Live (mostly rock) music is featured every night except Sunday, along with low-priced draft beer by the glass or pitcher. The rustic-and-woodsy Western decor is just right for the large-and-lively casual crowds.

★ **Slavey's**   *downtown at 280 Main St. N*   *726-5083*
Live entertainment is offered on weekends, but the real lure is the polished contemporary Western decor. An island bar, sculpted bar chairs, booths, ferns, fans, and high-tech lighting have been beautifully coordinated. In addition to an extensive drink list, wine by the glass can be enjoyed in the bar or the adjoining restaurant, or on a new rooftop deck with a super view of town and Bald Mountain.

★ **Sun Valley Lodge**   *1.5 mi. NE via Sun Valley Rd.*   *622-4111*
The resort's posh lounge features the wonderful grand piano stylings of Joe Fos, plus a picture window view of the ice rink, and a large stone fireplace with comfortable sofas. An adjoining patio terrace is a popular place for watching the action on the famed ice rink.

★ **Whiskey Jacques**   *downtown at 209 Main St. N*   *726-5297*
A mix of live country/western and rock music fills this big casual saloon most nights. Swinging doors connect the log cabin-style dance hall with a large, well-furnished pool hall.

RESTAURANTS

Ketchum has recently experienced a culinary quantum leap into the ranks of the gourmet havens in the West. Fine cuisine in a notable variety of styles, atmosphere ranging from frontier-rustic to timelessly elegant, and view or patio dining are readily available.

A Matter of Taste   *downtown at S. Main/River Sts.*   *726-8468*
L-D. Closed Sun.   *Moderate*
International gourmet specialties are served in an old log cabin that has been converted into a tiny Continental bistro and gourmet market, and on a flower-filled little patio.

★ **Andy's Cabin**   *downtown at 308 East Av. N*   726-4447
B-L-D.   *Moderate*
Carefully prepared American and Continental specialties are served indoors, or on a
flower-banked, tree-shaded deck with one of the best town and mountain views in the
area.

★ **Chez Michel**   *downtown at 200 Main St. S*   726-3032
L-D. Closed Sun.   *Moderate*
Authentic French cuisine is emphasized, accompanied by homemade baked goods. The
intimate dining rooms convey a casual elegance, and there is a charming deck for
creekside dining.

Christiania   *downtown at 303 Walnut Av. N*   726-3388
D only. Closed Sun.-Tues.   *Moderate*
Continental dinners are served in a congested dining room with a fine mountain view, or
on a patio in summer.

The Colonel's   *downtown at 391 Walnut Av. N*   726-5422
B-L.   *Moderate*
Omelets and pancakes are featured in a casual all-American restaurant that also offers
outdoor dining.

Creekside   *2.5 mi. W via Warm Springs Rd. at 317 Skiway Dr.*   726-8200
D only. Sun. brunch. Closed Mon.   *Moderate*
Contemporary American dinners are served in stylish Western atmosphere at one of
Ketchum's few creekside dining rooms. The adjoining view bar is also a crowd pleaser.

★ **Evergreen**   *downtown at 171 1st Av.*   726-3888
D only. Closed Mon.-Tues.   *Expensive*
Delicious Continental cuisine and home-baked breads and desserts are further enhanced
by a splendid wine list. The intimate dining room combines contemporary elegance with
a spectacular view of Bald Mountain.

Gurney's   *12 mi. S on ID 75 at 411 N. Main St. - Hailey*   788-3697
D only. Closed Sun.   *Moderate*
Continental dishes are served in the firelit dining room of an attractively converted house.

Ketchum Fish Market   *downtown at 312 East Av. N*   726-8360
L-D. Closed Sun. in summer.   *Moderate*
Fresh seafood is the specialty. There are two small, handsomely furnished dining areas
and an outdoor oyster bar.

The Kitchen   *downtown at 260 Main St. N*   726-3856
B-L.   *Moderate*
Homestyle omelets, soups, and sandwiches on homemade bread are featured in this
simple, pleasant coffee shop.

The Kneadery   *downtown at 216 Leadville Av. N*   726-9462
B-L.   *Moderate*
Distinctive omelets and homemade cinnamon rolls and soups are specialties served
amidst Western Gothic decor — old-fashioned mismatched wooden tables and chairs, old
photos, stained glass, and plants. A pot-bellied stove and patio are used during the
appropriate seasons.

★ **Le Club**   *downtown at 716 Main St. N*   726-4386
D only. Sun. brunch.   *Moderate*
Skillfully prepared Continental cuisine is served by firelight in cozy, romantic dining
rooms with beautifully-appointed tables.

Louie's   *downtown at 331 Leadville Av. N*   726-8325
L-D.   *Moderate*
Well-regarded Italian dinners and pizza are featured in a converted, historic Episcopal
church.

Pioneer Saloon   *downtown at 320 Main St. N*   726-3139
D only.   *Moderate*
Prime rib is the specialty in this down-home Western-style dining room behind a lively bar
with a stuffed wild animal collection.

★ **River Street Retreat**   *downtown at 120 River St. E*   726-9502
L-D.   *Moderate*
Six intriguing dishes plus nightly specials are served in a casual and intimate, wood-toned dining room with a fireplace. Guests are invited to select their wine in a uniquely atmospheric cellar reached by a mine shaft from the dining room. Lunch is also served on a deck by Trail Creek and wine is poured by the glass in a popular upstairs bar.

★ **Sun Valley Lodge**   *1.5 mi. NE via Sun Valley Rd.*   622-4111
D only. Sun. brunch.   *Expensive*
Continental specialties are served in one of the West's most illustrious examples of updated art deco opulence. Jackets are appropriately required for men in this imposing and resplendent dining room.

Warm Springs Restaurant   *1.5 mi. W on Warm Springs Rd.*   726-8238
L-D.   *Moderate*
Classic Western dishes, including sourdough scones (fry bread) are served in a large hunting lodge-style log cabin in the pines by Warm Creek.

Western Cafe   *downtown at 115 Main St. N*   726-3396
B-L-D.   *Moderate*
Huge homemade cinnamon rolls and biscuits accompany conventional Western fare in a modest cafe that is the favorite of early birds.

LODGING

For almost half a century, the Ketchum area has provided some of the West's most lavish accommodations — thanks to Sun Valley. Meanwhile, lodging in town was relatively scarce, plain, and aimed at action-oriented, budget-conscious recreationists. It still is. But recent construction has added some handsomely furnished accommodations in superb locations by the lifts at the base of Bald Mountain, plus contemporary lodgings with amenities downtown. Mid-winter rates are usually 30% to 50% higher than the summer rates shown, while spring and fall rates are normally at least 20% lower.

★ **Christiania Lodge - Best Western**   *downtown at 651 Sun Valley Rd. E*   726-3351
This contemporary Western-style motel has an outdoor pool and whirlpool. Each of the spacious, well-furnished rooms has a phone and cable color TV.

#219,#201,#101 — kitchen/bar, flagstone fireplace,   K bed...$62
regular room —   Q bed...$52

Heidelberg Inn   *1 mi. NW on Warm Springs Rd.*   726-5361
Off the beaten track, this modern motel has an outdoor pool with a slide, a whirlpool, and a sauna. Each large, well-furnished room has a phone, cable color TV, and a refrigerator.

#131,#130,#116,#115 — native stone wall/(duraflame log) fireplace,   K bed...$60
regular room —   Q bed...$39

Sun Inn   *downtown at Main/6th Sts.*   726-5183
This small, older **bargain** motel is conveniently located near the heart of town. Each of the rustic units has cable color TV.

regular room —   D bed...$25

★ **Sun Valley Lodge**   *1.5 mi. NE via Sun Valley Rd.*   622-4111
The "Queen Mother of American Ski Resorts" is operated by the Sun Valley Company, which also manages a newer inn and condominium apartments *(toll-free out-of-state calls: (800)635-8261)*. The well-maintained lodge is nearly half a century old. Still the largest single accommodation in the area, it is now surrounded by hundreds of clustered condominium units. The remarkable array of amenities includes a large outdoor pool, whirlpool, sauna, recreation and game rooms, plus (for a fee) an 18-hole golf course, indoor and outdoor ice-skating rinks, dozens of tennis courts, bicycle rentals, horseback riding, skeet shooting, and boat rentals for a tiny reservoir. In winter, downhill and cross-country skiing and sleigh rides are available. Other facilities include a grandiose dining room, plus a coffee shop and lounge. All of the beautifully decorated rooms have a phone and cable color TV.

#306 — top fl. suite, 2 lg. pvt. view decks, windows on 3 sides,
            corner fireplace, alabaster bathroom,   K bed..$146
deluxe unit — spacious,   K bed...$78
regular room —   Q bed...$58

★ **Tamarack Lodge**   *downtown at Sun Valley Rd./Walnut Av.*   726-3344
This contemporary motor lodge has a large glassed-in pool, a whirlpool, and an exercise room. Each room has a phone, cable color TV with movies, refrigerator, and either a patio or private balcony.
#210,#110 — spacious, tiny metal fireplace, wet bar, pvt. view balc.,   Q bed...$57
regular room —   Q bed...$49

★ **Warm Springs Resort**   *2.5 mi. W via Warm Springs Rd. on Skiway Dr.*   726-8274
The International Village condominiums offer contemporary overnight lodgings that can be reserved through Warm Springs Resort Properties *(toll-free out-of-state calls: (800)635-4404)*. This large, modern complex has an outstanding location next to both the Warm Springs Ski Lift and a rushing stream. There is an outdoor pool which is heated to whirlpool temperature in winter. Each spacious, well-furnished condominium rental has a phone, color TV, complete kitchen, and a patio or balcony.
#C11 — great creek view, fireplace, spiral staircase to view loft with   Q bed...$60
#'s F1,F3,F5,F7,F9 — 1 BR, greenhouse window in LR, patio, fireplace,   Q bed...$60
regular room — studio,   Q bed...$60

Wood River Motel   *.5 mi. W at 100 Buss Elle Rd.*   726-3341
Several **bargain** log cabin units with Western-style pinewood interiors are clustered in a quiet neighborhood in the midst of evergreen trees. Each room has a cable color TV.
regular room —   D bed...$30

CAMPGROUNDS
There are numerous primitive campgrounds in the majestic mountains north of town. However, the area's best combination of complete camping facilities, good recreation opportunities, and attractive shady sites by a river is right in town.

★ **Sun Valley Camping Resort**   *1.2 mi. S on ID 75*   726-3429
This privately owned campground has a fine shady location by Wood River. Trout fishing in the river, an outdoor pool, a rec room, and an outdoor game area are features. Teepees or tents may be rented. Flush toilets, hot showers, and hookups are available. Each of the grassy sites has a picnic table and fire ring. Some are tree-shaded. There is a separate tenting area.   base rate...$9.50

SPECIAL EVENT
Wagon Days   *downtown*   *Labor Day Weekend*
The highlight of this popular four-day celebration is one of the West's largest exclusively horse-and-wagon parades, which features the "Big Hitch." This train of authentic ore wagons that once rumbled over a nearby pass dwarfs even the enormous Belgian horses that pull it.

OTHER INFORMATION
Area Code: *208*
Zip Code: *83340*
Ketchum-Sun Valley Chamber of Commerce   *downtown at 4th & Main Sts.*   726-3423
Sawtooth Nat. Forest-Ketchum Ranger Station *.3 mi. E on Sun Valley Rd.*   622-5371
Sawtooth National Recreation Visitor Center   *N on ID 75*   726-8291

McCall, Idaho

Elevation:

5,030 feet

Population (1980):

2,188

Population (1970):

1,758

Location:

438 mi. NW
of Salt Lake City

McCall is a new year-round recreation hub for the northern Rocky Mountains. The village is in a luxuriant pine forest on the southern shore of a picture postcard lake framed by rugged peaks. Nearly a mile high, winter is normally long and cold with enough snowfall to support a major ski area on a nearby mountain. Cross-country skiing and snowmobiling areas are also well developed, and frozen lakes are popular for ice-skating and ice fishing. The season is highlighted by a popular winter carnival. Summer is the busiest season, however. This is partly because the weather is outstanding. Warm sunny days are ideal for every kind of outdoor activity. In town, picturesque lakefront parks feature scenic pine-shaded picnic sites, swimming areas, and sandy beaches. A pine-shaded golf course and tennis courts are also available. Surrounded by the Payette National Forest, McCall is a gateway to the rugged grandeur of the famed "River-of-No-Return" country. River running, fishing, boating, and swimming compete with hiking, backpacking, mountain climbing, hunting, and camping as popular visitor activities.

The town grew up on the southern shoreline of Payette Lake near the point where the Payette River flows out of the lake and meanders southward. A logging industry began here around the turn of the century to harvest vast pine forests in the area. A sawmill and logging railroad soon became the mainstays of the local economy. In recent years, both the lumber mill and railroad ceased operation. Their demise made it possible, in the 1970s, for the town to begin to fulfill its more distinguished destiny as an outdoor recreation capital of the West.

Both the mill site and the railroad right of way are being replaced with residences, parks, shops, and trails. Today, McCall has the kind of rustic, unspoiled charm that everyone thinks their favorite town had before it became famous and overcrowded. The tiny village center is still primarily a source of basic necessities, but new specialty shops and restaurants are oriented toward the more diverse needs of increasing numbers of visitors as well as residents. Nightlife includes an appealing mixture of rustic and rowdy older bars and contemporary lakeview lounges. Accommodations are relatively scarce, but include two of the state's finest facilities — a handsome lakefront resort hotel on the west side of town, and an extraordinarily picturesque lakefront campground on the eastern boundary.

McCall, Idaho

WEATHER PROFILE *Vokac Weather Rating*

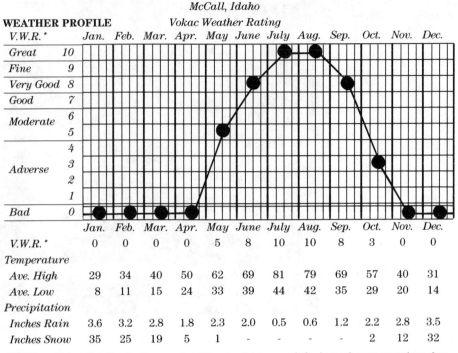

V.W.R.*	Jan.	Feb.	Mar.	Apr.	May	June	July	Aug.	Sep.	Oct.	Nov.	Dec.
V.W.R.*	0	0	0	0	5	8	10	10	8	3	0	0
Temperature												
Ave. High	29	34	40	50	62	69	81	79	69	57	40	31
Ave. Low	8	11	15	24	33	39	44	42	35	29	20	14
Precipitation												
Inches Rain	3.6	3.2	2.8	1.8	2.3	2.0	0.5	0.6	1.2	2.2	2.8	3.5
Inches Snow	35	25	19	5	1	-	-	-	-	2	12	32

V.W.R. = Vokac Weather Rating: probability of mild (warm & dry) weather on any given day.

Forecast

Month	V.W.R.*		Temperatures		Precipitation
			Daytime	Evening	
January	0	Bad	cold	frigid	frequent snowstorms
February	0	Bad	chilly	frigid	frequent snowstorms
March	0	Bad	chilly	cold	frequent snowstorms
April	0	Bad	cool	chilly	occasional snow flurries/showers
May	5	Moderate	cool	chilly	occasional rainstorms
June	8	Very Good	warm	cool	occasional rainstorms
July	10	Great	warm	cool	negligible
August	10	Great	warm	cool	infrequent showers
September	8	Very Good	warm	cool	infrequent showers
October	3	Adverse	cool	chilly	occasional rainstorms/snow flurries
November	0	Bad	chilly	cold	frequent snow flurries
December	0	Bad	cold	frigid	frequent snowstorms

Summary

Nearly a mile above sea level, McCall occupies a lush pine forest on the south shore of one of the most beautiful lakes in the Northwest. In this picture postcard setting, even the uncommonly rugged **winter** months have been turned into an asset. Days are cold and evenings are frigid, but frequent heavy snowstorms provide plenty of snow to assure outstanding conditions for the nearby major ski area and for all kinds of other winter sports facilities in and around town. Conventional **spring** weather doesn't arrive until almost Memorial Day. Earlier, cool temperatures and muddy terrain are accompanied by an unpredictable mixture of occasional showers and snow flurries. **Summer** is outstanding. Long warm days, cool evenings, and inconsequential showers contribute to easy enjoyment of both water and mountain sports in this delightful alpine playground. In **fall**, temperatures cool very rapidly and snow flurries begin again in earnest soon after Halloween.

ATTRACTIONS & DIVERSIONS

Beach Parks

Three picturesque public beaches are conveniently located in town. Art Roberts City Park, a tiny downtown grassy slope extending to the lake, is perfect for sunning and sightseeing. Public Beach, one mile west of downtown at the Payette River outlet, features pine-shaded picnic tables and a sandy-bottomed swimming area. Davis Beach, a half mile north at the western end of Lick Creek Road, has a long shady beach and pine-shaded picnic tables.

Bicycling

Follett's Mountain Sports   *downtown at 3rd/Lenora Sts.*   634-2150

Bicycles can be rented here for touring the relatively easy roads and byways around beautiful Payette Lake.

★ Boat Rentals

Sports Marina   *downtown at 1300 E. Lake St.*   634-5960

Fishing boats, ski boats, canoes and pontoons can be rented by the hour or day.

★ Boat Ride

Payette Lake Cruises   *1 mi. W on ID 55*   634-7726

One-hour scenic boat tours of Payette Lake leave several times daily in summer from the Shore Lodge dock. Closed Sun.

The Gardens   *5 mi. N via ID 55 on Warren Wagon Rd.*

Visitors are welcome to explore these lovely semi-natural private gardens during the summer. Follow Warren Wagon Road past Wagon Wheel Bay sign. At the next bend in the road look for a weathered sign on the right side.

Golf

McCall Golf Course   *1 mi. NE on Fairway Dr.*   634-7200

This scenic, relatively level 18-hole course was carefully carved out of a dense pine forest. It is open to the public with a pro shop, club and cart rentals, and a coffee shop.

Library   *downtown at Park/2nd Sts.*   634-5522

The McCall Public Library occupies a small contemporary building loaded with a surprising quantity of books and magazines. Visitors can enjoy the lake view from a few upholstered chairs.

★ North Beach State Rec. Area   *9 mi. N via ID 55 on Warren Wagon Rd.*   634-2164

The longest sandy beach in the area separates a dense pine forest from the north shore of Payette Lake. Nearby, the slow-moving, sandy-bottomed North Fork of the Payette River is well-suited to lazy river floats.

★ Payette Lake   *adjacent to town on the north*

The scenic sylvan gem of the central Idaho mountains is seven miles long. It is surrounded by luxuriant pine forests and an attractive mixture of public parks and residential areas. A scenic loop road (partly gravel) circles the lake and provides numerous overlooks and sandy beach accesses. Boating, water-skiing, swimming, and fishing are popular. Most recreation facilities are concentrated in or near McCall on the southern shore.

★ Payette National Forest   *surrounding town*   634-2255

This huge forest includes roads west of town that access awesome overlooks of the Grand Canyon of the Snake River, the world's deepest gorge. The highlight of the area east of town is the magnificent River of No Return Wilderness. This vast area of peaks and canyons, mountain lakes and streams, and forested hills offers some of the West's finest hiking, backpacking, pack trips, hunting, and fishing. It also includes a beautiful stretch of the Salmon River — the River of No Return — renowned as one of the world's great river running locations. The Brundage Mountain Ski Area, a major winter sports facility, is west of town. Cross-country skiing, snowmobiling and ice fishing are popular in the forest in winter.

★ Ponderosa State Park   *follow signs for 2 mi. NE on Payette Lake*   634-2164

Idaho has provided an outstandingly well-furnished park in one of the state's largest stands of unlogged ponderosa pines along the east shore of Payette Lake. Summer facilities include a visitor center, six miles of nature trails, a picturesque swimming area with a sandy beach, a boat launch, a five-mile scenic overlook drive, fishing sites, pine-shaded picnic facilities, and a full service campground with some delightful lake view sites. Winter activities include cross-country skiing, snowshoeing, sledding, ice-skating, ice fishing, and snowmobiling.

★ **River Running**

Salmon River Challenge   *45 mi. NW via ID 55 and US 95 - Riggins*   628-3270
Day trips are offered on a challenging twenty-mile stretch of the Salmon River between Riggins and Slate Creek, usually leaving around 10 a.m. daily during the summer. Several other companies also operate out of Riggins with daily and longer white-water trips.

Warm Water Features
McCall is in the midst of one of the West's greatest concentrations of geothermal springs. Some have been fully developed with swimming pools. Others remain sublime natural attractions of the high country wilderness.

★   **Gold Fork Hot Springs**   *26 mi. SE: 20 mi. S on ID 55 & 6 mi. E on Forest Rd.*
Very hot mineral water gradually cools in a series of large pools behind rustic log dams. This primitive hot springs is in a boulder-strewn area of wooded foothills. Nudity or clothing is left to the mutual consent of those present.

★   **Last Chance Hot Springs** *7 mi. NW: 6.5 mi. NW on ID 55 & .5 mi. N on Last Chance Rd.*
This small, unimproved hot springs is on the east bank of Goose Creek near Last Chance Campground. Hot mineral water flows from an overhead pipe into a little rock grotto deep in the forest. Nudity or clothing is left to the mutual consent of those present.

Waterhole #1   *5.5 mi. S: 5 mi. S on ID 55 & .5 mi. E of Lake Fork*   634-7758
Hourly rentals are available for six plain, wood-sided rooms with a redwood hot tub with jets, and a barn door that opens to a private panorama of forest and mountains. Beer or wine may be brought in from the adjoining funky bar — or you can bring your own.

Zim's Hot Springs   *17 mi. NW: 11 mi. NW on ID 55 & 6 mi. N on US 95*   347-2115
The nearest commercially developed swimming complex includes a large outdoor hot mineral water pool and an even hotter soaking pool. Modest picnic, dining, and camping facilities are also provided.

Winter Sports

★   **Brundage Mountain Ski Area**   *10 mi. NW via ID 55 & unnumbered road* 634-5650
The vertical rise is 1,600 feet and the longest run is about two miles. Elevation at the top is 7,600 feet. There are two chairlifts. Essential facilities, services and rentals are available at the base for downhill skiing. There are no restaurants, bars, or lodgings in the area. The ski season is mid-November to mid-April.

★   **Cross-Country Skiing**   *around town*
With an average of several feet of snow on the ground, cross-country skiing is excellent throughout the area during the winter. Well-groomed scenic trails are found at Ponderosa State Park, Little Ski Hill, Bear Basin, and other nearby sites. Maps, equipment rentals and sales, and lessons can be arranged at:

     David's of McCall   *1 mi. W at 500 W. Lake St.*   634-2171
     Follett's Mountain Sports   *downtown at 3rd/Lenora Sts.*   634-2150

★   Snowmobiling
     Medley Sports   *downtown at 809 3rd St.*   634-2216
An increasingly popular way to get farther, faster, into this outstanding snow country is on a snowmobile. There are hundreds of miles of groomed trails in the area. Snowmobiles can be rented here for a half day, day, or weekend tours.

SHOPPING
The tiny business district is beautifully located along the lake shore in a colorful mixture of old clapboard buildings and modern wooden structures. From the beginning, this has been the region's only complete shopping center. It still functions primarily as a place to buy basic supplies, but a few galleries and specialty shops have been added in recent years.

Food Specialties

★ **Danish Mill Bakery**   *downtown on Lenora St. between 1st & 2nd Sts.*   634-2827
European pastries and breads are specialties of this stylish newer bakery with a charming coffee shop and outdoor tables, as well as takeout service.

High Country Deli   *downtown at 308 Lake St.*   634-5327
A good selection of meats and cheese, plus homemade bagels, cheesecake and assorted desserts may be enjoyed here or taken out. Closed Sun.

McCall Rexall Drug Store   *downtown at 2nd/Lenora Sts.*   634-2433
This old-fashioned soda fountain provides a refreshing place to choose from a variety of flavors and styles of ice cream.

Specialty Shops

★ **Blue Lotus Books & Goods** *downtown on Park St. between 1st & 2nd Sts.* *634-5555*
A fine selection of books of regional interest is a highlight, and health foods are also sold
in this attractively converted home. An old-fashioned Franklin fireplace and soft music
lend to the relaxed atmosphere.

★ **Brown's Gallery** *1 mi. W at 402 W. Lake St.* *634-2302*
Western fine arts in a variety of media are beautifully displayed in a handsome
woodcrafted gallery.

NIGHTLIFE

Peace and quiet reign after the sun goes down over the lake. But, there are a few
distinctive places to drink, dance, or listen to music.

Cutty Sark *downtown at 317 E. Lake St.* *634-7049*
This contemporary lounge offers comfortably padded bar stools, tables on a sunny
lakeside patio, and premium beer on tap.

★ **Forester's Club** *downtown at 304 E. Lake St.* *634-2427*
Nightly live rock sessions, a big dance floor, and a bar embedded with hundreds of half
dollars make this casual old saloon an area favorite.

★ **Shore Lodge** *1 mi. W on W. Lake St.* *634-2244*
McCall's premier resort has a large lounge with a magnificent view of the lake and
mountains. Comfortably padded armchairs provide a perfect setting for a quiet drink by
the shore.

The Yacht Club *downtown at E. Lake/1st Sts.* *634-5745*
This big casual lounge offers a variety of live entertainment for dancing most nights, and
features a fine view of the lake.

RESTAURANTS

Most of the short list of local restaurants charge modest prices for hearty American fare
served in casual surroundings.

Cutty Sark *downtown at 317 E. Lake St.* *634-7049*
L-D. *Moderate*
A contemporary menu is offered in a newer restaurant where some of the comfortable
booths provide a view of the lake. A large lakeside patio is also used in summer, and there
is a popular lounge.

★ **Huckleberry** *downtown at 3rd St./Railroad Av.* *634-8477*
B-L. *Low*
Fine omelets and crepes reflect skillful use of fresh ingredients. Delicious homemade
sourdough biscuits are also featured in this cheerful newer cottage restaurant.

Lake Shore Lodge *1 mi. W on W. Lake St.* *634-2244*
B-L-D. *Moderate*
The Terrace Room restaurant offers hearty American dishes and an impressive salad bar
accompanied by a magnificent lakefront view. The room is a jungle of beautiful hanging
fuscias and ferns in summer. Downstairs, a coffee shop offers specialties like huckleberry
pancakes, and a flower-bordered lakeside terrace is used for meals when weather
permits.

Lardo Grill & Saloon *1.2 mi. W at 600 W. Lake St.* *634-7464*
B-L-D. *Moderate*
Hearty American breakfasts are served in a casual Western-style coffee shop adjoining a
saloon.

The Mill *.4 mi. S at 3rd/Stibnite Sts.* *634-7683*
D only. Closed Sun. *Moderate*
Steaks and prime rib are standouts on a contemporary American menu. Rustic hunting
lodge decor complements the hearty portions.

★ **The Pancake House** *.6 mi. S on 3rd St. near Floyde St.* *634-5849*
B-L. *Moderate*
Here is American homestyle cooking at its best. The cinnamon rolls and even the jams are
homemade, and regional specialties like huckleberry pancakes are featured in season.
Iron fireplaces in the dining rooms provide warmth in the area's finest rustic roadside
cafe.

LODGING

Accommodations are relatively scarce, but there are outstanding lakefront rooms in the town's premier resort. All of the other recommended facilities are nicely furnished and reasonably priced. Spring and fall prices may be as much as 20% less than the summer rates shown.

Riverside Motel   *1 mi. W at 400 W. Lake St.*   *634-5610*
This modern **bargain** motel is ideally situated by the Payette River across the street from the lake and a town beach. Each nicely furnished room has a color TV. Some kitchenettes are available.

#1 — end of single-level bldg., corner windows, good lake view,	Q bed...$29
#9 — view across parking lot of lake/mts.,	Q bed...$29
regular room —	Q bed...$29

Scandia Inn   *.4 mi. S on ID 55*   *634-7394*
One of McCall's newest motels is a **bargain,** featuring a Finnish sauna. The nicely furnished rooms have color TV.

regular room —	Q bed...$29

★ **Shore Lodge**   *1 mi. W on W. Lake St.*   *634-2244*
In a picture-postcard setting by Payette Lake, this large, modern resort motel has a big outdoor pool, tennis court, private sandy beach, boat dock, boat rentals, game room, and scenic dining and lounge facilities. Each well-furnished unit has a phone and color TV.

#224,#124 — spacious, rock wall fireplace, refr., fine lake/mt. view, 2 Q or K bed...$75
#322,#321 — spacious, fine panoramic lake/mt. view,	2 Q beds...$55
"Brundage Suite" — big, pvt. balc., lake/mt. view, wet bar,	K bed...$65
#222 (& 5 more 3rd fl. lakeview doubles) — fine pvt. view of lake/mts., 2 Q beds...$65
regular room —	Q bed...$44

Woodsman Motel   *.5 mi. S on ID 55*   *634-7671*
An older log cabin-style motel has **bargain** rooms with TV.

deluxe room — phone, color TV,	Q bed...$31
regular room — B/W TV,	D bed...$24

CAMPGROUNDS

It doesn't matter that campgrounds aren't numerous near McCall because one of the West's outstanding campgrounds adjoins town by the lake.

★ **Ponderosa State Park**   *2 mi. NE via E. Lake St. - follow signs*   *634-2164*
One of Idaho's finest state parks includes a large campground with a magnificent location in a forest of giant white pines by Payette Lake. Amenities include a sandy beach for swimming and sunbathing, a dock and ramp for boating and water-skiing, and fishing in the lake and nearby streams, plus well-tended nature trails and a visitor center. In winter, cross-country skiing, tobogganing and ice fishing are enjoyed. Flush toilets, hot showers, and hookups are available. Each well-spaced, pine-shaded site has a picnic table, fire area and grill. Some have spectacular lake views.   base rate...$5

SPECIAL EVENT

★ **Winter Carnival**   *downtown*   *early February*
Snow sculptures are a highlight, including one of monstrous proportions, in the downtown park. Festivities begin on Friday night with a torchlight parade and bonfire, welcoming ceremonies by the Mayor and Queen, and fireworks over the lake. During the weekend, a parade, ski and dogsled races, food booths, an art show, and dances are all well-attended.

OTHER INFORMATION

Area Code: *208*
Zip Code: *83638*
McCall Area Chamber of Commerce   *downtown at 903 N. 3rd St.*   *634-7631*
Payette National Forest-Smokejumpers Hqs.   *.5 mi. W on Lake St.*   *634-2255*

Sandpoint, Idaho

Elevation:

2,085 feet

Population (1980):

4,460

Population (1970):

4,144

Location:

353 mi. E
of Seattle

Sandpoint is a civilized complement to a naturally inspired setting. It occupies a superlative piece of shoreline along one of the West's finest large sylvan lakes. With a sheltered location surrounded by pine-forested mountains, the town has a four season climate. Summer is the most popular season. Warm sunny days practically assure comfortable enjoyment of nearby mountains, forests, lake, and rivers with a diversity of recreation opportunities, including hiking, backpacking, camping, boating, fishing, and swimming. In town, the major attraction is a large lakefront park next to downtown with sandy beaches, swimming areas, an adjoining marina with boat rentals and charter services, grassy lawns with shady picnic sites, and an assortment of other well-tended facilities. Since the completion of a major skiing complex in the adjacent mountains, the area has also become an increasingly popular destination for winter sports enthusiasts.

The town's evolution on the northwestern shore of Lake Pend Oreille where it flows into the Pend Oreille River has always been dominated by the lake. More than forty miles long and six miles wide, with about 110 miles of shoreline, this is one of the West's largest bodies of fresh water. Idaho's first permanent structure was built on the northeast shore of the lake in 1809 by David Thompson (a renowned geographer and explorer) for the Canadian-based Northwest Company. Because of the isolated location near the Canadian border, major settlement was forestalled for decades. It wasn't until the 1880s that Sandpoint began to develop following the completion of transcontinental railroad lines through the townsite coupled with the birth of this area's timber industry.

Transportation and forest products are still important. Today, however, with increasing appreciation of the splendid lakeside location and recent development of a major ski area nearby, plus high-tech contributions to improved clothing and equipment for winter and summer outdoor sports, Sandpoint is beginning to be "discovered" as a year-round leisure destination. Downtown has become a handsome synthesis of a frontier heritage and a contemporary Western outlook. Old and new buildings house a lively assortment of specialty shops and galleries offering locally-made gourmet foods and arts and crafts. The unique new Cedar Street Bridge shopping complex, spanning a waterway between the main street and the railroad depot, is a peerless wood-trimmed showcase for quality shops. A surprising number of stylish restaurants serving gourmet specialties are clustered in the heart of town. Most of the region's finest accommodations are also within a stroll of downtown and the lakefront.

WEATHER PROFILE — *Vokac Weather Rating*

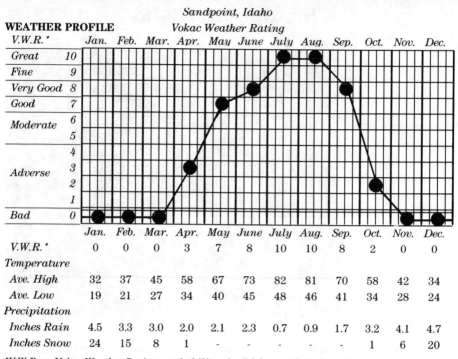

V.W.R. *	Jan.	Feb.	Mar.	Apr.	May	June	July	Aug.	Sep.	Oct.	Nov.	Dec.
V.W.R. *	0	0	0	3	7	8	10	10	8	2	0	0
Temperature												
Ave. High	32	37	45	58	67	73	82	81	70	58	42	34
Ave. Low	19	21	27	34	40	45	48	46	41	34	28	24
Precipitation												
Inches Rain	4.5	3.3	3.0	2.0	2.1	2.3	0.7	0.9	1.7	3.2	4.1	4.7
Inches Snow	24	15	8	1	-	-	-	-	-	1	6	20

*V.W.R. = Vokac Weather Rating: probability of mild (warm & dry) weather on any given day.

Forecast

Month	V.W.R. *		Temperatures Daytime	Evening	Precipitation
January	0	Bad	cold	cold	frequent snowstorms
February	0	Bad	chilly	cold	frequent snow flurries
March	0	Bad	chilly	chilly	frequent rainstorms/snow flurries
April	3	Adverse	cool	chilly	frequent showers
May	7	Good	warm	cool	frequent showers
June	8	Very Good	warm	cool	occasional rainstorms
July	10	Great	warm	warm	infrequent showers
August	10	Great	warm	cool	infrequent showers
September	8	Very Good	warm	cool	occasional showers
October	2	Adverse	cool	chilly	frequent rainstorms
November	0	Bad	chilly	chilly	frequent snowstorms/snow flurries
December	0	Bad	chilly	cold	frequent snowstorms

Summary

Only about two thousand feet above sea level, Sandpoint seems much higher because of its picturesque sylvan setting on the northern shore of one of the West's largest alpine lakes. The town enjoys a true four season climate tempered somewhat by a lakeside mountain-sheltered location. **Winter** is a combination of short, chilly days and cold nights. Frequent snowstorms and flurries usually provide ideal conditions at the major nearby ski area and other winter sports complexes. Damp but relatively mild weather begins around the first days of **spring**. Light sportswear is appropriate by May, except during frequent seasonal showers. **Summer** is outstanding, with long warm days, cool evenings, and very little rain. **Fall** weather soon becomes unpleasant. Rainfalls become heavy and frequent in October, and temperatures plummet in anticipation of gathering winter storms.

ATTRACTIONS & DIVERSIONS

★ **Boat Rentals**
  Carefree Houseboating   *1 mi. SW at 1005 S. US 2*   263-5710
Houseboat rentals are available for use on Lake Pend Oreille by the day or week.
  Windbag   *downtown at City Beach*   263-7811
Sailboats and windsurfer rentals and lessons are available at this lakefront location.
  Fishing Charters
★ **Sandpoint Charter Service**   *downtown at Sandpoint Marina*   263-8314
Day (or longer) sportfishing trips on Lake Pend Oreille, with all gear furnished, can be
reserved here.
  Flying
★   **Lake Pend Oreille Aviation**   *downtown just N of Sandpoint Beach Park*   263-8932
Scenic seaplane flights of various lengths give passengers a bird's-eye view of the beautiful
lake and mountains.
  Horsedrawn Carriage Rides   *downtown*
Old-fashioned town tours usually start from the bridge downtown.

★ **Kaniksu National Forest**   *surrounding town*
This huge preserve includes parts of both Lake Pend Oreille and Priest Lake, plus
numerous beautiful small lakes in an emerald empire of dense forests and rugged
mountains. In addition to excellent boating, fishing, and swimming opportunities, more
than 1,000 miles of scenic trails provide access for hikers, backpackers, and guided
hunting and fishing parties.

★ **Lake Pend Oreille**   *adjacent to town*
Idaho's largest lake was formed by glaciers that carved out a trough now filled for more
than forty miles by water that reaches a depth of 1,150 feet. The scenic lake is famous for
sportfishing with fourteen varieties of game fish, including record-sized kamloops (the
world's largest rainbow trout). For the average angler, the kokanee (a small, land-locked
salmon) is abundant. Recreation facilities dot the 111 miles of shoreline and provide
swimming, boating, water-skiing, camping, and hiking opportunities in summer.
  Lakeview Park   *.5 mi. SW on Lakeview Blvd.*
Bonner County Historical Museum, with exhibits depicting local history and a research
library, and War Memorial Field, the site of the summer festival and sporting events, are
located in this shady lakeside park.

★ **Sandpoint Beach Park**   *downtown at E end of Bridge St.*
A long sandy beach and splendid lake and mountain panoramas are highlights of a well-
tended park that covers the end of a little peninsula next to downtown. Landscaped
grounds include a bathhouse, boat launching facilities, public dockage, a tiled wading
pool, playground, tennis courts, picnic tables with fireplaces, and lifeguard services.

★ **Springy Point Recreation Area**   *4.5 mi. SW via US 95 on Lakeshore Dr.*   437-3133
Across Lake Pend Oreille from town is a sandy beach backed by a pine-shaded grassy
slope. In addition to fine swimming and sunbathing areas with panoramic views, there are
changing facilities, a boat launch and dock, picnic tables, and a campground.
  Winter Sports
★   **Schweitzer Ski Area**   *11 mi. NW off US 95*   263-9555
The vertical rise is 2,000 feet and the longest run is 2.5 miles. Elevation at the top is 6,400
feet. There are seven double chairlifts. All facilities, services, and rentals are available at
the area for both downhill and cross-country skiing. A lodge, restaurant, and bar are at
the base. The skiing season is late November to early April.

SHOPPING
Sandpoint has a picturesque downtown on an inlet of Lake Pend Oreille. Turn-of-the-
century landmarks have been carefully preserved and blend well with contemporary
structures highlighted by an inspired new complex of shops on a bridge over Sand Creek.
Galleries and specialty shops are proliferating, along with a remarkably sophisticated
cluster of restaurants and lounges.

Food Specialties

Chateau Wine Co. *downtown at Cedar St./N. First Av.* 263-1511
Premium wines and beers are well organized in this small shop.

Chilly Willy's *downtown at 102 Church St.* 263-9101
Fresh huckleberry milkshakes are a seasonal treat among many flavors and styles of ice cream. Homemade soups and sandwiches are also served in this pleasant little sit down or carryout shop.

★ **Hummdinger's** *downtown at 100 N. First Av.* 263-9021
A delicious assortment of pastries, including huckleberry turnovers and some splendid European specialties, are served in a plain little coffee shop, or to go. Closed Sun.

Pend Oreille Cheese Co. *downtown at 125 S. Second Av.* 263-2030
Mountain gem cheddar, colby, and jack cheese are made and sold, along with some non-local cheeses, at this casual little cheese factory. Closed Sun.

★ **The Smoke House** *2 mi. SE at US 95 & Lakeshore Dr.* 263-6312
Smoked salmon and other fish, plus smoked meats and cheeses, are prepared here with pure, natural ingredients. Carefully selected breads, salami, preserves, and other gourmet items from elsewhere in the West are also featured in this tantalizing carryout. Closed Wed.

Specialty Shops

★ **Book and Game Company** *downtown on Cedar St. Bridge* 263-1545
This small, new shop has both a good assortment of books and an interesting selection of adult games.

★ **Cedar Street Bridge** *downtown at E end of Cedar St.* 263-0502
More than thirty fascinating specialty shops, restaurants, and studio galleries have been incorporated onto a two-level pedestrian bridge over Sand Creek. The complex is a stunning achievement in Western-style contemporary architecture and interior decor. As an added attraction, several thousand square feet of glass windows provide tranquil views of the lake and mountains.

★ **The Cottage Craftsman** *downtown on Cedar St. Bridge* 265-4742
Arts and crafts by local and regional artists are beautifully displayed in an appealing new store.

Foster's Crossing Mall *.3 mi. W at 504 Oak St.* 263-5911
An old bottling company and freight house has been transformed into a collection of specialty shops, galleries and studios.

Vandeford's Books & Stationery *downtown at 201 Cedar St.* 263-2417
Western reference and field guide books are specialties in a combination book/office supplies store.

NIGHTLIFE

One of the most fun-loving towns in the Northwest has plenty of intriguing places to drink, dance, or listen to music. Both downtown and in nearby rustic roadhouses, the mood is casual, Western, and friendly.

★ **Bert's Place** *2.5 mi. NE on ID 200* 263-9992
This big, easygoing old roadhouse has some comfortable booths and frequently offers live country/western music for dancing or listening.

★ **Cowgirl Corral** *2 mi. NE on ID 200* 263-5193
Live music and dancing are featured every night in Sandpoint's largest nightclub. The cavernous roadhouse provides padded bar stools for safely watching the action on the mechanical bucking bull. Reasonable prices and a friendly attitude also help keep this place a favorite of goat ropers, pucky stompers, and all other true believers of the Western mystique.

Donkey Jaw *downtown at 212 Cedar St.* 263-5337
There is live entertainment on weekends in this comfortably furnished upstairs lounge. A good view of downtown, padded bar stools, and plants everywhere are features of the contemporary decor.

★ **Fireside Inn** *downtown at 215 Pine St.* 263-9959
Live country/western music and dancing are offered on weekends in a big Western-style saloon with two fireplaces and padded square bar stools. A separate area is outfitted with pool tables and shuffleboard.

★ **The Garden**   *downtown at 15 E. Lake St.*   *263-5187*
One of the West's most romantic lounges offers a perfect setting for a memorable tete-a-tete. Thoroughly opulent decor includes a grand piano, giant crystal chandeliers suspended from a greenhouse-sized skylight, a fireplace, overstuffed sofas and parlour chairs, and what has to be the world's largest fern.

★ **Kamloops**   *downtown at 302 N. First Av.*   *263-6715*
Serendipitous live music for listening attracts enthusiastic crowds on weekends to this handsome cabaret/cafe. Exposed brick walls and wood-and-plants decor is complemented by premium tap beer and wine by the glass.

Shenanigan's   *downtown at 206 N. First Av.*   *263-3238*
The meet-market concept thrives in an action-oriented lounge where live entertainment and dancing attract friendly crowds most nights.

RESTAURANTS
Culinary artistry is startlingly well represented, especially downtown, where gourmet cuisine is emphasized in a tantalizing cluster of distinctive dining rooms. The cost of fine dining is, surprisingly, uniformly reasonable.

★ **Donkey Jaw**   *downtown at 212 Cedar St.*   *263-5337*
B-L-D.   *Moderate*
Fine homemade cinnamon rolls accompany specialty omelets and other delicious American and Mexican fare. Contemporary wood/plants decor lends a charming intimacy to several small dining rooms.

Edgewater Lodge   *downtown at 56 Bridge St.*   *263-3194*
B-L-D.   *Moderate*
The Beach House features American fare and a salad bar in a handsome contemporary dining room. The lakefront views are outstanding. An adjoining outdoor patio is used in summer, and there is also a view lounge.

★ **The Garden**   *downtown at 15 E. Lake St.*   *263-5187*
L-D. No L on Sat.   *Moderate*
Gourmet American dishes include some outstanding specialties like sauteed halibut cheeks. Homemade baked goods and a soup-and-salad bar are included with meals served in a lovely greenhouse setting overlooking a marina on Lake Pend Oreille. A magnificent lounge adjoins.

Henry Villard   *downtown on Cedar Street Bridge*   *263-8587*
D only.   *Moderate*
Fresh fish is a specialty, along with steaks and Continental entrees, served in a plush, ultra-modern new restaurant on the Cedar Street Bridge.

Hoot Owl   *2 mi. NE on ID 200*   *263-9211*
B-L-D. Closed Sun.   *Low*
Homestyle breakfasts are served all day along with homemade cinnamon rolls and biscuits in this old-fashioned roadside cafe.

★ **Hydra**   *downtown at 115 W. Lake St.*   *263-7123*
D only.   *Moderate*
Contemporary American fare (seafood and prime rib with a salad bar) achieves distinction with regional specialties like halibut cheeks. Flourishing greenery complements several levels of cozy wood-crafted dining rooms. The wood-toned deck and lounge are also local favorites.

★ **Idaho Flynn & Co.**   *downtown at Pine St./Second Av.*   *265-4550*
L-D. No D on Sun.   *Moderate*
Continental gourmet specialties are capped by an elaborate list of fabulous homemade desserts. A singer/musician occasionally provides easy listening music with dinner on weekends in the casual dining room.

Ivanoe's   *downtown at 124 S. Second Av.*   *263-0211*
D only.   *Moderate*
Italian cuisine is emphasized in Sandpoint's newest adventure in gracious dining.

Lighthouse Restaurant   *17 mi. NE on ID 200 - Hope*   *264-5514*
D only.   *Moderate*
American dishes are offered along with a soup and dessert bar in a large, shoreline dining room with window wall views of Lake Pend Oreille. The salad dressings made here are shipped to many states.

Panhandler Pies   *downtown at 120 S. First Av.*   *263-2912*
B-L-D.   *Moderate*
A long list of fine pies are baked on the premises daily along with an assortment of carefully-made omelets and hearty American dishes. The big, wood-finished restaurant is casually furnished in Early American decor.

★ **The Pasta House**   *downtown at 526 N. Fourth Av.*   *263-6722*
D only. Closed Sun.   *Moderate*
Gourmet Italian cuisine and fine desserts are served amid casual elegance in a converted Victorian home, or outdoors in a garden during summer.

Trestle Creek Inn   *14 mi. NE on ID 200 - Hope*   *264-5443*
D only.   *Moderate*
American dishes are served in a surprisingly posh little creekside dining room tucked toward the back of a roadhouse saloon. A pleasant adjoining deck by the creek is used in summer.

LODGING

There are only about a dozen motels in the area. Recommended accommodations include some nicely furnished lakefront rooms and a good selection of reasonably priced rooms near both downtown and the beach. Fall through spring prices are usually at least 10% less than the summer prices shown.

★ **Edgewater Lodge**   *downtown at 56 Bridge St.*   *263-3194*
Sandpoint's finest beachfront rooms are in a modern, full service motor hotel adjacent to the splendid beachfront park. In addition to shaded lawns and a private sandy beach for swimming and sunning, there is also a dock, whirlpool, and saunas. Each nicely furnished room has a phone, cable color TV with movies, and a patio or balcony overlooking the lake and mountains.

    #232,#220,#257,#259 — spacious, pitched roof, balc., fine lake view,   K bed...$58
    #242 — balcony, fine lake view,   K bed...$58
    #243 — patio, fine lake view,   K bed...$58
    regular room —   Q or K bed...$54

Hupp Motel   *downtown at 521 N. Third Av.*   *263-3532*
This **bargain** motel in a quiet location has large pleasant rooms.

    regular room —   D bed...$22

K-2 Motel   *.3 mi. NW at 501 N. Fourth Av.*   *263-3441*
This **bargain** motel has a whirlpool and sauna. Each small, well-furnished room has a phone and cable color TV with movies.

    regular room —   Q bed...$28

★ **Lakeside Motel**   *downtown at 106 Bridge St.*   *263-3717*
By the marina adjacent to downtown and the lake is a modern motel with boat docking facilities and some new lakeside rooms. Each well-furnished room has a phone and cable color TV with movies.

    #63,#60 — spacious, good marina view across pvt. balc.,   Q bed...$42
    #32 — spacious, pvt. patio, view of marina,   Q waterbed...$42
    #34 — nice marina view beyond pvt. patio,   Q bed...$42
    #38,#36,#58,#56 — sm. windows, no view,   K bed...$35
    regular room — small, no views,   Q or K bed...$35

Sandpoint Inn   *2 mi. S on US 95*   *263-4195*
Each of the modest rooms in this modern **bargain** motel has a phone and cable color TV.

    deluxe room —   K waterbed...$31
    regular room —   D bed...$23

S & W Motel   *2 mi. NE on ID 200*   *263-5979*
This small, single-level modular motel is a **bargain.** Each attractively furnished room has a cable color TV and a refrigerator.

    regular room —   Q bed...$22

CAMPGROUNDS

Several excellent campgrounds have pine-shaded lakefront sites near town. The best offer fine scenery and all kinds of water recreation.

Garfield Bay *15 mi. SE: 6 mi. S on US 95 & 9 mi. E on County Rd.* 263-5111
This little Idaho Panhandle National Forest campground is on a lush pine-forested hill above Lake Pend Oreille. The wonderfully tranquil site is connected by a forest path to a grassy picnic area adjacent to a long, pebbly beach. Nearby are a boat ramp and a boat rental concession. Sunbathing, swimming, fishing, boating, water-skiing and hiking are popular activities. The campground has pit toilets, but no showers or hookups. Each pine-shaded site has a picnic table and fire pit/grill. A separate tent area has five luxuriously spaced, quiet sites deep in the forest.   base rate...no fee

Round Lake St. Park *10 mi. SW: 8 mi.S on US 95 & 2 mi. W on Cty. Rd.* 263-3489
A heavily pine-forested slope above a little lake accommodates this popular state park campground. Attractions include a small beach for sunbathing, a boat ramp, swimming, boating (no motors), fishing and nature trails. In winter, cross-country skiing, ice-skating and tobogganing are popular. Flush toilets and hot showers are provided, but there are no hookups. Each pine-shaded site has a picnic table and grill.   base rate...$5

★ **Springy Point**   *4.5 mi. SW via Lakeshore Dr.*   437-3133
The Corps of Engineers has provided a campground in a lush pine forest on a gentle slope by Lake Pend Oreille. Activities include sunbathing on a sandy beach, swimming, fishing, boating and water-skiing on the lake. A dock and ramp are provided. Flush toilets and (fee) hot showers are available, but there are no hookups. Each of the pine-shaded sites has a picnic table and grill.   base rate...$5

SPECIAL EVENTS

Fourth of July Celebration   *City Beach & Memorial Field*   *July 4th Weekend*
The Lion's Club sponsors a full day of old-fashioned festivities, including a carnival, pie eating contests, sack races, lakeside picnics, a variety show, and a fireworks display.

The Festival at Sandpoint   *Memorial Field*   *early August*
A stadium by the shore of Lake Pend Oreille is the site of this recently inaugurated celebration of the arts.

OTHER INFORMATION

Area Code: *208*
Zip Code: *83864*
Sandpoint Chamber of Commerce   *.5 mi. N on US 95*   263-2161
Idaho Panhandle Natl. Forest-Sandpoint Ranger Sta. *1 mi. SW on US 2*   263-5111

Bigfork, Montana

Elevation:

2,980 feet

Population (1980):

1,080

Population (1970):

500

Location:

264 mi. S
of Calgary

Bigfork is one of the hidden pleasures of the northern Rockies. The tiny village is sequestered along a picturesque bay in a remote corner of a huge high country lake. A handsome pine forest that conceals the town also covers increasingly precipitous mountains extending in waves eastward to glacier-dotted peaks. To the south, gentle slopes along several miles of shoreline are covered with fruit orchards. This idyllic setting features four relatively mild seasons. Summer is the most desirable season, when water-oriented outdoor recreation including swimming, sailing, boating, water-skiing, and fishing can be comfortably enjoyed in town along with a wealth of urbane diversions in the fledgling art colony. Hiking, backpacking, rock climbing, and river running are among the popular diversions available in the adjacent mountains. Blossom-time and the fruit harvest are highlights of spring and fall in the orchard-dotted countryside. Annual winter snowfall is heavy. There are no major skiing complexes in the immediate vicinity, but one of the state's finest ski areas is less than an hour away by car.

Bigfork adjoins the mouth of the Swan River by a little bay on the northeastern shore of Flathead Lake, the largest natural freshwater body in the West. In spite of the natural grandeur of the site, the town grew very slowly until recently because of its remote location and the absence of easily exploited mineral or lumber resources. By the early 1970s, it was still only a tiny crossroad serving the needs of a few nearby farms and ranches, and increasing numbers of sportsmen. Improved highways, high-tech recreation equipment, and an accelerating interest in outdoor recreation in the latest decade finally initiated the long-overdue "discovery" of one of the West's great leisure sites.

In only a few years, the tiny main street has developed a picture postcard appeal, with an attractively landscaped lineup of contemporary Western-style buildings. Behind rustic facades, startlingly sophisticated art galleries display museum-quality arts and crafts, much of it made here. Locally produced gourmet foods made from native huckleberries and other fruits are produced and sold in shops downtown. Several excellent restaurants serve gourmet meals in appealing dining rooms. A well-regarded summer theater and a cluster of saloons with beguiling Old West decor provide diverse evening entertainment. Accommodations are scarce, but a landmark in downtown has been carefully refurbished, and the area's finest condominium resort hotel was recently completed. Both are within a stroll of the main street and lake.

Bigfork, Montana

WEATHER PROFILE   *Vokac Weather Rating*

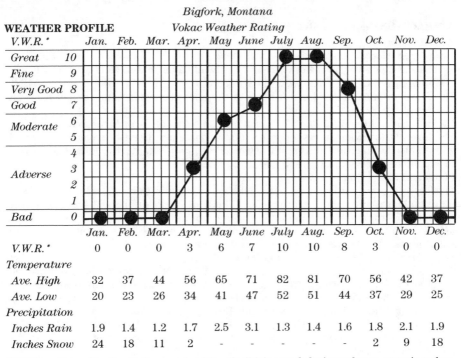

V.W.R.*	Jan.	Feb.	Mar.	Apr.	May	June	July	Aug.	Sep.	Oct.	Nov.	Dec.
V.W.R.*	0	0	0	3	6	7	10	10	8	3	0	0
Temperature												
Ave. High	32	37	44	56	65	71	82	81	70	56	42	37
Ave. Low	20	23	26	34	41	47	52	51	44	37	29	25
Precipitation												
Inches Rain	1.9	1.4	1.2	1.7	2.5	3.1	1.3	1.4	1.6	1.8	2.1	1.9
Inches Snow	24	18	11	2	-	-	-	-	-	2	9	18

V.W.R. = Vokac Weather Rating: probability of mild (warm & dry) weather on any given day.

Forecast

Month	V.W.R.*		Temperatures Daytime	Evening	Precipitation
January	0	Bad	cold	cold	frequent snowstorms
February	0	Bad	chilly	cold	occasional snowstorms
March	0	Bad	chilly	chilly	occasional snow flurries
April	3	Adverse	cool	chilly	occasional showers/snow flurries
May	6	Moderate	warm	cool	frequent rainstorms
June	7	Good	warm	cool	frequent rainstorms
July	10	Great	warm	warm	infrequent showers
August	10	Great	warm	warm	infrequent showers
September	8	Very Good	warm	cool	occasional showers
October	3	Adverse	cool	chilly	occasional rainstorms/snow flurries
November	0	Bad	chilly	chilly	occasional rainstorms/snow flurries
December	0	Bad	chilly	cold	frequent snow flurries

Summary

Bigfork is in a picturesque pine-shaded location on a tiny arm of Flathead Lake near Glacier National Park. Weather here is favorably influenced by the sheltering effect of the northern Rocky Mountains and the moderating influence of the West's largest freshwater lake. There are cold days in the middle of **winter**, but the town avoids most of the extremely cold nights common to Montana. There are enough snowfalls to assure fine conditions at a major ski area within easy driving distance. **Spring** is heralded by rapidly increasing temperatures and millions of blossoms in the orchards a few miles down-lake. Warm days are normal by May, as are frequent rainstorms that continue through June. **Summer** is outstanding. Warm days and evenings prevail, and there are only infrequent rainfalls. This is prime time for a remarkable range of water-and-mountain-oriented outdoor recreation. Temperatures plummet soon after **fall** begins. Brisk, damp days and more frequent snowfalls usually signal the return of wintry weather in November.

ATTRACTIONS & DIVERSIONS

★ **Boat Rentals**

Husky Station   *downtown at 437 Electric Av.*   *837-5146*

Sailboating is popular on Bigfork Bay and Flathead Lake. Rentals can be arranged here.

Woods Bay Marina   *5.5 mi. S via MT 35*   *837-4226*

This marina rents outboard motor boats by the hour or day for fishing and cruising on Flathead Lake.

Everit L. Sliter Memorial Park   *downtown on S side of Swan River Bridge*

This lovely little park features a playground and large new bandshell, picnic tables and grills shaded by huge pine and broadleaf trees. Precipitous steps up the adjacent dam lead to a great view of Bigfork Bay and Flathead Lake.

★ **Flathead Lake**   *adjacent to town on the west*

The largest freshwater lake west of the Mississippi is about thirty miles long and fifteen miles wide. During summer, numerous lakefront parks offer most kinds of water recreation. Summer silver salmon fishing is renowned. A scenic paved loop drive of approximately ninety miles provides panoramic views and access to numerous day use picnic areas, hiking trails, small villages, and orchards.

★ **Flathead National Forest**   *around town*   *837-5081*

The magnificent Bob Marshall, Great Bear and Mission Mountains Wildernesses are the major attractions in this huge preserve. Among the nation's largest and most spectacular, these areas offer more than a thousand miles of trails to hikers and backpackers during the summer. The Flathead Wild and Scenic River system is a major destination for river runners, and the Jewell Basin Hiking Area is another unusual attraction. In winter, cross-country skiing, snowmobiling, and ice fishing are popular, and Big Mountain is one of the state's major ski areas.

The Gatiss Gardens   *3 mi. N via MT 35 at jct. with MT 82*

Several acres of immaculately well-tended flower gardens, lawns, and streams are open to the public for strolling and picnicking. A series of pathways and identification signs are provided.

★ **Glacier National Park**   *38 mi. N via MT 35 & US 2*   *888-5441*

More than a million acres of the splendid northern Rocky Mountains are preserved much as they were long before man first saw them. Shimmering glaciers and emerald green lakes, cascading waterfalls, fields of wildflowers, dense forests and abundant wildlife are all part of the spectacle. The Going-to-the-Sun Highway is an unforgettable fifty mile drive over the Continental Divide. Roads, trails, and accommodations ranging from campgrounds to historic landmark lodges are usually open from June into September, depending on snow conditions.

★ **Jewell Basin Hiking Area**   *10 mi. NE via MT 35; MT 83 & Echo Lake Rd.*

A pristine little section of Rocky Mountain high country has been specially designated as a backcountry hiking area. Thirty-five miles of trails connect dozens of picturesque high mountain lakes accessible only to energetic walkers.

Orchards   *start 4 mi. S on MT 35*

For several miles, gentle slopes above the eastern shore of Flathead Lake are covered with cherry trees and other kinds of orchards. Roadside stands display and sell the harvest in summer.

★ **River Running**

Glacier Raft Company   *38 mi. N via MT 35 & US 2 - West Glacier*   *888-5541*

Half day and full day trips, plus overnight and multi-day excursions, are offered on the scenic North and Middle Forks of the Flathead River bordering Glacier National Park.

Village Square   *downtown on Electric Av.*   *837-6927*

A big, old wooden building in the heart of town has been converted into a small museum of Western memorabilia, an information center, and a gallery of local arts and crafts.

★ **Wayfarer State Recreation Area**   *1 mi. SW just W of MT 35*   *837-4196*

A dock, boat ramp, picnic and camping facilities have been added to a pine forest on the shore of Flathead Lake. Boating, swimming, fishing, and water-skiing are popular diversions.

SHOPPING

Bigfork has long been a source of basic supplies for guides and ranchers in the area. In recent years, the tiny downtown area has also blossomed into a first-rate center for the visual and culinary arts.

Food Specialties

★ **The Bread Board**   *downtown at 451 Electric Av.*   837-6644

Tucked inside a building off the main street is a woodsy little carryout bakery that has a real knack for turning whole wheat, cracked wheat, and sprouted wheat into a delicious assortment of breads, sweet rolls, bagels, pastries, and unusual specialties like huckleberry whole wheat Danish. A few tables are outside on a flower-strewn deck.

★ **Eva Gates Homemade Preserves**   *downtown on Electric Av.*   837-4356

Splendid homemade wild huckleberry and other preserves and syrups are displayed and sold in individual jars or gift packs. Visitors can watch the preserves being made. Samples are provided.

Judy B's Candy Shack   *1 mi. N on MT 35*   837-5349

Huckleberry candies, and regionally-made ice cream served in fresh Danish cones, are featured in this cheerful little shop.

★ **Rena's Kitchen**   *downtown on Bridge St.*   837-5700

Delectable huckleberry preserves lead a list of excellent fruit jellies, jams, and syrups made and sold in this little shop.

Specialty Shops

Bay House Books & Prints   *downtown at Grand St./Electric Av.*   837-4646

This small shop has a good selection of books of regional interest plus many historical volumes and prints.

★ **Flathead Lake Galleries**   *downtown on Electric Av.*   837-6633

A large collection of Western fine art by contemporary masters is balanced by an exhibit of quality pottery in another room. The stuffed Montana timberwolf near the door also contributes to the memorable Western atmosphere in this intriguing wood-finished gallery.

★ **Kootenai Galleries**   *downtown on Electric Av.*   837-4848

One of the West's most outstanding collections of Western paintings and sculpture is housed in a superlative two-story gallery. The beautiful complex also has a charming back patio/fountain area, plus a select array of gourmet foods.

The Osprey   *.5 mi. SW on MT 35*   837-6223

This art gallery/gift shop specializes in unusual minatures in wood, pewter and other materials.

★ **Seastar Gallery**   *downtown at 548 Electric Av.*   837-4254

A splendid collection of paintings and pottery is showcased in an artistically restored old shop that now includes a coffee/wine bar where several specials are served with pastries and beverages all day.

★ **The Weaver's Nest Art Gallery**   *10 mi. W on US 93 - Somers*   857-3318

Weaving is done on the premises. Shawls, sweaters and other hand-woven, knitted, and spun products, plus limited-edition prints and sculptures, are displayed in an attractive gallery setting. Closed Sun.

NIGHTLIFE

A remarkable quantity and diversity of live entertainment is packed into the robust little heart of town.

★ **Bigfork Inn Lounge**   *downtown at Grand/Electric Avs.*   837-6680

Live music and dancing are featured most weekends in a handsome old hunting lodge-style inn with an airy, rough-pine-log interior.

★ **Bigfork Summer Playhouse**   *downtown on Electric Av.*   837-4886

Broadway musicals are performed every night from late June to early September in a well-regarded little theater. Closed Sun.

Garden Bar   *downtown on Electric Av.*   837-4514

Tucked away by a garden off the main street is a tiny, contemporary wood/plant bar. An impressive assortment of beers and premium wines by the glass are available, and a good new deli adjoins.

★ **Mountain Lake Tavern**   *downtown on Electric Av.*   *837-6750*
Live music and dancing happen on weekends through summer, and there is a pool table.
But, the classic all-wood, split-level saloon is the star. A balcony drinking area, double-oil-barrel "object of art" fireplace/heater, high-tech juke box, and artistic barnwood mural etching bring it all together.

★ **Sam's Place (Buffalo Cafe)**   *downtown on Electric Av.*   *837-4585*
This old-time saloon features dancing and live music on weekends. Rustic pine-log decor includes a flagstone fireplace and a great iron stove.

The Water Works   *downtown just E of Electric Av.*   *837-5601*
Live entertainment is usually available on weekends in this popular little bar/pizza parlor with funky-woodsy decor. A separate room has a pool table.

RESTAURANTS

First-timers may wonder how a town this small can have such a diversity of notable dining places. Unfortunately, some of the best are only open in summer.

★ **Bigfork Inn**   *downtown at Grand Av./Electric Av.*   *837-6680*
D only.   *Moderate*
International gourmet specialties are prepared with seasonally fresh ingredients. The dining room in this small landmark hotel has been given a refined Western flair by tables set with colorful native wildflowers in a room well-outfitted with quality local art.

Buffalo Cafe   *downtown on Electric Av.*   *837-4639*
B-L. D on weekends only.   *Moderate*
Hearty American dishes and some Mexican specialties are offered in a rustic Old Western cafe in Sam's Place saloon.

★ **The Cellar**   *downtown at 548 Electric Av.*   *837-4254*
D only. Closed Sun.   *Moderate*
Gourmet meals are presented in an artistically furnished little dining room behind the Seastar Gallery.

Marina Cay Restaurant   *.3 mi. W on Bigfork Loop*   *837-5861*
L-D.   *Moderate*
Contemporary American dishes are featured in the resort's new poolside dining room.

★ **Red School House** *13 mi. W via MT 82 & US 93 - just N of Lakeside*   *844-3325*
L-D. No D on Sat. & Sun.   *Low*
A single entree is highlighted each evening and given abundant support from other carefully prepared dishes in a cheerfully decorated old red schoolhouse overlooking Flathead Lake.

The Sitting Duck   *5 mi. S on MT 35 - Woods Bay*   *837-5331*
L-D.   *Moderate*
Continental and American dishes are served in a beautiful new restaurant by Flathead Lake. The stylish oak-trimmed dining room has a huge fireplace and picture window views, plus a lakeside deck for alfresco dining.

★ **Stagecoach Restaurant and Saloon**   *11 mi. W at 25 Somers Rd. - Somers*   *857-3883*
D only.   *Moderate*
Gourmet American dining includes some classic Western delicacies like rattlesnake appetizers, brace of quail, pheasant, Flathead duck, buffalo steaks, and huckleberry cheesecake. Comfortably furnished dining rooms in a turn-of-the-century roadhouse complement the food. Next door, the saloon has an iron fireplace and a memorable artistic impression of three Indian nudes over the bar, plus occasional live entertainment and a stainless steel dance floor.

LODGING

Accommodations, like the town's other attributes, are distinctive and reasonably priced. Several of the best places are on the shore of Flathead Lake. Most are closed from late fall through spring. Rates are usually reduced by 20% or more apart from summer.

Bigfork Inn   *downtown at Grand/Electric Avs.*   *837-6680*
The town's landmark exudes an old hunting-lodge kind of charm in the heart of town. Above an excellent restaurant and lounge are a few simply furnished **bargain** guest rooms.

     regular room — private bath,   D bed...$25
     regular room — shared bath,   D bed...$22

★ **Flathead Lake Lodge**   *1 mi. S via MT 35*   *837-4391*
This long-established luxurious dude ranch occupies beautifully landscaped grounds
along the shore of Flathead Lake. Guests are pampered with an astonishing diversity of
leisure conveniences for one inclusive cost. A large outdoor heated pool, whirlpool,
saunas, tennis courts, rifle range, private beach, marina with all kinds of boating,
recreation room, and horseback riding are some of the features. All of the well-appointed
units are rented for a minimum stay of one week. The price below is with a full American
plan (three meals daily) per couple per week.

    regular room — in lodge, some have lake view,   Q bed...$1288

Holiday Motel   *13 mi. S on MT 35*   *982-3482*
A modern motel perched by the shore of Flathead Lake has a small marina with rental
boats for guests, plus a private dock, lawn and a swimming area. Each spacious unit has
a B/W TV and a large private lakeview deck.

    #16 — on water,   2 D beds...$39
    #14 — on water,   D bed...$39
    apartment — studio, full kitchen, on water,   D bed...$55
    regular room —   D bed...$39

Leivo's Lake Lodge   *downtown on Grand Av.*   *837-4656*
This small **bargain** motel over a cafe has several rooms with cable color TV.

    #2,#1 — fine Bigfork Bay views, window on front & side,   2 Q beds...$28
    regular room —   Q bed...$28

Levengood's Motel   *10 mi. W on US 93 - just N of Somers*   *857-3468*
A long indoor lap pool, an outdoor pool, two whirlpools, a sauna, a big restaurant with a
mountain view, and a lounge are attractions in this newer **bargain** motel. Each of the
small rooms has a phone and cable color TV with movies.

    regular room —   Q bed...$27

★ **Marina Cay Resort Motel**   *.3 mi. W on Bigfork Loop at 180 Vista Lane*   *837-5861*
An outstanding condominium resort was recently built adjacent to Bigfork Bay. Facilities
include a long outdoor pool, whirlpool, sauna, marina (with boats for rent), and a private
lawn/beach area on a sheltered bay of Flathead Lake. Each of the spacious new units is
beautifully decorated in plush contemporary furnishings. The rooms are distinguished by
pitched roofs, skylights, private balconies, floor-to-ceiling windows and numerous
refinements like grass-cloth wallpaper. Each unit has a phone and cable color TV.

    "studio on 3rd fl." — kitchen, raised gas fireplace, large pvt. balcony,
                bay/town view,   Q bed...$98
    "studio loft on 3rd fl." — as above, but loft BR with skylights,
                Flathead lake view,   Q bed...$98
    regular room —   Q bed...$44

Our Point of View Motel   *7 mi. S on MT 35*   *837-4742*
This rustic, older **bargain** cabin/motel complex occupies a ridge overlooking Flathead
Lake. There is a lawn area, and a marina at the base of the ridge with motor boat rentals
for guests. Each unit has a kitchenette and B/W TV.

    regular room —   D or Q bed...$25

Sunset Resort   *.6 mi. W via road on S side of Bigfork Bay*   *837-4532*
This older cabin/motel complex is on landscaped grounds adjacent to Flathead Lake.
There is a lake swimming area, grass areas for sunbathing, and a boat launch. Each simply
furnished unit has a kitchenette.

    regular room —   D bed...$32

Timbers Motel   *.5 mi. S on MT 35*   *837-6200*
An outdoor pool with mountain views, a whirlpool, and saunas are features of this
modern motel. Each nicely furnished unit has a phone and color TV.

    regular room —   Q or K bed...$38

Windjammer   *5 mi. S on MT 35 - Woods Bay*   *837-4414*
The old single-level motor court is frayed around the edges, but it is a **bargain,** and it is
across the road from Flathead Lake. Docking facilities, a restaurant and lounge are down
by the lake.

    regular room —   D bed...$24

CAMPGROUNDS

Surprisingly few campgrounds are nearby. The best is a scenic, primitive facility near the lake only a mile from town.

Wayfarer State Recreation Area *1 mi. SW of MT 35 on County Rd.*   *837-4196*
This small, state operated campground is on a pine-forested slope above Flathead Lake. Features include a boat ramp and dock, and a shady lakeside picnic area. Boating, swimming, fishing and water-skiing are popular on the lake. Flush toilets are available, but there are no showers or hookups. Each of the shady sites has a picnic table and a raised turret-style fireplace/grill.   base rate...$3

SPECIAL EVENT

★ **Whitewater Festival** *downtown and on the Swan River*   *3rd Weekend in May*
Kayakers from all over the country compete on Bigfork's challenging "Mile of Whitewater." Festivities also include an outdoor barbecue, games, and an exhibition of whitewater boats and equipment and boating skills.

OTHER INFORMATION

Area Code: *406*
Zip Code: *59911*
Bigfork Area Chamber of Commerce   *downtown on Electric Av.*   *837-4883*
Flathead National Forest-Bigfork Ranger Station *.5 mi. W on MT 35*   *837-5081*

Red Lodge, Montana

Elevation:

5,553 feet

Population (1980):

1,896

Population (1970):

1,844

Location:

480 mi. NE
of Salt Lake City

Red Lodge is an authentic Old West gateway to the heart of the Rocky Mountains. Colorful Victorian buildings still fill the pretty little valley, as they did a century ago. Just to the west, the sagebrush-covered rangeland that surrounds town hasn't changed much either. It still ends abruptly at the base of an awesome escarpment. Capped by the state's highest peak, the Beartooth Mountains shelter a seemingly endless number of lakes, streams, and waterfalls that share a vast wilderness with forests, tundras, and glaciers. A major skiing complex has developed close to town where snow sports of all kinds are now popular during long, cold winters. There is even a winter carnival to highlight the season. Summer is still the busiest time of year. Warm, sunny days accompany unlimited recreation opportunities in the magnificent surroundings and the town's two biggest annual celebrations — a major rodeo and a festival-of-nations.

Almost a century ago, the nation's first transcontinental railroad was completed through the northern Rockies. At about the same time, just to the south of the main line, coal was discovered at what is now Red Lodge. Mines proliferated to fuel locomotives that were opening the frontier, and agriculture flourished to support immigrants who came from all over Europe to work in the mines. It was an era of prosperity, and substantial businesses and homes were constructed. By the 1920s, however, the mines began to close. The Depression might have been a final blow, except that the Beartooth Highway was constructed during that time. This scenic masterpiece linked Red Lodge with Yellowstone National Park, and paved the way to the era of tourism. The town finally became a year-round travelers' destination after the Red Lodge Mountain ski area opened in 1960.

Today, the mines are all gone and the large creek is clean again as it flows past the town park. A legacy of Victorian structures endures downtown. A few now house galleries and specialty shops featuring local arts and crafts. Restaurants are numerous. Several are surprisingly good. The town's heritage of hard-working, hard-drinking European and American miners is remarkably well preserved on the main street, which sports one of the West's most outstanding concentrations of bars. Unpretentious saloons and dance halls almost a century old continue to echo with the sounds of Western music, and legal poker games regularly convene in the back rooms. Cowboys now blend with skiers as smoothly as the unspoiled historic buildings do with modest new motels and resort facilities that have been added to accommodate increasing numbers of visitors year-round.

Red Lodge, Montana

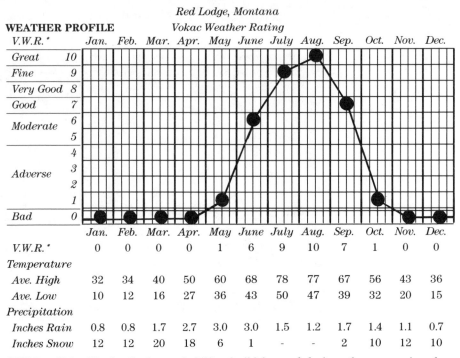

V.W.R.*	Jan.	Feb.	Mar.	Apr.	May	June	July	Aug.	Sep.	Oct.	Nov.	Dec.
Great 10												
Fine 9												
Very Good 8												
Good 7												
Moderate 6 / 5												
Adverse 4 / 3 / 2 / 1												
Bad 0												

	Jan.	Feb.	Mar.	Apr.	May	June	July	Aug.	Sep.	Oct.	Nov.	Dec.
V.W.R.*	0	0	0	0	1	6	9	10	7	1	0	0
Temperature												
Ave. High	32	34	40	50	60	68	78	77	67	56	43	36
Ave. Low	10	12	16	27	36	43	50	47	39	32	20	15
Precipitation												
Inches Rain	0.8	0.8	1.7	2.7	3.0	3.0	1.5	1.2	1.7	1.4	1.1	0.7
Inches Snow	12	12	20	18	6	1	-	-	2	10	12	10

V.W.R. = Vokac Weather Rating: probability of mild (warm & dry) weather on any given day.

Forecast

Temperatures

Month	V.W.R.*		Daytime	Evening	Precipitation
January	0	Bad	cold	frigid	infrequent snowstorms
February	0	Bad	chilly	frigid	infrequent snowstorms
March	0	Bad	chilly	cold	occasional snowstorms
April	0	Bad	cool	chilly	occasional snowstorms
May	1	Adverse	cool	chilly	frequent rainstorms/snow flurries
June	6	Moderate	warm	cool	frequent rainstorms
July	9	Fine	warm	cool	occasional showers
August	10	Great	warm	cool	infrequent showers
September	7	Good	warm	cool	occasional showers/snow flurries
October	1	Adverse	cool	chilly	infrequent showers/snow flurries
November	0	Bad	chilly	cold	infrequent snowstorms
December	0	Bad	chilly	cold	infrequent snowstorms

Summary

Near Yellowstone National Park, Red Lodge lies along a large creek cut into expansive sagebrush-covered rangelands far below the awesome Beartooth Plateau. **Winter** days are short and chilly, and evenings are often very cold. Still, properly dressed residents and visitors spend a lot of time outdoors in this season, enjoying the town's major nearby ski area made possible by infrequent but heavy snowfalls that begin in October and continue into May. **Spring** is cool, and the wettest time of year. Snow flurries and frequent rainstorms continue into June. All of the best weather is concentrated into **summer**. Warm days, cool evenings, and occasional showers are excellent for comfortably enjoying all outdoor activities. Shortly after **fall** begins, cool days, freezing nighttime temperatures, and unpredictable, heavy snowfalls usually foreshadow winter while it is still officially more than two months away.

ATTRACTIONS & DIVERSIONS

★ **Absaroka-Beartooth Wilderness** *13 mi. W via US 212 & Lake Fork Rd.* *446-2103*
The wilderness portion of Montana's Custer National Forest starts a few miles from town and extends almost to Yellowstone National Park. It is a ruggedly beautiful series of glacier-covered plateaus and jagged peaks that includes Granite Peak (12,799 feet), the highest point in the state. Hundreds of crystal clear lakes, shimmering glaciers, cascades and waterfalls, deep valleys, and dark forests appeal to hikers, backpackers, horseback riders, campers, hunters, and fishermen.

★ **Beartooth Highway** *US 212 for 70 mi. to Yellowstone Park*
"The most scenic drive in America," according to Charles Kuralt, among others, is a paved two-lane roadway that connects Red Lodge with Yellowstone National Park in sixty-nine breathtaking miles. Via a series of awesome switchbacks on a sheer canyon wall, travelers surmount the 11,000 foot Beartooth Plateau. For the next several miles the highway winds past snowfields, dozens of tiny lakes, and fields of flowers high above timberline. Further along, the roadway descends back into a dense pine forest rich with waterfalls, streams, and glimpses of jagged peaks. Picnic areas, campgrounds, trailheads, and fishing accesses are plentiful. The road is usually open from late May to mid-October.

City Park *.5 mi. S via Broadway & 19th St. bridge*
Shady picnic sites along Rock Creek attract visitors to this rustic little town park.

★ **Grasshopper Glacier** *70 mi. W via US 212 - N of Cooke City* *446-2103*
Millions of grasshoppers are embedded in the ice of a mile-long glacier high in the Beartooth Mountains. Hikers can reach it by taking a jeep road just east of Cooke City north from US 212 for about eight miles to the upper end of Goose Lake. A scenic trail extends the remaining two miles to the glacier. The rocky road is closed with snow most of the year. Check at the Red Lodge Ranger Station in July or August regarding conditions.

Historic District *downtown*
A self-guided walking tour of the town's historic district has been prepared by the Carbon County Historical Society. A brochure and map are available from the Chamber of Commerce.

Horseback Riding
 Paint Brush Trails *4.5 mi. S on US 212* *446-2376*
Horses can be rented here for hourly and longer rides into the Custer National Forest.

Winter Sports
★ **Red Lodge Mountain** *6 mi. W via US 212 & Forest Rd.* *446-2610*
The vertical rise is 2,016 feet and the longest run is over two miles. Elevation at the top is 9,400 feet. There are four chairlifts. All facilities, services and rentals are available at the base for downhill skiing, and there are cross-country trails. A cafeteria and bar are at the mountain, but all lodging is in town. The skiing season is mid-November to Easter.

★ **Yellowstone National Park** *69 mi. SW on US 212* *(307)344-7311*
America's oldest and largest national park attracts visitors from all over the world. Its predictable and erratic geysers, strange bubbling mud pots, beautiful hot springs terraces and geothermal pools, and thundering waterfalls are unforgettable. So are the snow-capped peaks, dense pine forests, and crystal clear rivers and lakes. This huge expanse of incomparable high country is also the home of a remarkable number and variety of wild animals. For those who want to get away from the inevitable crowds on the park's famed loop highway, a genuine wilderness adventure awaits just beyond the road in any direction. The park is open from early May to the end of October, weather permitting.

SHOPPING
Downtown is centered along a photogenic main street that still has most of the substantial brick buildings from the coal mining boom era before the turn of the century. The true-Western appearance is unmarred by parking meters or stop lights. Galleries and specialty shops are beginning to complement Western ware, sporting goods, and other stores that have served residents for decades.

Food Specialties

City Bakery *downtown at 104 S. Broadway* *446-2100*
The breads are good in a full-line conventional bakery with a few specialties like huge sticky buns. Closed Tues.

Harvest Haus   *downtown at 5 W. 11th*   *446-1907*
Several ice cream flavors from the local Carbon County Creamery are available in fountain treats served here or to go.

Specialty Shops
Carbon County Arts Guild   *downtown at Broadway/8th*   *446-1370*
The old railroad station has been converted into a showcase for local arts and crafts.

NIGHTLIFE
A reputation as an unspoiled, wild Western town is one of Red Lodge's most enduring attributes. The remarkable concentration of Victorian-era saloons and uninhibited drinking places that line the main street come alive with Western music, dancing, and legal gambling each evening as they have for nearly a century.

★ **Bogart's**   *downtown at 11 S. Broadway*   *446-9929*
A fine old back bar, mounted game animal trophies, comfortable booths, and padded bar chairs contribute to the popularity of this Western-style bar and restaurant. Several beers are on tap, and the pizza is the best in the area.

Bull n' Bear   *downtown at 17 N. Broadway*   *446-3468*
Live entertainment is offered most nights in this shaped-up Old Western bar.

★ **Pius & Karin's Place**   *downtown at 115 S. Broadway*   *446-1013*
High-tech recently arrived in Red Lodge in the form of a striking two-level lounge. Patrons can dance to live music, enjoy the quality of the sound-and-lights system, and relax in cushioned/chrome chairs.

★ **The Snag**   *downtown at 107 S. Broadway*   *446-9966*
Legal gambling and a pool table are among the attractions in this authentic Western saloon. The stamped tin ceiling and walls, a working pot-bellied iron stove, and a splendid corner hardwood back bar lend to the atmosphere.

★ **Snow Creek Saloon**   *downtown at 124 S. Broadway*   *446-2396*
A band plays most nights from a loft above a dance floor. In addition to an outsized mural in the back room, the large funky saloon has two bars and a Franklin stove.

Stoney's   *downtown at 2 S. Broadway*   *446-1105*
A pool table, darts and occasional live entertainment, plus two Franklin stoves, are features in a bar that is a local favorite.

RESTAURANTS
Restaurants are relatively scarce, reasonably priced, and surprisingly diverse both in food styles and atmosphere.

Natali's   *downtown at 115 S. Broadway*   *446-1013*
B-L-D.   *Moderate*
Homemade breakfast rolls and pies are baked fresh daily in this plain, popular restaurant. One of the world's largest Jim Beam bottle collections is on display in the next room.

Old Piney Dell   *4.5 mi. S on US 212*   *446-1196*
D only. B on Sat. & Sun. Closed Wed.   *Moderate*
Good food and a salad bar are enhanced by homemade baked goods. The pleasant dining room offers an intimate view of Rock Creek.

P.D. McKinney's Family Dining   *.3 mi. S at 407 S. Broadway*   *446-2523*
B-L-D.   *Low*
Large homemade cinnamon rolls are featured with hearty American fare in a plain and popular little cafe.

★ **Pius' International Room**   *downtown at 115 S. Broadway*   *446-1013*
D only.   *Moderate*
Continental gourmet dining is offered in a room that combines Old World comfort with a matchless collection of Jim Beam bottles artistically showcased in backlit trophy cabinets.

Red Lodge Cafe   *downtown at 16 S. Broadway*   *446-9977*
B-L-D.   *Moderate*
Buffalo is the highlight, when it is available, on an American menu. Homemade pastries and a salad bar accompany meals in an uncompromisingly old-fashioned, Western-style cafe that has been a family favorite for many years.

Round Barn Restaurant   *2 mi. N on US 212*   *446-1197*
D only. L-D on Sun. Closed Tues.   *Low*
An international entree is featured on the smorgasbord each night, along with homemade baked goods and an extensive salad bar. Waiters in Scandinavian costumes serve in an unusual dining room fashioned from a large, round, red brick barn.

Sundance Supper Club   *4 mi. S on US 212*   *446-1147*
D only.   *Moderate*
American dishes are accompanied by picture window views of the mountains in a large Western-style supper club.

★ **Sylvia's**   *1 mi. S at 1307 S. Broadway*   *446-2810*
L-D. No D on Sun. Closed Mon.   *Moderate*
Carefully prepared homestyle meals are served amidst comfortable Western decor in a rustic old cabin.

LODGING

There aren't many places to stay in or near Red Lodge. But the best accommodations offer a surprising array of amenities for a reasonable price. Winter rates are comparable to those of summer, while rates are usually reduced 20% or more in spring and fall.

Alpine Village   *.5 mi. N on US 212*   *446-2213*
This small **bargain** motel has a whirlpool and sauna. Large, older rooms were recently redecorated, and there are some new rooms. All have cable color TV.

#7 — older section,	K bed...$24
regular room — new section,	2 Q beds...$28
regular room — older section,	D bed...$24

Chateau Rouge   *1 mi. S on US 212*   *446-1601*
Each modern chalet-style unit has a phone, cable color TV, a complete kitchen, and a brick wood-burning fireplace.

#2B1 thru #2B14 — 2 level, fireplace in LR, some pvt. view,	K bed...$45
regular room —	Q bed...$36

Eagles Nest Motel   *.3 mi. S at 702 S. Broadway*   *446-2312*
This small older motel by Rock Creek is a nicely refurbished **bargain**. Each of the rooms has cable color TV and a refrigerator.

#11 — windows on 3 sides, some creek view,	D bed...$27
regular room —	D bed...$27

Lu Pine Inn - Best Western   *.4 mi. S at 702 S. Hauser*   *446-1321*
Red Lodge's only indoor pool, plus a whirlpool and game room are featured in this modern motel. Each well-furnished room has a phone and cable color TV.

regular room —	D bed...$39

Pollard Motor Hotel   *downtown at 2 N. Broadway*   *446-2860*
Red Lodge's turn-of-the-century, three-story landmark hotel has some **bargain** rooms. It was recently restored and now includes a whirlpool, sauna, and (for a fee) racquetball. Each of the refurbished rooms has a phone and a tub and shower.

deluxe room — cable color TV,	D bed...$31
regular room —	D bed...$28

★ **Rock Creek Mine Grizzly Condos**   *5 mi. S on US 212*   *446-1111*
Overlooking Rock Creek, the Grizzly Condos offer fishing, tennis, and volleyball in an attractively landscaped setting. A good restaurant adjoins. Each of the spacious units is well-furnished. Pitched beam ceilings and cheerful contemporary decor — bright reds and yellows — are used extensively.

#K2 & #K — pvt. balc. on river, spiral staircase, kitchen, metal fireplace, tall river-view windows,	K bed...$90
#L1&#L, #M2&#M, #N1&#N — all like #K2 & #K above,	K bed...$90
#F "Honeymoon Suite" — on river, kitchen, fireplace in LR,	Q bed...$65
#C&#C2 — kitchen, fireplace, sliding glass doors to deck, full river view,	K bed...$90
regular room — some have river view,	K bed...$38

Skyview Motel   *.5 mi. S at 811 S. Broadway*   *446-1510*
This small **bargain** motel is across the highway from the creek. Each room has a phone and cable color TV.
    regular room —   Q bed...$27
Valli Hi Motor Lodge   *.3 mi. S at 320 S. Broadway*   *446-1414*
Each room in this little **bargain** motel has a phone and cable color TV. Upstairs rooms have some mountain views.
    regular room —   Q bed...$27
Yodeler Motel   *.4 mi. S at 601 S. Broadway*   *446-1435*
Each of the rooms in this nicely furnished motel has a phone and cable color TV with movies.
    #8 — on lower fl., steambath,   Q bed...$32
    regular room — some have a steambath,   D bed...$32

CAMPGROUNDS

Several small, primitive campgrounds are scattered along clear streams in the magnificent canyons west of town. Complete facilities are available in a more prosaic campground a few miles north of town.

KOA - Red Lodge   *5 mi. N on US 212*   *446-2364*
This privately owned campground is in a rural setting beside two tiny streams. There is fishing in nearby Rock Creek, a recreation room, and a large outdoor pool. Flush toilets, hot showers, and hookups are available. Each of the sites has a picnic table and a fire area. Several sites are tree-shaded by the streams, and have a mountain view. A separate tenting area is provided.   base rate...$8.50

Parkside   *12 mi. SW: 11.5 mi. SW on US 212 & .5 mi. W on Forest Rd. 421*   *446-2103*
This tiny Custer National Forest campground is located near Rock Creek in an awesome canyon cut deep into the towering Beartooth Plateau. Attractions include stream fishing and marked nature trails. There are pit toilets only — no showers or hookups. Each of the well-spaced camp sites has a picnic table, fire area and grill.   base rate...$2

SPECIAL EVENTS

Winter Carnival   *in and around town*   *March*
Snowmobile races, a dog-pull contest, snow sculpturing, and a "torchlight" parade on skis are some of the events in this popular celebration of winter.

★ **Home of Champions Rodeo**   *downtown & rodeo grounds*   *around July 4th*
Many of the top cowboys on the rodeo circuit compete in a three-day event that also features daily parades.

Festival of Nations   *downtown*   *early August*
The European heritage of the early miners is celebrated in nine days of entertainment, foods, arts, and crafts reflecting various national cultures.

OTHER INFORMATION

Area Code: *406*
Zip Code: *59068*
Red Lodge Chamber of Commerce   *downtown at Broadway/8th*   *446-1718*
Custer National Forest-Red Lodge Ranger Station *1 mi. S on US 212*   *446-2103*

Whitefish, Montana

Elevation:

3,033 feet

Population (1980):

3,703

Population (1970):

3,349

Location:

251 mi. S
of Calgary

Whitefish is an uninhibited Western village in a classic northern Rocky Mountain setting. It occupies a luxuriant pine forest along the shore of a photogenic seven-mile-long lake rimmed by sylvan mountains. Nearby to the east are the ragged peaks of Glacier National Park. A four season climate assures good conditions for a wide range of recreation opportunities. The main street frames a spectacular view to the north of the carefully groomed slopes of Big Mountain, the state's largest skiing complex. All snow sports are popular, and the Winter Carnival is a major annual event. The most enjoyable weather occurs in summer, when both Whitefish Lake and the mountains attract visitors. Lakeside parks in town provide sandy beaches, swimming areas, scenic picnic sites, boat launching ramps, and fishing piers. Nearby, a public campground offers tree-shaded sites near the lake. The Whitefish River flows out of the lake and meanders through town toward giant Flathead Lake, thirty miles to the south. Canoeing and floating are favorite pastimes on the gentle little river. Golf is enjoyed on a large scenic lakeview course in town. Hiking, backpacking, horseback riding, rock climbing, fishing, boating, and river running are other popular summer activities in the area. Hunting is the favorite sport in the high country in fall.

Whitefish evolved slowly because of its remote location far from major cities. The town began to prosper after the arrival of the transcontinental railroad, as both a switchyard and logging center. Construction of the state's largest ski area within sight of downtown on Big Mountain finally established Whitefish as a year-round visitors' destination. In recent years, recreation and leisure-time pursuits have become the mainstays of the local economy.

Today, the enormous railroad switchyard downtown remains a jarring counterpoint to the beauty and tranquility of the surroundings. The town does benefit from being an Amtrak stop, however. Downtown is a handsome assortment of rustic wood-trimmed buildings where most of the area's businesses are still located. It includes an outstanding cluster of saloons featuring drinking, dancing, and legal gambling, plus some atmospheric restaurants that also typify the friendly, unpretentious spirit of Whitefish. Lodging is not plentiful. But, in recent years, attractive modern accommodations have been built overlooking the lake, on the lakefront, and at the base of the ski area.

WEATHER PROFILE *Vokac Weather Rating*

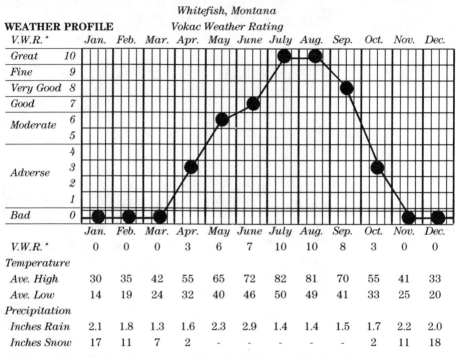

V.W.R.*	Jan.	Feb.	Mar.	Apr.	May	June	July	Aug.	Sep.	Oct.	Nov.	Dec.
V.W.R.*	0	0	0	3	6	7	10	10	8	3	0	0
Temperature												
Ave. High	30	35	42	55	65	72	82	81	70	55	41	33
Ave. Low	14	19	24	32	40	46	50	49	41	33	25	20
Precipitation												
Inches Rain	2.1	1.8	1.3	1.6	2.3	2.9	1.4	1.4	1.5	1.7	2.2	2.0
Inches Snow	17	11	7	2	-	-	-	-	-	2	11	18

V.W.R. = Vokac Weather Rating: probability of mild (warm & dry) weather on any given day.

Forecast

Temperatures

Month	V.W.R.*		Daytime	Evening	Precipitation
January	0	Bad	cold	frigid	frequent snow flurries
February	0	Bad	chilly	cold	occasional snow flurries
March	0	Bad	chilly	chilly	infrequent snow flurries
April	3	Adverse	cool	chilly	occasional showers/snow flurries
May	6	Moderate	warm	cool	frequent showers
June	7	Good	warm	cool	frequent rainstorms
July	10	Great	warm	warm	infrequent rainstorms
August	10	Great	warm	warm	infrequent showers
September	8	Very Good	warm	cool	occasional showers
October	3	Adverse	cool	chilly	occasional showers/snow flurries
November	0	Bad	chilly	chilly	occasional snow flurries
December	0	Bad	chilly	cold	frequent snow flurries

Summary

Whitefish is located in a luxuriant pine forest along the south shore of a beautiful lake near the western gateway to Glacier National Park. Only 3,100 feet above sea level, the area seems much higher because of the impressive alpine setting. **Winter** days are short and chilly, evenings are cold, and there are plenty of snowfalls to provide fine conditions for the large skiing complex nearby. **Spring** is a transition. Temperatures increase rapidly until warm days return in May. Unfortunately, rainfalls become heavier and more persistent in the year's wettest season. **Summer** weather is excellent. Long warm days and evenings, and infrequent rainfalls, complement a wide range of lake and mountain sports. **Fall** provides only a few weeks of pleasant weather before much cooler days, freezing nighttime temperatures, and occasional snowfalls portend the return of winter after Halloween.

ATTRACTIONS & DIVERSIONS

Aerial Tramway

★ **Big Mountain Chairlift**   *8 mi. N on County Road 487*   862-3511

From mid-June to Labor Day, visitors can ride a chairlift to the summit for panoramic views of the entire Flathead Valley plus spectacular peaks in Glacier Park and the Canadian Rockies. Hikers can opt to return via the Danny On Trail — a five mile mini-wilderness nature trail.

Bicycling

Glacier Mountaineering   *downtown at 15 Central Av.*   862-5169

Bicycles may be rented here during the summer for scenic tours of the relatively flat byways around town and in the nearby Flathead Valley.

★ **Flathead Lake**   *25 mi. S on US 93*

The largest freshwater lake west of the Mississippi is about thirty miles long and fifteen miles wide. This picturesque basin of water clear enough to drink becomes a vast playground in summer. Several lakefront parks off the scenic paved highway around the lake offer pine-shaded camping and picnic sites, as well as water recreation facilities. Fishing for silver salmon is especially popular in summer. Another bonus of the season is fresh fruit sold at roadside stands in the extensive orchards along the eastern shore.

★ **Flathead National Forest**   *surrounding town*   862-2508

This enormous national forest includes one of the state's largest skiing complexes, Big Mountain Ski Resort, plus major cross-country skiing, snowmobiling and ice fishing areas. The Bob Marshall, Great Bear, and Mission Mountains wildernesses are among the nation's largest and most spectacular. Collectively, they offer more than a thousand miles of trails to hikers, backpackers, and horseback riders during the summer. The Jewel Basin Hiking Area includes more than thirty miles of specially designated trails connecting dozens of scenic high mountain lakes. All 219 miles of the Flathead Wild and Scenic River system are also in the forest.

★ **Glacier National Park**   *26 mi. E via US 93 & MT 40 on US 2*   888-5441

More than a million acres of the majestic northern Rocky Mountains are preserved much as they were long before man first saw them. Shimmering glaciers and emerald-green lakes, cascading waterfalls, fields of wildflowers, dense forests, and abundant wildlife are all part of the spectacle. For fifty miles, the Going-to-the-Sun Highway is one of the world's most breathtaking drives. All roads and trails, and accommodations ranging from campgrounds to historic lodges, are usually open from June into September, depending on snow conditions.

Golf

★ **Whitefish Lake Golf Course**   *1 mi. W on US 93*   862-4000

Scenic mountain and lake views enhance this beautiful, pine-shaded 27-hole golf course on gentle slopes above the lake. It is open to the public, with all facilities, services, and rentals available.

★ **Holbrook Overlook**   *4 mi. N on County Rd. 487*

An outstanding panoramic picnic site has been carved out of a forested slope partway up the Big Mountain road. Several tables are positioned to maximize a grand view of Whitefish Lake and the town far below.

★ **Hungry Horse Dam**   *19 mi. SE via US 93 & MT 40*

Several miles south of a village called Hungry Horse on an unnumbered road is one of the world's highest (564 feet) concrete dams. A narrow roadway crosses the nearly half mile crest of the dam. A visitor center, self-guided tours, and displays are open every day in summer. Forested campgrounds and recreation sites are scattered along the thirty-four-mile-long reservoir.

★ **River Running**   *23 mi. E via US 93 & MT 40 on US 2 - West Glacier*

The national Wild and Scenic River system includes 219 miles of the North, Middle, and South Forks of the Flathead River east of town by Glacier National Park. Trips ranging from tranquil scenic floats to thrilling whitewater runs can be arranged in canoes or inflatables during July and August. The district ranger's office in town can provide maps and more information. For guided trips, contact:

Glacier Raft Co.   *24 mi. E on US 2 - West Glacier*   *888-5541*
Guided whitewater raft trips ranging from one-half to six days on the Flathead and other rivers are offered with all equipment provided. Raft rentals are also available.

Great Northern Float Trips   *23 mi. E on US 2 - West Glacier*   *387-5340*
Guided scenic and whitewater adventures on local rivers in inflatable rafts or dory boats are offered, along with guided fishing trips. All equipment is furnished.

★ **Whitefish Lake**   *1 mi. NW via County Rd. 487 & Skyles Place*
Dense forests surround the picturesque lake which is seven miles long and two miles wide. In town, City Beach Park provides a nicely maintained sandy beach overseen by lifeguards in summer. Swimming, sunbathing, sailing, sailboarding, fishing, and power boating are all popular.

★ **Whitefish State Recreation Area**   *3 mi. NW via West 2nd St. on State Park Rd.*
The view from the sandy beach across Whitefish Lake to the forested mountains epitomizes the natural grandeur of the Northwest. Pine-shaded picnic tables share the panorama with the well-maintained swimming and sunbathing beach, and a campground is just beyond. A boat ramp and dock are provided. Fishing and sailing are also popular.

Winter Sports

★ **The Big Mountain**   *8 mi. N on County Rd. 487*   *862-3511*
The vertical rise is 2,130 feet and the longest run is well over two miles. Elevation at the top is 7,000 feet. There are five chairlifts (including two triples) with the state's largest capacity. All facilities, services, and rentals are available at the area for both downhill and cross-country skiing. A few restaurants, bars, and lodging facilities are at the base. The skiing season is Thanksgiving to mid-April.

★ **Cross-Country Skiing**
Glacier Mountaineering   *downtown at 15 Central Av.*   *862-5169*
There are unlimited cross-country skiing opportunities in the area. Maps, equipment, sales, rentals, and lessons can be arranged here.

SHOPPING
The business district extends for several blocks along Central Avenue southward from the Amtrak Depot. This picturesque wood-trimmed main street, with its rustic Old West charm, is still the heart of the town's only complete shopping center. A few galleries and specialty shops have been added in recent years.

Food Specialties

★ **Geno's Village Bakery**   *downtown at 516 3rd St. E*   *862-6961*
Big whole wheat cinnamon rolls, cream cheese raisin swirls, and coffee cakes are delicious specialties accompanied by all kinds of breads and donuts. A couple of tables and coffee are available. Closed Sun.

Willow's Huckleberry Farm   *16 mi. E via US 93 & MT 40 - Hungry Horse*   *387-5564*
In a roadside complex that is a towering tribute to traditional tourism, there is one compelling reason to stop — huckleberries. They are used in pies, fruitcakes, pancakes, rolls, bread, and ice cream, and sold by the jar or in gift packs of preserves, jelly, syrup and candy! Free tastes are offered of jellies and preserves made from huckleberries and other local wild berries.

★ **The Wine and Cheese Seller**   *downtown at 401 1st St. E*   *862-7060*
An unusual assortment of mountain sausages and salami are featured along with locally-made French bread plus gourmet cheeses, and sandwiches by the inch. Both the wine and beer selections are excellent.

Specialty Shops

Art Unlimited   *downtown at 429 2nd St. E*   *862-5155*
Local wildlife and scenic photographs are featured, along with some oils, watercolors and bronzes.

Bebe Kezar   *downtown at 525 3rd St. E*   *862-5156*
Attractive displays of works by Montana artisans are featured in this two-story gallery.

Northwood Gallery   *downtown at 229 Central Av.*   *862-5122*
Many local artists' works can be found among the multimedia collection of arts and crafts displayed here.

NIGHTLIFE

Whitefish is a major center for old-fashioned action. While the nearest movie theater is miles away, there are plenty of saloons with dance halls and legal gambling dens. The notable cluster downtown keeps Whitefish's rambunctious Old Western spirit alive.

Bulldog Saloon   *downtown at 144 Central Av.*   862-5601
Occasional live music and full time casino action attract attention to an unpretentious saloon where the wild-Western atmosphere wasn't even planned.

Casey's   *downtown at 101 Central Av.*   862-9903
Legal gambling in the back room, plus pool tables and electronic games, are features of a popular "locals" bar.

Great Northern Bar   *downtown at 27 Central Av.*   862-2816
Pool, electronic games, and light food attract a young crowd to this modern bar.

Hanging Tree   *downtown at 10 Central Av.*   862-5196
Live country music and dancing on weekends, plus legal gambling, are offered in this big uninhibited saloon.

★ **Palace Bar**   *downtown at 125 Central Av.*   862-2428
Pool, ping-pong, darts and electronic games provide new and old lures for a saloon with an uncommercialized Old West feeling supported by the area's finest hardwood back bar.

The Place   *.7 mi. N at 845 Wisconsin Av.*   862-4500
This big rustic roadhouse offers a surprisingly diverse wine list, plus tap beers, pizza, and casual meals.

★ **The Remington**   *downtown at 130 Central Av.*   862-6303
Live entertainment and dancing are featured on weekends in a cavernous back room. Elsewhere, a casino offers poker, fun poker, and keno amidst freewheeling turn-of-the-century atmosphere.

RESTAURANTS

Restaurants in the area are relatively numerous, with an emphasis on reasonably priced, hearty American fare served in casual surroundings.

Alpinglow Inn   *8 mi. N on County Rd. 487*   862-3511
B-D.   *Moderate*
Homemade baked goods accompany American fare in a large, informal dining room at the ski area with a vast window wall overlooking the Flathead Valley.

Coupe de Ville Cafe   *downtown at 10 Central Av.*   862-6191
B-L-D.   *Low*
Homemade cinnamon rolls are a breakfast specialty and substantial Italian dishes are featured for dinner in this large and casual dining room.

★ **Frederic's**   *downtown at 130 Central Av.*   862-6303
D only.   *Moderate*
Carefully prepared American dishes are served in a comfortable newer dining room with Western decor.

La Dump   *7 mi. S on US 93*   257-1111
L-D. No L on Sun.   *Moderate*
Hearty American meals are emphasized. The big cheerful dining room has a fireplace, while a back alcove has booths outfitted with old sedan seats accessed by car doors.

Orient Express   *6 mi. S on US 93*   862-4613
D only.   *Moderate*
Steaks and seafoods are given an international flair. Well-appointed dining rooms have been created in two of the original Orient Express Railroad cars.

Stump Town Station   *downtown at 115 Central Av.*   862-4979
D only.   *Moderate*
Conventional Western fare (steak, prime rib, seafood) is served amid contemporary Western wood-trimmed decor in a popular eating and drinking place where patio dining is available when weather permits.

★ **3rd & Spokane**   *downtown at 3rd St. & Spokane Av.*   862-7820
B-L. Closed Sun.   *Moderate*
Fine omelets, biscuits, and croissants are among the delicious offerings in a stylish new restaurant with refreshingly modern atmosphere.

Viking Lodge　　*1.2 mi. N at 1360 Wisconsin Av.*　　　　　　*862-3547*
B-L-D.　　　　　　　　　　　*Moderate*
American fare predominates in homemade appetizers, soups, jams, cinnamon rolls, and desserts. The lodge's comfortable restaurant is the only dining room by beautiful Whitefish Lake. Meals are also served on a lakeside patio in summer, and there is a view lounge.

★ **Whitefish Lake Restaurant**　　*1 mi. W on US 93*　　　　　　*862-5285*
L-D.　　　　　　　　　　　*Moderate*
Well-prepared, ample American meals are served amidst gracious rusticity in a large old log lodge at the Whitefish Golf Club.

LODGING
Whitefish has relatively few places to stay, but there are impressive accommodations on and overlooking the lake and at the base of the ski lifts. Winter rates are comparable to those of summer, while rates in spring and fall are usually about 20% less.

★ **Alpenglow Inn**　　*8 mi. N on County Rd. 487*　　　　　　*862-6966*
Adjacent to the lifts on Big Mountain, this is *the* place to be in winter. Amenities include night skiing, a heated outdoor pool, sauna, restaurant, and bar. Rooms on the south side have panoramic views of Flathead Valley. Winter rates are about 80% more than those shown.
　　#309,#209,#109 — windows on 2 sides, superb valley view,　　　　Q bed...$35
　　#319,#219,#119 — window on S side, fine valley view,　　　　　Q bed...$35
　　#318 — window on N side, excellent ski run/base view,　　　　Q bed...$35
　　regular room —　　　　　　　　　　　　　　　　　　Q bed...$35

Chalet Motel　　*1.3 mi. S at 6430 S.US 93*　　　　　　*862-5581*
This attractive newer motel has an indoor pool, whirlpool, and sauna. Each spacious room has a phone and cable color TV.
　　regular room —　　　　　　　　　　　　　　　　2 Q beds...$40

Downtowner Motel　　*downtown at 224 Spokane Av.*　　　　　*862-2535*
The only motel near the heart of town is a **bargain.** Each of the well-furnished rooms has a phone and color TV.
　　deluxe room — new section,　　　　　　　　　　2 Q or K bed...$34
　　regular room — older section,　　　　　　　　　　Q bed...$27

★ **Grouse Mountain Lodge**　　*1 mi. W on US 93*　　　　　　*862-3000*
Whitefish's largest and most luxurious resort hotel opened in the summer of 1984. Landscaped grounds include an indoor pool, whirlpool, and sauna; two outdoor whirlpools; and there are tennis courts, a restaurant and a lounge across the highway. Each spacious, nicely furnished unit has a phone and cable color TV with movies.
　　deluxe room — balc., in-bath whirlpool, loft,　　　2 T & K beds...$100
　　deluxe unit — balc., kitchenette, loft,　　　　　2 T & K beds...$85
　　regular room —　　　　　　　　　　　　　　2 Q or K bed...$55

Mountain Holiday Motel　　*1 mi. S on US 93*　　　　　　*862-2548*
In a pleasant location near the river, this modern motel has a small outdoor pool and an indoor whirlpool. Each well-furnished room has a phone and cable color TV.
　　#304 — mountain view,　　　　　　　　　　　2 Q beds...$39
　　#114 — pvt., end unit on 1st fl., lawn & tree view,　　2 Q beds...$39
　　regular room —　　　　　　　　　　　　　　2 Q beds...$39

Rocky Mountain Lodging　　*1 mi. S on US 93*　　　　　　*862-2569*
A large indoor pool and saunas are featured in a nicely landscaped complex of modern motel rooms and refurbished older cabins. Each room has a cable color TV.
　　regular room — in motel, spacious, phone,　　　2 D beds...$36
　　regular room — cabin,　　　　　　　　　　　D bed...$36

★ **Viking Lodge**　　*1.2 mi. N at 1360 Wisconsin Rd.*　　　　　*862-3547*
Whitefish's only lakefront motor lodge is on the eastern shore of Whitefish Lake. Landscaped grounds include a large lake view pool (enclosed in winter) and a dock with rental boats. In the main building are a large whirlpool, sauna, dining room and lounge. Each spacious room has a phone, cable color TV, and either a private patio or balcony.
　　#211,#214,#217 — 2nd (top) fl., fine lake view, pvt. balc.,　　K bed...$46
　　#111 — end of lower fl., pvt. patio, lake view,　　　　2 Q beds...$46
　　#209,#207 — pvt. balc., fine lake view,　　　　　　2 Q beds...$46
　　regular room —　　　　　　　　　　　　　　2 Q beds...$42

Whitefish Motel   *.5 mi. S at 620 8th St.*   *862-3507*
Each of the humble **bargain** units in this rustic old single-level motel has a cable color TV
and kitchenette.
   regular room —   D bed...$30

CAMPGROUNDS

Campgrounds are surprisingly scarce nearby. The best is convenient to town, relatively
primitive and remarkably scenic.

★ **Whitefish State Recreation Area**   *3 mi. W on Hwy. 93 & State Park Rd.*   *No Phone*
This state operated campground is located by the heavily forested shore of picturesque
Whitefish Lake. It has a grassy, shaded picnic area, a sandy beach, and a boat ramp.
Swimming, boating, fishing and hiking are popular. There are pit toilets only — no showers
or hookups. Each of the pine-shaded sites has a picnic table and a raised rotating fire grill.
   base rate...$3

SPECIAL EVENTS

★ **Winter Carnival**   *in and around town*   *early February*
Weeks of celebration culminate in three days of mid-winter madness in a Mardi-Gras-of-
the-West. Floats and horse-drawn sleighs parade during the day. At night, torchlight
parades weave through downtown and in procession down the slopes of Big Mountain.
Hot-air balloons light the night sky with ghostly glows. A king and queen are feted with
fireworks, banquets and dances. Everyone parties to special entertainment at the local
night spots.

Regatta   *Whitefish Lake*   *late July*
This three-day event begins with a parade and the coronation of the "Queen of the
Waters." Championship power boat and sailboat races are featured, and there are street
dances, flea markets, and live entertainment.

OTHER INFORMATION

Area Code: *406*
Zip Code: *59937*
Whitefish Chamber of Commerce   *.3 mi. S on US 93 at 505 Spokane Av.*   *862-3501*
Flathead National Forest - District Ranger   *W on US 93*   *862-2508*

Santa Fe, New Mexico

Elevation:

7,000 feet

Population (1980):

48,953

Population (1970):

41,167

Location:

350 mi. S
of Denver

Santa Fe is the most unusual town in America. Here is the only significant community that has existed through the entire recorded history of the American West. For well over three centuries, Santa Fe has been a regional capital for a succession of nations. Today, it is the capital of New Mexico, a peerless repository of Southwestern lore, and a wonderfully cosmopolitan showcase for all of the arts. An astonishing assortment of museums, theaters, studios, galleries, restaurants and nightclubs display the artistry of residents in adobe structures that reflect the timeless beauty of Santa Fe-style architecture. The town is located at the edge of the vast Rio Grande basin amid gentle pinon pine-covered foothills of the southernmost Rocky Mountains. Although it is one of the highest towns in the country, there is a pleasant four season climate because of the southern location and sheltering peaks. Winters are relatively mild in town, yet a major ski area is only a short drive away in the mountains. The best weather usually occurs in spring and fall. Then, the town is uncrowded, and an invigorating crispness in the air is enhanced by the smell of pinon pine and juniper burning in thousands of kiva fireplaces. Summer is the busiest season. Hot days are relieved by frequent showers. Special events like rodeos, festivals, and fiestas are almost continuous, and the shops and attractions in town are filled with visitors. Nearby, the Sangre de Cristo Mountains offer a variety of outdoor recreation opportunities.

Don Pedro de Peralta founded Santa Fe in 1610, ten years prior to the pilgrims' arrival at Plymouth Rock. For more than two hundred years, this was the Presidio governing all Spanish lands between Florida and California, except for a brief period (1680-1692) when the Pueblo Indians revolted and drove out the Spaniards. Mexico gained independence from Spain in 1821 and governed until 1846, when General Kearny led troops into town and claimed the region (without resistance) for the United States. Because the transcontinental railroad bypassed Santa Fe, it was spared the explosive growth into a major city that would probably have occurred. Instead, the relative isolation and magnificent location began to attract artists and individualists who have done so much to portray and maintain the town's unique character.

Today, Santa Fe remains a perfectly-scaled walking town centered around the splendid centuries-old Plaza. Churches, public buildings, and historic businesses offer a picturesque treasury of Pueblo and Spanish-colonial architecture through the ages. Most have National Historic Landmark status, and all are protected by architectural controls. Ancient narrow streets and inviting adobe courtyards lead to an enchanting assortment of exceptional art galleries, craft studios, specialty shops, restaurants, lounges and lodging places — all within an easy stroll of the Plaza.

Santa Fe, New Mexico

Vokac Weather Rating

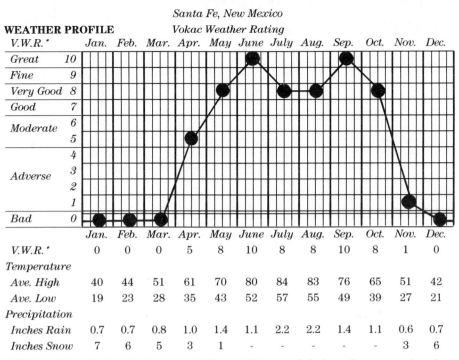

V.W.R.*	Jan.	Feb.	Mar.	Apr.	May	June	July	Aug.	Sep.	Oct.	Nov.	Dec.
V.W.R.*	0	0	0	5	8	10	8	8	10	8	1	0
Temperature												
Ave. High	40	44	51	61	70	80	84	83	76	65	51	42
Ave. Low	19	23	28	35	43	52	57	55	49	39	27	21
Precipitation												
Inches Rain	0.7	0.7	0.8	1.0	1.4	1.1	2.2	2.2	1.4	1.1	0.6	0.7
Inches Snow	7	6	5	3	1	-	-	-	-	-	3	6

*V.W.R. = Vokac Weather Rating: probability of mild (warm & dry) weather on any given day.

Forecast

Temperatures

Month	V.W.R.*		Daytime	Evening	Precipitation
January	0	Bad	chilly	cold	infrequent snow flurries
February	0	Bad	chilly	chilly	infrequent snow flurries
March	0	Bad	cool	chilly	infrequent showers/snow flurries
April	5	Moderate	cool	chilly	infrequent showers/snow flurries
May	8	Very Good	warm	cool	occasional showers
June	10	Great	warm	warm	infrequent showers
July	8	Very Good	hot	warm	frequent showers
August	8	Very Good	hot	warm	frequent showers
September	10	Great	warm	cool	occasional showers
October	8	Very Good	warm	cool	infrequent showers
November	1	Adverse	cool	chilly	infrequent showers/snow flurries
December	0	Bad	chilly	cold	infrequent snow flurries

Summary

Santa Fe blends beautifully into a scrub pine forest in low hills just west of the mighty Sangre de Cristo Mountains. In spite of a seemingly low profile, it is one of the largest of the West's towns and one of the highest—almost 7,000 feet above sea level. **Winter** days are chilly, evenings are cold, and snowfalls are erratic and relatively light. While these conditions aren't suitable for winter sports facilities in the immediate vicinity, good skiing is enjoyed at a major complex in the nearby mountains. **Spring** offers some of the finest weather of the year. Warm days begin in May. Infrequent showers bring out the aromatic tang of the ubiquitous pinon pine and juniper, and give a startling clarity to the expansive countryside. **Summer** is hot, with frequent showers contributing the year's heaviest rainfalls. **Fall** features some of the best weather in the Rocky Mountains. Warm days, cool evenings, and relatively little rainfall usually continue until almost Thanksgiving when unpredictable snowfalls signal the approach of winter.

ATTRACTIONS & DIVERSIONS

★ **Bandelier National Monument**   *46 mi. NW via US 84 on NM 4*   672-3861
Deep in Frijoles Canyon is a fascinating concentration of ruins of ancient pueblo and cliff dwellings. A great circular pueblo ruin on the floor of the canyon, cave rooms carved into soft cliff rock, and houses built out from the cliffs were probably occupied between 1200-1600 A.D. All are accessible from the museum/visitor center via a self-guided walking tour. There is also a campground.

★ **Bicycle Rentals**
Streets and byways in and around town are narrow and winding, but the terrain is gentle and the scenery is terrific. Bicycles may be rented with or without sightseeing tour guides.
> **Rob and Charlie's (rentals)**   *2 blocks S at 201 Galisteo St.*   988-2345
> **Santa Fe Trails (sightseeing tours)**   *downtown at 228 Ortiz St.*   984-1685

★ **Chimayo**   *32 mi. NE via US 84 on NM 76*
In the tiny historic village of Chimayo is an intriguing and renowned sanctuary. Many believe the dirt on the sanctuary's floor has miraculous healing power. The village is also well known for its blanket weavers and woodcarvers.

Christo Rey Church   *1.5 mi. E on upper Canyon Rd.*   983-8528
Built in 1939, this Catholic church is said to be the largest adobe structure in the country. It is the repository for ancient stone reredos (altar screens) from a chapel once located on the plaza.

Footsteps   *2 blks. SE at 211 Old Santa Fe Trail*   988-7625
A recently added attraction at the Inn at Loretto is a comfortable little theater where a high-tech slide show about northern New Mexico is screened using nine projectors and a raised-relief map of the state. An outstanding assortment of books about the local area are displayed and sold in an adjoining room.

Library   *1 block N at 120 Washington Av.*   982-4471
The Santa Fe Public Library is a large facility with brightly lighted, old-fashioned reading areas furnished with hardwood tables and chairs. There is a special reading list dealing with all aspects of Santa Fe, and a large record collection featuring opera selections from past local productions. The "Southwestern Room" is a showcase of regional furnishings.

★ **Loretto Chapel**   *1 block S on Old Santa Fe Trail*   982-3376
According to legend, workmen couldn't determine how to construct a staircase to the choir loft of this little gothic chapel (1878). A mysterious carpenter appeared and built a double-spiral stairway — without nails or central support. The famous staircase, a masterpiece of design and carpentry, may be viewed by the public year-round.

Los Alamos   *40 mi. NW via US 84 on NM 4*   667-4444
A boy's school on a high, remote plateau was taken over by the federal government during World War II as a site for secret research on the first atomic bombs. Today, the Los Alamos National Laboratory remains a classified installation (closed to the public), concentrating on peaceful applications of nuclear energy research and weaponry, laser technology, and the production of energy from fission, fusion, and geothermal sources. A science museum and a park with monuments commemorating the dawn of the Atomic Age attract visitors.

Museums

★   **Laboratory of Anthropology** *2 mi. S via Old Santa Fe Trail on Camino Lejo*   827-8940
The State displays a fine collection of Indian art and artifacts here, and a vast collection of folk art from around the world in the adjoining *Museum of International Folk Art.*

★   **Museum of Fine Arts**   *NW corner of the plaza*   827-4455
Recently restored to its early 1900s mission-style appearance, this state operated museum houses traditional and contemporary works by major Southwestern (especially Santa Fe and Taos) painters, photographers, and sculptors.

★   **The Palace of the Governors**   *N side of the plaza*   827-2454
Built in 1610, the oldest public building in continuous use in America was the seat of government in New Mexico for almost 300 years. When Lew Wallace was governor of the territory (1878-81) he wrote part of Ben Hur here. The long, low adobe structure is now a major state-operated museum, reflecting the history of New Mexico. On the porch-shaded sidewalk overlooking the plaza, Pueblo Indians display and sell their pottery and jewelry as they have for generations. They also sell delicious pueblo kiva bread.

★ **The Wheelwright Museum** *2 mi. S via Old Santa Fe Trail on Camino Lejo 982-4636*
Housed in a structure shaped like a Navajo hogan are a fascinating assortment of art objects reflecting Southwestern Indian culture. The Case trading post downstairs sells contemporary Indian artists' pottery, textiles, and jewelry.

Oldest House *3 blocks S on Old Spanish Trail*
This house, which is now a curio shop, is believed to include portions built by Indians more than 800 years ago.

★ **The Plaza**
The heart of Santa Fe was laid out in 1610 by decree of the King of Spain. It was the end of the famed Santa Fe Trail from Missouri and the El Camino Real from Mexico. The Plaza has been the site of more major historical events than any similar place in the Southwest. It remains the locale for the town's most colorful celebrations and fiestas.

Pueblos of the Rio Grande *for about 70 mi. N and S*
The flat land along the Rio Grande is dotted with fourteen pueblos which retain tribal customs and crafts. Many have changed remarkably little over hundreds of years.

★ **River Park** *2 blocks S along Alameda*
Ancient trees, well-tended lawns, and pathways along the tiny Santa Fe River make this a pleasant place to stroll or enjoy a picnic. Don't miss the whimsical fountain near the western end of the park.

River Running
  New Wave Rafting Co. *SE corner of the plaza* 984-1444
Half day, full day, and overnight whitewater float trips in the Rio Grande Canyon can be reserved from April to September in the La Fonda Hotel lobby.

★ **St. Francis Cathedral** *1 block E on San Francisco St.* 982-5619
A major landmark, this French Romanesque Cathedral was built under the direction of Santa Fe's first Archbishop (Lamy) in 1869.

★ **San Miguel Mission** *3 blocks S on Old Santa Fe Trail* 983-3974
The oldest church still in use in the United States was begun in 1610. The facade has changed substantially over time, but the interior contains Santa Fe's oldest (1798) wooden reredos (altar screens), plus other priceless relics and paintings.

★ **Santa Fe National Forest** *surrounding town* 988-6940
Major forest attractions include the southernmost peaks of the beautiful Sangre de Cristo Mountains, the Pecos Wilderness including the headwaters of the Pecos River, and the Santa Fe Ski Area. Camping, hiking, backpacking, hunting, fishing, and winter sports are seasonally popular.

State Capitol *4 blocks S on Old Santa Fe Trail* 827-2027
Santa Fe has both the oldest and the newest capitols in the United States. The Palace of the Governors, built in 1610, served for almost three centuries. Later, what is now named the Bataan Memorial Building served as the capitol until 1966. The legislative and executive branches were then transferred to the present capitol, a unique round building in modified territorial style that was inspired by Indian kivas and the Zia — an Indian sun sign.

Warm Water Features
★ **The Soak** *2 blocks N at 207 Lincoln Av.* 988-7625
A dozen artistically decorated private rooms each has a whirlpool, individually controlled lighting and music, relaxation deck, and a shower. Two private rooms are open to the sky. Food and beverages can be ordered to the rooms. Professional massage is also available by appointment.

★ **Ten Thousand Waves** *3 mi. NE on NM 475* 988-1047
One communal and seven nicely-designed private outdoor enclosures with whirlpools are secluded on one of the pine and juniper-covered foothills above town. Juices, teas, and pastries are available, as is professional massage.

Winter Sports
★ **Santa Fe Ski Area** *16 mi. NE on NM 475* 982-4429
With a vertical rise of 1,650 feet, the longest run is three miles. There are two chairlifts carrying skiers to spectacular views at 12,000 feet. All facilities, services, and rentals are available at the area for downhill skiing. There are two restaurants and a bar at the base but no lodging. The skiing season is from Thanksgiving to mid-April.

SHOPPING

Santa Fe's plaza, the heart of town from its beginning, is still the center of a remarkably vital business district. First-time visitors are delighted by the number of outstanding galleries, studios, and boutiques concentrated within a few blocks of the plaza in every direction. The appearance of the shops is also appealing, since they and other downtown buildings have all been architecturally patterned after the earthen pueblo and territorial styles of the area's many historic landmarks. Because this is one of the nation's greatest pedestrian-scaled shopping and sightseeing districts, the listings which follow are illustrative only. Additional scores of fine stores filled with visual and culinary delights await each shopper's discovery.

Food Specialties

Bagel and Lombard   *2 blocks S on Alameda at Springer Plaza*   988-7474
Many varieties of fresh bagels are served to go, or with breakfasts and lunches indoors or on the patio.

Becker's Delicatessen   *.4 mi. SW at 403 Guadalupe St.*   988-2423
Bagels, breads, and pastries are baked here fresh daily and served in a tiny patio, or to go.

★ **French Pastry Shop**   *SE corner of the plaza*   983-6697
French croissants, breads, and pastries are served to go, or with breakfast or lunch in an atmospheric little dining room in the La Fonda Hotel.

Haagen Dazs Ice Cream Shoppe   *on the plaza at 56 E. San Francisco St.*   988-3858
Various flavors of the chain's high-quality ice creams made from fresh natural ingredients are used in all kinds of treats served at the counter or tables in this bright little shop.

★ **Lickety Split**   *.4 mi. SW at 319 Guadalupe St.*   984-1334
Outstandingly rich, natural-flavored ice creams are served in many flavors and styles in a tiny Santa Fe-style ice cream parlor outfitted with handcrafted fixtures and soda fountain antiques.

★ **Palace Swiss Bakery**   *.4 mi. SW at 320 Guadalupe St.*   988-3737
Fine morning or dessert pastries can be taken out or enjoyed with light breakfast or lunch fare in an attractive dining room, or on an enclosed patio. Closed Sun.

★ **Sante Fe Cookie Company**   *1 block W at 110 W. San Francisco St.*   983-7707
Pinon nut shortbread is a delicious and unusual specialty of this little carryout cookie and brownie shop.

★ **Senor Murphy**   *SE corner of the plaza*   982-0461
Pinon candies, pinon nuts, and red or green chili jellies are some of the distinctive local specialties of a little candy shop in the La Fonda Hotel. There are two other outlets downtown. Closed Sun.

★ **Spirits, etc.**   *4 blocks S at 414 Old Santa Fe Trail*   984-0126
A good selection of California and other wines is displayed. Wine by the glass may be enjoyed in an adjoining small lounge, along with darts, chess, or backgammon. Closed Sun.

Swensen's Ice Cream Factory   *1 block S at 102 E. Water St.*   982-9251
The rich ice creams made here are used in assorted fountain treats served at the counter or in the ice cream parlor.

★ **The Winery**   *2 blocks SW at Galisteo & Water Sts.*   988-2984
Here is one of New Mexico's most extensive selections of wines, cheeses, and gourmet foods. Gift boxes are available and light meals are served in the store or on the patio. Closed Sun.

Specialty Shops

★ **Canyon Road**   *for about 1 mi. SE along Canyon Road*
A remarkable number of colorful art galleries, studios, specialty shops, and restaurants line a narrow winding street that was an Indian route before the coming of the Conquistadors. Working artisans abound, practicing their art in weaving, pottery, glass blowing, painting, sculpture, woodworking, and leather goods. A free map detailing Canyon Road shops is readily available at the Chamber of Commerce, bookstores, and hotels.

The Collected Works Bookstore   *2 blocks W at 208B W. San Francisco St.*   988-4226
This attractive bookstore has a fine selection of regional interest books as well as current best sellers.

★ **Los Llanos Bookstore**   *on the plaza at 72 E. San Francisco St.*   982-9542
Current bestsellers and Southwestern books, plus maps, globes, and art are nicely organized in this handsome store. Closed Sun.

★ **Nambe Mills**   *3 blocks E at 301 E. Alameda*   988-5528
Unique metal objects of art are made at the foundry (sixteen miles northwest on US 285) and sold there and at this retail outlet. Artistic Southwestern-style candles are sold next door to the foundry at the Luz de Nambe Candle Factory.

★ **Shidoni Foundry**   *6 mi. N on NM 22 - Tesuque*   988-8001
An innovative young arts and crafts colony has several acres of unique sculpture gardens displaying monumental works in metal. A gallery displays an intriguing assortment of bronzes and sculptures in other materials.

★ **Sunflower Book Store**   *1 block N at 105 E. Marcy St.*   988-9272
An unusually large collection of "New Age" books (dedicated to the whole person — mind, body, and spirit) is showcased in a tranquil environment with classical background music.

Villagra Book Shop   *1 block NE on E. Palace Av. in Sena Plaza*   982-0152
New Mexico's oldest book shop, featuring current and out-of-print Southwestern material, has packed a good assortment of books into a tiny shop.

★ **Wicked Wick**   *14 mi. N on US 285 - Pojoaque*   455-3448
One of America's largest makers of handcrafted designer candles sells factory seconds at wholesale prices in this retail shop.

NIGHTLIFE
Santa Fe offers a peerless diversity of nightlife, ranging from the contemporary grandeur of its renowned Opera to the frontier vitality of Old Western saloons. In addition to an outstanding selection of places featuring live entertainment and dancing, first-rate symphonies, concerts, and live theater are scheduled throughout the year. Romantic, intimate atmosphere is inevitably emphasized, rather than large or flashy facilities.

★ **The Armory for the Arts**   *1 mi. S at 1050 Old Pecos Trail*   988-1886
Professional companies present a full range of well-regarded theatrical events in a converted armory with several hundred plush seats and excellent sight lines. A sophisticated lobby/bar/gallery displays distinctive local works.

Club West   *2 blocks W at 213 W. Alameda*   982-0099
Jazz, rock, or soul are featured with dancing every night in a large nightclub with a contemporary Southwestern style.

★ **El Paso**   *1 block W at 123 W. San Francisco St.*   983-9671
This place is appropriately touted as an unusual "experience in environmental entertainment." An old movie theater was refurbished, and outfitted so that patrons can watch movies from sofas for couples, tables and chairs, or regular theater seating.

Inn of the Governors   *2 blocks S at 234 Don Gaspar Av.*   982-4333
Local jazz bands play and there is dancing nightly in the Forge Lounge, which has fireplaces and a patio. Rock groups play downstairs in the Cabaret on weekends, except in summer.

★ **Inn at Loretto**   *2 blocks SE at 211 Old Santa Fe Trail*   988-5531
Live easy listening music is played for dancing in this hotel's charming lounge. Native-contemporary decor complemented by a fireplace, an atmospheric balcony, and posh armchairs also provides a romantic setting for quiet conversation.

★ **La Fonda Hotel**   *SE corner of the plaza*   982-5511
La Fiesta Lounge offers varied live entertainment almost every night, even during "happy hour." El Greco is another lounge that is enthusiastically supported when flamenco dancing is offered.

The Line Camp   *15 mi. N on US 285 - Pojoaque*   455-7919
Live entertainment is offered nightly, with country/western music featured on Friday and Saturday nights. Nationally known acts occasionally play this nearly half-century-old saloon.

★ **Plaza Ore House**   *on the plaza at 50 Lincoln Av.*   983-8687
At the street level, a variety of live entertainment and dancing is offered most nights in a comfortable Santa Fe-style bar. Upstairs, a plush lounge offers piano music in a contemporary Southwestern setting accented by many sofas. An adjoining balcony drinking area has the town's best view of the plaza.

Ramada Inn   *3.9 mi. SW on US 85 at 2907 Cerrillos Rd.*   471-3000
In Mr. R's, country/western bands play next to one of the largest dance floors in town
every night.

★ **Vanessie**   *4 blocks W at 434 W. San Francisco St.*   982-9966
A well-played grand piano enhances the romantic mood each evening in this magnificent
new lounge. A cathedral-like room with a large fireplace has been exquisitely furnished
with fine local art works, plush sofas and armchairs, and an impressive bar. It is a tour de
force of native architecture and craftsmanship.

RESTAURANTS
Santa Fe is one of the ultimate gourmet capitals of the West, both in number and quality
of fine restaurants. The ubiquitous adobe-style architecture, handcrafted interiors, and
native fine art contribute to this distinction. Also, the unique flavors of "native New
Mexican" food like "posole" and "sopaipillas" evolved here. Best of all, Santa Fe is the cradle
of a newborn regional cuisine which creatively blends New Mexican, Continental, and New
California cookery. Several outstanding local restaurants are introducing the world to
this exciting "New Southwestern" cuisine.

Alfonso's   *1 mi. E at 724 Canyon Rd.*   982-3541
L-D.   *Moderate*
Santa Fe-style dishes and other specialties are given a light touch in a charming native-
contemporary restaurant with a fireplace patio and an attractive bar.

Beva's   *2 blocks SW at 125 W. Water St.*   983-1993
B-L.   *Moderate*
Carefully prepared fresh ingredients are used in generally light fare. The recently
remodeled dining room is a stylish contemporary showcase of artistic Santa Fe-style
decor, and there is a cozy sidewalk patio.

Bishop's Lodge   *3 mi. N on NM 22*   983-6377
B-L-D. Closed Nov.-Feb.   *Moderate*
An American menu is offered in the large, handsome old-fashioned dining room of this
famous resort. The romantic view across the terrace to the pinon-covered hills can be
enjoyed best apart from the busy, family-oriented summer season.

Bull Ring   *4 blocks S at 414 Old Santa Fe Trail*   783-3328
L-D. No L on Sat. & Sun.   *Moderate*
Assorted specialties are served in a rambling old adobe with several rooms with fireplaces,
or on a patio in summer. There is also a very popular lounge with live entertainment and
dancing.

★ **Chez Edouard**   *2 blocks NW at 239 Johnson St.*   982-9800
L-D. No D on Sun. Closed Mon.   *Moderate*
Fine French cuisine and New Southwestern specialties are served in several intimate
rooms opening onto a shady inner patio used for summer dining.

Chez Pancho   *4 blocks W at 409 W. Water St.*   983-9075
B-L-D. No D on Mon.-Wed.   *Low*
Several unusual breakfast specialties like sourdough pancakes or homemade black
molasses bread are reason enough to visit this casual Santa Fe-style cafe with an enclosed
garden patio.

★ **Comme Chez Vous**   *1 block S at 133 W. Water St.*   984-0004
L-D.   *Expensive*
French cuisine is featured in a splendid new dining landmark. Contemporary elegance is
reflected by a harpist playing in the waiting area, a rainbow fireplace, many flowers, and
gracious table settings in understated pastel-toned dining areas.

★ **The Compound**   *1 mi. E at 653 Canyon Rd.*   982-4353
L-D. Closed Mon.   *Expensive*
Well-regarded Continental cuisine is overshadowed by the strikingly elegant atmosphere
of this Santa Fe showplace in a century-old adobe residence. The formality of the setting
is reinforced by the town's only dress code. A walled, enchanting garden is used for
summer dining.

El Nido   *6 mi. N on NM 22 - Tesuque*   988-4340
D only.   *Moderate*
For more than half a century, this large restaurant has been serving steaks and native foods in firelit rooms. Live entertainment and dancing are featured in the lounge on weekends.

★ **El Paragua**   *25 mi. NW via US 285 at 603 NM 76 - Espanola*   735-3211
L-D. No L on Sun.   *Moderate*
Some of the state's finest native cuisine has come from the kitchen of this century-old adobe-and-stone building.

Ernie's   *1 mi. E at 731 Canyon Rd.*   982-4274
L-D. Closed Sun.   *Moderate*
Primarily American cuisine is served in a large restaurant featuring a delightful garden dining room under a translucent dome and an adjoining Santa Fe-style room.

★ **Fresco**   *1 block N at 142 Lincoln St.*   982-4583
L-D. No L on Sun.   *Moderate*
Delicious New Southwestern dishes are prepared over a mesquite grill in this classy new restaurant. Artistically updated Southwestern decor is accented by a dramatic copper bar near the entrance to the dining room. There are also several patio tables.

Guadalupe Cafe   *.4 mi. SW at 313 Guadalupe St.*   982-9762
L-D. No D Thurs. No L Sat. Closed Sun.   *Low*
Native New Mexican foods are featured, and dinner specials like breast of chicken relleno change nightly in an unassuming cafe.

★ **The Haven**   *1 mi. E at 613 Canyon Rd.*   988-5888
L-D.   *Moderate*
This is a fine place to explore the delectable subtleties of New Southwestern cuisine. The experience is enhanced by artistically decorated Santa Fe-style dining rooms with two fireplaces, and a patio for alfresco dining.

Josie's Casa de Comida   *1 block N at 95 W. Marcy St.*   983-5311
L only. Closed Sat.-Sun.   *Low*
Highly-regarded native foods like pear pie with sour cream are worth the wait in a line that usually extends onto the sidewalk. Don't be put off by the plain, plastic surroundings — this lunch spot is a local favorite.

La Fonda Hotel   *SE corner of the plaza*   982-5511
B-L-D.   *Moderate*
Native and American foods are offered in La Plazuela, a large glass-enclosed courtyard dining room in the romantic old hotel.

★ **La Tertulia**   *.5 mi. W at 416 Agua Fria St.*   988-2769
L-D. Closed Mon.   *Moderate*
A unique showplace for outstanding native New Mexican dishes has been created in a historic convent that now includes six comfortably furnished dining rooms, some with walls more than three feet thick. The unusual chapel-like lounge is a pleasant place to wait for a table, as is often necessary, in one of the West's most popular restaurants.

★ **Le Mirage**   *1 mi. E at 669 Canyon Rd.*   982-0388
D only. Sun. brunch.   *Expensive*
Innovative French gourmet cooking is featured. Inside, the atmosphere is intimate and elegant, while outside, a delightful flower-filled patio is used on summer evenings.

Ogelvie's Bar & Grille   *1 block N at Washington Av.*   988-3855
L-D.   *Moderate*
A contemporary menu is offered in an impressive new showcase of Santa Fe-style architecture and decor.

The Palace   *1 block W at 145 W. Palace Av.*   982-9891
L-D. Closed Sun.   *Moderate*
Continental specialties are served amidst rococo turn-of-the-century decor. The large, very Red Room is furnished with heavily upholstered banquettes and chairs, period pieces, and crystal chandeliers. A pianist plays most nights in the adjacent Victorian lounge under the enigmatic gaze of some well-executed paintings of nude ladies.

★ **The Periscope**   *2 blocks S at 221 Shelby St.*   *988-2355*
L only. D on Sat. only. Closed Sun.-Mon.   Very Expensive
Some of the West's best international and New Southwestern cuisine is served in cozy
dining rooms with understated Santa Fe decor. In this renowned chef-owned restaurant,
the prix fixe six course dinner is legendary, and usually requires reservations well in
advance.

★ **Pink Adobe**   *3 blocks S at 406 Old Santa Fe Trail*   *983-7712*
L-D. No L on Sat. & Sun.   *Moderate*
Continental and native specialties are served in several cozy and congested dining rooms
with fireplaces in a historic adobe. This well-known restaurant also has a garden
patio/bar.

Plaza Ore House   *SW corner of the plaza*   *983-8687*
D only.   *Moderate*
American fare, including homemade desserts, is offered amid comfortable, artistic Santa
Fe decor. A piano is played nightly in the plush upstairs lounge, and drinks are served on
a balcony with the best view of the plaza.

★ **Rancho de Chimayo**   *28 mi. N via US 285, NM 4 & NM 520*   *351-4444*
L-D. Closed Mon. & Jan.   *Moderate*
Classic native foods are carefully prepared, as are all of the baked goods made here. This
charming, famous restaurant, filled with local art and antiques, has retained the
authentic flavor of a large old hacienda. The patio dining area and bar are also distinctive.

★ **Rancho Encantado**   *8 mi. N via US 285 - Tesuque*   *982-3537*
B-L-D. Closed Jan.-Apr.   *Expensive*
American cuisine and on-premises baking enhance a strikingly beautiful, terraced dining
room in the area's most elegant resort. The restaurant is a tour de force of opulent Santa
Fe-style decor that also features an enchanting view of gardens and mountains.

★ **Santacafe**   *2 blocks N at 231 Washington Av.*   *984-1788*
L-D. Closed Sun.   *Expensive*
Carefully prepared New Southwestern cuisine is served sparingly, in keeping with the
refreshingly minimalist decor. The essence of a historic thick-walled adobe was
painstakingly retained as the building was artistically converted. The result is a series of
romantic dining rooms furnished with crisply elegant table settings surrounded by pastel-
colored walls accented with dramatic floral displays instead of paintings.

★ **The Shed**   *1 block E at 113½ E. Palace Av.*   *982-9030*
L only.   *Moderate*
Fine native New Mexican fare including homemade desserts and baked goods explains
the enduring appeal of this remarkably popular luncheon spot in one of the oldest
buildings in town. A patio is also used in summer.

The Soak   *1 block N at 207 Lincoln Av.*   *988-7625*
L-D.   *Low*
Homemade Italian specialties, soups, and desserts are served in a handsome dining room
and an outdoor sidewalk dining area. The restaurant adjoins twelve handcrafted hot tub
rooms that are rented by the hour.

The Staab House   *3 blocks E at 330 E. Palace Av.*   *983-6351*
B-L-D.   *Moderate*
American and native fare, plus a large salad bar, are offered in a converted Victorian
mansion that is the heart of the La Posada de Santa Fe resort. Meals are served amidst
contemporary New Mexican decor, in a cheerful Victorian-style conservatory, and on a
delightful fountain patio that is used in summer. The opulent lounge is a treat in itself.

Taro's   *3 blocks W at 321 W. San Francisco St.*   *984-0101*
L-D. Closed Sun.   *Low*
Popular Japanese specialties are featured in a tranquil setting that includes several
private low-table dining areas in addition to traditional American-style seating.

Tecolote Cafe   *1 mi. SE on US 85 at 1203 Cerrillos Rd.*   *988-1362*
B-L-D. Closed Tues.   *Moderate*
The omelets and huevos rancheros, plus biscuits, muffins, and other baked goods are all
made fresh daily in this cheerful little restaurant.

Tia Sophia's   *1 block W at 210 W. San Francisco St.*   *983-9880*
B-L. Closed Sun.   *Moderate*
Here is a pleasant place to learn about Santa Fe homestyle breakfasts — huevos with green or red chili, breakfast burritos, posole, etc. — amidst casual native decor.

Tinnie's Legal Tender   *18 mi. SE via I-25 & US 285 - Lamy*   *982-8425*
D only.   *Expensive*
An open-hearth grill is used to prepare steaks and other American dishes. This illustrious link in a leading New Mexican restaurant chain offers lavish reproduced Victorian atmosphere in a carefully converted century-old building. The saloon features an ornate cherrywood back bar.

★ **Victor's**   *4 blocks W at 423 W. San Francisco St.*   *982-1552*
L-D. No L on Sat. & Sun.   *Moderate*
Pastas, sauces, and breads are all made on the premises for fine traditional Italian meals served in contemporary Santa Fe-style dining rooms with kiva fireplaces, or in a small walled patio garden. The comfortably cushioned bar features interesting antipastos.

LODGING

All of the better lodgings reflect Santa Fe-style architecture, some with landmark success. Surprisingly, there are no really big facilities, in spite of the area's renown. Instead, almost all of the major hotels and resorts reflect the enchanting human scale and artistic temperament of the town itself. Rooms are relatively expensive downtown, but there are bargains on "motel row" (Cerrillos Road — US 85) south of downtown. During special events, on weekends, and throughout summer, vacancies are inevitably scarce. Apart from these times, rates are typically reduced by 25% and more from those shown.

Alamo Motel   *2.8 mi. SW on US 85 at 1842 Cerrillos Rd.*   *982-1841*
This small, older Santa Fe-style motel is a **bargain.** Each unit has a phone and color TV.
   deluxe room —   Q bed...$31
   regular room —   Q bed...$27

★ **Bishop's Lodge**   *3 mi. N on NM 22*   *983-6377*
Attractively landscaped grounds surround this famous old resort in the rolling foothills near town. Amenities include a large outdoor pool with beautiful views, a whirlpool, and saunas, as well as a handsome old-fashioned dining room and lounge. Oriented toward families during the summer, rates include a summertime children's program. A fee is charged for tennis, horseback riding, and skeet or trap shooting. Each room has a phone, and TV is available. In the summer, rates are American plan (3 meals daily) only.
   #57 — spacious, in older bldg., nice view of countryside,   K bed..$175
   #71 — spacious, in newer complex, garden/hills view, kiva fireplace, 2 Q beds...$225
   regular room — in older building,   Q bed..$175

★ **El Rey Motel**   *2.8 mi. S on US 85 at 1862 Cerrillos Rd.*   *982-1931*
Low level buildings of Santa Fe-style architecture are scattered around a large outdoor pool on landscaped grounds. Each well-furnished unit has a phone and color TV.
   #50 — new, spacious, kitchenette, fireplace,   Q bed...$62
   #32 — raised corner fireplace watchable from   2 Q beds...$47
   #45,#49 — newer units, spacious, corner fireplace, refr.,   K bed...$58
   regular room —   Q bed...$41

Grant Corner Inn   *2 blocks NW at 122 Grant Av.*   *983-6678*
A large older home has been converted into a handsome bed-and-breakfast inn. Each of the well-furnished rooms has a phone and cable color TV. A full complimentary breakfast is served in the morning, as is wine in the evening.
   #8 — porch, pvt. bath,   K bed..$100
   regular room — shared bath, small,   D bed...$65

★ **Inn at Loretto - Best Western**   *2 blocks S at 211 Old Santa Fe Trail*   *988-5531*
This recently-built pueblo-style adobe hotel features intriguing Southwestern decor in all public rooms, including the restaurant, lounge, and an arcade of shops. There is a large outdoor pool. Each well-furnished room has a phone and cable color TV.
   #317,#217 — fireplace, decks, fine views,   2 D beds...$115
   #453 — spacious, pvt. balc., town/mt. view,   K bed...$108
   regular room —   2 D beds...$98

★ **Inn of the Governors**   *2 blocks S at 234 Don Gaspar Av.*   *982-4333*
Santa Fe's architectural style is reflected in this modern motor inn, which has a small outdoor pool, plus a dining room and lounge. Each room has a phone and color TV. Many of the rooms also have a wood-burning fireplace and refrigerator.

#243 — lg., Santa Fe River view, refr., kiva fireplace,	K bed...$85
regular room —	2 D or K bed...$65

★ **La Fonda**   *SE corner of the plaza*   *982-5511*
Santa Fe's most famous pueblo-style landmark anchors a corner of the plaza. An outdoor pool, three whirlpools, and distinctive restaurants, lounges, and shops are part of this well-maintained old complex. Each room has a phone and cable color TV with movies.

suite — 1 BR, spacious, fireplace,	K bed...$150
regular room —	Q or K bed...$85

Lamplighter - Best Western   *3.3 mi. SW on US 85 at 2405 Cerrillos Rd.*   *471-8000*
This modern motel has a large indoor pool and a whirlpool. Each unit has a phone and cable color TV.

deluxe room — spacious,	K bed...$47
regular room —	D bed...$42

★ **La Posada de Santa Fe**   *3 blocks E at 330 E. Palace Av.*   *983-6351*
Scattered over six acres of landscaped grounds in a quiet and convenient location is a picturesque older motor hotel with a large outdoor pool. Fine Santa Fe-style dining rooms and an opulent Yankee Victorian-style lounge complete with conservatory occupy the old Staab mansion at the center of the complex. Adjoining adobe buildings house handsomely furnished rooms, each with a color TV.

#108 — spacious, skylighted, secluded, fireplace,	K bed...$69
#302,#159 — spacious, fireplace,	Q bed...$69
#308 — spacious, corner room,	K bed...$69
#144 — spacious, corner fireplace,	K bed...$65
#138 — small, fireplace,	D bed...$46
regular room —	D bed...$35

Linda Motel   *3.4 mi. SW on US 85 at 2505 Cerrillos Rd.*   *471-8471*
There are some **bargain** rooms in an older, single-level section of this motel with cable color TV.

regular room —	D bed...$27

Motel 6   *4 mi. SW on US 85 at 3007 Cerrillos Rd.*   *471-2442*
The **bargain** in modern motel chains is represented with a large facility in the middle of "motel row." There is an outdoor pool, and (fee) TV is available.

regular room —	D bed...$22

★ **Preston House**   *3 blocks NE at 106 Faithway St.*   *982-3465*
Santa Fe's first bed-and-breakfast inn is located in a large turn-of-the-century converted home on a quiet street. All rooms feature Victorian and Santa Fe furnishings. A Continental breakfast is included.

#5 — spacious, upstairs corner, fireplace, pvt. bath,	K bed...$90
#1 — spacious, downstairs corner, fireplace, pvt. bath,	K bed...$90
#3 — regular room, upstairs, shared bath,	D bed...$35

★ **Rancho Encantado**   *8 mi. N via US 285 - near Tesuque*   *982-3537*
This small, renowned resort is nestled in rolling pinon pine-covered hills at the rim of the vast Rio Grande Valley. Classic Santa Fe-style adobe architecture prevails in low-profile buildings that have been carefully coordinated with splendid Southwestern decor and art objects. A large outdoor pool includes sun and shade view decks in a landscaped garden. A whirlpool, tennis courts, and horseback riding are also available, plus one of the loveliest restaurants and lounges in the West. Each lavishly furnished room has a phone. Closed Jan.-Mar.

#32 — 1 BR, spacious, end unit, corner fireplace, refr., mt. view,	K bed..$150
#15 — cottage, spacious, end unit, pvt. pine view, fireplace,	K bed..$115
regular room — in lodge,	Q bed...$95

Sheraton-Santa Fe Inn   *1.3 mi. NW via US 285 at 750 N. St. Francis Dr.*   *982-5591*
Some of the best panoramic views in the region are the feature of this large newer motor hotel. Amenities include a large outdoor pool, a restaurant, and a lounge. Each well-furnished room has a phone and color TV.

#204,#206,#208,#330,#320 — panoramic town/mt. views,		K bed...$89
regular room —		2 D or K bed...$89

Silver Saddle Court   *3.7 mi. SW on US 85 at 2810 Cerrillos Rd.*   *471-7663*
This small, older single-level motel has rooms with color TV.

regular room —   Q bed...$32

Stage Coach Motor Inn   *4.4 mi. S on US 85 at 3360 Cerrillos Rd.*   *471-0707*
Each of the rooms in this small, older motel has a phone and color TV.

regular room —   Q bed...$31

CAMPGROUNDS
There are several campgrounds in the area. The best offer either primitive facilities in a pine forest by a tiny stream, or complete facilities in less picturesque surroundings.

Camel Rock Campground   *8 mi. N on US 285*   *455-2661*
This privately operated campground near a freeway has a distant mountain view. Flush toilets, hot showers, and hookups are available. Each of the gravel sites has a picnic table, and many have a grill.   base rate...$9

Hyde Memorial State Park   *8.5 mi. NE on NM 475*   *827-2726*
This state park campground is by a small creek in a pine forest. Features include marked nature trails in summer and, in winter, an ice-skating rink and tobogganning. Only pit toilets are available. There are no showers or hookups. Each pine-shaded site has a picnic table and grill.   base rate...$3

KOA - Ranchero de Santa Fe   *10 mi. SE via I-25 to exit 290*   *983-3482*
This large, privately owned campground is in a wooded area near the base of the Sangre de Cristo Mountains. An outdoor pool, whirlpool, and rec room are on the premises, and motorbike trails are nearby. Flush toilets, hot showers, and hookups are available. Each site has a picnic table, fire ring, and grill. Some sites are shaded.   base rate...$9

SPECIAL EVENTS
★ **Santa Fe Film Festival**   *several locations in town*   *late April*
This film festival is only a few years old, but it attracts famous guests for premieres of new films, plus screenings of classics and silent films.

★ **Santa Fe Rodeo**   *rodeo grounds*   *mid-July*
Cowboys from all over the West compete in a major four-day rodeo, preceded by a parade through downtown.

★ **Indian Market**   *the plaza*   *mid-August*
Tribes from all over the country display their arts and crafts in one of the West's largest and most colorful Indian markets. It is a popular once-a-year shopping opportunity.

★ **Santa Fe Opera**   *7 mi. N on US 285*   *July-August*
The renowned company presents classic and contemporary works in an inspired semi-open-air theater. Reservations are essential. Backstage tours are also offered. (Schedule and prices: 982-3851.)

★ **Santa Fe Fiesta**   *the plaza*   *early September*
This is the largest fiesta and the oldest community celebration of its kind in America, dating back to 1712. Three days of parades, costumed pageantry, street dancing, food booths, and arts and crafts shows begin on a Friday night with the burning of a memorable forty-foot tall puppet named Zozobra ("Old Man Gloom").

OTHER INFORMATION
Area Code: *505*
Zip Code: *87501*
Santa Fe Chamber of Commerce   *2 blocks N at 200 W. Marcy St.*   *983-7317*
Santa Fe National Forest-Supervisor's Office *1220 St. Francis Dr.*   *988-6940*

Taos, New Mexico

Elevation:

6,950 feet

Population (1980):

3,369

Population (1970):

2,475

Location:

280 mi. S
of Denver

Taos is an ancient village with an enchanting presence. It is a unique reflection of a spectacular location, diverse cultures, and an artistic temperament. Almost 7,000 feet above sea level, Taos lies near the edge of an enormous river basin at the base of the state's highest mountains. The elevation lends an inevitable crispness to the air and a remarkable clarity to the evening sky. In spite of the altitude, the town has a normal four season climate due in part to the sheltering effect of nearby mountains. Spring and fall are especially pleasant, with mild days, and cool evenings warmed by fragrant pinon pine and juniper burned in kiva fireplaces in every building. Summer is the most popular season. Hot days are relieved by frequent showers, and the town is normally full of visitors enjoying the wealth of shops and attractions, plus special events like a rodeo, music and art festivals, and Indian fiestas. A few miles to the west, the dramatic Rio Grande River gorge provides exciting whitewater rafting experiences. The Sangre de Cristo Mountains just east of town are the most popular locale for backpacking, horseback riding, camping and other outdoor recreation during the warm months. These mountains are also the location of some of the Southwest's best skiing areas.

Indians had lived in a nearby pueblo for hundreds of years when Taos, one of America's oldest towns, was established around 1615 as Spain's northernmost colony. By the early 1800s, it was the West's largest fur trading center. Mexico gained independence from Spain in 1821 and ruled Taos until 1846, when it became part of American territory. The transcontinental railroad bypassed this area in the late nineteenth century, and the town briefly settled into quiet rural life. However, the splendid isolation and natural grandeur began to attract artists and dreamers in the 1890s. They are still coming.

The tiny village's great charm lies in the memorable concentration of ancient adobes, romantic courtyards shaded by enormous old elm and cottonwood trees, and narrow winding streets all within an easy stroll of the venerable little plaza at the heart of town. Newer buildings are so carefully blended with historic structures that the ubiquitous Spanish-pueblo adobe style of architecture conveys a timeless enchantment. Downtown has a fascinating array of museums, arts and crafts studios, and galleries. Many feature works by renowned Western artists. In addition, the best of the bars, restaurants and lodging places on and near the plaza convey a unique blending of Old World charms in memorable frontier settings.

Taos, New Mexico

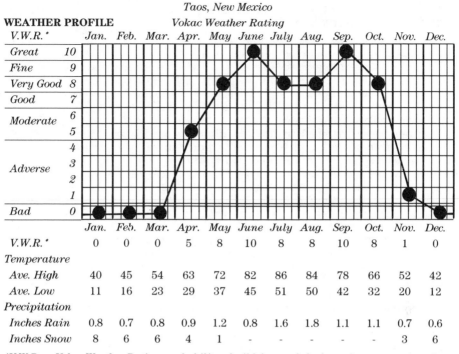

WEATHER PROFILE — Vokac Weather Rating

V.W.R.*		Jan.	Feb.	Mar.	Apr.	May	June	July	Aug.	Sep.	Oct.	Nov.	Dec.
Great	10						●			●			
Fine	9												
Very Good	8					●		●	●		●		
Good	7												
Moderate	6												
	5				●								
	4												
Adverse	3												
	2												
	1											●	
Bad	0	●	●	●									●

	Jan.	Feb.	Mar.	Apr.	May	June	July	Aug.	Sep.	Oct.	Nov.	Dec.
V.W.R.*	0	0	0	5	8	10	8	8	10	8	1	0
Temperature												
Ave. High	40	45	54	63	72	82	86	84	78	66	52	42
Ave. Low	11	16	23	29	37	45	51	50	42	32	20	12
Precipitation												
Inches Rain	0.8	0.7	0.8	0.9	1.2	0.8	1.6	1.8	1.1	1.1	0.7	0.6
Inches Snow	8	6	6	4	1	-	-	-	-	-	3	6

*V.W.R. = Vokac Weather Rating: probability of mild (warm & dry) weather on any given day.

Forecast

Month	V.W.R.*		Temperatures Daytime	Evening	Precipitation
January	0	Bad	chilly	cold	infrequent snowstorms
February	0	Bad	chilly	cold	infrequent snow flurries
March	0	Bad	cool	chilly	infrequent snow flurries/showers
April	5	Moderate	cool	chilly	infrequent showers/snow flurries
May	8	Very Good	warm	cool	occasional showers
June	10	Great	warm	cool	infrequent showers
July	8	Very Good	hot	warm	frequent showers
August	8	Very Good	hot	warm	frequent showers
September	10	Great	warm	cool	infrequent showers
October	8	Very Good	warm	chilly	infrequent rainstorms
November	1	Adverse	cool	chilly	infrequent snow flurries/rainstorms
December	0	Bad	chilly	cold	infrequent snow flurries

Summary

Almost 7,000 feet above sea level, Taos seems tiny—lost in the vast scrub-covered plains of the upper Rio Grande River valley just west of the towering Sangre de Cristo Mountains. **Winter** days are chilly, nights are cold, and snowfalls infrequently disrupt activity. The nearby mountains accommodate some of the best skiing facilities in the West. Really good **spring** weather begins in May with the return of warm days and cool evenings. A few light showers settle the dust and bring out the special tang of pinon pine and juniper. **Summer** is pleasant. Hot days and warm evenings are accompanied by frequent light rains that clear the air for maximum enjoyment of grand panoramic views for which the area is justifiably famed. **Fall** features some of the finest weather in the Rocky Mountains. Comfortably warm days and little shower activity continue until after Halloween when freezing temperatures and erratic snowfalls foretell the return of winter.

ATTRACTIONS & DIVERSIONS

★ **Carson National Forest**   *surrounding town*   *758-2237*
The most prominent attraction in this forest is Wheeler Peak. At 13,161 feet, it is the highest point in the state and in the Wheeler Peak Wilderness Area, which can be accessed from Taos Ski Valley a few miles northwest of town. Other sections of the majestic Sangre de Cristo Mountains are also popular for hiking, backpacking, hunting, fishing, and winter sports. Information and maps may be obtained at the Supervisor's Office in town.

D.H. Lawrence Ranch and Shrine   *about 20 mi. NE via NM 3*   *776-2245*
D.H. Lawrence lived here briefly in the 1920s. His widow passed it on to the University of New Mexico when she died, and it is now used by writers in residence, and as a conference and education facility. The shrine is open to visitors.

Ernest L. Blumenschein Home   *1 block SW at 13 Ledoux St.*   *758-4741*
This National Historic Landmark, with portions of the building dating back to 1790, was the home of the co-founder of the famous Taos Society of Artists. In addition to containing original antique furnishings, it also showcases paintings by Taos artists. Closed Sun.

Governor Bent House   *2 blocks N on Bent St.*   *758-2376*
New Mexico's first American governor, after the territory was annexed to the U.S. in 1846, was killed here in his home by an angry mob protesting American rule. Today the old adobe houses an interesting museum of his and Southwestern memorabilia.

★ **The Harwood Museum and Library**   *2 blocks SW at 25 Ledoux St.*   *758-3063*
A group of adobe buildings including portions of some of the oldest residences in Taos is now a distinctive cultural center operated by the University of New Mexico. The complex houses an excellent public library and research library of the Southwest, a collection of books by and about D.H. Lawrence, and a gallery which includes many paintings by some of the famous early artists of Taos.

Horseback Riding
   Loba Ranch & Taos Equestrian Center *12 mi. N via NM 3 - Arroyo Hondo* 776-8526
One hour and longer trail rides into Kit Carson National Forest can be arranged here.

★ **Kit Carson Home and Museum**   *2 blocks E on Kit Carson St.*   *758-4741*
From 1843 until he died in 1868, this was the permanent residence of one of the West's most famous frontiersmen. Several rooms have been furnished as they might have been, and there are many momentoes of the period.

Kit Carson Memorial State Park   *4 blocks NE on N. Pueblo Rd.*
This lovely shaded park includes the old cemetery where Kit Carson and other historic figures are buried. Picnic tables and grills are available.

★ **Millicent Rogers Memorial Museum**   *4.2 mi. N via NM 3*   *758-2462*
An outstanding collection of Spanish-colonial and Indian arts and crafts is located in a well-preserved Spanish adobe hacienda overlooking the valley.

★ **Rio Grande Gorge Bridge**   *11 mi. NW on US 64*
One of the highest highway bridges in the country spans a precipitous chasm 650 feet above the Rio Grande. Elevated sidewalks, observation platforms, and picnic areas have been provided.

River Running
Whitewater raft trips through the rock-strewn Rio Grande Gorge and the "Taos Box" can be reserved in spring and summer.
   Rio Grande Rapid Transit   *15 mi. S on NM 68 - Pilar*   *758-9700*
   Sierra Outfitters and Guides   *3 blocks S at 307 S. Pueblo Rd.*   *758-9556*

★ **St. Francis of Assisi Mission Church**   *4 mi. S on NM 68*   *758-2754*
Here is a magnificent example of early Spanish mission architecture. The massive, heavily buttressed building, constructed between 1710 and 1755, is one of the oldest continuously-used churches in the West. The interior contains many religious art objects and a mystery painting. In daylight, "The Shadow of the Cross" portrays the barefoot Christ. In complete darkness, the portrait becomes luminescent, outlining the figure while clouds over the left shoulder form into a shadow of a cross. The artist disclaimed any knowledge of the reason for the change, and after many tests the painting remains a mystery.

★ **Taos Indian Pueblo**   *2 mi. N on N. Pueblo Rd.*   758-8626
This is not a ruinsite of ancient peoples. It is an occupied village of more than 1,000 Taos Indians that has been inhabited continuously for at least 800 years. A masterpiece of Indian architecture, it has changed little since the first Spaniards saw it in 1540. The two large, five-level adobe structures are the oldest "apartment buildings" and the highest pueblos in the country. Visitors are admitted daily. There is a parking fee and an additional fee for any camera use.

★ **Taos Plaza**
The town began to develop around the present plaza about 1615. Homes were built so that the rear of the buildings formed a continuous wall, making a fortress-like structure. There have been modifications over the centuries, but that historic interior space still remains the principle gathering place for the entire area, and it is still surrounded by solid blocks of Spanish-pueblo style buildings.

Winter Sports
★   **Angel Fire** *26 mi. E: 22 mi E. on US 64 & 4 mi. S on NM 38*   377-2301
With a vertical drop of 2,180 feet, the longest run is 3.5 miles. Two triple and four double chairlifts serve the area. All facilities, services, and rentals are available at the base for both downhill and cross-country skiing. Snowmobiling and ice-skating are also enjoyed. There are bars at the slope, and restaurants and lodgings nearby.

★   **Taos Ski Valley**   *18 mi. NE via NM 3 & NM 150*   776-2291
The vertical drop is 2,612 feet and the longest run (5.2 miles) is one of the West's longest. Six double chairlifts serve the area. All facilities, services, and rentals are available at the area for downhill skiing. Numerous restaurants and bars are at the base.

SHOPPING
The compact business district around the plaza has been the commercial heart of the area for centuries. Today, dozens of excellent galleries and studios, and specialty shops as charming as their picturesque adobe facades suggest, define the spirit of the area. The narrow, poorly maintained streets and ubiquitous parking meters will not gladden the hearts of motorists. However, endlessly intriguing architecture, decor, and arts and crafts delight pedestrians in one of the West's most extraordinary settlements.

Food Specialties
Dori's   *4 blocks N on N. Pueblo Rd.*   758-9222
An eclectic mixture of good international pastries, breads, and pies are served to go, or with meals in a rustic little dining area.

★ **Le Bunnerie**   *3 blocks S on S. Santa Fe Rd.*   758-1637
Delicious French pastries are served to go, or with all meals in a polished new example of contemporary Taos decor.

★ **Michael's Kitchen**   *.3 mi. N on N. Pueblo Rd.*   758-4178
Outstanding breads and pastries in limited variety are made fresh daily and served to go, or with all meals in a handcrafted Taos-style coffee shop. Don't miss the delicious "Taos Spanish Bread" or the cinnamon rolls.

Senor Murphy Candymaker   *N side of the plaza*   758-1990
Pinon nuts in chocolate candy or shelled and roasted, plus chili jellies, are notable regional specialties of this tiny shop.

★ **Taos Candy Factory**   *on the plaza*   758-4000
All kinds of chocolates and fudges are made here, including chocolate-covered pinon nuts. Some candy is prepared on a display table.

Specialty Shops
Fernandez de Taos Book Store   *N side of the plaza*   758-4391
Magazines — particularly those with an emphasis on art — are featured along with paperbacks in this small shop.

Maxae's Books   *2 blocks N on Bent St.*   758-4018
This is a charming place to relax and browse through a good selection of new, used, and rare books while listening to fine music. Topographic maps are also available.

★ **Overland Sheepskin Co.**   *1 mi. N on NM 3*   758-8822
Sheepskin apparel is manufactured here and sold at reasonable prices in a large, fascinating store filled with sheeplined jackets, coats, gloves, hats, and other clothing.

★ **Stables Art Center**   *2 blocks N on N. Pueblo Rd.*   *758-2036*
The Taos Art Association has established a community art center in a converted stables. First-rate arts and crafts in all media by Taos artists are displayed. Lectures and demonstrations, plus concerts, plays, and movies, are scheduled throughout the year.

★ **Taos Art Galleries**   *throughout downtown*
There are about forty galleries and studios within three blocks of the plaza in one of the West's most outstanding concentrations of fine art. Emphasis is appropriately on works reflecting the unique heritage of the Taos area. To understand why "art is a way of life in Taos," visitors must "discover" for themselves the many superb galleries on the plaza, down narrow adjoining streets, and hidden in picturesque courtyards.

★ **Taos Book Shop**   *1 block E on E. Kit Carson St.*   *758-3733*
The books in this long-established shop fill many rooms in a beautiful old adobe. Two fireplaces (much used except in summer) and background music contribute to the tranquil setting. D.H. Lawrence and Southwest Americana are specialties.

★ **Twining Weavers**   *9 mi. NE on NM 150*   *776-8367*
Handwoven wool rugs, tapestries, vests, purses, handknit sweaters, and hats, all in extraordinarily colorful contemporary designs, are sold at this direct outlet shop. Visitors can watch the artistic weavers at work daily. Closed Sun.

NIGHTLIFE
Musical events and artist's receptions periodically enliven evenings in Taos. In addition, there are a few romantic little lounges with live entertainment, and some authentic Old West bars that carry on the town's frontier spirit.

Kachina Lodge   *.5 mi. N on US 64*   *758-2275*
Cabaret entertainment and dancing are featured on Friday and Saturday nights, and there is live music nightly in the spacious Zuni Lounge.

★ **Ogelvie's**   *E side of the plaza*   *758-8866*
A large view deck overlooks the plaza, and there is a cheerful fireplace along with comfortable seating in a charming, contemporary Taos-style lounge.

★ **Sagebrush Inn**   *3 mi. S on NM 68*   *758-2254*
Live music is offered nightly in a perennial favorite with comfortable native furnishings and a big fireplace accenting the massive adobe-and-rough-beam interior.

★ **Taos Inn**   *2 blocks N on N. Pueblo Rd.*   *758-2233*
Live entertainment is offered almost every night in the beautifully handcrafted Adobe Bar, furnished with Taos-style art objects. Ice cream and custom margarita drinks are a specialty. For a private tete-a-tete, drinks are even served on cozy balconies overlooking a spectacular two-story lobby.

RESTAURANTS
Restaurants in Taos, at their best, capture the essence of the combination of Old World charm and frontier spirit that is the most compelling feature of this ancient village. "Native food" is emphasized, and it can be as delicious as it is regionally distinctive.

★ **Apple Tree Restaurant**   *2 blocks N at 21 Bent St.*   *758-1900*
B-L-D.   *Moderate*
The delicious New Southwestern-style cuisine of Santa Fe is served here in a charming old adobe house with romantic fire-and-candlelit rooms, and on an enclosed garden patio.

Casa Cordova   *8 mi. NE on NM 150*   *776-2200*
D only. Closed Sun.   *Expensive*
A Continental menu and on-premises baking are featured in this award-winning restaurant. The spare elegance of the dining room and cocktail lounge in this lovely old adobe home are fine examples of Taos-style decor.

Fagerquist's   *4.1 mi. N on NM 3*   *776-2448*
D only.   *Moderate*
Hearty American dinners and homemade baked goods are served family-style in casual dining rooms in a converted house, or on an outdoor dining patio.

The Fountain at El Patio   *just N of NW corner of the plaza*   *758-2121*
L-D. No D on Sun.   *Moderate*
Italian and native foods and casually elegant table settings are offered in a room with a skylit working fountain in one of the oldest buildings in Taos.

★ **Garden Restaurant**   *N side of the plaza*   *758-9483*
B-L-D.   *Moderate*
Fine omelets and homemade cinnamon rolls are well-regarded, along with other home-baked goods and native dishes, in this stylish woodcraft-and-plants dining room.

La Dona Luz   *1 block E on E. Kit Carson Rd.*   *758-3332*
L-D. No D on Wed. Closed Tues.   *Expensive*
Continental entrees are offered in a historic adobe building.

★ **Michael's Kitchen**   *.3 mi. N on N. Pueblo Rd.*   *758-4178*
B-L-D.   *Moderate*
Superb cinnamon rolls and other excellent pastries made here accompany hearty American dishes in an acclaimed old-Taos-style family coffee shop and bakery.

Ogelvie's Bar and Grille   *E side of the plaza*   *758-8866*
L-D.   *Moderate*
A contemporary menu is offered, and some homemade baked goods are served in a large updated-Taos-style dining room or on an outdoor balcony overlooking Taos Plaza.

Roberto's Restaurant   *2 blocks E on E. Kit Carson Rd.*   *758-2434*
L-D. Closed Tues.   *Low*
Highly-regarded native New Mexican specialties are served in an ancient building.

Sagebrush Inn   *3 mi. S on NM 68*   *758-2254*
B-L-D.   *Moderate*
Native and American foods are served all day in the large main dining room. Steaks are featured in the (dinner only) Los Vaqueros room. Both rooms have traditional Taos atmosphere, as does the lounge.

The Stakeout at Outlaw Hill   *8.5 mi. S on NM 68*   *758-2042*
D only. Closed Mon.   *Moderate*
Steaks are the specialty. American fare and a salad bar are also available in this remote pueblo-style building.

Taos Inn   *2 blocks N on N. Pueblo Rd.*   *758-2233*
B-L-D.   *Moderate*
Contemporary American and native dishes, plus a salad bar, are served in Doc Martin's, the inn's handsome Taos-style dining rooms.

Villa de Don Peralta   *.3 mi. S on S. Santa Fe Rd.*   *758-2111*
L-D. No L on Sat. Closed Sun.   *Low*
Territorial-style New Mexican cooking is featured in a plain and popular converted house.

★ **Whitey's**   *3 mi. N on NM 3*   *776-8545*
D only. Closed Mon.   *Moderate*
A short list of distinctive international specialties is noted on a chalkboard menu that changes according to the availability of fresh ingredients. Homemade baked goods include magnificent cheesecakes and other pastries. Classical piano music blends well with artistic and gracious furnishings in a lovely converted home where several tables and the small patio have enchanting mountain views.

LODGING

There aren't many places to stay in Taos. However, the better accommodations capture some of the unconventional appeal of this area. Rooms are inevitably scarce in summer and during the prime winter skiing season. Rates are usually at least 15% cheaper during spring and fall in most places.

Adobe Wall Motel   *.3 mi. E on US 64*   *758-3972*
This old pueblo-style motor court in the midst of an ancient stand of enormous cottonwood trees has **bargain** rooms with cable color TV.
   regular room —   K bed...$30

★ **El Pueblo Motor Lodge**   *.5 mi. N on US 64*   *758-8641*
A year-round pool (covered in winter) and a whirlpool are features of this modern pueblo-style motel. Each well-furnished unit has a phone and color cable TV, and there are some modern condominiums with full kitchens.
   #243,#244 — spacious, kitchenette, fireplace, mt. view,   Q bed...$55
   #240,#247 — spacious, kitchenette, fireplace,   Q bed...$55
   "condo" — 2 BR, kitchen, LR, fireplace, in-loft   Q bed..$128
   regular room —   Q bed...$48

Kachina Lodge - Best Western   *.5 mi. N on US 64*   *758-2275*
This large modern motel was carefully constructed in the Taos style. Landscaped grounds include a very large outdoor view pool, dining room, lounge, and cabaret. Each spacious, well-furnished room has a phone and cable color TV.

    #262 — end unit, semi-pvt. balc., mt. view,   K bed...$60
    regular room —   D bed...$55

★ **Sagebrush Inn**   *3 mi. S on NM 68*   *758-2254*
The area's most well-known motor hotel is a wonderfully atmospheric old adobe complex with a large outdoor pool, whirlpool (winter), and two tennis courts, plus charming restaurants and a lounge. Each of the comfortably furnished pueblo-style rooms has a phone and cable color TV with movies.

    fireplace room —   Q bed...$60
    suite — LR, fireplace in BR, refr.,   Q bed...$70
    regular room —   D bed...$35

Silvertree Lodge   *1.5 mi. E on US 64*   *758-3071*
A tiny stream lends to the tranquility of this small, older, single-level motel with an outdoor pool. Each room has cable color TV and a mural by a Taos artist.

    regular room —   K bed...$36

★ **Taos Inn**   *2 blocks N on N. Pueblo Rd.*   *758-2233*
Downtown's landmark inn, on the National Register of Historic Places, was recently exquisitely restored. Interior courtyards house an outdoor pool and whirlpool, and delightful public rooms include a restaurant and lounge. Each beautifully furnished room has a phone and cable color TV with movies.

    #111 — spacious, kiva fireplace, pvt. mt. view from corner windows,   K bed...$70
    #303 — bright, spacious, in single-level bldg., kiva fireplace,   Q bed...$70
    regular room —   D bed...$50

★ **Tennis Ranch of Taos**   *5 mi. NE on NM 150*   *776-2211*
This newer pueblo-style condominium complex has a year-round pool (covered in winter), whirlpool, sauna, six outdoor tennis courts and (for a fee) two lighted indoor tennis courts and two racquetball courts, plus a restaurant and lounge. Each of the beautifully furnished units has a phone, color TV, and a fireplace.

    #155, #158, #160 — spacious studio, kitchenette, fireplace,   Q bed...$70
    regular room —   Q bed...$55

CAMPGROUNDS

Few campgrounds are near town. Most have relatively primitive facilities in scenic locations. The best has complete facilities a few miles from town in a pretty little canyon by a stream.

Sierra Campground   *5.6 mi. SE on US 64*   *758-3660*
This privately operated campground in the Carson National Forest is by an attractive little stream in Taos Canyon. Fishing and hiking are featured. Flush toilets, hot showers, and hookups are available. Each of the closely-spaced sites is grassy. Many have a picnic table, and some are in tree-shaded locations by the stream.   base rate...$6.50

SPECIAL EVENTS

New Mexico Music Festival   *Taos Community Auditorium*   *mid-July to mid-August*
The Taos School of Music sponsors chamber music concerts and seminars downtown and at Taos Ski Valley for a month in mid-summer.

Taos Fiesta   *on the plaza and elsewhere*   *last weekend in July*
A Fiesta Queen is crowned on the plaza, and dances and trade fairs are held downtown and at the nearby Taos Indian Pueblo.

★ **Taos Arts Festival**   *around town*   *first week in October*
A medley of arts and crafts exhibits and sales on the plaza, studio tours, gallery shows, musical and theatrical events, and poetry readings highlight the year's major art event.

OTHER INFORMATION

Area Code: *505*
Zip Code: *87571*
Carson National Forest-Supervisor's Office *2 mi. S via NM 68 on Cruz Alta* 758-2237
Taos Chamber of Commerce   *2 mi. S via NM 68 on Teresina*   *758-3873*

Ashland, Oregon

Elevation:

1,951 feet

Population (1980):

14,943

Population (1970):

12,342

Location:

268 mi. S
of Portland

Ashland has become a great Western crossroads of culture and recreation. One of the nation's finest theatrical complexes and Shakespearean festivals is the driving force behind this refined community. The location is also special. In a luxuriant mixed forest of broadleaf and evergreen trees high on the southern rim of the Rogue River country, the town overlooks a scenic valley surrounded by impressive peaks. Complementing the lovely natural setting is one of the mildest climates in the Northwest. Temperatures are pleasant from spring (when blossoms cover the orchards in the valley below) through fall (when roadside stands offer the bountiful harvest). During summer there is almost no rainfall to mar enjoyment of all kinds of outdoor recreation at nearby rivers, lakes, and mountains. Warm evenings normally complement both the Shakespearean Festival and the Peter Britt Music Festival, which are staged outdoors under star-studded skies. The town is usually filled to capacity with enthusiastic theater-goers throughout the summer season. In winter, snowfall is light in town, but there is plenty of snow on nearby Mt. Ashland to support a major skiing complex.

Gold was first discovered in Oregon in 1851 in the Jacksonville area a few miles northwest of town. Ashland was founded a year later. It never experienced a gold boom. Instead, it grew slowly at first with conventional businesses — a sawmill, flour mill, and general store. Development was more rapid after the arrival of passenger train service in 1884. By the turn of the century, the diversified local economy included railroading, fruit growing, and lumbering. Pursuit of the town's ultimate destiny began inauspiciously in 1935, when a local Professor, Angus Bowmer of Southern Oregon State College, won support for using an abandoned Chatauqua site for a Shakespearean production as part of a Fourth of July celebration. Success soon led to the organization of the Oregon Shakespearean Festival Association, and Ashland was on its way toward becoming a culture capital for the West.

Today, the Festival runs from February to early November in a complex of three fine live theaters. Tourism and education are now the town's principle industries. Lithia Park (superbly landscaped by the designer of Golden Gate Park in San Francisco) adjoins the Festival grounds, and lends great charm to the heart of town. Numerous distinctive shops and galleries feature local and regional arts, crafts, and specialty foods. Among the many restaurants in town are several gourmet dining rooms serving outstanding international specialties. A proliferation of bed-and-breakfast inns is a welcome recent development, as are several new motor inns and a handsomely restored landmark hotel that was once the tallest building between San Francisco and Portland.

Ashland, Oregon

WEATHER PROFILE   *Vokac Weather Rating*

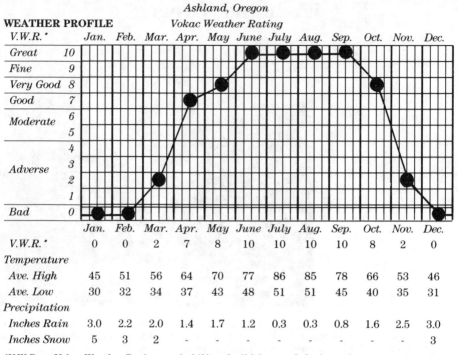

V.W.R.*	Jan.	Feb.	Mar.	Apr.	May	June	July	Aug.	Sep.	Oct.	Nov.	Dec.
Great 10												
Fine 9												
Very Good 8												
Good 7												
Moderate 6 / 5												
4												
Adverse 3 / 2												
1												
Bad 0												

	Jan.	Feb.	Mar.	Apr.	May	June	July	Aug.	Sep.	Oct.	Nov.	Dec.
V.W.R.*	0	0	2	7	8	10	10	10	10	8	2	0
Temperature												
Ave. High	45	51	56	64	70	77	86	85	78	66	53	46
Ave. Low	30	32	34	37	43	48	51	51	45	40	35	31
Precipitation												
Inches Rain	3.0	2.2	2.0	1.4	1.7	1.2	0.3	0.3	0.8	1.6	2.5	3.0
Inches Snow	5	3	2	-	-	-	-	-	-	-	-	3

V.W.R. = Vokac Weather Rating: probability of mild (warm & dry) weather on any given day.

Forecast

Temperatures

Month	V.W.R.*		Daytime	Evening	Precipitation
January	0	Bad	chilly	chilly	frequent rainstorms/snow flurries
February	0	Bad	cool	chilly	frequent showers/snow flurries
March	2	Adverse	cool	chilly	frequent showers
April	7	Good	cool	cool	occasional showers
May	8	Very Good	warm	cool	occasional showers
June	10	Great	warm	cool	infrequent showers
July	10	Great	hot	warm	negligible
August	10	Great	hot	warm	negligible
September	10	Great	warm	cool	infrequent showers
October	8	Very Good	warm	cool	occasional showers
November	2	Adverse	cool	chilly	frequent rainstorms
December	0	Bad	chilly	chilly	frequent rainstorms/snow flurries

Summary

Ashland is near the upper end of one of the broad tributary valleys of the Rogue River. It is nestled along the fringe of a splendid mixed-forest of pines and shade trees in low hills at the base of beautiful Mt. Ashland. The area enjoys the mildest four season climate in the Northwest. **Winter** is relatively short, chilly, and damp. Almost half of the year's precipitation occurs in frequent rainfalls and a few snow flurries. A few miles away and thousands of feet higher, a well-regarded skiing complex offers fine conditions for winter sports. **Spring** is delightful. Good weather arrives in April and is heralded by a fragrant profusion of blossoms in nearby orchards. Days are warm by May, and rainfalls are infrequent. **Summer** is faultless. Long warm-to-hot days, warm evenings, and negligible rainfalls are perfect for enjoying the areas water features during the day and outdoor theaters at night. In **fall**, mild weather continues through Halloween and provides ideal conditions for savoring fall colors and the bountiful nearby fruit harvest.

ATTRACTIONS & DIVERSIONS

Applegate River Canyon   *starts 25 mi. W via OR 99 & OR 238*

Near the town of Ruch, the road forks south and winds for several miles along the scenic reaches of the upper Applegate River Canyon toward the California border. Numerous clear pools in idyllic settings have caused this remote portion of the river to be popular for nude bathing.

★ **Bicycling**

    Siskiyou Cyclery   *1.7 mi. SE on OR 99 at 1729 Siskiyou Blvd.*   *482-1997*

Bicycles may be rented here by the hour or longer to explore miles of scenic byways in the lush, gentle valley.

★ **Crater Lake National Park**   *80 mi. NE via I-5 & OR 62*

Oregon's only national park features one of the world's most beautiful lakes. It lies nestled in a huge bowl created when volcanic Mt. Mazama collapsed into a caldera hollowed out by climactic eruptions about 6,000 years ago. The mountainous rim of Crater Lake rises more than 2,000 feet above the water in places, and the lake is nearly 2,000 feet deep (America's deepest). A magnificent thirty-two-mile rim drive around the lake doesn't open until about the Fourth of July, except in years of light snowfall. The highway (OR 62) to Rim Village is kept open year-round, however, in spite of normal snowfalls totalling fifty feet each year. Daily boat tours in summer are another way to explore the lake and see majestic Wizard Island up close. Scenic spur roads and well-marked trails extend from many viewpoints along the rim drive.

Emigrant Lake   *5 mi. S on OR 66*

The nearest major water body to town is a reservoir with a swimming area, plus boating, water-skiing, and fishing. Several shaded picnic areas with barbecues and an improved campground have been provided.

★ **Howard Prairie Lake**   *20 mi. E via Dead Indian Rd.*   *482-1979*

This six-mile-long lake, surrounded by a pine forest, has four county parks on the western shore. Boats may be rented at the marina. Boating, fishing, water-skiing, swimming, picnicking, and camping are popular.

★ **Jacksonville**   *15 mi. NW via OR 99 & OR 238*   *899-8118*

Gold was discovered here in 1851 in one of the state's first strikes. But the town was bypassed later when the first railroad went through Medford. When the gold played out in the 1920s, Jacksonville even lost its county seat (in 1927) to Medford. It is now a National Historic Landmark. Many well-preserved original buildings now house specialty stores, galleries, and restaurants. The old County Courthouse (1884) is now a museum displaying Oregon history. A self-guided walking tour of town is detailed on a brochure available at the old Rogue River Valley Railway Depot Information Center at Oregon and C Streets. There is also a pioneer village at 725 N. 5th Street with relocated Victorian buildings, memorabilia, a melodrama theater, and dinner house. The Bella Union Bar on MainStreet features authentically creaky floorboards and a picturesque sheltered courtyard.

Library   *downtown at Siskiyou Blvd./Gresham St.*   *482-1151*

The Ashland Public Library occupies a 1912 Carnegie Library building regally positioned above the main street in a lovely small park. Closed Fri.-Sun.

★ **Lithia Park**   *downtown along Ashland Creek on Pioneer St.*   *482-9215*

One of the West's grandest achievements among town parks borders the theater complex downtown and extends for more than a half mile along Ashland Creek. An enchanting forest shelters formal rose and rhododendron gardens, a landscaped pond with resident swans, meandering pathways, a band shell, tennis courts, imaginative play equipment, emerald green lawns and playing fields, and secluded picnic sites.

★ **Lithia Spring Water**   *downtown at Winburn Way/N. Main St. in Town Plaza*

For about sixty years, drinking fountains on the plaza have provided Lithium water from the nearby mountains. It *is* different.

★ **Orchards**   *starts 3 mi. N via OR 99*

Vast pear and peach orchards are joined by other fruit and nut trees to transform the Bear Creek valley below Ashland into a blossom-time spectacle in April. In the fall, the delectable harvest is displayed and sold at roadside stands.

★ **Rogue River**   *19 mi. N on I-5*
The renowned Rogue River offers, in its relatively short length, a greater diversity of
outdoor recreation opportunities than any river in the West. Between its spectacular
beginnings in the high Cascades near Crater Lake and its broad outlet in the ocean at Gold
Beach, the Rogue has a nationally classified Wild and Scenic River section, several pine-
clad man-made lakes, and limitless sandy beaches, deep clear pools, riffles, and rapids. It
is the primary destination of an increasing number of river runners in a remarkable
variety of still or rough watercraft, as well as hordes of swimmers, sunbathers, hikers,
picnickers, and campers; and it is world famous for salmon and trout fishing.

★ **Rogue River National Forest**   *NE and SW of town*   *482-3333*
This large forest includes the scenic headwaters of the Rogue River. The Sky Lakes Area
features numerous heavily forested lakes. A major winter sports area is on the slopes of
Mt. Ashland. A good system of highways and dirt roads plus hundreds of miles of trails,
including a picturesque segment of the Pacific Crest National Scenic Trail, provide access
for hiking, backpacking, horseback and pack trips, swimming, excellent fishing and
boating, camping, and skiing in winter. Information and maps may be obtained at the
Ashland Ranger District Office.

Scenic Flights
   Above it All   *1 mi. SE on OR 99 at 1257 Siskiyou Blvd.*   *482-8301*
Balloons depart daily at dawn, weather permitting, in summer. The approximately hour-
long flight provides a spectacular view of the Rogue River Valley. Complimentary light
refreshments are served upon your return.

Winery
   Valley View Vineyard   *23 mi. W via OR 238 at 1000 Applegate Rd. - Ruch* *899-8468*
Several styles of premium grape wine, plus pear wine, are in limited production at the
area's first serious winery. Informal tours are offered and the tasting room is open daily
11-5. From Jan. 2-Apr. 14, only open 1-5 on weekends.

Winter Sports
   Mt. Ashland Ski Area   *19 mi. SW via I-5 and Mt. Ashland Rd.*   *482-2897*
The vertical rise is 1,150 feet and the longest run is approximately one mile. Elevation at
the top is 7,500 feet. There are two chairlifts. All essential services, facilities, and rentals
are available at the base for downhill skiing. There is a cafeteria and lounge at the base,
but no lodging facilities. The skiing season is December through April.

SHOPPING
A lively and compact downtown is centered around the plaza. Specialty shops are
thriving, along with theaters and an increasing number of distinctive restaurants, lounges,
and lodging places. Parking on the street and in municipally-owned lots is free.

Food Specialties
Ashland Bakery Cafe   *downtown at 38 E. Main St.*   *482-2117*
A full line of pastries and breads is displayed in a cheerful new bakery/cafe overlooking
Main Street.

★ **Ashland Wine Cellar**   *downtown at 38 C St.*   *488-2111*
A fine selection of Northwestern wine is displayed, sold, and offered for limited tasting,
along with many other premium wines, in an impressive cellar beneath a very complete
liquor store. Closed Sun.

★ **Bear Creek Store**   *10 mi. NW at 2836 S. OR 99*   *776-2277*
The retail outlet for the Bear Creek Orchards of Harry and David fame showcases
gourmet foods and kitchenwares in a large gift shop. In an adjacent market, delicious
Comice pears and other kinds of locally grown fruit are packaged in season for purchase
or shipment anywhere in gift packs. There is also a new dining area specializing in locally
produced light gourmet foods. Tours of the vast facility are offered from October into
December. In late summer, the Jackson and Perkins Rose Test Garden on adjoining
property is a radiant and fragrant feast for the senses.

★ **Manna from Heaven**   *.3 mi. E at 542 A St.*   *482-5831*
Some of the West's best pastries and breads are the tantalizing lure of an out-of-the-way
little carryout bakery that is hard to find, but well worth it.

★ **Rogue River Valley Creamery**   *18 mi. N at 311 N. OR 99 - Central Pt.*   664-2233
The cheddar and jack cheeses made here are very good. This is one of the few places in the country where blue cheese is also made. Samples are served upon request. Closed Sat.-Sun.

★ **Rosie's Sweet Shoppe**   *downtown at 303 E. Main St.*   488-0179
Dozens of flavors of premium ice cream by several manufacturers, plus chocolates and other candy treats, can be enjoyed in the large, comfortable parlor, or packaged to go.

★ **Second Hand Rose Ice Cream Parlour**   *downtown at 40 N. Main St.*   482-9962
Locally-made butter-rich ice cream from natural ingredients, plus popular Umpqua ice cream, are served in all kinds of fountain treats in a pleasant, plant-filled parlor.

★ **The Wizard's Den**   *downtown at 59 N. Main St.*   482-4867
This eclectic, culinary tour de force is the place to put together a picnic with delicious French bread and pastry made here, fine pates and cheeses, plus other gourmet foods and wines. The sights and smells of this quintessential Northwestern deli can also be enjoyed at your leisure in a comfortable dining area built into the cellar of a Victorian building.

Specialty Shops

★ **Bloomsbury Books**   *.3 mi. SE on OR 99 at 505 Siskiyou Blvd.*   488-0029
A handsome Eastlake-style Victorian home has been carefully restored to house an excellent full-line bookstore and an art gallery featuring works by Northwestern artists. Background music, coffee or tea, and a comfortable chair contribute to the store's appeal.

Casa del Sol   *downtown at 82 N. Main St.*   482-5443
Fine pottery is emphasized in this studio/gallery, plus poster art and other items.

The Golden Mean Bookstore   *downtown at 42 E. Main St.*   482-9771
Self-help books are emphasized in a mellow bookstore with classical music and reading chairs.

★ **Lithia Creek Arts**   *downtown at 49 N. Main St.*   488-1028
Art work and handicrafts by Rogue River Valley artists are showcased in an inviting little shop.

★ **Myrtlewood Chalet**   *downtown at 11 N. Main St.*   482-5263
This shop is devoted to a wide assortment of artistic and functional items made from myrtlewood — the prized hardwood of the Northwest.

Nimbus   *downtown at 25 E. Main St.*   482-3621
This large, intriguing store features many objects of art in pottery and glassware.

Paddington Station   *downtown at 125 E. Main St.*   482-1343
A large old building has been updated into a fascinating two-level gift shop crammed with regional foods and wines, gourmet cookware, and much more.

★ **Tudor Guild Gift Shop**   *downtown at 15 S. Pioneer St.*   482-0940
In the theater complex is a small shop that caters to lovers of Elizabethan lore with many books on Shakespeare and his plays, slides of Ashland productions, patterns for Elizabethan costumes, Shakespeare and theater posters, and many Old English items. Closed Mon.

NIGHTLIFE
Live theater is *the* vital force in Ashland, and it is presented in more than one theater on most nights of the year. Numerous restaurants, gourmet dessert places, and lounges cater especially to after-theater crowds. Several distinctive nightclubs provide a diversity of live entertainment for dancing.

★ **Ashland Hills Inn**   *3 mi. SE on OR 66 at 2525 Ashland St.*   482-8310
Live music for dancing is provided most nights in the resort's plush contemporary lounge.

Backstage IV   *downtown at 166 E. Main St.*   482-8114
Behind the Varsity Theater (reached by an adjoining walkway off Main Street) is a little cabaret/movie theater. Classic films, live theater, poetry readings, and musicals are among the appealing events offered with beer, wine, coffee and tea.

Beau Club   *downtown at 347 E. Main St.*   482-4185
A pool table in the back room, a jukebox, a back bar with stained glass murals, and comfortably padded stools and booths make this a good place to drop in for casual refreshments.

Brooklyn   *downtown at 33 Water St.*   488-2867
Hard rock is featured most evenings in this dark, funky club.

Cooks Tavern   *downtown at 66 E. Main St.*   482-5145
This lively contemporary tavern offers disco dancing in a rear area, and a good
assortment of tap beers.

★ **Jazmin's**   *downtown at 180 C St.*   488-0883
An eclectic mixture of popular live entertainment is showcased in a large, handsome
lounge with comfortable seating and a dance floor. International specialties are served for
dinner earlier in the evening.

★ **Log Cabin Tavern**   *downtown at 41 N. Main St.*   482-9701
Pool, foosball, and electronic games are provided, but the most notable feature in this
handsome tavern with a distinctive back bar and wooden armchairs is that it has the
elusive feeling of a classic "town bar."

★ **Mark Antony Hotel**   *downtown at 212 E. Main St.*   482-1721
The landmark hotel's spacious lobby is a favorite rendezvous for theater-goers and actors.
A pianist entertains on weekend evenings. The comfortable adjoining lounge is a good
place to enjoy a quiet drink and a Main Street view.

★ **Oregon Shakespearean Festival**   *downtown at 15 S. Pioneer St.*   482-4331
Three live theaters offer a remarkable variety of productions from February into
November in the complex that won the 1983 Tony Award for America's best regional
theater. As many as three plays may be staged on any given evening.

Vintage Inn   *downtown at 31 Water St.*   482-1120
Live country/western music is often featured in this casual, woodsy saloon. All meals are
served during the day.

RESTAURANTS

Local restaurants have flourished with Ashland's growing acclaim as a theater town.
Some of Oregon's most exciting and distinguished dining can be experienced in this
burgeoning gourmet haven.

Arbor House   *5.5 mi. N via OR 99 at 103 W. Wagner St. - Talent*   535-6817
D only. Sun. brunch. Closed Mon.-Tues.   Low
An around-the-world tour of various countries' specialties is the feature of this cozy little
restaurant.

Ashland Hills Inn   *3 mi. SE on OR 66 at 2525 Ashland St.*   482-8310
D only. Sun. brunch.   Moderate
The resort's Cascade Restaurant features Continental specialties in a gracious
contemporary dining room with a tranquil picture window view of the countryside.

★ **Banbury Cross Creperie**   *downtown at 55 N. Main St.*   482-3644
L only.   Moderate
Delicious crepes are the highlight in a bright and pretty little dining room by Ashland
Creek.

The Breadboard   *1 mi. N on OR 66 at 744 N. Main St.*   488-0295
B-L. Closed Sun.   Moderate
Good breakfasts (omelets, sourdough pancakes, etc.) and homemade baked goods are
served in a cheerful little roadside cafe with a mountain view and a fireplace.

Brother's   *downtown at 95 N. Main St.*   482-9671
B-L-D. Closed Mon.   Low
Awesome homemade cinnamon rolls are the star attraction. Breakfast is served all day in
this casual New York kosher-style deli/restaurant.

Callahan's Lodge   *10 mi. S on I-5 (Mt. Ashland exit) at 7100 OR 99*   482-1299
D only. Closed Mon.   Moderate
Family-style Italian dinners are featured, including a relish tray, soup, salad, spaghetti, an
entree, dessert, and beverage. Many windows provide high country views.

★ **Change of Heart**   *downtown at 139 E. Main St.*   488-0235
D only.   Expensive
Gourmet Continental cuisine is served in an elegant, romantic setting overlooking the
Elizabethan theater, Main Street, and the mountains beyond.

★ **Chata**   *4 mi. N at 1212 S. OR 99 - Talent*   535-2575
D only. Closed Mon.-Tues. from Oct. to May. Closed Jan.   Moderate
The Eastern European cuisine is superb. All dishes are prepared with skill, discipline, and
the freshest possible ingredients in a charming, casually elegant little roadside house.

★ **Chateaulin** *downtown at 50 E. Main St.* *482-2264*
D only. Closed Mon. *Expensive*
Traditional and Nouvelle French dishes are carefully prepared with seasonally fresh ingredients. The polished, wood-trimmed little bistro is inevitably crowded with theater-goers and others here to enjoy good food and sophisticated ambiance.

★ **Clark Cottage Restaurant** *.3 mi. SE on OR 99 at 568 E. Main St.* *482-2293*
B-L. D in summer only. *Moderate*
Fresh homemade croissants and cinnamon rolls are among the delicious specialties that accompany some of the West's finest homestyle cooking in a converted cottage with comfortable old-time decor.

Copper Skillet *2 mi. SE at 2270 OR 66* *482-2684*
B-L-D. *Low*
Breakfasts, including homemade cinnamon rolls or biscuits, are served with unlimited omelet variations. Pies are also homemade in this pleasant, family-oriented coffee shop.

Geppetto's *downtown at 345 E. Main St.* *482-1138*
B-L-D. *Moderate*
In addition to good Italian foods, some unusual specialties (chicken in currant sauce, scrambled eggs with pepperoncini and cheddar, pesto, and homemade cinnamon rolls) are served in a popular, casual cafe.

Gourmet Underground Deli *downtown at 125 E. Main St.* *482-9111*
B-L-D. *Moderate*
Homemade pastries and jams are highlights in a well-decorated cellar deli.

Hamlet's Rooste *downtown at 58 E. Main St.* *482-5955*
B-L-D. *Low*
Homestyle American cooking, including homemade sweet rolls and pies, is the feature of this modest neo-Elizabethan coffee shop.

Jacksonville Inn *15 mi. NW at 175 E. California St. - Jacksonville* *899-1900*
L-D. *Moderate*
Very complete multi-course American dinners are served amidst Victorian elegance in a refurbished Civil War-era building.

Omar's *1.2 mi. SE on OR 99 at 1380 Siskiyou Blvd.* *482-1281*
L-D. No L on Sat. & Sun. *Moderate*
There are some distinctive dishes on a seafood and steak menu. Everything is carefully prepared in this casual, long-established restaurant.

Pioneer House *15 mi. NW via OR 99 at 725 N. 5th St. - Jacksonville* *899-1683*
D only. Sun. brunch. Closed Mon.-Tues. *Moderate*
Seasonally fresh ingredients are used to prepare very complete table d'hote dinners. The casually elegant dining room is decorated with local antiques.

Seasons at Oak Knoll *3.3 mi. SE at 3070 OR 66* *482-4312*
L-D. Closed Mon. *Moderate*
Homestyle American cooking is featured in an attractive dining room at the Oak Knoll Golf Course.

Tommy's the Restaurant *downtown at 47 N. Main St.* *482-3556*
B-L-D. *Moderate*
The omelets are a highlight on a comprehensive menu offered in a pleasant, wood-brick-and-plant-trimmed restaurant.

★ **The Winchester Inn** *downtown at 35 S. 2nd St.* *488-1113*
L-D. Closed Mon. *Moderate*
Skillfully prepared Continental cuisine is served in a lavishly restored Victorian mansion that was recently converted into a charming bed-and-breakfast inn. Guests are also treated to a colorful view of an adjoining flower garden in summer.

★ **Yorgo's** *1 mi. SE on OR 99 at 1209 Siskiyou Blvd.* *482-9410*
L-D. *Moderate*
Authentic Greek specialties are served in a casual and congested, lively little restaurant.

Young's Pantry　　*5.5 mi. N on OR 99 at 109 Talent Hwy. - Talent*　　　*535-2673*
D only. Closed Sun.　　　　　　　　　　　*Low*
All-American fare, including several homemade pies and cakes nightly, is carefully prepared and nicely presented. The casual and pleasant restaurant is a local favorite.

LODGING

Good accommodations have recently proliferated in Ashland. In addition to contemporary motels, a remarkable number of bed-and-breakfast places have been added. Accommodations anywhere near the festival complex are relatively expensive in summer. However, there are still some bargains on the main highway through town — OR 99 and OR 66. Most places reduce their summer prices (shown below) by about 15% in early fall, 30% in late fall and winter, and 15% in spring.

★ **Ashland Hills Inn**　　*3 mi. SE on OR 66 at 2525 Ashland Av.*　　　*482-8310*
Ashland's largest accommodation is a contemporary resort hotel with a big outdoor pool, whirlpool, putting green, two (fee) tennis courts, and an elegant dining room and lounge. Each spacious, well-furnished room has a phone, cable color TV, and a private balcony.
　　#275 — corner, bay windows, fine mt. view,　　　　　　K bed...$75
　　#366,#266,#375 — corner, bay windows, fine mt. view,　　2 Q beds...$63
　　regular room —　　　　　　　　　　　　　　　　　Q bed...$61

Ashland Motel　　*.9 mi. SE on OR 99 at 1145 Siskiyou Blvd.*　　　*482-2561*
An outdoor pool is a feature of this small motel. Each room has a phone and cable color TV with movies.
　　regular room —　　　　　　　　　　　　　　　　　Q bed...$40
　　regular room —　　　　　　　　　　　　　　　　　D bed...$32

Bard's Inn - Best Western　　*downtown at 132 N. Main St.*　　　*482-0049*
This newer motel has a convenient location and a small outdoor pool. Each room has a phone and color TV with movies.
　　regular room —　　　　　　　　　　　　　　　　　K bed...$48

Cedarwood Inn　　*2 mi. SE on OR 99 at 1801 Siskiyou Blvd.*　　　*488-2000*
The outdoor pool is notably accented by palm trees in this modern motel. Other amenities include a whirlpool, sauna, and steam room. Each room has a phone and cable color TV with movies.
　　courtyard room — wet bar, deck or patio,　　　　K waterbed...$44
　　regular room —　　　　　　　　　　　　　　　　　Q bed...$34

★ **Chanticleer Inn**　　*downtown at 120 Gresham St.*　　　*482-1919*
In this large bed-and-breakfast inn, each room is beautifully furnished with antiques and fresh flowers, and has a private bath. A full breakfast is served in a sunny dining room, or by request in bed.
　　"Aerie" — sunny corner room overlooking the valley,　　T & Q beds...$59
　　regular room —　　　　　　　　　　　　　　　　　Q bed...$59

Columbia Hotel　　*downtown at 262½ E. Main St.*　　　*482-3726*
A small refurbished turn-of-the-century hotel in the heart of town is a **bargain.**
　　"large front room" — share bath,　　　　　　　　2 D beds...$29
　　regular room — pvt. bath,　　　　　　　　　　　　2 D beds...$40
　　regular room — share bath,　　　　　　　　　　　　D bed...$25

Jackson Hot Springs　　*2.3 mi. N at 2253 OR 99*　　　*482-3776*
A large outdoor mineral pool is operated in summer free to guests. Private rooms for hot mineral tub baths are available. Each of the rustic old cabin units is a **bargain** with a complete kitchen and private bath. Some have color TV.
　　regular room —　　　　　　　　　　　　　　　　　D bed...$25

Knights Inn Motel　　*2.5 mi. SE on OR 99 at 2359 Ashland St.*　　　*482-5111*
This modern **bargain** motel has an outdoor pool. Each nicely furnished unit has a phone and cable color TV.
　　regular room —　　　　　　　　　　　　　　　　　Q bed...$25

Main St. Inn　　*downtown at 142 N. Main St.*　　　*488-0969*
A renovated Victorian house is now a small bed-and-breakfast inn. Each room has color TV and a private bath. A complimentary Continental breakfast is served to the room.
　　"Blue Room" — view toward downtown, bay window, semi-pvt. deck,　　D bed...$52
　　regular room —　　　　　　　　　　　　　　　　　D bed...$52

Manor Motel   *.7 mi. N at 476 N. Main St.*   *482-2246*
This small, old motor court is a **bargain**. Each plainly furnished, small room has a cable color TV.

regular room —   D bed...$26

★ **Mark Antony Hotel**   *downtown at 212 E. Main St.*   *482-1721*
Ashland's National Historic Landmark hotel in the heart of town was once the tallest building between San Francisco and Portland. Recently renovated, there is a large landscaped outdoor pool, plus a dining room with a grand chandelier, and a comfortable lounge. Each room has a phone, B/W TV, and a private bath.

#911 — fine theater/mt. view from the top (9th) fl. corner,   K bed...$60
#907,#905 — corners, top fl., fine town views,   Q bed...$55
regular room —   D bed...$50

The Morical House   *1.2 mi. N at 668 N. Main St.*   *482-2254*
A century-old home was recently restored to reflect its Victorian heritage and to serve as a bed-and-breakfast inn surrounded by an acre of lawns and gardens. Each room features some antiques and a private bath. A full complimentary breakfast is served.

#5 — whole top (3rd) floor,   Q bed...$56
regular room —   Q bed...$56

★ **Romeo Inn**   *.4 mi. S at 295 Idaho St.*   *488-0884*
A charming Cape Cod-style house is now an outstanding bed-and-breakfast inn set amid noble trees on an expansive lawn. Landscaped grounds also include a tranquil outdoor pool and a whirlpool. Each spacious, beautifully furnished bedroom has a private bath. A full complimentary breakfast is served in the morning, and tea is offered in the afternoon.

#1 — pvt. entrance, splendid fireplace, windows on 3 sides,   K bed...$59
regular room —   K bed...$59

Stratford Inn   *.3 mi. SE at 555 Siskiyou Blvd.*   *488-2151*
This handsome newer motel has a small indoor pool and whirlpool. Each well-furnished room has a phone and cable color TV.

regular room —   Q bed...$52

Vista-6 Motel   *3 mi. SE via OR 66 to 535 Clover Lane*   *482-4423*
The freeway adjoins this modern little single-level motel, which has a tiny outdoor pool. Each of the plain **bargain** rooms has a cable color TV.

regular room —   Q bed...$22

★ **The Winchester Inn**   *downtown at 35 S. 2nd St.*   *488-1113*
One of Ashland's newest bed-and-breakfast inns is a large, spectacularly restored century-old home that is an easy stroll from the theaters. An elegant dining room is used for full complimentary breakfasts exclusively for guests. Fine dinners are served to the public as well. Each beautifully furnished room has a private bath.

"Sylvan Room" — fine view of adjacent oak trees,   Q bed...$63
"Garden Room" — windows on 2 sides,   Q bed...$63
regular room —   Q bed...$63

CAMPGROUNDS

An outstanding assortment of water-related campgrounds are within a half hour drive of town. All of the best feature complete facilities in shady locations by a scenic lake or a hot springs pool.

Emigrant Lake Campground   *5 mi. SE on OR 66*   *776-7001*
The county operates a facility by an attractive little reservoir with lake swimming, boating, fishing, and water-skiing. Flush toilets and hot showers are available, but there are no hookups. Each site has a picnic table, fire ring, and grill. Some sites are tree-shaded.

base rate...$5.50

★ **Howard Prairie Lake Resort**   *24 mi E via OR 66 on Hyatt Lake Rd.*   *773-3619*
This big, private facility includes a campground in a pine forest by a large reservoir. There is a beach, a boat ramp and dock, and rental boats. Lake swimming, boating, water-skiing, and fishing are popular. Flush toilets, hot showers (fee), and hookups are available. Each site has a picnic table and grill, and some are pine-shaded. There is a separate tenting area.

base rate...$5

★ **Hyatt Lake** *20 mi. E: 16 mi. SE on OR 66 & 4 mi. N on Hyatt Lake Rd.*   *776-3728*
The Bureau of Land Management operates a small campground near a scenic little reservoir. Features include a boat ramp, lake swimming, boating, and fishing, plus marked nature trails. Cross-country skiing and snowmobile trails are attractions in winter. Flush toilets and hot showers are available, but there are no hookups. Each site has a picnic table and grill.   base rate...$4

Jackson Hot Springs   *2.3 mi. N at 2253 OR 99*   *482-3776*
A private motel and trailer park adjoin an Olympic-sized outdoor pool. Sunbathing, swimming, and private hot mineral baths are featured. Flush and pit toilets, hot showers, and hookups are available. Each shaded closely-spaced site has a picnic table. Grills are shared. There is a separate tenting area.   base rate...$6

SPECIAL EVENTS

★ **Oregon Shakespearean Festival** *downtown in Lithia Park*   *late Feb. to early Nov.*
Classic and contemporary plays are professionally staged outdoors in a uniquely beautiful replica of an Elizabethan Theatre (1,200 seats) and indoors in the well-proportioned Angus Bowmer (600 seats) and intimate Black Swan (150 seats) theaters. Backstage tours can also be reserved.

Fourth of July   *downtown*   *4th of July*
Here is a classic old-fashioned fourth of July celebration with a parade, fiddlers' jamboree, live entertainment in Lithia Park, and a fireworks display.

★ **The Peter Britt Music Festival**   *in Jacksonville*   *late July to late August*
Two weeks of full-orchestra concerts are performed on the handsome new Peter Britt Pavilion stage before outdoor audiences each evening, and during the day on selected weekends. Benches with backs are provided, but many patrons prefer to bring a blanket to the lovely wooded setting and lie on the grassy slope and stargaze while listening. A three-day bluegrass festival takes place in late July, and there is a three-day jazz festival in late August.

OTHER INFORMATION

Area Code: *503*
Zip Code: *97520*
Ashland Chamber of Commerce   *downtown at 110 E. Main St.*   *482-3486*
Rogue River National Forest-Ashland Ranger *2 mi. SE at 2200 Ashland St.*   *482-3333*

Bend, Oregon

Elevation:

3,628 feet

Population (1980):

17,263

Population (1970):

13,710

Location:

160 mi. SE
of Portland

Bend is the heart of a year-round recreation wonderland. Nearby, majestic glacier-clad peaks overlook an evergreen forest that shades a seemingly endless assortment of lakes and streams. Symmetrical cinder cones, lava tubes and flows, and other bizarre remnants of recent volcanism also punctuate the area. Coupled with these dramatic surroundings is a surprisingly pleasant four season climate. Winters are relatively mild in town, but heavy snowfall on nearby Mt. Bachelor provides ideal conditions for both downhill and cross-country skiing at the state's finest snow sports complex. In spring, skiing remains excellent on the mountain even after warm weather begins to attract crowds to golf courses, tennis courts, swimming pools and other outdoor recreation facilities in Bend. Summer is the busiest season, when uniformly warm and sunny weather attracts throngs of visitors to a remarkable diversity of outdoor recreation opportunities.

The town's name is attributed to an early immigrant who said "Farewell, Bend!" as he reluctantly continued westward across the Deschutes River that runs through town. The lush pine forest and the good water at this bend in the river were the first that pioneers from the east saw after hundreds of miles of dry, open prairie. Although the initial exploration of the area was by John C. Fremont in the 1840s, Farewell Bend wasn't founded until 1900. (Postal authorities soon dropped the "Farewell.") The railroad arrived in 1911 and lumber milling became the dominant industry. Meanwhile, as roads and recreation equipment improved, Bend gradually developed as a tourist destination. With the recent completion of several major resort complexes in and near town, and the development of a superb skiing complex (including a just-completed lift to the top of beautiful Mt. Bachelor), Bend's ultimate destiny as a year-round leisure center is being fulfilled.

Today, a bend of the Deschutes River is showcased in one of the West's loveliest parks. The center of town is only a block away with a small but increasing number of interesting shops, restaurants, lounges and theaters. The compact district has recently been outfitted with colorful landscaping, eye-catching supergraphics, and one of the most whimsical sculptures anywhere. Accommodations are plentiful, ranging from budget motels to lavish resorts. Many of the best facilities feature picturesque riverside locations, and views of distant volcanic peaks. Lakeside and riverfront campgrounds are also plentiful in the forests near town.

Bend, Oregon

WEATHER PROFILE — *Vokac Weather Rating*

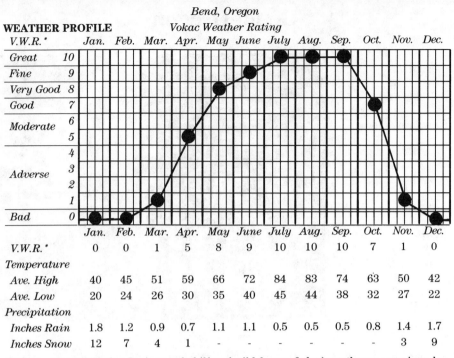

V.W.R.*	Jan.	Feb.	Mar.	Apr.	May	June	July	Aug.	Sep.	Oct.	Nov.	Dec.
V.W.R.*	0	0	1	5	8	9	10	10	10	7	1	0
Temperature												
Ave. High	40	45	51	59	66	72	84	83	74	63	50	42
Ave. Low	20	24	26	30	35	40	45	44	38	32	27	22
Precipitation												
Inches Rain	1.8	1.2	0.9	0.7	1.1	1.1	0.5	0.5	0.5	0.8	1.4	1.7
Inches Snow	12	7	4	1	-	-	-	-	-	-	3	9

V.W.R. = Vokac Weather Rating: probability of mild (warm & dry) weather on any given day.

Forecast

Month	V.W.R.*		Temperatures Daytime	Evening	Precipitation
January	0	Bad	chilly	cold	occasional snow flurries
February	0	Bad	chilly	chilly	occasional snow flurries
March	1	Adverse	cool	chilly	infrequent snow flurries/showers
April	5	Moderate	cool	chilly	infrequent showers
May	8	Very Good	warm	cool	infrequent showers
June	9	Fine	warm	cool	infrequent showers
July	10	Great	hot	cool	negligible
August	10	Great	hot	cool	negligible
September	10	Great	warm	cool	negligible
October	7	Good	cool	chilly	infrequent showers
November	1	Adverse	cool	chilly	infrequent showers/snow flurries
December	0	Bad	chilly	cold	occasional snow flurries

Summary

Bend straddles the Deschutes River on a vast pine-forested plain accented by volcanic hills and distant glacier-capped peaks. The rugged grandeur of the setting, matched by a surprisingly mild four season climate, has resulted in one of the West's most desirable year-round playgrounds. Even in **winter**, when all of the year's nominally bad weather occurs, bitter cold or heavy snowstorms are rare. Instead, days are typically chilly, but sunny. While occasional snowfalls are relatively light in town, they are heavy enough on nearby Mt. Bachelor to support the state's finest winter sports complex. **Spring** starts with cool temperatures that increase rapidly. Warm days arrrive in May. Light sportswear is appropriate in town while good skiing continues into late spring on the mountain. **Summer** is splendid, with warm days, cool evenings, and a few sprinkles. Brisk sunny weather in early **fall** contributes to carefree enjoyment of all kinds of outdoor recreation through Halloween.

ATTRACTIONS & DIVERSIONS

★ **Bicycling**

There is a lot of scenic, relatively level terrain in the pine forests around Bend. Two bicycle paths with a combined distance of more than nine miles start downtown and extend westward to recreation areas. Many additional miles of picturesque separated bikeways are available to guests and bicycle renters at Sunriver Resort. Bicycles can be rented by the hour or longer at:

Century Cycles	*.6 mi. W at 1135 NW Galveston Av.*	*389-4224*
Sunriver Resort	*16 mi. S off US 97 - Sunriver*	*593-1221*

Boat Rentals

★ **Sunriver Marina**   *19 mi. S off US 97 - Sunriver*   *593-2161*

For nearly forty miles, the crystal clear Deschutes River meanders slowly through luxuriant forests and meadows. Canoes may be rented here by the hour or longer, and downstream pickups can be arranged.

★ **Cascade Lakes**   *start 25 mi. SW via Century Drive Hwy.*

Dozens of small, clear lakes are nestled in a vast pine forest near the base of glacier-shrouded volcanic peaks along a thirty mile section of the Century Drive Highway. Cultus and Elk Lakes are the most picturesque and best developed, with rustic resorts, launching ramps, sandy beaches, swimming areas, picnic facilities, and campgrounds.

★ **Cove Palisades State Park**   *39 mi. N off US 97*   *546-3412*

One of central Oregon's most popular parks borders the southern shore of Lake Billy Chinook near the confluence of the Crooked and Deschutes Rivers. Volcanic cliffs tower above narrow watery fingers that stretch back to shaded campgrounds, picnic and swimming areas, and a marina (546-3521 for reservations) where visitors can rent catamarans and motorboats. Fishing and water-skiing are also popular on the reservoir.

★ **Deschutes National Forest**   *S & W of town*   *382-6922*

This giant forest includes Century Drive — a 100-mile paved scenic loop past some of the Northwest's finest peaks and lakes; several notable volcanic areas; parts of the Mt. Jefferson, Mt. Washington, Three Sisters, and the Diamond Peak wilderness areas; and the state's biggest winter sports facility — the Mt. Bachelor Ski Area. A good system of paved and dirt roads is backed by hundreds of miles of trails. The Pacific Crest National Scenic Trail lies along part of the western boundary of the forest. Hiking, backpacking, horseback and pack trips, boating, fishing, swimming, river running, and camping are popular. All kinds of snow sports are enjoyed in winter. Information and maps may be obtained at the Supervisor's Office in town.

★ **Drake Park**   *downtown on Riverside Blvd.*

Pine-shaded lawns slope to a placid stretch of the Deschutes River and frame splendid views of distant peaks. This is an enchanting place for a picnic by the heart of town. Canoeing is also popular. A half mile downstream is another picturesque haven, Pioneer Park, with shaded lawns and flower beds by the river.

Golf

    Bend Golf and Country Club   *3.5 mi. S at 20399 Murphy Rd.*   *382-3261*

This attractively landscaped, private 18-hole golf course does allow visitor play. A pro shop, club and cart rentals, and a restaurant and lounge are available.

★ **Sunriver Resort**   *16 mi. S off US 97 - Sunriver*   *593-1221*

Two scenic 18-hole championship courses have been built into broad meadows and forests near the Deschutes River. All facilities are open to the public, including a pro shop, driving range, putting green, club and cart rentals, plus view restaurants and a lounge.

★ **Horseback Riding**

Several area stables rent horses by the hour or longer. Some will also arrange extended pack trips into the national forest wilderness areas. For information and reservations, contact:

High Cascade Stables	*25 mi. NW - Sisters*	*549-4972*
The Inn at Seventh Mountain	*7 mi. SW on Century Drive Hwy.*	*382-8711*
Lake Creek Lodge (unguided, too)	*25 mi. NW - Sisters*	*595-6158*
Sunriver Resort	*15 mi. S off US 97 - Sunriver*	*593-1221*

★ **Lava Lands**   *12 mi. S on US 97*   382-5668
The Lava Lands Visitor Center has automated displays and slide shows describing the
remarkable geology of the area. There are also interpretive trails. A road winds to the top
of Lava Butte, a cinder cone more than 500 feet high, just north of the center. At the top,
an observation tower rewards visitors with breathtaking panoramic views of the central
Cascades. About 1.5 miles south, across the highway, another paved road leads to the lava
river caves, where the highlight is a lava tunnel a mile long. Lanterns may be rented. There
are also ice-filled caves. Two miles further south on US 97 and east on Forest Road 195 is
the eerie lava cast forest, a fascinating collection of tree molds — or casts — which were
formed when flowing molten lava surrounded and destroyed living trees some 6,000 years
ago. It can be viewed from a mile-long paved interpretive trail.

Library   *downtown at 507 NW Wall St.*   388-6677
The Deschutes County Library is a modern facility with upholstered chairs in a spacious,
well-stocked periodical reading area. Closed Sun.

★ **Newberry Crater**   *39 mi. S: 25 mi. S on US 97 & 14 mi. E on Forest Rd. 2129*
Within the caldera (giant crater) of this enormous extinct volcano are waterfalls, streams,
and two pretty little lakes. Boat ramps and rentals, campgrounds, rustic resorts, and
hiking trails have been provided. A magnificent panoramic view is enjoyed from the easily
reached summit of Paulina Peak. One of the world's largest obsidian (volcanic glass) flows
is accessed by a short interpretive trail.

★ **Oregon High Desert Museum**   *7 mi. S on US 97*   382-4754
The cultural and natural history of the arid region of central and eastern Oregon is the
focus of an impressive "living museum" opened in 1982. Among unusual features, visitors
experience a variety of different tactile sensations at "touch tables," and they are
encouraged to take part in demonstrations like wool-carding, and grinding corn with an
ancient mano. There are several buildings in addition to the large orientation center,
including a Forestry Learning Center where a tree's entire root system dangles
dramatically overhead. A highlight among wildlife exhibits is an otter pond with both
underwater and den viewing areas.

★ **Pilot Butte State Park**   *1 mi. E on US 20*
A paved road circles up symmetrical slopes to the summit of an extinct volcanic cinder
cone. There, visitors have a 360° unobstructed view across town to all of central Oregon,
including most of the majestic volcanic peaks of the central Cascade Range.

★ **River Running**
Several river guide services offer two hour, all day, or longer rafting trips on the Deschutes
River near town and on other nearby streams during the summer. All equipment and
meals are provided for scenic, whitewater, and moonlight trips. For information and
reservations, contact:

    The Factory Outlet (sells/rents rafts)   *3 mi. S at 61297 US 97*   389-6070
    Hunter Expeditions (guided trips)   389-8370
    The Inn of the Seventh Mountain (guided trips)   382-8711
    Sun Country Tours (guided trips)   382-6277

Warm Water Features
★   **Juniper Aquatic Center**   *.6 mi. E at 800 NE 6th St.*   389-7665
Big adjoining indoor and outdoor pools are the centerpieces of an imposing recreation
complex that also includes a sauna, whirlpool, and gym. In the surrounding park are
tennis courts and attractively sited picnic tables.

★   **Sunriver Resort**   *15 mi. SW via US 97 - Sunriver*   593-1221
An Olympic-sized pool with a beautifully furnished scenic deck area is open to the public
daily.

Winter Sports
★   **Mt. Bachelor**   *22 mi. SW on Century Drive Hwy.*   382-8334
With a newly completed chairlift to the top of the mountain, the vertical rise in Oregon's
biggest skiing complex is 3,100 feet and the longest run is several miles. There are ten
chairlifts, including five triple chairs. All services, facilities, and rentals are available at the
base for both downhill and cross-country skiing. Restaurant and lounge facilities have
been provided at the area, but no lodgings. The skiing season is one of the longest in the
West — from November into June.

★　**Mt. Bachelor Nordic Sports Center**　　*22 mi. SW on Century Drive Hwy.*　*382-8334*
More than fourteen miles of cross-country ski touring trails are marked, patrolled, and maintained in quiet forests and meadows at the base of Mt. Bachelor. Rentals and classes are offered from November through May.

Snowmobile Rentals
The Yamaha Store　　*.8 mi. N at 1841 NW Division St.*　　　*389-8686*
Snowmobiles can be rented here, and guided tours are available.

SHOPPING
The compact downtown, centered just east of the Deschutes River and Drake Park, still primarily serves the everyday needs of residents and visitors. But, a growing number of galleries, gourmet food stores, and other distinctive shops are opting for this especially picturesque location instead of the big ordinary shopping malls that have proliferated in recent years.

Food Specialties
The Bagel Stop　　*.6 mi. E at 661 NE Greenwood Av.*　　*389-3363*
A variety of good bagels are made at this small shop daily. Several kinds of tasty croissants are brought in from elsewhere.

Coffee & Company　　*downtown at 835 NW Wall St.*　　*389-6464*
Coffee and tea are served by the glass at a coffee bar. All kinds of coffee beans and products, teas, and Italian sodas are sold.

Don's Wines, Inc.　　*downtown at 709 NW Wall St.*　　*388-3667*
A good selection of premium wines, plus beers and cheeses, are sold. Closed Sun.

★　**Flanagan's**　　*downtown at 801 NW Wall St.*　　*382-1455*
Many flavors and styles of premium ice cream are served in an inviting plant-filled parlor. Cinnamon rolls, bagels, and sandwiches are also served here, or to go.

★　**Pi's**　　*1.1 mi. SE at 325A SE Wilson Av.*　　*382-2747*
Outstanding breakfast and dessert pastries (including Old World Kolaches) and breads are served to go, or with their own excellent coffee blend at a few tables in this newer bakery.

★　**Sandi's Cookery**　　*downtown at 917 NW Wall St.*　　*389-7385*
In this charcuterie, delicious pastries and breads are made fresh daily and served in a demonstration kitchen with fine complimentary coffee, or to go. Cooking classes, gourmet foods, and cookware are also offered.

★　**Sweetheart Donuts**　　*.4 mi. E on US 97 at 505 NE 3rd St.*　　*389-7928*
Donuts in a remarkable assortment of flavors, textures, fillings, and styles are sold fresh daily in this tiny takeout shop.

Wildwood Delicatessen　　*downtown at 932 NW Bond St.*　　*389-1118*
A fine selection of Northwestern and other premium wines, plus deli specialties, are served here or to go.

Specialty Shops
Blue Spruce Pottery　　*4.4 mi. S at 61021 S. US 97*　　*389-7745*
Assorted handcrafted pottery items are showcased in a roadside studio/gallery.

★　**The Book Barn**　　*downtown at 124 NW Minnesota Av.*　　*389-4589*
A fine selection of books about the Northwest is a major attraction of this well-organized two-level store. A rental library, collectable older books, seating for browsers, and background music are also featured.

★　**Oregon's Own**　　*downtown at 233 NW Oregon Av.*　　*382-9041*
Exclusively Oregon products — gourmet foods, books, arts, and crafts — are the specialty of this unusual little shop.

Vortex　　*downtown at 811 NW Wall St.*　　*382-8346*
Unique handcrafted objects are produced and sold in an inviting little glass blowing studio/gallery. All items will be individually gift-packaged and shipped anywhere.

NIGHTLIFE
There is plenty of life after dark in Bend, where places to go for the fun of it are scattered but numerous. In addition to live entertainment, music and dancing, Bend has the distinction of being one of the West's cinema centers, both in number of theaters and in unusual facilities offered to patrons.

Bend Woolen Mill   *.8 mi. NE at 1854 NE 1st St.*   *382-6767*
Live music and dancing are offered several nights each week in a large funky tavern, along
with pool tables, foosball, electronic games, and assorted tap beers.

★ **Brandy's**   *.8 mi. SE on US 97 at 197 NE 3rd St.*   *382-2687*
Live entertainment for dancing and listening is especially popular on weekends in a stylish
cabaret with an adjoining restaurant.

China Ranch Bar   *1.3 mi. SE on US 97 at 1005 SE 3rd St.*   *389-5888*
Country/western and other live music for dancing is featured several nights weekly in this
large casual bar.

Community Theatre of the Cascades *downtown at 134 NW Greenwood Av.*   *389-0803*
Live theatrical productions ranging from tragedies to musicals are offered in a new, nicely
furnished little playhouse.

Cooper Room Downtown   *downtown at 125 NW Oregon Av.*   *382-1800*
Live music and dancing are offered nightly in a contemporary, comfortable bar. There is
a restaurant upstairs. Closed Sun.

Dejola's   *downtown at 61 NW Oregon Av.*   *388-1288*
Live entertainment is offered on weekends, but this is a favorite place for meeting people
anytime. The modern, plant-filled lounge has seating on two levels and an island bar with
premium beer on tap. A casual Italian restaurant adjoins.

★ **Deschutes Station Tavern**   *4 mi. S at 61219 S. US 97*   *389-7574*
The action ranges from live country/western music and dancing to occasional pro boxing
matches in this large and lively roadhouse tavern. A big stone fireplace, pool tables,
electronic games, half a dozen tap beers, burgers and chili are also crowd-pleasers.

Inn of the Seventh Mountain   *7 mi. SW at 18575 Century Drive Hwy.*   *382-8711*
Live entertainment and dancing are offered several nights each week in the resort's
strikingly contemporary lounge. A delightful fireplace/conversation area is the
centerpiece.

★ **Pat & Mike's Cinema Restaurant**   *downtown at 918 NW Wall St.*   *382-5006*
Primarily film classics are screened in an intimate theater/dining room where patrons sit
at tables with director's chairs, or in traditional theater seats. Light meals, tap beer, wine,
and homemade desserts can be enjoyed while watching the movie, or in an adjoining
dining area.

★ **Riverhouse Motor Inn**   *1.3 mi. N at 3075 N. US 97*   *389-3111*
At the Riverhouse Lounge, live music and dancing are available nightly in a handsome
room with plush contemporary furnishings. Outside, drinks are served on an umbrella-
shaded view deck overlooking the picturesque Deschutes River.

RESTAURANTS
Hearty American fare is flourishing here, along with several delightful alternatives.
Restaurant decor ranges from plain and casual to elegant and formal. Surprisingly few
dining rooms offer picture window views of the area's natural grandeur.

Beef and Brew   *1.4 mi. N at 3194 N. US 97*   *388-4646*
D only.   *Moderate*
Steaks and prime rib are featured. A center fireplace lends distinction to contemporary
wood-trimmed decor in the large dining room.

★ **Black Forest Inn**   *1 mi. SW at 25 SW 14th St.*   *389-3138*
D only.   *Low*
German specialties, delicious homemade pastries, and Continental dishes are served in a
charming Bavarian-style dinner house.

Brandy's   *.8 mi. SE on US 97 at 197 NE 3rd St.*   *382-2687*
B-L-D.   *Low*
Breakfasts are a specialty, enhanced by linen napkins and stoneware in a large,
comfortably furnished modern restaurant adjoining a popular nightclub.

★ **Cafe South Center**   *2.5 mi. SE at 61419 S. US 97*   *382-5946*
B-L-D. No D on Sun. & Mon.   *Low*
Homemade biscuits, cinnamon rolls, and pies accompany an assortment of American
dishes made from scratch in a cheerful contemporary restaurant with comfortably
padded booths.

★ **Cyrano Restaurant**   *downtown at 828 NW Wall St.*   *389-6276*
D only. Closed Sun.-Tues.   *Expensive*
Five-course international gourmet dinners, skillfully prepared from the freshest
ingredients, are served in an intimate dining room outfitted in country-French decor. The
restaurant is hidden in an alley, but worth finding.

Dandy's Drive-Inn   *.6 mi. NE on US 97 at 1334 NE 3rd St.*   *382-6141*
L-D. Closed Sun.   *Low*
For nostalgia buffs, the 1950s lingers on in this classic burger and milkshake drive-in
where the food and prices are better than in latter-day versions, and the service is by
roller skating car hops.

★ **Dillon's Restaurant**   *2 mi. N at 63011 N. US 97*   *388-3545*
D only.   *Moderate*
Fine seafood is presented in delicious and creative dishes. Nicely appointed tables are
well-spaced and screened for intimacy in a pleasant dining room with a salad bar.

Frieda's Restaurant   *.9 mi. N at 1955 NE Division St.*   *382-3790*
L-D. Closed Sun.   *Moderate*
American dishes and some German specialties such as potato pancakes and apple fritters
are served in this long-established, casual dinner house.

Juniper Cafe   *1.1 mi. SE on US 97 at 603 SE 3rd St.*   *382-6873*
B-L.   *Low*
Fine homemade biscuits and cinnamon rolls (fresh in the late morning) enhance
homestyle breakfasts served in this plain, popular cafe.

Kayo's   *2.4 mi. S at 61363 S. US 97*   *389-1400*
D only.   *Moderate*
Continental specialties are accompanied by a salad bar in a polished contemporary setting.

★ **Le Bistro**   *.5 mi. NE on US 97 at 1203 NE 3rd St.*   *389-7274*
D only. Closed Sun.-Mon.   *Moderate*
Skillfully prepared French cuisine is served in a remodeled church that now sports
sidewalk cafe atmosphere with an open kitchen. Downstairs, an intimate piano lounge
has been comfortably furnished in posh velvet Victorian-style chairs.

The Ore House   *downtown at 1033 NW Bond St.*   *388-3891*
D only.   *Moderate*
Steaks are the specialty among contemporary American dishes offered with a salad bar
in this comfortably furnished newer restaurant. The lounge has live music on weekends.

The Pine Tavern   *downtown at 967 NW Brooks St.*   *382-5581*
L-D. No L on Sun.   *Moderate*
Sourdough scones are a specialty served with American dishes in a beautifully
refurbished historical landmark. Two giant living ponderosa pines have been
incorporated into the decor of the main dining room that also has an outstanding view of
Drake Park and the Deschutes River.

The Riverhouse Motor Inn   *1.3 mi. N at 3075 N. US 97*   *389-3111*
B-L-D. Closed Sun.   *Moderate*
Continental dishes and flambe desserts are finished at tableside in a handsome
contemporary dining room overlooking the Deschutes River. A lounge and deck with a
fine view adjoin the hotel's restaurant.

Roszak's   *.6 mi. NE on US 97 at 1230 NE 3rd St.*   *382-3173*
L-D. No. L on Sat. Closed Sun.   *Moderate*
Prime rib is a highlight on a contemporary menu in this sleek newer restaurant.

Sargent's Cafe   *1.1 mi. SE at 719 SE 3rd St.*   *382-3916*
B-L-D.   *Low*
Hearty portions of homestyle all-American dishes are complemented by big fluffy biscuits
and (in late morning) cinnamon rolls made here. Diners have a choice of booths, tables,
or counter service in an unabashedly old-fashioned roadhouse cafe.

Tumalo Emporium   *6 mi. NW at 64619 US 20*   *382-2202*
L-D.   *Moderate*
Homestyle food is prepared for a short list of house specialties, and a conventional buffet
is also displayed in a large, family-oriented restaurant furnished in Victorian rococo
decor. A very comfortable Old Western-style piano bar is in the next room.

Victorian Pantry   *.8 mi. W at 1404 NW Galveston Av.*   *382-6411*
B-L-D.   *Moderate*

Fresh home-cooked dishes, including an impressive variety of omelets, are served with delicious fluffy scones or other pastries in a recycled house with booths and cheerful decor.

LODGING

There are plenty of places to stay. Most of the area's finest facilities are on the Deschutes River in or near town. One of the West's greatest concentrations of bargain motels line 3rd Street (US 97) which is the main north-south highway through town. Most places reduce their rates by 15% or more apart from summer. A few increase their rates during the prime skiing season.

★ **Bend Riverside**   *.4 mi. N at 1565 NW Hill St.*   *382-3802*
A large motel complex occupies a choice site by the Deschutes River next to Pioneer Park. Landscaped grounds include a large indoor pool, whirlpool, saunas, and a tennis court. Each spacious unit has a phone and cable color TV with movies. There are **bargain** rooms.

    #258,#257,#253 — in one-level bldg., superb falls/rapids view,   K bed...$32
    #321 — kit., gas fireplace, fine view over rapids/falls,   Murphy Q bed...$44
    #238,#242,#237,#241 — balc. next to falls, kit., gas fireplace,   Murphy Q bed...$44
    regular room —   Q bed...$28

Cascade Lodge   *.9 mi. SE on US 97 at 420 SE 3rd St.*   *382-2612*
An outdoor pool is a feature of this modern single-level **bargain** motel. Each room has a phone and cable color TV with movies.

    regular room —   Q bed...$30

Chaparral Motel   *1.5 mi. S at 1300 S. US 97*   *389-1448*
The highway is close by this modern little motel with an outdoor pool. Each **bargain** room has a phone and cable color TV.

    regular room —   Q bed...$22

Cimmaron Motel   *.8 mi. E on US 97 at 201 NE 3rd St.*   *382-8282*
This is a newer **bargain** motel with an outdoor pool. Each room has a phone and cable color TV.

    regular room —   Q bed...$26

City Center Motel   *downtown at 509 NE Franklin Av.*   *382-5321*
This modest little **bargain** motel has plain rooms with cable B/W TV.

    regular room —   Q bed...$17

Entrada Lodge - Best Western   *4 mi. SW at 19221 Century Drive Hwy.*   *382-4080*
A pine forest surrounds this appealing motel with an outdoor pool, whirlpool, and sauna. Each well-furnished room has a phone and cable color TV with movies.

    #32 — end of single-level bldg., good view of Mt. Bachelor,   Q bed...$37
    regular room —   Q bed...$37

Hill Crest Motel   *2.3 mi. SE at 61405 S. US 97*   *389-5910*
This is a little single-level **bargain** motel with cable color TV in each room.

    regular room —   Q bed...$23
    regular room —   D bed...$18

★ **Inn of the Seventh Mountain**   *7 mi. SW on Century Drive Hwy.*   *382-8711*
One of Bend's largest resort hotel/condominium complexes has an extensive array of leisure facilities and services, including two large outdoor pools, whirlpools, saunas, seven tennis courts, a putting green, miniature golf, a recreation room, and (for a fee) an outdoor roller/ice rink, rental bicycles, moped trips, guided river rafting, and horseback riding. There are also dining rooms and a lounge with live entertainment. Each well-furnished unit has a phone and cable color TV.

    #719,#701 — 1 BR, kitchen, fireplace, balcony, mt. view,   Q bed...$94
    #724,#706 — deluxe room, pvt. balc., mt. view,   Q bed...$58
    regular room — forest view,   Q bed...$42

Maverick Motel   *.6 mi. E on US 97 at 437 NE 3rd St.*   *382-7711*
An outdoor pool is available at this newer **bargain** motel. Each room has a phone and cable color TV.

    regular room —   Q bed...$27

Motel West   *.5 mi. E at 216 NE Irving Av.*   389-5577
In this newer **bargain** motel, each room has a phone and cable color TV.
   regular room —   Q bed...$26
★ **Mt. Bachelor Village**   *3 mi. SW at 19717 Mt. Bachelor Dr.*   389-5900
On a bluff above the Deschutes River is an imposing condominium complex that includes
a large outdoor pool, whirlpool, six tennis courts (two lighted), and a nature trail to the
river. Each nicely decorated, spacious unit has a phone, color TV, kitchen, and a fireplace.
   #241,#244 — 2 BR suite, balc., loft with Q beds, fine mt. views,   3 Q beds...$85
   #141,#144 — 1 BR suite, balc., good views,   2 Q beds...$65
   regular room — 1 BR suite,   Q bed...$55
Pilot Butte Motor Inn   *downtown at 1236 NW Wall St.*   382-1411
This older single-level **bargain** motel has units with a phone and cable color TV with
movies.
   regular room —   Q bed...$21
Plaza Motel   *.4 mi. N at 1430 NW Hill St.*   382-1621
Across from Pioneer Park is an older single-level **bargain** motel. Each small room has a
phone and cable color TV with movies.
   regular room —   Q bed...$21
Poplar Motel   *.8 mi. SE at 163 SE 3rd St.*   382-6571
In this little old one-level **bargain** motel, each spacious unit has cable color TV and a
kitchen.
   regular room —   Q bed...$15
Rainbow Motel   *.4 mi. E at 154 NE Franklin Av.*   382-1821
This small single-level motel is a **bargain.** Each room has a phone and cable color TV with
movies.
   regular room —   Q bed...$21
★ **Riverhouse Motor Inn**   *1.3 mi. N at 3075 N. US 97*   389-3111
One of Bend's largest and finest lodgings is a contemporary motor hotel delightfully
located by the Deschutes River. Amenities include a large scenic pool, whirlpool, and
saunas, plus a view dining room and a lounge with entertainment. Each spacious,
attractively furnished unit has a phone and cable color TV with movies.
   #223 thru #226 — pvt. window wall & balc. over river rapids,   2 Q beds...$47
   "Whirlpool Suite" — mirrored whirlpool rm., wet bar, mirrored   K waterbed...$95
   regular room —   Q bed...$39
Royal Gateway Motel   *.9 mi. SE on US 97 at 415 SE 3rd St.*   382-5631
Each modest room in this modern single-level **bargain** motel has a phone and cable color
TV with movies.
   regular room —   Q bed...$22
   regular room —   D bed...$20
Sonoma Lodge   *1 mi. SE on US 97 at 450 SE 3rd St.*   382-4891
This is a small modern **bargain** motel. Each room has a phone and cable color TV.
   regular room —   Q bed...$23
Sportsman's Motel   *2 mi. N. at 3705 N US 97*   382-2211
An outdoor pool and whirlpool are features of this modern **bargain** motel. Each room has
a phone and cable color TV with movies.
   deluxe room — spacious,   Q bed...$29
   regular room —   D bed...$22
★ **Sunriver Resort**   *15 mi. SW via US 97 - Sunriver*   593-1221
One of the West's outstanding contemporary resorts is at the edge of a large meadow
surrounded by a vast pine forest. Many of the lodge/condominium units have panoramic
views of distant snow-capped peaks. A remarkable assortment of leisure facilities
includes a giant scenic pool, several whirlpools, saunas, a recreation room, exercise room,
dock and fishing on the Deschutes River, and (a fee for) five racquetball courts, bicycles
(miles of separated scenic bikeways), golf (36 holes), eighteen tennis courts (three
indoors), horseback riding, and canoes. The Meadows is a posh dining room with a
spectacular view, and there are several other restaurants, plus lounges with
entertainment. Each spacious, handsomely appointed suite has a phone, cable color TV,

a large stone fireplace, and a private deck. Most of the units have twin beds.

#104,#110 — fine meadow/mt. views,	K bed...$70
#208 — good view,	K bed...$70
regular room — lodge bedroom,	2 T or K bed...$70

Westward Ho Motel   *1.3 mi. SE at 904 SE 3rd St.*   *382-2111*
A large enclosed swimming pool and whirlpool are features of this modern **bargain** motel.
Each nicely furnished room has a phone and cable color TV with movies.

#166 — impressive stonework fireplace in full view of	Q bed...$34
regular room —	Q bed...$29

CAMPGROUNDS

Numerous campgrounds are in the forests west of town. The best of these offer primitive facilities on picturesque little lakes with all kinds of water and high country recreation. In addition, one of the West's finest campgrounds, beautifully sited by the Deschutes River near town, offers complete camping and recreation facilities in a luxuriously furnished park.

★ **Cultis Lake** *45 mi. SW via OR 46 & Forest Rd. 2025*   *382-6922*
This Deschutes National Forest campground is located near a beautiful little high country lake in a lush pine forest. Boat launching and rental facilities are nearby. Swimming, fishing, boating, water-skiing, and hiking are deservedly popular. There are pit toilets only — no showers or hookups. Each pine-shaded site has a picnic table and a fire area.
                                                                    base rate...$4

★ **Elk Lake Recreation Area**   *30 mi. W on OR 46*   *382-6922*
This Deschutes National Forest facility is in a heavily wooded area by a little lake backed by a spectacular snow-capped peak. Rental boats and a boat ramp are nearby, and swimming, fishing, and boating are enjoyed. There are pit toilets only — no showers or hookups. Many of the pine-shaded sites have a picnic table and fire area.   base rate...$5

★ **Tumalo State Park** *5.5 mi. NW via US 20 & County Rd.*   *382-3586*
The state operates this superb facility by the pretty little Deschutes River. The beautifully landscaped park features a large picnic area by the river, grassy play areas, an outdoor theater, and nature trails in addition to a campground. Swimming and fishing in the river, and hiking are popular. Flush toilets (B Loop), solar-powered hot showers, and hookups are available. Each of the well-spaced, shady sites has a picnic table and fire grill/pit. Several sites are by the river.   base rate...$7

OTHER INFORMATION

Area Code: *503*
Zip Code: *97701*

Bend Chamber of Commerce	*downtown at 164 NW Hawthorne Av.*	*382-3221*
Deschutes Nat. Forest-Supervisor's Off.	*.7 mi. NE at 211 NE Revere Av.*	*382-6922*

Cannon Beach, Oregon

Elevation:

25 feet

Population (1980):

1,187

Population (1970):

779

Location:

80 mi. NW
of Portland

Cannon Beach is a charming little art center in a magnificent coastal setting. Whitewashed and weathered-wood cottages and shops are surrounded by captivating natural features. The shoreline includes one of the world's largest free-standing monoliths just off a "singing sands" beach, plus miles of broad sandy beaches and low coastal dunes. Inland, a natural amphitheater extends to a massive seaward headland. State parks and forests that encircle the village assure preservation of the wealth of scenic attractions in the area, while providing an impressive variety of recreation opportunities. Beachcombing, clamming, fishing, beach driving, horseback riding, hiking and camping attract capacity crowds during summer. On warm sunny days, ocean swimming and surfing are popular enough to justify lifeguards on the town's beaches. Temperatures are surprisingly moderate year-round. Freezes and snow are scarce. However, almost continuous rainstorms during winter and spring, and the drama of wind-whipped storm surf, provide a compelling spectacle. Increasing numbers of visitors come to experience the phenomenon — from the comfort of firelit oceanfront motel rooms.

The attributes of this superb coastal setting were first admired by American explorers with the Lewis and Clark expedition of 1805. But, the potential for a townsite was ignored for nearly a century. The tiny village was named after a cannon loosed from the shipwrecked U.S. schooner "Shark" was hauled to high ground here in 1898. Settlement was very slow until the 1960s, when increasing numbers of artists and craftsmen, attracted by the spectacular location, began to work and live here year-round.

Cannon Beach is still a tiny village. The special kind of boom that has occurred recently has been one of quality, not quantity. The artistry of the residents is apparent in details of architectural craftsmanship, in an abundance of flowers and carefully-tended landscapes, and in several memorable public sculptures. A proliferation of studios and galleries display locally handcrafted products. Winsome shops abound, including two of the most unconventional grocery stores anywhere. Restaurants are numerous and surprisingly ordinary, while bars and lounges are scarce, atmospheric, and reflect the tranquility of the setting. Picture window views of memorable sunsets on the Oregon coast can be enjoyed in a couple of places. Accommodations range from carefully maintained tourist cabins that have been here for decades to luxurious contemporary ocean view units in facilities loaded with amenities. All of the best lodgings are close to the beach, and several are also within an easy stroll of the center of town.

Cannon Beach, Oregon

WEATHER PROFILE
Vokac Weather Rating

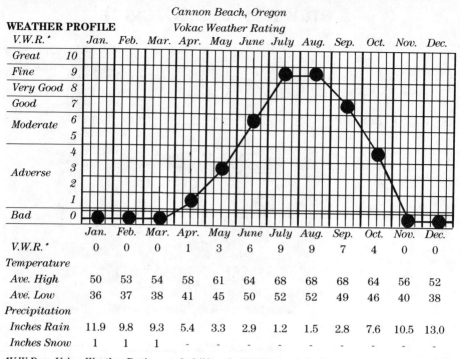

V.W.R.*		Jan.	Feb.	Mar.	Apr.	May	June	July	Aug.	Sep.	Oct.	Nov.	Dec.
Great	10												
Fine	9												
Very Good	8												
Good	7												
Moderate	6												
	5												
	4												
Adverse	3												
	2												
	1												
Bad	0												

	Jan.	Feb.	Mar.	Apr.	May	June	July	Aug.	Sep.	Oct.	Nov.	Dec.
V.W.R.*	0	0	0	1	3	6	9	9	7	4	0	0
Temperature												
Ave. High	50	53	54	58	61	64	68	68	68	64	56	52
Ave. Low	36	37	38	41	45	50	52	52	49	46	40	38
Precipitation												
Inches Rain	11.9	9.8	9.3	5.4	3.3	2.9	1.2	1.5	2.8	7.6	10.5	13.0
Inches Snow	1	1	1	-	-	-	-	-	-	-	-	-

*V.W.R. = Vokac Weather Rating: probability of mild (warm & dry) weather on any given day.

Forecast

Month	V.W.R.*		Temperatures Daytime	Evening	Precipitation
January	0	Bad	cool	chilly	continual downpours
February	0	Bad	cool	chilly	continual rainstorms
March	0	Bad	cool	chilly	continual rainstorms
April	1	Adverse	cool	chilly	continual rainstorms
May	3	Adverse	cool	cool	continual showers
June	6	Moderate	cool	cool	frequent showers
July	9	Fine	warm	cool	infrequent showers
August	9	Fine	warm	cool	infrequent showers
September	7	Good	warm	cool	frequent rainstorms
October	4	Adverse	cool	cool	frequent downpours
November	0	Bad	cool	chilly	continual downpours
December	0	Bad	cool	chilly	continual downpours

Summary

Tiny ocean-fronting Cannon Beach is sequestered within a lush pine-forested amphitheater dramatically anchored by a massive headland jutting into the Pacific north of town. Because of the tempering influence of the ocean, the area enjoys one of the longest growing seasons in the West outside of California while it endures one of the nation's heaviest annual rainfalls. **Winter** is uniformly cool and very wet. Because the temperature seldom drops to freezing, snowfall is rare. Continual rainstorms preclude casual enjoyment of outdoor recreation. However, **spring** remains cool and damp with gradually increasing temperatures and diminishing rainfall through June. Fine weather finally arrives in **summer** when, for two very special months, warm days, cool evenings, and infrequent showers make exploring this wonderfully scenic hideaway easy. **Fall** is accompanied by the return of cool days and continual rain.

ATTRACTIONS & DIVERSIONS

Bicycling
Mike's Bike Shop   *downtown at 248 N. Spruce*   436-1266

Coastal highways and byways give bicyclists access to countryside that is relatively gentle and remarkably scenic. Bicycles may be rented by the hour or longer at this small shop. Closed Tues.

★ **Cannon Beach**   *borders downtown on W side*

One of the most magnificent beaches anywhere forms the town's three-mile-long western boundary. Sand on the broad flat beach is so hard that drivers are allowed to take their automobiles on it during winter months. Above the high tide line, low dunes of dry and powdery "singing sands" provide a picturesque backdrop.

★ **Ecola State Park**   *1 mi. N via Ecola Park Rd.*   436-2844

This large natural park occupies most of the southern slopes of Tillamook Head — the massive promontory between Cannon Beach and Seaside. Several well-spaced picnic tables overlook breathtaking coastline views from a highland meadow. Two picturesque sandy beaches line the southern portion of the park's nearly six miles of protected coastline. Rock fishing, tide pool exploring, sunbathing, and surfing are popular. Hiking trails lead to beaches and to coastal overlooks where sea lion and bird rookeries can be observed on offshore rocks. Tillamook Rock Light, a century-old lighthouse abandoned in 1957, can also be seen offshore.

Golf
★ **Neah-Kah-Nie Golf Course**   *18 mi. S on US 101*

This remarkably scenic 9-hole course is situated on the slopes of a mountain where every hole has a dramatic ocean view. It is open to the public and includes a pro shop, plus club and pull-cart rentals.

Haystack Gardens   *.6 mi. S at 148 E. Gower St.*   436-1161

In the late summer, manicured gardens behind the nursery/flower shop are ablaze with brilliant colors of roses, fuscias, and other blooms. There are also small plots set aside for fragrance, succulents, and other specialized plantings.

★ **Haystack Rock**   *.6 mi. S - just offshore*

The third largest coastal monolith in the world rises 235 feet from the surf adjacent to Cannon Beach. Its natural scenic beauty is a major source of local pride. While the rookery and tide pools around the base of the rock are protected, observing the small marine life that abounds there is a favorite pastime.

Library   *downtown on Hemlock St. near 1st St.*

The Cannon Beach Library is housed in a contemporary wood-toned building on the main street. A fireplace dominates a charming reading area with an interesting display of oversized volumes, pictures, and information about the town and region. Unfortunately, the library is only open a few afternoons each week.

★ **Oswald West State Park**   *11 mi. S on US 101*   238-7488

This state park memorializes the farsighted governor who, in 1912, preserved Oregon's coastal beaches for all of the people. An outstanding walk-in campground one-quarter mile from the parking lot provides tent sites set in a lush coastal rain forest. A sheltered cove and tide pools are a short walk beyond.

Winery
Nehalem Bay Winery   *19 mi. SE: 18 mi. S via US 101 & 1 mi. E on OR 53*   368-5300

Fruit, berry, and grape wines are produced and sold in a building that was one of the original Tillamook cheese factories. The tasting room is open daily 10-5.

SHOPPING

A compact downtown area, centered along Hemlock Street just inland from the beach, is housed in a picturesque cluster of weathered-wood buildings. Collectively, the low-profile cottage-style architecture and numerous fanciful handcrafted touches reflect the town's artistic charm and intimate scale. Galleries and shops emphasizing locally produced fine arts and crafts in all media, plus stores specializing in regional gourmet foods, set the tone for this flourishing district.

Food Specialties

★ **Blue Heron French Cheese Factory**   *42 mi. S on US 101 - Tillamook*   *842-8281*
French-style brie and camembert cheeses are produced, sold, and available for sampling here daily. A fine assortment of international cheeses is also featured, and samples are offered. Regional wines, jams, and other gourmet specialties are displayed, sampled, and sold. Oregon-made chocolate candies are sold next door at La Bonbonniere.

Bruce's Candy Kitchen   *downtown at 256 N. Hemlock St.*   *436-2641*
A variety of fancy chocolates including some shaped like the famed "haystack" are made on the premises. Samples are available.

★ **C & W Meats (Art and Dick's)**   *34 mi. S on US 101 - Bay City*   *377-2231*
Sausage, pepperoni, jerky, and smoked salmon are made and sold here every day. Samples are provided on request.

★ **Cannon Beach Bakery**   *downtown at 144 N. Hemlock St.*   *436-2592*
Famous for its bread loaf in the shape of Haystack Rock, this outstanding bakery offers a full line of fine breads, pastries, cookies, and some unusual treats like Chinese fruit pockets. There are a few tables, and coffee is available. Closed Tues.-Wed.

Cannon Beach Seafood Co.   *downtown at 123 S. Hemlock St.*   *436-2272*
Fresh Dungeness crab and smoked salmon are specialties. The little carryout shop also has a good selection of seasonally fresh fish and other shellfish, plus seafood cocktails.

★ **Karla's Krabs**   *23 mi. S on US 101 - Rockaway*   *355-2362*
All kinds of fresh, smoked, and canned fish and shellfish are sold at this long-popular roadside takeout. Custom fish smoking can also be arranged.

★ **Mariner Market**   *downtown at 139 N. Hemlock St.*   *436-2442*
Grocery stores aren't usually regarded as whimsical, but this one is. A chess board is set in a corner beside a pot-bellied stove, a museum-load of memorabilia hangs overhead, unique signwork and handcrafted furnishings are used throughout, contemporary classical music wafts down the aisles, and books are sold along with magazines and newspapers — and groceries.

★ **Old Trapper Sausage**   *42 mi. S on US 101 - Tillamook*   *842-2622*
Jerky, pepperoni, beer sausage, and other fine beef sausages are made, displayed, and sold in a tantalizing takeout shop by the Blue Heron Cheese Factory. Samples are offered.

★ **Osburn's Grocery & Ice Creamery**   *downtown at 240 N. Hemlock St.*   *436-2234*
This is a fine place to assemble a gourmet picnic with pate, fresh pasta salad, premium cheeses and wines, whole wheat fruit bar cookies, and more. The adjoining ice creamery is easily located by the lineup of contented customers in chairs on the porch and sidewalk savoring cones, shakes, and sundaes.

★ **Phil and Joe's Crab Co.**   *31 mi. S on US 101 - Garibaldi*   *322-3410*
Different sizes of carryout crab and shrimp cocktails star in an extensive display of fresh, smoked, and canned seafoods to go in a large, well-organized shop.

★ **Tillamook Cheese Factory**   *41 mi. S on US 101 - Tillamook*   *842-4481*
One of the world's largest cheese-processing plants produces the West's most renowned cheddar cheese. Visitors can watch through picture windows. Minimal samples are offered. A large regional foods and gifts shop and a coffee shop featuring Tillamook dairy products adjoin.

Wine Shack   *downtown at 263 N. Hemlock St.*   *436-1100*
A surprising number of premium Northwestern, California, and imported wines are packed into this inviting little shop. Closed Tues.

Specialty Shops

Cannon Beach Book Co.   *downtown at 132 N. Hemlock St.*   *436-1301*
A good selection of books is augmented by attractive decor and classical background music in this small bookstore.

★ **Greaver Gallery**   *.3 mi. S on Hemlock St.*   *436-1185*
Watercolors and prints of local scenes are artistically displayed in a small fireside gallery.

★ **Haystack Gallery**   *downtown at 183 N. Hemlock St.*   *436-2547*
This intriguing little gallery features watercolors, paintings, musical wall hangings using coastal materials, and sculptures by Northwestern artists.

★ **The Weathervane Gallery**   *downtown at 130 N. Hemlock St.*   *436-2808*
Graceful and unusual three-dimensional wire sculptures are produced and sold in this studio/gallery.

★ **White Bird Gallery**   *downtown at 251 N. Hemlock St.*   *436-2681*
This large two-story gallery showcases multimedia fine arts — weaving, pottery, etc. — primarily by Western artists.

★ **Worchester Glassworks**   *.5 mi. S at Hemlock/Gower Sts.*   *436-2377*
Unique objects and functional pieces in glass are casually displayed in a bright, personalized studio/gallery.

NIGHTLIFE

After dark, the loudest noise in town is usually the sound of waves breaking on Cannon Beach. Casual live entertainment is available, however, and more elaborate "action" can be found a few miles north in Seaside.

★ **Bill's Tavern**   *downtown at 188 N. Hemlock St.*   *436-2202*
The quintessential Cannon Beach tavern features woodcrafted decor with skylights, a pot-bellied stove, pool, and darts. Half a dozen beers are on tap to wash down the homemade chili and hamburgers.

Coaster Theater   *downtown at 108 N. Hemlock St.*   *436-1242*
Live theater productions, concerts, ballet, lectures, and films are presented at various times in a versatile little auditorium.

Harpoon Room Lounge   *downtown at 200 N. Hemlock St.*   *436-2821*
Behind the Whaler Restaurant, live piano and/or organ music are occasionally played for dancing. The cozy, nautical bar has comfortable booths and armchairs by an unusual raised fireplace.

★ **Tolovana Inn**   *2 mi. S at 3400 S. Hemlock St.*   *436-1111*
Live music and dancing are offered several nights weekly in Daggett's, a comfortably furnished fireside lounge with an ocean view.

RESTAURANTS

Restaurants are relatively numerous. Not surprisingly, most feature seafood. The artistic decor and ocean views are usually more notable than the cuisine.

The Brass Lantern   *.6 mi. S at 1116 S. Hemlock St.*   *436-2412*
D only. Sun. brunch. Closed Wed.-Thurs.   Moderate
Several well-prepared fresh seafood entrees, plus delicious rolls and pastries, are highlights of this casual dinner house.

The Driftwood Inn   *downtown at 179 N. Hemlock St.*   *436-2439*
L-D. Closed Mon.-Tues.   *Moderate*
Fresh seafood and homemade specialties including bread and deep dish berry pies are served in a popular family restaurant.

Lazy Susan Cafe   *downtown at 126 N. Hemlock St.*   *436-2816*
B-L. Closed Mon.-Tues.   *Moderate*
Breakfast omelets are featured, using Tillamook cheese, and there are some unusual specialties like oatmeal waffles. Seating is on two levels in a handcrafted wood-toned dining room where fresh flowers and fine raspberry jam in glass jars enhance the cheerful decor.

Morris Fireside Restaurant   *downtown at 207 N. Hemlock St.*   *436-2917*
B-L-D.   *Moderate*
American fare, including seafood specialties, is offered. The distinctive log cabin-style room with a stone fireplace is a local favorite for casual dining.

Tolovana Inn   *2 mi. S at 3400 S. Hemlock St.*   *436-1111*
Daggett's, the large restaurant at the Tolovana Inn, features seafood as an accompaniment to an expansive beachfront view from every seat in the plush contemporary dining room.

Wayfarer Restaurant   *.6 mi. S at 1190 Pacific Dr.*   *436-1108*
L-D.   *Moderate*
An interesting selection of regional seafood specialties — like crab casserole — is served in a casual dining room. The adjoining lounge has a fine view of Haystack Rock and the beach.

The Whaler   *downtown at 200 N. Hemlock St.*   *436-2821*
B-L-D.   *Moderate*
Extra-small oysters and steamed littleneck clams are among the dinner specialties, and homemade cinnamon rolls are a morning delight in this casual family-oriented restaurant.

LODGING

Many accommodations in town are convenient to both downtown and the beach. All but two are small and well-scaled to the intimate, romantic setting. Behind weathered wood exteriors, many of the best accommodations offer remarkably elegant furnishings and craftsmanship. Most lodgings reduce their rates by at least 10% apart from summer, when some require a three day or longer minimum stay.

Bell Harbor Motel   *.3 mi. N at 208 5th St.*   *436-2776*
An ocean view is the feature of a small **bargain** motel near the mouth of Ecola Creek. Each of the older, spacious units has cable color TV.

#8 — 1 BR, unusual round kitchen with a fine ocean view, fireplace,	Q bed...$60
regular room #20 & #21 — some ocean view,	D bed...$30

Blue Gill Motel   *.3 mi. S at 632 S. Hemlock St.*   *436-2714*
The beach is an easy stroll from this old, single-level **bargain** motel. Each simply furnished unit has a cable color TV.

#14 — large, knotty pine decor,	Q bed...$28
#16 — old kit., brick fireplace,	Q bed...$38
#6a,#5a — small, rustic,	K waterbed...$30
regular room —	2 T or Q beds...$28

The Cove   *downtown at W. 2nd & N. Larch Sts.*   *436-2300*
The Cove is a conveniently located little oceanfront cottage colony. Several units have views, kitchens, and fireplaces. All of the comfortably furnished units have cable color TV.

"Surf Crest" — fronts on ocean/forest, brick fireplace, kitchen,	Q bed...$57
regular room — kitchenette, no view,	D bed...$32

★ **Ecola Inn**   *.6 mi. S at 1169 Ecola Court*   *436-2457*
Haystack Rock is near this modern oceanside motel. Each spacious unit fronts on the beach, and has a color TV.

#2 — corner, Franklin (presto log) fireplace, kitchen, fabulous many-window beach view,	2 Q beds...$46
#3 — Franklin (presto log) fireplace, kitchen, fine beach view from several windows,	2 Q beds...$41
regular room —	Q bed...$34

Hidden Villa Motel   *.4 mi. S at 188 E. Van Buren St.*   *436-2237*
A beautifully landscaped garden enhances this tiny older cottage colony. Each modest unit is a **bargain** with cable color TV.

regular room —	D bed...$28

★ **Lands End Motel**   *downtown at 263 W. 2nd St.*   *436-2264*
This contemporary beachfront motel has a whirlpool. Several rooms have fine oceanfront views. Each unit has a (sterno log) fireplace, cable color TV, and a kitchen.

#6 — 1 BR, fine ocean view from LR and BR,	Q bed...$64
#5,#4 — 1 BR, fine ocean view from LR,	Q bed...$64
regular room —	Q bed...$46

Major Motel   *1.6 mi. S at 2863 Pacific St.*   *436-2241*
The beach adjoins this small modern motel. Each plainly furnished unit has a cable color TV with movies.

#18 — corner, raised brick fireplace, pvt. balc., kit., ocean view,	K bed...$52
#17 — raised brick fireplace, pvt. balc., kit., ocean view,	Q bed...$48
regular room — ocean view, public deck,	Q bed...$40

McBee Court   *.4 mi. S at Hemlock/Van Buren Sts.*   *436-2569*
This tiny, single-level, older motel is a recently redecorated **bargain** only a block from the beach. Each simply furnished unit has cable color TV.

#10 — end unit, fireplace, kit., partial ocean view,	D bed...$42
regular room —	D bed...$25

★ **New Surfview Resort Motel** *.3 mi. S at 1400 S. Hemlock St.* *436-1566*
A beachfront bluff overlooking Haystack Rock provides a dramatic site for one of the finest resort motels in the Northwest. A beautifully enclosed big indoor pool with a slide, a whirlpool, and a sauna are other amenities in this large new motel. Each unit has lavish contemporary furnishings, cable color TV with movies, a refrigerator, and a phone. Most have a wood-burning fireplace and a balcony overlooking the ocean.

#333,#233 — spacious, raised fireplace, pvt. balc., in-room spa, floor-to-ceiling
  window wall with Haystack/ocean view,   K bed...$115
#342 — spacious, corner, raised fireplace, pvt. balc., floor-to-ceiling
  window wall with a fine ocean view,   K bed...$79
#242 — as above,   Q bed...$79
#343 — raised fireplace, ocean/town view,   Q bed...$62
regular room — no ocean view,   Q bed...$40

★ **Surfsand - Best Western** *.5 mi. S at W end of Gower St.* *436-2274*
This modern beachfront motel has a large indoor pool and a whirlpool. Each unit has a phone and cable color TV.

#216 — end unit, fireplace, pvt. balc., refr., oceanfront view, K bed...$79
#221 — end unit, fireplace, pvt. balc., oceanfront view, 2 Q beds...$79
#220,#219 — as above, but not end units,   Q bed...$74
regular room — no ocean view,   Q bed...$39

★ **Tolovana Inn** *2 mi. S at 3400 S. Hemlock St.* *436-2211*
Wood-trim and shingles distinguish the three-story buildings of the area's largest and most complete motor hotel. In addition to a choice location on the beach, amenities include a large indoor pool, a whirlpool, saunas, and a well-furnished game room with table tennis and pool tables, plus a view restaurant and lounge. Each spacious, nicely refurbished unit has a phone and cable color TV.

#328,#327,#332,#330 — studio, kitchen, glass-front (presto log) fireplace,
  pvt. balc., great beach/ocean view, Murphy Q bed...$60
#323,#322,#320,#319 — studio, kitchen, glass-front fireplace, pvt. balc.,
  nice ocean view,   Murphy Q bed...$60
regular room — mt. view,   Q bed...$35

★ **The Viking Motel** *1.5 mi. S off Hemlock St.* *436-2269*
This small oceanfront motel has a newer complex with some excellent units. Each has a phone, cable color TV, and a small refrigerator.

#16,#13 — studio, raised fireplace, kit., awesome beach &
  Haystack Rock view from lg. corner windows, Q bed...$68
#14,#11 — studio, as above but no Haystack Rock view, Q bed...$68
regular room — older, ocean view,   Q bed...$44

★ **The Waves** *downtown at 2nd/Larch Sts.* *436-2205*
Artistically handcrafted newer units are featured in the loveliest little cottage colony on the beach next to the heart of town. Each beautifully decorated and furnished unit has cable color TV. Most have a wood-burning fireplace and an electric kitchen.

"South Flagship" — free-standing metal fireplace, kitchen,
  pvt. ocean view balc.,   Q bed...$69
"North Flagship" — metal fireplace, kitchen,
  pitched roof, great ocean view,   Q bed...$59
"Sunscoop" #3 & #4 — split level, fireplace, kitchen, many view windows,
  skylights, pvt. decks,   Q bed...$72
regular room — some ocean view,   D bed...$38

Webb's Scenic Surf *downtown on Larch St. N of 2nd St.* *436-2706*
Near the heart of town on the beach is a small motel with some fine ocean views. Each plainly furnished unit has a cable color TV and refrigerator.

#6 — brick fireplace, kitchen, pvt. beach-view deck, 2 T & Q beds...$84
#11 — gas fireplace, patio, beach view,   Q bed...$74
regular room — oceanfront deck,   Q bed...$64

CAMPGROUNDS

There are few campgrounds near town. Visitors have a choice of either a rustic, private campground with complete facilities a stroll from town and the beach, or a wonderfully picturesque walk-in campground with relatively primitive facilities near the ocean an easy drive south of town.

★ **Oswald West State Park** *11 mi. S on US 101*   *238-7488*

This state owned facility includes a tenting campground located in a luxuriant rain forest near a secluded ocean beach. It can only be reached by a quarter-mile trail from a parking lot where wheelbarrows are provided to transport your gear. Sunbathing, beachcombing, cold-ocean swimming, and shore fishing are popular. There are flush toilets, but no showers or hookups. Each of the well-spaced pine-shaded sites has a picnic table and a fire area.   base rate...$4

Sea Ranch Trailer Village *.3 mi. N on US 101A*   *436-2815*

This privately owned campground is by an attractive stream a short walk from a superb ocean beach. Fishing in Ecola Creek, plus guided horseback rides on the beach, are features at the site. Flush toilets, hot showers, and hookups are available. Each of the closely-spaced sites has a rustic picnic table and a fire area. Some are shaded.

SPECIAL EVENT   base rate...$7

★ **Sand Castle Contest** *on the beach in town*   *early June*

More than 10,000 spectators watch participants from all over the country produce short-lived architectural masterpieces and fanciful sculptured figures from wet sand during this one-day celebration of Cannon Beach's greatest attraction.

OTHER INFORMATION

Area Code: *503*

Zip Code: *97110*

Cannon Beach Chamber of Commerce *downtown at 201 E. 2nd St.* *436-2623*

Grants Pass, Oregon

Elevation:

948 feet

Population (1980):

15,032

Population (1970):

12,455

Location:

230 mi. S
of Portland

Grants Pass is the West's ultimate river town. The Rogue River is calm and clear as it flows past the heart of town. A few miles upstream, several small dams have created scenic lakes. Downstream, the river dashes wildly down breathtaking gorges, and it meanders slowly through forested valleys surrounded by gentle mountains. Grants Pass occupies a broad valley midway along the fabulous stream. Noted for one of the mildest climates in the Northwest, the town is further enhanced by a profusion of broadleaf and pine trees, and flowers. Rhododendron bushes twenty feet high flourish near what may be the continent's most northerly palm trees. Daytime temperatures are already warm by early spring. During the normally hot sunny days of summer, pretty little upstream lakes, peaceful stretches in town, and downstream "wild river" sections entice the year's largest crowds to sample the wonderful diversity of water recreation available on the Rogue River. Nearby, a large national forest, a wilderness area and several state and local parks provide additional outdoor recreation opportunities from spring through fall. In winter, temperatures are relatively moderate and there is very little snowfall, but rainfall is almost continuous.

Tortuous mountain passes and unfriendly Indians discouraged pioneers who came West over the Oregon Trail from settling in this area during the 1840s. However, with the first discovery of gold in Oregon in the nearby Jacksonville area in 1851, hordes of soon-to-be-disappointed prospectors arrived. After the last major Indian battle in 1854, homesteaders began to move here to take advantage of the area's fertile soil and mild climate. The town was probably named after General U.S. Grant during the Civil War, when this area was being surveyed. With a diversified economy that included (and still includes) lumbering, dairying, and farming, growth has been steady since that time.

Residents' pride in their river remains the town's binding force, and sharing it with visitors has become a major industry in recent years. Guide and rental services now offer jet boats, inflatable kayaks, and wind sailboards, plus old favorites like fishing boats and whitewater rafts, for people to experience the river. One of the West's finest riverside parks is a short stroll from the heart of town. Downtown is an unpretentious commercial center with a large number of conventional shops, bars, and restaurants. Accommodations are concentrated along the business routes into town, and — like everything else in Grants Pass — they are plain, plentiful, and very reasonably priced. Nearby along the river are some of the West's most picturesque campgrounds.

WEATHER PROFILE

Grants Pass, Oregon
Vokac Weather Rating

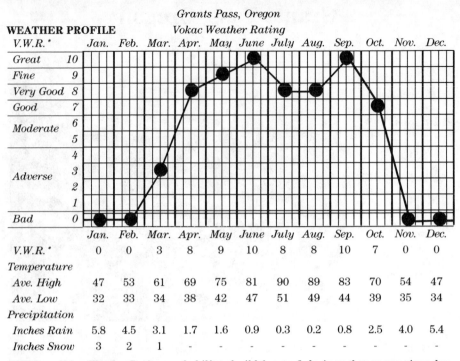

V.W.R.*	Jan.	Feb.	Mar.	Apr.	May	June	July	Aug.	Sep.	Oct.	Nov.	Dec.
V.W.R.*	0	0	3	8	9	10	8	8	10	7	0	0
Temperature												
Ave. High	47	53	61	69	75	81	90	89	83	70	54	47
Ave. Low	32	33	34	38	42	47	51	49	44	39	35	34
Precipitation												
Inches Rain	5.8	4.5	3.1	1.7	1.6	0.9	0.3	0.2	0.8	2.5	4.0	5.4
Inches Snow	3	2	1	-	-	-	-	-	-	-	-	-

V.W.R. = Vokac Weather Rating: probability of mild (warm & dry) weather on any given day.

Forecast

Temperatures

Month	V.W.R.*		Daytime	Evening	Precipitation
January	0	Bad	chilly	chilly	continual rainstorms/snow flurries
February	0	Bad	cool	chilly	frequent rainstorms
March	3	Adverse	cool	chilly	frequent rainstorms
April	8	Very Good	warm	cool	occasional showers
May	9	Fine	warm	cool	occasional showers
June	10	Great	warm	cool	infrequent showers
July	8	Very Good	hot	warm	negligible
August	8	Very Good	hot	warm	negligible
September	10	Great	hot	cool	infrequent showers
October	7	Good	warm	cool	occasional rainstorms
November	0	Bad	cool	chilly	frequent rainstorms
December	0	Bad	chilly	chilly	continual rainstorms

Summary

Grants Pass is located in the heart of the beautiful Rogue River Valley in a luxuriant pine-and-broadleaf forest. Only about 900 feet above sea level, it is framed by the Coast Range mountains of southwestern Oregon. The area enjoys one of the West's mildest four season climates outside of California. All of the nominally bad weather is confined to **winter** which is very cool and wet. More than half of the year's precipitation occurs during this season in continual rainstorms and rare snow flurries. **Spring** is delightful, with warm days, cool evenings, and occasional showers. From Easter through Memorial Day, outdoor activities are further enhanced by blossom-time, when nearby orchards and noble shade trees throughout town lend fragrance and beauty to the setting. **Summer** days are usually hot, evenings are warm, and there's almost no rainfall. These are ideal conditions for enjoying the West's most usable river. In **fall**, comfortably warm days, cool evenings, and occasional rainstorms continue through Halloween, when a brilliant foliage spectacle highlights the season.

ATTRACTIONS & DIVERSIONS

★ Boat Rides

An exciting and popular way to enjoy the spectacular Rogue River in summer is via jet boat. Trips involve some whitewater and range from one hour, to five hours for the round trip to Hellgate Canyon. Some trips include a champagne brunch or country dinner by the river. For more information and reservations, contact:

Hellgate Excursions	*on SE 7th St. near Riverside Motel*	*479-7204*
Morrison's Lodge Jet Boat Trips	*17.3 mi. NW at 8500 Galice Rd.*	*476-3825*
Rogue River Jet Boat Trips	*10 mi. E on OR 99*	*582-3101*

★ Crater Lake National Park *80 mi. NE via I-5 & OR 234 on OR 62*

Oregon's only national park has as its centerpiece Crater Lake. The clear, brilliant blue waters of this magnificent mountain-rimmed lake are 1,932 feet deep — America's deepest. The renowned six-by-five-mile water body was formed when rain and snow filled what was left of volcanic Mount Mazama more than 6,000 years ago after violent eruptions collapsed the mountaintop. A breathtakingly beautiful thirty-two-mile rim drive around the lake doesn't open until approximately the 4th of July except in years of light snowfall. The main highway (OR 62) is kept open to Rim Village year-round, in spite of a normal snowfall of fifty feet each winter. Boat tours leave daily during the summer to Wizard Island, a symmetrical cinder cone that rises about 760 feet above the lake's surface. Scenic panoramas and, in summer, fields of wildflowers line spur roads and well-marked trails that extend from many points along the rim drive.

★ Hellgate *14.4 mi. NW on Galice Rd.*

The Rogue River's phenomenal entrance into the Coast Range is a narrow passage with sheer rock walls more than 250 feet high. It is an especially popular section for river trips. Far above, a panoramic viewpoint has been provided by the road that parallels the river.

Hop Yards *5 mi. W on Upper and Lower River Roads*

Some of the largest hop fields in the Northwest are found west of town. These unique perennial plants start growing in May and reach the top of seventeen-foot-tall strings by mid-July. They are harvested in September for blossoms used primarily in the production of beer.

★ Library *downtown at 200 NW C St.* *474-5480*

The handsome Josephine County Library has an extensive display of periodicals and upholstered reading chairs in a large and cheerful room that also showcases a big globe. Closed Sat.-Sun.

Mint Farms *8 mi. SW via US 199 on Riverbanks Rd.*

The Fry Mint Farms consist of more than one square mile of picturesque emerald green mint. The plants are harvested in August and made into pure mint oil concentrate on the premises.

★ Oregon Caves National Monument *49 mi. SW via US 199 on OR 46*

Visitors can explore many dramatic and beautiful chambers in the "Marble Halls of Oregon." Guide service is required and available year-round. For the strenuous cave tours, children under six are not permitted. Visitors should have a jacket since the average temperature is only 42°F, and non-slip walking shoes. There are hiking trails and picnic and camping facilities nearby in the lush mountain forest.

★ Palm Tree *downtown at 7th/G Sts.*

The diverse and luxuriant vegetation of the Rogue River Valley is perhaps best symbolized by a palm tree casually located by a downtown thoroughfare. Benches near the palm give visitors a chance to contemplate the fact that palm trees can and do grow year-round outdoors in the Northwest.

River Running

★ Rogue River - downstream *west of town*

In 1968, an eighty-four-mile segment of the Rogue River was designated as a "National Wild and Scenic River." The segment begins a few miles west of town at the junction of the Rogue and Applegate Rivers, and extends almost to the ocean. The stretch between Grave Creek and Illahe is the most remote. It has been classified as "Wild River" and is inaccessible except by trail or man-powered boat. Gentler parts of the designated segment are classified as "Scenic" or "Recreational," and are accessible by the Galice Road which parallels the river for nearly thirty miles, and by jet boats which join rafts and other oar-powered craft on these stretches. An extraordinary diversity of river experiences is available. Scenic, whitewater, or fishing trips ranging from a half day to nine days can be arranged in crafts ranging from jet boats to individual inflatable kayaks. Several rustic lodges and picturesque campgrounds are scattered along the river. Visitors bringing their own raft can easily arrange to be left off and picked up at prearranged spots. Excellent maps, books, and complete lists of guide services can be obtained at the Chamber of Commerce. Some of the local guide services and their specialties are:

Galice Raft Trips (do-it-yourself rafts)	*12221 Galice Rd.*	*476-8051*
The Galice Resort (do-it-yourself rafts)	*11744 Galice Rd.*	*476-3818*
Grants Pass Float Co. (inflatable kayaks, rafts)		*479-2455*
Orange Torpedo Trips (inflatable kayaks)	*777 Debrick Wy.*	*479-5061*
Osprey River Trips (inflatable kayaks, rafts)	*6109 Fish Hatchery Rd.*	*479-4215*
River Adventure Float Trips (rafts, McKenzie boats)		*476-6493*
Robertson's Guide Service (drift fishing, rafts)	*3424 Amber Lane*	*479-9554*
Sundance Expeditions (kayaks, rafts, drift fishing)	*14894 Galice Rd.*	*479-8508*
Wilderness Water Ways Inc. (rafts, inflatable kayaks)	*12260 Galice Rd.*	*479-2021*

★ **Rogue River - upstream**   *east of town*

Several small scenic reservoirs have been created behind dams upstream from town. The smooth waters are popular for speed boating and water-skiing as well as for most watercraft. Picturesque areas for picnicking, sunbathing, swimming, and fishing abound. Riverside campgrounds, lodges, and motels are also numerous along the Rogue River Highway (OR 99) which parallels the river east of town.

★ **Riverside Park**   *.5 mi. S on E. Park St.*

Well-maintained lawns sloping down to the Rogue River delight sunbathers, and swimmers enjoy calm, clear pools just offshore. Above, noble trees provide shade for picnic tables. Imaginative play equipment (like a large wooden maze), formal flower gardens, and playfields are other attractions of this outstanding riverfront park.

★ **Rogue River Hiking Trail**   *starts 23 mi. NE on Galice Rd. at Grave Creek*

The "Wild River" segment of the Rogue River is paralleled by a scenic hiking trail along the entire north bank. The forty-mile-long trail begins at Grave Creek on the Galice Road and ends at Illahe. It is closed to motorized vehicles, horses, and pack animals. Hiking the entire distance normally takes about five days.

★ **Siskiyou National Forest**   *S & W of town*   *479-5301*

This vast forest includes most of the southwestern corner of the state. The only redwood trees outside of California are an unusual feature. The Kalmiopsis Wilderness Area, at the rugged heart of the forest, is a botanist's paradise of rare and unusual plants. Nearly half of the designated National Wild and Scenic River portion of the Rogue River is in the forest, as is Oregon Caves National Monument. A good system of paved and dirt roads and hundreds of miles of trails provide access for river running, swimming, fishing, hiking, backpacking, horseback riding, pack trips, and camping. Information and maps may be obtained at the Forest Supervisor's Office in town.

SHOPPING

Grants Pass has a lively downtown oriented primarily toward meeting the conventional needs of residents and outdoor recreation enthusiasts. Attractively landscaped buildings and parking lots and an abundance of shade trees enhance the area.

Food Specialties

★ **The Cake Shop**   *8.8 mi. NW at 215 Galice Rd.*   *476-7087*

In addition to beautifully decorated cakes, this roadside bakery offers outstanding breads (like sheepherder, earth, and sourdough), plus old-fashioned cinnamon rolls and other delicious treats on weekends. Closed Mon.-Tues.

Grants Pass Pharmacy   *downtown at 414 SW 6th St.*   *476-4262*

In the center of an old-fashioned pharmacy is an island ice cream bar where a variety of flavors and styles are served to go or at some tables overlooking the main street.

★ **Jim's Ice Cream Factory**   *downtown at 203 SE H St.*   *476-1462*

Many flavors of chemical-free, natural ingredient ice cream are made here and served in all kinds of delicious creations along with some pastry desserts in a cheerful little parlor, or to go.

Rogue Gold Dairy   *downtown at 234 SW 5th St.*   476-7786
Locally made cheeses are sold in this small retail outlet, along with assorted teas and spices.

Specialty Shops
The Book Stop   *downtown at 420 SW 6th St.*   479-1587
This inviting store features books about southern Oregon and the Rogue River in a large collection of well-organized books.
Myrtlewood Products, Inc.   *downtown at 6th/D Sts.*   479-6664
Artistic and functional pieces from Oregon's most sought hardwood tree are displayed in this small shop. Closed Sun.
The Train Gallery   *2 mi. SW via US 199 at 1951 Redwood Av.*   476-1951
Downstairs, one of the largest model railroad exhibits in the Northwest is evolving. There is a casual art gallery upstairs.

NIGHTLIFE
Many casual bars, lounges, and roadside taverns are scattered in and around town. Several offer live music and dancing. Two overlook the Rogue River.
Larry's Kashmir Lounge   *.6 mi. SE at 515 SE Rogue River Hwy.*   479-2631
Live music and dancing are featured most nights in a casual, comfortable lounge next to a coffee shop/restaurant.
Merlin Mining Company   *8.5 mi. W at 330 Merlin Rd.*   479-2849
Live music and dancing are offered most nights in an Old West-style saloon. Live theater is presented in another room on weekends.
The Owl Club   *downtown at 125 SE G St.*   476-7559
A high-tech light display behind the dance floor is featured in this large, very casual disco bar.
★ **Pastime Cafe**   *downtown at 121 SW G St.*   479-0332
A spectacular hardwood back bar lends distinction to this frayed relic from the turn of the century. Pool, ping-pong, and darts provide the action in an authentic old-time workingman's bar.
R-Haus   *2.3 mi. SE at 2140 Rogue River Hwy.*   476-4287
The antique-filled Liberty Lounge overlooking the Rogue is a tranquil spot for a quiet conversation above a restaurant.
★ **Riverside Motel Lounge**   *.4 mi. S at 971 SE 6th St.*   476-2488
Classy, comfortable furnishings and a picture window view of the river and town park give distinction to the motel's lounge. Refreshments are also served on a sunny riverside deck.
Woodshed Lounge   *1.2 mi. SW on US 199 at 690 Redwood Hwy.*   474-6211
Live music and dancing are offered several nights each week in a large, rustic, Western-style saloon and restaurant complex.

RESTAURANTS
Most of the local dining rooms offer hearty American fare and conventional Western decor. The plain, plentiful food and casual surroundings are well-suited to the town's preoccupation with robust outdoor activity focused on the river. Prices at most of the recommended restaurants are among the lowest among great towns in the West.
A Lunch Inn   *downtown at 422 SW 5th St.*   476-1641
B-L. Closed Sun.   *Low*
Good homestyle meals (including homemade biscuits, cinnamon rolls, and pies) served here are remarkably inexpensive. Dining in the tiny room is like eating in someone's cozy kitchen. Windows frame a palm tree growing on the front lawn.
The Brewery   *downtown at 509 SW G St.*   479-9850
L-D. No L on Sat. Closed Sun.   *Moderate*
Contemporary American dishes are served in comfortably furnished dining rooms with an old-time brewery theme. An inviting bar adjoins.
Erik's   *.5 mi. E at 1067 Redwood Spur*   479-4471
L-D. No L on Sat.   *Moderate*
This newer restaurant features a comprehensive assortment of American specialties amidst appealing wood-and-plants decor.

Galice Restaurant and Store   *21 mi. W at 11744 Galice Rd.*   *476-3818*
B-L-D.   *Low*
Giant homemade cinnamon rolls are a specialty among hearty American dishes served in a rustic cafe with a big fireplace, or on an inviting deck where occasional steak cookouts accompany a great view of some of the best riffles of the Rogue. The place is perfectly geared for river-users.

Hamilton House Restaurant   *1 mi. E at 344 NE Terry Lane*   *479-3938*
L-D. Closed Mon.   *Moderate*
A variety of carefully prepared American entrees highlights abundant, family-style meals served in an out-of-the-way restaurant that is a local favorite. The pleasant dining rooms have garden views.

Honeycutt's Restaurant   *downtown at 432 NW 6th St.*   *479-3725*
B-L-D.   *Low*
Homemade biscuits, cinnamon rolls, pastries, and pies are featured in a plain recently-enlarged coffee shop.

L'Allegro's   *downtown at 205 NW E St.*   *479-7607*
D only. Closed Sun.-Mon.   *Low*
Italian food is served family-style in an appealingly refurbished little yellow house.

Merlin Mining Co.   *8.5 mi. NW at 330 Merlin Rd.*   *479-2849*
L-D.   *Moderate*
Steaks and seafood are served in a Western-style dining room. Several wines are available by the glass on an unusual all-Oregon wine list. Dinner theater is offered in an adjoining room on weekends.

Pee Bee's   *.5 mi. S at 201 E. Park St.*   *474-2541*
B-L-D. No D on Sun.   *Low*
Homestyle American favorites like huge cinnamon rolls are emphasized in this unassuming coffee shop.

Riverside Motel Restaurant   *.4 mi. S at 971 SE 6th St.*   *476-2488*
B-L-D.   *Moderate*
American dishes are served in a plush contemporary dining room with splendid picture window views of the Rogue River and the town park on the other bank.

Shepp's Sportsman Inn   *2 mi. E at 1883 Rogue River Hwy.*   *479-2832*
D only.   *Moderate*
Steak and family-style hearty American meals are served in a casual dining room. The adjoining lounge features live music and dancing on weekends.

Three Oaks Restaurant   *7 mi. E at 6801 Rogue River Hwy.*   *582-0810*
L-D. B on Sat. & Sun. Closed Mon.   *Moderate*
Homemade soup, chili, and sandwiches are served with malts and sundaes in a little roadside cafe built into a restored 1853 house. The soda fountain is delightful.

★ **Wolf Creek Tavern**   *20 mi. N on I-5*   *866-2474*
L-D.   *Low*
Carefully prepared, classic American fare is served family-style in a large, wonderfully authentic 1850s stagecoach stop that has been painstakingly restored and furnished in period pieces. Upstairs, eight antique-filled rooms provide overnight accommodations. A handsome bar and exquisitely detailed parlour adjoin the nostalgic dining rooms.

Yankee Pot Roast   *.4 mi. N at 720 NW 6th St.*   *476-0551*
L-D. Sun. brunch.   *Low*
An abundance of down-home all-American cooking is offered amidst old-time atmosphere in several cozy dining rooms of a recycled old house.

LODGING

There are plenty of places to stay in and around town. The best have riverfront views. A remarkable number of bargain motels are located on 6th and 7th Streets between downtown and Interstate 5. Many of the recommended accommodations offer 10% and greater rate reductions apart from summer.

Bridge Motel   *.4 mi. S at 986 SW 6th St.*   476-7788
This modern single-level motel by the Rogue River is a **bargain** with a large landscaped
outdoor pool. Each spacious room has a phone and cable color TV.
   #20 — end unit, good river view (but near a noisy bridge),   Q bed...$28
   #5,#6,#15,#17 — nice river views beyond public balc.,   Q bed...$28
   regular room — some have river views beyond public balc.,   Q bed...$28

★ **Del Rogue Motel**   *2.7 mi. E at 2600 Rogue River Hwy.*   479-2111
This beautifully landscaped little motel has a delightfully tree-shaded location by the river.
Each well-furnished unit has cable color TV and a private screened porch. A kitchen may
be added for $7.
   #D,#C,#A — fine river views,   Q bed...$35
   regular room —   Q bed...$35

Egyptian Motel   *.4 mi. N at 728 NW 6th St.*   476-6601
There is a large landscaped outdoor pool in this **bargain** single-level motel. Each room has
a phone and cable color TV.
   regular room —   Q bed...$26
   regular room —   D bed...$22

Fireside Motel   *.5 mi. N at 839 NE 6th St.*   474-5558
An outdoor pool is a feature of this small, older **bargain** motel. Each simply-furnished
room has cable color TV.
   regular room —   2 D or Q bed...$22

★ **Half Moon Bar Lodge**   *27 mi. W on the Rogue River*   476-4002
The small lodge has no access road. It can only be reached by boat, plane, or on foot. The
rate includes gourmet home-cooked meals prepared from their own garden-fresh
produce and served to (at most) sixteen guests sharing the Rogue River wilderness. Rates
include three family-style meals plus Oregon wines at dinner. (Additional nights are 20%
less.) Business office: 410 NW E St. in Grants Pass.
   regular room —   D bed...$150

Motel 6   *1.4 mi. N at 1800 NE 7th St.*   476-9096
The nationwide **bargain** chain is represented here by a large modern motel with an
outdoor pool. Each no-frills room has (fee) B/W TV.
   regular room —   D bed...$22

Oregon Motel   *1.1 mi. N at 1464 NW 6th St.*   476-2555
This smaller, older, single-level **bargain** motel has an outdoor pool with a slide. Each of the
plain rooms has a color TV.
   regular room —   Q bed...$26
   regular room —   D bed...$22

Regal Lodge   *1 mi. N at 1400 NW 6th St.*   479-3305
A small outdoor pool is a feature of this modern **bargain** motel. Each room has a phone
and cable color TV.
   regular room —   D or Q bed...$26

★ **Riverside Motel - Best Western**   *.4 mi. S at 971 SE 6th St.* 476-6873
A riverfront location across from the town park is a splendid site for this large modern
three-level motor hotel. Facilities include two outdoor pools (the large one overlooks the
river) and a whirlpool, plus (for a fee) jet boat rides. The stylish dining room and a deck
have fine river views, and there is a comfortable lounge. Each spacious, well-furnished
room has a phone and cable color TV.
   #205 — on top fl., great view from pvt. balc.,   2 Q beds...$68
   #150 — end unit, pvt. balc., fine river view,   K bed...$70
   #140,#146 — pvt. balc., fine river view,   K bed...$48
   #189,#192,#199,#202 — pvt. balc., fine river view,   Q bed...$45
   regular room —   Q bed...$41

Uptown Motel   *.9 mi. N at 1253 NE 6th St.*   *479-9217*
In this small, single-level **bargain** motel, each room has cable color TV with movies.
   regular room —   Q bed...$26
   regular room —   D bed...$24

CAMPGROUNDS

The West's greatest recreational river and an unusually long season of warm weather make this a special destination for campers. Numerous public and private campgrounds offer complete facilities and all kinds of water recreation. The best are remarkably scenic, complete, and well-situated by the river.

Circle W Campground   *9 mi. SE at 8110 Rogue River Hwy.*   *582-1686*
This small, private campground on the Rogue River offers water-skiing, swimming, and fishing. Flush toilets, hot showers, and hookups are available. Each closely-spaced site has a picnic table. There are two fine shady sites on grass by the river.   base rate...$7.50

★ **Indian Mary** *16 mi. NW: 3.4 mi. N on I-5 & 12.6 mi. NW on Galice Rd.*   *474-5285*
Josephine County has provided an outstanding campground on a beautifully landscaped site among pines and hardwoods by the Rogue River. Features include river swimming, boating (plus a boat ramp), fishing, and marked nature trails. Flush toilets, hot showers, and hookups are available. Each shaded, well-spaced site has a picnic table and fire grill.
                                                                                    base rate...$6

Riverfront Trailer Park   *7.4 mi. SE at 7060 Rogue River Hwy.*   *582-0985*
This private facility by the Rogue River features swimming, boating, water-skiing, fishing, and a (fee) boat launch. Flush toilets, hot showers, and hookups are available. All sites are shaded and each has a picnic table. Two tent sites are beautifully positioned by the river.
                                                                                    base rate...$9

★ **Schroeder Campground** *3.5 mi. W via US 199 & Willow Ln.*   *474-5285*
Josephine County has provided a well-landscaped campground and park by the Rogue River. Features include boating (and ramp), fishing and swimming in the river, plus tennis courts and large lawn areas. Flush toilets, hot showers, and hookups are available. The hardwood and pine-shaded sites each have a picnic table and fire grill/ring.
                                                                                    base rate...$6

SPECIAL EVENT

★ **Boatnik Festival**   *downtown and Riverside Park*   *late May*
Boat races highlight an extended Memorial Day weekend celebration of the Rogue River. The fun-filled "boatnik" run ends at the beautiful riverside park near downtown, and the thrilling whitewater race to Hellgate Canyon both starts and ends there. Festivities begin with a downtown parade. A carnival, concessions, craft displays, a beer garden, and live entertainment are featured in the park.

OTHER INFORMATION

Area Code: *503*
Zip Code: *97526*
Grants Pass Chamber of Commerce   *1 mi. N at 1439 NE 6th St.*   *476-7717*
Siskiyou National Forest-Sup. Off. *1.5 mi. N at 200 NE Greenfield Rd.*   *479-5301*

Newport, Oregon

Elevation:

130 feet

Population (1980):

7,519

Population (1970):

5,188

Location:

114 mi. SW
of Portland

Newport is the keystone of the Pacific Northwest coast. The town covers a scenic peninsula where the Yaquina River flows into the Pacific Ocean. For a century, people have been attracted to this favored site bordered by broad sandy ocean beaches and a calm harbor sheltered by bluffs near the river's mouth. Over the years, the best features around town have been enhanced by an assortment of beach-fronting state parks and harborside marinas. Nearby, gentle forested slopes of Coast Range mountains are part of a large national forest. All of the area's features attract enthusiastic crowds during the normally sunny days of summer. Beachcombing, clamming, crabbing, shore and sportfishing, (and even swimming and surfing for a hearty few) are popular leisure activities. Golf, tennis and bicycling are enjoyed in town, and the colorful waterfront district is the most unspoiled and exhilarating maritime attraction on the Northwest coast. Temperatures year-round are surprisingly moderate. Freezes are unusual in town, and no snow is recorded during some years. However, there are almost continuous rainstorms from fall through spring.

Maritime activities have always been the compelling attraction of Newport, which was named after the resort in Rhode Island during the 1880s. By the early twentieth century, it was a rustic coastal tourist destination for Willamette Valley residents who lived in tents in what is now the Nye Beach neighborhood. The splendid Yaquina Bay bridge was completed during the Depression. It was a final link on the national highway that opened the entire magnificent Oregon coast to travelers. Tourism continues as a major segment of the local economy — along with commercial fishing and forest products industries.

Today, most of the area's conventional businesses are scattered along the main highway on the blufftop through town. Below, in the shadow of the bridge, is the compact bayfront district known as Old Town. This unspoiled historic enclave is the real heart of town. A captivating hodgepodge of shops, restaurants and bars share refurbished Victorian buildings amidst a mosaic of unpretentious canneries and other maritime businesses. Newport is the self-proclaimed Dungeness Crab capital of the world. Canneries, seafood markets, cafes and restaurants in Old Town do an outstanding job of showcasing this gourmet crustacean. Visitors can opt to stay at a plush contemporary resort hotel on the bay a short stroll from Old Town. Reasonably priced motels are plentiful along the highway through town. Several luxurious accommodations offer splendid oceanfront views along secluded coves and broad ocean beaches on the west side of town.

WEATHER PROFILE — *Vokac Weather Rating*

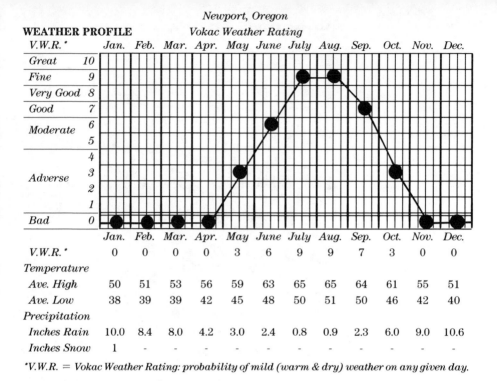

V.W.R.*	Jan.	Feb.	Mar.	Apr.	May	June	July	Aug.	Sep.	Oct.	Nov.	Dec.
V.W.R.*	0	0	0	0	3	6	9	9	7	3	0	0
Temperature												
Ave. High	50	51	53	56	59	63	65	65	64	61	55	51
Ave. Low	38	39	39	42	45	48	50	51	50	46	42	40
Precipitation												
Inches Rain	10.0	8.4	8.0	4.2	3.0	2.4	0.8	0.9	2.3	6.0	9.0	10.6
Inches Snow	1	-	-	-	-	-	-	-	-	-	-	-

V.W.R. = Vokac Weather Rating: probability of mild (warm & dry) weather on any given day.

Forecast

		Temperatures		
Month	V.W.R.*	Daytime	Evening	Precipitation
January	0 Bad	cool	chilly	continual downpours
February	0 Bad	cool	chilly	continual rainstorms
March	0 Bad	cool	chilly	continual rainstorms
April	0 Bad	cool	chilly	continual rainstorms
May	3 Adverse	cool	cool	frequent rainstorms
June	6 Moderate	cool	cool	occasional rainstorms
July	9 Fine	warm	cool	infrequent showers
August	9 Fine	warm	cool	infrequent showers
September	7 Good	cool	cool	occasional rainstorms
October	3 Adverse	cool	cool	frequent rainstorms
November	0 Bad	cool	chilly	continual rainstorms
December	0 Bad	cool	chilly	continual downpours

Summary

Newport occupies a handsome peninsula above the Oregon coast's finest beach-and-harbor. While it enjoys one of the longest growing seasons in the West outside of California because of the ocean's moderating influence, it endures one of the nation's heaviest annual rainfalls. **Winter** is cool and very wet. Since freezing temperatures are unusual, snowfall is rare, but continual rainstorms preclude many kinds of outdoor recreation. **Spring** remains unpleasantly cool and wet with only slightly higher temperatures and fewer rainstorms lasting through Memorial Day. **Summer** is the special season. Relatively warm days, cool evenings, and surprisingly infrequent showers provide suitable conditions for comfortably enjoying this water wonderland. **Fall** weather deteriorates rapidly, with cooler weather and increasingly frequent rainstorms before Halloween.

ATTRACTIONS & DIVERSIONS

Bicycling

Mike's Bikes   *downtown at 202 E. Olive St.*   *265-7212*

The hills are easy and the coastal scenery is magnificent for bicycle tours in and about town. Bike rentals, repairs, and sales are available in this casual little shop. Closed Sun.

★   **Parkway Grocery**   *6.7 mi. N on US 101 - Beverly Beach*   *265-9822*

Many types of bicycles may be rented at this convenient starting point for scenic coastal rides.

★ Boat Rentals

There are several places on Yaquina Bay where boats and gear may be rented by the hour or day. Among the most convenient are:

Embarcadero Marina   *.7 mi. E of Old Town at 1000 SE Bay Blvd.*   *265-5435*
South Beach Marina   *1.8 mi. S via US 101 on Oceanography Rd.*   *867-3800*

★ Depoe Bay   *14 mi. N on US 101*

An appealing village has grown up around a tiny rock-bound harbor that may be the nation's smallest. A sea wall promenade and bridge are the best places for watching sportfishing and pleasure boats negotiate the remarkably narrow, rock-lined channel between the harbor and the sea. Just west of the promenade are "spouting horns" — natural rock formations throwing geyserlike sprays of surf high in the air. Various sightseeing and deep sea fishing trips depart from the north wharf.

★ Devil's Punch Bowl State Park   *8 mi. N on US 101*

A huge bowl-shaped rock formation fills from below with a roar at high tide. Scenic picnic sites, a long spectacular curve of clean sandy beach, swimming (for the hearty), tide pools, and ocean-carved caves are other features of this delightful day use park.

Flying

Newport Aviation, Inc.   *3 mi. S via US 101 at Newport Airport*   *867-3615*

Scenic flights along the coast, and beyond for whale watching, are offered as frequently as every half hour. Charter service and rentals are also available.

Golf

Agate Beach Golf Course   *2.4 mi. N at 4100 Golf Course Dr.*   *265-7331*

Located on a relatively flat bluff inland from the ocean, this 9-hole course is open to the public. Facilities include a pro shop, clubs and cart rental, a driving range, and a cafe.

★   **Salishan Golf Course**   *19 mi. N via US 101 - Gleneden Beach*   *764-2471*

The famed resort's magnificent 18-hole championship golf course provides panoramic ocean views and lush fairways in picturesque sylvan frames. It is open to the public and includes a pro shop, club and cart rentals, a driving range, and a fine view restaurant and lounge.

Lincoln County Historical Museum   *downtown at 545 SW 9th St.*   *265-7509*

Two buildings, the Burrows House (1895) and a log cabin, display Newport area memorabilia and relics from Victorian and later times. Closed Mon.

★ Ona Beach State Park   *8 mi. S on US 101*

A bathhouse and boat ramp contribute to this day use park's attraction for swimming and fishing. There are many scenic picnic sites on a grassy lawn with shade trees overlooking the mouth of a creek and a sandy ocean beach.

★ OSU Marine Science Center   *1.8 mi. S on Oceanography Rd.*   *867-3011*

Oregon State University operates a large coastal research center on Yaquina Bay. The public is invited to view marine fish and invertebrates in tanks that simulate their natural environments. There is a handling pool where visitors can pick up and examine starfish and other intertidal creatures. Exhibits explain coastal geology, tides, and harbor life. During the summer, marine workshops, field trips, lectures, and films are offered to the public in the Seatauqua program. Nearby on Yaquina Bay is the Salmon Ocean Ranch, where visitors may view salmon in holding tanks.

★ Rock Hunting   *beaches north and south of town*

Tide-polished gem stones, agates, petrified wood, and coral may be found on the sand wherever streams cross coastal beaches.

★ **Sea Lion Caves**   *37 mi. S on US 101*

Here is the only year-round home for wild sea lions on the mainland. An elevator takes visitors down to a mammoth wave-carved grotto, more than a quarter mile long, at the base of the cliff. The viewing area is open during daylight hours all year.

★ **Siuslaw National Forest**   *NE and SE of town*   547-3289

This is the only coastal national forest in the Northwest. Cape Perpetua Visitor Center (27 mi. S on US 101) offers a movie and exhibits about the Oregon coast. Ten miles of scenic hiking trails branch out from the center into lush rain forests, driftwood-strewn beaches, and rock-bound tide pool formations. The view from the top of Cape Perpetua is magnificent and accessible by car. This is the highest point on the Oregon coast. Nearby are some fascinating rock and sea attractions — the Devil's Churn and Cook's Chasm. Inland, luxuriant forests blanket Coast Range mountains that reach elevations over 4,000 feet above sea level.

★ **South Beach Marina**   *1.8 mi. S via US 101 on Oceanography Rd.*   867-3800

One of the Northwest's largest and most complete marina facilities recently opened near the outlet of Yaquina Bay. In addition to a huge moorage and complete marine services, there is a public fishing pier with fine bay views, a bait and tackle store, deep sea charters, a picnic area with barbecues, and a crab cooking facility.

South Beach State Park   *2 mi. S on US 101*

Expansive low dunes and a broad sandy beach lie between a campground and picnic facilities, and the ocean. Fishing and beachcombing are popular.

★ **Sportfishing**

Salmon fishing is one of the major attractions off the Oregon coast. Newport is home port to several sportfishing charters located along the Old Town waterfront. Salmon trolling, tuna and deep sea fishing, and whale watching excursions are featured by:

Barnacle Bill's *Old Town at 839 SW Bay Blvd.*		265-7777
Embarcadero Marina *.7 mi. E of Old Town at 1000 SE Bay Blvd.*		265-5435
Newport Tradewinds *Old Town at 653 SW Bay Blvd.*		265-2101
Sea Gull Charters *Old Town at 343 SW Bay Blvd.*		265-7441
South Beach Charters *1.8 mi. S via US 101 on Oceanography Rd.*		867-7200

Undersea Gardens   *Old Town at 267 SW Bay Blvd.*   265-7541

Thousands of marine creatures can be viewed in their natural habitat through more than 100 underwater viewing windows. There are scuba diving shows hourly.

Warm Water Feature

Newport Swimming Pool   *1.2 mi. NE at 1212 NE Fogarty St.*   265-7770

Lap, recreational, and family swimming sessions are open to the public year-round in a large heated indoor pool.

★ **Yaquina Bay State Park**   *.6 mi. SW on US 101 at N end of bridge*

Dozens of scenic picnic sites are positioned on a well-landscaped blufftop with panoramic views of ocean beaches and the mouth of Yaquina Bay. Sunbathing, beachcombing, fishing, and swimming (for the hearty) are also popular. The park also includes the historic Yaquina Bay Lighthouse (1871). This combined lighthouse/residence has been restored and refurnished in period style and is open to the public Thursday through Monday.

SHOPPING

Intriguing shops are clustered in several locations in town. Downtown offers a small, growing cluster of newer shops near the civic buildings along US 101 on the bluff. It lies between two contemporary specialty shopping complexes that prove that new suburban shopping centers are not inevitably boring. Below the bluff about half a mile south of downtown is one of the West's liveliest and most distinctive shopping and strolling districts — Old Town — along the colorful Yaquina Bay waterfront.

Food Specialties

Arrow Food Market   *downtown at 425 SW US 101*   265-2132

In addition to groceries and magazines, this place features a gourmet deli that serves a wide assortment of sandwiches, and wine or beer from extensive collections, in a surprisingly pleasant dining area.

Aunt Belinda's   *Old Town at 663 SW Bay Blvd.*   265-9540
Tillamook ice cream is featured in a variety of flavors and styles in a small carryout shop.

★ **Bridge Bakery**   *.4 mi. SW at 1006 SW US 101*   265-8067
This popular full-line bakery offers a variety of outstanding pastries, donuts, cookies, pies, and breads to go, or with coffee at a few tables. Closed Sun.

Cape Perpetua Seafoods   *Old Town at 839 SW Bay Blvd.*   265-5661
Fresh seafoods, including live Dungeness crabs and fresh smoked seafoods, are featured in this market.

David's Donuts   *downtown on US 101 at 715A SW Hurbert St.*   265-7231
A variety of good donuts are served with coffee, or to go. Closed Sun.

★ **Depoe Bay Fish Market**   *14 mi. N on US 101 - Depoe Bay*   765-2287
Fresh, frozen, smoked, or canned seafoods are enticingly displayed and sold in a fish market that provides samples on request.

★ **Fish Peddler's Market**   *Old Town at 617 SW Bay Blvd.*   265-7057
From the viewing area of the Depot Bay Fish Co., visitors can watch the processing of fish, crab, and shrimp. In the retail market, seafood is sold fresh, frozen, smoked, or canned, and in special gift packs.

★ **Gino's Seafood & Deli**   *Old Town at 808 SW Bay Blvd.*   265-2424
This large, clean fish market features fresh, smoked, and canned seafoods, plus a good assortment of cheeses and other food items.

★ **Jack's Sea Food Inc.**   *Old Town at 456 SW Bay Blvd.*   265-5442
A large assortment of all types (fresh-packed, alder-smoked, barbecued, etc.) of canned seafoods is attractively displayed. They will also custom smoke your fish. "Sea Pak gift boxes" can also be purchased, ready for mailing.

JC's Ice Cream Parlor   *downtown at US 101/US 20*   265-3040
All natural ingredients and an unusually high cream content are featured in a variety of fine ice cream flavors and styles served to go or in a modern parlor.

Latta's Oregon Delicacies   *downtown on US 101 near Alder St.*   265-7675
Oregon gourmet foods are emphasized, including canned salmon, wild berry jams, nuts, candies, and other items packaged for carryout or in gift packs.

Rich Maid Ice Cream   *1 mi. N at 1514 N. US 101*   265-7392
A variety of good homemade ice creams are used in all kinds of creations in this little roadside cafe.

★ **Swafford's Oregon Specialties**   *1.1 mi. N at 1630 N. US 101*   265-7675
Oregon specialties — wine, cranberry candies, seafoods, wild berry preserves, etc. — are beautifully displayed along with local crafts. Many gift pack varieties will be shipped anywhere from this tantalizing contemporary shop in Sea Towne Shopping Center. In an adjoining dining area, fine pastries, desserts, and light fare are served for lunch. Closed Sun.

Tom Lazio Fish Co., Inc.   *Old Town at 623 SW Bay Blvd.*   265-5762
Smoked, fresh, or canned (Bell Buoy) seafoods are available in this casual fish market.

★ **West Candies Mfg.**   *.8 mi. N at 1329 N. US 101*   265-7317
Saltwater taffy, homemade chocolates, and cranberry candies are among the distinctive candies made and sold in this long-established candy store. Custom packed boxes will be shipped anywhere.

Specialty Shops

Bay Bridge Mall   *.5 mi. SW on US 101 at Minnie St.*
Just north of the bridge and Yaquina Bay Park, a small new shopping center has showcased some good specialty shops in buildings with appealing contemporary architecture and decor.

★ **Canyon Way Restaurant & Bookstore**   *downtown at 1216 SW Canyon Way*   265-8319
A large and eclectic assortment of books, arts, and crafts fills several rooms adjoining an unusually distinctive restaurant featuring delicious homemade soups, breads, pastries, and other light fare, along with beer, wine and espresso.

Land's End Gifts   *1.1 mi. N at 1610 N. US 101*   265-7526
Many of the beautifully displayed arts and crafts, candies, and nautical items have a Northwestern flair in this inviting contemporary shop in Sea Towne Mall.

The Myrtlewood Chalet   *Old Town at 325 SW Bay Blvd.*   *265-6979*
A fascinating assortment of myrtlewood items made elsewhere in Oregon are nicely displayed in a shop that also has a fine bay view.
★ **Sea Gulch**   *9 mi. S on US 101*
All kinds of large chain-sawed wood sculptures are the highlight of this unusual roadside business. Visitors can watch the motorized artists at work most days.
★ **Sea Towne Mall**   *1.1 mi. N at US 101/16th St.*
A classy cluster of specialty shops lends vitality to nautically-themed contemporary decor in this handsome shopping center.
★ **The Wood Gallery**   *Old Town at 818 SW Bay Blvd.*   *265-6843*
A superb selection of unique wood creations and pottery is featured in a captivating gallery.

NIGHTLIFE

One of the West's most refreshing "action" centers is the wonderful jumble of adult diversions that come alive after dark along historic Old Town's Bay Boulevard. Scruffy bars and legal gambling dens are interspersed with big whitewashed canneries, cozy cafes and contemporary restaurants, gift shops and galleries, and sleek lounges with spectacular bay views and live entertainment in a vibrant potpourri of businesses that suggest what Fisherman's Wharf in San Francisco may have been like in the "old days."

Barge Inn   *Old Town at 358 SW Bay Blvd.*   *265-8051*
The "Home of winos, dingbats and riffraff" is a frayed tavern that is a local favorite with pool, shuffleboard, and premium beer on tap.
Bay Haven Inn   *Old Town at 608 SW Bay Blvd.*   *265-7271*
Occasional jam sessions attract crowds to the funky bar. The short order grill, open for all meals, is popular with the natives.
★ **Captain Kidd's**   *downtown at 706 SW Hurbert St.*   *265-5114*
Pool, ping-pong, darts, foosball, and legal electronic gambling contribute to the popularity of a fanciful tavern outfitted with swing seats, boat seats, and captain's chairs.
Embarcadero Hotel Lounge   *.7 mi. E of Old Town at 1000 SE Bay Blvd.*   *265-8521*
Nightly entertainment and dancing are offered in a comfortable lounge with a bayfront view.
★ **The Inn at Otter Crest**   *9 mi. N on US 101 at Otter Rock*   *765-2111*
While live music for dancing is furnished most nights in the resort's plush modern lounge, the spectacular window wall view of the Oregon coast is the main attraction.
★ **Neptune's Wharf**   *Old Town at 325 SW Bay Blvd.*   *265-5316*
Fine bay and bridge views, plus live entertainment and dancing in summer, are features in a large contemporary lounge above a bayfront restaurant.
★ **Newport Hilton**   *2 mi. N at 3019 N. US 101*   *265-5341*
Casey's provides live entertainment for dancing most nights. The hotel's polished, contemporary lounge also has a fireplace and a panoramic view of Agate Beach.
★ **Pip Tide**   *Old Town at 836 SW Bay Blvd.*   *265-3138*
Live music and dancing are offered every night in a large and inviting lounge, while upstairs, Yaquina Fats Game Room features gambling (legal poker, etc.). The complex also has a firelit dining room and a coffee shop serving complete meals twenty-four hours daily.

RESTAURANTS

Seafood is appropriately emphasized, since fishing is a major local industry. Readily available local fresh fish and extraordinary shellfish like Yaquina Bay oysters and Dungeness crab reinforce Newport's status as the gourmet center of the coastal Northwest. Several dining rooms also provide enchanting views of the ocean or bay.
★ **The Bridge Company**   *.5 mi. SW at 1164 SW US 101*   *265-9551*
B-L-D.   *Moderate*
Carefully prepared homestyle meals are featured on a contemporary American menu. There is also a salad bar backed by a memorable mural of the Yaquina Bay Bridge in this handsome, high-tech dining room in the Bay Bridge Mall.

Casey's Bar and Grill   *2 mi. N at 3019 N. US 101*   *265-9411*
B-L-D. Sun. brunch.   *Moderate*
At the Newport Hilton, salmon is cooked over alder wood on the front lawn. But, the seafood specialties take a back seat to the panoramic view of Agate beach from the large, plush, contemporary dining room.

★ **The Centre at Canyon Way**   *downtown at 1216 SW Canyon Way*   *265-8319*
L-D. No D on Tues. & Wed. Closed Sun.-Mon.   Moderate
Delicious and unusual international specialties like the "French quickie," and fine homemade pastries, are served in several eclectic dining areas or in a garden patio. Fine coffees and teas, premium wines, and tap beers are also available. An outstanding bookstore adjoins.

★ **Champagne Patio**   *1.1 mi. N at 1630 N. US 101*   *265-7675*
L only. Closed Sun.-Mon.   *Moderate*
Carefully prepared soups, salads, sandwiches, and delectable homemade pastries are served in a small, nicely furnished dining room. Northwest wines selected from the outstanding Oregon specialty foods store in the next room will be poured for a low corkage fee.

The Chowder Bowl   *.4 mi. NW at 728 NW Beach Dr.*   *265-7477*
L-D. Closed Mon.   *Low*
Clam chowder is the well-regarded specialty of this casual, comfortable dining room near Nye beach.

★ **The Experience**   *19 mi. SE via US 101 at 3750 OR 34*   *563-4555*
D only. Closed Tues. (and Mon. in winter).   Moderate
The main course is exclusively seafood for the outstanding gourmet dinners served here, and it may be such seasonal specialties as Yaquina Bay oysters or halibut cheeks. Everything from soup to desserts, like an awesome cashew-kumquat pie, is skillfully homemade. The casually elegant little dining room has a fine forest view and an unusual world map mural wall. By reservation only.

The Flying Dutchman   *8 mi. N via US 101 - Otter Rock*   *765-2111*
B-L-D.   *Moderate*
At the Inn at Otter Crest, conventional Continental dishes are accompanied by homemade breads and pastries. The meals give patrons an excuse to linger over a magnificent panoramic view of the Oregon coast from the large, plush dining room. An adjoining view lounge features live music and dancing.

★ **The Moorage**   *.7 mi. E of Old Town at 1000 SE Bay Blvd.*   *265-8521*
B-L-D.   *Moderate*
Dungeness crab and salmon are among local specialties prepared with a gourmet flair at the Embarcadero Hotel. The Friday seafood buffet extravaganza is unforgettable in this large handsome dining room on picturesque Yaquina Bay.

Mo's   *Old Town at 622 SW Bay Blvd.*   *265-2979*
L-D.   *Low*
The clam chowder is renowned, and homestyle cooking lends distinction to fresh fish dishes and pies. This noisy little no-frills fish shack was the first of a redoubtable restaurant empire started by an Indian named Mohava Niemi.

★ **Mo's Annex**   *Old Town at 657 SW Bay Blvd.*   *265-7512*
L-D.   *Moderate*
Fresh fish casseroles join the acclaimed clam chowder as notable specialties. Across the street from the original cafe, Mo's Annex features a casual bayside dining room with delightful views of waterfront activity, and an excellent collection of Oregon wines.

Neptune's Wharf   *Old Town at 325 SW Bay Blvd.*   *265-2532*
L-D. Sun. brunch.   *Moderate*
The fresh sauteed seafood and a house bouillabaisse are good in this contemporary, casually elegant dining room with a delightful view by Yaquina Bay.

Peter's Place   *Old Town at 669 SW Bay Blvd.*   *265-8047*
L-D.   *Low*
Northern New Mexican specialties like blue corn tortillas, sopaipillas, and chile verde, plus seafoods are prepared Santa Fe-style in a casual upstairs cafe with a bayside view.

Pip Tide   *Old Town at 836 SW Bay Blvd.*   *265-7797*
B-L-D.   *Moderate*
Homestyle cooking is highlighted by magnificent pastries (when they're fresh) like huge cinnamon rolls, double pineapple surprise, etc. Breakfasts feature hundreds of omelet possibilities and some distinctive specialties like hangtown fry, and razor clams and eggs. The bright and cheerful twenty-four-hour coffee shop has a cannery/bay view. A firelit dining room adjoins.

★ **Salishan Lodge**   *19 mi. N on US 101 - Gleneden Beach*   *764-2371*
D only.   *Expensive*
Continental cuisine is formally presented nightly in the large, well-regarded Gourmet Dining Room. All three dining levels in this showplace of contemporary opulence overlook the resort's artful landscaping and, in the far distance, the ocean.

Vic's on the Wharf   *Old Town at 839 SW Bay Blvd.*   *265-8907*
B-L-D. Closed Tues.   *Low*
"Vic's (deservedly) famous biscuits and gravy" and very good homestyle fare are served in an unassuming little bayside cafe with a delightful view of the waterfront and bridge. For dinner, a limited menu offers exclusively seafood entrees — with local specialties featured.

★ **Whale's Tale**   *Old Town at 452 SW Bay Blvd.*   *265-8660*
B-L-D. Closed Jan.   *Low*
Breakfasts are notable, including specialties like poppyseed pancakes from stone-ground flour, and oyster omelets. Local artwork enlivens the handcrafted wood-toned interior, and there is occasional live entertainment in the evening.

LODGING

Several of the best accommodations overlook the ocean or the bay. Numerous motels, ranging from old and modest to posh and contemporary, are inland along US 101 through town. Many offer 25% and greater rate reductions apart from summer.

★ **Channel House**   *15 mi. N on US 101 - Depoe Bay*   *765-2140*
Perched on the rocks above the tiny Depoe Bay outlet is a superb little contemporary inn above a stylish ocean view dinner house. Each beautifully furnished unit has a cable color TV with movies. There is one **bargain** room. A Continental breakfast is included.

#3 — oceanfront suite, kitchen, 2 fireplaces, wood deck with whirlpool &
      awesome marine view,   Q bed...$95
#5 — top fl. oceanfront suite, kitchen, 2 fireplaces, in-bath
      whirlpool, large deck, awesome marine view,   Q bed...$95
#4 — remarkable ocean and bay view,   Q bed...$45
regular room #2 — partial ocean view,   D bed...$30

City Center Motel   *downtown at 538 SW US 101*   *265-7381*
In this small, older **bargain** motel, each room has a cable color TV.
regular room — movie channel on TV,   Q bed...$27
regular room —   D bed...$24

★ **Dunes Ocean Front Motel**   *.4 mi. SW at 536 SW Elizabeth St.*   *265-7701*
A large indoor pool and a whirlpool are features of this large modern oceanfront motel. Each room has a phone and cable color TV.
#133,#148 — great ocean views,   Q bed...$45
regular room —   Q bed...$41

★ **Embarcadero Resort Hotel**   *.7 mi. E of Old Town at 1000 SE Bay Blvd.*   *265-8521*
Newport's largest condominium motor hotel fronts on Yaquina Bay. Nicely landscaped grounds include several contemporary wood-toned buildings, a large indoor pool with a bay view, whirlpool, sauna, fishing and crabbing piers, outdoor barbecue and crab cooking facilities, a marina with rental boats, plus a fine restaurant and lounge. Each spacious well-furnished unit has a phone, cable color TV, and a private balcony.
Building C — 1 BR bayside suite, kitchen, fireplace in LR,
      fine bay/bridge view,   Q bed...$79
Buildings D,E,F,G — as above, but bay view only (no bridge),   Q bed...$79
regular room —   2 T or Q bed...$49

★ **Inn at Otter Crest**   *9 mi. N on US 101 - Otter Rock*   765-2111
Majestically located in a pine forest high above the ocean, this large contemporary condominium hotel offers a private sandy cove, a large outdoor pool with splendid views, a whirlpool, saunas, a putting green, (fee) indoor tennis courts, plus a spectacularly located restaurant, and a lounge with live entertainment and dancing. Each well-furnished unit has a phone, cable color TV with movies, refrigerator, and deck.

#189,#405 "honeymoon loft suites" — fireplace, kitchen, stunning views,
loft with   K bed...$85
regular room —   2 D beds...$55

★ **Little Cove Creek**   *2.3 mi. N via US 101 at 3641 NW Ocean View*   265-8587
A secluded beachfront cove has been transformed with perfectly-scaled naturalistic buildings and landscaping into an enchanting little condominium motel. Each beautifully furnished unit has a phone, cable color TV with movies, fireplace, kitchen, and a private deck.

#29 — 1 BR, magnificent ocean/beach views,   K bed...$62
#3 — studio, magnificent ocean view,   Murphy Q bed...$52
regular room — studio, some ocean view,   Murphy Q bed...$52

★ **Moolack Shores Motel**   *4.9 mi. N on US 101*   265-2326
This contemporary single-level motel is in a secluded spot at the edge of a bluff above the beach. Each room is artistically decorated in a different theme and has cable color TV.

#10A — corner, Franklin (duraflame log) fireplace, kitchenette,
ocean view windows,   Q bed...$46
#4,#5A,#9 — as above, but not a corner unit,   Q bed...$46
regular room — small, (duraflame) fireplace, kit., no view,   Q bed...$33

Newport Inn   *1 mi. N at 1311 N. US 101*   265-8516
Each room in this modern **bargain** motel has a phone and cable color TV with movies.
regular room —   Q bed...$24

★ **Newport Hilton**   *2 mi. N at 3019 N. US 101*   265-9411
Overlooking picturesque Agate Beach is a large, modern six-story hotel with a big outdoor pool and a whirlpool, plus a view restaurant, and a view lounge with entertainment. Each well-furnished room has a phone and cable color TV.

#630,#620,#612,#610,#602 — balc., outstanding pvt. ocean view,   K bed...$72
regular room — faces a hillside,   Q bed...$47

Park Motel   *.3 mi. SW via US 101 at 1106 SW 9th St.*   265-2234
This is a modern, single-level **bargain** motel. Each room has a phone and cable color TV with movies.
regular room —   Q bed...$24

Penny Saver Inn   *.6 mi. N at 710 N. US 101*   265-6631
One of the area's newest **bargain** motels features a phone and cable color TV with movies in each room.
regular room —   Q bed...$30

★ **Salishan Lodge**   *19 mi. N on US 101 - Gleneden Beach*   764-2371
Exquisite sensitivity was shown in blending contemporary opulence into a natural Oregon landscape. This large, world famous resort motel sprawls in low profile across many acres of manicured grounds. Amenities include a big indoor pool, whirlpool, saunas, exercise room, putting green, playground, nature trails, and (for a fee) a championship 18-hole golf course and four tennis courts (three indoors), plus lavish dining and lounge facilities. The nearest ocean beach is a half mile away. Each beautifully decorated, spacious room has a phone, cable color TV, a fieldstone fireplace and a balcony with a view of either the nearby golf course or distant bay and ocean.

"Chieftain Deluxe North" (several) — refr., bay view,   K bed..$126
regular room —   2 D or K bed...$88

Sands Motor Lodge   *.3 mi. N at 206 N. US 101*   265-5321
A sauna is featured in a **bargain** motel where each plainly furnished room has a phone and cable color TV with movies.
regular room —   Q bed...$28
regular room —   D bed...$26

Seven Seas Motel   *.3 mi. SW at 861 SW US 101*   *265-2277*
This modern **bargain** motel is by the highway in a convenient location. Each of the plain rooms has a phone and cable color TV.

regular room —   Q bed...$28

Summer Wind Motel   *.6 mi. N at 728 N. US 101*   *265-5722*
This small, single-level older motel is a **bargain**. Each of the simply furnished rooms has a cable color TV.

regular room —   Q bed...$22

Surf 'n Sand   *4.6 mi. N on US 101*   *265-2215*
In this tiny oceanfront motel, each unit is nicely furnished and has cable color TV and a refrigerator.

#16,#17 — fine ocean view from 2 sides, free-standing fireplace, kit.,   K bed...$42
#11,#15 — fine corner window ocean views, free-standing fireplace, kit.,   Q bed...$42
regular room —   Q bed...$34

★ **Surfrider**   *15 mi. N on US 101 - Depoe Bay*   *764-2311*
High on a bluff overlooking the ocean just north of Fogarty Creek State Park is a handsome contemporary motel with a large indoor pool, whirlpool, sauna, and a ping-pong room, plus an ocean view restaurant and lounge. Each nicely furnished, spacious unit has a phone and cable color TV with movies.

#40,#47 — Bridal Suites, semi-pvt. balcony, raised fireplace, lg. sunken
         tub, splendid ocean view,   K bed...$52
#12,#23 — fireplace, pvt. deck, fine ocean view,   Q bed...$42
#50,#57 — 1 BR, semi-pvt. balc., fireplace, kit., great ocean view,   Q bed...$52
#51,#56 — semi-pvt. balc., fireplace, fine ocean view,   Q bed...$48
regular room — ocean view,   2 D or Q bed...$40

West Wind Motel   *.3 mi. SW at 747 SW US 101*   *265-5388*
An indoor pool and a whirlpool are features of this small, single-level **bargain** motel. Each plain room has a phone and cable color TV.

regular room —   Q bed...$28

The Whaler Motel   *.3 mi. W at 155 SW Elizabeth St.*   *265-9261*
Newport's newest seaside motel is a three-story complex across a street from the ocean. Each attractively furnished room has a phone and cable color TV.

#79,#59 — corner windows, ocean view,   2 Q beds...$49
#77 — (chem-log) fireplace, good ocean view,   2 Q beds...$54
#41,#40 — (chem-log) fireplace, good ocean view,   Q bed...$45
regular room —   Q bed...$38

★ **The Windjammer - Best Western**   *.4 mi. SW at 744 SW Elizabeth St.*   *265-8853*
All of the units in this attractive contemporary motel on a bluff above the ocean have a fine beachfront view. Each nicely furnished unit has a phone and cable color TV.

#444 — raised brick fireplace, great corner window with ocean views,   Q bed...$53
#435 — fireplace, kitchen, huge ocean view window, loft,   2 Q beds...$68
regular room —   Q bed...$43

CAMPGROUNDS
Several campgrounds are scattered along the coast near town. The best is a nearly perfect combination of an easy drive to town, complete facilities, and a scenic sheltered location a short stroll from a picturesque sandy beach.

★ **Beverly Beach State Park**   *6.7 mi. N on US 101*   *265-9278*
The state operates this big facility located in a lush forest along a little stream near a fine sandy ocean beach. Features include saltwater or freshwater swimming and fishing in the ocean or Spencer Creek, beachcombing, and marked nature trails. Flush toilets, hot showers, and hookups are available. Each of the well-spaced, tree-shaded sites has a picnic table and a fire ring/grill. A scenic day use picnic area adjoins.   base rate...$6

South Beach State Park   *2 mi. S on US 101*   *867-4715*
This large state operated facility is in scrub pines across some low dunes from a long ocean beach. Beachcombing and fishing are within walking distance. Flush toilets, hot showers, and hookups are available. Each site has a picnic table and fire ring/grill.

base rate...$6

SPECIAL EVENTS

★ **Seafood and Wine Festival**   *.7 mi. NE at Fairgrounds*   *late February*
In only a few years, this weekend festival has become one of the largest of its kind on the West Coast. Oregon wines and seafoods are featured, with music and arts and crafts as sidelights.

Loyalty Days and Sea Fair Festival   *around town*   *first weekend in May*
A parade, sailing regatta, military ship tours, art and seafood booths, a chicken barbecue, and live entertainment are popular highlights of this long-established four-day celebration.

OTHER INFORMATION

Area Code: *503*
Zip Code: *97365*
Newport Chamber of Commerce   *downtown at 555 SW US 101*   *265-8801*

Seaside, Oregon

Elevation:

13 feet

Population (1980):

5,193

Population (1970):

4,402

Location:

81 mi. NW
of Portland

Seaside is the premier coastal playground of the Pacific Northwest. For more than a century, vacationers have been attracted to the broad sandy beach that links the ocean with a massive forested headland at one of the most dramatic sites on the Northwest coast. Unfortunately, almost continuous rainfall reduces the area's usability from fall through spring. However, long warm days and relatively little rain attract capacity crowds during summer, the year's only busy season. Popular activities include beachcombing, clamming, and fishing, plus horseback riding and automobile driving on miles of hard beach sand. Bicycle paths, hiking trails, and campgrounds are available in nearby state parks. While the ocean water is always relatively cold, it is used for swimming and surfing by hearty visitors in summer. Attractive facilities for golf, tennis, and indoor swimming have been provided in town, and there are a few old-fashioned commercial "fun zone" amusement places downtown. The most noteworthy man-made attraction, however, is a scenic two-mile-long concrete promenade bordering the beach. For many decades, this has been the place to stroll, ride a bicycle, people-watch, or enjoy a sunset.

Seaside is at the end of the Lewis and Clark Trail. Members of that expedition boiled water to obtain salt here in the winter of 1806. Settlement didn't really start until the 1870s, however, when travelers began to journey here because of the site's handsome coastal location. The promenade, amusement facilities and elaborate accommodations were soon constructed, establishing Seaside as the first major coastal resort in the Northwest. In recent years, a civic center and convention facilities were added.

Today, Seaside is undergoing a renaissance. Several major improvements have just been completed in the heart of town. A well-landscaped pedestrian-and-auto mall on the main street is attracting distinctive new specialty shops and restaurants, and the remaining amusement concessions are being upgraded. Several atmospheric bars on the mall offer live entertainment. A new multistoried landmark hotel anchors the mall and promenade at the main street turnaround by the beach. Numerous other contemporary lodgings are also concentrated downtown and along the beach. Several of these feature oceanfront views and plush amenities within an easy stroll of the heart of town.

WEATHER PROFILE — *Vokac Weather Rating*

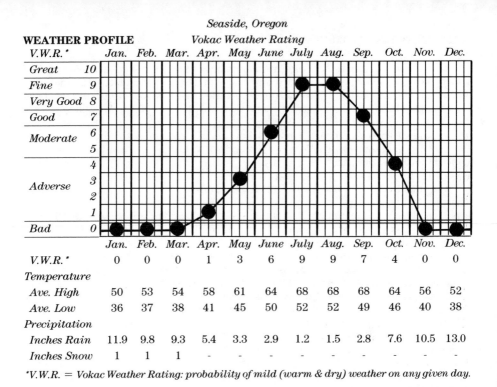

V.W.R.*		Jan.	Feb.	Mar.	Apr.	May	June	July	Aug.	Sep.	Oct.	Nov.	Dec.
Great	10												
Fine	9												
Very Good	8												
Good	7												
Moderate	6												
	5												
	4												
Adverse	3												
	2												
	1												
Bad	0												

	Jan.	Feb.	Mar.	Apr.	May	June	July	Aug.	Sep.	Oct.	Nov.	Dec.
V.W.R.*	0	0	0	1	3	6	9	9	7	4	0	0
Temperature												
Ave. High	50	53	54	58	61	64	68	68	68	64	56	52
Ave. Low	36	37	38	41	45	50	52	52	49	46	40	38
Precipitation												
Inches Rain	11.9	9.8	9.3	5.4	3.3	2.9	1.2	1.5	2.8	7.6	10.5	13.0
Inches Snow	1	1	1	-	-	-	-	-	-	-	-	-

*V.W.R. = Vokac Weather Rating: probability of mild (warm & dry) weather on any given day.

Forecast

Month	V.W.R.*		Temperatures		Precipitation
			Daytime	Evening	
January	0	Bad	cool	chilly	continual downpours
February	0	Bad	cool	chilly	continual rainstorms
March	0	Bad	cool	chilly	continual rainstorms
April	1	Adverse	cool	chilly	continual rainstorms
May	3	Adverse	cool	cool	continual showers
June	6	Moderate	cool	cool	frequent showers
July	9	Fine	warm	cool	infrequent showers
August	9	Fine	warm	cool	infrequent showers
September	7	Good	warm	cool	frequent rainstorms
October	4	Adverse	cool	cool	frequent downpours
November	0	Bad	cool	chilly	continual downpours
December	0	Bad	cool	chilly	continual downpours

Summary

Backed by low evergreen mountains, Seaside stretches north from a massive headland along one of the Northwest's most magnificent beaches. Because of the ocean's moderating influence, the area enjoys one of the longest growing seasons in the West outside of California, while it endures one of the nation's heaviest annual rainfalls. **Winter** days are uniformly cool, and continual rainstorms preclude many kinds of outdoor recreation. **Spring** remains unpleasantly cool and damp, with only gradually increasing temperatures and diminishing rainfall through June. For two delightful months in mid-**summer**, fine weather prevails. Warm days, cool evenings, and surprisingly infrequent showers make it easy to comfortably enjoy the splendid beach and nearby highlands. **Fall** weather deteriorates rapidly into cool days and frequent heavy rainstorms by October.

ATTRACTIONS & DIVERSIONS

★ **Astoria**   *17 mi. N on US 101*
The oldest settlement in Northwestern America has numerous historical sites including a Victorian mansion/museum and an impressive maritime museum; the 123-foot-high Astoria Column on Coxcomb Hill (with an observation platform more than 600 feet above the Columbia River), and the four-mile-long Columbia River Bridge to Washington.

★ **Beach Drive**   *starts 2 mi. N - Gearhart*
The expansive, hard sand beach from Gearhart north for ten miles to Fort Stevens State Park is open to automobile traffic when the tide is low. It is an exhilarating, scenic drive and an unusual experience.

★ **Bicycling**
  Prom Bike Shop   *downtown at 325 S. Holladay Dr.*   *738-8251*
There is a lot of flat coastal terrain in the Seaside area that can be toured on miles of paved separated bikeways including a nearly two-mile-long concrete promenade for leisurely rides, as well as scenic highways and byways. All kinds of bicycles and roller skates are rented here by the hour or longer.

★ **Fort Clatsop National Memorial**   *17 mi. N: 12 mi. N on US 101 & 5 mi. E*   *861-2471*
A full-scale reconstructed log fort is on the site of the Lewis and Clark expedition's headquarters during the winter of 1805. An adjacent visitor center houses a museum and audio-visual programs, and has a good selection of books and maps for sale. Living history demonstrations of frontier skills and tasks are presented by rangers in period costumes during summer. Short trails lead to the camp's freshwater spring and to a canoe landing with a replica of a dugout canoe of that period.

★ **Fort Stevens State Park**   *17 mi. N via US 101*   *861-2000*
The park features remnants of military installations that protected the mouth of the Columbia River from the Civil War through the end of World War II. This is the only military post in the lower forty-eight states to have been fired on by foreign sources since 1812. (A Japanese submarine fired its five-inch gun on the fort in 1942.) There is an interpretive center in the War Games Building and self-guided trails to batteries, guardhouses, and earthworks. The "Peter Iredale," a schooner that went aground here in 1906, may be seen on the beach. Camping and picnicking facilities are plentiful, and hiking, bicycling, boating, clamming, fishing, and swimming are enjoyed.

★ **Fun Zone**   *downtown on Broadway*
Skill games, electronic amusements, and rides are offered in a cluster of commercial entertainment places on the main street between the river and the beach.

Golf Course
  Gearhart Golf Course   *2.5 mi. N on N. Marion Av. - Gearhart*   *738-8331*
This 18-hole golf course is the oldest in the Pacific Northwest. Open to the public, it features long challenging straightaways. Facilities include a pro shop, club and cart rentals, a restaurant and a lounge.

Horseback Riding
  Circle Creek Trail Rides   *1 mi. S on US 101*   *738-9263*
Guided rides along inland rivers and mountain trails are offered.
  Gearhart Stables   *4 mi. N via US 101 - Gearhart*
Horses are ridden on the beach, but only in conjunction with guided trail rides.

★ **Mopeds**
  Arco Gas Station   *downtown at 231 S. Holladay Dr.*   *738-7015*
Mopeds can be rented here by the hour or longer for relatively effortless tours of the scenic countryside.

★ **The Promenade**   *N & S from downtown*
Built in 1920, this concrete walkway borders the beach for nearly two miles. It is a delightful place to stroll, skate, or ride a bicycle with sand and surf views on one side and impressive beach homes on the other. Near the midpoint, "the Turnaround" at the west end of Broadway is the designated "End of the Lewis and Clark Trail." Near the south end of the Promenade (on Lewis and Clark Way) a reconstructed Salt Cairn marks the place where expedition members boiled sea water to obtain salt during the winter of 1805.

Saddle Mountain State Park   *14 mi. E via US 26*
A three-mile trail leads to the top of 3,283 foot Saddle Mountain, one of the higher peaks in the Coast Range. From the summit, there is an outstanding view on clear days. Unusual alpine wildflowers are tucked amid rocky crags along the way. Picnicking and primitive camping facilities are also available.

Seaside Aquarium   *downtown at 200 N. Prom*   *738-6211*
Marine life from the North Pacific is displayed, and you can feed the trained seals seen and heard from the Promenade. Open daily in summer. Closed Mon.-Tues. in winter.

★ **Seaside Beach**   *W of downtown*
Bordering the west side of town is a broad beach of hardpacked sand backed by low sand dunes extending to the Promenade. Lifeguard services are provided in summer. While the surf looks inviting, the water is inevitably cold, so sunbathing and beachcombing are the most popular activities. Surfing is not permitted within Seaside's city limits. However, one of the most popular "breaks" along the entire Northwest Coast is adjacent to town on the south side near Sunset Boulevard.

★ **Sportfishing**   *16 mi. N off US 101 - Hammond*
Numerous charter boat services feature salmon fishing over the nearby Columbia River Bar. Each provides bait and tackle and arranges for freezing or canning your catch. The nearest to the ocean are:

Corkey's *1180 Pacific Dr. - Hammond*		*861-2668*
Fort Stevens Salmon Charters *918 Pacific Dr. - Hammond*		*861-1211*
Surf Charters *890 Pacific Dr. - Hammond*		*861-2208*
Tiki Salmon Charters *897 Pacific Dr. - Hammond*		*861-1201*

★ **Tillamook Head**   *5 mi. SW via Sunset Blvd.*
The area's most impressive landmark is a massive quarter-mile-high cape jutting into the sea between Seaside and Cannon Beach. Tillamook Head Trail, which is six miles each way, rewards energetic hikers with memorable coastal panoramas while attaining a height of nearly 1,200 feet above sea level.

Warm Water Feature
Sunset Pool   *.3 mi. E at 1140 Broadway*   *738-9446*
This large indoor heated pool is open to the public most days.

SHOPPING
Seaside's compact business district is concentrated along Broadway on both sides of the Necanicum River. This main business thoroughfare was recently converted to an attractively landscaped, one-way-drive mall where old-fashioned arcades and amusements are still intermixed with a growing assortment of gift shops, restaurants and lounges.

Food Specialties

★ **Bell Buoy Crab Co.**   *.9 mi. S at 1800 S. Holladay Dr.*   *738-6354*
Delicious fresh or canned Dungeness crab, and fresh or smoked salmon are specialties in an impressive line of seasonally available fresh, smoked, and canned seafoods. Custom smoking or canning can also be arranged. Various seafood cocktails are displayed to go.

Fenton's Farmer's Market   *7 mi. N on US 101*   *738-7332*
Locally grown fruits, vegetables, and flowers are featured here in season.

★ **Harrison's Bakery**   *downtown at 608 Broadway*   *738-5331*
For seventy years, this full line takeout bakery has offered an excellent selection of coffee cakes and Danish pastries, plus breads and cookies. It is still deservedly popular. Closed Tues.

★ **Kristina's Health Foods & Bakery**   *.7 mi. S at 1445 S. Holladay Dr.*   *738-9211*
An impressive array of European specialty breads, and pastries (such as Kolache), rolls, and muffins are featured in a large, well-organized, health-oriented store.

Lunch Basket   *downtown at 604 Broadway*   *738-8840*
Homemade chowders, soup, and desserts are offered along with all other items necessary for a gourmet beach picnic, or a meal in the cozy dining room. Closed Sun. in winter.

★ **Phillips Candy Kitchen**   *downtown at 217 Broadway*   *738-5402*
Saltwater taffy made here has been the specialty since before the turn of the century. Gift packages will be mailed anywhere.

Specialty Shops

Bee Gee Studio   *downtown at 1005 Broadway*   *738-8298*
Handcrafted ceramic, earthtone dishes and vessels are made here from volcanic ash and various native clays of the Northwest. Tours are available, and the entire line is displayed and sold in an adjoining showroom.

Oregon Woods   *4.4 mi. S at US 101/US 26*   *738-5676*
Redwood and myrtlewood art objects are displayed in polished and unpolished forms in an inviting roadside shop.

The Weary Fox   *downtown at 8 N. Downing St.*   *738-3363*
This contemporary two-level gallery features quality arts and crafts in a variety of media.

NIGHTLIFE

After dark, a notable concentration of bars and lounges on downtown Broadway cater to adult crowds with comfortable, casual furnishings, live music and dancing. Meanwhile, a similarly notable assortment of amusement parlors on the same street beckon to anyone with an interest in old-fashioned (or electronically updated) games of skill or chance.

The Bounty   *downtown at 504 Broadway*   *738-7342*
Live music for dancing is furnished on weekends in a cozy fireside lounge with comfortable sofas and armchairs. Seafood is featured in the adjoining grill.

The Bridge Tender   *downtown at 554 Broadway*   *738-8002*
Pool tables, foosball, and a view of the river are some of the attractions in this popular, casual tavern.

El Toucan   *downtown at 334 Broadway*   *738-8417*
Live entertainment and dancing happen most nights in the back of a conventional cantina-style saloon.

The Frontier Club   *downtown at 405 Broadway*   *738-9921*
After the dinner hours, this casual place usually provides live music for dancing.

RESTAURANTS

Most area restaurants offer conventional American fare in family-oriented surroundings. A few exceptions serve fresh seafoods and other Northwestern regional specialties in distinctive surroundings, and even fewer have ocean views.

Bounty Bar and Grill   *downtown at 504 Broadway*   *738-7342*
D only. Closed Mon. in winter.   *Moderate*
Local seafoods are featured on a conventional American menu in a pleasant, contemporary dining room.

Crab Broiler   *4.4 mi. S at jct. US 101 & US 26*   *738-5313*
L-D.   *Moderate*
A full range of American dishes includes seasonally fresh seafoods and homemade baked goods. The long-established restaurant has grown into several expansive dining rooms surrounded by tranquil Japanese-style gardens. A fireside lounge and a gift shop are also included in this large roadside landmark.

★ **Dooger's**   *downtown at 505 Broadway*   *738-3773*
B-L-D. No B in winter.   *Moderate*
Delicious regional seafoods and other American fare are featured in from-scratch specialties ranging from homemade blue cheese dressing to peanut butter pie. This pleasant, newer restaurant is already an area favorite.

Hara's Dining Room   *downtown at 227 Broadway*   *738-6701*
D only. Closed Tues.-Wed. in winter.   *Moderate*
An American menu emphasizing local seafoods is offered in a darkly handsome firelit dining room adjoining a comfortable lounge.

Lumpy's Fishworks   *downtown at 104 Broadway*   *738-7176*
B-L-D.   *Low*
Breakfast and seafood specialties from fresh ingredients are highlights in a casually attractive newer restaurant.

Norma's   *downtown at 20 N. Columbia St.*   *738-6170*
L-D. Closed Nov.-Feb.   *Low*
Clam chowder, razor clams, and other seafood, plus homemade treats like peanut butter pie, are featured. The long-popular, family-oriented restaurant recently moved into a cheerful new dining room with casual nautical decor.

Oceanside   *3 mi. N on N. Marion Av. - Gearhart*   738-3554
D only. Closed Mon.   *Moderate*
Fresh seafood is featured on a changing menu in an informal beachfront dining room with
a panoramic view of the ocean.

Pig 'n Pancake   *downtown at 323 Broadway*   738-7243
B-L-D.   *Moderate*
All kinds of well-made pancakes are offered twenty-four hours a day in summer, along
with a variety of plain American fare. This family-oriented coffee shop is part of a regional
chain.

LODGING

An impressive assortment of accommodations has been an area feature for many
decades. Tiny motels, elaborate motor hotels, and condominiums are all represented on
beachfront sites. Numerous bargains are available in older inland facilities. A special part
of the town's appeal is that most of the best lodgings are clustered an easy stroll from
downtown, the Promenade, and the beach. Many places reduce their rates by 20% and
more apart from summer.

Bungalow City   *.5 mi. NE at 930 N. Holladay Dr.*   738-7911
In this older, single-level **bargain** motel, each of the small, simply furnished rooms has a
cable TV with movies.

  #2 — color TV, in Bungalow City section,   K bed...$32
  regular room — in Chief Motel section,   D bed...$27

City Center Motel   *downtown at 250 1st Av.*   738-6377
A large indoor pool and a sauna are featured in a conveniently located modern motel.
Each nicely furnished room has a phone and cable color TV with movies.

  regular room —   Q bed...$33
  regular room —   D bed...$31

★ **Ebb Tide Motel**   *downtown at 300 N. Prom*   738-8371
This modern three-story motel has an indoor pool, whirlpool, and saunas. Each
beautifully furnished unit has a phone, cable color TV with movies, refrigerator, gas
fireplace, and an oceanfront view.

  #221,#321 — corner windows, kitchenette, great views,   K bed...$48
  #223,#225 — as above, handsome blue decor,   K bed...$48
  #323,#325 — as above, handsome green decor,   K bed...$48
  regular room —   D bed...$35

★ **Gearhart by the Sea** *2.5 mi. N at Marion Av./10th St. - Gearhart*   738-8331
Two large indoor pools, a whirlpool, and an 18-hole golf course are features of this newer
condominium resort complex above the beach. Each spacious unit has a phone, cable
color TV with movies, a kitchenette, and a private balcony.

  #633 — 1 BR, kit., free-standing (presto-log) fireplace, good ocean view, K bed...$65
  #673 — 1 BR, as above,   Q bed...$65
  regular room — 1 BR, limited ocean view,   Q bed...$60

★ **Hi-Tide Motel**   *downtown at 30 Av. G*   738-8414
This oceanfront motel has an indoor pool and a whirlpool. Each well-furnished unit has
a phone, cable color TV with movies, and a refrigerator.

  #305,#205 — corner, kitchenette, gas fireplace, great beach view, K bed...$50
  #319,#219 — as above,   2 Q beds...$55
  regular room — older, no view,   K bed...$40

Holladay Motel   *downtown at 426 S. Holladay Dr.*   738-6529
This older, single-level motel is a **bargain.** Each modest room has a cable color TV.

  regular room —   Q bed...$23

The Lanai   *1.6 mi. S at 3140 Sunset Blvd.*   738-6343
On Sunset Beach, this modern motel has a small outdoor pool. Each spacious room has
a phone, cable color TV with movies, and a kitchenette.

  #41,#32 — lg. pvt. balc., fine corner window ocean view, Q bed...$49
  #42 thru #47,#33 thru #38 — lg. pvt. balc., fine ocean view, Q bed...$49
  regular room —   D bed...$38

Landmark Motor Inn   *downtown at 441 2nd Av.*   *738-9581*
This newer motel has a small indoor pool, whirlpool, and sauna. Each attractively furnished room has a phone and color cable TV with movies.
    regular room —   Q bed...$39

Royale Motel   *downtown at 531 Av. A*   *738-9541*
This newer motel is a small, conveniently located **bargain.** Each room has a phone and cable color TV with movies.
    regular room —   Q bed...$29
    regular room —   D bed...$27

★ **Sand and Sea**   *downtown at 475 S. Prom*   *738-8441*
Seaside's highest lodgings are in this six-level modern oceanfront condominium/motel with a small round indoor pool and saunas. Each spacious suite has a phone and cable color TV.
    regular room — 1 BR, kitchen, gas log fireplace, floor-to-ceiling
              windows, pvt. balc. with ocean view,   Q or K bed...$65

★ **Seashore Resort Motel - Best Western**   *downtown at 60 N. Prom*   *738-6368*
By the beach and Promenade in the heart of town, this modern motel has a large indoor pool, whirlpool, and sauna. Each nicely furnished room has a phone and cable color TV.
    #38 — corner, fine beach/ocean view,   Q bed...$48
    regular room —   Q bed...$42

★ **Shilo Inn**   *downtown on Broadway at the Turnaround*   *738-9571*
Seaside's newest and largest motor hotel features an indoor pool, whirlpool, steam bath, sauna, and exercise room, plus a restaurant and lounge. Each beautifully furnished unit has a phone and cable color TV with movies.
    deluxe suite — 1 BR, kitchen, oceanfront view,   K bed...$115
    suite — oceanfront view,   K bed...$95
    regular room — view of town/mountains,   Q bed...$59

Sundowner Motor Inn   *downtown at 1250 Oceanway*   *738-8301*
This small modern motel has a tiny indoor pool with a whirlpool, and a sauna. Each unit has a phone and cable color TV with movies.
    apartment — 1 BR, kitchenette,   Q bed...$52
    regular room —   Q bed...$33

Surfside-Windward Condominiums   *3 mi. N at N. Marion Av. - Gearhart*   *738-6384*
On the beach at Gearhart, this single-level condominium complex has access to a nearby outdoor pool and an 18-hole golf course. Each of the plainly furnished one-bedroom units has a phone, cable color TV, kitchen, and a wood-burning fireplace.
    #209 — great beach view,   K bed...$64
    #207 — fine beach view,   Q bed...$64
    regular unit —   Q bed...$64

★ **The Tides**   *1 mi. S at 2316 S. Beach Dr.*   *738-6317*
This modern motel/condominium has some fine beachfront units plus **bargain** units. There is a large outdoor pool. Each spacious well-furnished unit has a phone and cable color TV with movies.
    #60,#50 — 2 BR, kit., fireplace, pvt. ocean view from corner window, 2 Q beds...$66
    #53,#54,#43,#44 — studio, kit., fireplace, pvt. beach/ocean view,   K bed...$48
    #51 — 2 BR, kit., fireplace, fine beach/ocean view from corner window, K bed...$66
    regular room — no view,   D or Q bed...$27

White Caps   *.5 mi. N at 120 9th Av.*   *738-5371*
This small older motel has some **bargain** units almost on the beach. Each simply furnished unit has cable color TV with movies.
    #12 — 1 BR, kitchenette, good ocean view from LR,   Q bed...$44
    #5 — good ocean view,   Q bed...$30
    regular room #7 — small, some ocean view,   D bed...$22

CAMPGROUNDS
There are only a couple of campgrounds in the area. Fortunately, the best has complete camping and recreation facilities in an unusual setting a stroll from the beautiful Oregon coast.

★ **Fort Stevens St. Pk.** *14 mi. N: 9 mi. N on US 101 & 5 mi. NW on Co. Rd.* 861-1671
Oregon's largest state park includes a giant campground near the ocean. In addition, ocean beaches, two tiny lakes, a boat ramp, bicycle paths, hiking trails, and sand dunes provide opportunities for beachcombing, fishing, clamming, boating, swimming, bicycling, and hiking. Flush toilets, hot showers (fee) and hookups are available. Each well-spaced site has a picnic table and a fire area.   base rate...$7

Riverside Lake Resort *3 mi. S on US 101* 738-6779
This private facility is by a tiny river which is used for swimming and fishing. Flush toilets, hot showers, and hookups are available. Most of the closely spaced sites have a picnic table. There is a shady, separated tent area.   base rate...$7

SPECIAL EVENT

4th of July Fireworks *at the Turnaround* *July 4th*
Traditional 4th of July festivities are climaxed on the beach at the Turnaround with a fireworks display that can be easily seen and enjoyed by all. The Miss Oregon Pageant always takes place here on the next weekend.

OTHER INFORMATION
Area Code: *503*
Zip Code: *97138*
Seaside Chamber of Commerce *downtown at Broadway/Roosevelt Dr.* 738-6391

St. George, Utah

Elevation:

2,880 feet

Population (1980):

11,350

Population (1970):

7,097

Location:

301 mi. SW
of Salt Lake City

St. George is a peaceful, picturesque link between the Southwestern desert and the Rocky Mountains. Utah's lowest town sprawls across a small basin far below the mountainous northern edge of America's hottest desert. Towering forested peaks, multicolored domes and precipices in Zion National Park, and enormous red sandstone cliffs are highlights of the spectacular backdrop. Pink sand dunes, ancient lava beds, hot springs pools and attractive little reservoirs are some of the features within the basin. Hiking, backpacking, horseback riding, swimming, boating and fishing are popular. In and around town, one of the West's noteworthy concentrations of golf courses has developed. St. George has the unique distinction of being the only town in the Rocky Mountain area where hard freezes and snowfalls are scarce enough that palm trees can grow outdoors year-round. Winter days are normally cool, but by spring the weather is idyllic. Increasingly, vacationers are opting to come here in spring or fall, when all of the area's outdoor attractions can be comfortably enjoyed while much of the rest of the West is cold or wet. Surprisingly, summer is still the busiest season, in spite of the relentless heat.

Recognizing that cotton would grow here and nowhere farther north in the Rockies, the Mormon colonizer Brigham Young began the settlement of this area during the Civil War when Utah had to produce its own cotton. A textile mill was built, and production continued in what residents called "Dixie" until the South could again cheaply supply cotton. The first Mormon Temple in Utah was built here (1871-1877) of hand-quarried red sandstone. Plastered a brilliant white, the 175-foot-high building remains the town's outstanding landmark. Other symbols of the early Mormon era include an impressive tabernacle and Brigham Young's colonial-style winter home. The town grew slowly until the 1950s, when modern air conditioning began to make the great Southwestern desert livable, even in summer.

Today, St. George is developing facilities appropriate to a leisure destination. Several scenic golf courses and a major aquatic complex are recent additions. The downtown area is being refurbished. It now includes a tree-shaded mini-mall and a small new complex of specialty shops on the main street. An abundance of very plain cafes and restaurants lines the business route through town. The same thoroughfare is a "motel row" offering many ordinary inexpensive accommodations, and the town's most elaborate motor hotel. In a quiet section near downtown, St. George's unusual heritage is preserved in a charming new bed-and-breakfast inn that is the area's finest.

WEATHER PROFILE Vokac Weather Rating

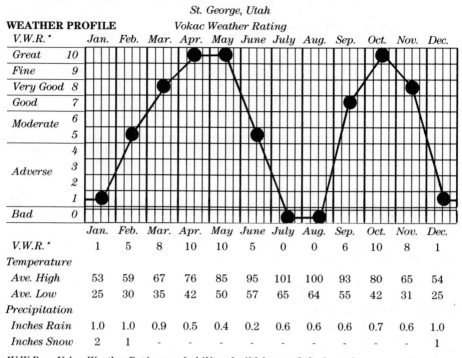

V.W.R.*	Jan.	Feb.	Mar.	Apr.	May	June	July	Aug.	Sep.	Oct.	Nov.	Dec.
V.W.R.*	1	5	8	10	10	5	0	0	6	10	8	1
Temperature												
Ave. High	53	59	67	76	85	95	101	100	93	80	65	54
Ave. Low	25	30	35	42	50	57	65	64	55	42	31	25
Precipitation												
Inches Rain	1.0	1.0	0.9	0.5	0.4	0.2	0.6	0.6	0.6	0.7	0.6	1.0
Inches Snow	2	1	-	-	-	-	-	-	-	-	-	1

*V.W.R. = Vokac Weather Rating: probability of mild (warm & dry) weather on any given day.

Forecast

Month	V.W.R.*		Temperatures Daytime	Evening	Precipitation
January	1	Adverse	cool	chilly	infrequent rainstorms/snow flurries
February	5	Moderate	cool	chilly	infrequent rainstorms
March	8	Very Good	warm	cool	infrequent showers
April	10	Great	warm	cool	infrequent showers
May	10	Great	hot	warm	negligible
June	5	Moderate	torrid	warm	negligible
July	0	Bad	torrid	hot	infrequent showers
August	0	Bad	torrid	hot	infrequent showers
September	6	Moderate	hot	warm	infrequent showers
October	10	Great	warm	cool	infrequent showers
November	8	Very Good	warm	chilly	infrequent showers
December	1	Adverse	cool	chilly	infrequent rainstorms

Summary

St. George is both a northern outpost of the great Southwestern deserts and a gateway to the Rocky Mountains. In this unusual setting the climate is almost as distinctive as the awesome surroundings. In **winter**, cool days and chilly evenings are common, and there are infrequent rainstorms, plus rare snow flurries. **Spring** is the year's most appealing season. Warm sunny days begin around the vernal equinox. By Easter, the weather is ideal for playing golf and tennis, and for exploring the area's natural wonders—at a time when heavy snow is still the rule to the north. Unfortunately, **summer** is essentially unusable for many outdoor activities. Even the evenings are hot after relentlessly sweltering days. **Fall**, like spring, is delightful. Warm sunny days and infrequent showers usually continue almost to Thanksgiving.

ATTRACTIONS & DIVERSIONS

★ **Bicycling**

    Spoke & Pedal Shop   *downtown at 90 S 100 E*   673-4492

The gentle basin around town offers fine bicycling opportunities on paved byways. Dramatic rock formations, sand dunes, hot springs, and ghost towns are some of the worthwhile destinations. Bike rentals, repairs, accessories, and topographic maps of the area are available here.

★ **Brigham Young's Winter Home**   *downtown at 200 N 100 W*   673-5181

The second President of the Mormon Church used this as his winter residence for several years. Its spacious, modified colonial style set it apart from the rough pioneer dwellings of the time (1870s). Both the grounds and building have been meticulously restored and outfitted with authentic period furnishings. Guided tours are offered daily.

Dixie National Forest   *approx. 30 mi. N via UT 18*   673-3431

The Pine Valley Mountains that tower over St. George are thought to be the world's largest intrusion of igneous lava. A paved road provides access to the mountain village of Pine Valley and beyond to forested campgrounds near the tiny Santa Clara River and a picnic site at the Pine Valley Reservoir. In addition to camping and picnicking, hiking, horseback riding, and fishing are popular summer activities.

Golf

Several public golf courses have been constructed around town in recent years. Each has distinctive landscaping, picturesque backdrops, a clubhouse, pro shop, carts, and equipment rentals. Among the best are:

★   **Bloomington Country Club**   *4 mi. S on Ft. Pierce Rd.*   673-4922

This relatively level 18-hole golf course winds through a posh residential area rimmed by colorful sandstone cliffs. It is open to the public year-round with all facilities.

★   **Lava Hills**   *3 mi. SW at 1975 S. Toniquint Dr.*   628-0000

This 18-hole golf course was carefully built into sloping terrain to maximize panoramic "color country" views. It is open to the public year-round with all facilities.

Gunlock Lake State Recreation Area   *18 mi. NW off UT 18*

A small scenic reservoir has been created on the Santa Clara River to provide year-round boating, fishing, and primitive camping. Swimming and water-skiing are enjoyed from spring to fall. In the spring, the waterfalls created by heavy runoff overflowing down red sandstone cliffs near the southern shore become picturesque hiking and picnicking destinations.

★ **Library**   *downtown at 50 S. Main St.*   628-3621

The Washington County Library occupies a large, strikingly contemporary building. A well-lighted, spacious interior is enhanced by a high open-beam ceiling and many large windows. The comfortably furnished reading area with an extensive selection of magazines and newspapers is a pleasant place to relax. Closed Sun.

★ **St. George L.D.S. Temple**   *.5 mi. S at 440 S 300 E*   673-5181

St. George's most impressive man-made landmark is a 175-foot-high Latter Day Saints (Mormon) Temple constructed of red sandstone covered with gleaming white plaster. Its size and condition belie the fact that it was dedicated more than a century ago. The Temple visitor center, which is open year-round, offers guided tours of the center and beautifully landscaped grounds — complete with palm trees.

St. George Tabernacle   *downtown at Main & Tabernacle Sts.*   673-5181

The native red sandstone tabernacle was completed during the 1870s in the style of a New England church, with a steeple 140 feet high. It is open year-round. The surprisingly spacious interior and the handcrafted unsupported spiral staircase are fine examples of pioneer skill and dedication.

★ **Snow Canyon State Park**   *8 mi. NW via UT 18*   628-2255

A wonderfully photogenic, flat-bottomed gorge has been cut deeply into multicolored sandstone, capped in places by a black mantle of lava spewed from extinct nearby volcanoes. Hiking trails abound amid massive rock outcroppings and sand dunes that have been featured in numerous major motion pictures. Tree-shaded picnic sites are thoughtfully located, and a picturesque campground with complete facilities is heavily used year-round.

Warm Water Features

★ **Pah Tempe Hot Mineral Springs** *19 mi. NE on UT 9 - Hurricane* 635-2879
The large volume of hot mineral water flowing out of the rugged south side of the Virgin River canyon is being used in an unusual, privately owned spa. There is a small, rustic semi-enclosed outdoor pool. But, the real attraction is down a path several hundred feet further into the canyon. There, several tranquil soaking pools have been created on terraces by the river and in cave grottos in the rocky cliffs.

★ **St. George Swimming Pool** *1 mi. S at 250 E 700 S* 673-6276
A hydro-slide (a long plastic tubular water slide) provides refreshing high-tech relief from the desert heat. The complex also includes an Olympic-sized outdoor pool with large concrete decks for sunbathing. Closed Sun.

★ **Zion National Park** *41 mi. E on UT 9* 772-3256
Deep, narrow multicolored canyons and gigantic stone masses make this one of the world's most magnificent natural attractions. A paved roadway follows the Virgin River for several miles along Zion Canyon, where sheer cliffs and awesome rock formations soar to great heights above the gentle floor of the narrow chasm. Scenic trails lead climbers, hikers, and horseback riders into a silent realm of secluded canyons resplendent with emerald pools and veiled waterfalls. The Zion Visitor Center has a museum and an information office. Large, dramatically sited campgrounds are open all year.

SHOPPING
St. George has a prosaic little business district between century-old landmarks downtown. With the recent development of both a landscaped semi-mall on the main shopping street and the first contemporary shopping complex in the heart of town, a nucleus of distinctive stores is beginning to develop.

Food Specialties

★ **Andelin's Shaved Ice Stand** *downtown at St. George Blvd./200 E*
The extreme heat of summer is made more bearable because refreshing, authentic shaved ice (smoother than a snow cone) is available in a variety of flavors at this tiny roadside stand.

Dixie Drug *downtown at 28 E. Tabernacle St.* 673-3231
A conventional pharmacy has a little, old-fashioned soda fountain that serves a variety of ice cream treats, even on Sunday.

Linden's Ice Cream *downtown at 2 W. St. George Blvd.* 628-2680
Many flavors of ice cream are prepared in a variety of ways to be enjoyed here with other light fare or on an adjoining patio in Ancestor Square. Closed Sun.

Nielson's Bakery *downtown at 110 E. St. George Blvd.* 673-2861
A full range of pastries and breads is produced in this old-fashioned bakery. Closed Sun.

Sunrise Donuts *downtown at 2 W. St. George Blvd.* 673-9875
Apple fritters are a highlight of the good assortment of donuts made at this inviting shop in Ancestor Square. There are coffee tables. Closed Sun.

Specialty Shops

★ **Ancestor Square Shopping Center** *downtown at Main St./St. George Blvd.*
The new heart of downtown is this recently established cluster of specialty shops and restaurants housed in an appealing blend of contemporary buildings and Victorian restorations surrounded by attractive gardens, fountains, and sculpture.

Book Cellar *downtown at Main St./St. George Blvd.* 628-0380
This small shop in Ancestor Square has a good assortment of books, including many about the area. Closed Sun.

St. George Arts Center *downtown at 86 S. Main St.* 628-1635
Works of local artists in all media are displayed for sale. Traveling exhibits, workshops, and classes are also provided.

★ **Spearex Western Gallery** *downtown at 2 W. St. George Blvd.* 673-6669
Western paintings, sculptures, and other fine art objects are beautifully displayed in a handsome contemporary gallery in Ancestor Square. Closed Sun.-Mon.

NIGHTLIFE

Peace and quiet reign each evening in St. George. But, there are a remarkable number of movie theaters for a town of this size, plus a live summer theater, and a very few places with drinking and entertainment.

Four Seasons Lounge   *.7 mi. E at 747 E. St. George Blvd.*   *673-4804*
Live music on Friday and Saturday nights is offered in a plain little downstairs lounge in the Four Seasons Motor Inn.

Millhouse Cantina   *downtown at 2 W. St. George Blvd.*   *628-3685*
Live entertainment is featured on weekends, along with exotic drinks. Mexican and American food is served for lunch and dinner beneath the clock tower at Ancestor Square.

Pioneer Courthouse Players   *downtown at 97 E. St. George Blvd.*   *628-1658*
During July and August, a century-old building that was once the courthouse is used for a series of repertory theater productions staged "in the round." Closed Sun.-Mon.

RESTAURANTS

Restaurants are plentiful, plainly furnished, reasonably priced, and family-oriented. Conventional Western-style cooking predominates. Almost all are closed on Sunday, do not serve wine, and have nonsmoking sections.

★ **Andelin's Gable House**   *downtown at 206 E. St. George Blvd.*   *673-6796*
L-D. Closed Sun.   *Expensive*
St. George's most distinguished restaurant features very good American cuisine, including homemade rolls and desserts, in three or five course table d'hote dinners. An old gabled house has been attractively converted into several cozy dining areas with Early American decor, antiques, and costumed staff.

Homespun *16 mi. NE via I-15 & Frontage Rd. N off Exit 22 - Leeds*   *673-4054*
D only. Closed Sun.-Tues.   *Moderate*
Bountiful five course German meals are served family-style in a handsome ranch-style setting. Reservations are necessary.

The Rafters   *.7 mi. E at 747 E. St. George Blvd.*   *673-6797*
B-L-D.   *Moderate*
Conventional American dishes are served in a contemporary dining room in the Four Seasons Motor Inn.

Sullivan's Rococo Steak House   *1.2 mi. W at 511 S. Airport Rd.*   *673-3305*
D only.   *Moderate*
Steaks are the best bet on an ordinary American menu, and there is a salad bar. The food and the large neo-rococo dining room are incidental to the magnificent panoramic town and mountains view beyond the window wall of this blufftop restaurant.

LODGING

With few exceptions, accommodations are numerous, well-maintained, conventional motels conveniently located along St. George Boulevard. All recommended facilities have air conditioning and most have nonsmoking rooms. Rates are reduced by 20% and more in many places from fall through early spring on weekdays, and 10% and more on weekends.

Browers Vacation Hometel   *.5 mi. E at 525 E. St. George Blvd.*   *673-6137*
This newer apartment motel has an outdoor pool with a slide and some **bargain** units. Each unit has a phone and cable color TV.

suite — 1 BR, modern compact kitchen,	Q bed...$35
regular room —	2 Q beds...$29

Chalet Motel   *.6 mi. E at 664 E. St. George Blvd.*   *673-9902*
This small, older **bargain** motel has an outdoor pool. Each modest room has a cable color TV.

regular room —	Q bed...$24

★ **Four Seasons Motor Inn**   *.7 mi. E at 747 E. St. George Blvd.*   *673-4804*
St. George's best in-town resort motel has a large, landscaped pool (covered with a dome in winter), whirlpool, sundeck, putting green, two lighted tennis courts, and a game room. The Rafters restaurant serves all meals, and is one of the few places in town open on

Sunday. Each spacious, nicely decorated room has a phone and cable color TV with movies.

#423,#426,#427 — mirrored in-bath steam bath, valley views,   K bed...$44
regular room —   Q bed...$38

Hilton Inn   *1.5 mi. S on I-15 at 1450 Hilton Inn Dr.*   *628-0463*
St. George's newest and most expensive resort motel has a large outdoor pool, whirlpool, sauna, two lighted tennis courts, a dining room serving all meals every day, and a lounge. There are (fees for) golf privileges at a nearby course and racquetball in the health club. Each spacious, well-furnished room has a phone and cable color TV with movies.

regular room —   2 D or K bed...$52

Motel 6   *1 mi. E at 205 N 1000 E*   *673-6666*
The West's biggest **bargain** motel chain has a large, modern facility here, with an outdoor pool. TV is available (for a fee).

regular room —   D bed...$22

★ **Seven Wives Inn**   *downtown at 207 N 100 W*   *628-3737*
Southern Utah's first bed-and-breakfast inn is a real winner that even includes some **bargain** rooms. A large, historic home was lovingly renovated and is now resplendent in period decor and furnishings. The finest breakfast in town is a delicious complimentary meal served to guests in the elegant dining room each morning.

"Melissa" — spacious, windows on 3 sides, stone fireplace,
         pvt. bath (tin tub),   Q bed...$50
"Sarah" — lg., corner, stone fireplace, semi-pvt. bath,   Q bed...$45
"Susan" — sm., corner, pvt. entrance, pvt. bath, Franklin fireplace,   D bed...$30
regular room "Clarinda" — tiny, bath across hall,   D bed...$25

Stardust Motel   *.6 mi. E at 651 E. St. George Blvd.*   *673-3103*
This single-level **bargain** motel has a small outdoor pool. Each room has a B/W TV.

regular room —   Q bed...$24
regular room —   D bed...$22

Thunderbird - Best Western   *1 mi. E at 150 N 1000 E*   *673-6123*
This large modern motel has an outdoor pool, a whirlpool, and saunas. Each nicely furnished room has a phone and cable color TV with movies.

#458 — spacious, pvt. panoramic view of Dixie Valley,   K bed...$40
regular room — south side rooms view Dixie Valley,   Q or K bed...$40

Western Safari Motel   *.3 mi. W at 310 W. St. George Blvd.*   *673-5238*
This older single-level motel is a real **bargain.** Each room has a color TV.

regular room —   K bed...$20
regular room —   Q bed...$19

Weston's Lamplighter Motel   *.5 mi. E at 460 E. St. George Blvd.*   *673-4861*
A large outdoor pool with a slide, a whirlpool, and saunas are features of this modern **bargain** motel. Each spacious, nicely furnished unit has a phone and cable color TV.

#221,#218 — blue decor, refr. and wet bar, view of red rocks,   K bed...$36
regular room —   Q bed...$28

CAMPGROUNDS

There are several campgrounds in the area. The best offer a choice of either a spectacularly scenic locale and relatively primitive facilities, or complete facilities in a less picturesque setting nearer town.

★ **Redlands Recreational Vehicle Park** *3 mi. NE on I-15 (Washington Exit)*   *673-9700*
This large privately operated facility near the freeway is attractively landscaped with small trees and grassy sites. An outdoor pool, whirlpool, rec room, and outdoor game area are featured. Flush toilets, hot showers, and hookups are available. Some of the grassy sites have a picnic table and shade. There is a separate tenting area.   base rate...$8.50

★ **Snow Canyon State Park**   *8 mi. NW on UT 18*   *628-2255*
Utah has provided a small campground deep in a colorful sandstone canyon. Hiking trails provide access to strange rock formations, sand dunes, and panoramic views. Flush and pit toilets and hookups, but no showers, are available. Each well-spaced site has a scenic view and a picnic table. Some sites are shaded.   base rate...$5

SPECIAL EVENT

St. George Arts Festival   *downtown*   *Easter Weekend*

The main street and Ancestor Square are transformed into festival grounds for the visual and performing arts. Art exhibits and demonstrations, live entertainment, food booths, a mini-carnival, a classic car show, and concerts contribute to the festivities.

OTHER INFORMATION

Area Code: *801*

Zip Code: *84770*

Dixie National Forest - Office *downtown at 196 E. Tabernacle St.*   *673-3431*

St. George Chamber of Commerce *downtown at 97 E. St. George Blvd.*   *628-1658*

Utah State Tourist Information Center   *4 mi. S on I-15*   *673-4542*

Chelan, Washington

Elevation:

1,208 feet

Population (1980):

2,802

Population (1970):

2,837

Location:

178 mi. E
of Seattle

    Chelan is the gateway to America's most extraordinary big lake. The little town is ideally situated among apple orchards along the sunny eastern end of Lake Chelan in an area backed by small, grass-and-brush-covered hills. Remarkably, the other end of this long, narrow and very deep lake is surrounded by glacier-clad peaks, lush pine forests, streams and waterfalls in the magnificent North Cascades. The lake's great reach gives Chelan a special closeness with an enormous complex of national forests, parks and recreation areas beyond the towering mountain backdrop to the west. The lake even moderates the weather in town, except during winters, which are relatively cold and snowy. There are no major winter sports facilities in the nearby mountains — yet. Spring features warm clear days early in the season, and the fragrance of apple blossoms in orchards along the lake shore. Early fall is also relatively mild. It is an uncrowded time to relish the beauty of the apple-laden countryside, and to savor the quality of the fruit grown here. Summer is the only season when Chelan is filled with visitors, drawn by perfect weather and the clear warm lake. Swimming, boating, water-skiing, fishing and lake excursions are popular. Hiking, camping, backpacking, rock climbing, horseback riding and pack trips are enjoyed in the nearby mountains. Golf, tennis, a major new water slide complex, and fine shoreline parks with sandy beaches are the favorite attractions in town.

    The area around the state's longest, biggest and deepest lake remained unsettled until 1879, when the U.S. government established a short-lived army post to protect settlers who were beginning to come into the valley. The townsite was platted in 1889. Passenger boat service and lake traffic were important to the local economy from the beginning. Gold and other precious metals were discovered around the turn of the century in mountains near the lake. Ore was shipped down-lake to the railroad at Chelan until 1957, when the state's largest producing mine closed. As mining and lumber declined in importance, apple growing and tourism have become the mainstays of the area's economy.

    Picturesque apple orchards increasingly blanket the lower slopes of gentle hills along the lake adjacent to town. An attractively landscaped park overlooks sandy beaches and marinas near the heart of town. Downtown still reflects a peaceful, hard-working past with a limited assortment of ordinary shops, restaurants and nightlife. Numerous fine accommodations, some with luxurious resort amenities, have recently been constructed along the lakefront. Most are within an easy stroll of the small business district.

Chelan, Washington

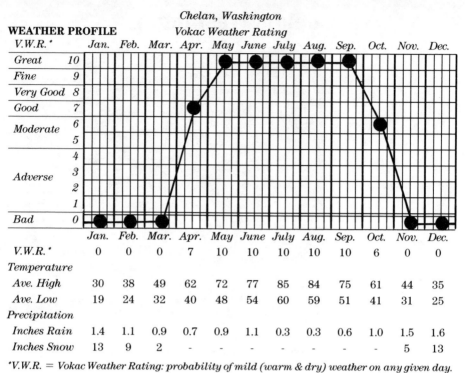

V.W.R.*	Jan.	Feb.	Mar.	Apr.	May	June	July	Aug.	Sep.	Oct.	Nov.	Dec.
V.W.R.*	0	0	0	7	10	10	10	10	10	6	0	0
Temperature												
Ave. High	30	38	49	62	72	77	85	84	75	61	44	35
Ave. Low	19	24	32	40	48	54	60	59	51	41	31	25
Precipitation												
Inches Rain	1.4	1.1	0.9	0.7	0.9	1.1	0.3	0.3	0.6	1.0	1.5	1.6
Inches Snow	13	9	2	-	-	-	-	-	-	-	5	13

*V.W.R. = Vokac Weather Rating: probability of mild (warm & dry) weather on any given day.

Forecast

Month	V.W.R.*		Temperatures		Precipitation
			Daytime	Evening	
January	0	Bad	cold	frigid	occasional snowstorms
February	0	Bad	chilly	cold	occasional snow flurries
March	0	Bad	chilly	chilly	infrequent showers/snow flurries
April	7	Good	cool	cool	infrequent showers
May	10	Great	warm	cool	infrequent showers
June	10	Great	warm	warm	infrequent rainstorms
July	10	Great	hot	warm	negligible
August	10	Great	hot	warm	negligible
September	10	Great	warm	cool	infrequent showers
October	6	Moderate	cool	cool	infrequent rainstorms
November	0	Bad	chilly	chilly	occasional showers/snow flurries
December	0	Bad	chilly	cold	occasional snowstorms

Summary

Chelan lies at the eastern end of the West's most uniquely fiord-like lake. About 1,200 feet above sea level, the town is surrounded by fruit orchards along the lake and backed by dry sagebrush-covered hills. To the west, the orchards and hills end abruptly where the lake enters the awesome escarpment of the North Cascade Range. The dramatic setting is coupled with one of the West's most usable four season climates. Almost all of the bad weather occurs in **winter**, with chilly days and cold evenings. Occasional snowstorms provide enough snow to support winter sports, although no major skiing facilities are available in the nearby mountains—yet. Temperatures increase very rapidly in **spring**. Good weather accompanies blossom-time starting in April, and comfortably warm weather prevails by May. **Summer** is outstanding. Long, hot sunny days and warm evenings are ideal for enjoying the crystal clear lake and the alpine grandeur along its upper reaches. Cool dry weather accompanies the apple harvest in early **fall**. Conditions deteriorate to chilly days, plus occasional showers and snowfalls after Halloween.

ATTRACTIONS & DIVERSIONS

★ **Boat Rentals**

M & M Marina   *1 mi. SW on US 97 at 1228 W. Woodin Av.*   682-4333

Pleasure, skiing and fishing boats can be rented at this small marina.

N.W. Para-Sails & Watersports *1 mi. SW on US 97 at 1328 W. Woodin Av.* 682-5324

Surf jet rentals and para-sailing equipment can be reserved at this casual lakefront location in summer.

Boat Rides

Charter Chelan Boat Service   *operates from downtown*   682-5986

Boats can be chartered (hourly and destination rates) for sightseeing tours, water-skiing, or para-sailing.

★   **Lake Chelan Boat Co.**   *1.1 mi. SW at 1418 W. Woodin Av.*   682-2224

"The Lady of the Lake" is a large excursion boat that takes passengers the entire length of Lake Chelan. After cruising past orchard-covered slopes and shorelines, the boat enters a narrow canyon in the Cascade Range. Glacier-clad peaks tower overhead, and lush pine forests, waterfalls, and occasional big game seem even nearer because the lake is never more than two miles wide. At the north end, fifty-five miles from town, passengers can have lunch or explore the tiny village of Stehekin before returning. The boat operates from 8:30 a.m.-6 p.m. daily May 15-Oct. 15, and on Sundays, Mondays, Wednesdays, and Fridays the rest of the year.

★   **The Stehekin Journey**   *starts downtown on the lake*   682-2224

During an unforgettable all-day adventure, a minimum of four participants enjoy: a scenic float plane ride the length of Lake Chelan to Stehekin, a shuttlebus up Stehekin Valley, a whitewater raft trip down the Stehekin River, time out for lunch at the North Cascades Lodge in Stehekin, and a cruise of the entire lake on an excursion boat back to town.

Chelan Butte   *5 mi. S via Chelan Butte Rd.*

From the lookout tower at the top, visitors have a splendid panoramic view of Lake Chelan, orchard-covered slopes, the Cascades, the Columbia River gorge, and tawny wheat fields stretching endlessly to the east.

Chelan Falls Gorge   *4 mi. SE via WA 151*

The Chelan River is only four miles long, but it has cut an impressive gorge through rock cliffs on its 405-foot drop from the lake to the Columbia River. The old Chelan River Bridge is the best viewpoint for the river and falls.

Flying

Chelan Airways   *downtown on the lakeshore*   682-5555

Scenic seaplane flights over the magnificent Cascade Range to Stehekin at the other end of Lake Chelan can be chartered here any time.

Golf

★   **Lake Chelan Municipal Golf Course** *1.5 mi. N via N. Lakeshore Rd.*   682-5421

A challenging 18-hole championship golf course is located on a relatively level terrace above town with fine lake and mountain views. It is open to the public, and includes a pro shop, driving range, club and cart rentals, and a snack bar.

Horseback Riding

Washington Creek Trails, Inc. *8 mi. NE via US 97 & Howard Flats Rd.*   682-4670

Horses can be rented daily for trail rides, with or without a guide, in the open hilly country northeast of town.

★ **Lake Chelan**

One of the world's most extraordinary lakes is also the largest, longest, and deepest in the State of Washington. Well over fifty miles long and less than two miles wide, it was formed by a gigantic glacier that carved out a trough now filled by water to a depth of more than 1,400 feet. At its deepest point, the lake is actually below sea level. The town of Chelan occupies a small portion of an enormous natural dam created by the ancient glacier. No other lake on the continent has the variety of topography and climate found here. The town of Chelan, at the lake's eastern end, is surrounded by orchards and rangeland in a near-desert setting. At the lake's western end, lush pine forests line the shore, and glacier-shrouded peaks of the North Cascade Mountains rise abruptly from the water. All kinds of outdoor activities are already available on and near the crystal clear lake, yet the area's awesome recreation potential has only been lightly tapped.

★ **Lake Chelan National Recreation Area**   *access by Lake Chelan*
The rugged mountains of the North Cascade Range that enclose the northern end of Lake Chelan are included in this natural preserve. The scenic Stehekin River and Rainbow Falls are favorite destinations in a vast expanse of lush pine forests and towering glacier-shrouded peaks. The only access to the area is by boat, seaplane, or hiking trails.

★ **Lake Chelan State Park**   *9 mi. SW via US 97 & S. Lakeshore Rd.*
Spectacular up-lake views are a feature in a large, well-landscaped lakeshore park. A grassy slope overlooks a sandy beach and a protected swimming area that has lifeguards in summer. Excellent docking, picnicking, and camping facilities are also provided.

★ **Lakeshore Park**   *downtown on WA 150*
On the west side of downtown is a delightful park with superb lake views. Lawn-covered slopes rise above a sandy beach and a popular swimming area on Lake Chelan. Well-positioned picnic tables, plus a marina and a campground, are nearby. Miniature golf and imaginative play equipment are also available.

★ **Moped Rentals**
  M & M Marina   *1 mi. SW on US 97 at 1228 W. Woodin Av.*   682-4333
Mopeds can be rented here by the hour or longer for lakeshore jaunts and tours of the apple orchards and surrounding hills.

★ **North Cascades National Park**   *90 mi. NW via US 97: WA 153 & WA 20*   682-2549
There are no roads in this park, but a highway (WA 20) was completed between the park's two sections in 1972 through some of the most rugged mountains in the West. Numerous trails extend from this highway into both sections of the park. The major access to the southern section is via passenger ferry from Chelan to Stehekin and shuttle bus service from there to the park entrance. Within the park, many miles of trails are threaded throughout a wilderness of jagged peaks with more than 300 active glaciers, jewel lakes hidden in luxuriant forests, and deep canyons with clear rushing streams and beautiful waterfalls. Hiking, climbing, backpacking, pack trips, fishing, and camping are popular activities.

★ **Ohme Gardens**   *35 mi. S near jct. US 97/US 2*   662-5785
On a promontory overlooking the Wenatchee Valley, nine acres of impressive mountain greenery have been skillfully nurtured on natural basalt formations. Stone pathways meander past fern grottos, trickling waterfalls, a wishing well, and a lookout point. The gardens have been evolving for more than half a century. Closed November-March.

★ **Orchards**   *NW on WA 150 & SW on US 97*
For several miles, gentle slopes along the eastern shores of Lake Chelan are speckled with apple orchards. The nine-mile drive along the north shore to the farming community of Manson is especially delightful because of the picturesque orchards and the many spectacular up-lake views from the road. Roadside stands near town start displaying the new harvest, primarily of red and golden delicious apples, in late summer.

★ **Rocky Reach Dam**   *29 mi. S on US 97*   663-7522
The visitor information center for this dam on the Columbia River has an underwater fish-viewing gallery. Even more impressive are the self-guided tours of interpretive museums within the dam's power house. The Gallery of Electricity has inventive displays explaining the whole history of electricity from Ben Franklin's kite to space age microcircuitry. Visitors can cause all kinds of electrical contrivances to make noise or give light. The Gallery of the Columbia has exhibits that highlight the geologic and cultural evolution of the area. Fifteen acres of colorful gardens and shady lawns by the dam provide attractive picnic sites.

  St. Andrews Episcopal Church   *downtown at 120 E. Woodin Av.*   682-2851
The design for this log church (1898) is attributed to the noted architect, Stanford White. It is reportedly the only log church building in the Northwest in continuous use since before the turn of the century.

★ **Stehekin**   *55 mi. NW via Lake Chelan*
One of the nation's most isolated communities can be accessed only by seaplane or boat from Chelan, or on foot. The tiny village is the gateway to the heart of North Cascades National Park. There are nightly park-related programs in summer. Food, lodging, and camping facilities are available. Hiking, climbing, backpacking, horseback riding, river running, and boating are some of the activities based here.

Warm Water Feature

★ **Lake Chelan Waterslide**   *1 mi. SW via US 97*

With a splendid view from a slope near the lake, this new water slide complex offers slides ranging from slow and tame to fast and scary. Whirlpools, picnic areas, a viewing deck, and a fast food concession have also been provided. Closed from late September into May.

★ **Wenatchee National Forest**   *W of town*   682-2576

This vast forested area of rugged mountains includes most of Lake Chelan and part of the majestic Glacier Peak Wilderness Area. Highways and dirt roads, and an excellent trail system (including a stretch of the Pacific Crest National Scenic Trail) provide access to a myriad of brilliant glaciers and jagged peaks, streams and waterfalls, and sparkling lakes. Hiking, backpacking, climbing, boating, fishing, hunting, camping, and winter sports are seasonally popular.

SHOPPING

Chelan's small downtown area is concentrated along Woodin Avenue just east of Lake Chelan. It is an unassuming, old-fashioned town center oriented toward fulfilling the everyday needs of residents and visitors.

Food Specialties

Ingram's Harvest Land Fruit   *1 mi. SW at 1328 W. Woodin Av.*   682-5122

Fresh, locally grown fruits and vegetables, and cold cider, are sold at this roadside market in season.

★ **Judy-Jane Bakery**   *downtown at 216 W. Manson Rd.*   682-2151

Delicious pastries, donuts, and specialty breads are displayed in Chelan's fine full line bakery. Customers can also buy chicken snacks and other light meals to eat at several coffee tables, on a patio with lake views, or to go.

Specialty Shops

Gallery Chelan   *downtown at 136 E. Woodin Av.*   682-4364

Handcrafted items in a variety of media by regional artists are displayed and sold here, along with furniture made behind the store.

NIGHTLIFE

There isn't much life after dark in Chelan, apart from a cluster of bars downtown and a couple of comfortable lounges by the lake.

★ **Campbell's Lodge Lounge**   *downtown at 104 W. Woodin Av.*   682-2441

A delightful Victorian-style parlor with sofas and upholstered chairs and a flower-rimmed deck with a lake view attract patrons to the lounge in Campbell's Lodge.

★ **Cosina del Lago**   *2.5 mi. NW on WA 150*   682-4071

Here is a fine place to enjoy an expansive view of apple orchards, Lake Chelan, and the Cascades. The handsome new lounge also offers comfortable seating in front of a tiled fireplace. Upstairs, a stylish restaurant offers conventional Mexican-style dishes.

Town Tavern   *downtown at 104 E. Woodin Av.*   682-2436

A card room area, several pool tables, pinball, and short order foods are available in a plain and popular, 1950s-style tavern.

RESTAURANTS

There are more than a dozen restaurants in Chelan and most are located downtown. Almost all serve conventional American fare in family-oriented, plain surroundings.

Campbell's Lodge   *downtown at 104 W. Woodin Av.*   682-2561
B-L-D.   *Moderate*

American dishes are served in the large, pleasant dining room of an enduring hotel that has been a landmark since the turn of the century.

Katzenjammer's   *8 mi. NW via WA 150 at Wapato Point*   687-9541
D only. Sat. & Sun. brunch.   *Moderate*

Steak is a specialty, and there is a salad bar in a casually elegant dining room with a panoramic Lake Chelan backdrop. Flowering plants enhance the inviting new deck that adjoins this contemporary restaurant in the Inn at Wapato Point.

Musical Chairs   *downtown at 105 N. Emerson St.*   682-4456
L-D.   *Moderate*

International dishes are featured in a new upstairs restaurant outfitted with antique musical chairs.

LODGING

Several excellent resorts have choice lakefront locations, and a good assortment of motels are in and near town. Most of the area's best accommodations are next to downtown along the eastern end of Lake Chelan. From fall through spring, rates are usually at least 30% less than those shown below.

Apple Inn Motel   *.5 mi. E at 1002 E. Woodin Av.*   682-4044
This small modern motel has a few **bargain** rooms with a phone and cable color TV.
    regular room —   D bed...$27

★ **Campbell's Lodge**   *downtown at 104 W. Woodin Av.*   682-2561
A historic turn-of-the-century lodge remains the major landmark downtown. Accommodations now also include cottages and modern motel units by Lake Chelan. In addition to a beach, landscaped grounds include two large outdoor pools (one beautifully sited for outstanding views by the lake), a whirlpool, a dock, plus restaurant and lounge facilities. Each spacious, well-furnished unit has a phone and cable color TV.
    #314,#313,#312,#311 — pvt. balc., great lake/mt. view from   K bed...$84
    #214,#316,#210,#110,#310 — as above,   2 Q beds..$88
    #14 (in Lodge #4) — balc., fine lake views,   Q bed...$78
    #16 (in Lodge #4) — 1 BR, kitchen, patio, fine lake views,   Q bed...$91
    regular room —   Q bed...$78

★ **Caravel Motor Hotel**   *downtown at 322 W. Woodin Av.*   682-2715
This modern lakefront motel has a large outdoor pool by the lake, and a dock. Each spacious unit has color TV with movies.
    #58,#54 — in new addition, pvt. balc. over water, fine lake/town view,   Q bed...$60
    #111,#112 — studio, kitchenette, pvt. balc., fine lake/mt. view,   Q bed...$85
    regular room —   Q bed...$60

★ **Darnell's Resort Motel**   *1 mi. NW at 901 Spader Bay Rd.*   682-2015
A sandy beach on Lake Chelan is a feature, along with a boat launch, moorage, and a swimming area with a diving and slide platform. Landscaped grounds include a large outdoor pool with a lake view, a whirlpool, two tennis courts, pitch and putt golf, and complimentary bicycles. Each spacious unit has cable color TV and a kitchen. In summer, no maid service is provided, units are rented to families only, and a minimum stay of one week is required. The rates below apply before June 15 and after September 10 when singles and couples are welcomed.
    #1,#10 (A Bldg.) — 1 BR suite, ground level, lake view,   K bed...$60
    #6 — pvt. balc., splendid lake/mt. view,   Q bed...$60
    #8 — pvt. balc., fine lake/mt. view,   Q bed...$68
    regular room —   Q bed...$54

★ **Inn at Wapato Point**   *8 mi. NW off WA 150*   687-9511
The neck of a peninsula on Lake Chelan has become a big lakeside condominium resort with a large indoor pool and two outdoor pools; a whirlpool; six tennis courts; a sandy beach and dock; rental canoes, rowboats, sailboats, and bicycles; plus a spectacularly located restaurant and lounge. Each nicely furnished, spacious unit has a phone, cable color TV, wood-burning fireplace, kitchen, and a balcony or patio overlooking the lake.
    regular room — 1 BR, splendid lake/mts. view,   Q bed...$100

North Cascade Lodge *55 mi. NW at other end of Lake - Stehekin*   682-4711
Operated as a leased concession by the National Park Service, this recently remodeled complex includes a two-story alpine lodge, cabins, and motel units on a hill overlooking Lake Chelan and the Stehekin Valley. A rustic dining room; a boat dock; and boat, bicycle, and car rentals are available.
    lodge room — spacious, lake view,   Q bed...$60
    housekeeping unit — spacious, lake view, kitchenette,   Q bed...$63
    regular room — small,   D bed...$41

Parkway Motel   *downtown at 402 N. Manson Rd.*   682-2822
Across from Lakeshore Park, this single-level **bargain** motel has modest units with color TV.
    deluxe room — kit., some lake view,   Q bed...$45
    regular room — no view,   D bed...$25

★ **Spader Bay Condominium Resort**   *.9 mi NW at 102 Spader Bay Rd.*   *682-5818*
This modern lakeshore condominium complex has a private sandy beach, a very large outdoor pool with a panoramic lakefront view, whirlpool, sauna, and dockage. Each well-furnished unit has cable color TV and a patio or balcony. In summer, daily maid service is not provided, and the minimum stay is at least three nights.

#30,#40 — studio, kitchen, excellent lake views from corner windows,	Q bed...$85
#8B — studio, fireplace, good lake view,	Q bed...$90
#10,#11 — 1 BR, fireplace, kitchen, good lake view,	D bed...$125
regular room —	Q bed...$60

CAMPGROUNDS

There are several campgrounds in the area. One of the West's finest is a short drive from town with complete camping and recreation facilities in a picturesque setting by Lake Chelan.

★ **Lake Chelan St. Pk.** *9 mi. W: 4 mi. W on US 97 & 5 mi. W on Shore Dr.*   *687-3710*
The state has provided a large, outstanding campground along a scenic south shore beach by Lake Chelan. Attractions include a designated swimming area with a sandy beach, a grassy slope that is a favorite of sunbathers, a boat ramp and dock, boating, fishing, and water-skiing, plus nature trails. Flush toilets, hot showers (fee) and hookups are available. Well-spaced lake-view sites have a picnic table and fire grill/ring. Several especially scenic, tree-shaded tent sites by the lake are a few steps down a slope near the eastern end of the campground.   base rate...$5.50

SPECIAL EVENT

Harvest Festival   *Chelan City Park*   *mid-September*
Apple-oriented displays, exhibits, concessions, live entertainment, and contests are all part of a weekend celebration of the apple harvest.

OTHER INFORMATION

Area Code: *509*
Zip Code: *98816*
Lake Chelan Chamber of Commerce *downtown at 208 E. Johnson Av.*   *682-2022*
North Cascades Natl. Park-Dist. Office *downtown at 206 Manson Rd.*   *682-2549*
Wenatchee Natl. For.-Chelan Ranger Stn. *downtown at 428 W. Woodin Av.*   *682-2576*

Port Townsend, Washington

Elevation:

100 feet

Population (1980):

6,067

Population (1970):

5,241

Location:

about 50 mi. NW
of Seattle

Port Townsend is a showcase for the arts in a town that time forgot. Here on the remote northeastern tip of the Olympic Peninsula is the finest collection of Victorian architecture in the Northwest. The appealing human scale of the unspoiled old town, and a sublime waterfront location backed by lush pastoral countryside, contribute to the magic of this special place. Even the climate is a pleasant surprise. During the mild winters, snowfall and hard freezes are unusual. Precipitation is relatively light throughout the year because the area is in the "rain shadow" of the nearby Olympic Mountains. Vacationers fill the town nightly in summer when warm sunny days are perfect for comfortably enjoying the area. Nearby to the southwest is the rugged grandeur of Olympic National Park. To the east, a remarkable diversity of open water, natural canals, and tiny hidden harbors have been developed with parks, beaches and marinas offering every kind of maritime recreation. Boating, fishing, clamming, beachcombing, hiking and camping are popular near town, and there are several scenic golf courses in the area.

In 1792, Captain George Vancouver came ashore and named this site Port Townsend in honor of an English nobleman. Almost sixty years went by before settlers erected the area's first log cabin. By the 1880s, the town was booming with logging and maritime activity. New wealth was quickly translated into substantial brick and stone buildings in the waterfront business district and mansions on the adjacent bluff. During the 1890s, however, the boom collapsed as Port Townsend lost the race for shipping and railroad preeminence to Seattle and other towns. Intermittent activity at the adjoining fort and construction of a paper mill two miles away kept the town alive through a period of benign neglect which lasted for well over half a century. In 1972, the Army deeded its turn-of-the-century military complex to the Washington State Parks and Recreation Commission. Artists and craftsmen began to rediscover the natural beauty of the area at about the same time, and to restore and use the legacy of Victorian structures.

Today, solid rows of nineteenth century brick buildings on the waterfront house studios and shops displaying locally produced arts and crafts. Lending additional distinction are a cluster of restaurants with a special penchant for fine breakfasts, plus several atmospheric bars. Even the adjoining fort site has been converted into a major cultural and recreational asset. It is now the home for Port Townsend's arts festivals and symposiums. There are almost no conventional lodgings in town. Instead, many of the splendid century-old homes and mansions on the blufftops have been carefully restored to serve as charming bed-and-breakfast inns filled with authentic period pieces or locally made art objects.

WEATHER PROFILE

Vokac Weather Rating

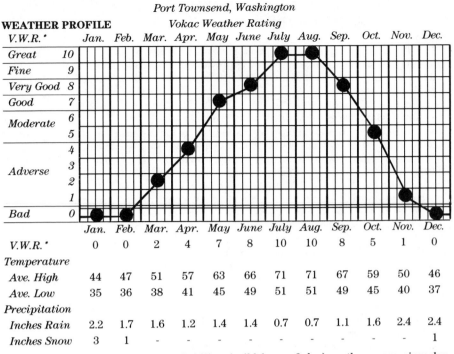

V.W.R.*	Jan.	Feb.	Mar.	Apr.	May	June	July	Aug.	Sep.	Oct.	Nov.	Dec.
Great	10											
Fine	9											
Very Good	8											
Good	7											
Moderate	6											
	5											
	4											
Adverse	3											
	2											
	1											
Bad	0											

	Jan.	Feb.	Mar.	Apr.	May	June	July	Aug.	Sep.	Oct.	Nov.	Dec.
V.W.R.*	0	0	2	4	7	8	10	10	8	5	1	0
Temperature												
Ave. High	44	47	51	57	63	66	71	71	67	59	50	46
Ave. Low	35	36	38	41	45	49	51	51	49	45	40	37
Precipitation												
Inches Rain	2.2	1.7	1.6	1.2	1.4	1.4	0.7	0.7	1.1	1.6	2.4	2.4
Inches Snow	3	1	-	-	-	-	-	-	-	-	-	1

V.W.R. = Vokac Weather Rating: probability of mild (warm & dry) weather on any given day.

Forecast

		Temperatures		
Month	V.W.R.*	Daytime	Evening	Precipitation
January	0 Bad	chilly	chilly	frequent showers/snow flurries
February	0 Bad	chilly	chilly	frequent showers
March	2 Adverse	cool	chilly	frequent showers
April	4 Adverse	cool	chilly	frequent showers
May	7 Good	cool	cool	occasional showers
June	8 Very Good	warm	cool	occasional showers
July	10 Great	warm	cool	infrequent showers
August	10 Great	warm	cool	infrequent showers
September	8 Very Good	warm	cool	occasional showers
October	5 Moderate	cool	cool	frequent showers
November	1 Adverse	cool	chilly	frequent showers
December	0 Bad	chilly	chilly	frequent showers

Summary

Carved out of a splendid evergreen forest at the isolated northeastern tip of the Olympic Peninsula lies Port Townsend. The town has a surprisingly mild four season climate including one of the West's longest growing seasons outside of California. The location is warmed by the adjoining strait, and it is in the rain shadow of the nearby Olympic Mountains. All of the bad weather occurs in **winter**, which is chilly and damp from frequent showers and snow flurries. **Spring** temperatures are cool, but frequent drizzles support all kinds of delicate new growth throughout the season. **Summer** weather is excellent. Long warm days, cool evenings, and infrequent sprinkles encourage exploration of this tranquil seaside hideaway. In **fall**, cool days return along with frequent showers.

ATTRACTIONS & DIVERSIONS

★ **Bicycling**

Port Townsend Emporium   *downtown at 1102 Water St.*   385-5900
An excellent system of tree-shaded byways provides easy access to hidden harbors, sandy beaches, and tiny coastal villages. For leisurely explorations, bicycles can be rented here by the hour or day.

Boat Ride

★ **Whidbey Island Ferry**   *downtown off Water St.*   (800)542-0810
The Port Townsend-Keystone ferry leaves frequently for the half hour trip to Whidbey Island — the largest in Puget Sound. Numerous scenic byways may be explored by car, bicycle, or on foot. A few miles north of the ferry terminal is Coupeville, a quaint historic town with an intriguing assortment of shops along the waterfront.

★ **Chetzemolka Park**   *.7 mi. N at Blaine/Jackson Sts.*
On a bluff overlooking Admiralty Inlet is a large town park named after a friendly Indian Chief. It features panoramic marine views with snow-capped Mt. Baker in the distance; access to a long rocky beach; well-spaced picnic facilities and beautifully landscaped grounds with meandering streams, ponds, flower gardens, and a gazebo.

★ **Courthouse**   *.5 mi. SW at Jefferson/Cass Sts.*
Built in 1891, this monumental brick building is a masterwork of Victorian overstatement. The 100-foot-tall clock tower is an enduring source of pride for residents, and a landmark for mariners. One of the two oldest courthouses in the state, the building still serves as it always did. Visitors marvel at the expansive interior spaces and unadulterated Victorian craftsmanship that convey a museum-like quality in contrast with the building's continuing governmental role.

★ **Customs House**   *downtown at Washington/Van Buren Sts.*
This imposing stone building, constructed in 1893, is another showcase of "living history." The post office and federal offices are housed behind public areas that remain relatively untouched by time — with polished wood trim, inlaid stone floors, curved glass windows, and elaborate wrought iron staircases. Topping stone columns at the south entrance are faces of the friendly Indian Chief "Duke of York" and his wife.

Fort Flagler State Park *20 mi. SE off WA 20 on Morrowstone Island*   385-1259
Established in the 1890s, the fort was deactivated in 1937. The waterfront site features sandy beaches, picnic facilities, a campground, boat launch and moorage (rental boats are available), nature-study trails, and a lighthouse. Recreation opportunities include beachcombing, saltwater swimming, fishing, and boating.

★ **Fort Worden State Park**   *2 mi. N via Walker & Cherry Sts.*   385-4730
The state now operates the fort, built just before the turn of the century, as a center for cultural workshops and symposiums. Restored structures lining the parade ground include a number of large Victorian houses that were officers' quarters. They are available for vacation rentals. Within easy walking distance are lush forests and long expanses of beach. Gun emplacements overlooking Puget Sound, and the Point Wilson Lighthouse (built in 1870 and operated by the Coast Guard), are highlights of shore hikes. A popular campground has been provided near the beach.

Golf

★ **Port Ludlow Golf Course**   *18 mi. SE off WA 20 - Port Ludlow*   437-2222
Lush fairways are flanked by towering firs at this beautifully designed 18-hole championship golf course overlooking Admiralty Inlet. It is open to the public and includes a pro shop, putting green, driving range, club and cart rentals, and a restaurant and lounge in the Admiralty Resort.

★ **Haller Fountain**   *downtown at Washington/Taylor Sts.*
At the bottom of a long scenic stairway that connects downtown with the blufftop is a tiny garden park with a wonderfully old-fashioned fountain sculpture. The bronze lady "Innocence" has been here since 1909.

★ **Historic Buildings**
Authentic Victorian structures are everywhere. Many are listed on the "National Register of Historic Places." Most are still in use either for their original purpose or for compatible adaptations. An easily-followed brochure with a map and descriptions of historical sites is available at the Chamber of Commerce.

★ **Library**   *.3 mi. NW at 1220 Lawrence St.*   *385-3181*
The Port Townsend Public Library, one of the few Carnegie libraries still used as a public
building, was built in 1913. It exudes nostalgia, especially in the periodical reading area,
with upholstered sofa and chairs in front of a wood-burning brick fireplace. Closed Sun.-
Mon.

★ **Moped Rentals**
    Brick and Sons Motor Co.   *.2 mi. SW at 1615 Sims Way*   *385-4290*
Mopeds can be rented here by the hour or longer for exhilarating explorations of the
peninsula's tree-shaded byways.

★ **Olympic National Forest**   *28 mi. SW via WA 20 & US 101*   *753-9535*
Surrounding Olympic National Park are lush rain forests; one of the world's heaviest
stands of Douglas fir; abundant wildlife — including Roosevelt elk; and sparkling lakes,
streams and rivers in picturesque canyons far below glacier-capped peaks. Hundreds of
miles of hiking trails and self-guided nature trails lead to camping, hiking, hunting, fishing,
river running, and swimming sites.

★ **Olympic National Park**   *50 mi. SW via WA 20 & US 101*   *452-4501*
More than 1,400 square miles of awe-inspiring wilderness extends from glacier-clad peaks
to ocean shores. The wettest climate in the coterminous United States (averaging 140
inches of precipitation a year) has created luxuriant coniferous rain forests in the
western river valleys. From the spectacular Hurricane Ridge Highway, there are
breathtaking panoramas of Mt. Olympus (the highest peak at 7,965 feet) and dozens of
glaciers that lend a shimmering brilliance to the extremely rugged mountains at the top
of the peninsula. Wildlife is abundant, including elk, bear, deer, and bald eagles. Seals are
common on the rocky fifty-seven-mile strip of primitive Pacific coastline. Hundreds of
miles of trails (including many self-guided nature trails) provide access to scores of lakes,
streams, and waterfalls. Hiking, backpacking, mountain climbing, horseback and pack
trips, fishing, and camping are popular, as is swimming at Sol Duc Hot Springs.

★ **Port Gamble**   *28 mi. SE via WA 20 & WA 104*
Founded in 1853, this tiny nineteenth century town was built by a logging company that
still owns it. What may be the oldest continuously operating sawmill in America is here.
The company has restored more than thirty homes, churches, and commercial buildings.
Even street lights have been replaced with gas lamp replicas. There is a historical
museum, and a sea-and-shore museum with an outstanding shell collection.

Poulsbo   *35 mi. SE via WA 20, WA 104 & WA 3*
This picturesque little harborside community has a distinctive Scandinavian flair. There
are numerous specialty shops and an old landmark, the Olympic Inn, has been converted
into a handsome restaurant.

Sportfishing
Charter boat services feature salmon fishing in season, and year-round bottom fishing. All
bait and tackle are provided. For reservations, contact:
    Calm Sea Charters   *downtown at Boat Haven*   *385-5288*
    Dogfish Charters   *downtown at Boat Haven*   *385-3575*

★ **Whitney Rhododendrons Garden**   *37 mi. S on US 101 - Brinnon*   *796-4411*
Especially in May when these giant shrubs are in fullest bloom, this garden nursery is a
floral wonderland.

SHOPPING
Downtown, on Washington and Water Streets between the waterfront and a nearby bluff,
is one of the most picturesque concentrations of Victorian structures anywhere. Rows of
solid brick buildings now house distinctive gift and gourmet shops, antique stores, and
arts and crafts studios, as well as restaurants, bars, and lodgings.

Food Specialties
★ **Bread and Roses Bakery**   *downtown at 230 Quincy St.*   *385-1044*
The beauty of the roses out front is matched by the quality of the breads and pastries
made in this fine new full line bakery. Scones, galettes, and traditional baked goods, like
cinnamon rolls and croissants, are available to go, or they may be enjoyed with coffee on
a pleasant rear deck. Closed Mon.

★ **Elevated Ice Cream Co.** *downtown at 627 Water St.* *385-1156*
Many flavors of homemade ice cream, fruit-based Italian ices, and baked goods are served to go, or in a charming parlor with artwork lining the walls. There is also an espresso bar and a sundeck overlooking the bay.

Neuharth Fine Dinner Wines *32 mi. W on US 101 - Sequim* *683-9652*
Classic varieties and several specialty grape wines are produced in the nation's most northwesterly winery. A tasting cellar is open 12-5 Wed.-Sun.

★ **Showcase Bakery** *downtown at 229 Taylor St.* *385-2500*
This outstanding full line carryout bakery features splendid pastries (including delicious cinnamon rolls in the afternoon), cookies, donuts, and breads.

★ **Water Street Deli** *downtown at 634 Water St.* *385-2422*
Northwestern wines are featured along with a fine selection of homemade soups (like clam bisque), sandwiches, and delicious desserts. All items are packaged to go or served in comfortable seating areas for lunch in a handsomely restored 1885 building.

The Wine Seller *downtown at 227 Adams St.* *385-7673*
A fine selection of Northwestern wines heads an extensive premium wine collection, and there are imported beers and roasted coffees. A wine taste is available daily in this attractive little shop.

Specialty Shops

★ **Earthenworks** *downtown at 630 Water St.* *385-0328*
A collection of fine things created by local and regional artists is beautifully exhibited in a large, century-old building.

Eng and Eng Magazines *downtown at 922 Water St.*
This narrow little shop features an excellent selection of magazines and pottery.

Imprint Bookstore *downtown at 820 Water St.* *385-3643*
Books of regional interest are a feature among many well-organized displays in an inviting shop.

★ **Jamesware Ceramics** *downtown at 237 Monroe St.* *385-2129*
Molded "greenware" (unglazed, unfired pottery) ranging from functional cookware to art objects is the specialty of this gallery/workshop. You can purchase it to finish yourself, or have it finished to your color and use specifications. Some finished pieces are also displayed for sale.

Liz's Loft *downtown at 1010 Water St.* *385-0773*
A Northwestern theme unites a potpourri of arts and crafts by regional artists and others in a historic building.

North by Northwest *downtown at 630 Water St.* *385-0955*
Indian arts and crafts ranging from baskets to wool sweaters and hats, plus a good collection of books regarding Northwestern Indians, are nicely displayed in a converted Victorian building.

★ **Port Townsend Art Gallery - Bookstore** *downtown at 725 Water St.* *385-1926*
Multimedia art works and a fine selection of books on the Northwest are highlights. The full line bookstore is in a high-ceilinged, brick-walled room with a waterfront view.

Waterfront Gallery *downtown at 225 Taylor St.* *385-0566*
This is a cooperative showcase for the multimedia works of a number of local artists and craftsmen. Closed Mon.

NIGHTLIFE
Distinctive places for evening entertainment and refreshments range from casual, comfortably furnished taverns in restored century-old buildings to posh view lounges in contemporary resorts.

★ **Admiralty Resort** *18 mi. SE off WA 20 - Port Ludlow* *437-2222*
Downstairs from the Harbor Master Restaurant is the Wreck Room, a large modern lounge with a window wall overlooking a picturesque bay. Live music for listening or dancing is offered almost every night.

Back Alley Tavern *downtown at 923 Washington St.* *385-6536*
Live entertainment is offered most nights in this hideaway tavern, and there is an outdoor beer garden.

Chandler's   *1.5 mi. SW at 1200 Sims Way*   385-5210
Live music and dancing are featured in a contemporary lounge with high-backed armchairs and a bay view, next to a family restaurant.

★ **Manresa Lounge**   *1.7 mi. SW at Sheridan/7th Sts.*   385-5750
The Manresa Castle has a romantic little Victorian bar with polished wood everywhere (walls, ceiling, back bar, etc.), comfortable sofas, and a memorable overview of the town and bay through tall windows. A large conventional restaurant adjoins.

★ **Town Tavern**   *downtown on Water St.*   *no phone*
Live entertainment and dancing draw crowds on weekends to Port Townsend's classic old-time tavern. This unspoiled Victorian showplace captures the community's spirit with its well-worn wooden floor, high ceilings and tall windows adorned with hanging plants, resplendent polished wood back bar, much-used pot-bellied stove, cozy balcony seating area, and an arresting painting of a nude lady, plus pool tables, a half dozen beers on tap, and wines by the glass.

RESTAURANTS

Recent years have witnessed a notable improvement in the quality of local restaurants. Port Townsend has become one of the West's gourmet havens of homestyle American cuisine emphasizing fresh local seafood and produce. Several of the best restaurants are in artistically restored Victorian structures, and some dining rooms provide fine views of Puget Sound.

★ **Ace of Cups**   *.3 mi. N at 1025 Lawrence St.*   385-4561
B-L-D.   *Moderate*
Croissants, pastries, and outstanding homemade desserts highlight light fare served along with premium coffees, teas, and espresso in a relaxed and funky coffee house where wood trim and fresh flowers reign. Up front, a well-stocked little reading nook with sofas lends to the casual charm.

★ **The Bayview**   *.3 mi. SW at 1590 Water St.*   385-1461
B-L-D.   *Low*
Homemade breakfasts, including an assortment of tasty crepe-style omelets, contribute to the enduring popularity of this wood-and-fabric, contemporary cafe/dining room. The restaurant was built over the water, and the panoramic view is one of the most beguiling anywhere.

★ **Conway's Farmhouse**   *2 mi. NW on 49th St. - North Beach*   385-1411
D only. Closed Tues.-Wed. & Dec.-Jan.   Expensive
Extraordinary prix fixe five-to-seven-course international dinners, changing monthly, are presented with gracious formality in a Victorian building with splendid views of the mountains and straits. Dinner is by reservation only.

★ **Landfall Restaurant**   *downtown at 412 Water St.*   385-5814
B-L.   *Moderate*
Fresh ingredients are used in a delicious assortment of unusual specialties like crab or oyster omelets. A handcrafted "greenhouse" room was recently added to the rustic little cafe that provides an intimate view of an adjacent marina.

Mom's   *downtown at 711 Water St.*   385-2777
B-L. No L on Sun.   *Low*
You can select from many ingredients for your omelet, or order an unusual specialty like fresh fruit Norwegian pancakes, in this modest little cafe.

★ **Nancy's Place**   *8 mi. SE at 2380 Rhody Dr. - Hadlock*   385-5285
B-L-D.   *Low*
Scrumptious homemade breakfast pastries, breads, and dessert pies call attention to an all-American roadside coffee shop where "from scratch" still means something.

Quilcene Cafe   *25 mi. S on US 101 - Quilcene*   765-3541
B-L-D.   *Low*
Superb homemade almond rolls, plus cinnamon rolls, biscuits, pies, and breads (many available to go), are specialties of this casual old-fashioned roadside coffee shop.

★ **The Salal Cafe**   *downtown at 634 Water St.*   385-6532
B-D.   *Moderate*
Fresh local ingredients are skillfully prepared with a light touch. A cheerful new solarium-style back room is decorated with excellent locally produced wall hangings.

★ **Sally's**   *downtown at 920 Washington St.*   *385-5794*
L-tea. Closed Sun.   *Moderate*
Delicious and distinctive light fare and daily dessert specials are featured in a charming little teahouse/restaurant housed in a converted 1889 building.

Sea Galley   *downtown at Water/Taylor Sts.*   *385-2992*
L-D.   *Moderate*
Seafoods, steaks, and a salad bar are offered, along with nautical decor and marine views from the contemporary wharfside dining room. Lunches are also served in a comfortable lounge which has an even better view of Puget Sound.

★ **Sheba's Lido**   *downtown at 925 Water St.*   *385-1132*
L-D.   *Moderate*
Uncommon dishes emphasizing fresh regional seafoods, plus homemade pastas and desserts, are well-liked in a casually elegant dining room that is one of the area's favorites.

★ **Starrett House**   *.3 mi. N at 744 Clay St.*   *385-2976*
D only. Closed Tues.-Thurs.   *Moderate*
Continental specialties made with seasonally fresh ingredients are prepared and served with distinction. The ornate grandeur of the dining room is the centerpiece for one of the Northwest's most extraordinary Victorian mansions.

Three Crabs   *38 mi. W: 33 mi. W via US 101 & 5 mi. N - Dungeness*   *683-4264*
L-D.   *Low*
Local Dungeness crab is the specialty — cracked, on toast, in omelets, etc. It is served fresh in season (October-March) along with other fresh seafood, including geoduck — a giant local clam. A family-oriented fish shack has grown into a large, easygoing restaurant with several cheerful dining rooms and a bay view beyond the parking lot.

Timber House Restaurant   *26 mi. S on US 101 - Quilcene*   *765-3339*
L-D.   *Moderate*
Local oysters and other seafoods are featured, along with steaks. Linen tablecloths, candles, captain's chairs, and ferns lend casual elegance to the hand-milled wood-toned structure. There is a pleasant forest view from many windows.

LODGING

With an unsurpassed collection of Victorian structures, it is not surprising that Port Townsend has become one of the West's bed-and-breakfast capitals. There are very few conventional motels or other accommodations. From late fall through early spring, rates are usually at least 10% less than those shown apart from weekends.

★ **Admiralty Resort**   *18 mi. SE via WA 20 & Oak Bay Rd. - Port Ludlow*   *437-2222*
Naturalistic contemporary architecture and decor distinguish this large bayside resort. Amenities include two pools (an indoor pool, and a large outdoor pool with a fine bay view), sauna, squash court, recreation room with pool and ping-pong tables, seven tennis courts, beach and saltwater swimming lagoon; plus (a fee for) an 18-hole championship golf course, rental bicycles, rental boats of all kinds, fishing gear, and sail or powered boat charters at the marina. There is also a large and elegant harbor-view dining room and a view lounge with entertainment. Each beautifully furnished unit has a phone and cable color TV.

   #610 — 1 BR loft suite, stone fireplace, pvt. deck, kitchen, fine bay view, Q bed...$110
   #223,#158 — deluxe waterside BR, excellent bay view, pvt. deck,   K bed...$80
   #607,#611 — deluxe waterside BR, fine water view, pvt. deck,   Q bed...$90
   regular room — view of landscaped grounds,   Q bed...$70

Bishop Victorian   *downtown at 714 Washington St.*   *385-6122*
An old apartment building in the heart of town was recently thoroughly upgraded. Each spacious unit has some period pieces, plus a phone, cable color TV, and a kitchen.

   #18,#20 — 1 BR, corner, intimate town/water view,   D bed...$55
   #22 — 1 BR, corner, fine bay view,   D bed...$55
   regular room —   D bed...$50

Fort Worden State Park   *2 mi. N via Walker & Cherry Sts.*   *385-4730*
This beautifully sited ex-military base includes a remarkably intact cluster of turn-of-the-century buildings. Several of the large officer's houses (ranging from two to six bedrooms) have been refurbished as vacation rentals. While you can't rent the commanding officer's

house (now a museum), you can get a wonderfully isolated, refurbished blue bungalow that overlooks it and has a panoramic view of Admiralty Inlet.

"Blissful Vista" — 1½ BR cottage, kit., raised brick fireplace, LR with view windows on 3 sides, tiny extra BR, sea view from   T & Q beds...$45
regular unit — 2 BR house, some water views,   2 D beds...$55

Griffith House   *1 mi. N at 2030 Monroe St.*   *385-4922*

A Victorian residence on the crest of a hill with a fine water view has been attractively restored as a bed-and-breakfast inn. Breakfast is complimentary. The two well-furnished guest rooms share a big tile tub and a sauna.

"Blue Room" — superb pvt. 3-window town/harbor view,   D bed...$45
regular room "Corner Room" — 3-window view to Olympic Mts.,   D bed...$45

★ **The James House**   *downtown at 1238 Washington St.*   *385-1238*

This grand Victorian mansion may have been the first bed-and-breakfast inn in the Northwest. All rooms are nicely furnished in period antiques. Several have fine views of town and the waterways. A complimentary Continental breakfast is served.

"Bridal Suite" — pvt. balc., bay windowed sitting room, clawfoot tub bath, fireplace, complimentary champagne, bay view,   D bed...$80
#3 — shared bath, several windows, fine harbor views,   D bed...$55
regular room — shared bath,   D bed...$48

Lizzie's   *.4 mi. W at 731 Pierce St.*   *385-9826*

An Italianate Victorian residence has been carefully restored into a charming bed-and-breakfast inn. All rooms feature period furnishings, and a complete breakfast is complimentary.

"Lizzie's Room" — fireplace, bay window alcove, clawfoot tub, half-canopied   D bed...$79
"Daisy's Room" — shared bath, bay view from 4-window alcove,   K bed...$55
regular room "Hope's Room" — shared bath,   D bed...$42

Manresa Castle   *1.7 mi. S at Sheridan/7th Sts.*   *385-5750*

The town's largest lodging facility is a landmark mansion with more than thirty rooms. Built by the town's first mayor, it was acquired by Jesuits in the 1920s and enlarged to serve as a seminary. In the last decade, it has been restored to some of its turn-of-the-century distinction, with formal gardens, antiques, a restaurant, and a wonderful Victorian lounge. Each room has some period furnishings, a phone, color TV, and a private bath.

#302 "Skyline Tower Suite" — extraordinary round room with 5 large rounded windows, brass bed overlooks town/harbor,   D & Q beds...$80
#200 "Honeymoon Tower Suite" — stately round room with 3 rounded windows,   Q bed...$80
regular room —   D bed...$56

Palace Hotel   *downtown at 1004 Water St.*   *385-0773*

A handsome, nearly century-old brick building in the heart of town is now a small Victorian-style hotel. All rooms, including the **bargain** room, feature antiques and have a cable color TV.

"Marie's Suite" — lg. BR/parlour, kitchenette, fireplace, great main st. & harbor view,   Q bed...$58
#9A — pvt. bath,   D bed...$35
regular room — shared bath,   D bed...$30

Quimper Inn   *.3 mi. W at 1306 Franklin St.*   *385-1086*

A century-old Georgian-style Victorian residence has been creatively restored as a bed-and-breakfast inn. Country antiques and whimsical local arts and crafts are appealing furnishings. A homemade Continental breakfast is complimentary.

"Gaff Schooner" — antique tin tub, brass bed in bay window alcove, bay/town views,   D bed...$69
"Rose Thistle" — shared bath, iron bed in window alcove, mt. view,   Q bed...$60
regular room "Brasspyglass" — shared bath, bright corner, some bay view,   D bed...$47

★ **Starrett House**   *.3 mi. N at 744 Clay St.*   385-2976
One of the most photogenic three-story Victorian brick mansions in the Northwest is now
a captivating bed-and-breakfast inn. A silver tea service at the room and a full breakfast
in the opulent dining room are complimentary. Fine antique furnishings are used
throughout. (Public tours are given in the afternoons.)
"Bridal Suite" — half bath, windows on 3 sides, sitting alcove,
               parlor stove, canopied   D bed...$75
"The Master's Quarters" — shared bath, spacious, opulent blue tones, sitting
               alcove, parlor stove, great water/town views,   D bed...$75
"Ann's Parlor" — pvt. balc., windows on 3 sides, parlor stove,
               great water/Mt. Baker view,   D bed...$68
regular room "The Carriage Room" — shared bath,   2 T beds...$50

★ **The Tides Inn**   *.4 mi. SW at 1807 Water St.*   385-0595
This modern little single-level motel offers the only conventional accommodations right
on the water. Each unit has a phone and cable color TV.
#19 — kitchenette, shared deck, several windows view downtown/bay,   Q bed...$60
#25 — pvt. water view from corner windows,   Q bed...$42
#26,#27,#28 — front windows have pvt. water view,   Q bed...$42
regular room #31 — pvt. corner window view of water,   D bed...$42

CAMPGROUNDS
There are few campgrounds in the area. The best adjoins town and offers complete
camping and recreation facilities on a picturesque sandspit next to Puget Sound.

★ **Fort Worden State Park**   *2 mi. N via Walker & Cherry Sts.*   385-4730
The state has provided a beautifully situated campground at the base of a heavily wooded
hill between two sandy beaches overlooking Puget Sound. Features include saltwater
swimming and fishing, scuba diving, beachcombing, clamming, boating, a boat ramp, and
nature trails. Flush toilets, hot showers, and hookups are available. All sites have a picnic
table and fire ring/grill.   base rate...$8

SPECIAL EVENTS
★ **Rhododendron Festival**   *in and around town*   *mid-May*
A flower show; coronation and dance; sports events; arts and crafts fair; sailing, balloon,
and bed races; parades; fireworks; and a fish fry are all included in a nine day celebration
that coincides with the peak bloom of the Northwest's loveliest shrubs.

★ **Celebration of American Arts**   *Fort Worden St. Pk.*   *mid-June to early September*
A series of special events attracts nearly one thousand professional and amateur
participants from around the U.S. and Canada to workshops conducted by luminaries in
the disciplines of dance, poetry and fiction writing, jazz, chamber music, and traditional
folk music. The public is invited to attend exhibits, readings, dances, and performances.

★ **Wooden Boat Festival**   *on the waterfront in town*   *mid-September*
A fine display of boats is the highlight of a celebration that brings seafarers and marine
craftsmen together for nautical festivities and a series of workshops.

OTHER INFORMATION
Area Code: *206*
Zip Code: *98368*
Port Townsend Chamber of Commerce   *.8 mi. SW at 2437 Sims Way*   385-2722

Cody, Wyoming

Elevation:

5,018

Population (1980):

6,790

Population (1970):

5,161

Location:

440 mi. NE
of Salt Lake City

Cody is the eastern gateway to a Rocky Mountain wonderland. The town is located a mile high near the edge of a vast sagebrush-covered basin. Towering mountains along the western skyline are within one of the nation's largest wildernesses. Weather is capricious most of the year in this wide-open high country. There are no major snow sports facilities because of relatively light snowfalls and periodic strong winds during winter. The weather is normally fine during summer, however, when visitors flock here to experience the West. Three spectacularly scenic highways provide access to all kinds of recreation amidst unspoiled lakes, rivers, streams, waterfalls and glaciers tucked into pine-forested mountain ranges that extend for more than fifty miles into Yellowstone National Park. The world's foremost museum of Western lore is in Cody, and a famed rodeo takes place almost every summer night by a scenic canyon on the west side of town. The Shoshone River has cut deeply into colorful benchlands in the same area, and now provides a popular river run. Nearby, undisturbed tepee ring stones remain as haunting reminders of a far different civilization not long gone, and a fascinating array of massive extinct geyser cones, pits, and terraces in "Colter's Hell" suggests how much like Yellowstone Park this area once was.

Colonel William F. "Buffalo Bill" Cody and several friends came here in the 1890s to build a community. The town was named Cody at the insistence of his fellow developers in 1895. In 1902, he opened his landmark hotel (the Irma) and the Burlington Railroad built a spur into town. Cody's friendship with Teddy Roosevelt helped him to persuade the then-president to establish the Bureau of Reclamation and build the Shoshone (later Buffalo Bill) Dam and Reservoir near town. It also helped secure the nation's first national forest (the Shoshone) and ranger station (Wapiti) for the spectacular high country between Cody and the nation's first national park (Yellowstone).

Today, a diversified economy based on tourism, ranching, farming, and petroleum explains the prosperous appearance of the classic New Western town. The outstanding museum/gallery complex dedicated to Western lore is the town's major attraction. This incomparable tribute to Buffalo Bill and the unspoiled grandeur of the "Cody Country" are attracting renowned artists and fine art galleries. Restaurants and bars are numerous and surprisingly conventional. Buffalo Bill's own Irma Hotel still offers the most distinguished accommodations in town. Fortunately, numerous historic lodges in the mountains west of town retain the authentic spirit and decor of their thoroughly Western settings.

WEATHER PROFILE   *Vokac Weather Rating*

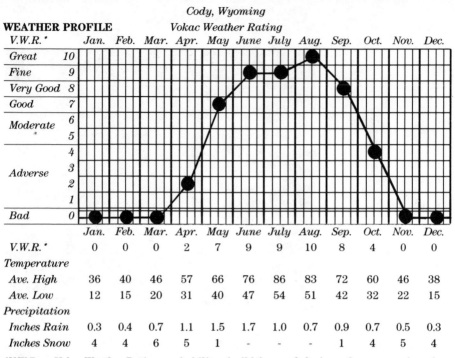

V.W.R.*	Jan.	Feb.	Mar.	Apr.	May	June	July	Aug.	Sep.	Oct.	Nov.	Dec.
V.W.R.*	0	0	0	2	7	9	9	10	8	4	0	0
Temperature												
Ave. High	36	40	46	57	66	76	86	83	72	60	46	38
Ave. Low	12	15	20	31	40	47	54	51	42	32	22	15
Precipitation												
Inches Rain	0.3	0.4	0.7	1.1	1.5	1.7	1.0	0.7	0.9	0.7	0.5	0.3
Inches Snow	4	4	6	5	1	-	-	-	1	4	5	4

*V.W.R. = Vokac Weather Rating: probability of mild (warm & dry) weather on any given day.

Forecast

		Temperatures		
Month	V.W.R.*	Daytime	Evening	Precipitation
January	0 Bad	chilly	frigid	infrequent snow flurries
February	0 Bad	chilly	cold	infrequent snow flurries
March	0 Bad	chilly	chilly	infrequent snow flurries
April	2 Adverse	cool	chilly	occasional showers/snow flurries
May	7 Good	warm	cool	occasional showers
June	9 Fine	warm	cool	occasional showers
July	9 Fine	hot	warm	occasional showers
August	10 Great	hot	warm	infrequent showers
September	8 Very Good	warm	cool	infrequent showers
October	4 Adverse	cool	chilly	infrequent showers/snow flurries
November	0 Bad	chilly	chilly	infrequent snow flurries
December	0 Bad	chilly	cold	infrequent snow flurries

Summary

Cody is dramatically situated a mile high on sagebrush-covered benchlands far below the eastern sentinels of mountain ranges which extend westward into Yellowstone National Park. **Winter** days are short and chilly, and evenings are cold. Snowfall in the area is surprisingly infrequent, light, and unusable for winter sports except in the distant mountains. **Spring** weather becomes pleasant in May, with the arrival of warm days, cool evenings, and occasional showers. **Summer** is delightful, with long, relatively hot days and warm evenings occasionally disrupted by brief thundershowers. All of the wonderful natural attractions of the Cody County are comfortably accessible in this season. **Fall** usually begins with the return of cool days and unpredictable snow flurries, mixed with agreeable periods of relatively warm, dry "Indian Summer" weather.

ATTRACTIONS & DIVERSIONS

★ **Buffalo Bill Dam**   *6 mi. W on US 20*
When the Shoshone Dam (renamed in 1947) was completed in 1910, it was the world's highest. The concrete-arch structure is 328 feet high, with a crest length of only 200 feet. The canyon view from the crest is spectacular — and unsettling. From the visitor parking lot, access is via a solid rock tunnel and a lot of steps.

★ **Buffalo Bill Historical Center**   *.4 mi. W at 720 Sheridan Av.*   587-4771
This is the nation's most comprehensive treasure house of Western Americana. From a small museum started in memory of Col. William Cody, it has grown into a preeminent four-part complex housing the finest collection of Western art and memorabilia ever assembled. Open daily in summer, it is closed on Monday the rest of the year, and closed December thru February. Included are the:

   ★ **Whitney Gallery of Western Art** — The world's most inclusive collection of nineteenth century Western art is highlighted by superb exhibits of works by both Charles M. Russell and Frederic Remington.

   ★ **Buffalo Bill Museum** — Thousands of his personal belongings are artistically displayed to provide a feeling for the life and times of the legendary frontiersman and showman.

   ★ **Winchester Museum** — Recently transferred from its original home in New Haven, Connecticut, are 5,000 firearms and accessories dating back as much as two thousand years. Here is one of the world's most prestigious and comprehensive collections of weapons.

   ★ **Plains Indian Museum** — Personal belongings of some of the nineteenth century's most renowned Indians are showcased among notable exhibits of tribal costumes, weapons, jewelry, and other artifacts.

★ **Buffalo Bill Monument**   *.4 mi. W at Sheridan Av./8th St.*
Photogenically positioned at the western end of the main street is one of the largest bronze equestrian statues in the world. This monument to Buffalo Bill and the adjoining acreage occupied by the Historical Center were donated to Cody by Gertrude Vanderbilt Whitney in 1924.

Buffalo Bill State Park   *9 mi. W on US 20*   587-9227
A several-mile-long reservoir behind Buffalo Bill Dam is the feature of this park. Along the shore are naturalistic picnicking and day use facilities and a campground, plus a commercial marina and boat ramp. Boating and trout fishing are popular.

Cody Mural   *.5 mi. NE at Wyoming Av./17th St.*   587-3290
Edward Grigware, a famous Cody artist, completed this dramatic painting of the early history of the Mormon religion in 1949. It may be viewed in the domed foyer of the Church of Jesus Christ of Latter-Day Saints any day (except Sunday morning) in summer.

Cody Park   *downtown at Sheridan Av./10th St.*
This tree-shaded, block-square park has picnic tables, drinking fountains, restrooms, a bandshell, a tennis court, a talking soda pop machine, and a miniature golf course.

Flying

★   **Cody Aero Service**   *3 mi. SE on US 20 at Cody Airport*   587-5095
Airplane flights ranging from twenty minutes to an hour can be reserved here. Passengers are given thrilling bird's-eye views of the majestic wilderness between Cody and Yellowstone Park.

Golf

   Olive-Glenn Country Club   *.8 mi. S via 11th St. at 802 Meadow Ln.*   587-5551
Panoramic views are a feature of this relatively level 18-hole golf course. It is open to the public, and has a pro shop, club and cart rentals, plus lighted tennis courts, and a restaurant and bar.

Library   *downtown at 1057 Sheridan Av.*   587-6204
The Park County Library is in a handsome contemporary building that includes a bright and comfortable periodical reading room. Closed Sun.

Newton Lake   *5 mi. NW: 2 mi. NW via WY 120 & 3 mi. W along Cody Canal*
This hard-to-find little lake, reached by a well-graded dirt road, is locally popular for swimming, sunbathing, boating, and fishing. The picturesque view of nearby Red Butte is impressive.

★ **North Fork Valley**   *for approx. 50 mi. W on US 20*
Snow-capped peaks provide a dramatic backdrop for Buffalo Bill Reservoir; the "Chinese Wall," "Holy City," and other strange lava formations; the nation's first ranger station; and an outstanding assortment of lodges, guest ranches, campgrounds, picnic areas, hiking and horseback trails, and fishing sites along the valley of the North Fork of the Shoshone River. An unforgettably scenic paved highway parallels the river between Buffalo Bill Dam and the eastern entrance of Yellowstone Park.

★ **Old Trail Town**   *3 mi. W via US 20*   *587-5302*
Historic buildings and relics of the Wyoming frontier are authentically displayed adjacent to still-visible ruts of a wagon trail through the original Cody townsite. A saloon, general store, schoolhouse, and other structures were obtained from remote locations throughout the northwestern part of the state and carefully reassembled here. An outlaw cabin from the "Hole-in-the-Wall" Country used by Butch Cassidy and the Sundance Kid, and the grave of Jeremiah "Liver Eating" Johnson are highlights. The memorable complex is the continuing life's work of Bob Edgar, a local historian and artist.

★ **River Running**
The excitement of whitewater is coupled with the enjoyment of a scenic river during two-hour float trips through a picturesque red rock canyon near town. Reservations can be made daily in summer at:
Cody's Shoshone River Float Trips *.3 mi. E at Sheridan Av./16th St.*   *587-3535*
Wyoming River Trips   *.3 mi. E at Sheridan Av./17th St.*   *587-6661*

★ **Shoshone National Forest**   *W of town*   *527-6241*
The nation's oldest national forest frames the entire eastern side of Yellowstone National Park and extends for another hundred miles to the south. Major attractions include the scenic Southfork, Northfork, and Sunlight valleys; Buffalo Bill's Wapiti hunting lodge; Wapiti Ranger Station, the first built with government funds; North Absaroka, South Absaroka, Stratified Glacier, and Popo Agie Wilderness Areas; and most of the Dinwoody Glacier (the largest in the American Rockies). Innumerable trails give hikers, backpackers, and fishermen access to a myriad of peaks, canyons, lakes, rivers, and streams throughout the forest. An outstanding variety of wilderness pack trips are another way for visitors to experience the vastness and unspoiled grandeur of this superlative high country in summer. Big game attracts sportsmen from all over the world in the fall, and cross-country skiing and snowmobiling are popular in winter.

★ **Southfork Valley**   *for approx. 40 mi. SW on WY 291*
The unspoiled little valley carved by the South Fork of the Shoshone River fulfills everyone's fantasy of what the Old West looked like at its best. Deer and antelope still graze sagebrush-covered rangelands beneath awesome snow-capped peaks. A mostly-paved highway provides easy access to long-established guest ranches, and to campgrounds, picnic areas, and hiking trails well-situated to give visitors an excuse to linger.

★ **Sunlight Country**   *approx. 40 mi. NW via WY 120 & WY 296*
A graded dirt road over a high pass is the shortest route between Cody and the breathtaking natural beauty of a remote mountain-rimmed wonderland of rivers, forests, and meadows with an abundance of scenic campgrounds, picnic areas, hiking trails, and fishing sites.

Warm Water Features

★   **Colter's Hell** *3 mi. W via US 20 & dirt rds. on N side of Shoshone River*
It is believed that, in 1808, John Colter (of the Lewis and Clark Expedition) became the first white explorer to pass through this area and Yellowstone Park. The now-extinct geyser basin just west of Cody may have been active enough then to have been the "Colter's Hell" of his description — with geysers, hot pools, and bubbling mud. Today the area is poorly publicized, difficult to find, unmarked from the dirt access roads, and thoroughly fascinating because it is so unspoiled. Features include giant dry hot springs craters; dry geyser cones that dwarf Old Faithful's; tiny bubbling hot springs and Indian soaking pools at the base of a cliff by the river; and tepee rings undisturbed since the nineteenth century when tribes gathered in this "neutral area" for therapeutic bathing in the springs. Adjacent to the parking lot for Shoshone River float trips is the remnant of historic DeMaris Hot Springs. The foundation of the original swimming pool is still filled with warm effervescent mineral springs water issuing from a natural vent in the pool's deep end.

★ **Thermopolis Hot Springs State Park** *84 mi. SE on WY 120 - Thermopolis* *864-2636*
The world's largest single mineral hot springs is located on the banks of the Big Horn River at the north edge of Thermopolis. Millions of gallons pour forth daily at a constant 135°F. This and other springs result in an enchanting area of mineral deposits and pools called Rainbow Terrace. A nearby State Bathhouse has indoor and outdoor pools overlooking the colorful mineral deposits. Another complex, the Star Plunge, has big indoor and outdoor pools, a hot soaking pool, a delightful steam grotto hollowed into a cliff, and a new, long, and exciting warm water slide. Elsewhere in the park are giant mineral deposit cones, a herd of bison, shady picnic facilities, a motor lodge, and a campground. Contact the Thermopolis Chamber of Commerce (864-2636) for more information.

★ **Yellowstone National Park** *53 mi. W on US 20* *344-7381*
The nation's first (1872) and largest (3,472 square miles) national park in the lower forty-eight states is about an hour's drive west of town. The world's most unusual natural preserve is symbolized by "Old Faithful," the famous relatively predictable geyser. Thousands of other thermal spectacles are scattered throughout the enormous park, ranging from clear hot geothermal pools; boiling, bubbling mud pots; and beautiful hot springs terraces; to a river made warm and swimmable by the many hot springs pouring into it. A scenic loop drive provides panoramic views of snow-capped peaks, vast pine forests, meadows with a remarkable variety of wild animals, crystal clear rivers, spectacular waterfalls, and one of the world's largest and clearest high mountain lakes. Just beyond the heavily-trafficked loop highway, the largest continuous wilderness south of Canada awaits the adventurous. Park roads are usually open from May 1 to October 31. For most of the remainder of the year, these roads offer an unforgettable experience to snowmobilers and cross-country skiers.

SHOPPING
Cody has a compact downtown concentrated along Sheridan Avenue east of the courthouse. Handsome rows of shops offer a full range of conventional goods and services. In keeping with the town's developing role as a preeminent treasury of Western lore, several Western fine art galleries have opened in recent years.

Specialty Shops
★ **Big Horn Gallery** *downtown at 1167 Sheridan Av.* *587-6762*
Limited editions and collector prints, plus original paintings and sculpture by Western artists, are attractively and informatively displayed.

★ **Buffalo Bill Historical Center** *.4 mi. W at 720 Sheridan Av.* *587-3243*
Prints of some of the famed Russell and Remington paintings displayed in the Whitney Gallery are sold, along with original Western art and crafts, Indian jewelry, and books.

Cody Country Art League *.3 mi. W at 836 Sheridan Av.* *587-3597*
Original works by local artists are nicely displayed in a historic log building. Closed Sun.

Post Office Store *downtown at 1121 13th St.* *587-3351*
A selection of books on the West and topographic maps of the area, plus a good assortment of magazines and newspapers, are carried in this eclectic little store.

★ **Sage Brush Gallery** *downtown at 1215 Sheridan Av.* *527-6518*
First-rate Western paintings and bronzes by prominent local artists are featured.

★ **Thunder Horse Gallery** *.6 mi. W at 720 Allen Av.* *587-4549*
This handsome new gallery offers a variety of museum-quality paintings and sculpture by contemporary Western artists.

Wagon Wheel Gallery *downtown at 1414 Sheridan Av.* *527-7196*
Western originals and prints by local and regional artists are featured.

NIGHTLIFE
An excellent night rodeo is the highlight of most summer evenings in town. There are also a few places with live music and dancing, and melodramas are presented during the summer.

Buffalo Bill Village Theater *.3 mi. E at 1701 Sheridan Av.* *587-5555*
Family-oriented melodramas and musicals are staged nightly in a tourist complex.

★ **Cassie's Supper Club** *1.7 mi. W on US 20* *587-3383*
Live music and dancing are featured most nights in a rambling old-time roadhouse. The rustic, unabashedly real-West saloon atmosphere makes this the favorite of natives and visitors.

Daisy Belle Lounge   *.3 mi. E at 1701 Sheridan Av.*   *587-5544*
The casual, comfortable lounge in the Holiday Inn has a well-known Western painting, "Bottoms Up," by Cody's Ed Grigware. Live music and dancing are offered most nights.

Silver Saddle Lounge   *downtown at 1192 Sheridan Av.*   *587-4221*
The lounge in the Irma Hotel was "modernized" years ago and lost Buffalo Bill's splendid cherrywood bar to the hotel's family-oriented coffee shop, but it's still a convenient gathering place in the heart of town.

RESTAURANTS
Restaurants in town are plentiful, plain, and tourist family-oriented. Fortunately, several dining rooms with authentic Western decor and furnishings, and homestyle meals, are open to the public in the historic lodges west of town.

★ **Brannon's Wilderness Lodge**   *32 mi. W via US 20 & (3.5 mi.) dirt rd.*   *527-7817*
D only. Closed Sun.-Wed.   *Very Expensive*
Gourmet Italian cuisine, in many-course prix fixe dinners, is featured in the Cody Country's most unusual dining experience. A maximum of twenty people are served amidst romantic elegance in an artfully remodeled log cabin high in the mountains — by reservation only.

Cassie's Supper Club   *1.7 mi. W on US 20*   *587-3383*
D only.   *Moderate*
Good steaks and hearty portions have been the hallmark of this rustic roadhouse for decades. Old-fashioned American specialties are complemented by casual Western decor in several dining rooms. A notable bar adjoins.

Goff Creek Lodge   *41 mi. W on US 20*   *587-3753*
B-L-D.   *Moderate*
Homestyle meals and fresh baked breads and pies are served to the public and lodge guests in an authentic Old Western dining room. Large stone fireplaces distinguish both the restaurant and atmospheric bar.

The Green Gables   *downtown at 937 Sheridan Av.*   *587-4640*
B-L-D.   *Moderate*
The favorite place in town for breakfast specializes in many kinds of pancakes and several flavors of syrups. Buffets are offered for lunch and dinner. A pleasant picture window view of the park across the street contributes to the casual dining room's popularity.

Griff's Place   *19 mi. W on US 20*   *587-3701*
D only.   *Moderate*
Steaks are a specialty in a historic log building that now houses a restaurant with three wood-trimmed Western-style dining rooms. Live music is an added treat on weekends.

Hidden Valley Ranch Supper Club   *15 mi. SW via WY 291*   *587-5090*
D only.   *Moderate*
Homemade meals and baked goods are emphasized in a big dining room outfitted with classic Western decor and furnishings at a guest ranch in Southfork Valley. A handsome bar adjoins.

Shoshone Lodge   *48 mi. W on US 20*   *587-4044*
B-L-D.   *Moderate*
Homestyle meals are occasionally accompanied by freshly baked breads. But the real crowd-pleaser is the genuine sixty-year-old hunting lodge-style dining room with its great stone fireplace, polished pine wood floors, and rough log walls displaying trophy animals.

LODGING
Accommodations in Cody are plentiful and disappointingly plain. However, America's greatest concentration of historic Western lodges and guest ranches is located in the scenic valleys west of town. Most of the lodges and ranches are closed in winter and spring. Most motels in town stay open year-round and reduce prices by at least 20% apart from summer.

Big Bear Motel   *3 mi. W on US 20*   *587-3117*
This single-level modern motel has a large outdoor pool. Each room has a cable TV.
   #34,#36 —   K bed...$32
   regular room —   D bed...$32

Brannon's Wilderness Lodge *32 mi. W via US 20 & (3.5 mi.) dirt rd.* *527-7817*
Several newly remodeled half-century-old cabins are spaced along a mountain stream near the area's finest dining room. Each cabin has a wood-burning fireplace. A Continental breakfast is brought to the room.

    deluxe room — 1 BR, 2 T & 2 D beds...$50
    regular room — cabin, D bed...$40

Buckaroo Motel *.5 mi. E on US 20 at 1701 Central Av.* *587-4295*
This small single-level **bargain** motel has cable color TV in each simply furnished room.

    regular room — D bed...$29

Cedar Mountain Lodge *.3 mi. W at 803 Sheridan Av.* *587-2248*
Within a stroll of the Historical Center and downtown, this **bargain** single-level log cabin-style motel has the area's only indoor pool. Each room has a TV.

    motel unit — phone, color TV, Q bed...$37
    regular room — small cabin, B/W TV, D bed...$27

Cody Athletic Club & Motel *3 mi. W on US 20* *527-7131*
A large outdoor mineral springs pool is surrounded by a modern, single-level motel. Guests have free use of the pool, plus the saunas, whirlpool, steam room, racquetball courts, and exercise room in an adjoining athletic club. Each simply furnished room has a phone and color TV.

    regular room — Q bed...$38

Colonial Inn *1 mi. SW on US 20* *587-4208*
An outdoor pool with a mountain view is the feature of this modern single-level motel. Each room has a phone and cable color TV.

    #39 — pvt. view to the canyon from Q bed...$40
    regular room — Q bed...$40

★ **Irma Hotel** *downtown at 1192 Sheridan Av.* *587-4221*
Still the most illustrious landmark downtown, Buffalo Bill's turn-of-the-century hotel is being restored. There is a large, family-oriented dining room/coffee shop with Buffalo Bill's splendid cherrywood back bar, and a lounge. All of the restored rooms have a phone, cable color TV, a private bath, and some period furnishings.

    "Buffalo Bill" #12 — suite, spacious, corner view of main st., 2 T & D beds...$47
    "Colonel Cody" #20 — suite, spacious, good main st. view, 2 D beds...$47
    regular room — in hotel annex, D bed...$36

Mountaineer Court *downtown at 1015 Sheridan Av.* *587-2221*
Convenient to everything in town, this modern single-level motel has a small outdoor pool. Each room has a phone and cable color TV.

    regular room — Q bed...$35

★ **The Skytel Ranch** *21 mi. W on US 20 at 2978 North Fork Hwy.* *587-4029*
A large outdoor view pool, a tennis court, and a nearby 5,000 foot airstrip are features of this working ranch. In addition to various ranch activities, there is a casual restaurant in the headquarters building with the best panoramic views on the Northfork. Rustic (duplex) log cabins have color TV and a tub/shower with an in-tub steam bath.

    #1,#2 — 2 BR, spacious, kit., metal fireplace in LR, 2 T & 2 D beds...$70
    #9,#8 — small windows on 3 sides, mt. views, 2 D beds...$50
    regular room — D bed...$38

Sunset Motor Inn - Best Western *.7 mi. SW on US 20 at 1601 8th St.* *587-4265*
An outdoor pool is a feature of this large modern single-level motel near the Buffalo Bill Historical Center. Each of the nicely furnished rooms has a phone and cable color TV.

    regular room — Q bed...$45

Super 8 Motel *1 mi. SW on US 20* *527-6214*
This new **bargain** motel is part of a major chain. Each room has a phone and cable color TV with movies.

    regular room — D bed...$30

Trail Inn *23 mi. W on US 20* *587-3741*
The older (duplex) log cabin rooms here are a **bargain** located halfway along the North Fork Valley. A small rustic restaurant serves all meals.

    #8,#9 — some mt. view, off hwy., D bed...$30
    regular room — D bed...$30

UXU   *34 mi. W on US 20*   *587-2143*

Secluded along the North Fork River, this older guest ranch offers fishing, horseback riding, and hiking trails. The Western-style dining room has mountain views. Simply furnished rustic log cabins all have showers.

#1 — kit., fireplace, windows on 3 sides, remote locale by river,   D bed...$46

regular room —   D bed...$32

Wapiti Valley Inn   *18 mi. W on US 20*   *587-3961*

Deep in the North Fork Valley is a plain little **bargain** motel with a small pool, (fee) horseback riding, and a restaurant. Each no-frills cabin has a bathroom and TV.

regular room —   D bed...$30

Wise Choice Motel   *22 mi. W on US 20*   *587-5004*

This newer **bargain** motel is located about halfway along the North Fork Valley. There is a whirlpool, and each room has color TV.

regular room —   Q bed...$30

CAMPGROUNDS

There are numerous small, relatively primitive campgrounds in the mountains west of town. The best are in splendid locations by a river surrounded by towering peaks. Campgrounds in and near town offer complete facilities in less picturesque surroundings.

Buffalo Bill State Park   *11 mi. W on US 20*   *587-9227*

This large state operated facility by Buffalo Bill Reservoir features boating, water-skiing, and fishing. Boat rentals and a boat ramp are available at a nearby marina. The campground has pit toilets only — no showers or hookups. Each site has a picnic table and a fire area. Most are shaded by cottonwood trees near the reservoir's high-water shoreline.   base rate...$5

Gateway Motel and Campground   *1.8 mi. W on US 20*   *587-2561*

A plain, private campground is located in a level, shaded area behind some cabins. Rental horses and trail rides are featured. Flush toilets, hot showers, and hookups are available. Each closely spaced, tree-shaded site has a picnic table. There is a separate tenting area.
                                                                      base rate...$7

Hitching Post Campground   *19 mi. W on US 20*   *587-4149*

This privately operated facility is on open benchlands in the middle of the expansive North Fork Valley. There is a private fishing pond (fee), fishing on the nearby river, an outdoor pool, rec room, mini-golf, pony rides, and horse trails/rentals. Flush toilets, hot showers, and hookups are available. Level grassy sites have scenic mountain views, picnic tables, and fire areas. Some are tree-shaded.   base rate...$6.75

Wapiti   *29 mi. W on US 20*   *587-3291*

This Shoshone National Forest campground is beautifully situated by the North Fork River in the heart of the Wyoming Rockies. River fishing and hiking are popular activities. Pit toilets are provided, but there are no showers or hookups. Each of the well-spaced, tree-shaded sites has a picnic table and fire area.   base rate...$3

SPECIAL EVENTS

★ **The Cody Stampede**   *Stampede Grounds and downtown*   *4th of July*

The spirit of the "Old West" thrives during a three day celebration that includes a mile-long parade downtown, a carnival in the park, and a fireworks display on the night of the 4th visible from many places in town. But the main event is the Stampede, one of the West's major rodeos. Top cowboys from all over compete in a large arena with a perfect Old West setting.

★ **The Cody Night Rodeo**   *Stampede Grounds*   *early June to late August*

This authentic little rodeo offers all of the major rodeo events every evening (except during the Stampede) in summer. For more than a third of a century, visitors and residents have enjoyed the action from bleachers with a panoramic mountain backdrop. The Night Rodeo and the Stampede are the basis for Cody's claim to the title — "the Rodeo Capital of the World."

OTHER INFORMATION

Area Code: *307*

Zip Code: *82414*

Cody Country Chamber of Commerce   *.3 mi. W at 836 Sheridan Av.*   *587-2297*

Shoshone Natl. For.-Sup. Ofc. *3 mi. W on US 20 at 225 W. Yellowstone Av.*   *527-6241*

Jackson, Wyoming

Elevation:

6,234 feet

Population (1980):

4,511

Population (1970):

2,688

Location:

267 mi. NE
of Salt Lake City

Jackson is a year-round rendezvous for leisure pursuits in the heart of the Rocky Mountains. An astonishing number of diversions are packed into the little town at the edge of a broad grass-and-sage-covered valley between the two highest ranges in Wyoming. At an elevation well over a mile above sea level, winters are long, cold, and snowy enough to support an outstanding diversity of winter sports facilities in the area, including a major ski area in town and another on the nearby Tetons. Jackson is always filled with visitors in summer. The weather is usually fine for exploring both Grand Teton National Park and Yellowstone National Park with their spellbinding alpine and thermal attractions, and their countless outdoor recreation opportunities. Scenic golf courses and elaborate tennis complexes compete with unusual diversions like Old Western stagecoach rides, high-tech alpine slides and picturesque hot springs pool, plus a host of first-rate Western art galleries and specialty shops in and around town. Fall is uncrowded, and the high country is unforgettably beautiful after the first snows whiten the peaks and set the aspens ablaze with color.

The town was named for Davey Jackson, who had an unwritten fur trading right to the broad Snake River valley at the base of the Tetons. The valley became known as "Jackson's Big Hole," which was eventually shortened to Jackson Hole. Permanent settlers didn't arrive until the 1880s. The townsite was laid out in 1897 in a location convenient to ranches and homesteaders in the valley. "Dude ranching" also quickly became popular as cattle ranchers began to offer guide services and lodging after big game hunting became famous in the area. Grand Teton National Park was created in 1929. By the time the park was greatly expanded in 1950, the "Hole" was already a famous summer recreation site. Since then, expansion of skiing facilities on the mountain in town and development of world-class downhill runs nearby on the Tetons have confirmed Jackson's role as a year-round visitor destination. Also in recent decades, many well-known Western artists have made their homes here, and their works are displayed in numerous outstanding galleries.

Downtown Jackson reflects residents' desire to retain the town's original frontier spirit and appearance. Elkhorn arches, board sidewalks, and clapboard and log buildings enhance the compact business district that surrounds the well-landscaped town square. A phenomenal assortment of fine art galleries, Western ware shops, live theaters, atmospheric bars and gourmet restaurants are all within an easy stroll of the square. An abundance of accommodations, including some of the town's finest, share the same area. Nearby, backed by views of the Teton Range, several of the West's most luxurious resorts feature amenities appropriate to the majestic alpine setting.

Jackson, Wyoming

WEATHER PROFILE *Vokac Weather Rating*

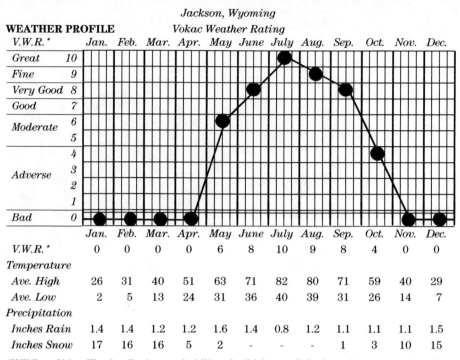

V.W.R.*	Jan.	Feb.	Mar.	Apr.	May	June	July	Aug.	Sep.	Oct.	Nov.	Dec.
V.W.R.*	0	0	0	0	6	8	10	9	8	4	0	0
Temperature												
Ave. High	26	31	40	51	63	71	82	80	71	59	40	29
Ave. Low	2	5	13	24	31	36	40	39	31	26	14	7
Precipitation												
Inches Rain	1.4	1.4	1.2	1.2	1.6	1.4	0.8	1.2	1.1	1.1	1.1	1.5
Inches Snow	17	16	16	5	2	-	-	-	1	3	10	15

*V.W.R. = Vokac Weather Rating: probability of mild (warm & dry) weather on any given day.

Forecast

Month	V.W.R.*		Temperatures		Precipitation
			Daytime	Evening	
January	0	Bad	cold	frigid	occasional snowstorms
February	0	Bad	cold	frigid	occasional snowstorms
March	0	Bad	chilly	cold	occasional snowstorms
April	0	Bad	cool	chilly	occasional snow flurries/showers
May	6	Moderate	cool	chilly	occasional showers/snow flurries
June	8	Very Good	warm	cool	occasional showers
July	10	Great	warm	cool	infrequent showers
August	9	Fine	warm	cool	occasional showers
September	8	Very Good	warm	cool	infrequent showers
October	4	Adverse	cool	chilly	infrequent snow flurries/showers
November	0	Bad	chilly	cold	infrequent snowstorms
December	0	Bad	cold	frigid	occasional snowstorms

Summary

More than 6,200 feet above sea level, Jackson is just south of Grand Teton National Park. It is on the edge of the broad floor of Jackson Hole where sagebrush-rangeland abuts pine clad mountains. **Winter** days are short and cold, and evenings are bitter cold. Coupled with occasional snowstorms, conditions are fine for hardy hordes of winter sports enthusiasts here to enjoy famed winter sports complexes in town and on the nearby Tetons. Good **spring** skiing continues through April. Then, the area becomes unusable when snow cover turns to mud and slush as a result of freezing and thawing, frequent showers, and snow flurries which continue through Memorial Day. **Summer** is fine, with long warm days, cool evenings, and occasional light thundershowers. This is the only time to get out and explore the area's matchless natural attractions in light sportswear. **Fall** begins with warm days. But, before Halloween, cool days, freezing nights, and snow flurries foretell the return of winter.

410

ATTRACTIONS & DIVERSIONS

Aerial Tramways

★ **Snow King Mountain Chairlift** *.5 mi. S at King St./Snow King Av.*   *733-5200*
During the summer, a double chairlift takes passengers up Snow King Mountain to splendid panoramic views of town and the Tetons.

★   **Teton Village Gondola** *12 mi. NW via WY 22 & WY 290 in Teton Village*   *733-2291*
Large gondolas carry passengers 2.5 miles from the valley floor to the top of 10,446 foot Rendezvous Mountain. The view of the Teton Range and all of Jackson Hole is breathtaking. Guided nature walks and hiking trails are provided at the summit, which is also used as a trailhead by backpackers. The tram operates daily from June into Sept.

★ **Alpine Slide**   *.7 mi. SE at 400 E. Snow King Dr.*   *733-7680*
A chairlift on a slope of Snow King Mountain offers a fine view of the Tetons and Jackson Hole. From the top of the lift, two parallel slide paths wind around trees and through meadows. Riders guide an easily-braked, toboggan-like sled down either fiberglass path at the speed of their choice for an exhilarating or leisurely ride.

★ Bicycling

There are no exclusive bikeways, but bicycling is very popular in summer. Some of the roads in Jackson Hole have wide shoulders, and all provide sensational views of mountain scenery. Bicycle rentals and tour suggestions are available at:

Hoback Sports	*downtown at 40 S. Millward St.*	*733-5335*
Teton Cyclery	*downtown at 175 N. Glenwood St.*	*733-4386*
Wildernest Sports	*12 mi. NW in Teton Village*	*733-4297*

★ Boat Rentals

Motorboats and canoes can be rented at:

Colter Bay Marina	*38 mi. N on US 89*	*543-2811*
Leek's Marina	*30 mi. NW via US 89 on Teton Park Rd.*	*543-2494*
Teton Boating Co.	*20 mi. NW via US 89 on Teton Park Rd.*	*733-2703*
Jackson Hole Ski & Sports (inflatables)	*.3 mi. W at 485 W. Broadway*	*733-4449*

Boat Rides

Colter Bay Marina	*38 mi. N on US 89*	*543-2811*

Scenic cruises or guided fishing trips on Jackson Lake are offered. Motorboat and canoe rentals are also available.

★   **Teton Boating Company**   *20 mi. NW via US 89 on Teton Park Rd.*   *733-3703*
A cruise across the southern end of Jenny Lake gives passengers awe-inspiring views of the Tetons, and ends at a trail to picturesque Hidden Falls. A boat leaves every twenty minutes daily in summer.

★ **Bridger-Teton National Forest**   *surrounding town*   *733-2752*
This giant forest is the nation's largest outside of Alaska. Features include the Gros Ventre Slide — the result of a massive earth slide which created a dam more than 200 feet high and a lake nearly five miles long. The Teton Wilderness is a vast tract of unspoiled high country between Grand Teton and Yellowstone National Parks. The Bridger Wilderness to the southeast includes the west slopes of the Wind River Range, with more than 1,000 lakes scattered beneath the state's highest mountain (Gannett Peak) and the Rocky Mountain's largest system of glaciers outside of Canada. An extensive network of backcountry roads provides access to trailheads for hundreds of miles of scenic wilderness trails. Camping, hiking, backpacking, mountain climbing, pack trips, hunting, fishing, and winter sports are seasonally popular.

Climbing

★   **Exum Mountain Guides**   *20 mi. NW via US 89 on Teton Park Rd.*   *733-2297*
Mountain climbing courses both for beginners and experienced mountaineers are taught on the rock faces and glaciers of the Grand Teton and other peaks in the Teton Range.

★ Flying

Visitors can now achieve an eagle's perspective of the high country when they fly through the canyons of the Tetons, or hover close by the shoulders of the awesome peaks, or float silently over the "Hole." For information and reservations call:

Jackson Hole Aviation (airplane)	*9 mi. N off US 89 at Airport*	*733-4767*
Kjerstad Helicopters (helicopter)	*1.5 mi. SW on US 89*	*733-2435*
Red Baron Flying Service (hot-air balloon, glider)		*733-7961*

Golf

★ **Jackson Hole Golf & Tennis Club**   *6 mi. N off US 89*   *733-3111*
Sporting a fabulous view of the Teton Range, this relatively level 18-hole championship course (redesigned by Robert Trent Jones) is open to the public. There is a pro shop, club and cart rentals, and a fine restaurant, bar, and patio that overlook the links and Tetons. Several tennis courts and a swimming pool are also available.

★ **Grand Teton National Park**   *begins 3 mi. N on US 89*   *733-2800*
Founded in 1929 and greatly expanded in 1950, this has become one of the nation's most popular parks. The renowned centerpiece — the Grand Teton (13,770 feet) — is the highest peak this far north in the Rocky Mountains, and one of the world's most photographed mountains. Majestic peaks with granite cliffs, glaciers, waterfalls, streams, lakes, and forests provide a superb playground. Hundreds of miles of scenic trails entice hearty backpackers, hikers, rock climbers, horseback riders, campers, and fishermen to leave their cares, and cars, behind. Far below, the Snake River accommodates a remarkable number of scenic float trips as it meanders through the park. Boating, fishing, and cruises are enjoyed on twenty-mile-long Jackson Lake, and swimming is surprisingly popular in mid-summer at a pebbly beach with a magnificent backdrop near Colter Bay, and in nearby String Lake.

★ **Horseback Riding**
In addition to guided scenic trail rides, there are breakfast rides, evening campfire rides, steak fry rides, and hayrides destined for cowboy cookouts. Arrangements can be made at several area corrals, including:

Bar-T-Five Outfitters *.7 mi. SE at 400 E. Snow King Av.*		*733-3534*
Jackson Hole Trail Rides *12 mi. NW in Teton Village*		*733-5047*
Jackson Lake Lodge Corrals *31 mi. N on US 89*		*733-2811*
Rising Sage Stables *2 mi. N on US 89*		*733-6558*
Scott's Horse Palace (guides not required) *9 mi. S on US 89*		*733-2590*
Teton Trail Rides *20 mi. N via US 89 on Teton Park Rd.*		*733-2108*

★ **Jackson Hole**   *66 mi. loop via US 89 & Teton Park Rd.*
The first panoramic view of the entire Teton Range as the highway crests a hill three miles north of Jackson is unforgettable. From there northward for about fifty miles, the Rockefeller Parkway provides continuous panoramas of the awesome Tetons and glimpses of the Snake River etched into sagebrush-covered rangeland. Returning by the Teton Park Road offers more intimate close-ups of peaks and glaciers, the Park's biggest lakes, and wildlife. A side road to the top of Signal Mountain rewards travelers with one of the most-photographed vistas in the nation.

★ **Library**   *downtown at 320 S. King St.*   *733-2164*
The Teton County Library occupies a handsome log cabin-style building. A magazine reading area, outfitted with comfortably upholstered chairs, has a picture window view of Snow King Mountain, as well as a number of fine Western paintings and sculptures.

★ **River Running**
Jackson is the base for one of the world's most popular rivers for both whitewater and scenic float trips. The Snake River is relatively gentle throughout Jackson Hole, and easygoing scenic floats beneath the magnificent Grand Teton are deservedly acclaimed. South of town, an eight mile stretch through the spectacular Snake River Canyon offers thrilling whitewater runs. In between, dory fishing expeditions for native cutthroat trout are popular. Nearly twenty professional companies offer half day, full day, and overnight river trips, and they provide all equipment and food. The Chamber of Commerce has a complete list, and brochures on each outfit.

★ **Snake River Canyon**   *begins 20 mi. S on US 89*
The highway parallels the Snake River southwestward from its junction with the Hoback River. Mountains tower thousands of feet on either side as the river plunges through a narrow defile. River runners can be watched as they maneuver through rapids hundreds of feet below the highway, which is carved into precipitous canyon walls.

★ **Town Square**   *Broadway/Cache St.*
The heart of town is a handsomely landscaped block square park featuring four walk-thru elk horn arches, picturesque boardwalks, and a stagecoach stop.

Warm Water Features

    Astoria Hot Springs   *15 mi. S on US 89*   733-2659

Warm mineral water is used to fill a large outdoor pool located by the Snake River. A well-maintained picnic area and a private campground are nearby.

★   **Firehole River** *109 mi. NW on US 89 - about 2 mi. S of Madison Jct.*

One of the West's most unusual attractions is near the western border of Yellowstone Park. An entire crystal clear river is warmed by hundreds of geothermal springs flowing into it. Fearless fun-lovers have discovered a picturesque little gorge where swimming the rapids to a calm pool downstream is an unforgettable experience. Pine-shaded grassy banks and dramatic rock formations lend an idyllic feeling to the enchanting setting.

★   **Granite Hot Springs** *30 mi. SE via US 89, US 189 & Granite Creek Rd.*

A concrete dam across a hot springs creek has created a memorable little pool backed by giant granite boulders surrounded by a pine forest. Forest Service campgrounds, picnic areas, and a dramatic waterfall are nearby. This is also a favorite cross-country skiing and snowmobile destination in winter.

    Teton Hot Pots   *downtown at 365 N. Cache St.*   733-7831

Private hot tub rooms with music can be rented by the hour. Guests also have access to a large public tub, a sauna, and showers.

Winter Sports

★   **Cross-Country Skiing**

From November to May, the broad floor of Jackson Hole becomes a brilliant snowscape, while geothermal features in Yellowstone Park seem even more impressive surrounded by enormous clouds of steam. Cross-country tours of these areas are becoming increasingly popular. All necessary equipment may be rented at several places, including:

    Jackson Hole Ski and Sports   *.3 mi. W at 485 W. Broadway*   733-4449

    Skinny Skis   *downtown at 65 W. Deloney Av.*   733-6094

    Teton Mountaineering   *downtown at 86 E. Broadway*   733-3595

    Dogsled Rides

★   **Nanook Dogsled Adventures** *downtown at NE corner of the square*   733-4821

Professional guides and registered sled dogs take guests on half day or full day trips, and on moonlit adventures for adults only.

★   **Grand Targhee Resort** *47 mi. NW via WY 22 & ID 33 - E of Driggs*   *(208)353-2304*

On the backside of the Teton Range, the vertical rise is 2,200 feet and the longest run is 2.5 miles. Elevation at the top is 10,200 feet. There are three double chairlifts. All facilities, services, and rentals are available at the base for both downhill and cross-country skiing. A restaurant, bar, and lodges are located at the base. The skiing season is late November to late April.

★   **High Mountain Helicopter Skiing**   *12 mi. NW in Teton Village*   733-3274

Heli-skiing and cross-country tours in the untracked snow of Jackson Hole's backcountry are offered on five mountain ranges.

★   **Jackson Hole Ski Area**   *12 mi. NW in Teton Village*   733-2292

The vertical rise is 4,140 feet which is the nation's highest, and the longest run is five miles. Elevation at the top is 10,450 feet. There is an aerial tramway, a triple chairlift, and five double chairlifts. All facilities, services, and rentals are available at the base for both downhill and cross-country skiing. Several restaurants, bars, and lodges are located at the base. The skiing season is December to mid-April.

★   **Sleigh Rides**   *5 mi. NE via E. Broadway*   733-9212

A horsedrawn sleigh takes passengers into an expansive snowy meadow that is the winter home of the largest elk herd in North America. Rides can be reserved daily from Christmas thru March.

★   **Sleigh Rides with Dinner**   *12 mi. NW in Teton Village*   733-3657

Lap robes are provided for a ride in a horsedrawn sleigh to a heated tent cabin where a steak dinner is served. Reservations must be made in advance at the Sojourner Inn.

★   **Snow King Mountain**   *.5 mi. S via Cache St. on Snow King Av.*   733-5200

The area's oldest major downhill skiing complex has a vertical rise of 1,550 feet, and the longest run is about one mile. Elevation at the top is 7,800 feet. The panorama of Jackson and the Teton Range is breathtaking. There are two double chairlifts. All facilities, services, and rentals are available at the base and downtown for both downhill and cross-country skiing. Restaurants, bars, and lodges are located at the base, and there are many more within five blocks. The skiing season is December to mid-April.

★ **Snowmobile Rentals**

From December to May, Jackson Hole, Granite Hot Springs, and Yellowstone Park are among the West's most popular destinations for guided or self-guided tours by snowmobile. Several places offer rentals and/or guided tours:

Flagg Ranch Village	*54 mi. N on US 89*	*733-4818*
Grand Teton Lodge Co.	*12 mi. N on US 89 - Moose*	*733-3449*
High Country	*.7 mi. SE at 400 E. Snow King Av.*	*733-5017*
Weeks Motor Co.	*1 mi. E at 1185 E. Broadway*	*733-2237*

★ **Yellowstone National Park**   *57 mi. N on US 89*   *344-7311*

The nation's first and most unusual national park has been a renowned destination for more than a century. "Old Faithful" is only the most predictable among many geysers. Collectively, the thousands of geothermal pools, bubbling mud pots, and hot springs terrace formations are unforgettable. The photogenic Grand Canyon of the Yellowstone is highlighted by two spectacular waterfalls, one twice as high as Niagara. Yellowstone Lake is the highest big lake on the continent. All of these attractions are located on an enormous sky-scraping plateau covered by a vast pine forest interspersed with meadows and snow-capped peaks extending well above timberline. Wildlife is abundant, and includes some of the nation's largest herds of buffalo, elk, and moose, as well as endangered species like grizzly bear and trumpeter swan. Just beyond the Park's famed loop drive to the southeast lies the nation's largest continuous wilderness area outside of Alaska.

SHOPPING

Boardwalks, log and natural wood buildings, rustic courtyards, and ubiquitous pine trees contribute to the distinctive "frontier atmosphere" of the compact downtown. Some of the West's finest art galleries, sporting goods, and Western wear stores, plus an outstanding array of specialty shops, are within two blocks of the delightful town square.

Food Specialties

★ **Beck Sausage**   *3 mi. S via US 89 on South Park Route*   *733-8343*
Excellent buffalo meat products are prepared and sold here. Buffalo sticks, salami, and jerky are specialties. A variety of gift packs can be shipped anywhere.

Jackson Drug Co.   *downtown at 15 E. Deloney Av.*   *733-2442*
Homemade ice cream sodas, shakes, and sundaes have attracted customers to the little soda fountain ever since this pharmacy was opened in 1912.

★ **Moose Wine Shop**   *12 mi. N via US 89 - Moose*   *733-2415*
Wyoming's most impressive wine collection has been drawing enophiles to this surprisingly remote location for many years.

Old West Wine Shop   *downtown at 49 W. Broadway*   *733-4695*
A good selection of wines, beers, and liquors is nicely displayed.

★ **Patty-Cake Patisserie**   *downtown at 135 W. Broadway*   *733-7864*
This tiny newer bakery features excellent sticky buns, plus croissants, strudel, and other pastries served to go — or at the coffee bar.

★ **Peppermint Parlour**   *downtown at 49 W. Broadway*   *733-3753*
Many delicious flavors of ice cream are made here and served in a red-and-white replica of an old-time ice cream parlour.

★ **Pub Wine & Liquors Shop**   *3 mi. S on US 89*   *733-6977*
In addition to excellent selections of wines, beers, and liquors, this store sells the outstanding breads made fresh daily in the Steak Pub upstairs.

★ **Star Valley Cheese Co.**   *54 mi. SW on US 89*   *883-2510*
The West's finest swiss cheese is made here. This and other cheeses are displayed and sold in a large retail shop adjoining the factory. Samples are offered.

★ **Sugar Mountain Taffy Co.**   *downtown at 60 E. Broadway*   *733-6168*
A dozen kinds of taffy are made here fresh daily. You can watch all of the steps, from pulling to wrapping, in their display window. They also make fudge and brittle.

Specialty Shops

★ **Galleries**

The unsurpassed scenery of the Teton Country has attracted working artists for years. Many have chosen Jackson Hole as their home. Today, well over a dozen excellent galleries, mostly concentrated within two blocks of the square, display an outstanding variety of pictures in all media, plus sculptures and jewelry. Contemporary and past masters have captured the spirit of the high country with art to suit every taste and price range. The following galleries illustrate the scope and quality of locally available works, but many others also merit attention by everyone interested in Western art.

★ **Made in Jackson Hole**   *downtown at 49 W. Broadway*   733-7710

Every item in this small shop is made in the area. The selection ranges from arts and crafts to foods and music.

★ **Overland Trail Galleries**   *downtown at 98 N. Center St.*   733-6534

Fine bronzes and paintings are displayed in several well-furnished rooms.

★ **Teton Book Shop**   *downtown at 10 W. Broadway*   733-9220

One of the West's finest bookstores has a large selection of general interest books and an outstanding display of material on Western Americana. Background music and comfortable chairs enhance the contemporary Western decor.

★ **Trailside Galleries**   *downtown at 105 N. Center St.*   733-3186

Museum-quality Western fine art is beautifully displayed in Jackson's most illustrious gallery.

★ **Two Grey Hills Gallery & Indian Arts** *downtown at 110 E. Broadway*   733-2677

The area's finest collection of authentic Indian jewelry, rugs, arts and crafts is artistically exhibited.

★ **Under the Willow Photo Gallery**   *downtown at 50 S. Cache St.*   733-6633

Original photographs that capture the grandeur and intimacy of the Tetons and Jackson Hole are featured.

★ **The Valley Book Store**   *downtown at 125 N. Cache St.*   733-4533

This inviting, well-organized shop specializes in Western Americana and books of regional interest. Browsers enjoy background music and complimentary tea.

★ **Western Ware**   *downtown around the town square*

Fronting on the Town Square is the West's most notable concentration of shops specializing in Western sportswear, hardware, recreation equipment, and supplies. Among the best are:

Jackson Hole Hardware *downtown at 48 E. Broadway*		733-2640
Jackson Sporting Goods *downtown at 25 W. Broadway*		733-3461
Ranch Shops *downtown at 10 E. Broadway*		733-3332
Wyoming Outfitters *18 E. Deloney Av.*		733-3877

NIGHTLIFE

The shootout on the town square every evening in summer sets the tone for a night on the town. The flavor of the Old West extends to melodramas presented in three local playhouses, a nightly rodeo, and distinctive bars featuring first-rate Western music for dancing. Classic Music Festival performances are an alternative on summer evenings.

★ **Alpenhof Lodge**   *12 mi. NW in Teton Village*   733-3242

Deitrich's Bar and Lounge is a popular place for conversation, live music, and dancing. Contemporary decor is complemented by a rock fireplace and plush furnishings, and there is a mountain-view sundeck.

Live Theater

There are three well-outfitted stage theaters downtown. Unfortunately, all play exclusively family-oriented melodramas and musical comedies. The productions are inevitably lightweight, but the acting can be good, the casts are enthusiastic, and the atmosphere is fine.

Dirty Dick's Wild West Theater *downtown at 140 N. Cache St.*	733-4775
Jackson Hole Playhouse *downtown at 145 W. Deloney Av.*	733-6994
Pink Garter Theater *downtown at 49 W. Broadway*	733-3670

★ **Log Cabin Saloon**   *.5 mi. N at 505 N. Cache St.*   733-7525

Live Western music for dancing is featured nightly in a newer split-level rustic-wood bar.

Mangy Moose Saloon *12 mi. NW via WY 22 & WY 390 in Teton Village*   *733-4913*
Live entertainment and dancing are offered most nights in this popular, two-level watering hole. A restaurant adjoins. Closed Apr.-May and Oct.-Nov.

★ **Million Dollar Cowboy Bar**   *downtown at 25 N. Cache St.*   *733-2207*
This vast Western showplace is the ultimate frontier-style saloon. Unique bentwoods and burls accent matchless pine log decor. Western saddles are used as bar stools. Hundreds of silver dollars are imbedded in the state's longest bar. Trophy animals and oil paintings cover the walls. Country/western music, dancing, and huge crowds are the rule each evening as they have been for decades.

★ **Pub Tavern**   *3 mi. S on US 89*   *733-6977*
One of Jackson's newest bars offers a luxurious mix of oak, brass, leather, and plants as an accompaniment to a picture window view of the Teton Range. It is a delightful spot for a quiet conversation. Outstanding steaks are served in the next room.

★ **Rancher Bar & Lounge**   *downtown at 20 E. Broadway*   *733-3886*
Various popular groups provide live music for dancing almost every evening in a durable lounge where padded booths and comfortable chairs are blended with modern Western decor.

★ **Shady Lady Saloon**   *.7 mi. SE at 400 E. Snow King Av.*   *733-5200*
In the Americana Snow King Resort, nightly entertainment and dancing are offered in a comfortable, contemporary Western-style lounge. Closed Sun.

★ **Silver Dollar Bar**   *downtown at Broadway/Glenwood St.*   *733-2190*
Live entertainment, including occasional "big name" floor shows, and dancing nightly during the summer have been popular for decades in the big showroom of the rebuilt Wort Hotel. Novel decor in the adjacent barroom might be described as "Western art deco," highlighted by a gracefully curved bar counter inlaid with more than two thousand silver dollars.

RESTAURANTS

In recent years, Jackson has become one of the West's gourmet havens. Dozens of tantalizing restaurants serve dishes ranging from prime cowboy-cut steaks to Continental gourmet specialties in rustic or refined dining rooms that capture the area's frontier spirit in unconventional ways.

Alice's Restaurant   *downtown at 145 N. Glenwood St.*   *733-4020*
B-L-D.   *Moderate*
American fare is accompanied by big homemade cinnamon rolls, biscuits, breads, and desserts, plus some Mexican specialties in an unassuming little cafe that is open twenty-four hours daily.

Alpenhof Garden Room *12 mi. NW via WY 22 & WY 390 in Teton Village*   *733-3242*
B-L-D.   *Expensive*
A Continental menu is offered. Many plants and Western paintings enhance the polished contemporary decor of several well-furnished dining areas in the hotel's large restaurant.

Americana Snow King Resort   *.7 mi. SE at 400 E. Snow King Av.*   *733-5200*
D only.   *Moderate*
American dishes are served in the large, contemporary Outlook Restaurant, appropriately named for expansive windows overlooking the ski slopes on Snow King Mountain. This updated, Western-style dining room adjoins a bright and cheerful coffee shop serving all meals. The hotel also has a casual steak house and a fine lounge.

★ **Anthony's Italian Restaurant**   *downtown at 50 S. Glenwood St.*   *733-3717*
L-D. No L on Sat. & Sun.   *Moderate*
Skillfully prepared authentic dishes and homemade bread are offered in the region's best Italian restaurant. Don't be put off by the very casual surroundings.

★ **Blue Lion**   *downtown at 160 N. Millward St.*   *733-3912*
L-D. Sun. brunch.   *Moderate*
Fine French cuisine and homemade desserts are served in an elegantly restored old house, and outdoors on an inviting deck.

★ **The Bunnery**   *downtown at 130 N. Cache St.*   *733-5474*
B-L.   *Moderate*
Homemade pastries, desserts, and breads are featured. They are served as a delicious accompaniment to fine omelets and other specialties in a pleasant dining room, or to go.

The Cadillac Grill   *downtown at 55 N. Cache St.*   *733-3279*
B-L-D.   *Moderate*
French-style donuts and fine cinnamon rolls are standouts among the many pastries made here (they're all available to go). This large, newly remodeled restaurant/bakery is a classy update of 1940s decor. Maroon and grey colors, mahogany trim and marble floors, and comfortable booths have been artistically used to create a pleasant new style in one of Jackson's most durable dining rooms.

★ **Dornan's Chuckwagon at Moose**   *12 mi. N via US 89 - Moose*   *733-2415*
B-L-D.   *Moderate*
Western Dutch-oven-style cooking and steaks are the right stuff for this enduring rustic cookhouse. When the weather is good, no one complains about the outdoor picnic table seating, because the awe-inspiring view of the Grand Teton is a heavyweight contender for the finest restaurant backdrop in the West. The wine selection in an adjacent shop is also outstanding.

Greminger House   *downtown at 170 N. Millward St.*   *733-2393*
L-D. No L on Sat. & Sun.   *Moderate*
American and Mexican specialties are offered amidst reproductions of Old Western decor and furnishings in this newer restaurant.

Heidelberg Inn   *8 mi. W on WY 22 - Wilson*   *733-3728*
L-D.   *Moderate*
German and American dishes are served in a large, comfortably furnished Bavarian-style lodge. A downstairs bar has ping-pong, pool, darts, and electronic games.

★ **Jedediah's Original House of Sourdough** *downtown at 135 E. Broadway*   *733-5671*
B-L-D.   *Moderate*
Sourdough cookery from biscuits to desserts is the specialty in this popular newer restaurant. Multicourse dinners (a soup tureen, salad, entree, fresh vegetable, potato, dessert, bread, and beverage) are featured in the evening. A pioneer log cabin was carefully remodeled into several nostalgic dining rooms, and there is outdoor dining when weather permits.

★ **Jenny Lake Lodge**   *25 mi. NW via US 89 on Teton Park Rd.*   *733-4647*
B-L-D.   *Very Expensive*
Skillfully prepared six-course gourmet dinners are offered from a short menu that varies according to seasonal availability of fresh ingredients. The spacious dining room is a study in plush frontier-style decor enhanced by fine Western paintings.

★ **Lost Horizons** *40 mi. NW via WY 22 & ID 33 - 6 mi. E of Driggs*   *(208)353-8226*
D only. Sun. brunch in summer. Closed Sept.-early Oct.   Very Expensive
Eight-course gourmet meals are served in a setting that lives up to the idea of a Rocky Mountain Shangri-La. A maximum of sixteen people spend several hours in the thoroughly adult environment of a unique restaurant in a spacious home overlooking the backside of the Grand Teton. Guests may also enjoy a romantic downstairs lounge furnished with sophisticated erotic art.

The Mangy Moose *12 mi. NW via WY 22 & WY 390 in Teton Village*   *733-4913*
D only. Closed Apr.-May & Oct.-Nov.   Moderate
American specialties include some surprising treats like smoked chicken breasts, and homemade peanut butter pie. The large, two-level dining room is very popular, and so are the tempting pastries in "Your Just Dessert" downstairs.

Peppermill Gourmet *36 mi. NW via WY 22 & ID 33 - E of Driggs*   *(208)354-2962*
D only.   *Expensive*
Oriental specialties are featured in leisurely six or eight-course dinners served in the simply furnished, intimate dining room of a contemporary home on the road to Grand Targhee Ski Area.

Ridenaur's Blue Room   *downtown at 75 N. Cache St.*   *733-3544*
D only.   *Low*
American and Continental specialties are served in a well-furnished dining room with a soup and salad bar adjoining the plush Open Range Restaurant.

★ **Ridenaur's Open Range Restaurant** *downtown at 75 N. Cache St.* *733-3544*
D only. Closed mid-Nov. to mid-Dec. *Moderate*
Delicious Continental and American specialties are preceded by an excellent complimentary pate. Elegant Western decor lends charm to Jackson's premier gourmet restaurant.

Spring Creek Ranch *2 mi. NW on Spring Gulch Rd.* *733-8731*
Contemporary American fare is served with a splendid view of the Tetons. This new resort's stylish Granary Restaurant is perched on a hill several hundred feet above the valley floor.

★ **The Steak Pub** *3 mi. S on US 89* *733-6977*
D only. *Moderate*
Some of the West's finest steaks command the center of attention among delicious American dishes served with a salad bar and three kinds of fresh homemade bread. Cozy dining rooms adjoin an ingratiating new lounge with splendid Teton views in a frontier-style log building. A spacious view deck is also used in summer.

★ **The Strutting Grouse Restaurant** *8 mi. N via US 89* *733-7788*
L-D. No D on Mon. Closed Oct.-May. *Expensive*
Gourmet Continental fare is served amidst contemporary Western elegance at the Jackson Hole Golf and Tennis Club.The view of the Teton Range from the gracious dining room, outdoor patio, and handsome window-walled lounge is sublime.

Sweetwater Deli & Restaurant *downtown at 85 King St.* *733-3553*
L-D. *Moderate*
An eclectic assortment of well-prepared dishes is served in an intimate, antique-laden log cabin or on a pleasant outdoor deck.

Vista Grande *8 mi. NW via WY 22 on WY 390* *733-6964*
D only. *Low*
Mexican specialties attract impressive crowds to this big modern roadside restaurant and cantina.

Wort Hotel *downtown at 50 W. Deloney Av.* *733-2190*
D only. Only brunch on Sun. *Moderate*
A traditional assortment of American dishes is served in casual elegance in the recently remodeled Gold Piece Dining Room. Elsewhere in the hotel are a coffee shop serving all meals, a lounge, and a cabaret.

LODGING

Rough logs, natural wood, and shake shingles are hallmarks of the numerous frontier-style accommodations in Jackson Hole. Furnishings usually carry out the Old Western theme without sacrificing modern conveniences or comfort. Many of the better facilities are within a stroll of the town square. While there are few bargains in summer, most motel prices are reduced by at least 30% from fall through spring. However, the lodges near the ski lifts at Teton Village increase their rates by as much as 20% in winter.

★ **Alpenhof - Best Western** *12 mi. NW via WY 22 & WY 390 in Teton Village* *733-3242*
This luxurious lodge in the heart of Teton Village is an appealing mixture of Old West and Old World styles. An outdoor view pool, whirlpool, and sauna are featured, and the rooms are only a few steps from outstanding skiing. There is (a fee for) horseback riding in summer. In addition to a popular restaurant, the lodge also has a picturesque lounge. Each spacious, nicely decorated room has a phone and cable color TV.

#44 — pvt. balc., mt. view windows on 2 sides,   K bed...$98
#25 — pvt. balc., mt. view windows,   2 Q beds...$98
#48 — pvt. balc., view to mts.,   K bed...$98
regular room —   Q bed...$70

★ **Americana Snow King Resort** *.7 mi. SE at 400 E. Snow King Av.* *733-5200*
Jackson Hole's largest year-round resort hotel is at the base of Snow King Mountain. The multilevel, Western-style contemporary lodge has a fine set of restaurants, a lounge, an outdoor pool and a whirlpool, plus (a fee for) an alpine slide and horseback riding. In winter, there are (fees for) ski lifts, rental equipment, skiing instruction, and snowmobiles.

Each spacious, well-furnished room has a phone, cable color TV, and a view of Jackson Hole or Snow King Mountain.

#601 — fine view of ski slopes,	Q bed..$80
7th or 6th fl. (south wing) — ski slope view,	2 D or Q beds...$85
regular room —	2 D or Q bed...$75

Antler Motel   *downtown at 43 W. Pearl Av.*   *733-2535*

This modern Western-style motel is in the heart of town, and has a sauna. Each well-furnished room has a phone and cable color TV.

#209,#214,#156,#160 — spacious, stone fireplace,	K bed...$56
#138,#147,#155,#161,#208,#215 — spacious, stone fireplace,	2 Q beds...$70
regular room — .	D bed...$40

49er Motel   *downtown at 330 W. Pearl Av.*   *733-7550*

There are no amenities, but each spacious, nicely furnished room has a phone and cable color TV with movies.

#219,#220 — corner, lg. stone fireplace, valley view,	2 Q beds...$70
#218 — lg. stone fireplace, semi-pvt. mt. view,	K bed...$60
#123,#122 — lg. stone fireplace, mt. view,	2 Q beds...$70
#121 — big stone fireplace, ski slope view beyond public balc.,	K bed...$60
regular room —	2 Q beds...$54

Golden Eagle Motor Inn   *downtown at 325 E. Broadway*   *733-2042*

This small, modern Western-style motel is in a quiet location and has an outdoor pool. Each well-furnished room has a phone and cable color TV.

#8 "Fireplace Suite" — flagstone fireplace, LR has town/ski slope view,	2 Q beds...$70
regular room —	Q or K bed...$54

★ **The Inn at Jackson Hole** *12 mi. NW via WY 22 & WY 390 in Teton Village*   *733-2311*

At the base of the ski area in Teton Village, this motor hotel offers a large outdoor pool, whirlpool, tennis court, and a restaurant and lounge. Each spacious unit has a phone and cable color TV. All of the recommended rooms are in condominium units in the "Mountain Wing."

#343,#348,#349 — fireplace, kitchenette, pvt. balc.,	K bed...$70
#433,#438,#439 — loft, fireplace, kitchenette, pvt. balc.,	*K bed...$80*
regular room —	*2 D beds...$60*

★ **Jackson Hole Racquet Club Resort**   *9 mi. NW via WY 22 on WY 390*   *733-3990*

This large complex of contemporary Western-style condominiums is on extensively landscaped grounds with two heated pools (including one indoor lap pool), whirlpool, saunas, and (for a fee) tennis courts (two indoor) and racquetball courts, plus a restaurant and lounge. Each spacious, luxuriously decorated unit has a phone, cable color TV, complete kitchen, fireplace, washer and dryer, and a private patio or balcony.

#3322 — 1 BR loft, fine mt. view,	Q bed...$105
#3414 — 1 BR, good mt. view,	Q bed...$95
#3412 — 1 BR, good mt. view,	D bed...$95
#3424 — 2 BR loft, good mt. view,	2 Q beds...$130
regular unit — studio,	Q bed...$80

★ **Jackson Lake Lodge**   *35 mi. N on US 89*   *543-2811*

On a bluff overlooking Jackson Lake, this famous resort hotel complex has an awesome view of the Teton Range. Extensively landscaped grounds include a large outdoor pool and nature trails. There is (for a fee) horseback riding, bicycles, and (nearby) fishing and float trips, and boat or bus tours. An inspired contemporary Western lobby/lounge is flanked by two huge fireplaces and sixty-foot picture windows framing the Tetons. The Mural Room, the resort's main dining room, is vast and well furnished, but the expensive meals served there can't compete with the panoramic view. Visitors should insist on one of the large, handsomely decorated rooms "with a Teton view" in either the main lodge or motor lodge buildings. (Closed Oct.-May.)

#46 — in lodge, awesome view,	K bed...$86
regular room — in one of several motor lodge buildings, no view,	2 D beds...$58

★ **Jenny Lake Lodge** *25 mi. N via US 89 on Teton Park Rd. loop* *733-4647*
Solitude is the feature in this ultra-exclusive cluster of individual log cabins nestled in a tranquil pine-shaded meadow near the base of the Tetons. Horseback riding, fishing, and bicycles are included in the rate. The charming, frontier-style main building houses a beautifully appointed gourmet restaurant. Each comfortably furnished cabin has a private patio and bath. Modified American plan rates include breakfast and dinner. (Closed Oct.-May.)

"suite" — lg. cabin, fireplace,   2 T & D beds...$260
"cabin" —   2 T or D bed...$195

Kudar's Motel *downtown at 260 N. Cache St.* *733-2823*
An older log cabin-style motel near the heart of town offers modest rooms with B/W or color TV.

regular room —   D bed...$35

Motel 6 *1.8 mi. SW on US 89* *733-9666*
One enormously popular representative of a major motel chain provides most of Jackson's **bargain** rooms. This large, modern motel has an outdoor pool. Each simply furnished room has a (fee) TV.

regular room —   D bed...$22

Pines Motel *downtown at 360 W. Broadway* *733-9823*
This older single-level motel has cable color TV.

regular room —   D or K bed...$35

Prospector Motel *downtown at 155 N. Jackson St.* *733-4858*
In a quiet location, this older motel offers small rooms with cable color TV.

regular room —   Q bed...$32

★ **Signal Mountain Lodge** *27 mi. N via US 89 on Teton Park Rd.* *733-5470*
Jackson Hole's only major lakeside accommodations are in a motor hotel complex that includes marina facilities and boat rentals on Jackson Lake, plus a family dining room and a view lounge. Each spacious unit has a phone.

#164,#168,#166,#170 — 1 BR, semi-pvt. balc., sm. kitchen, fine
                     Teton/lake view,   K bed...$76
#162,#158 — 1 BR, kitchenette, semi-pvt. view balc.,
                     fine lake/Teton views,   2 D beds...$81
regular room — rustic log cabin in the pines,   D bed...$38

Snow King Lodge Motel *.4 mi. S at 470 King St.* *733-3480*
In a quiet area near the Snow King Ski Area, this motel has rooms with color TV.

regular room —   Q bed...$34

★ **Sojourner Inn** *12 mi. NW via WY 22 & WY 390 in Teton Village* *733-3657*
The largest hotel in Teton Village is only a few yards from the ski lifts. The modern facility, a blend of Old World and Old West styles, includes a large outdoor pool, an indoor whirlpool and sauna, a large game room, and a restaurant and lounge. Each spacious room has cable color TV.

#416,#316 — balc., mt. view,   Q bed...$70
regular room —   D or K bed...$60

★ **Spring Creek Ranch** *2 mi. NW via WY 22 & Spring Gulch Rd.* *733-8833*
The nearest accommodations with a superb Teton view are in a new condominium resort several hundred feet up the side of an isolated butte west of town. Features include an outdoor pool and a whirlpool, two tennis courts, hiking trails, (a fee for) horseback riding, plus a view restaurant and lounge. Each beautifully decorated unit has a phone, cable color TV, refrigerator, and a fireplace.

lodge room — pvt. balc., fabulous view of Teton Range,   2 Q or K bed...$80
apartment — 2 BR, kitchen, 2 fireplaces, pvt. balc.,
                     some Teton view,   2 Q or K bed...$130
regular room — in lodge, pvt. balc., some Teton view,   2 Q or K bed...$70

Stagecoach Motel *downtown at 291 N. Glenwood St.* *733-3451*
This Old Western-style motel is in a quiet location. Each attractively furnished room has cable color TV.

regular room —   D bed...$38

Banff, Alberta

WEATHER PROFILE *Vokac Weather Rating*

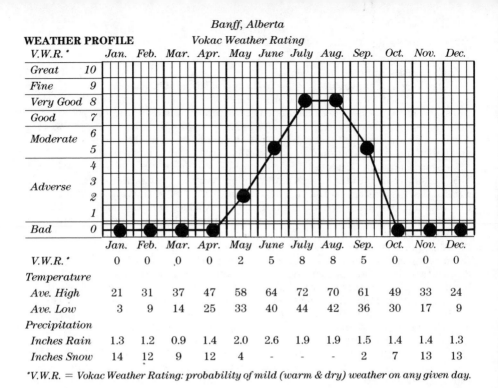

V.W.R.*	Jan.	Feb.	Mar.	Apr.	May	June	July	Aug.	Sep.	Oct.	Nov.	Dec.
V.W.R.*	0	0	0	0	2	5	8	8	5	0	0	0
Temperature												
Ave. High	21	31	37	47	58	64	72	70	61	49	33	24
Ave. Low	3	9	14	25	33	40	44	42	36	30	17	9
Precipitation												
Inches Rain	1.3	1.2	0.9	1.4	2.0	2.6	1.9	1.9	1.5	1.4	1.4	1.3
Inches Snow	14	12	9	12	4	-	-	-	2	7	13	13

*V.W.R. = Vokac Weather Rating: probability of mild (warm & dry) weather on any given day.

Forecast

Month	V.W.R.*		Temperatures Daytime	Evening	Precipitation
January	0	Bad	frigid	frigid	frequent snow flurries
February	0	Bad	cold	frigid	frequent snow flurries
March	0	Bad	chilly	cold	frequent snow flurries
April	0	Bad	chilly	chilly	frequent snow flurries
May	2	Adverse	cool	chilly	frequent showers/snow flurries
June	5	Moderate	cool	cool	continual showers
July	8	Very Good	warm	cool	frequent showers
August	8	Very Good	warm	cool	frequent showers
September	5	Moderate	cool	chilly	frequent showers
October	0	Bad	chilly	chilly	frequent showers/snow flurries
November	0	Bad	chilly	cold	frequent snow flurries
December	0	Bad	frigid	frigid	frequent snow flurries

Summary

Almost a mile above sea level, Banff is situated in the heart of one of the world's most renowned alpine playgrounds. It straddles the Bow River in a broad pine-forested valley surrounded by majestic snow-capped peaks. Unfortunately, the weather is almost as demanding as the location is awe-inspiring. **Winter** temperatures are extremely cold, days are very short at this latitude, and there are frequent snow flurries. In spite of this, hardy individuals willing to dress appropriately are rewarded by a variety of excellent winter sports facilities nearby. **Spring** skiing continues through April, but mild weather doesn't arrive until June. **Summer** weather is very good in July and August. Days are long and warm, evenings are cool, and frequent light showers bring out the refreshing pine-scent of the spectacular countryside. In **fall**, cool days and frequent showers are quickly replaced by freezing nights and frequent snow flurries—months in advance of the official start of winter.

ATTRACTIONS & DIVERSIONS
Aerial Tramways
★   **Lake Louise Gondola Lift**   *35 mi. NW on TC-1*   *522-3555*
Canada's longest tramway takes riders to the top of Mount Whitehorn in twenty minutes via glass-enclosed gondolas. The view from the sundeck is astounding. A cafeteria, hiking trails, and picnic facilities are maintained at the top from mid-June to Labor Day.
★   **Mt. Norquay Gondola Lift**   *3 mi. N via Mt. Norquay Rd.*   *762-4421*
A glass-enclosed gondola takes riders to the summit in seven minutes between mid-May and Labor Day. The panorama from the cliffhouse restaurant is splendid.
★   **Sulphur Mountain Gondola Lift**   *2 mi. S on Mountain Av.*   *762-2523*
This has long been one of the area's most popular year-round attractions. Glass-enclosed gondolas whisk riders to the top of a mountain next to town in eight minutes. Breathtaking panoramic views of Banff and the Rockies can be enjoyed from broad terraces or a large new circular restaurant with multilevel seating and a dramatic window-wall. Several short scenic hiking trails start at the top of the tram.
★ **Banff-Jasper Highway**   *177 mi. each way via TC-1 & C 93*
Often called the world's most scenic alpine highway, this broad, well-graded, paved road is the state of the art in displaying mountain grandeur. The entire drive offers breathtaking panoramas of rivers, lakes, waterfalls, and forests below majestic snow-cap   d peaks and glaciers along the Continental Divide. Just off the highway is Lake Louise - one of the world's most photographed spectacles. Farther along, the road passes near the tongue of Athabasca Glacier, a mile-long extension of the enormous Columbia Icefield. Specially designed snowcoaches take guests on forty-five minute tours across the ice. The narrow gorge carved by thunderous Athabasca Falls is another highlight. Short scenic hiking trails with interpretive signs and trailheads for backpackers are thoughtfully located along the entire route. Mountain sheep, moose, and other wild animals are frequently seen from the highway.
★ **Banff National Park**   *surrounding town*   *762-3324*
Canada's first national park (1885) includes the town of Banff, the hot springs that caused a park to be created, and many miles of the beautiful Bow River Valley. Surrounding mountain wildernesses offer more than one thousand miles of scenic hiking trails leading to a wonderful array of lakes, glaciers, streams, and waterfalls. World famous Lake Louise and Victoria Glacier are natural park highlights, while Chateau Lake Louise and the Banff Springs Hotel are enormous, world-class complements to their inspiring settings. In winter, three major ski areas provide excellent skiing amidst the awesome grandeur of the Canadian Rockies.
★ **Banff Natural History Museum**   *downtown at 93 Banff Av.*   *762-4747*
Grizzly bears and other animals you'd rather get close to here than in the wilderness are artistically displayed, along with birds of Western Canada, in a large wooden building operated by Parks Canada.
★ **Bicycling**
Pedaling has become an enthusiastically supported way to experience the grandeur of the Canadian Rockies on the well-designed highways and byways around Banff. Quality rental bicycles are invitingly displayed in great numbers, and tour suggestions are plentiful at:
     Park 'n Pedal   *downtown at 229 Wolf St.*   *762-3191*
     Spoke 'n Edge   *downtown at 214 Banff Av.*   *762-2854*
Boat Rentals
★   **Rocky Mountain Raft Tours**   *downtown at Bow Av./Wolf St.*   *762-3632*
The scenic meanders of the glacial-green Bow River through town and upstream were made to be explored by canoe. This concession, conveniently located on the water in town, rents canoes by the hour or longer.
★ **Boat Rides**
     Bow River Raft Tours *1 mi. S on Spray Av. in Banff Springs Hotel*   *762-3632*
Scenic three-hour river floats down the Bow River are offered from July thru mid-September.

Minnewanka Tours   *7 mi. NE at Minnewanka Lake*   762-3473
Guided hour-and-a-half cruises on scenic Minnewanka Lake are offered daily in summer.
Canoes and other boats can also be rented at the lake.

★ **Buffalo Paddocks**   *2 mi. NE on TC-1*
Plains bison were first transplanted to the Banff Reserve in 1897. Visitors may drive into
a large, fenced area to observe the herd in a natural setting between May and October.

★ **Cascade Rock Gardens**   *downtown at S end of Banff Av.*
One of the West's most delightful public gardens is adjacent to the Park Administration
building. Rock terraces covered with beautiful flowers and shrubs are accented by small
cascades and pools, rustic bridges and flagstone walks, and pavilions. The spectacle is
framed by a pine forest backed by towering peaks of the Canadian Rockies.

Climbing
★   **Banff Alpine Guides**   *downtown at 120 Banff Av.*   762-4277
Classes and climbing trips for both beginners and skilled climbers interested in
experiencing the Canadian Rockies up close originate here.

Flying
     Summit Vacations, Ltd.   *downtown at 204 Caribou St.*   762-5383
An uplifting and effortless way to experience the Canadian Rockies is via lighter-than-air
craft. Daily balloon flights, complete with champagne, can be reserved here.

Golf
★   **Banff Springs Hotel Golf Course**   *1.2 mi. S via Spray Av.*   762-2962
Ranked among the most scenic golf courses in the world, this relatively level 18-hole
course is open to the public. A pro shop, club and cart rentals, and a driving range are
available, plus the complete facilities of the adjacent Banff Springs Hotel.

★ **Horseback Riding**
Horseback rides ranging from a one hour scenic trail ride to a several-day pack trip in to
the wilderness can be easily arranged at several stables. Unfortunately, no hired hors
may be ridden in the park without a guide. For details about trips, times, and charges, ca

Banff Springs Hotel	*1 mi. S on Spray Av.*	762-221
Chateau Lake Louise	*35 mi. NW off TC-1*	522-351
Martins Stables Ltd.	*.5 mi. SW on Birch Av.*	762-283
Warner and MacKenzie	*downtown at 132 Banff Av.*	762-4551
Natural History Museum	*downtown at 112 Banff Av.*	762-4747

This new museum uses films and slide shows to portray the geological development of the
Rocky Mountains. Displays include a dinosaur exhibit and a lifelike model of Sasquatch,
the legendary "Big Foot," as well as exhibits explaining the geology and plant life of the
area.

★ **Peter & Catherine Whyte Foundation**   *downtown at 111 Bear St.*   762-2291
Banff's cultural center includes a handsome contemporary Western-style building
housing an art gallery, the public library, and extensive archives on the history of the
Canadian Rockies. Displays featuring well-known Canadian artists are changed
frequently. Special events are programmed all summer. Several historic cabins dot the
nicely landscaped grounds.

Warm Water Feature
★   **Upper Hot Springs**   *2 mi. S via Mountain Av.*   762-2966
The natural sulphur springs water is too hot for serious swimming. But, the outdoor pool
does offer sensational views from a mountainside location, it is remarkably relaxing, and
it is open year-round. Massage is also offered by appointment.

Winter Sports
★   **Helicopter Skiing**
Untracked powder is readily available to more adventurous and experienced skiers by
helicopter service. For reservations, contact:

Canadian Mountain Holidays	762-4531
Cariboo Helicopter Skiing	762-5548
Mountain Canada Purcell Helicopter Skiing	762-5383

★ **Lake Louise** *36 mi. NW on TC-1* 522-3555

At Canada's largest ski area, the vertical rise is 3,250 feet and the longest run is five miles. Elevation at the top is 8,650 feet. A gondola, a triple, and four double chairlifts operate daily. All facilities, services, and rentals are available at the base for both downhill and cross-country skiing. There are about fifty miles of cross-country trails. Sleigh riding, ice-skating, and tobogganing are also enjoyed. A restaurant is located at the base, and numerous bars and lodgings are two miles west. The skiing season is early December to early May.

★ **Mt. Norquay Ski Area** *3 mi. N on Mt. Norquay Rd.* 762-4421

The vertical rise is 1,350 feet, and the longest run is more than one mile. Elevation at the top is 7,050 feet. Two chairlifts operate daily. All facilities, services, and rentals are available at the base for downhill skiing. Ski jumping and tobogganing are also enjoyed. A cafeteria is located at the base, and restaurants, bars, and lodging are plentiful in nearby Banff. The skiing season is early December to mid-April.

★ **Sunshine Village** *9 mi. W via TC-1* 762-3383

The vertical rise is 3,500 feet and the longest run is about five miles. Elevation at the top is 8,950 feet. A gondola, one triple, and four double chairlifts operate daily. All facilities, services, and rentals are available at the base for both downhill and cross-country skiing. A few restaurants and bars are located at the mountain, and there is a lodge above the gondola in the alpine village. The skiing season is mid-November to late May.

SHOPPING

One of the world's most photogenic downtowns occupies a compact site on a flat valley floor surrounded by towering peaks of the Canadian Rockies. Just north of a beautiful stone bridge over the Bow River, handsome, human-scaled buildings along and near Banff Avenue house a notable array of intriguing shops, and galleries specializing in Canadian arts and crafts.

Food Specialties

Alberta Liquor Store *downtown at 316 Marten St.* 762-2518

This official provincial store is the best local source of Canadian, American and European wines.

Pop's Bakery *downtown at 319 Banff Av.* 762-2337

Various Canadian and European-style breads and pastries are sold in this takeout bakery.

★ **Scoop Ice Cream and Donut House** *downtown at 207 Banff Av.* 762-2928

This remarkably popular little shop serves a variety of hard and soft ice cream treats; plus fresh-squeezed orange or grapefruit juice, or lemonade; and homemade donuts and pastries.

Welch's Chocolate Shop *downtown at 126 Banff Av.* 762-3737

Homemade sponge toffee is the odd-looking specialty among an impressive assortment of chocolates and other candy, nuts, popcorn, and ice cream sold here.

★ **Ye Olde Fudgery Ltd.** *downtown at 215 Banff Av.* 762-3003

You can watch fudge being made through display windows, and select from a notable assortment of fudges and chocolates. Candied apples are another specialty. Gift boxes will be prepared and mailed anywhere.

Specialty Shops

Banff Book and Art Den *downtown at 110 Banff Av.* 762-3919

This store has a fine assortment of books of current and regional interest, a good selection of posters, and topographic maps of the region.

★ **Canada House** *downtown at Bear/Caribou Sts.* 762-3757

Exclusively Canadian fine art, including one of the West's finest selections of Eskimo and Indian art, is beautifully displayed.

★ **The Quest** *downtown at 105 Banff Av.* 762-2722

Purely Canadian handicrafts are exquisitely showcased in one of the West's most distinguished galleries.

★ **Stone's** *downtown at 215 Banff Av.* 762-4744

Original Eskimo soapstone sculptures are featured, along with jade, ivory and turquoise carvings and jewelry.

NIGHTLIFE

Numerous places downtown and nearby offer live music for dancing and drinking in facilities ranging from rustic to opulent. Festival of the Arts productions also enliven most summer evenings.

★ **Banff Park Lodge**   *downtown at 222 Lynx St.*   *762-4433*
Live folk music is a frequent attraction in the Glacier Lounge. Romantic contemporary decor and furnishings include plush sofas and armchairs, a native rock fireplace, and picture window views of the mountains. Closed Sun.

★ **Banff Springs Hotel**   *1 mi. S on Spray Av.*   *762-2211*
The Rob Roy Room offers sophisticated dance music and dinner in a setting of baronial splendor. In the Mount Rundle Lounge, furnished with luxurious sofas and easy chairs, huge windows overlook the terrace gardens, Bow River, and magnificent Mt. Rundle.

Cascade Inn   *downtown at 124 Banff Av.*   *762-3311*
The Buffalo Paddock Lounge features a buffalo head over a fireplace, comfortable booths, and live entertainment. Downstairs, the Great Divide offers loud, live music for dancing to blinking colored lights.

Magpie and Stump   *downtown at Caribou/Bear Sts.*   *762-2014*
Folk music is offered most nights, along with casual, rough-hewn decor and Mexican food.

Rimrock Inn   *2 mi. S on Mountain Av.*   *762-3356*
The cozy, contemporary Topaz Lounge has picture windows overlooking the Canadian Rockies from a lofty mountain slope.

★ **Silver City Saloon** *downtown on Banff Av. in Clock Tower Mall*   *762-3337*
Live music and dancing are offered every night in this large and popular cellar saloon.

Timberline Lodge   *1 mi. NW off TC-1 on Mt. Norquay Rd.*   *762-2281*
The Quilted Bear Lounge offers armchaired comfort, occasional live music, and a panoramic view of town and the mountains. A big fireplace is much used except in summer.

RESTAURANTS

Banff has an abundance of restaurants. Many are associated with hotels. The best are in a cluster downtown. The food has only begun to compete with the spectacular views provided in many of the town's better places.

Athena Pizza & Spaghetti House   *downtown at 112 Banff Av.*   *762-4022*
D only, plus L on Sat. & Sun.   *Moderate*
Pizzas and Italian dishes are emphasized. Ribs and sirloin are also served in this plain, popular restaurant.

Banff Park Lodge   *downtown at 222 Lynx St.*   *762-4433*
D only.   *Expensive*
Continental dishes are offered in the Terrace Dining Room. Plush table settings enhance the contemporary elegance of a room with a large glass skylight for dining under the stars.

Banff Springs Hotel   *1 mi. S on Spray Av.*   *762-2211*
B-L-D.   *Expensive*
Multi-course prix fixe meals are featured in the Alhambra — a spacious, elegant dining room with live background music. In the Rob Roy Room, conventional dishes are no match for the baronial presence of the room or the view of the Bow River Valley from a window table. Dinner is accompanied by live music for listening or dancing. There are seven other restaurants in the renowned hotel.

Caboose Co., Ltd.   *.5 mi. N at Elk/Lynx Sts.*   *762-3622*
D only.   *Moderate*
A contemporary Western menu and a self-serve salad cart are offered in a converted railway depot adjoining the present train station. The dining room and lounge are attractively decorated with railroad memorabilia.

Cafe la Ronde   *downtown at 209 Banff Av.*   *762-5122*
L-D.   *Moderate*
International dishes are featured, plus a variety of homemade European pastries and desserts. Dining areas in natural woods-and-greenery decor are furnished with a choice of booths, armchairs, or director's chairs. Live music is occasionally offered.

★ **Giorgio's La Casa**   *downtown at 219 Banff Av.*   *762-5116*
D only. Closed Mon.   *Expensive*
Fine Italian cuisine is presented in intimate, elegant rooms that are as tranquil as the
downstairs dining room, La Pasta, is lively.

★ **Giorgio's La Pasta**   *downtown at 219 Banff Av.*   *762-5114*
D only.   *Moderate*
The pasta dishes and pizza served here are so good that occasional overcrowding can be
easily forgiven in this sleek newer trattoria.

Grizzly House   *downtown at 207 Banff Av.*   *762-4055*
L-D.   *Moderate*
Several fondues and steaks are offered in a large, wood-toned restaurant that has been
subdivided into intimate areas accented by an eclectic collection of carvings and totem
poles. The adjoining lounge has live entertainment and dancing.

Guido's Spaghetti Factory   *downtown at 116 Banff Av.*   *762-4002*
D only.   *Moderate*
An assortment of conventional Italian dishes are featured in a cedar-paneled dining
room.

Inns of Banff Park   *.9 mi. NE at 600 Banff Av.*   *762-4581*
B-L-D.   *Expensive*
Reflections, the hotel's restaurant, specializes in five course table d'hote dinners served in
a plush, modern dining room with window wall views of the mountains.

Joshua's   *downtown at 204 Caribou St.*   *762-2833*
L-D.   *Moderate*
A Continental menu is offered in an intimate dining room decorated in an early-Canadian
theme.

★ **Le Beaujolais**   *downtown at 212 Buffalo St.*   *762-2712*
D only.   *Expensive*
French gourmet cuisine is presented in an atmosphere of formal elegance. Windows
provide views of the main street and Bow River from an upstairs location.

Magpie & Stump   *downtown at 203 Caribou St.*   *762-2014*
D only.   *Moderate*
The Mexican food is well regarded in this casual Canadian-style cantina.

Melissa's   *downtown at 218 Lynx St.*   *762-5511*
B-L-D.   *Moderate*
With a few unusual offerings like Swiss apple pancakes, this may be the most popular of
the surprisingly few places that serve a complete breakfast in town. An eclectic dinner
menu ranges from steak and seafood to deep dish pizza. Comfortably rustic decor is
appropriate for the large old log building that also houses an upstairs bar.

Paris Restaurant   *downtown at 114 Banff Av.*   *762-3554*
L-D.   *Moderate*
Continental and Canadian dishes are offered in a wood-paneled dining room enhanced
by paintings and classical music.

Rimrock Inn   *2 mi. S on Mountain Av.*   *762-3356*
D only.   *Expensive*
The Eagle's Nest features Continental dishes in a stylish contemporary dining room with
an expansive view of the Bow River Valley. A cozy view lounge adjoins.

Sulphur Mountain Restaurant   *2 mi. S via Mountain Av.*   *762-2523*
L-D.   *Moderate*
A dramatic circular restaurant was recently added at the top of the gondola lift.
Conventional Canadian dishes and casual decor accompany magnificent panoramic
views of the entire area. Tiered seating lets everyone enjoy the awesome scene from the
large, modern, self-service dining room.

★ **Ticino Swiss-Italian Restaurant**   *downtown at 205 Wolf St.*   *762-3848*
D only.   *Moderate*
This cosmopolitan dining room serves skillfully prepared meat dishes and fondues at
tables set with fresh flowers and crisp linens.

LODGING

The premier destination of the Canadian Rockies has an abundance of accommodations, including several with some of the finest views and furnishings in the West. Baronial splendor, chic contemporary elegance, and rustic Old Western atmosphere are all well represented. Most of the best lodgings are an easy stroll from the heart of town. There are very few bargains in summer, but most places reduce their prices by at least 25% from fall thru late spring.

★ **Banff Park Lodge**   *downtown at 222 Lynx St.*   762-4433

This large, luxuriously contemporary motor hotel is conveniently located downtown near the river. Amenities include a large indoor pool, a whirlpool, and saunas, plus heated underground parking, strikingly modern restaurants, and a fine view lounge. Each spacious, beautifully furnished room has a phone, cable color TV with movies, and a balcony.

"suites"(there are 12) — in-room whirlpool,	K bed..$140
#313 — good Bow River view,	K bed...$80
#325,#333 — good mt. views,	2 Q beds...$80
regular room —	2 Q beds...$80

★ **Banff Springs Hotel**   *1 mi. S on Spray Av.*   762-2211

One of the world's renowned architectural triumphs has a photogenic location overlooking the Bow River. The scenic natural grandeur is wonderfully complemented by the vaulting interiors, polished hardwoods and stone, and museum-quality furnishings in the palacial hotel. Expansive, flower-bedecked grounds include a remarkable array of facilities — giant indoor and outdoor pools with alpine views; a whirlpool; saunas; exercise, recreation, and game rooms; and (for a fee) a spectacular championship 18-hole golf course; putting green; five tennis courts; bicycle rentals; horseback riding; guide services; and arrangements for fishing, canoeing, or mountain climbing. Within the hotel are nine separate dining rooms and several lounges, plus many excellent shops. Each room has a phone and cable color TV. Surprisingly (perhaps because of the hotel's convention and tour group orientation), most of the 550 rather plain rooms have twin beds. Double beds are scarce, and king beds are currently available only in a few of the suites (starting at $185) with the two exceptions noted below.

#301,#201 — corner, big windows on 2 sides, great pvt. view of town/mts.,	K bed...$104
regular room — ask for valley side, N half of bldg., fine Bow River & mt. view,	2 T or D bed...$104

★ **Bow View Motor Lodge**   *downtown at 228 Bow Av.*   762-2261

The accommodations nearest to the Bow River are in a modern, three-story motel in a secluded location — yet convenient to downtown. An outdoor pool, a sauna, and a small restaurant are features. Each spacious, luxuriously furnished room has a phone, color TV, and large windows.

#304,#305 — tree & river view from floor/ceiling windows,	K bed..$60
#306,#307 — floor/ceiling windows, pvt. balc., view of mts.,	Q bed...$60
regular room — some have balc., tree view,	Q bed...$60

Charlton's Cedar Court   *.6 mi. NE at 513 Banff Av.*   762-4485

A small indoor pool is a feature of this contemporary Western-style motel, and there is covered parking. Each well-furnished room has a phone and color TV.

#133,#125,#101 "Loft Suites" — gas fireplace,	K bed...$56
regular room —	D bed...$48

★ **Chateau Lake Louise**   *38 mi. NW via TC-1*   522-3511

The site, by the shore of a small lake backed by a shimmering glacier suspended in an amphitheater of towering peaks, is one of the world's most photographed. The renowned chateau, a large hotel that is being renovated, includes a recently opened indoor pool. Horseback riding and canoeing are available (for a fee). There are nine dining and drinking places in the imposing building, including the majestic Victoria Dining Room, one of the West's great interior dining spaces. The Fairview Supper Club also provides an elegant setting for enjoying the exquisite view. Each room has a phone. Surprisingly, perhaps because of the hotel's tour group orientation, only a few rooms currently have large beds — almost all are twins.

#859,#759,etc.to #159 "executive suites" — 4 windows,

breathtaking panorama,	Q bed...$140
"view suite" — good view of lake/mts.,	2 T or D bed...$116
regular room — forest view,	2 T or D bed...$104

★ **Douglas Fir Resort**   *1 mi. NE on Tunnel Mountain Rd.*   762-5591

This large, contemporary Western-style resort motel complex sprawls over a pine-shaded hillside. Amenities include a small indoor pool, whirlpool, sauna, tennis court, and (for a fee) racquetball and squash. Each of the spacious, handsomely furnished units has a phone, color TV, fireplace, kitchen, and private balcony.

#321,#322 — studio, corner, extra (pvt.) side window, mt. view,	Q bed...$60
#421 — 1 BR loft, corner windows, mt. view,	2 Q beds...$80
#419,#417,#415,#413 — as above, but no side window,	2 Q beds...$80
regular room — studio, some mt. views,	Q bed...$60

Hidden Ridge   *1.5 mi. NE via Tunnel Mountain Rd.*   762-3544

In a quiet location high above town is a small cluster of two-level, arch-frame, cedar chalets. Each spacious, comfortably furnished unit has a cable color TV, kitchenette, and a large private porch, plus three bedrooms (one downstairs).

#106 — fireplace, superb panoramic valley/mt. view,	3 D beds...$76
#105,#107 — fabulous panoramic valley/mt. view,	3 D beds...$68
#112,#110 — fireplace, fine panoramic valley/mt. view,	3 D beds...$76
regular unit — 1 BR in lodge, fireplace, some mt. view,	2 Q beds...$60

★ **Inns of Banff Park**   *.9 mi. NE at 600 Banff Av.*   762-4581

A striking Western design distinguishes this large newer motor hotel. Amenities include a small indoor pool, whirlpool, saunas, exercise room, and a (fee) squash court; plus a heated underground parkade, a plush view restaurant, and a lounge. Each of the spacious, luxuriously furnished earth-toned bedrooms has a phone, color TV, a large private balcony, and floor-to-ceiling windows.

#A400,#A402,#A404,#A406,#B408,#B410 — fine pvt. mt. view,	K bed...$80
regular room — some mt. view,	Q bed...$80

Irwin's Motor Inn   *.4 mi. NE at 429 Banff Av.*   762-4566

This modern motel is a **bargain** with an underground garage and a restaurant. Each spacious, well-furnished room has a phone and cable color TV, plus a high-tech decor bathroom.

#346 — pitched roof, pvt. balc., mt. view,	Q bed...$32
#338,#339 — pitched roof, sm. pvt. balc., mt. view,	2 Q beds...$37
regular room —	Q bed...$29

King Edward Hotel   *downtown at 137 Banff Av.*   762-2251

One of Banff's landmarks in the heart of town is this older **bargain** hotel. Most of the plainly furnished rooms share hall baths.

#214 — corner, pvt. bath, phone, color TV, view of mts./main st.,	2 D beds...$34
regular room — small, shared bath,	D bed...$21

Mount Royal Hotel   *downtown at 138 Banff Av.*   762-3331

This landmark hotel, at the main intersection in the heart of town, has a restaurant and lounge. Plain, modern rooms each have a phone, color TV and a bathroom, but there are currently no large beds.

#338 — corner, outstanding town/mt. views from windows on 2 sides,	D bed...$60
regular room —	D bed...$60

Red Carpet Motor Inn   *.4 mi. NE at 425 Banff Av.*   762-4184

This modern motel is a **bargain**. Each nicely furnished unit has a phone and cable color TV. The third (top) floor units have mountain views.

regular room —	Q bed...$30

★ **Rimrock Inn**   *2 mi. S on Mountain Av.*   762-3356

High on a mountain slope above town is a large contemporary hotel with a spectacular view overlooking the Bow River Valley. Facilities include a view dining room and lounge.

Each of the spacious rooms has luxurious furnishings and floor-to-ceiling windows with mountain views, plus a phone and cable color TV.

#1115 — perhaps the most astounding pvt. mt. views in
      the West from windows on 2 sides,   Q bed...$80
#1017,#919 — awesome pvt. mt. views from windows on 2 sides,   Q bed...$71
regular room — fine mt. view,   Q bed...$71

Timberline Lodge   *1 mi. NW off TC-1 on Mt. Norquay Rd.*   *762-2281*

This Western-style motor lodge high above town has a dining room and lounge with panoramic views. Each spacious unit has a phone and color TV.

#211 — balc., 3 big windows with awesome mt. view, lg. stone fireplace, Q bed...$76
#214 — balc., elaborate wood furnishings, good mt. views, 4 poster   Q bed...$76
#201 thru #204 — lg. pvt. balc., corner window, fine Mt. Rundle views, 2 Q beds...$56
regular room —   Q bed...$56

★ **Tunnel Mountain Chalets**   *1 mi. NE on Tunnel Mt. Rd.*   *762-4515*

A cluster of contemporary cedar and stone chalets is located in a secluded pine forest above town. Features include an indoor pool, whirlpools, saunas, and a steam room. Each of the large, handsomely furnished units has a phone and cable color TV, plus a living room, kitchen, impressive stone wood-burning fireplace, and a balcony or patio.

#264,#267 — 2 BR, new bldg., pvt. balc., in-bath whirlpool,
      fine mt. view, loft,   2 T & Q beds...$74
#164,#167 — 1 BR, new bldg., pvt. patio, in-bath whirlpool,
      fine mt. view,   Q bed...$70
#123,#125 — 2 BR, sep. chalet, panoramic mt. view . from LR,   D & Q beds...$78
#126 thru #128 — 2 BR, superb view of mts. from LR,   D & Q beds...$74
regular room — 1 BR,   Q bed...$68

CAMPGROUNDS

There are only a few campgrounds near town, but they have many hundreds of sites. A campground in a pine forest by a lake, and another along a scenic ridgetop near town, are extremely popular.

Tunnel Mountain   *1.2 mi. NE on Tunnel Mt. Rd.*   *762-3324*

This enormous Banff National Park campground extends for well over a mile along a heavily wooded ridgetop above town. Flush toilets, hot showers, and hookups are available. Each of the close, pine-shaded sites has a picnic table. Some sites have spectacular mountain views. There is a separate tent area.   base rate...$4.50

Two Jack Lakeside *7.5 mi. NE:5 mi. E via TC-1 & 2.5 mi. N on park road*   *762-3324*

This Banff National Park facility is located near a small lake. A much larger campground is nearby. Fishing and boating on Two Jack Lake, a nature program, and marked nature trails are features. Flush toilets are available, but there are no showers or hookups. Each site has a picnic table and a fire area.   base rate...$4

SPECIAL EVENT

★ **Banff Festival of the Arts**   *.6 mi. E at Banff Centre*   *late May-August*

Productions and workshops in drama, musical theater, concerts, opera, dance, poetry, and visual arts are presented in an impressive three-theater complex. This annual summer-long celebration has showcased young talent for more than half a century.

OTHER INFORMATION

Area Code: *403*

Zip Code: *TOL OCO*

Banff/Lake Louise Chamber of Commerce   *downtown on Banff Av.*   *762-3777*
Banff Park Information Centre   *downtown at 224 Banff Av.*   *762-4256*
Travel Alberta Travel Information Centre *downtown at 224 Banff Av.*   *762-2777*

Courtenay, British Columbia

Elevation:

20 feet

Population (1981):

8,992

Population (1971):

7,152

Location:

83 mi. (plus ferry trip) NW of Vancouver

Courtenay is the year-round recreation center for the West's largest island. It has all of the advantages of both a scenic coastal location and proximity to glacier-shrouded mountains. Winters are cool and very wet. But, spectacular scenery and heavy snowfall on mountains a few miles west of town attract crowds to the largest downhill skiing complex on Vancouver Island. The view to the west from the main street includes a giant glacier that shimmers along the crest of one of the mountains between town and Strathcona Provincial Park, the huge island's largest wilderness area and park. Below the glaciers, luxuriant pine forests shade a wealth of waterfalls, rivers, streams and lakes. Two of these rivers merge in town to become the Courtenay River, which serves as a snug harbor by the Strait of Georgia. Waterfront parks have been developed in town and nearby. As a result, the public has convenient access to both fresh and saltwater swimming, boating, and fishing in summer, which is Courtenay's busiest season. Long, warm days with surprisingly little rain are also fine for beachcombing, clamming, hiking, backpacking, horseback and pack trips, and many other outdoor activities.

The town was named for an admiral, George Courtenay, who took his frigate up the river estuary in 1848 for gunnery practice. It was many years before the advantage of this site at the junction of the Puntledge and Tsolum Rivers at the northern end of Comox Harbor was recognized. The location is unusual in that it is the only freshwater anchorage for deep sea fishing boats on the entire island. About a century ago, the Courtenay Hotel was constructed and a settlement began to grow up around it. A new townsite on the west side of the river grew steadily after 1890, with the development of forest products, farming, and maritime industries. Courtenay's role as the island's year-round hub of recreation began only recently, as ferry and highway access improved.

Major nearby recreation facilities now include the island's first big ski area and an impressive community recreation center with an indoor ice-skating rink and a large swimming pool. Attractive landscaping and furnishings have been added to create a mall on the main street that enhances views of the phenomenal Comox Glacier to the west and the Courtenay River bridge to the east. A convention center and park improvements also distinguish downtown, and a "mile of flowers" is proudly tended on the main highway nearby. A small but growing number of distinctive restaurants, pubs and cabarets lend vitality to the handsome little business district. Across the river, the Courtenay Hotel remains a lively landmark. Several gourmet restaurants and luxuriously furnished motor hotels have scenic locations on the outskirts of town.

WEATHER PROFILE

Courtenay, British Columbia

Vokac Weather Rating

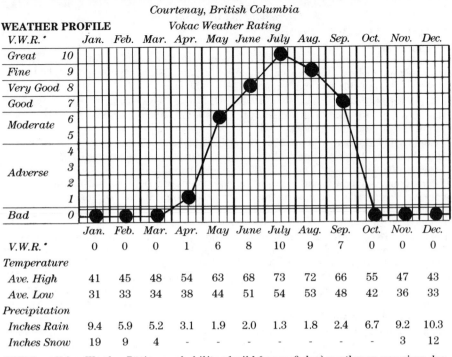

V.W.R.*	Jan.	Feb.	Mar.	Apr.	May	June	July	Aug.	Sep.	Oct.	Nov.	Dec.
V.W.R.*	0	0	0	1	6	8	10	9	7	0	0	0
Temperature												
Ave. High	41	45	48	54	63	68	73	72	66	55	47	43
Ave. Low	31	33	34	38	44	51	54	53	48	42	36	33
Precipitation												
Inches Rain	9.4	5.9	5.2	3.1	1.9	2.0	1.3	1.8	2.4	6.7	9.2	10.3
Inches Snow	19	9	4	-	-	-	-	-	-	-	3	12

*V.W.R. = Vokac Weather Rating: probability of mild (warm & dry) weather on any given day.

Forecast

Month	V.W.R.*		Temperatures		Precipitation
			Daytime	Evening	
January	0	Bad	chilly	chilly	continual downpours/snow flurries
February	0	Bad	chilly	chilly	continual rainstorms/snow flurries
March	0	Bad	chilly	chilly	continual rainstorms/snow flurries
April	1	Adverse	cool	chilly	frequent showers
May	6	Moderate	cool	cool	frequent showers
June	8	Very Good	warm	cool	frequent showers
July	10	Great	warm	cool	occasional showers
August	9	Fine	warm	cool	occasional rainstorms
September	7	Good	warm	cool	frequent rainstorms
October	0	Bad	cool	chilly	continual rainstorms
November	0	Bad	chilly	chilly	continual rainstorms/snow flurries
December	0	Bad	chilly	chilly	continual downpours/snow flurries

Summary

Halfway up the east coast of Vancouver Island, Courtenay has a beautifully pastoral location accented by an awesome glacier-capped peak. The adjacent Strait of Georgia moderates temperatures year-round. **Winter** days and evenings are inevitably chilly and wet from almost continuous rainstorms and snow flurries. Nevertheless, the island's best winter sports facilities are nearby for those willing to dress appropriately. Snowfalls in town are usually over by **spring**, but uncomfortably cool, wet days persist into May. The year's best weather is concentrated into **summer**. Long warm days, cool evenings, and only occasional rainfalls provide excellent conditions for exploring outstanding water and mountain features. Warm days continue through September, but by early **fall**, unpleasant weather has returned, with chilly days and continual rainfalls.

ATTRACTIONS & DIVERSIONS

★ **Boat Rentals**

Bates Beach Boathouse *10 mi. NE via Island Hwy. on Coleman Rd.* *334-4154*
Outboard motor boats with a swiveling armchair and fishing equipment can be rented here for salmon fishing on the adjoining Georgia Strait.

Bates Beach Resort *10 mi. NE via Island Hwy. on Coleman Rd.* *334-2151*
Outboard motor boats and all necessary fishing equipment can be rented here for salmon fishing on the adjoining Georgia Strait.

Comox Bay Marina *4 mi. E at foot of Port Augusta - Comox* *339-4664*
Motor boats and fishing tackle rentals, and guide services can be arranged at the marina.

Gordon Greer Ltd. *4 mi. E at 1797 Comox Av. - Comox* *339-4914*
Fishing boats, sail boats, and windsurfing equipment can be rented at a large modern store which also sells a good assortment of marine supplies and clothing.

Boat Ride

Powell River Ferry *6 mi. NE via Ryan & Ellenor Rds.* *339-3310*
The most northerly direct access to the mainland is provided to Powell River from the B.C. Ferry Terminal near town. The scenic trip across Georgia Strait takes an hour and forty minutes, and leaves four times daily.

Comox Lake *9 mi. SW via Cumberland & Comox Lake Rds.*
A sylvan park by this large freshwater lake has a coarse sand beach and a log-bordered swimming area. Picnicking, sunbathing, fishing, and water-skiing are popular. Nearby, some well-spaced campsites have lake views.

Comox Valley Sports Centre *1.5 mi. N via Headquarters Rd.* *334-2458*
Both a large swimming pool and an ice-skating rink are enclosed within this big, modern recreation center. Swimming is open to the public year-round, with some adults-only swim times most days. The ice rink is open to the public from fall through spring.

Courtenay and District Museum *downtown at 360 Cliffe Av.* *334-3881*
This museum is located on the top floor of the Native Sons Hall, reputed to be Canada's largest log cabin. Replicas of a longhouse with Indian artifacts, a Chinese store and a pioneer kitchen, and a large collection of dolls, animals, and birds are displayed.

Flying

★ **Coval Air Ltd.** *4 mi. E at 1800 Beaufort Av. - Comox* *339-6711*
Seaplane flights can be chartered for sightseeing, photography, or fishing trips. Fly-in fishing is a specialty.

★ **Kye Bay** *8 mi. E past Comox via Lazo and Kye Bay Rds.*
This is a locally popular saltwater swimming site on the Georgia Strait. At low tide, several hundred yards of sandy bottom is exposed beyond a narrow sloping sandy beach where sunbathing and picnicking are enjoyed. On a clear day, the panoramic view of glacier-capped mountains across the Strait is grand.

Lewis Park *downtown on Island Hwy.*
A downtown park has been thoughtfully developed at the confluence of the valley's two major rivers. The deep, lazy currents are good for swimming and access has been provided for launching canoes and other small boats. A large outdoor pool, expansive grassy play areas, tennis courts, walking and jogging paths by the rivers, and picnic facilities are other features.

★ **Puntledge Park** *.5 mi. W on 1st St.*
Mature shade trees overhang pathways along a lovely creek. When salmon are spawning, this tiny, crystal clear stream becomes a fascinating natural setting in which to observe their remarkable determination up close. Nearby, the Puntledge River offers exciting riffles and a swift current to challenge swimmers and casual river runners. A cluster of picturesque boulders attracts sunbathers to the far bank.

Railroad Trip

★ **E & N Railway** *.4 mi. S at Cumberland Rd./10th St.*
Courtenay is the northern terminus for a scenic dayliner railroad that has been bringing passengers here from Victoria daily for almost a century.

★ **Sportfishing**
   Nighthawk Charters   *4 mi. E at 72 Jane Place - Comox*   339-6465
Experienced guides and all equipment are provided for salmon fishing, or for digging
clams and picking oysters on secluded island beaches.
   Tide Winder Charters   *downtown at 1590 Cliffe Av.*   338-7811
Experienced guides are available for salmon fishing charters (day or overnight) and for
scuba diving.

★ **Strathcona Provincial Park**   *15 mi. W via Forbidden Plateau Rd.*   337-5121
Vancouver Island's largest park is a wilderness of mountains and lakes with some
extraordinary attractions. Della Falls, one of the world's highest waterfalls, is a remote
and hidden wonder. The island's highest peak, Golden Hinde (7,219 feet) is nearby. A
douglas fir nearly 300 feet tall, perhaps Canada's tallest tree, grows in a lush virgin forest
near the headwaters of the Puntledge River. The park also has many glaciers, including
the phenomenal Comox Glacier which looms over the Forbidden Plateau and is
spectacularly visible from town. Wildlife is abundant, including rare wolverines, wolves,
and the island's last elk herd. Hiking, backpacking, mountain climbing, fishing, swimming,
and camping are popular in summer. Skiing is enjoyed in winter.

Winter Sports
   Forbidden Plateau Ski Area   *15 mi. W on Forbidden Plateau Rd.*   334-4744
The vertical rise is 1,150 feet and the longest run is about 1.5 miles. Elevation at the top
is 3,450 feet. One chairlift operates daily. All facilities, services, and rentals are available at
the base for both downhill and cross-country skiing. There are many miles of groomed
cross-country trails. A cafeteria, lounge, and lodge are near the lifts. The skiing season is
early December to late April.

★   **Mt. Washington Ski Resort** *18 mi. NW via Condensory & Piercy Rds.*   338-1386
Vancouver Island's foremost ski area has a vertical rise of 1,700 feet, and the longest run
is about 2.5 miles. Elevation at the top is 5,200 feet. Four chairlifts operate daily, including
two triples. At this major new area, services and rentals are available for both downhill
and cross-country skiing, along with day lodges for both alpine and cross-country skiing,
a ski school, and many miles of groomed cross-country trails. A restaurant and bar are
near the lifts, but lodging is in Courtenay. The skiing season is November thru May.

SHOPPING
Downtown is concentrated along 5th Street west of the Courtenay River Bridge. There are
no parking meters along this handsome, landscaped semi-mall which also frames a
delightful view of the Comox Glacier to the west. A few specialty stores contribute to the
distinctiveness of the region's most complete shopping district.

Food Specialties
The Courtenay Bakery   *downtown at 267 5th St.*   334-4234
Meat pies, pasties, and sausage rolls are some of the unusual items displayed in this full
line bakery. A self-service coffee shop also has sandwiches and soup.

★ **The Farmer's Market**   *1 mi. S at 2270 S. Island Hwy.*
This cheerful collage of shops tucked into a big contemporary cedar barn is a fine place
to assemble a memorable picnic. Fresh regional fruits and seafood, smoked salmon,
Canadian cheeses, homemade sausages, and desserts are usually available.

Portuguese Joe's Fish Market   *2 mi. E at 3025 Comox Rd.*   339-2119
Fresh Dungeness crab, shrimp, oysters, and other local seafoods are displayed and sold in
season. On-premises smoked salmon is featured. They will also smoke your salmon.

★ **Runge's Delicatessen**   *downtown at 347 4th St.*   338-8621
An impressive selection of cheese, meats, and homemade sausage distinguish this inviting
delicatessen, along with all kinds of gourmet foods, teas, and coffees. Closed Sun.

Specialty Shops
Central Island Arts Alliance   *downtown at 367 4th St.*   338-6211
This cooperative displays artworks in a variety of media by several local artists, plus a
rotating exhibition of an individual artist's work.

Laughing Oyster Book Shop   *downtown at 250 6th St.*   334-2511
A good selection of new books is well organized in a handsome little book shop that caters
to general and regional interests.

NIGHTLIFE

Distinctive places for live entertainment and dancing, or for a drink and quiet conversation, are scattered in and around town.

Arbutus Travelodge Lounge   *downtown at 275 8th St.*   338-7089
Darts, shuffleboard, foosball, pool, and electronic games all get attention in this big casual sports-style pub.

★ **Courtenay House Hotel**   *.3 mi. NE at 498 Island Hwy.*   334-4401
Entertainment offered several nights each week in the large pub of the historic hotel ranges from live bands to exotic dancers. The Garden of Eden Lounge is uniquely decorated with boldly erotic pictures in illuminated colored glass.

★ **Fanny Bay Inn**   *16 mi. S on Island Hwy.*
Authentic pub furnishings — highback wooden chairs, darts, and a fireplace — accompany a view of Denman Island and premium Canadian beers on tap in this handsome roadside pub.

The 5th Ave. Club   *downtown at 90 5th St.*   334-3354
An eclectic mix of entertainment, from live rock bands and big screen video music to exotic dancers, is featured almost every night in the casual cabaret.

Loft Cabaret   *4.5 mi. E at 2100 Guthrie Rd. - Comox*   339-6612
Live entertainment and dancing are offered in a large cabaret. Closed Sun.-Mon.

★ **The Pointe**   *5.5 mi. SE at 4330 S. Island Hwy. - Royston*   338-5456
Easy listening live music, posh armchair comfort, tables made from polished free-form wood sections, and a view of Georgia Strait distinguish the resort's handsome lounge.

★ **Westerly Hotel**   *.5 mi. S at 1590 Cliffe Av.*   338-7741
The large Spinnaker Pub offers live entertainment and dancing nightly in a casual setting. In the Windjammer Lounge, live piano stylings, plush chairs, a solarium with intimate conversation areas, a fireplace, and an aquarium-wall have been beautifully blended into the most luxurious contemporary lounge in the area.

The Whistle Stop Pub   *1.2 mi. SE at 2355 Mansfield Ct.*   334-4500
Pool and darts are featured in a popular pub with a railroad theme. Closed Sun.

RESTAURANTS

Included among a surprisingly large number of area restaurants are two of the finest restaurants in the West.

Bridgehouse Restaurant   *.5 mi. S at 1675 Cliffe Ct.*   334-4425
L-D. No L on Sat.   *Moderate*
Fresh ingredients and a light touch are used in this plush, contemporary new restaurant.

★ **Gaff Rig Restaurant**   *4 mi. E at 1984 Buena Vista Av. - Comox*   339-7181
D only. Closed Mon.   *Moderate*
Local seafoods and all support dishes are deliciously fresh and skillfully prepared in this outstanding new restaurant. The capacious dining room, a tasteful extension of an old house, overlooks lovely gardens and Comox Harbor.

Gourmet-by-the-Sea   *15 mi. N on Island Hwy. - Oyster Bay*   923-5234
D only. Closed Tues.   *Expensive*
Continental cuisine, including some unusual specialties, is featured along with homemade desserts. A pleasant view of Georgia Strait is the highlight in a comfortable, nautically-furnished dining room.

★ **La Cremaillere**   *.3 mi. E at 975 Comox Court*   338-8131
L-D. No L on Sat. & Sun. Closed Mon.-Tues.   *Moderate*
French cuisine is served amidst charming French provincial decor in several rooms of a Tudor-style building by the Courtenay River. Call ahead for the romantic room-for-two.

★ **Old House Restaurant**   *.6 mi. S at 100 17th St.*   338-5406
D only. Sun. brunch. Closed Mon.   *Expensive*
Superb Continental cuisine emphasizing seafoods and wild game is prepared from the best and freshest local meats, fruits, vegetables and herbs. All of the delicious pastries and desserts are made on the premises. A transformed pioneer mansion with acres of lovely grounds includes an upstairs dinner house with elegant table settings amid rough-hewn beams and fireplaces. Windows overlook lawns and gardens, and a riverscape with a small working sawmill. Splendid, moderately priced lunches and dinners (prepared in a separate kitchen) are served in cozy, informal dining rooms downstairs.

The Pointe   *5.5 mi. SE at 4330 S. Island Hwy. - Royston*   *338-5456*
D only.   *Moderate*
International cuisine including homemade pastries is featured. Picture window views of
Georgia Strait and plush table settings enhance the resort's charming dining room.

Rodello's Restaurant   *4 mi. E at 2082 Comox Av. - Comox*   *339-6311*
B-L-D.   *Moderate*
Homestyle breakfasts are a highlight. Fresh fish is emphasized in the evening in this
pleasant coffee shop.

Tulio's   *downtown at 625 Cliffe Av.*   *338-6031*
L-D. No L on Sat. & Mon. Closed Sun.   *Moderate*
International specialties are served in a Mediterranean bistro setting.

★ **The William Van Horn Restaurant**   *1 mi. S at 2270 Island Hwy.*   *334-3102*
L-D. No L on Sun. Closed Mon.   *Moderate*
Fresh seafoods, plus meats and produce from the adjacent Farmer's Market, are used in
innovative Continental specialties in a stylish, skylit dining room with a working fireplace.

LODGING

Several luxurious motor hotels have recently been added to a good selection of
accommodations in town and along nearby beaches. Spring and fall rates are usually at
least 10% less than the summer rates shown below.

Anco Slumber Lodge   *.7 mi. S at 1885 Cliffe Av.*   *334-2451*
An outdoor pool is an attraction of this modern **bargain** motel. Each room has a phone
and cable color TV with movies.
    regular room —   D or Q bed...$27

Bates Beach Resort   *10 mi. N via Island Hwy. & Coleman Rd.*   *334-2151*
This modern little motel has a tranquil beachfront location overlooking Georgia Strait. An
adjoining boat and tackle rental is available for salmon fishing. Each large, simply
furnished unit has a kitchenette, living room, and a balcony or patio. Most have a fine view
of the Strait beyond the lawn.
    regular room — 1 BR, Strait view,   D bed...$36

★ **Bennett's Point Resort**   *15 mi. N on Island Hwy. - Oyster Bay*   *923-4281*
In addition to a woodsy waterfront setting, this small resort has an indoor pool, whirlpool,
and sauna, plus a tennis court. Next door is a well-regarded restaurant, and a lounge.
Each unit has a phone and cable color TV. Several have glimpses of the Strait through
Douglas fir, and there are **bargain** rooms.
    apartment — kitchenette,   Q bed...$37
    regular room — water view,   Q bed...$42
    regular room — tree view,   Q bed...$27

Collingwood Inn   *.5 mi. S at 1675 Cliffe Av.*   *338-1464*
There are some **bargain** units in an older single-level section of this contemporary motor
hotel, plus a good restaurant and lounge. Each unit has a phone and cable color TV.
    suite — modern 1 BR, kitchenette,   Q bed...$37
    regular room — small, older building,   D bed...$22

Courtenay House Hotel   *.3 mi. N at 498 Island Hwy.*   *334-4401*
For more than a century, this three-story hotel has been a local landmark. The restaurant
and pubs are still popular gathering places. All of the frayed rooms are a **bargain** and
humbly outfitted, although they were modernized at some point in recent decades.
    regular room — cable color TV, pvt. bath,   D bed...$16

Economy Inns Ltd.   *1.5 mi. S at 2605 Cliffe Av.*   *334-4491*
This modern **bargain** motel has an enclosed pool and a sauna. Each room has color TV.
    regular room —   D bed...$18

★ **The Pointe - Best Western**   *5.5 mi. SE at 4330 S. Island Hwy.*   *338-5456*
Well-landscaped grounds on a bluff above George Strait provide a handsome setting for
a small contemporary resort with a picturesque outdoor pool, whirlpool, sauna, and a
tennis court, plus a stylish dining room and lounge with Strait views. All arrangements
can be made for salmon fishing (for a fee). Each spacious, nicely furnished room has a
phone, cable color TV, a patio or balcony, stove/ refrigerator, and a Strait view.
    #201,#203,#103 — excellent water views,   2 D beds..$38
    #202,#209 — good water view,   Q bed...$37
    regular room —   D or Q bed...$37

★ **Port Augusta Motel**   *4 mi. E at 2082 Comox Av. - Comox*   *339-2277*
A distant view of Comox Bay, plus an indoor pool, a sauna, and a restaurant are features of this modern **bargain** motel. Boat rentals, salmon fishing charters, and scuba diving are available nearby (for a fee). Each unit has a phone and cable color TV.

#70 thru #74 — kitchenette, pvt. balc., some bay view,	Q bed...$31
#75 — pvt balc., some bay view,	2 Q beds..$29
regular room —	D or Q bed...$29

Sleepy Hollow Motel   *downtown at 1190 Cliffe Av.*   *334-4476*
This **bargain** motel has an indoor pool and a sauna. Each room has a phone and cable color TV. A Continental breakfast is complimentary.

regular room —	D bed...$24

★ **The Washington Inn**   *1 mi. NE at 1001 Ryan Rd.*   *338-5441*
Amenities in this contemporary **bargain** motor hotel include a large indoor pool, whirlpool, sauna, and steam bath, plus a restaurant, lounge, and pub. Each spacious, well-furnished room has a phone, cable color TV with movies, and a balcony.

#300,#304,#308,#312 — fine view across a meadow to mts.,	2 D beds...$28
#341,#337 — top floor, fine countryside view,	2 Q beds...$36
regular room —	2 D beds...$28

★ **Westerly Hotel**   *.5 mi. S at 1590 Cliffe Av.*   *338-7741*
Courtenay's most luxurious accommodations are in a large, strikingly contemporary hotel on the banks of the Courtenay River. Amenities include a small indoor pool, whirlpool, sauna, tennis court, and gym facilities, plus a handsome dining room, lounge, and pub with live entertainment. Each of the spacious, well-furnished rooms has a phone and cable color TV with movies.

#402,#409,#309 — pvt. balc. over river,	K bed...$42
#408,#410,#310,#308 — pvt. balc. over river,	Q bed...$42
regular room —	Q bed...$42

CAMPGROUNDS
Among several campgrounds in the area, the best are in a lush forest by Georgia Strait with a choice of either primitive or complete facilities, in addition to all kinds of water recreation.

Maple Pool Campsite *.8 mi. N via Island Hwy. & Headquarters Rd.*   *338-6992*
This private campground is in a quiet, grassy spot by the Tsolum River. Features include river swimming and fishing. Flush toilets, hot showers, and hookups are available. All of the closely spaced sites have picnic tables and fire rings. Some are tree-shaded and by the river. There is a separate tenting area.   base rate...$5

★ **Miracle Beach**   *14.6 mi. NE via Island Hwy. & Miracle Beach Rd.*
This large provincial campground is in a lush mixed forest near a rocky beach on Georgia Strait. Fishing and swimming are popular, and there are picturesque hiking trails. Flush and pit toilets are available, but there are no showers or hookups. Each widely-spaced site, separated by spectacular ferns and undergrowth and shaded by a luxuriant forest, has a picnic table and a fire ring/grill.   base rate...$4

★ **Miracle Beach Resort** *15 mi. NE via Island Hwy. & Miracle Beach Rd.*   *337-5171*
This privately operated waterfront facility features saltwater swimming, boating, and fishing, and has a ramp and motor boat rentals. Flush toilets, hot showers (fee), and hookups are available. All sites have picnic tables and fire rings. Some sites are tree-shaded and surrounded by lush ferns, while others overlook the Strait. There is a separate tenting area.   base rate...$6.50

SPECIAL EVENTS
Winter Carnival   *in town and on nearby mountain*   *first week in February*
Since 1964 this mid-winter festival has grown into a nine-day event with a parade, ski races, curling and hockey games, a queen crowning, live entertainment, and dances.

Canada Day Celebrations   *downtown*   *July 1*
The national holiday is celebrated with a parade, beer garden, shows and displays, a canoe race, and the volunteer fire department's water ball game with fire hoses.

★ **Renaissance Faire**　　*1 mi. N by Comox Valley Sports Centre*　　*mid-July*
For three days, Courtenay attracts musicians and craftsmen from all over the island. Arts, crafts and exotic foods are displayed and sold in about one hundred booths.

★ **Courtenay Youth Music Centre Presentations** *Civic Theatre　mid-July to mid-August*
Dozens of professional musicians gather to teach hundreds of gifted students from around the country in this acclaimed summer festival. Artists of international stature appear with the local festival orchestra in a series of symphony performances, in solo recitals, and in choral, jazz, and chamber music.

OTHER INFORMATION
Area Code: *604*
Zip Code:　*V9N*
Courtenay-Comox Chamber of Commerce　　*1 mi. S at 2040 Cliffe Av.*　　*334-3234*

Penticton, British Columbia

Elevation:

1,150 feet

Population (1981):

23,181

Population (1971):

18,146

Location:

250 mi. E
of Vancouver

Penticton is the year-round lakeside paradise of the Northwest. The town is bordered on two sides by fine sandy beaches. Beyond, deep clear lakes share a lovely valley with a cornucopia of orchards and vineyards for almost one hundred miles. Sheltered by the Coast Ranges to the west and the Canadian Rockies to the east, the idyllic setting gains further distinction from one of the mildest climates in Canada. Winters aren't very cold and snowfall is remarkably light in comparison to most Canadian towns. However, nearby mountains support a major skiing complex that attracts enthusiastic crowds each winter. Warm sunny days are continuous from spring, when orchards all around town become an extravanganza of fragrant blossoms, through the fall fruit harvest. Faultless weather in summer accompanies capacity crowds of vacationers. Many miles of picturesque shoreline and gentle forested mountains rising beyond a profusion of orchard-covered slopes give everyone an opportunity to exercise their playful moods. Lakeside parks with long sandy beaches, expansive lawns, and shady picnic sites; scenic golf courses; tennis complexes; and a noteworthy recreation center with an enclosed Olympic-sized pool, ice-skating, and other facilities are available in town. In addition, Penticton is the hub of the West's greatest concentration of water slide park complexes. These exhilarating high-tech facilities seem especially appropriate in a place where water recreation has always been preeminent.

Penticton's name is derived from an Indian word translated as "the ideal meeting place." The first permanent settler, Thomas Ellis, established headquarters for a vast cattle empire in 1865 in what is now the heart of town on an alluvial plain between two lakes. He planted the area's first fruit trees in 1872, and set aside a townsite in 1892 when he put a seventy-foot boat "the Penticton" on eighty-five-mile-long Okanagan Lake and established freight service. Shortly after the turn of the century, an irrigation system was built and major fruit growing was underway. Soon, railroads arrived, and the municipality grew steadily as a freight, fruit growing, and lumbering terminus. After World War II, vacation travel accelerated as highway and airline facilities improved.

Today, the beautifully landscaped main street has a nucleus of distinctive shops. Recent improvements to the civic and convention centers, recreation complex, parks, and beaches have spurred private development of fine restaurants, pubs and cabarets downtown and nearby. An abundance of contemporary lodgings is available throughout town. A large new luxury hotel on the south shore of Okanagan Lake is downtown Penticton's major landmark, and a worthy symbol of the town's emerging status as a world class leisure destination.

WEATHER PROFILE   *Vokac Weather Rating*

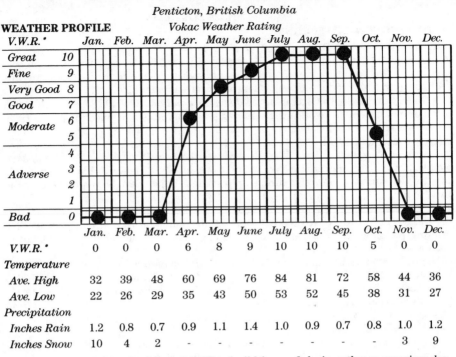

V.W.R.*		Jan.	Feb.	Mar.	Apr.	May	June	July	Aug.	Sep.	Oct.	Nov.	Dec.
V.W.R.*		0	0	0	6	8	9	10	10	10	5	0	0
Temperature													
Ave. High		32	39	48	60	69	76	84	81	72	58	44	36
Ave. Low		22	26	29	35	43	50	53	52	45	38	31	27
Precipitation													
Inches Rain		1.2	0.8	0.7	0.9	1.1	1.4	1.0	0.9	0.7	0.8	1.0	1.2
Inches Snow		10	4	2	-	-	-	-	-	-	-	3	9

V.W.R. = Vokac Weather Rating: probability of mild (warm & dry) weather on any given day.

Forecast

Month	V.W.R.*		Temperatures Daytime	Evening	Precipitation
January	0	Bad	cold	cold	frequent snow flurries
February	0	Bad	chilly	cold	occasional snow flurries
March	0	Bad	chilly	chilly	occasional showers/snow flurries
April	6	Moderate	cool	chilly	occasional showers
May	8	Very Good	warm	cool	occasional showers
June	9	Fine	warm	cool	occasional showers
July	10	Great	hot	warm	infrequent showers
August	10	Great	warm	cool	infrequent showers
September	10	Great	warm	cool	infrequent showers
October	5	Moderate	cool	chilly	occasional showers
November	0	Bad	chilly	chilly	occasional showers/snow flurries
December	0	Bad	chilly	cold	frequent snow flurries

Summary

Penticton is Canada's Shangri-La. Nestled among orchards and vineyards, the town lies between two of the West's finest lakes in a gentle valley rimmed by sylvan mountains. Less than 1,200 feet above sea level, the area enjoys one of Canada's best climates. In **winter**, days are short and chilly and evenings are cold. Normally, almost all of the year's surprisingly light snowfall is concentrated in this season. Good snow conditions prevail at the major skiing complex in nearby mountains. **Spring** warms quickly. By May, warm days, cool evenings, and occasional light showers complement the delicate beauty and fragrance of millions of blossoms in surrounding orchards. **Summer** is remarkable, with some of the best weather in the West. Very long, warm days and evenings, plus infrequent light rains, ensure comfortable enjoyment of this bountiful water wonderland. In early **fall** the weather cools rapidly, but brisk sunny days are suitable for pursuing fall colors and sampling fruits and wines of the local harvest.

ATTRACTIONS & DIVERSIONS

★ **Agricultural Research Station**   *7 mi. N on BC 97*   *494-7711*
An ornamental garden displays a wide variety of trees, shrubs, and flowers on an eye-catching site above Okanagan Lake. It is an inviting place to learn about current technology in fruit production, enjoy a stroll, or have a quiet picnic.

Art Gallery of the South Okanagan   *downtown on Lakeshore Dr.*   *493-2928*
A major new gallery, the world's first utilizing solar energy, is scheduled to open in 1985. Major national touring exhibits will be featured.

★ **Bicycle & Moped Rental**
    Riverside Rentals   *.8 mi. W at Riverside/Lakeshore Drs.*   *493-2426*
Gentle hills and lakeside terraces covered with orchards and vineyards have a network of byways well suited to leisurely touring. Bicycles and mopeds can be rented here by the hour or longer.

★ **Boat Rentals**
Several places in town offer different kinds of boats for rent by the hour or longer for cruising, paddling, water-skiing, sailing, or fishing while enjoying the scenic grandeur of Okanagan Lake or Skaha Lake. Among these are:
    Happy Hour Boat Rentals   *4.5 mi. S on BC 97 on Skaha Lake*   *492-2848*
    Okanagan Lake Marina *.6 mi. NE at 293 Front St. on Okanagan Lake*   *492-0600*
    Recreation West   *4.5 mi. S at 124 S. Beach Dr. on Skaha Lake*   *492-7019*
    Roli's Windsurfing   *downtown at 75 Front St.*   *493-0244*

Golf Course
    Penticton Golf & Country Club   *.6 mi. W on W. Eckhardt Av.*   *492-0727*
This nicely landscaped 18-hole golf course is relatively level and offers impressive mountain views. It is open to the public with a pro shop, club and cart rentals, and a dining room and lounge.

Horseback Riding
    Circle M Ranch   *1 mi. W on BC 97*   *492-8064*
Horses can be rented by the hour or longer at this stable.

Library   *.4 mi. S at 785 Main St.*   *492-0024*
The Penticton Public Library is a large, plain facility (with an excellent children's area) in a well-landscaped complex that includes an art gallery and museum.

Okanagan Game Farm   *5 mi. SW on BC 97*   *497-5405*
Set against the tawny hillsides of the Okanagan valley, the farm provides a naturalistic habitat for viewing animals. Rare and endangered species like Siberian tigers are on display, as well as grizzly bears and timber wolves and about 700 animals from all over the world.

★ **Okanagan Lake**   *downtown at N end of Main St.*
This sublime eighty-five-mile-long lake has an endless variety of captivating bays, coves, and sandy beaches. Grassy, ponderosa pine-speckled hills and towering rock outcroppings provide dramatic natural backdrops. Most of the gentle slopes surrounding the lake are carpeted with orchards and vineyards which give the valley a remarkably lush appearance. Dozens of roadside stands operate when Canada's most bountiful fruit bowl is being harvested. In only a few years, the area has also become the country's second most important wine producing district. The southern end of the lake, framed by a splendid mile-long sandy beach backed by a tree-shaded park with lawns and picnic areas, is adjacent to downtown Penticton. Numerous provincial and local parks assure easy access to limitless freshwater recreation opportunities along most of the shoreline to the north. One of the West's most enchanting highways parallels the lake for more than seventy miles. Panoramic viewpoints; picturesque communities; lakeside parks; and a cornucopia of fruit stands, distinctive wineries, and some epicurean surprises like Old World sausage shops line the route. Midway, travelers cross the lake on Canada's longest floating bridge.

★ **Penticton Community Centre**   *.5 mi. W at 401 Power St.*   *493-4171*
Queen's Park includes one of the most outstanding recreation complexes in the West. The recently constructed center houses an Olympic-sized swimming pool, whirlpool, sauna, gym, racquetball courts, three tennis courts, and a multipurpose theater.

Warm Water Features

Penticton has recently earned additional distinction by becoming the water slide capital of the West. Three major complexes are in or near town and others are within an hour's drive north and south.

★ **Whitewater West Recreations** *3.3 mi. S at Skaha Lake Rd./Waterford Av.* *493-8466*
A variety of water slides dip, drop, and spiral amidst a succession of waterfalls, pools, and fountains in a new complex that also has a whirlpool, sundeck, food patio, and video arcade. Adjoining is a large tent and trailer park. Closed mid-Sept. to mid-May.

★ **Wild n' Wet Amusement Park** *26 mi. N on BC 97 - Westbank* *768-5141*
This large and diverse hillside water complex includes "the Skimmer" — a long, straight, fast slide ending in a skim across a pool, as well as more conventional twisting and spiral water slides. The centerpiece is a thrilling "River Ride" down a wide and turbulent 500-foot flume. There are also two large whirlpools, a food concession, and picnic tables. Closed mid-Sept. to mid-May.

★ **Wonderful Waterworld** *3.5 mi. S at 225 Yorkton Av.* *493-8121*
Seven major slides twist and dip for nearly one-half mile in this large new complex. A whirlpool, 18-hole mini golf course, electronic games, food concession, and a picnic area have also been provided, and a tent and trailer park adjoins. Closed mid-Sept. to mid-May.

Wineries

In only a few years, several wineries have been established in the southern Okanagan area. Among the most interesting are:

Casabello Wines *2 mi. S at 2210 Main St.* *492-0621*
Established in 1966, this winery is now one of the largest producers in the country. The modern complex includes a wine shop where the full line is sold and limited tastes are offered. Tasting, tours, and sales 10-6. Closed Sun.

Sumac Ridge Winery *12 mi. N at 17403 BC 97 - Summerland* *494-0451*
This tiny estate winery was established in 1980 on the Sumac Ridge Golf Course. Careful modifications were made to retain the beauty and challenge of the golf course while adding the vineyard. A short list of wines is available for tasting and sales. Closed Sun.

Winter Sports

★ **Apex Alpine** *22 mi. SW* *493-3200*
The vertical rise is 2,000 feet and the longest run is approximately 1.5 miles. Elevation at the top is 7,250 feet. There are four chairlifts, including two triple chairs. All necessary services, facilities, and rentals are available at the base for both downhill and cross-country skiing. The novice run is used for night skiing. Two restaurants and lounges, plus condominium rentals, are located at the hill. The skiing season is late November to mid-April.

SHOPPING

Main Street is the vital heart of downtown. It is a well-landscaped semi-mall with the area's best assortment of shops, including a few that specialize in local arts, crafts, and gourmet produce.

Food Specialties

★ **Continental Pastry Bakery** *downtown at 354 Main St.* *493-5959*
Delicious local and Continental breakfast and dessert pastries, plus fine sausage rolls, are offered in this outstanding new takeout pastry shop. Closed Sun.

Edible Dried Goods *downtown at 407 Main St.* *493-4093*
An unusual specialty — "fruit leather" (a dried fruit snack) — is featured here. No preservatives or additives are used in the "fruit stix" and other edible dried foods made locally from various Okanagan fruits and honey.

Sunset Bakery *downtown at 540 Main St.* *493-5266*
This takeout bakery displays the area's most diverse assortment of baked goods, including some tantalizing specialties like sausage rolls and "rootin-tootins." Closed Sun.

Specialty Shops

Okanagan Books *downtown at 239 Main St.* *493-1941*
A large selection of books on many topics, including books about the region, are displayed along with a good assortment of magazines.

Terwilliger P. Jones Gifts *downtown in Courtyard One on Main St.* *439-9221*
This inviting little shop features crafts made exclusively by local artists.

NIGHTLIFE

Distinctive places with evening entertainment and refreshments are plentiful, ranging from casual taverns to plush high-tech lounges. Most of the best are located downtown.

★ **Barley Mill Pub**   *2.2 mi. S at 2460 Skaha Lake Rd.*   *493-8000*
This new roadside pub has a delightfully authentic feeling enhanced by darts and pool and a great stone fireplace, and comfortably updated furnishings that include posh contemporary chairs and sofas. Fine pub grub is served with appropriate English and Canadian beers and other beverages. Closed Sun.

★ **Delta Lakeside**   *downtown at 21 E. Lakeshore Dr.*   *493-8221*
The Leading Edge is a sleek, high-tech lounge in Penticton's leading hotel. Grand piano stylings, or groups playing mellow sounds for dancing, are offered most evenings. Overstuffed sofas and armchairs overlook a magnificent view of Okanagan Lake. A fireplace nook and a view terrace are seasonally popular.

Lacey's Cabaret   *downtown at 511 Main St.*   *493-8311*
Live entertainment and dancing attract crowds to this big, casual downstairs nightclub.

Nite Moves   *downtown at 333 Main St.*   *493-1222*
Hard rock and dancing are featured in this large subterranean cabaret.

Penticton Inn   *downtown at 333 Martin St.*   *493-0333*
Jiggers is a large and lively nightclub that provides music with a heavy beat for dancing most nights. The hotel also offers easy listening music and comfortable armchairs in an adjoining lounge.

★ **Three Gables Hotel**   *downtown at 353 Main St.*   *492-3933*
The Gables Pub features live mellow sounds and dancing, plus shuffleboard, pool, and electronic games. Individual musicians or vocalists occasionally entertain guests relaxing in armchair comfort in the adjoining wood-toned Tudor Lounge.

Tiffany's   *downtown at 535 Main St.*   *493-1023*
Hard rock music and dancing happen nightly in a contemporary, cavern-like cabaret with an elaborate lighting system.

RESTAURANTS

Restaurants are plentiful and diverse in and around town. A surprising lack of good breakfast places is balanced by a selection of dinner houses notable for quality and variety of cuisine as well as distinctive decor.

Charlie Malcolm's   *.4 mi. W at 795 W. Westminster Av.*   *493-6364*
L-D.   *Moderate*
Steak, seafood, and pizza are the odd mix in an unusual and relaxed dining room where old-time movie favorites are screened nightly for diners.

The Chelsea House   *downtown at 510 Main St.*   *492-4585*
B-L-D. No B on Sat. & Sun.   *Low*
Traditional British fish and chips are taken seriously in this pub-style coffee shop.

★ **Country Squire**   *10 mi. NE via Naramata Rd. on 1st St. - Naramata*   *496-5416*
D only. Closed Mon.-Tues.   *Expensive*
Expertly prepared Continental cuisine is served to about thirty guests each evening in an elegant house overlooking Okanagan Lake. Guests are given an opportunity to compose their own fixed price meal when they phone for reservations, as required, at least a day in advance.

The Delta Lakeside Hotel   *downtown at 21 E. Lakeshore Dr.*   *493-8221*
D only.   *Moderate*
Ripples, the main dining room of Penticton's largest hotel, offers conventional hotel fare that is no match for the plush contemporary setting with a waterfront view of Okanagan Lake. The adjoining Peaches and Cream Coffee Shop serves plain, pricey breakfasts, lunches, and dinners with the best lakeside view in the area.

★ **Granny Bogner's Restaurant**   *.4 mi. S at 302 W. Eckhardt Av.*   *493-2711*
D only. Closed Sun. & Mon.   *Moderate*
European specialty dishes made with the freshest available ingredients are given splendid attention in a handsome Tudor-style house. Elegant furnishings, authentic antiques, and many plants provide a romantic setting for memorable dining.

Micky Finn's   *downtown at 57 E. Padmore Av.*   *493-3883*
L-D. No L on Sat. & Sun.   *Moderate*
A contemporary American menu and seasonal homemade desserts are offered in a relaxed and pleasant restaurant.

★ **The 1912 Restaurant** *9 mi. SW via BC 97 at 100 Alder Av. - Kaleden*   *497-8555*
D only. Sun. brunch. Closed Mon.-Tues.   *Moderate*
Continental cuisine is served in an artistically converted general store. From the casually elegant dining room or the beautiful adjoining garden (used on warm evenings and for Sunday brunch in summer), the view of nearby Skaha Lake is splendid.

Rossi's   *downtown at 123 Front St.*   *492-7717*
L-D.   *Low*
This new trattoria does nice work with a short list of pastas and nightly specials, plus a variety of delicious cakes and pastries, in a romantic little dining room.

Rubin's Bistro   *downtown at 101 Westminster Av.*   *492-4404*
L-D. No L on Sun.   *Moderate*
Contemporary Canadian fare is served in this popular restaurant's casually inviting dining room, or on an outdoor patio. A comfortable lounge adjoins.

Stonehouse Inn   *12 mi. NW at 14015 Rosedale Av. - Summerland*   *494-9293*
L-D. No L on Sat.   *Moderate*
Continental dishes are served in a comfortably old-fashioned stone house with a fireplace in the main dining room.

★ **Theo's Restaurant**   *downtown at 687 Main St.*   *492-4019*
L-D. No L on Sun.   *Moderate*
Tantalizing Greek specialties are exuberantly paired with a bright and lively split-level dining area outfitted with an atmospheric fireplace, a Mediterranean-style bar, and casually elegant table settings amidst an abundance of greenery.

★ **Three Mile House**   *4.5 mi. NE at 1507 Naramata Rd.*   *492-5152*
D only. Closed Sun.   *Moderate*
Continental cuisine and attentive tableside preparation are featured. A home in a garden surrounded by some of the finest orchard country on Okanagan Lake has been skillfully converted into a charming dinner house with several cozy dining rooms.

LODGING

In keeping with its status as the heart of the Canadian sunbelt, Penticton has a remarkable diversity of accommodations, including some delightful lakefront places. Many of the best require a minimum stay of three or more days in summer. During the remainder of the year, rates are usually reduced by 25% and more from those shown.

Beachside Motel   *3.8 mi. S at 3624 Parkview St.*   *492-8318*
Opposite a beachfront park and tennis courts near Skaha Lake, this small **bargain** motel has an indoor pool and a sauna. Each room has cable color TV.
    regular room —   D bed...$24

Bel-Air Flag Inn —   *2.3 mi. S at 2670 Skaha Lake Rd.*   *492-6111*
This well-landscaped, modern motel has an outdoor pool, whirlpool, and saunas. Each room has a phone and cable color TV.
    regular room —   Q bed...$34

Blue Ridge Motel   *2.2 mi. S at 2406 Skaha Lake Rd.*   *492-3029*
This small single-level motel is a **bargain** with a large pool. Each room has a cable color TV.
    regular room —   Q bed...$30

The Bowmont Motel   *.8 mi. W at 80 Riverside Dr.*   *492-0112*
Okanagan Beach is nearby, and a large outdoor pool, whirlpool, and sauna are features of this modern motel. Each room has a phone and cable color TV.
    regular room —   Q bed...$32

★ **The Delta Lakeside**   *downtown at 21 E. Lakeshore Dr.*   *493-8221*
Penticton's largest and tallest hotel is a recently completed six floor structure with the best location in the Okanagan Valley — adjacent to the mile-long beach park on the south shore of Okanagan Lake. In addition to a fine sandy beach, amenities include a large indoor pool with an up-lake view, whirlpool, saunas, two tennis courts, an exercise room,

and rental boats, plus restaurants and a superb lounge. Each spacious, beautifully appointed room has a phone, cable color TV, and a private balcony.

#643,#543,#443 — corner, magnificent lake view, K bed...$84

#624,#626,#632,#524,#526,#532,#424,#426,#432 — superb lake views, K bed...$71

regular room — view toward downtown, K bed...$55

El Rancho Motel *.5 mi. W at 877 Westminster Av.* *492-5736*

This modern **bargain** motel has a large outdoor pool, three tennis courts, bicycles for guests, plus a restaurant and cocktail lounge. Each room has a phone, cable color TV, and a refrigerator.

regular room — D or Q bed...$30

Flamingo Motel *2.2 mi. S at 2387 Skaha Lake Rd.* *492-8333*

A large outdoor pool is a feature in a modern motel with some **bargain** units. Each room has a phone and cable color TV.

regular room — Q bed...$28

Kreekside Motel *1.5 mi. S at 1706 Main St.* *492-3829*

This modern motel has a large indoor pool, whirlpool, and sauna. Each room has a phone, cable color TV, and a refrigerator.

regular room — Q bed...$32

Lakeland Motel *.9 mi. W at 190 Riverside Dr.* *492-0610*

Some **bargain** rooms are available in this small motel with an outdoor view pool. Each room has a cable color TV.

regular room — D bed...$26

Meadow Lark Motel *2.4 mi. S at 2730 Skaha Lake Rd.* *492-3994*

In this tiny single-level **bargain** motel, each unit has a kitchenette and a B/W TV.

regular room — 1 BR, kit., D bed...$21

Penticton Inn *downtown at 333 Martin St.* *493-0333*

A large five-story hotel in the heart of town has an indoor pool and saunas, plus a restaurant, lounge, and pub with entertainment. Each **bargain** room has a phone and cable color TV with movies.

regular room — Q bed...$30

★ **Penticton TraveLodge** *.6 mi. W at 950 Westminster Av.* *492-0225*

A new 250-foot water slide (for guests only) is the main attraction in a modern motel that also has an outdoor pool, a whirlpool, and a sauna. Each nicely decorated room has a phone and cable color TV.

regular room — Q bed...$34

★ **Pilgrim House** *.7 mi. W at 1050 Eckhardt Av.* *492-8926*

The Penticton Golf Course adjoins the spacious, attractively landscaped grounds of this modern single-level motor hotel. There is a large scenic outdoor pool, plus an architecturally unusual dining room, and a lounge and pub. Each spacious room has a phone, cable color TV, and a private patio.

regular room — most have a refr., Q bed...$40

Riverside Motel *.9 mi. W at 110 Riverside Dr.* *492-2615*

This modern **bargain** motel with an outdoor pool is near Okanagan Beach. Each room has cable color TV and a kitchenette.

regular room — D bed...$28

Royal Anchor Resort Motel *10 mi. NE - Naramata* *496-5492*

Across a street from a sandy beach on Okanagan Lake is a tiny single-level **bargain** motel set on shady spacious lawns. Canoes, paddle and row boats, and bicycles are complimentary to guests, along with shuffleboard, ping-pong, and other games.

#2,#4 — kitchen, some lake view, D bed...$30

regular room — kitchen, no view, D bed...$30

★ **Sandman Inn** *.6 mi. W at 939 Burnaby Av.* *493-7151*

This large newer motor hotel has an indoor pool in an enclosed courtyard, whirlpool, sauna, and two tennis courts, plus (a fee for) racquet and squash courts. A dining room and a handsome lounge are also available. Each room has a phone and cable color TV.

regular room — Q bed...$35

★ **Sandy Beach Lodge**   *10 mi. NE via Naramata Rd. - Naramata*   *496-5765*
The area's most charming little resort is set amidst orchards by a splendid private sandy beach on Okanagan Lake. An outdoor pool and tennis courts are surrounded by colorful gardens and fruit tree-shaded lawns. Each unit is large and comfortably furnished.
    #11,#12 — lakeshore cottages, patio, kitchenette, superb lake view,   D bed...$45
    regular room — in lodge, lake view,   D bed...$40

Shoreline Motel   *.5 mi. W at 926 Lakeshore Dr.*   *492-7113*
Across the street from the mile-long beachfront park by Okanagan Lake, this motel has a small outdoor pool. Each room has a phone, cable color TV, and refrigerator.
    #20 — spacious, fine lake view,   Q bed...$32
    regular room —   Q bed...$32

Slumber Lodge   *downtown at 274 Lakeshore Dr.*   *492-4008*
Across a street from the park by Okanagan Lake, this modern motel has a large indoor pool with a lake view, saunas, and an upstairs view dining room. Each room has a phone and cable color TV.
    #56 — corner windows, up-lake view,   Q bed...$40
    regular room —   Q bed...$40

★ **Telstar Motor Inn - Best Western** *3.3 mi. S at 3180 Skaha Lake Rd.*   *493-0311*
Pleasant landscaped grounds around this contemporary motel include both large outdoor and indoor pools, a whirlpool, and an inviting restaurant. Each spacious, well-furnished room has a phone and cable color TV.
    "Honeymoon Suite" (4 of these) — mirrored ceiling, sunken Roman tub,   Q bed...$58
    regular room —   D bed...$39

Western Motel   *1.8 mi. S near Main St. at 38 Warren Av.*   *493-1677*
This single-level **bargain** motel has a small outdoor pool and a quiet location off the highway. Each simply furnished room has cable color TV.
    regular room —   Q bed...$26

CAMPGROUNDS
Of the many campgrounds surrounding town, the best offer some of the most distinctive locations in the West. Campers can opt to be by a sandy beach, in an orchard overlooking the lake, or next to a water slide complex.

★ **Camp-along Tent and Trailer Park**   *6 mi. S on BC 97*   *497-5584*
This privately operated campground occupies the top and slopes of an orchard-covered hill overlooking Skaha Lake. A beautifully landscaped kidney-shaped pool with a panoramic view is an outstanding feature. Flush toilets, hot showers (fee), and hookups are available. Well-separated grassy sites occupy several hillside terraces. Each is shaded by mature apricot and other fruit trees and has a picnic table. Tent sites are separated.
    base rate...$7.50

★ **Okanagan Lake Provincial Park**   *15 mi. NW on BC 97*
This large provincial campground, spectacularly situated on the west shore of Okanagan Lake, has a sandy beach, boat ramp, and nature trails. Swimming, sunbathing, boating, water-skiing, fishing, and hiking are popular. There are flush toilets, but no showers or hookups. Each of the sites has a picnic table and fire area.   base rate...$4

Water World Tent & Trailer Park *3.5 mi. S on BC 97 at Yorkton Av.*   *492-4255*
This privately owned facility is adjacent to a large new (fee) water slide park, and has a swimming pool and therapy pool. Flush toilets, hot showers, and hookups are available. Each closely spaced, grassy site has a picnic table.   base rate...$8

★ **Wright's Beach Camp**   *4.5 mi. S on BC 97*   *492-7120*
The only campground adjacent to Skaha Lake in town is a privately owned facility with a long sandy beach for sunbathing and swimming. Boating and fishing are also popular. Flush toilets, hot showers, and hookups are available. All of the closely-spaced sites are shaded by poplars, and each has a picnic table. Most border the sandy beach.
    base rate...$9.50

SPECIAL EVENTS
★ **Mid-Winter Breakout**   *in town and on Apex Mountain*   *mid-February*
This week-long festival features ice sculptures, a "Polar Bear Dip," a costumed bed race, and a "Mad Dash" multi-sport event from Apex Mountain to Okanagan Lake, as well as dances and live entertainment.

★ **Peach Festival**   *in town*   *last week in July*
A giant Peach Festival parade, plus a queen coronation, live entertainment, dancing, sand castle judging, and sailing races highlight the year's biggest celebration — a week-long tribute to the peach harvest.

★ **British Columbia Square Dance Jamboree**   *in King's Park*   *early August*
Thousands of square dancers from all over the continent dance in the streets in the morning, and on the world's longest outdoor floor under the stars. There are also lakeside events and a fun parade.

★ **Septober Wine Festival**   *in town*   *last week in September*
Penticton hosts (with other communities in the Okanagan Country) public wine tastings; winery and vineyard tours; entertainment; and dances in celebration of the valley's increasingly significant grape harvest and crush.

OTHER INFORMATION
Area Code: *604*
Zip Code: *V2A*
Penticton Chamber of Commerce .   *downtown at 185 W. Lakeshore Dr.*   *492-4103*

Vernon, British Columbia

Elevation:

1,190 feet

Population (1981):

19,987

Population (1971):

13,283

Location:

320 mi. NE
of Vancouver

Vernon is an urbane hideaway in a wonderland of lakes and mountains. At the northern end of the enchanting Okanagan Lake country, the town occupies a little basin at the confluence of several valleys. Midway between the Coast Ranges on the west and the Canadian Rockies to the east, the protected setting has a mild climate compared to most of Canada. Snowfall is relatively light in town, but there is enough to support a major winter sports complex on nearby mountains. From late spring through the busy summer season, warm sunny days are the norm. Swimming, boating, fishing, hiking, backpacking, horseback and pack trips, and camping are some of the popular outdoor activities enjoyed on the surrounding lakes and mountains. Beautifully landscaped parks, scenic golf courses, one of the West's finest recreation centers (with a splendid multi-building complex including an Olympic-sized pool, ice-skating, tennis, and other facilities), and a large new water slide park are available in town.

Fur trading, mining, and cattle in turn provided early opportunities for settlement in the area. But it was the advent of sternwheeler ships on eighty-five-mile-long Okanagan Lake in 1886 and the railroad in 1891 that marked the beginning of real growth. Incorporated in 1892, Vernon is the oldest town in the Western Canadian interior. It may also be the most cosmopolitan, with a population that includes large minorities of Eastern European and of Oriental ancestry. Large-scale irrigation was introduced in 1908. Orchards, vegetable farms, and dairies soon began to transform the valleys into a pastoral heartland. Highway and rail access improved enough that lake barge and steamer service ended in 1936. As transportation systems throughout the province have developed, Vernon has begun to gracefully respond to its inevitable role as a major leisure destination.

Several major civic improvements give the town an especially urbane appearance, including an outstanding civic center, an enormous recreation/cultural complex, and two enchanting downtown garden parks — each with one of the West's most ingenious fountains. A well-landscaped main street mall has also helped concentrate a small but growing assortment of distinctive shops, good restaurants, and lively pubs and cabarets downtown. International specialties are featured in restaurants throughout the area. Numerous lodgings are well-situated in town, including two of the Northwest's most extraordinary motor hotels.

WEATHER PROFILE

Vokac Weather Rating

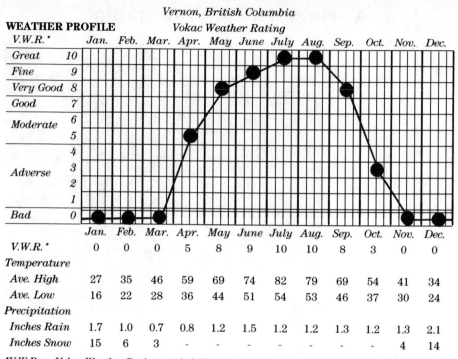

V.W.R.*	Jan.	Feb.	Mar.	Apr.	May	June	July	Aug.	Sep.	Oct.	Nov.	Dec.
Great	10											
Fine	9											
Very Good	8											
Good	7											
Moderate	6											
	5											
	4											
Adverse	3											
	2											
	1											
Bad	0											

	Jan.	Feb.	Mar.	Apr.	May	June	July	Aug.	Sep.	Oct.	Nov.	Dec.
V.W.R.*	0	0	0	5	8	9	10	10	8	3	0	0
Temperature												
Ave. High	27	35	46	59	69	74	82	79	69	54	41	34
Ave. Low	16	22	28	36	44	51	54	53	46	37	30	24
Precipitation												
Inches Rain	1.7	1.0	0.7	0.8	1.2	1.5	1.2	1.2	1.3	1.2	1.3	2.1
Inches Snow	15	6	3	-	-	-	-	-	-	-	4	14

*V.W.R. = Vokac Weather Rating: probability of mild (warm & dry) weather on any given day.

Forecast

Month	V.W.R.*		Temperatures		Precipitation
			Daytime	Evening	
January	0	Bad	cold	frigid	frequent snow flurries
February	0	Bad	chilly	cold	frequent snow flurries
March	0	Bad	chilly	chilly	occasional showers/snow flurries
April	6	Moderate	cool	chilly	occasional showers
May	8	Very Good	warm	cool	occasional showers
June	9	Fine	warm	cool	frequent showers
July	10	Great	warm	warm	occasional showers
August	10	Great	warm	warm	occasional showers
September	8	Very Good	warm	cool	occasional showers
October	3	Adverse	cool	chilly	frequent showers
November	0	Bad	chilly	chilly	occasional showers/snow flurries
December	0	Bad	chilly	cold	frequent snow flurries

Summary

Vernon lies deep in the folds of gentle brush-covered hills near the north end of the magnificent Okanagan Lake country. Only about 1,200 feet above sea level, the area enjoys a surprisingly mild four season climate. **Winter** is cold, with frequent snow flurries providing enough snow to support a major winter sports complex nearby. **Spring** warms quickly, and by May, mild weather settles in with warm days, cool evenings, and light, frequent rainfalls. **Summer** is outstanding. Delightfully long warm days and evenings and occasional showers assure that light sportswear and swimsuits are appropriate for this splendid lake country. After the beginning of **fall**, temperatures cool very rapidly and shower activity increases. However, brisk sunny days early in the season are the right weather for indulging in the fruits and wines of nearby harvests.

ATTRACTIONS & DIVERSIONS

Adventureland   *17 mi. S on BC 97 - Winfield*   766-2980
This old-fashioned roadside amusement park includes an impressive rug slide, among more prosaic attractions for kids.

★ **Boat Rentals**
Several places in and near town rent boats by the hour or longer to fish, water-ski, sail, or cruise while enjoying the scenic grandeur of Okanagan Lake. Among these are:
   Seymour Marina   *4 mi. SW on Okanagan Landing Rd.*   542-6466
   Western Service & Marina   *4 mi. SW on Okanagan Landing Rd.*   542-2043
★ **Ellison Park**   *10 mi. SW on Okanagan Landing Rd.*   545-6940
Granite cliffs surround sheltered bays edged with sandy beaches on Okanagan Lake. In addition to fine swimming and sunbathing areas, fishing and boating are popular. Pine-shaded picnic tables and campsites offer panoramic lake and mountain views.

Golf Courses
   Spallumcheen Golf & Tennis Club   *8 mi. N on BC 97*   545-5824
Visitors are welcome to play an attractive 18-hole golf course. Other facilities include a pro shop, driving range, club and cart rentals, plus four tennis courts and food service.
   Vernon Golf and Country Club   *2 mi. S on Kalamalka Lake Rd.*   541-9126
This 18-hole golf course is open to the public. Facilities include a pro shop, club and cart rentals, and a dining lounge.

★ **Justice Court Park**   *downtown at 30th Av. & 27th St.*
One of the West's most distinctive walk-under waterfall/sculptures is the highlight of an appealing little park in front of an imposing turn-of-the-century granite courthouse.

★ **Kalamalka Lake Provincial Park** *6 mi. S via Kalamalka & Cosens Bay Rds.*
The Okanagan Valley's natural vegetation (grassy slopes interspersed with ponderosa pines) assures easy hiking, panoramic views, and scenic picnic sites throughout this park. The beautiful lake is clear and warm enough that swimming is popular in summer. Rock outcroppings separate the shoreline into a number of picturesque small bays and beaches.

★ **Okanagan Lake**   *4 mi. W via Okanagan Landing Rd.*
The centerpiece of the Canadian sunbelt is a beautiful 85-mile-long freshwater lake with an endless variety of alluring bays, coves, and sandy beaches. Ponderosa pine-speckled hills and towering rock outcroppings provide dramatic natural backdrops in several areas, while vast orchards blanket slopes and terraces along the lake. During the summer, dozens of roadside stands display fresh-picked fruits from Canada's most luxuriant fruit bowl. The valley is also becoming one of the country's most important wine producing districts. Recreation opportunities abound in provincial and local lakeside parks. A wonderfully scenic highway parallels the lake for most of its length, giving travelers access to panoramic viewpoints, picturesque communities and parks, distinctive wineries and fruit stands, and some surprises like fine old country sausage shops and a lake crossing on Canada's longest floating bridge.

★ **O'Keefe Ranch**   *8 mi. N on BC 97*   542-7868
From 1867 to 1977, this historic ranch was occupied by members of the O'Keefe family. Their self-contained cattle empire had a store, post office, church, and blacksmith shop. Carefully preserved original buildings, period furnishings, and memorabilia may be viewed daily. Extensive, landscaped grounds also include a restaurant, gift shop, and picnic area.

★ **Polson Park**   *downtown at 25th Av. & 32nd St.*
This enchanting park features a beautifully landscaped stream, a meticulously accurate and detailed floral clock, colorful Japanese gardens, large expanses of tree-shaded lawns, and several picturesque ponds. Don't miss the whimsical Ogopogo fountain on one of the ponds. Tennis courts, scenic bikeways and paths, romantic little bridges, and tranquil picnic sites round out the facilities.

★ **Vernon Civic Centre**   *downtown at 32nd Av. & 31st St.*
This award-winning complex of contemporary public buildings includes the city hall, museum and archives, library, and an art gallery. Beautifully landscaped grounds also showcase numerous fountains, sculptures, and a graceful clock tower.

★ **Vernon Recreation Complex**   *.3 mi. NW at 3310 37th Av.*   545-6035
One of the most outstanding recreation complexes in the West is on landscaped grounds
by Swan Lake Creek. Handsome contemporary buildings house an Olympic-sized
swimming pool, ice-skating rinks, a gym, arts center, arenas, and an auditorium. Outdoor
tennis courts are converted to public ice rinks in winter.

Warm Water Features

★   **Atlantis World of Water**   *3 mi. N on BC 97*   549-4121
A river slide is the highlight among an assortment of twisting and spiraling water slides in
Vernon's big new aquatic playground. Drop slides, a giant hot tub, a sundeck, food patio,
and picnic areas have also been provided at the sunny hillside complex.

★   **Cedar Springs**   *6 mi. NE via Silver Star Rd. on Dixon Dam Rd.*   542-5477
The biggest hot tub in the West, filled with hot mineral water bubbling in from over a dozen
jets, is on a large cedar deck nestled in a tranquil pine forest. Several small tubs, including
a private tub in the skylit Cedar Room, may also be rented by the hour.

Winery

★   **Grey Monk Cellars** *22 mi. S on Camp Rd. - 4 mi. W of Winfield*   766-3168
The first estate winery was recently established on slopes of the northern section of
Okanagan Lake. An inviting new tasting room, beautifully sited amidst the vineyards, has
an enchanting overview of the lake. Tasting, tours and sales daily 10-5. Closed Sun.

Winter Sports

★   **Silver Star**   *14 mi. NE via BC 97*   542-0224
The vertical rise is 1,600 feet and the longest run is approximately two miles. There are
three chairlifts. Elevation at the top is 6,280 feet. All necessary services and rentals are
available at the base for downhill skiing, along with cafeterias, a bar, and lodge. The skiing
season is mid-November to mid-April.

★   **Snowmobiling**   *downtown at 3311 30th Av.*   542-6124
The head office of the British Columbia Snow Vehicle Association (address and phone
number above) will explain why Vernon is known as the snowmobile capital of British
Columbia. They can also supply information on areas, rentals, and guides.

SHOPPING
The main street (30th Avenue) is a well-furnished partial mall that is the heart of a
compact downtown bounded by the Civic Centre, Justice Court park, and Polson Park.
Here is the area's most complete assortment of shops, including several that feature
locally produced crafts and gourmet food items.

Food Specialties

★ **Armstrong Cheese** *16 mi. N via BC 97 on Pleasant Valley Rd.*   546-3084
A fine selection of cheddar cheeses, plus ice creams, are sold at this popular cheese
factory. There are limited samples and a viewing area for visitors. Closed Sun.

Greyhound Bus Terminal   *downtown at 3102 30th St.*   542-3118
Surprisingly, the area's most authentic and delicious Ukranian pyrogys and borscht are
featured in a terminally plain depot where the best table (the one with the view of a minipark) is reserved for bus drivers.

★ **H & P Ranch Sausages & Meats**   *10 mi. S on BC 97*   545-7796
An outstanding selection of European-style sausages is displayed and sold in a little meat
market on a picturesque ranch. Closed Sun.

★ **Okanagan Sausage Ltd.**   *13 mi. S on BC 97 - Oyama*   548-3564
Many kinds of excellent European-style sausages are made and sold in a well-stocked
roadside meat market that is a long-time favorite of the region.

★ **Rogers Foods Ltd.**   *10.5 mi. N via BC 97 on Larkin Rd.*   546-3155
An extraordinary selection of whole grains, natural foods, and candies are sold in an
authentic, old-fashioned mill. Closed Sat.

★ **Roxy Bakery and Delicatessen**   *downtown at 3008 31st St.*   542-6126
Delicious egg-rich apple fritters and sausage rolls are specialties of this European-style
bakery/deli where all baking is done on the premises. Hot and cold drinks and light fare
are also served in the shop, or to go.

★ **Valley Fruit Stand**   *.8 mi. N at 2902 43rd Av.*   542-3830
Okanagan "fruit leather" and fruit candy are specialties. Fresh vegetables and fruits —
even fresh fruit milkshakes — are sold in season in a big, bright open-air market.

★ **Vernon Bakery**   *downtown at 3413 30th Av.*   *542-2780*
This bakery offers a full line of European-style breads and pastries, including outstanding scones, sausage rolls, and other specialties. Closed Sun.

★ **Walloschek Sausage Ltd.**   *downtown at 3402 31st Av.*   *542-9288*
Flavorful sausages like Ukranian salami, kolbasa, and pepperoni are made on the premises. Visitors can have them packaged to go or served in sandwiches in the nicely decorated coffee shop.

Specialty Shops

Bookland   *downtown at 3101 30th St.*   *545-1885*
A large selection of books and magazines is attractively displayed in this bright and inviting bookstore.

Eskila Arts and Crafts   *1.3 mi. N at 4412 27th St.*   *542-4593*
A charming potpourri of local and regionally produced arts and crafts is displayed in this roadside gallery.

Galerie Gagnon   *downtown at 2901 30th Av.*   *545-5408*
A contemporary gallery above a frame shop sells works of British Columbia artists.

NIGHTLIFE
Many places, ranging from casual taverns to elegant lounges, come alive after dark along the main thoroughfares of town.

Brass Rail   *downtown at 2828 30th Av.*   *549-1771*
Country/western or rock music set the tone for dancing almost every night in a casual, woodsy nightclub with some comfortable alcoves.

The Lakeside Motor Inn   *4 mi. SW at Okanagan Landing Rd.*   *542-2377*
The motel's Quarterdeck Lounge has live entertainment and casual nautical atmosphere overlooking Okanagan Lake. Barnacles offers cabaret-style entertainment nightly, ranging from exotic dancers to live band music and dancing. Closed Sun.

★ **29/29 Nite Club**   *downtown at 2900 29th Av.*   *545-4242*
Disco or live music for dancing is featured nightly. This high-tech showplace has comfortable chairs surrounding a lighted dance floor backed by a giant video screen. A pool room adjoins. Closed Sun.

★ **The Vernon Lodge**   *.4 mi. N at 3914 32nd St.*   *545-3385*
The hotel's unique Garden Lounge offers live entertainment in a jungle-like plant-filled setting amidst an expansive courtyard that encloses a portion of a large natural stream. Elsewhere, Squeeks features dancing in a whimsical-Canadiana disco setting. Closed Sun.

Village Green Inn   *1.4 mi. N on BC 97 at 4801 27th St.*   *542-3321*
The El Cantina is a piano bar with comfortable couches and chairs in a sort-of Spanish-style bar. Elsewhere in the hotel, exotic dancers strut their stuff nightly in a cabaret. The Patio Lounge offers poolside drink service in summer.

RESTAURANTS
Restaurants are plentiful and plain, with a few notable exceptions. Several feature uncommon dishes that reflect the Ukranian heritage of many area residents.

Cafe Europa   *downtown at 3202 31st Av.*   *545-8538*
L-D. No L on Sat. Closed Mon.   *Moderate*
Carefully prepared Continental dishes are served amidst casual elegance in a cozy and romantic dining room.

Hy's Steak House   *1.4 mi. N on BC 97 at 4801 27th St.*   *545-1777*
D only.   *Moderate*
In the Village Green Inn, steak is the specialty of the main restaurant. This formally elegant dining room is a popular representative of one of Canada's most highly regarded contemporary restaurant chains.

Intermezzo Restaurant   *downtown at 3206 34th Av.*   *542-3853*
D only. Closed Tues. (& Mon. non-summer).   *Moderate*
Pasta dishes and selected Italian specialties are offered in several nicely furnished dining rooms.

★ **Jamieson Booker's**   *.4 mi. N at 3915 32nd St.*   *545-4451*
L-D. No L on Sat. & Sun.   *Moderate*
Continental and Canadian specialties are skillfully prepared, and served amidst informal Old World decor in a handsome dining room.

Lakeside Motor Inn   *4 mi. SW on Okanagan Landing Rd.*   *542-2377*
D only.   *Moderate*
Steak and seafood are accompanied by a salad bar and an unobstructed view of
Okanagan Lake from the motor hotel's casual lakeshore dining room. Evening barbecues
on the lakeside patio are a specialty during the summer.

★ **Mister D's**   *downtown at 3210 30th Av.*   *549-2565*
L-D. Closed Sun.   *Moderate*
Contemporary fare is highlighted by delicious homemade desserts and pastries in a
cheerful upstairs restaurant. Unusual beverages are also offered along with frequent live
background music in the comfortable dining areas.

Sundowner   *1.6 mi. N at 2501 53rd Av.*   *542-5142*
L-D. No L on Sat. & Sun.   *Moderate*
A variety of international dishes (usually including selected Ukranian specialties)
accompanies the area's finest soup and salad bar. The Sunday buffet is especially notable
in this casual, modern restaurant.

Vernon Lodge Hotel   *.4 mi. N at 3914 32nd St.*   *545-3385*
B-L-D.   *Moderate*
In the casually elegant Pepper House Restaurant, Canadian fare is served all day, and
Continental dishes are featured in the evening. Patrons in restful banquettes or armchairs
overlook an enclosed tropical courtyard with a natural stream running through it in this
novel dining room.

White Rose   *downtown at 3209 30th Av.*   *545-8600*
B-L-D.   *Low*
Some homemade baked goods and several Ukranian specialties are featured in this
modest coffee shop.

Woodslake Inn   *17 mi. S on BC 97 - Winfield*   *766-4544*
L-D. No L on Sat. & Sun.   *Moderate*
Several Old English dishes are featured on a Continental menu in a charming new country
inn with elegant furnishings and decor.

LODGING

Accommodations are fairly numerous. Disappointingly few are on either of the splendid
nearby lakes. Several newer motels do offer surprising numbers of amenities, however.
From fall through spring, rates are often reduced by 20% or more from the prices noted
below.

Blue Stream Motel   *.6 mi. N at 4202 32nd St.*   *545-2221*
In this small **bargain** motel, each simply furnished room has a phone and cable color TV.
   regular room —   D bed...$20

The Globe Motel   *.4 mi. N at 3900 33rd St.*   *542-2327*
This modern **bargain** motel has a large outdoor pool and a picnic area, plus a sauna. Each
spacious, plainly furnished room has a phone and cable color TV.
   "courtyard" room — pvt. patio/balc. over pool, refr.,   Q bed...$30
   regular room —   Q bed...$27

Hegler's Lakeshore Resort   *3 mi. S at 12408 Kalamalka Rd.*   *545-0677*
Vernon's beach park adjoins this older **bargain** motel that has its own private sandy beach
on beautiful Kalamalka Lake. Power boats and rowboats can be rented. Each rustic unit
has a color TV and kitchen.
   regular room —   D bed...$29

Highwayman Motel   *downtown at 3500 32nd St.*   *545-2148*
This small single-level **bargain** motel is convenient to both the heart of town and the
recreation center. Each room has a phone and cable color TV.
   deluxe room —   K waterbed...$34
   regular room —   D bed...$26

Hillside Plaza Inn   *.5 mi. N at 4100 32nd St.*   *549-1211*
A large indoor pool, whirlpool, and sauna are features of this modern motel. Each
spacious, well-decorated room has a phone and cable color TV with movies.
   regular room —   Q bed...$35

Lakeside Motor Inn   *4 mi. SW on Okanagan Landing Rd.*   *542-2377*
Vernon's only lodging on Okanagan Lake is a plain two-level **bargain** motel with a sandy beach and docking facilities, an indoor pool and whirlpool, plus a lakeview restaurant, a lounge, and a cabaret. Each simply furnished room has a phone, cable color TV, and a balcony or patio with a lake view.
　　regular room —   2 D beds...$30

Midway Motel   *.5 mi. N at 4006 32nd St.*   *549-1241*
This newer **bargain** motel has a large indoor pool with a slide, plus a whirlpool and sauna. Each nicely furnished room has a phone and cable color TV with movies.
　　regular room —   Q bed...$28

Park Royal Motel   *downtown at 3200 25th Av.*   *545-0544*
Across the highway from lovely Polson Park, this **bargain** motel has an outdoor pool and a sauna. Each simply furnished room has a phone, cable color TV, and a private balcony or patio.
　　regular room —   D bed...$26

Sandman Inn   *.6 mi. N at 4201 32nd St.*   *542-4325*
This modern motel has a large indoor pool and sauna, plus a coffee shop. Each room has a phone and cable color TV.
　　regular room —   D bed...$31

Schell Motel   *downtown at 2810 35th St.*   *545-1351*
In addition to **bargain** units, this modern motel has a large outdoor pool with a slide and a sauna. Each room has a phone and cable color TV. Most have private balconies.
　　#115 — spacious, kitchenette, pvt. balc. over creek, creek view from   Q bed...$30
　　regular room —   Q bed...$26

Silver Star Motel   *.3 mi. N at 3700 32nd St.*   *545-0501*
This small **bargain** motel, adjacent to the recreation complex, has a sauna. Each room has a phone and cable color TV.
　　regular room —   Q bed...$21

Slumber Lodge   *.3 mi. N at 3602 32nd St.*   *545-2195*
A large outdoor pool, an indoor pool, saunas, a recreation room, and a coffee shop are features of a modern **bargain** motel. Each room has a phone and cable color TV.
　　regular room —   Q bed...$30
　　regular room — small,   D bed...$26

★ **Tiki Village Motor Inn**   *.3 mi. S at 2408 34th St.*   *545-2268*
A garden courtyard provides a tranquil setting for an outdoor pool with a slide in a modern Polynesian-style motel that also has a sauna, a whirlpool, and a well-regarded dining room. Attractively furnished rooms each have a phone, cable color TV, and a patio or balcony.
　　regular room —   Q bed...$33

★ **Vernon Lodge Hotel**   *.4 mi. N at 3914 32nd St.*   *545-3385*
One of the West's most novel lodgings is a large motor hotel with a remarkable enclosed courtyard. Within the airy skylit interior, a large pool, a whirlpool, and an appealing lounge and restaurant are set amidst lush tropical plants growing along the banks of a channeled natural creek that flows through the courtyard. The hotel also has a sauna and a cabaret. Each spacious, well-furnished room has a phone and cable color TV with movies.
　　#117,#217,#317 — by the corner where the creek comes in,   Q bed...$41
　　#301,#303,#305,#307,#309,#311,#313, — good pvt. courtyard view, Q bed...$41
　　regular room —   Q bed...$39

★ **The Village Green Inn**   *1.4 mi. N at 4801 BC 97*   *542-3321*
The area's most complete lodging facility is a six-story, neo-Spanish-style motor hotel with both large outdoor and indoor pools, a whirlpool, saunas, and a tennis court, plus a restaurant, lounge, and cabaret. Each large, well-decorated room has a phone, cable color TV, and a private balcony or patio.
　　#628 — pvt. balc., good town/mts. view,   K bed...$55
　　#622,#626,#522,#526,#422,#426 — pvt. balc., good town view,   2 Q beds...$50
　　regular room —   Q bed...$48

Westgate Motor Inn   *.6 mi. N at 4204 32nd St.*   *542-0314*
This contemporary **bargain** motel has a large glass-walled indoor pool, plus a whirlpool, sauna, and game room. Each spacious, well-furnished room has a phone, cable color TV with movies, and a private balcony.
    regular room —   Q bed...$28

Willy's Motor Inn   *.4 mi. N at 3309 39th Av.*   *545-3351*
In a quiet creekside location, this **bargain** motel has a large, nicely landscaped outdoor pool. Each room has a phone, cable color TV, and a private balcony or patio.
    regular room —   D bed...$26

CAMPGROUNDS
Among several nearby campgrounds, the best have picturesque lakeside locations and complete facilities.

Crystal Waters Resort   *10 mi. S on BC 97*   *548-3332*
This large private camping and cabin complex above Kalamalka Lake features a pier, boat launch (fee), and boat rentals. Swimming, boating, and fishing are popular. Flush toilets, hot showers (fee), and hookups are available. Each site has a picnic table, and there are many sandy beachfront sites.   base rate...$6

★ **Ellison Provincial Park**   *10 mi. SW on Okanagan Landing Rd.*   *545-6940*
One of the prettiest campgrounds on Okanagan Lake is in a park where granite cliffs shelter calm bays edged by sandy beaches. Sunbathing, swimming, boating, and fishing are extremely popular. There are flush and pit toilets, but no showers or hookups. Each site is on a bench above the lake and has a picnic table and a fire area.   base rate...$4

Newport Beach Rec. Park *7 mi. NW via BC 97 & Westside Rd.*   *542-7131*
This private facility near the northern end of Okanagan Lake has a boat ramp, dock, and rentals. Swimming, fishing, boating, and water-skiing are popular. Flush and pit toilets, hot showers, and hookups are available. Each site has a picnic table and fire ring. There are shaded sites by the lake, and a separate tenting area.   base rate...$5

SPECIAL EVENT
★ **Winter Carnival**   *in and around town*   *early February*
The entire community is involved in the largest winter carnival in Western Canada. A big parade, queen coronation, many themed dances, live entertainment, wine and cheese tasting parties, beer gardens, ice sculptures, wind surfing races on ice, a polar bear swim, and bed races are some of the highlights of this ten day celebration.

OTHER INFORMATION
Area Code: *604*
Zip Code: *V1T*
Vernon & District Chamber of Commerce   *.3 mi. N at 3700 33rd St.*   *545-0771*

Index

About the Author

David Vokac, born in Chicago, grew up on a ranch near Cody, Wyoming. His enthusiasm for the West has continued in a career coupled to locations throughout the region. During summers while an undergraduate, he served as an airborne fire-spotter for the Shoshone National Forest in Wyoming. He taught courses in land economics while completing a Master's degree in geography at the University of Arizona in Tucson. In Denver, Colorado, Vokac was in charge of economic base analysis for the city's first community renewal program, and later became Chief of Neighborhood Planning. He moved to the West coast during the mid-1970s to prepare San Diego County's first local parks plan, and stayed to act as Park Development Director.

Mr. Vokac is now a full-time writer, and founder of a Western travel and leisure advisory service. During the past three years, he logged more than ninety thousand miles in a silver Audi criss-crossing eleven states and two provinces while identifying and researching all of the great towns of the West. When not gathering new material, speaking, consulting, or traveling for the sheer joy of it somewhere in the West, he resides in San Diego, California.

ORDER FORM

West Press
Dept. B
P.O. Box 99717
San Diego, CA 92109

Please send me _____ copies of *THE GREAT TOWNS OF THE WEST* at $16.90 each, which includes the $14.95 book plus $1.95 for postage, handling and sales tax.

Total amount enclosed $_____
(Make check or money order payable to West Press.)

Name _____

Address _____

City _____ State _____ Zip _____